Methodology of Educational Measurement and Assessment

[1] This work was conducted while M. von Davier was employed with Educational Testing Service.

This new book series collates key contributions to a fast-developing field of education research. It is an international forum for theoretical and empirical studies exploring new and existing methods of collecting, analyzing, and reporting data from educational measurements and assessments. Covering a high-profile topic from multiple viewpoints, it aims to foster a broader understanding of fresh developments as innovative software tools and new concepts such as competency models and skills diagnosis continue to gain traction in educational institutions around the world. Methodology of Educational Measurement and Assessment offers readers reliable critical evaluations, reviews and comparisons of existing methodologies alongside authoritative analysis and commentary on new and emerging approaches. It will showcase empirical research on applications, examine issues such as reliability, validity, and comparability, and help keep readers up to speed on developments in statistical modeling approaches. The fully peer-reviewed publications in the series cover measurement and assessment at all levels of education and feature work by academics and education professionals from around the world. Providing an authoritative central clearing-house for research in a core sector in education, the series forms a major contribution to the international literature.

More information about this series at http://www.springer.com/series/13206

Detlev Leutner • Jens Fleischer
Juliane Grünkorn • Eckhard Klieme
Editors

Competence Assessment in Education

Research, Models and Instruments

Springer

Editors
Detlev Leutner
Faculty of Educational Sciences,
Department of Instructional Psychology
University of Duisburg-Essen
Essen, Germany

Jens Fleischer
Faculty of Educational Sciences,
Department of Instructional Psychology
University of Duisburg-Essen
Essen, Germany

Juliane Grünkorn
German Institute for International
Educational Research (DIPF)
Frankfurt/Main, Germany

Eckhard Klieme
German Institute for International
Educational Research (DIPF)
Frankfurt/Main, Germany

ISSN 2367-170X ISSN 2367-1718 (electronic)
Methodology of Educational Measurement and Assessment
ISBN 978-3-319-50028-7 ISBN 978-3-319-50030-0 (eBook)
DOI 10.1007/978-3-319-50030-0

Library of Congress Control Number: 2017935541

Printed on acid-free paper

This Springer imprint is published by Springer Nature
The registered company is Springer International Publishing AG
The registered company address is: Gewerbestrasse 11, 6330 Cham, Switzerland

Contents

1 **Competence Assessment in Education: An Introduction** 1
Detlev Leutner, Jens Fleischer, Juliane Grünkorn, and Eckhard Klieme

Part I Modeling and Assessing Student Competencies

2 **Science-P I: Modeling Conceptual Understanding in Primary School** 9
Judith Pollmeier, Steffen Tröbst, Ilonca Hardy, Kornelia Möller, Thilo Kleickmann, Astrid Jurecka, and Knut Schwippert

3 **Science-P II: Modeling Scientific Reasoning in Primary School** 19
Susanne Koerber, Beate Sodian, Christopher Osterhaus, Daniela Mayer, Nicola Kropf, and Knut Schwippert

4 **The Heidelberg Inventory of Geographic System Competency Model** 31
Kathrin Viehrig, Alexander Siegmund, Joachim Funke, Sascha Wüstenberg, and Samuel Greiff

5 **An Extended Model of Literary Literacy** 55
Christel Meier, Thorsten Roick, Sofie Henschel, Jörn Brüggemann, Volker Frederking, Adelheid Rieder, Volker Gerner, and Petra Stanat

6 **Self-Regulated Learning with Expository Texts as a Competence: Competence Structure and Competence Training** 75
Joachim Wirth, Melanie Schütte, Jessica Wixfort, and Detlev Leutner

Part II Modeling and Assessing Teacher Competencies

7 Investigating Pre-service Teachers' Professional Vision Within University-Based Teacher Education ... 93
Tina Seidel, Kathleen Stürmer, Manfred Prenzel, Gloria Jahn, and Stefanie Schäfer

8 Teacher Knowledge Experiment: Conditions of the Development of Pedagogical Content Knowledge ... 111
Thilo Kleickmann, Steffen Tröbst, Aiso Heinze, Andrea Bernholt, Roland Rink, and Mareike Kunter

9 Teachers' School Tracking Decisions ... 131
Ines Böhmer, Cornelia Gräsel, Sabine Krolak-Schwerdt, Thomas Hörstermann, and Sabine Glock

10 Modeling, Measuring, and Training Teachers' Counseling and Diagnostic Competencies ... 149
Mara Gerich, Monika Trittel, Simone Bruder, Julia Klug, Silke Hertel, Regina Bruder, and Bernhard Schmitz

11 Development and Evaluation of a Competence Model for Teaching Integrative Processing of Texts and Pictures (BiTe) ... 167
Annika Ohle, Nele McElvany, Britta Oerke, Wolfgang Schnotz, Inga Wagner, Holger Horz, Mark Ullrich, and Jürgen Baumert

Part III Modeling and Assessing Vocational Competencies and Adult Learning

12 Multidimensional Competency Assessments and Structures in VET ... 183
Tobias Gschwendtner, Stephan Abele, Thomas Schmidt, and Reinhold Nickolaus

13 Professional Competencies of Building Trade Apprentices After Their First Year of Training ... 203
Kerstin Norwig, Cordula Petsch, and Reinhold Nickolaus

14 Assessing Tomorrow's Potential: A Competence Measuring Approach in Vocational Education and Training ... 221
Viola Katharina Klotz and Esther Winther

Part IV Competency Development: Modeling of Change and Training of Competencies

15 The Development of Students' Physics Competence in Middle School ... 247
Susanne Weßnigk, Knut Neumann, Tobias Viering, David Hadinek, and Hans E. Fischer

16 Modeling and Fostering Decision-Making Competencies Regarding Challenging Issues of Sustainable Development 263
Susanne Bögeholz, Sabina Eggert, Carolin Ziese, and Marcus Hasselhorn

17 Metacognitive Knowledge in Secondary School Students: Assessment, Structure, and Developmental Change 285
Wolfgang Schneider, Klaus Lingel, Cordula Artelt, and Nora Neuenhaus

18 Development of Dynamic Usage of Strategies for Integrating Text and Picture Information in Secondary Schools 303
Wolfgang Schnotz, Inga Wagner, Fang Zhao, Mark Ullrich, Holger Horz, Nele McElvany, Annika Ohle, and Jürgen Baumert

19 Training in Components of Problem-Solving Competence: An Experimental Study of Aspects of the Cognitive Potential Exploitation Hypothesis 315
Florian Buchwald, Jens Fleischer, Stefan Rumann, Joachim Wirth, and Detlev Leutner

20 An Intensive Longitudinal Study of the Development of Student Achievement over Two Years (LUISE) 333
Gizem Hülür, Fidan Gasimova, Alexander Robitzsch, and Oliver Wilhelm

Part V Innovations in Psychometric Models and Computer-Based Assessment

21 Multidimensional Structures of Competencies: Focusing on Text Comprehension in English as a Foreign Language 357
Johannes Hartig and Claudia Harsch

22 Multidimensional Adaptive Measurement of Competencies 369
Andreas Frey, Ulf Kroehne, Nicki-Nils Seitz, and Sebastian Born

23 Development, Validation, and Application of a Competence Model for Mathematical Problem Solving by Using and Translating Representations of Functions 389
Timo Leuders, Regina Bruder, Ulf Kroehne, Dominik Naccarella, Renate Nitsch, Jan Henning-Kahmann, Augustin Kelava, and Markus Wirtz

24 Relating Product Data to Process Data from Computer-Based Competency Assessment 407
Frank Goldhammer, Johannes Naumann, Heiko Rölke, Annette Stelter, and Krisztina Tóth

25 **Dynamic Problem Solving: Multiple-Item Testing Based on Minimally Complex Systems** 427
Joachim Funke and Samuel Greiff

Part VI Feedback From Competency Assessment: Concepts, Conditions and Consequences

26 **Formative Assessment in Mathematics Instruction: Theoretical Considerations and Empirical Results of the Co²CA Project** 447
Katrin Rakoczy, Eckhard Klieme, Dominik Leiß, and Werner Blum

27 **Arguing Validity in Educational Assessment** 469
Simon P. Tiffin-Richards and Hans Anand Pant

28 **Evaluating Prerequisites for the Development of a Dynamic Test of Reading Competence: Feedback Effects on Reading Comprehension in Children** 487
Tobias Dörfler, Stefanie Golke, and Cordula Artelt

Chapter 1
Competence Assessment in Education: An Introduction

Detlev Leutner, Jens Fleischer, Juliane Grünkorn, and Eckhard Klieme

Abstract In this chapter, the structure and the specific research areas of the German DFG-Priority Program "Competence Models for Assessing Individual Learning Outcomes and Evaluating Educational Processes" are briefly described, in order to provide a background for the following chapters, which describe various individual projects of this Priority Program. The chapters have been organized into six thematic parts.

Keywords Competencies • Assessment • DFG-Priority Program "Competence Models for Assessing Individual Learning Outcomes and Evaluating Educational Processes"

1.1 The German DFG-Priority Program "Competence Models for Assessing Individual Learning Outcomes and Evaluating Educational Processes"

In the past few decades, educational systems worldwide have been moving towards evidence-based policy and practice (e.g., Slavin 2002), where "evidence" often implies empirical assessment of students' competencies as the main outcome of education at school. Thus, the assessment of competencies plays a key role in optimizing educational processes and improving the effectiveness of educational systems. However, the theoretically and empirically adequate assessment of competencies in educational settings is a challenging endeavor that is often underestimated by policy makers and practitioners.

D. Leutner (✉) • J. Fleischer
Faculty of Educational Sciences, Department of Instructional Psychology, University of Duisburg-Essen, Essen, Germany
e-mail: detlev.leutner@uni-due.de; jens.fleischer@uni-due.de

J. Grünkorn • E. Klieme
German Institute for International Educational Research (DIPF), Frankfurt/Main, Germany
e-mail: gruenkorn@dipf.de; klieme@dipf.de

D. Leutner et al. (eds.), *Competence Assessment in Education*, Methodology of Educational Measurement and Assessment, DOI 10.1007/978-3-319-50030-0_1

To cope with these challenges, and to promote and coordinate scientific efforts in the field of competence assessment across disciplines in Germany, the German Research Foundation (DFG) funded the Priority Program "Competence Models for Assessing Individual Learning Outcomes and Evaluating Educational Processes", which started in 2007 and ended in 2013. Over the six-year funding period, the Priority Program coordinated the work of a large number of research projects (see http://kompetenzmodelle.dipf.de/en/projects) with experts from psychology, educational science, and subject didactics.

The main point of reference for all projects of the DFG-Priority Program is the concept of "competencies", which are defined as "context-specific cognitive dispositions that are acquired and needed to successfully cope with certain situations or tasks in specific domains" (Koeppen et al. 2008, p. 62; see also Hartig et al. 2008, and Shavelson 2010). According to this definition, "competencies" differ from other constructs such as "intelligence", as competencies refer to the mastering of sets of specific challenges in specific situations in specific domains, whereas intelligence refers to mental abilities that can be used to master challenges in general. In addition, intelligence is generally not considered to be influenced by school education, whereas the development of competencies is at the core of school education. The definition of competencies as "cognitive" dispositions is in line with the way in which the term "competence" is used in international large-scale assessment studies such as PISA, TIMSS, or PIRLS (e.g., OECD 2001), as motivational and volitional aspects of competencies–in order to begin with research in this field–are excluded from being studied in those studies (Weinert 2001).

1.2 Research Areas of the DFG-Priority Program

The research addressed by the DFG-Priority Program covers different aspects of competence assessment, and is organized into four consecutive main research areas (Fig. 1.1): (1) The development and empirical testing of theoretical competence models is at the core of the research program. These theoretical models are complemented by (2) psychometric models, which in turn inform the construction of measurement procedures for the empirical assessment of competencies (3). The program is finally rounded off by (4) research on how best to use diagnostic information.

The following chapters of this book present the findings of 24 DFG-Priority Program projects. All projects have a primary focus on one of these four research areas; several projects moved consecutively through several areas. In the following sections, the research areas are described briefly, and an overview is given of projects within the areas.

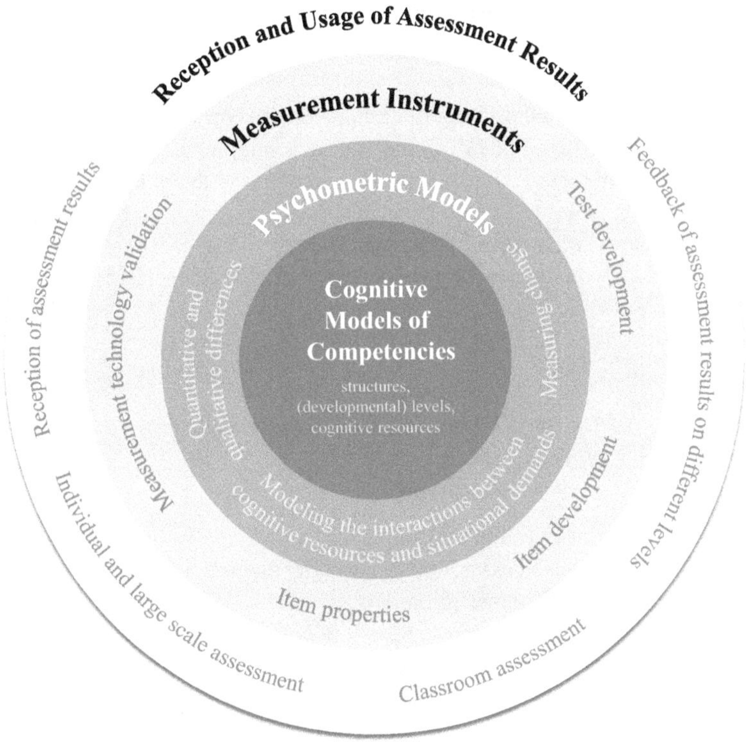

Fig. 1.1 Research areas of the DFG-Priority Program "Competence Models for Assessing Individual Learning Outcomes and Evaluating Educational Processes"

1.2.1 Cognitive Modeling and Assessment of Competencies

Research in the area of cognitive modeling asks how competencies can be modeled adequately with regard to those situations or tasks where they are needed in specific domains. As such, models of competencies are necessarily domain-specific, and the research program covers a broad variety of domains.

A first group of domains (Part I: Modeling and assessing student competencies) concerns competencies of students at school, ranging from conceptual understanding and scientific reasoning in primary school, through geography and literary literacy, to self-regulated learning at high school (Chaps. 2, 3, 4, 5 and 6).

A second group of domains (Part II: Modeling and assessing teacher competencies) concerns the competencies of teachers, in areas such as professional vision, pedagogical content knowledge, tracking decisions, counseling, and teaching the integrative processing of text and pictures (Chaps. 7, 8, 9, 10 and 11).

A third group of domains (Part III: Modeling and assessing vocational competencies and adult learning) concerns vocational competencies and adult learning in fields such as car mechatronics, electronics, building trades, and industrial management (Chaps. 12, 13 and 14).

Modeling of change and training of competencies represents a fourth, very challenging area of research (Part IV: Competency development: Modeling of change and training of competencies). Projects are concerned with students' physics competencies, decision making regarding sustainable development, metacognitive competencies, strategies for integrating text and picture information, problem-solving competencies, language and mathematics competencies (Chaps. 15, 16, 17, 18, 19 and 20).

1.2.2 Innovations in Psychometric Models and Computer-Based Assessment

Research in the area of psychometric models (Part V: Innovations in psychometric models and computer-based assessment) asks how theoretical models of competencies can be linked to psychometric models in order to develop assessment instruments. Innovative approaches are presented concerning multidimensional IRT models for English as a foreign language, multidimensional adaptive measurement for large-scale assessments, adaptive assessment of competencies regarding multiple representation of mathematical functions, relating product and process data from computer-based assessments, and dynamic problem solving (Chaps. 21, 22, 23, 24 and 25).

1.2.3 Reception and Usage of Assessment Results

Research in the area of assessment results (Part VI: Feedback from competency assessment: Concepts, conditions and consequences) asks what kinds of information from competence assessments can be used by practitioners in the educational system, and in which ways. A specific focus of the projects is on feedback, such as the role of feedback in formative assessment, in arguing validity and standard setting, as well as feedback effects in a dynamic test of reading competence (Chaps. 26, 27 and 28).

1.3 Conclusion

As outlined in this introduction, the assessment of competencies plays a key role in optimizing educational processes and improving the effectiveness of educational systems. However, to adequately assess competencies in educational settings is a challenging endeavor, and the German DFG-Priority Program "Competence Models for Assessing Individual Learning Outcomes and Evaluating Educational Processes" has been an attempt to move the field onto a broad national footing by funding basic scientific research on modeling competencies.

The Priority Program has had significant influence, not only in terms of scientific publications (a complete list of publications is provided at http://kompetenzmodelle.dipf.de/en/publications/km_literatur_e.html), but also in terms of stimulating additional, more-applied large-scale research programs funded by the German Federal Ministry of Education and Research (BMBF). One example of these latter is the Research Program KoKoHs: "Modeling and Measuring Competencies in Higher Education" (Zlatkin-Troitschanskaia et al. 2014, 2015, 2016). Another example is the Research Program ASCOT: "Technology-based Assessment of Skills and Competencies in Vocational Education and Training" (BMBF 2012).

As a result of both the more basic research (DFG-Priority Program) and the more-applied research (BMBF Programs), a large number of theoretical models, psychometric approaches, and assessment instruments are now available. These allow practitioners in the educational field to assess competencies in a great variety of domains. Furthermore, these models, approaches, and instruments that were developed within specific domains, can be used as a blueprint for developing models, approaches, and instruments in other domains. Thus, there are good grounds for optimizing educational processes and improving the effectiveness of the educational system in Germany through adequately assessing student competencies.

Acknowledgments The preparation of this chapter was supported by grants KL 1057/9–1 to 9–3 and LE 645/11–1 to 11–3 from the German Research Foundation (DFG) in the Priority Program "Competence Models for Assessing Individual Learning Outcomes and Evaluating Educational Processes" (SPP 1293). The chapter is based on papers by Fleischer et al. (2012, 2013), Klieme and Leutner (2006), Koeppen et al. (2008), and Leutner et al. (2013).

References

BMBF (German Federal Ministry of Education and Research). (2012). *Vocational skills and competencies made visible: The ASCOT research initiative*. Bonn: Federal Ministry of Education and Research (BMBF), Training Policy Division.

Fleischer, J., Leutner, D., & Klieme, E. (2012). Modellierung von Kompetenzen im Bereich der Bildung: Eine psychologische Perspektive [Modeling of competencies in education: A psychological perspective] (Editorial). *Psychologische Rundschau, 63*, 1–2. doi:10.1026/0033-3042/a000111.

Fleischer, J., Koeppen, K., Kenk, M., Klieme, E., & Leutner, D. (2013). Kompetenzmodellierung: Struktur, Konzepte und Forschungszugänge des DFG-Schwerpunktprogramms [Modeling of competencies: Structure, concepts, and research approaches of the DFG-Priority Program]. *Zeitschrift für Erziehungswissenschaft*, Special Issue *18*, 5–22. doi:10.1007/s11618–013-0379-z.

Hartig, J., Klieme, E., & Leutner, D. (Eds.). (2008). *Assessment of competencies in educational contexts*. Göttingen: Hogrefe.

Klieme, E., & Leutner, D. (2006). Kompetenzmodelle zur Erfassung individueller Lernergebnisse und zur Bilanzierung von Bildungsprozessen: Beschreibung eines neu eingerichteten Schwerpunktprogramms der DFG [Competence models for assessing individual learning outcomes and evaluating educational processes: Description of a new priority program of the German Research Foundation, DFG]. *Zeitschrift für Pädagogik, 52*, 876–903.

Koeppen, K., Hartig, J., Klieme, E., & Leutner, D. (2008). Current issues in competence modelling and assessment. *Zeitschrift für Psychologie/Journal of Psychology, 216*, 61–73. doi:10.1027/0044-3409.216.2.61.

Leutner, D., Klieme, E., Fleischer, J., & Kuper, H. (2013). Kompetenzmodelle zur Erfassung individueller Lernergebnisse und zur Bilanzierung von Bildungsprozessen: Aktuelle Diskurse im DFG-Schwerpunktprogramm [Competence models for assessing individual learning outcomes and evaluating educational processes: Current discussions in the DFG-Priority Program] (Editorial). *Zeitschrift für Erziehungswissenschaft, Special Issue 18*1–4. doi:10.1007/s11618-013-0378-0.

OECD (Organisation for Economic Co-operation and Development). (2001). *Knowledge and skills for life: First results from the OECD Programme for International Student Assessment (PISA) 2000*. Paris: OECD Publications.

Shavelson, R. J. (2010). On the measurement of competency. *Empirical Research in Vocational Education and Training, 2*, 41–63.

Slavin, R. E. (2002). Evidence-based education policies: Transforming educational practice and research. *Educational Researcher, 31*, 15–21.

Weinert, F. E. (2001). Concept of competence: A conceptual clarification. In D. S. Rychen & L. H. Salganik (Eds.), *Defining and selecting key competencies* (pp. 45–65). Seattle: Hogrefe.

Zlatkin-Troitschanskaia, O., Kuhn, C., & Toepper, M. (2014). The German research program KoKoHs: Theoretical concept, assessment design, and validation approach in modeling and measuring competencies in higher education. *The Brunswik Society Newsletter, 29*, 56–59. http://www.albany.edu/cpr/brunswik/newsletters/2014news.pdf.

Zlatkin-Troitschanskaia, O., Shavelson, R. J., & Kuhn, C. (2015). The international state of research on measurement of competency in higher education. *Studies in Higher Education, 40*, 393–411. doi:10.1080/03075079.2015.1004241.

Zlatkin-Troitschanskaia, O., Pant, H. A., & Coates, H. (2016). Assessing student learning outcomes in higher education: Challenges and international perspectives (Editorial). *Assessment and Evaluation in Higher Education, 41*, 655–661. doi:10.1080/02602938.2016.1169501.

Part I
Modeling and Assessing Student Competencies

Chapter 2
Science-P I: Modeling Conceptual Understanding in Primary School

Judith Pollmeier, Steffen Tröbst, Ilonca Hardy, Kornelia Möller, Thilo Kleickmann, Astrid Jurecka, and Knut Schwippert

Abstract In the Science-P project (*Science* Competency in *P*rimary School), we aimed at modeling scientific literacy in two dimensions—scientific reasoning and conceptual understanding—to describe science learning in primary school. The present chapter focuses on conceptual understanding exemplified by two content areas: floating and sinking (FS) and evaporation and condensation (EC). Drawing on results from conceptual change research in developmental psychology and science education, we devised a model with three hierarchically ordered levels of understanding—naïve, intermediate and scientifically advanced—as the foundation of item and test construction. The two content areas engendered a two-dimensional structure in our test instrument. A validation study underscored that responses to our paper-pencil items were systematically related to responses obtained in interviews. Our test instrument was used to capture the development of primary school students' conceptual understanding from second to fourth grade, in both a cross-sectional and a longitudinal study. For cross-sectional data, students' proficiency in scientific reasoning was found to predict their conceptual understanding. In future analyses, we will test this finding with our longitudinal data.

Keywords Conceptual understanding • Science competency • Primary school • Development

J. Pollmeier (✉) • S. Tröbst • T. Kleickmann
Kiel University, Kiel, Germany
e-mail: pollmeier@paedagogik.uni-kiel.de; troebst@paedagogik.uni-kiel.de; kleickmann@paedagogik.uni-kiel.de

I. Hardy • A. Jurecka
Goethe University Frankfurt, Frankfurt/Main, Germany
e-mail: Hardy@em.uni-frankfurt.de; Jurecka@em.uni-frankfurt.de

K. Möller
University of Münster, Münster, Germany
e-mail: molleko@uni-muenster.de

K. Schwippert
University of Hamburg, Hamburg, Germany
e-mail: knut.schwippert@uni-hamburg.de

D. Leutner et al. (eds.), *Competence Assessment in Education*, Methodology of Educational Measurement and Assessment, DOI 10.1007/978-3-319-50030-0_2

2.1 The Assessment of Science Competency in Primary School

In recent years, science learning has been described within the construct of scientific literacy, which has been conceptualized with various facets, distinguishing a component of conceptual understanding from a component of procedural understanding (Bybee 1997). While there are theoretical and empirically validated models of science competency for secondary schools, corresponding efforts are rare within the growing body of research on competency development for primary schools (e.g., Walpuski et al. 2011). Hence, in our project we aimed to model the development of science competency in primary school in the two dimensions of scientific reasoning (e.g., Koerber et al. 2017, in this volume) and conceptual understanding. The latter is the focus of this chapter.

To derive a theoretically plausible and empirically testable competency model of conceptual understanding in primary school science, it appears suitable to resort to the findings of conceptual change research in developmental psychology and science education. This research has revealed that students bring a wide range of individual content-specific ideas and conceptions to the science class; these have potential to hinder or foster formal science learning. Aside from the nature of students' naïve conceptions, conceptual change research has also explored the pathways along which these evolve (e.g., Schneider and Hardy 2013). In this context, we pursued three main goals: (a) modeling primary school students' conceptual understandings in the content areas of FS and EC with paper-pencil tests to empirically validate a competency model using large groups of students, (b) investigating the development of conceptual understanding over the course of primary school and (c) examining the relation between students' conceptual understanding and scientific reasoning.

2.2 Modeling Conceptual Understanding in Primary School Science

2.2.1 *Model Specification and Item Construction*

In the first place, we hypothesized a competency model with three hierarchical levels of increasing understanding: At the *naïve* level students hold scientifically inadequate conceptions which, through processes of restructuring or enrichment may possibly result in *intermediate* conceptions. These contain partly correct conceptualizations and are applicable in a broader range of situations than are naïve conceptions. At the *scientifically advanced* level, eventually, students hold conceptions in accordance with scientifically accepted views (Hardy et al. 2010). Within this framework, we designed a construct map as the foundation for item development (Wilson 2005). For each content area, this contained detailed descriptions of possible student conceptions at each level of understanding. These conceptions were extracted from conceptual change research (e.g., Hsin and Wu 2011; Tytler 2000).

The translation of the conceptions identified in conceptual change research into a paper-pencil instrument suitable for testing groups of primary school students, posed a considerable challenge for item development. Specifically, the test instrument had to incorporate and represent different levels of conceptual understanding without inducing artificial response tendencies and preferences. Using the construct map, we designed items with mainly closed response formats; response alternatives represented varying levels of conceptual understanding. Response formats were either forced-choice (select the better of two alternatives), multiple-choice (select the best of three to six alternatives) or multiple-select (judge three to six alternatives consecutively as true or false). In addition, a few items with open and graphical response formats were constructed (Kleickmann et al. 2010).

For all items, the stems consisted of descriptions of physical phenomena relevant to the two content areas. Of these phenomena, those which could be presented in a classroom, were demonstrated during administration of the test (see Fig. 2.1). After presentation of a specific phenomenon, students had to select or, in the rare case of open response formats, produce an explanation for that phenomenon. For multiple-select items, students could select several explanations simultaneously (see Fig. 2.1). To minimize the impact of reading ability on students' performance, descriptions of phenomena and response alternatives were read out aloud. Students in participating classes proceeded simultaneously through the test within 90 min. The majority of items represented explanations on the naïve level, due to the wealth of naïve conceptions identified by previous research. In general, primary school students were considered to demonstrate proficient conceptual understanding by the dismissal of naïve explanations and the endorsement of intermediate or scientifically advanced explanations.

2.2.2 *Conceptual Understanding: Dimensions and Levels*

To examine the dimensionality of our test instrument, we fitted one-parametric logistic item response models with varying dimensionality to the data of a cross-sectional study with 1820 s, third and fourth graders, using ACER Conquest 2.0 (Wu et al. 2005). A likelihood ratio test of relative model fit demonstrated that a model featuring the two content areas as separate dimensions, fitted the data better than did a uni-dimensional model ($\Delta\chi^2(2) = 246.83$, $p < .001$, $\Delta AIC = 242.88$, $\Delta BIC = 231.71$; Pollmeier 2015; Pollmeier et al. in prep.). This finding supported the notion that competency in certain content areas might develop separately from that in other content domains. Thus, further analyses for the cross-sectional data were performed separately for each content area. The two-dimensionality established for the cross-sectional data set was consistent with the results of preliminary studies (Pollmeier et al. 2011).

The Cold Glass

Instruction:

You fill a glass with cold water and ice cubes. At first the glass is dry on the outside. But after a couple of minutes you can see little droplets on the outside.

Let's try this by ourselves.

(*Demonstration of phenomenon with corresponding material.*)

Why do the droplets appear on the outside of the glass?

Select either "true" or "false" after each explanation!

	true	false
The water droplets came from inside the glass through small pores.	*naïve*	
The water droplets condensed in the air, as the air cooled.	*scientific*	
Water from the air became visible because of the cold.	*intermediate*	
The water from the glass is now on the outside.	*naïve*	

Fig. 2.1 Sample item: condensation

To clarify the influence of the hypothesized levels of understanding and subfacets of content areas defined in the construct map on students' performance, we devised explanatory item response models, using the R-package lme4 (De Boeck and Wilson 2004; De Boeck et al. 2011). These models explored the impact of specific person and item characteristics on students' responses (Pollmeier et al. 2013). In particular, the analyses revealed differential proficiency in subgroups of students with regard to levels of understanding in the two content areas. We found an overall gender effect for the content area of FS, with boys outperforming girls. Furthermore, girls exhibited specific weaknesses for items on density and displacement, compared to items on buoyancy. They also, relative to boys, had a preference for explanations on the intermediate level, whereas they neglected explanations based on scientifically advanced conceptions. In contrast, for the content area of EC, overall performance did not differ between girls and boys. Yet girls also displayed a relative preference for items featuring intermediate conceptions in the content area of EC, although they did not neglect scientifically advanced conceptions (Pollmeier et al. 2013).

To explain additional variance in item difficulties, we explored the relevance of characteristics derived from the classification of item stems. Again, we employed explanatory item response models, both for the cross-sectional data and for one further experimental study, in which certain contextual features were varied systematically across item stems (Pollmeier 2015). For the content area of FS we identified *congruence* as an important explanatory characteristic for items associated with the concepts of density and displacement: With these items, students had to compare two objects and decide which was made of the denser material or displaced more water. Items featuring congruent objects—that is, the denser object was also the heavier object, or the heavier object displaced more water—were easier to solve than incongruent items—that is, where the denser object was the lighter object or the lighter object displaced more water.

For the content area of EC we obtained no single explanatory characteristic of central importance. However, we found that the specific content used in items accounted for a large portion of the variance in item difficulties. The most difficult content for the facet of evaporation was a naïve conception: the anthropomorphic interpretation of the physical phenomena to be explained. Items with scientifically advanced content—that is, with the correct explanation for phenomena of evaporation in age-appropriate language—were not as difficult to solve as these items, or items proposing a mere change of matter as the explanation for evaporation phenomena. Items conveying a false description of the change of matter, a description of change of location, and non-conservation of matter as explanations for evaporation phenomena, were comparatively easy to solve. For the facet of condensation, items featuring a faulty description of a cause, a change of location, a change of matter and a scientifically advanced explanation for condensation phenomena, constituted an order of decreasing difficulty of content (Pollmeier 2015).

2.2.3 *Validity*

To assess the convergent and discriminant validity of our instrument, we conducted a validation study with four third grade classes (FS: $N = 41$, EC: $N = 32$). For each content area we presented two classes with 13 item stems, both as paper-pencil items with closed response format and as interview items with open response format (Pollmeier et al. 2011). Students were randomly assigned to an order of presentation of the two forms of item. Additionally, reading ability (Lenhard and Schneider 2006) and cognitive ability (Weiß 2006) were measured. We found substantial correlations between the two modes of assessment for each content area, but also systematic differences in the responses: Students produced a wider range of answers on the naïve and intermediate levels, and fewer answers on the scientifically advanced level for interview items than for paper-pencil items. As expected, the production of explanations was more demanding than merely endorsing correct response alternatives. Apart from that, knowledge in the content area of FS, as assessed with the interviews, appeared to be more fragmented and context dependent than corresponding knowledge in the content area of EC; a discrepancy not evident in the paper-pencil items.

Moreover, for the content area of EC, performance on paper-pencil items was independent of reading ability and cognitive ability. This finding supports the claim that our instrument measured a form of science competency that was more specific than those general abilities. The substantial relation found between the test of cognitive ability and performance on the paper-pencil items for the content area of FS probably was induced by the similarity between items covering the facet of density and items assessing cognitive ability. The impact of socio-economic status on proficiency in the content of FS was evident both for interview and for paper-pencil items.

In sum, there was a systematic difference between responses to interview and paper-pencil items that can be readily explained by the discrepancy between free retrieval and recognition and that thus was not caused by a difference in the constructs assessed by the items. In other words, the positive associations between responses to interview and paper-pencil items indicate that our test instrument for assessment of conceptual understanding captured a form of science competency that is plausibly parallel to the conceptual understanding found in classic conceptual change research.

2.3 The Development of Conceptual Understanding in Primary School Science

Analyses of the cross-sectional data set (see Sect. 2.2.2 above) by means of explanatory item response models also yielded insights into the differences in average conceptual understanding between grade levels: Third and fourth graders outperformed students from second grade in terms of conceptual understanding, and we further unveiled the specific strengths of third and fourth graders. Within the content area of FS, third and fourth graders performed particularly well on items covering the facets of density and displacement and on items featuring scientifically advanced conceptions. In the content area of EC, students from third and fourth grade displayed a specific strength in items concerned with the facet of evaporation.

A longitudinal study with a total of 1578 students in 75 classes from primary schools in two federal states of Germany (Baden-Wuerttemberg, North Rhine-Westphalia) concluded our project. Students completed our tests on science

Table 2.1 Descriptive statistics for the longitudinal study

	Grade 3, end of school year			Grade 4, end of school year		
Content area	M(SD)	Min	Max	M(SD)	Min	Max
Descriptive item statistics						
Floating and sinking	.50(.43)	.16	.96	.56(.45)	.30	.90
Evaporation and condensation	.52(.47)	.30	.86	.59(.47)	.33	.92
Descriptive person statistics						
Floating and sinking	11.40(4.48)	2	23	14.39(4.87)	0	23
Evaporation and condensation	24.63(5.53)	10	42	27.92(6.30)	2	46

competency at the end of third and fourth grade. For the preliminary analyses we used 48 individual items from 23 anchoring item stems, of the total 27 stems that were used in this study.

For both content areas, on average, the solution rates of anchor items increased in fourth grade and were accompanied by relatively large standard deviations (see Table 2.1, item statistics); a first hint that our instrument covered a sensible amount of variety. Also, the number of correctly solved items reveals that students on average solved more items at posttest than at pretest (see Table 2.1, person statistics). In relation to the number of anchor items assigned to each content area, this implies a relatively smaller gain in conceptual understanding for the content area of EC.

In sum, our preliminary explorations suggest that we succeeded in assessing naturally occurring growth in conceptual understanding in this longitudinal study. In future analyses based on all items, we will examine whether the small growth in the content area of EC is attributable to the general difficulty of this content or rather to deficiencies in the amount and quality of formal instruction. Furthermore, we will investigate students' performance with regard to the various characteristics of items and item stems (e.g., the assigned level of conceptual understanding). Finally, future analyses will focus on investigating the conjoint development of conceptual understanding and scientific reasoning.

2.4 Conceptual Understanding and Scientific Reasoning

The issue of the relation between conceptual understanding and scientific reasoning was also tackled with the cross-sectional study data (for detailed analyses of primary school students' competency in scientific reasoning see Koerber et al. 2017, in this volume). After calibrating our tests by the use of simple Rasch models, we retrieved weighted likelihood estimates of person ability for subsequent analyses. Multilevel analyses revealed substantial associations between scientific reasoning and conceptual understanding in both content areas that were not readily explained by relevant covariates like fluid intelligence, reading ability, interest in science, socioeconomic status, and immigrant status. Furthermore, in the content area FS, the predictive effect of scientific reasoning on conceptual knowledge slightly increased with grade, even after controlling for fluid ability. These findings hint at the possibility that proficient scientific reasoning facilitates the acquisition of conceptual understanding. Specifically, having a command of the processes of scientific reasoning could enhance the evaluation of evidence with respect to existing conceptions, which could take the role of hypotheses or even theories. This could also account for the possibly cumulative effect of proficient scientific reasoning on conceptual understanding, suggested by its interaction with the content area FS in the cross-sectional data. Future analyses of the longitudinal data will yield deeper insights into this issue.

Acknowledgements The preparation of this chapter was supported by grants to Kornelia Möller (MO 942/4-1, MO 942/4-2 and MO 942/4-3), from the German Research Foundation (DFG) in the Priority Programme "Competence Models for Assessing Individual Learning Outcomes and Evaluating Educational Processes" (SPP 1293).

References

Bybee, R. W. (1997). Toward an understanding of scientific literacy. In W. Gräber & C. Bolte (Eds.), *Scientific literacy* (pp. 37–68). Kiel: IPN.

De Boeck, P., & Wilson, M. (Eds.). (2004). *Explanatory item response models: A generalized linear and nonlinear approach*. New York: Springer.

De Boeck, P., Bakker, M., Zwitser, R., Nivard, M., Hofman, A., Tuerlinckx, F., & Partchev, I. (2011). The estimation of item response models with the lmer function from the lme4 package in R. *Journal of Statistical Software, 39*(12), 1–28.

Hardy, I., Kleickmann, T., Koerber, S., Mayer, D., Möller, K., Pollmeier, J., … Sodian, B. (2010). *Die Modellierung naturwissenschaftlicher Kompetenz im Grundschulalter: Projekt Science-P* [Modeling science competence in primary school: The project Science-P.]. *Zeitschrift für Pädagogik, Beiheft 56*, 115–125.

Hsin, C., & Wu, H.-K. (2011). Using scaffolding strategies to promote young children's scientific understandings of floating and sinking. *Journal of Science Education and Technology, 20*, 656–666. doi:10.1007/s10956-011-9310-7.

Kleickmann, T., Hardy, I., Möller, K., Pollmeier, J., Tröbst, S., & Beinbrech, C. (2010). Die Modellierung naturwissenschaftlicher Kompetenz im Grundschulalter: Theoretische Konzeption und Testkonstruktion [Modeling science competence in primary school: Theoretical conception and test construction]. *Zeitschrift für Didaktik der Naturwissenschaften, 16*, 265–283.

Koerber, S., Sodian, B., Osterhaus, C., Mayer, D., Kropf, N., & Schwippert, K. (2017). Science-P II: Modeling scientific reasoning in primary school. In D. Leutner, J. Fleischer, J. Grünkorn, E. Klieme, *Competence assessment in education: Research, models and instruments* (pp. 19–29). Berlin: Springer.

Lenhard, W., & Schneider, W. (Eds.). (2006). *ELFE 1–6. Ein Leseverständnistest für Erst- bis Sechstklässler* [A reading literacy test for Grades 1–6]. Göttingen: Hogrefe.

Pollmeier, J. (2015). *Kontextmerkmale und die Bearbeitung von Aufgaben in einem Test naturwissenschaftlicher Kompetenz in der Grundschule* [Contextual features of items in a test of science competence in primary school] (Unpublished doctoral dissertation). WWU Münster, Münster, Germany.

Pollmeier, J., Hardy, I., Koerber, S., & Möller, K. (2011). Lassen sich naturwissenschaftliche Lernstände im Grundschulalter mit schriftlichen Aufgaben valide erfassen [Valid assessment of scientific knowledge in primary school with written tests]? *Zeitschrift für Pädagogik, 57*, 834–853.

Pollmeier, J., Tröbst, S., & Möller, K. (2013, August). *Conceptual competence in science in primary school*. Paper presented at the 15th Biennial EARLI Conference, München, Germany.

Pollmeier, J., Tröbst, S., Hardy, I., Osterhaus, C., Koerber, S., Mayer, D., … Sodian, B. (in preparation). *The effect of scientific reasoning on conceptual scientific understanding in the course of primary school (Grade 2–4).*

Schneider, M., & Hardy, I. (2013). Profiles of inconsistent knowledge in children's pathways of conceptual change. *Developmental Psychology, 49*, 1639–1649. doi:10.1037/a0030976.

Tytler, R. (2000). A comparison of year 1 and year 6 students' conceptions of evaporation and condensation: Dimensions of conceptual progression. *International Journal of Science Education, 22*, 447–467. doi:10.1080/095006900289723.

Walpuski, M., Ropohl, M., & Sumfleth, E. (2011). Students' knowledge about chemical reactions development and analysis of standard-based test items. *Chemistry Education Research and Practice, 12*, 174–183. doi:10.1039/C1RP90022F.

Weiß, R. H. (2006). *Grundintelligenztest Skala 2–Revision (CFT 20-R)* [Test for general mental capacity]. Göttingen: Hogrefe.

Wilson, M. (2005). *Constructing measures: An item response modeling approach*. Mahwah: Erlbaum.

Wu, M., Adams, R., & Wilson, M. (2005). *ACER ConQuest*. Camberwell: ACER Press.

Chapter 3
Science-P II: Modeling Scientific Reasoning in Primary School

Susanne Koerber, Beate Sodian, Christopher Osterhaus, Daniela Mayer, Nicola Kropf, and Knut Schwippert

Abstract Basic scientific reasoning abilities in primary-school children have been documented in numerous studies. However, an empirically tested competence-structure model has not been developed, most likely due to the difficulty of capturing conceptual understanding in paper-and-pencil tasks. The Science-P project contributes to this research area by constructing and testing a theoretical model of the development of scientific reasoning in primary school. Based on our own competence-structure model, derived from developmental research, we constructed a comprehensive inventory of paper-and-pencil tasks that can be used in whole-class testing. This chapter provides an overview of the development of our inventory, and reports three central findings: (1) the convergent validity of our inventory, (2) the significant development of scientific reasoning in primary school from Grades 2 to 4, and (3) empirical proof of our competence-structure model.

Keywords Scientific reasoning • Primary school • Competence modeling

3.1 Science-P

The Science-P project (*Science* competencies in *P*rimary school) investigated the development of two central dimensions of science understanding: general scientific reasoning, and conceptual understanding in physics in primary school. This chapter focuses on the dimension "scientific reasoning" and reports central findings regarding the development of this form of reasoning from Grades 2 to 4. The

S. Koerber (✉) • C. Osterhaus
Freiburg University of Education, Freiburg, Germany
e-mail: susanne.koerber@ph-freiburg.de; osterhaus@ph-freiburg.de

B. Sodian • D. Mayer • N. Kropf
University of Munich (LMU), Munich, Germany
e-mail: sodian@psy.lmu.de; daniela.mayer@psy.lmu.de; nicola.kropf@psy.lmu.de

K. Schwippert
University of Hamburg, Hamburg, Germany
e-mail: knut.schwippert@uni-hamburg.de

D. Leutner et al. (eds.), *Competence Assessment in Education*, Methodology of Educational Measurement and Assessment, DOI 10.1007/978-3-319-50030-0_3

development of conceptual understanding in physics is described in the chapter by Pollmeier et al. (2017) in this volume.

Whereas early studies of scientific reasoning focused primarily on secondary-school students, modern developmental research indicates the presence of basic scientific reasoning abilities in primary-school children (Zimmerman 2007) and even of beginning skills and understanding in preschool children (e.g., Koerber et al. 2005). The literature contains descriptions of two research approaches: (1) theory-oriented research focused on the developmental function and on qualitative change, mainly using interview-based studies (e.g., Carey et al. 1989; Kuhn 2010; Lederman 2007) and (2) research focusing on the psychometric modeling of science understanding (e.g., TIMSS, PISA), which usually involves large-scale assessments and complex models based on post-hoc-determined hierarchical levels of competence. Science-P aimed to bridge the gap between these two approaches by developing and empirically testing a theory-based model of scientific reasoning competence.

In line with the common conceptualization (e.g., Zimmerman 2007), we regard scientific reasoning as intentional knowledge seeking (Kuhn 2010) involving the generation, testing, and evaluation of hypotheses and theories, and reflecting on this process (e.g., Bullock et al. 2009). The resulting wide range of scientific reasoning tasks includes those related to experimentation strategies (e.g., control of variables [COV]), data interpretation and the evaluation of evidence (e.g., Kuhn et al. 1988), and the process of scientific knowledge construction (i.e., understanding the nature of science [NOS]). Despite the apparent variety of tasks, it is commonly assumed that understanding the hypothesis-evidence relation is fundamental to these diverse scientific reasoning tasks (Kuhn 2010; Zimmerman 2007); this assertion however has not been tested empirically.

3.2 Development of Our Inventory

Our inventory was constructed in three project phases (see Fig. 3.1). Based on an extensive literature review of interview-based and experimental studies, Phase 1 developed a series of paper-and-pencil tasks (see e.g., Koerber et al. 2011) that could be used in whole-class testing. In Phase 1a, we conducted several studies,

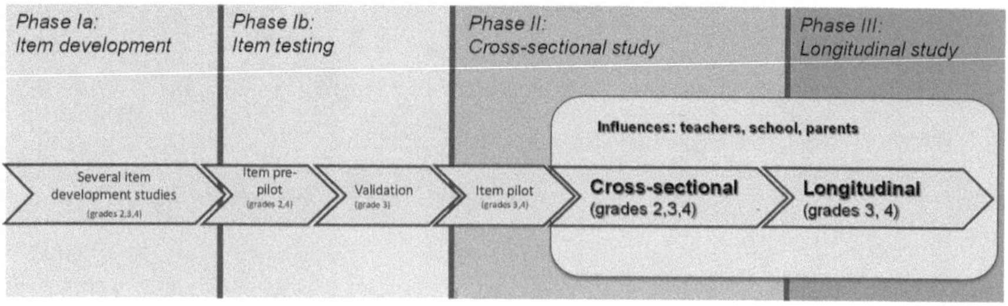

Fig. 3.1 Phases of the project Science-P

using multiple-choice (MC), forced-choice (FC), multiple-select (MS), and short open-answer tasks in one-on-one sessions. Each closed response format entailed answer options that corresponded to two or three hierarchical levels of competence, as postulated by the model (for an example of an MS task, see Fig. 3.2 from Koerber et al. 2015b). After designing and iteratively refining the tasks in several small studies, the first large-scale rotated-design study, involving 379 second and fourth

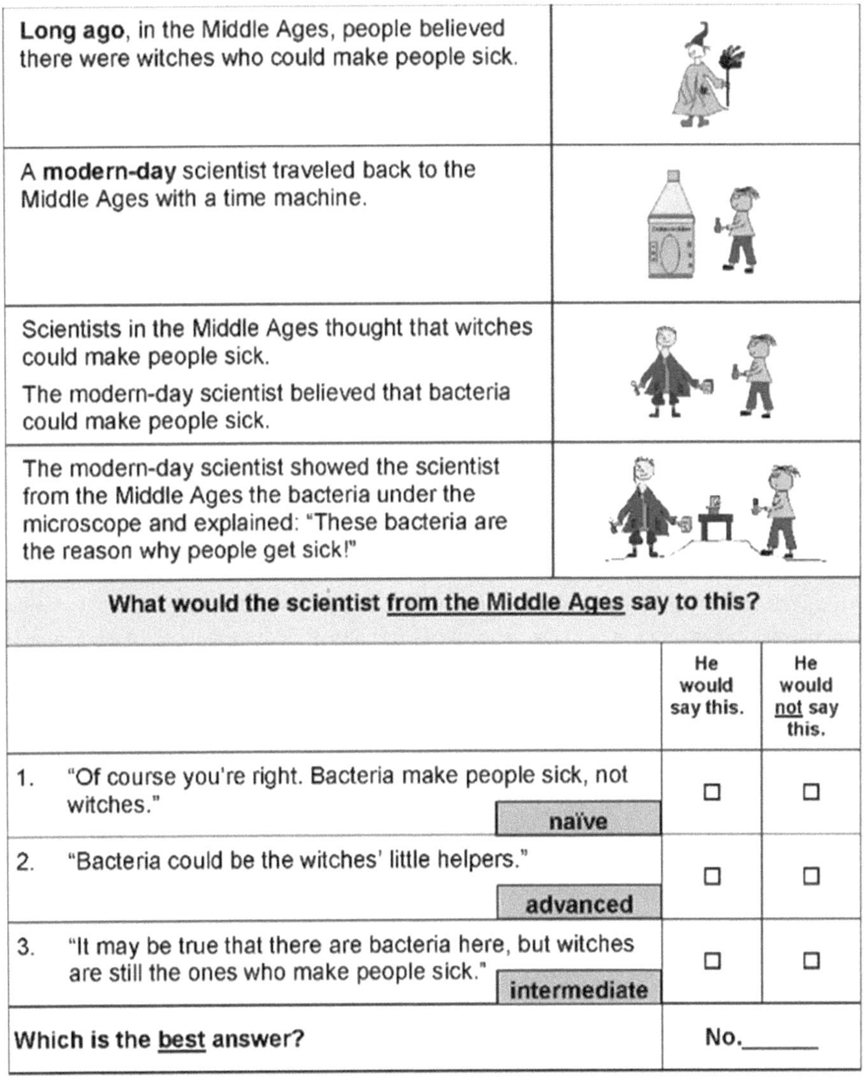

Long ago, in the Middle Ages, people believed there were witches who could make people sick.

A **modern-day** scientist traveled back to the Middle Ages with a time machine.

Scientists in the Middle Ages thought that witches could make people sick.
The modern-day scientist believed that bacteria could make people sick.

The modern-day scientist showed the scientist from the Middle Ages the bacteria under the microscope and explained: "These bacteria are the reason why people get sick!"

What would the scientist from the Middle Ages say to this?

		He would say this.	He would not say this.
1.	"Of course you're right. Bacteria make people sick, not witches." naïve	☐	☐
2.	"Bacteria could be the witches' little helpers." advanced	☐	☐
3.	"It may be true that there are bacteria here, but witches are still the ones who make people sick." intermediate	☐	☐
	Which is the best answer?	No.______	

Fig. 3.2 Example of an item assessing NOS (understanding theories) (Reprinted from Koerber et al. (2015b) with permission from Wiley & Sons. (C) The British Psychological Society)

graders, was conducted in order to test the fit of tasks ($N = 47$) and the applicability of the inventory in whole-class testing procedures (item pre-pilot). Phase 1b finished with a validation study of representative items of the inventory (see Kropf 2010, and below, Sect. 3.3). After constant improvement and extension of the item pool, Phase 2 comprised a large item pilot study involving 996 third and fourth graders. Based on item fits, biserial correlations, difficulty, and discrimination, 13 out of 83 tasks were excluded. The resulting item pool formed the basis for the further optimization and selection of tasks for the cross-sectional study (see below, Sect. 3.4), which also took place in Phase 2 and which tested more than 1500 second, third, and fourth graders. Phase 3 of the project was a longitudinal study (with two measurement series to date) that began with testing more than 1500 third graders (see below, Sect. 3.5).

Taking into account the diverse aspects of scientific reasoning, we aimed to provide a comprehensive inventory of scientific reasoning competence comprising five components: (1) a knowledge of experimentation strategies (e.g., the COV strategy), (2) an understanding of conclusive experimental designs for hypothesis testing, and (3) the ability to test hypotheses by interpreting data and evidence, and—on a more general level—to assess the understanding of NOS concerning (4) the goals of science and (5) how sociocultural frameworks influence theory development.

3.3 Convergent Validity of Paper-and-Pencil Inventory and Interviews

Whether the designed tasks adequately captured children's scientific reasoning competence was tested in a validation study comparing performance in a set of tasks with performance in an established interview (cf. Carey et al. 1989). The evidence for convergent validity is crucial, since a potential criticism of the use of paper-and-pencil tests is that they increase the probability of responding correctly by guessing (Lederman 2007). Indeed, paper-and-pencil tests might lead to arbitrary responses, and significant relations between children's answers in interviews and parallel MC tests are not always found. Whereas a slightly better performance might be expected in paper-and-pencil tests rather than interviews, due to the lower cognitive and language demands in the former, interindividual differences should be stable across the two methods when testing convergent validity. Because standardized interviews do not exist for all aspects of scientific reasoning, we exemplarily chose understanding NOS to establish the instrument's validity (see also Kropf 2010 for a related analysis of the instruments' validity, incorporating the component experimentation strategies).

3.3.1 *Method*

3.3.1.1 Participants

The participants comprised 23 third graders (*M* = 8.10 years, *SD* = 5 months) recruited from two primary schools in a rural part of Germany.

3.3.1.2 Material

Interview The Nature of Science Interview (NOSI; Carey et al. 1989; Sodian et al. 2002) focuses on the hypothesis-evidence relation: that is, the metaconceptual understanding of ideas (i.e., hypotheses, theories) underlying scientific activities and their differentiation from evidence. NOSI consists of several questions investigating children's understanding of science in general (e.g., "What do you think science is all about?") and of its central elements (e.g., ideas, hypotheses, experiments) as well as their relations (e.g., "What happens when scientists are testing their ideas, and obtain a different result from the one they expected?"). Based on prior research (Kropf 2010), the present study used a reduced version of NOSI, (nine of the 18 questions).

A three-level coding scheme was adapted from Carey et al. (1989, see also Bullock et al. 2009; Sodian et al. 2006) and further differentiated into the lowest level due to the youth of our participants and our focus on beginning abilities. The answers at Level 0 (the lowest naïve level, Level 1a, according to Sodian et al.) reflect a naïve understanding in which science is understood in terms of activities and without reference to ideas as formative instances of knowledge (e.g., "the goal of science is to make things work"). At Level 0.3, again a naïve level (Level 1b according to Sodian et al.), children regard science as information-seeking, but do not yet display an understanding of the hypothesis-evidence relation. Answers at Level 1 (the intermediate level) reflect a basic but not yet elaborated understanding of the differentiation between ideas and activities (e.g., "scientists consider things and think about why things are as they are; then they do research, perhaps they read what others have done, and then they probably ask a question why something is as it is, and they just do science"). Answers at Level 2 (the scientifically advanced level) indicate a beginning understanding of the relations between theories, hypotheses, and experiments, sometimes including an implicit notion of the role of a theoretical framework (e.g., "scientists have a certain belief or hypothesis, and then they try to confirm it by doing experiments or tests").

Paper-and-Pencil Tasks This study used five paper-and-pencil tasks presented in the format of FC, MC, or MS questions.

Control Variables Textual understanding was assessed using the ELFE 1–6 German reading proficiency test (Lenhard and Schneider 2006). Intelligence was assessed using the working-memory, logical-reasoning, and processing-speed subtests of HAWIK-IV, which is the German version of the WISC intelligence test (Petermann and Petermann 2008).

3.3.1.3 Procedure

Each child was tested twice. Half of the participants received the paper-and-pencil tasks first (whole-class testing) followed by the individual interview, with the order reversed for the other half. In the whole-group session, each child completed an individual test booklet under step-by-step guidance from an administrator using a PowerPoint presentation. Furthermore, a test assistant helped in the answering of comprehension questions.

3.3.2 *Results*

3.3.2.1 Pre-analyses

Pre-analyses revealed no significant effect either of order of presentation (interviews before paper-and-pencil tasks or vice versa), $F(1, 21) = 0.22$, *ns*, for the paper-and-pencil test, $F(1, 21) = 0.07$, *ns*, for the interview, or of gender, $F(1, 21) = 0.60$, *ns* and $F(1, 21) = 0.15$, *ns*.

3.3.2.2 Convergent Validity

We found a significant correlation between the scores for the paper-and-pencil test and NOSI ($r = .78$, $p < .01$). Whereas NOSI especially differentiated lower competencies (i.e., naïve conceptions at Level 0 or 0.3), the spread in the paper-and-pencil test was much larger (see Fig. 3.3). When partialing out intelligence and reading ability, the correlation between scores for NOSI and the paper-and-pencil test remained strong ($p_r = .70$, $p < .01$; partial correlation).

We also found that the level of difficulty differed significantly between NOSI and the paper-and-pencil test, in that children showed a significantly lower score in NOSI ($M = 0.22$, $SD = 0.14$) than in the paper-and-pencil test ($M = 0.95$, $SD = 0.43$; $t(22) = 10.20$, $p < .001$).

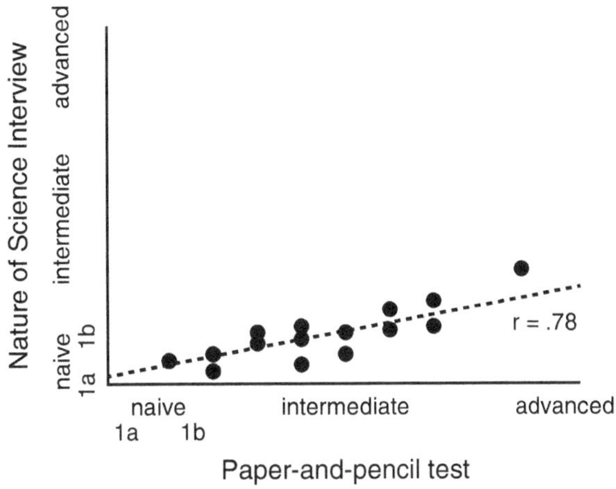

Fig. 3.3 NOS interview and paper-and-pencil test; Data visualizing their relation

3.3.3 Discussion

This study aimed to test the validity of paper-and-pencil tasks. The strong correlation between the scores for the paper-and-pencil test and for NOSI supports our hypothesis that children seriously reflected on the choice of answers before selecting the best one, rather than simply guessing.

The performance was lower when interview questions had to be answered, but even in this format there was individual variation between two naïve levels of understanding, which was correlated with the level of understanding attained in the paper-and-pencil test. Our finding that children perform better in the paper-and-pencil test than in NOSI is consistent with previous research (e.g., Bullock et al. 2009; Pollmeier et al. 2011). Two factors facilitating children's performance might account for this finding: (1) the questions included in NOSI were embedded in our paper-and-pencil test in a contextual format, and (2) presenting children with a choice of answers and asking them to select the best one (MC tasks), or alternatively requiring them to reflect on each proposition (at different levels) and to accept or reject it (MS tasks), helped them to structure their ideas and elicited answers that they might not have given had they been required to answer spontaneously. We consider this format a suitable framework for helping them to express their ideas and to compensate for their restricted eloquence. Primary-school children are not yet used to verbally reflecting on certain issues, and so a paper-and-pencil test might be more suitable than an interview for research studies aiming at detecting basic competence.

3.4 Scientific Reasoning: Development from Grades 2 to 4

After constructing a reliable scale and establishing its validity, we used the instrument (1) to systematically investigate the development of scientific reasoning from Grades 2 to 4, and (2) to investigate whether components of scientific reasoning are conceptually connected (for a more detailed description see Koerber et al. 2015a; Mayer 2012; Mayer et al. 2014).

In a rotated design, we presented more than 1500 children from Grades 2 to 4 with 66 paper-and-pencil tasks comprising several components of scientific reasoning. The children were also presented with an intelligence test (CFT) and a test of text comprehension (see Sect. 3.2). Furthermore, the parents completed a questionnaire about their socioeducational status (SES).

A unidimensional Rasch model revealed a good fit to our data, with only six items being excluded due to undesirable item fit statistics. The reliability was found to be good (EAP/PV = .68). Several multidimensional model comparisons supported the divergent validity of scientific reasoning, intelligence, problem-solving, and textual understanding, although these constructs are closely related to scientific reasoning, as indicated by strong correlations (between .63 and .74). Furthermore, different components of scientific reasoning (see Sect. 3.2) could be scaled together, indicating that they constituted a unitary construct. The results for the entire sample were the same as those for each grade separately. Identifying scientific reasoning as a unitary construct is especially impressive, given that the children were only second graders and that we used a comprehensive test with tasks involving different scientific-reasoning components in a single test.

Significant development was observed from Grades 2 to 3 and from Grades 3 to 4: this was independent of intelligence, textual understanding, and parental educational level. Previous studies of scientific reasoning in primary schools have employed single tasks from only one or two scientific-reasoning components, and the present study is the first to trace the development of scientific reasoning across different components using multiple tasks. The use of this inventory revealed development from Grades 2 to 4, despite scientific-reasoning competence not being explicitly and continuously addressed in the curricula.

Similarly to intelligence and textual understanding, the parental educational level and the time of schooling significantly impacted the children's scientific reasoning competence. However, since the obtained data are purely correlational, the direction and possible causation of these variables should be addressed in a future longitudinal study.

3.5 Competence-Structure Model of Scientific Reasoning: Hierarchical Levels of Competence

A central aim of the Science-P project was to develop and empirically test a competence-structure model. More specifically, our model is based on accounts of scientific reasoning that posit distinct hierarchical levels of naïve and intermediate understanding that children pass through before developing more advanced conceptions of science and the scientific method (Carey et al. 1989). Up to this point, testing such models has posed methodological difficulties, since these levels had not been implemented a priori in the tasks used in any previous large-scale study.

This was the first longitudinal study to test the competence structure described herein. In our refined inventory, the answer options for each item included all three hierarchical levels (naïve, intermediate, advanced), and the children were asked to consider each answer option individually (MS format) and also to choose the best answer option (MC format). From the resulting eight possible patterns of rejection and acceptance of each of the three answer options, the lowest level answer was identified as the final level. That is, an answer was coded as being naïve whenever the child endorsed a naïve level (regardless of the other answer options) and performance was coded as advanced only when the child accepted the advanced answer option and simultaneously refuted the naïve and intermediate options. An intermediate score was given in the case of acceptance of the intermediate and rejection of the naïve option, regardless of the acceptance of the advanced option. This form of MS assessment reduces the probability of correctly answering the items by guessing, which is a known problem of MC assessment.

The first measurement series of the longitudinal study (see Osterhaus et al. 2013) included a sample of more than 1300 third graders—a different sample from that in the cross-sectional study (reported in Sect. 3.3)—who answered 23 MS tasks on scientific reasoning (see Fig. 3.2). Again, intelligence and textual understanding were assessed.

A partial-credit model revealed a good fit to the data, supporting the hypothesized competence-structure model, which postulated that the three distinct levels represent the theorized hierarchical difficulties. For all but eight tasks, this assumption was supported by three indicators: (1) higher point-biserial correlations for higher categories (e.g., intermediate and advanced conceptions), (2) increasing ability level per category (naïve < intermediate < advanced conception), and (3) ordered delta parameters. This instrument, which includes hierarchical levels, exhibited acceptable reliability, and its divergent validity with respect to intelligence and textual understanding confirmed the results of the cross-sectional study presented in Sect. 3.3. The items differentiated sufficiently between children, although changing the item format to an MS format, and the stricter coding, made the items generally more difficult than in the cross-sectional study.

Together, these results confirm the validity of our competence-structure model, which posits three hierarchical levels. Therefore, we have succeeded in combining the methodological scrutiny of competence modeling with developmental accounts of the conceptual development of scientific reasoning (Carey et al. 1989).

3.6 Outlook

Future studies will include the results of the second measurement series, and will use multilevel analyses and structural models to determine competence gains and conceptual development, taking into account multiple factors of different levels of influence (e.g., intelligence, socio-economic status, teacher competence). Analyses of the developmental paths with respect to the hierarchical levels are currently underway.

An important future next step is to investigate the assumed mutual influence of content-specific science understanding (Pollmeier et al. 2017, in this volume) and scientific reasoning in development. The cross-sectional study of Pollmeier et al. found a close relation between both dimensions, and the results obtained in the present longitudinal study will facilitate identifying the direction of the influences.

In summary, the Science-P project contributes to our understanding of the relation between scientific reasoning and content-specific science understanding and its development in primary school. In addition, it has produced a competence-structure model of scientific reasoning in primary school and shed light on many of the important factors influencing the development of scientific reasoning, including intelligence, parental educational level, and school.

Acknowledgments The preparation of this paper was supported by grants to Susanne Koerber (KO 2276/4-3), Beate Sodian (SO 213/29-1/2); and Knut Schwippert (SCHW890/3-1/3) from the German Research Foundation (DFG) in the Priority Program "Competence Models for Assessing Individual Learning Outcomes and Evaluating Educational Processes" (SPP 1293).

References

Bullock, M., Sodian, B., & Koerber, S. (2009). Doing experiments and understanding science: Development of scientific reasoning from childhood to adulthood. In W. Schneider & M. Bullock (Eds.), *Human development from early childhood to early adulthood. Findings from the Munich Longitudinal Study* (pp. 173–197). Mahwah: Erlbaum.

Carey, S., Evans, R., Honda, M., Jay, E., & Unger, C. (1989). An experiment is when you try it and see if it works. A study of junior high school students' understanding of the construction of scientific knowledge. *International Journal of Science Education, 11*, 514–529.

Koerber, S., Sodian, B., Thoermer, C., & Nett, U. (2005). Scientific reasoning in young children: Preschoolers' ability to evaluate covariation evidence. *Swiss Journal of Psychology, 64*, 141–152. doi:10.1024/1421-0185.64.3.141.

Koerber, S., Sodian, B., Kropf, N., Mayer, D., & Schwippert, K. (2011). Die Entwicklung des wissenschaftlichen Denkens im Grundschulalter: Theorieverständnis, Experimentierstrategien, Dateninterpretation [The development of scientific reasoning in elementary school: Understanding theories, experimentation strategies, and data interpretation]. *Zeitschrift für Entwicklungspsychologie und Pädagogische Psychologie, 43*, 16–21. doi:10.1026/0049-8637/a000027.

Koerber, S., Mayer, D., Osterhaus, C., Schwippert, K., & Sodian, B. (2015a). The development of scientific thinking in elementary school: A comprehensive inventory. *Child Development, 86*, 327–336. doi:10.1111/cdev.12298.

Koerber, S., Osterhaus, C., & Sodian, B. (2015b). Testing primary-school children's understanding of the nature of science. *British Journal of Developmental Psychology, 33*, 57–72. doi:10.1111/bjdp.12067.

Kropf, N. (2010). *Entwicklung und Analyse von Messinstrumenten zur Erfassung des wissenschaftlichen Denkens im Grundschulalter* [Development and analysis of instruments for the measurement of scientific reasoning in elementary school] (Unpublished doctoral dissertation). LMU München, München.

Kuhn, D. (2010). What is scientific thinking and how does it develop? In U. Goswami (Ed.), *Handbook of childhood cognitive development* (2nd ed., pp. 472–523). Oxford: Blackwell.

Kuhn, D., Amsel, E., & O'Loughlin, M. (1988). *The development of scientific thinking skills*. San Diego: Academic Press.

Lederman, N. G. (2007). Nature of Science: Past, present, and future. In S. K. Abell & N. G. Lederman (Eds.), *Handbook of research on science education* (pp. 831–880). Mahwah: Erlbaum.

Lenhard, W., & Schneider, W. (2006). *ELFE 1–6. Ein Leseverständnistest für Erst- bis Sechstklässler* [ELFE 1–6. A reading proficiency test for children in Grades 1–6]. Göttingen: Hogrefe.

Mayer, D. (2012). *Die Modellierung des wissenschaftlichen Denkens im Grundschulalter: Zusammenhänge zu kognitiven Fähigkeiten und motivationalen Orientierungen* [Modeling scientific reasoning in elementary school: Relations with cognitive abilities and motivational orientations]. Doctoral dissertation. Retrieved from http://edoc.ub.uni-muenchen.de/14497/

Mayer, D., Sodian, B., Koerber, S., & Schwippert, K. (2014). Scientific reasoning in elementary school children: Assessment and relations with cognitive abilities. *Learning and Instruction, 29*, 43–55. doi:10.1016/j.learninstruc.2013.07.005.

Osterhaus, C., Koerber, S., Mayer, D., Schwippert, K., Sodian, B. (2013, August). *Scientific reasoning: Modelling hierarchical levels of understanding*. Poster presented at the 15th biennial EARLI conference, München.

Petermann, F., & Petermann, U. (Eds.). (2008). *Hamburg-Wechsler-Intelligenztest für Kinder IV (HAWIK-IV)* [Hamburg-Wechsler intelligence test for children IV (HAWIK IV)]. Bern: Huber.

Pollmeier, J., Möller, K., Hardy, I., & Koerber, S. (2011). Naturwissenschaftliche Lernstände im Grundschulalter mit schriftlichen Aufgaben valide erfassen [Do paper-and-pencil tasks validly assess elementary-school children's knowledge of natural sciences]? *Zeitschrift für Pädagogik, 6*, 834–853. doi:10.3262/ZP1106834.

Pollmeier, J., Troebst, S., Hardy, I., Moeller, K., Kleickmann, T., Jurecka, A., & Schwippert, K. (2017). Science-P I: Modeling conceptual understanding in primary school. In D. Leutner, J. Fleischer, J. Grünkorn, & E. Klieme (Eds.), *Competence assessment in education: Research, models and instruments* (pp. 9–17). Berlin: Springer.

Sodian, B., Thoermer, C., Kircher, E., Grygier, P., Günther, J. (2002). Vermittlung von Wissenschaftsverständnis in der Grundschule [Teaching the nature of science in elementary school]. *Zeitschrift für Pädagogik*, Beiheft *45*, 192–206.

Sodian, B., Thoermer, C., Grygier, P., Wang, W., Vogt, N., Kropf, N. (2006). *Coding scheme to the nature of science interview (BIQUA NOS)*. Unpublished paper, LMU München, München.

Zimmerman, C. (2007). The development of scientific thinking skills in elementary and middle school. *Developmental Review, 27*, 172–223. doi:10.1016/j.dr.2006.12.001.

Chapter 4
The Heidelberg Inventory of Geographic System Competency Model

Kathrin Viehrig, Alexander Siegmund, Joachim Funke, Sascha Wüstenberg, and Samuel Greiff

Abstract The concept "system" is fundamental to many disciplines. It has an especially prominent place in geography education, in which additionally, the spatial perspective is central. Empirically validated competency models dealing specifically with geographic systems—as well as adequate measurement instruments—are still lacking. Therefore, based on the theoretically-guided development of a Geographic System Competency (GSC) model, the aim was to build and evaluate such a measurement instrument, with the help of probabilistic measurement models. The competency model had three dimensions: (1) "comprehend and analyze systems", (2) "act towards systems" and (3) "spatial thinking", whereby dimension (2) was changed to "evaluating possibilities to act towards systems" after a thinking-aloud study. A Cognitive Lab (CogLab) and two quantitative studies (Q1 n = 110, Q2 n = 324) showed divergent results. Dimension (2) could not be identified in both quantitative studies. Whereas Dimensions (1) and (3) constituted separate dimensions in Q1, in Q2 the two-dimensional model did not fit significantly better than the one-dimensional model. Besides showing the close relationship between spatial and systemic thinking in geographic contexts, which are thus both needed in modeling GSC, the project highlights the need for more research in this central area of geography education.

K. Viehrig (✉)
School of Education, University of Applied Sciences and Arts Northwestern Switzerland, Windisch, Switzerland
e-mail: kathrin.viehrig@fhnw.ch

A. Siegmund
Heidelberg University of Education, Heidelberg, Germany
e-mail: siegmund@ph-heidelberg.de

J. Funke
Heidelberg University, Heidelberg, Germany
e-mail: funke@uni-hd.de

S. Wüstenberg • S. Greiff
University of Luxembourg, Esch-sur-Alzette, Luxembourg
e-mail: sascha.wuestenberg@uni.lu; samuel.greiff@uni.lu

D. Leutner et al. (eds.), *Competence Assessment in Education*, Methodology of Educational Measurement and Assessment, DOI 10.1007/978-3-319-50030-0_4

Keywords Systems thinking • Spatial thinking • Competence model • University students • Geography

4.1 The Role of Geographic System Competency in Geography Education

Geography often deals with complex human-environment systems that are seen as important to society and business. Whether it is a matter of extreme weather events, transformations in the energy sector or resource conflicts, learning to understand (geographic) systems has been a central part of the overall objective of geographic education for decades (e.g., DGfG 2010; Köck 1993).

Because the concept "system" is regarded as one of the most important cognitive constructs of science (e.g., Klaus 1985; Smithson et al. 2002), research looking at how learners and/or experts understand systems is undertaken in different subjects (e.g., physics: Bell 2004; mathematics: Ossimitz 2000; biology: Sommer 2005; economics: Sweeney and Sterman 2000), in interdisciplinary areas such as education for sustainable development (e.g., Rieß and Mischo 2008) and in the area of complex problem solving (e.g., Funke 1990). Thus, the research spans a wide age range from kindergarten to adults/university.

Geographic inquiry deals with "[…] the whys of where […]" (Kerski 2013, 11). Consequently, to understand geographic systems, both systemic (why) and spatial thinking skills (where) seem necessary.

In general, systemic and spatial thinking would appear to be researched mostly independently of each other. Moreover, despite their longstanding importance in the German geography education discourse, the specific geographic competencies necessary to understand *geographic* systems seem not to have been empirically identified as yet, especially with regard to the relationship of systemic and spatial thinking. Additionally, there seem to be only few validated, psychometrically and geographically adequate, assessment instruments.

Consequently, in recent years, two DFG-funded projects have started to test competency models empirically for geographic system competency. The model by Rempfler and Uphues (see e.g., 2010, 2011, 2012) is based on a socio-ecological approach and focuses on systemic thinking. In contrast, the Heidelberg Inventory of Geographic System Competency (HEIGIS) model explicitly includes both systemic and spatial thinking (Table 4.1).

Hence, in line with the general competency definition in the Priority Program (SPP 1293), and based on existing works (see overview in Viehrig et al. 2011; Viehrig et al. 2012), geographic system competency (GSC) has been defined as "[…] the cognitive achievement dispositions […] that are necessary to analyze, comprehend geographic systems in specific contexts and act adequately towards them" (Viehrig et al. 2011, p. 50, translated).

Table 4.1 Original HEIGIS model[a]

	Dimension 1: Comprehend and analyze systems	Dimension 2: Act towards systems	Dimension 3: Spatial thinking
Level 3	Identification and understanding of the complex network of relationships	Also take into account side effects and autoregressive processes	Use several spatial thinking skills in a structured way
Level 2	Identify and understand relationships between the system elements	Take into account multiple effects	Use several spatial thinking skills in an unstructured way
Level 1	Identify and understand system elements	Take into account main effects	Use only one spatial thinking skill in an unstructured way

Largely based on Ben-Zvi Assaraf and Orion (2005), Gersmehl and Gersmehl (2006), Greiff and Funke (2009), and Hammann et al. (2008)
[a]Viehrig et al. (2011, p. 51, translated)

The original model (Table 4.1) comprised three dimensions: *comprehend and analyze systems*, *act towards systems* and *spatial thinking*, with differentiation between Dimensions 1 and 2 based both on geographic education theory (e.g., Köck 1993, p. 18, translated, speaks of "thinking and acting in geo-ecosystems") and empirical results in problem solving (e.g., Greiff 2010). An overview of the basis for development can be found, for example, in Viehrig et al. (2011) and Viehrig et al. (2012). The spatial thinking skills in Dimension 3 refer to those identified by Gersmehl and Gersmehl (2006), namely: "Defining a Location […]" (p. 12), "Describing Conditions […]" (p. 13), "Tracing Spatial Connections […]" (p. 14), "Making a Spatial Comparison […]" (p. 14), "Inferring a Spatial Aura […]" (p. 15), "Delimiting a Region […]" (p. 15), "Fitting a Place into a Spatial Hierarchy […]" (p. 16), "Graphing a Spatial Transition […]" (p. 17), "Identifying a Spatial Analog […]" (p. 18), "Discerning Spatial Patterns […]" (p. 19) and "Assessing a Spatial Association […]" (p. 20) (partly bold-enhanced in the original).

To test the HEIGIS model empirically, three different studies were conducted. The studies were targeted at university students in subjects including geography, geography education and other subjects, such as psychology. However, the first one in particular was constructed with thought to its applicability to high school in mind.

4.2 Study Overview

The three studies conducted within the project (2009–2011) consisted of a video-graphed thinking-aloud cognitive lab study (CogLab) split into two rounds, and two quantitative studies (labeled Q1 and Q2). An overview over the samples used for analysis can be seen in Table 4.2.

The CogLab aimed at further developing the competency model as well as exploring possible similarities in domain-general problem solving. The CogLab

Table 4.2 Sample overview used for analysis[a]

	CogLab Round 1 & 2	Q1	Q2
n	10	110 (questionnaire)	324
		67 (MicroDYN)	
Students	100 %	98.2 %	96.6 %
Type of students	Pre-service teacher geography 90.0 %	Psychology 33.6 %	psychology 17.9 %
	Pre-service teacher other 10.0 %	Pre-service teacher geography 60.9 %	Pre-service teacher geography 37.0 %
		Geography 2.7 %	Geography 34.9 %
		Other 0.9 %	Other geo-sciences 4.9 %
			Pre-service teacher other 0.6 %
			Other 1.2 %
Male	50.0 %	32.7 % (1 missing)	39.2 %
M age (*SD*)	23.8 (2.3)	23.2 (7.2) (1 missing)	23.9 (6.1)
M GPA		2.1 (0.8) (8 missing)	2.3 (0.7)
GPA better than 2.5		55.5 % (8 missing)	53.4 %

GPA grade point average (school leaving certificate, with 1.0 considered the best and 4.0 considered passed)

[a]The description for Q1 refers to the 110 participants of the questionnaire

was conducted in two rounds. The first round ($n = 5$) used fictitious examples, while the second round ($n = 5$) used real world examples. Moreover, the two rounds differed in the items used.

Q1 aimed at a first quantitative exploration of the modified model and the relationship between GSC and problem solving. Thus, the study consisted of two parts: a questionnaire containing background variables, and including the geographic system competency items, and a MicroDYN to measure problem solving (for an introduction to the MicroDYN testing environment see the chapter by Funke and Greiff (2017, in this volume)). The GSC used real world examples. In Q1, 137 participants filled out the questionnaire, of which 110 were included in the analysis because they filled out at least one of the GSC items (only 81 returned complete questionnaires). In the MicroDYN part, there were 81 participants, of which 67 could be included in the analysis. The rest were excluded either because data was not saved properly or, for more than 25 % of the items, questions were not answered.

Q2 aimed at further exploring the structure of GSC, with the help of a revised questionnaire and a larger sample. In Q2, there were over 600 participants, of which 324 were included in the analysis. Excluded participants included those who returned incomplete answers, and those reporting a below-B1[1] language level in German.

[1]Using a simplified self-report scale (A1 to C2 plus an option for native speaker), based on the "Common European Framework of Reference for Languages" (CEFR, see e.g. Council of Europe 2001)

This chapter focuses on the results related to the structure of GSC. The relationship of achievement to various variables included in the studies will be reported elsewhere.

4.3 CogLabs

4.3.1 Description of the Measurement Instruments

The CogLabs contained different item formats, especially MicroDYN, concept maps and short answer tasks in the first round, and MicroDYN, multiple-choice and "add to a started concept map" tasks in the second round (see details in Viehrig et al. 2011; Viehrig et al. 2012). Based on the national educational standards (DGfG 2010), items were generated in three areas, that is: physical and human geography, and human-environment interactions.

Concept maps are frequently used to measure domain-specific systemic thinking, both in the geo-sciences (e.g., Ben-Zvi Assaraf and Orion 2005) and in other subjects, such as biology (e.g., Sommer 2005). Short answer questions are often used in educational courses and have also been used in systemic thinking research (e.g., Sommer 2005). MicroDYN items have been used to measure problem solving and have shown good psychometric properties. They consist of minimally complex systems, with students first having three minutes to find out the structure of the system and then one and a half minutes to achieve a specified aim by manipulating system variables (e.g., Greiff 2010). A brief discussion of the advantages and disadvantages of some item formats can be found, for example, in Viehrig et al. (2011). In both rounds the systems used were very simple, in order to fit with the minimally complex structure of MicroDYN.

The first CogLab round started with a general introduction by the respective interviewer, the signing of a consent form and a short questionnaire collecting basic demographic data. Then the measurement instrument proper began with an example and explanation of the MicroDYN format for the students to explore. Afterwards, the students had to respond to six MicroDYN items, to measure their problem solving skills. This part was followed by three MicroDYN items using geographic contexts to measure Dimension 1 (part: model building) and Dimension 2 (part: prognosis). The geographic system competency and the problem solving items had identical structures. The second part started with an example and explanation of CMapTools, software that can be used to create concept maps (available from http://cmap.ihmc.us/). The three tasks created consisted of a short informational text, a Dimension 1 item, which asked students to create a concept map, and a short answer item, approximating Dimension 2. This was followed by three tasks to measure Dimension 3. Students were presented with a number of simple thematic maps and had to use a concept map to describe their answers to a spatial question. Besides being asked to think aloud while responding to the items, there were specific questions, for example regarding their problems with a task, or what procedure they used to solve the task during the CogLab. Furthermore, there were some general questions after all tasks were completed: for example, what kind of similarities and differences they noticed in their thinking processes, between explicitly spatial and not explicitly spatial tasks. At the end, formalities regarding the participant's payment were taken care of. Sample items can be seen in Fig. 4.1.

The second CogLab round also started with a general introduction by the respective interviewer, the signing of a consent form and a short questionnaire collecting some basic demographic data. Afterwards, after a brief introduction, there were three tasks, with three items each for Dimension 1. After reading an informational text, the students had to answer two multiple-choice tasks (one correct answer) and

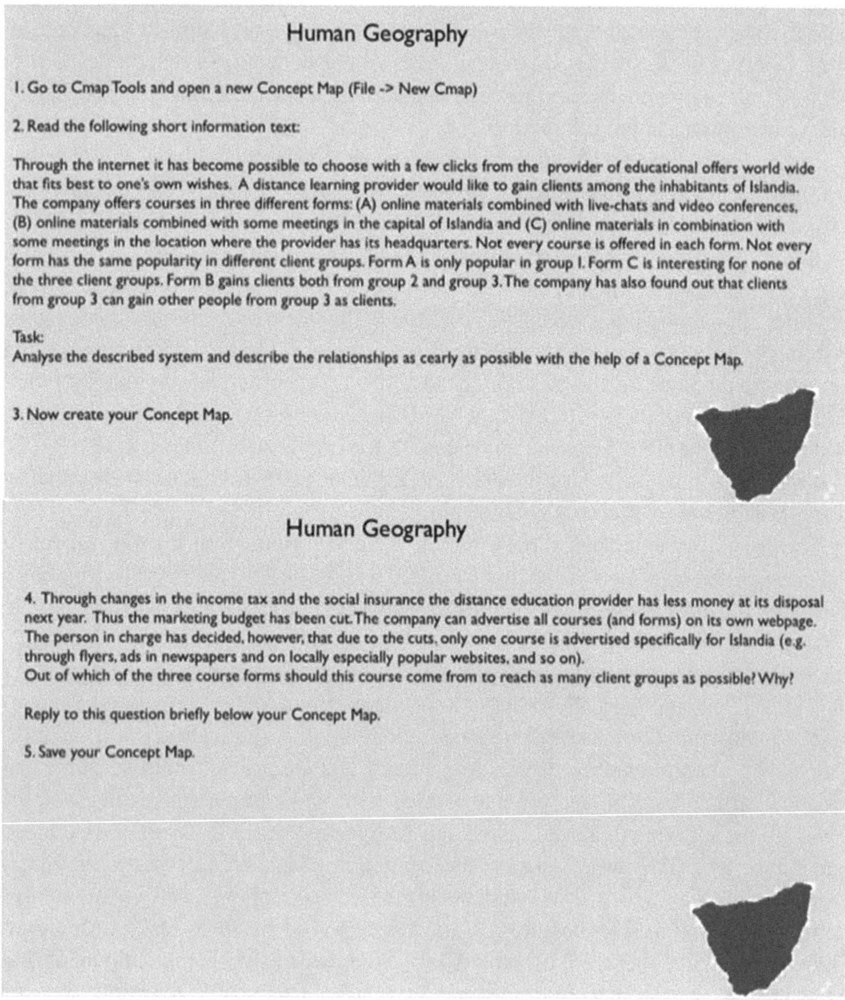

Fig. 4.1 Sample items from the CogLab Round 1: Concept map and short answer (Dimensions 1 and 2, translated)

Climate

Galveston is located on the coast of the Gulf of Mexico, in the South of the USA, in Texas.
In the media a lot is discussed about the global warming and its consequences. One possible consequence is the rise of the sea level[1].
Several factors can contribute to the rise of the sea level. This includes e.g. the expansion of the seawater through an increase in water temperature. Also the melting of the glaciers and ice caps on land can contribute to sea level rise.

Item 3: Complete the following graphic based on the text. Use only one of the following phrases per blank. For that write the suitable number in the blank.
(1) melting of ice on the land (e.g. glacier); (2) melting of ice bergs that swim on the water; (3) contributes to the rise of; (4) contributes to the lowering of the; (5) Gulf of Mexico Golf; (6) expansion of the seawater at warmer water temperature; (7) does not contribute to the rise of

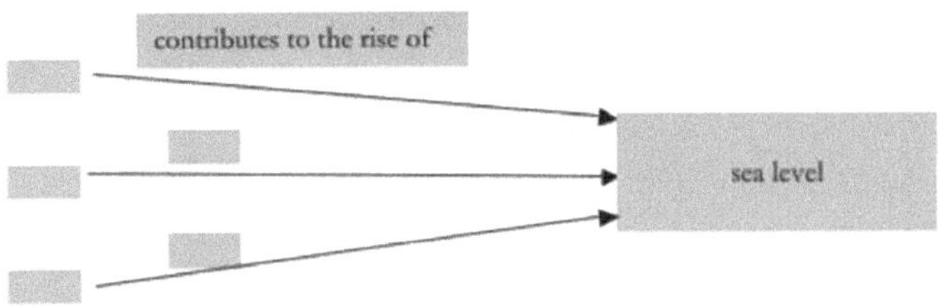

Fig. 4.2 Sample item from the CogLab Round 2: Item group stem and "add to a started concept map " task (Dimension 1, translated)

one "add to a started concept map" task (concepts, relationship descriptions and structure provided). Then came the MicroDYN part, consisting of three geographic items to measure Dimensions 1 (part: model building) and 2 (part: prognosis). This was followed by three tasks, each consisting of a short informational text and two maps with three multiple-choice items (one correct answer), to measure the students' spatial thinking skills. Because these items dealt with real-world examples, the students had to locate 19 countries on a world map and indicate that two were not a country, as a basic indicator of geographic pre-knowledge (spatial framework of reference). The last part consisted of four MicroDYN items to measure problem solving. The CogLab ended with some general questions and again, taking care of the formalities. A sample item can be seen in Fig. 4.2.

4.3.2 *Selected Results*

In the first CogLab, fictitious places were used as examples to reduce the influence of pre-acquaintance with a specific location (similar to e.g., Ossimitz 1996). In the second round, real places were used as examples. In summary, the CogLabs indicated a better suitability of real world examples to assess GSC, in terms of item generation and processing. Moreover, some of the participants emphasized the importance of the authenticity/real world relevance of the tasks. Participants also

Table 4.3 HEIGIS model after the CogLabs (translated)

	Dimension 1: Comprehend and analyze systems	Dimension 2: Evaluate possibilities to act towards systems	Dimension 3: Spatial thinking
Level 3	Identification and understanding of the complex network of relationships	Also take into account side effects and autoregressive processes	Can use 8 or more spatial thinking skills
Level 2	Identify and understand relationships between the system elements	Take into account multiple effects	Can use 6 or 7 spatial thinking skills
Level 1	Identify and understand system elements	Take into account main effects	Can use up to 5 spatial thinking skills

Largely based on Ben-Zvi Assaraf and Orion (2005), Gersmehl and Gersmehl (2006), Greiff and Funke (2009), and CogLab results

indicated, however, that the country example used in a task makes a difference, even if the essential information is given.

In general, the CogLabs hinted at the separability of Dimensions 1 and 3. However, the CogLabs resulted in two key changes to the competency model (see Table 4.3 and Viehrig et al. 2012). Firstly, the CogLabs indicated that MicroDYN is well suited to measuring general dynamic problem solving but not to content- specific systemic thinking. One example is Participant 9, who stated for instance (excerpt, translated):

> […] I really don't need my pre-knowledge and I also don't need to think about anything. […] So, I can simply try out. Then I see what happens there. That means I don't need to supply pre-considerations. I can try out as much as I want. That means I'm not forced at all to think for myself. […] Because I can, well, execute. I can simply look, how, with what controller moves […] the value. That means, I don't need to at all, eh, that could also be Chinese now, which I don't understand. I still would know which value has an effect on it. And I wouldn't know what's behind it. […] Without that I've understood it. Solely through the technicality. I put the controller up and that one changes and this one doesn't change, thus it's that one […].

Without MicroDYN, acting towards systems was no longer possible as an item format. This made it necessary to change Dimension 2 to proximal estimation, via the evaluation of several possibilities for acting towards systems.

Secondly, the CogLabs indicated that the levels of spatial thinking (assumptions based on Hammann et al. 2008) could not be observed in the concept maps. Moreover, while multiple choice items seemed to work for Dimension 1, the levels of Dimension 3 would hardly be representable by multiple choice tasks. Consequently, the levels were replaced by a preliminary quantitative graduation: that is, how many spatial thinking skills could be used, based on rounded 50 % and 75 % cutoffs. Gersmehl and Gersmehl (2007) state that "[t]he human brain appears to have several 'regions' that are structured to do different kinds of spatial thinking" (p. 181) and that "[p]arallel research by child psychologists and educational specialists tends to reinforce one main conclusion of the neuroscientists: the brain areas that are devoted to different kinds of spatial thinking seem to develop in very early childhood" (p. 188). Thus, there was no basis for assuming a systematic ranking in difficulty of the spatial thinking skills that could have been used for a more qualitative description of the levels.

4.4 First Quantitative Study (Q1)

4.4.1 Description of the Measurement Instruments

The first quantitative study (Q1) comprised two parts, namely, MicroDYN and a limesurvey questionnaire. The MicroDYN part consisted of six items and used geographic contexts. The limesurvey questionnaire contained background variables, eight items measuring interest in various aspects of geography on a five-point scale, as well as a geographic pre-knowledge task asking students to write the names of twelve countries marked on a world map, and three geographic pre-knowledge items asking students to choose one of five places (or none) where they would expect a specified condition to be fulfilled. This was followed by four GSC tasks for Dimensions 1–2 and six tasks for Dimension 3. Thus, the tasks contained 12 items to measure Dimension 1, 4 items to measure Dimension 2, and 14 items to measure Dimension 3. To get a credit, respondents had to check several correct and zero incorrect answers, bring answers into the correct sequence, etc. At the end, the participants were asked for their feedback, both in an open comment field and with the help of specific questions that they had to rate on a four point scale (e.g., regarding how much reading literacy the questionnaire requires). A sample item for the limesurvey questionnaire can be seen in Fig. 4.3.

4.4.2 Dimensions of the Competency Model

Firstly, each of the dimensions was tested separately for one-dimensionality using a CFA (confirmatory factor analysis) in Mplus (Muthén and Muthén 2007; Table 4.4) and a Rasch Analysis in Conquest (Wu et al. 2007). Thereby, for the analysis in Mplus, items with a small factor loading ($r_{it} < 0.40$) were excluded. The analysis in Mplus showed a good model fit in Dimension 1. There was a bad model fit for Dimension 3, which might have been caused by having only one item for each spatial thinking skill (except for "condition"; see overview of all skills in Gersmehl and Gersmehl 2006), due to test time considerations (see Table 4.4).

Because Dimension 2 was not identifiable/did not converge, it had to be excluded in further analyses of the data. The Rasch Analysis of the remaining items in Conquest showed acceptable WMNSQ (weighted mean square)- and *t*-values.

Spatial Thinking 1

In front of the Chilean coast runs a plate boundary. Therefore, Chile is often rocked by earthquakes. On 27.02.2010 in Chile there was an earthquake with a magnitude of 8.8. The epicenter was located in front of the coast of the Chilean region Maule (between Talcahuano and San Antonio).

https://www.cia.gov/library/publications/the-world-factbook/geos/ci.html

Severe earthquakes are often associated with great destructions, e.g., collapsing buildings and bridges. Earthquakes can also cause Tsunamis, whose flood waves can cause damages even on distant coasts.

Which of the following places were probably affected very strongly from the earthquake in Chile? Which rather to a lesser extent? Number the place from 1 (most) to 5 (least).

Click on an element in the list on the left, start with the element most highly rated by you and continue to the lowest.

Your selection	**Your rank order**
Concepción	1:
Puerto Montti	2:
the vicinity around Curanipe in the Maule region	3:
the islands of French Polynesia in the Pacific Ocean	4:
Germany	5:

Click on the scissors to the right of each element to delete the last entry form the rank order.

Fig. 4.3 Sample item from Q1: Limesurvey—Spatial thinking item stem and one of the associated items, namely, the one for the skill "Aura" (translated)

Secondly, a two- and a one-dimensional model were tested for the remaining dimension 1 and 3 items. As assumed, the two-dimensional model was to be preferred, both based on an analysis in Mplus and an IRT analysis in Conquest (Table 4.5) The χ^2 -test of difference for the Mplus analysis was calculated according to Muthén and Muthén (2007). The separability of the two dimensions is supported by a latent correlation of $r = 0.776$. This is fairly high. However, in PISA for example, even constructs with latent correlations >0.90 have been seen as separable (see Klieme et al. 2005).

Table 4.4 Results of the separate tests for one-dimensionality for each dimension in Q1 (Mplus)

	Dimension 1: Comprehend and analyze systems	Dimension 2: Evaluate possibilities to act towards systems	Dimension 3: Spatial thinking
Number of items	12	4	14
Number of items without excluded items	8	–	12
χ^2	15.138		42.093
df	13		26
p	>0.10		0.024
CFI	.98		.87
RMSEA	.04		.08
Conclusion	Remaining items fit one-dimensional model well	Model did not converge with all 4 items; model was not identifiable when excluding items	remaining items fit one-dimensional model barely acceptable

CFI Comparative Fit Index, *RMSEA* Root Mean Square Error of Approximation

Table 4.5 Results of the test for dimensionality (Dimensions 1 and 3) for the remaining items in Q1

Mplus	Two-dimensional model	One-dimensional model	χ^2 test of difference	
χ^2	53.727	56.915	χ^2	7.814
df	41	41	*df*	1
p	0.088	0.050	*p*	0.005
CFI	.92	.90		
RMSEA	.05	.06		
Conclusion	Two-dimensional to be preferred			
Conquest	Two-dimensional model	One-dimensional model	χ^2 test of difference	
Final deviance	1932.69	1945.51	χ^2	12.82
Number of estimated parameters	23	21	*df*	2
			p	0.002
Conclusion	Two-dimensional to be preferred			

4.4.3 Levels of the Competency Model

The GSC levels could only be examined on the basis of the remaining items of Dimensions 1 and 3. The item map, showing the difficulty of the items based on a two-dimensional Rasch model, can be seen in Fig. 4.5. "Condition" was the only spatial thinking skill for which more than one item was included, with "Condition 1" being assumed the easiest and "Condition 4" the hardest.

For Dimension 1, levels could not be confirmed, with the Level 1 items being unexpectedly difficult. There are several possible explanations (see also discussion in Viehrig 2015). Firstly, this could have been caused by the items used. Secondly, the empirically derived levels of Ben-Zvi Assaraf and Orion (2005) could possibly hold only in the context of recall tasks, and not in tasks in which information is provided in the item stem. Thirdly, item difficulty might be influenced by differences in terms of the sample's (German vs. Israeli, university vs. school students) prior educational experiences.

For Dimension 3, an analysis of the raw data sum score of the remaining Level 3 items indicated the possibility for using the number of spatial thinking skills as a graduation. Thereby, "condition" was counted if any of the tasks were solved. It must be kept in mind that one spatial thinking skill had to be excluded and that only 81 respondents could be included in the analysis. Level 1 was reached by 76.5 % of the sample, Level 2 by 18.5 % and Level 3 by the remaining 5 %. The item map (Fig. 4.4) shows differences in difficulty between the spatial thinking skill items. Moreover, the spatial thinking skill "condition" showed a graduation in difficulty

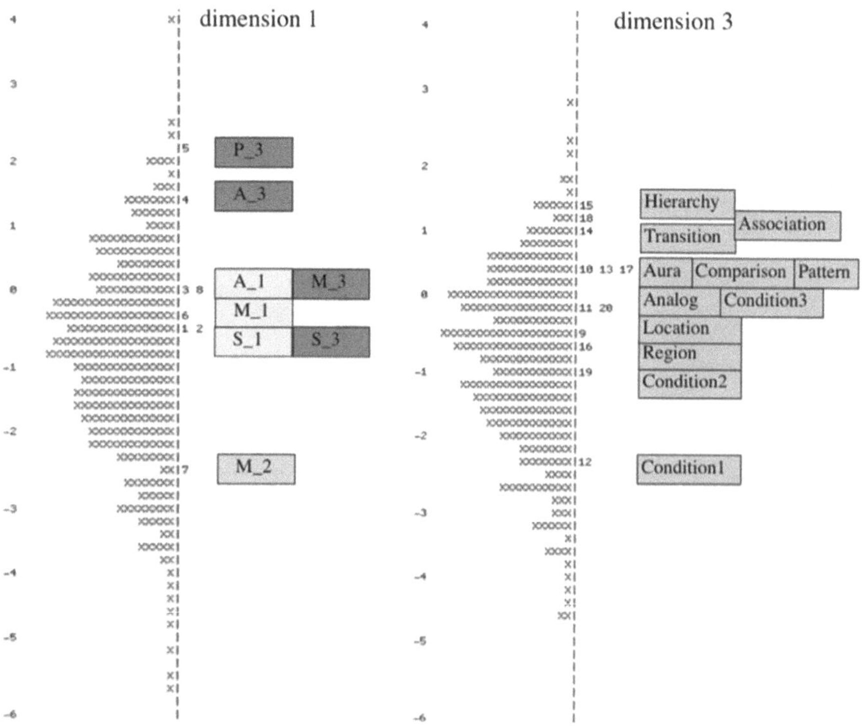

Fig. 4.4 Item map for Q1 without the excluded items
Dimension 1: the letter indicates the item stem, the number the assumed level
Items for "condition" in Dimension 3: a greater number indicates greater assumed complexity

according to complexity in the item map, as expected. These both point to future possibilities of a more qualitative graduation.

4.5 Second Quantitative Study (Q2)

4.5.1 Description of the Measurement Instruments

The second quantitative study used revised items. Q1 had shown that having to check several answers to get a credit was problematic. Consequently, in Q2, participants only had to choose one option to get full credit. Moreover, in contrast to earlier studies, the items were only drawn from one of the three areas of geography education specified by the national educational standards (DGfG 2010): that is, human-environment interaction. The items focused on the topic agriculture. Individual students, as well as a small number of experts were provided with draft versions of (some of) the items to get feedback and further improve the assessment instrument.

The questionnaire was implemented in Limesurvey. It contained background variables, a geographic pre-knowledge task asking students to write the names of seven countries marked on a world map, 13 items asking students to rate their own knowledge of different geographic aspects on a four-point scale, 13 items measuring their interest in these aspects on a five-point scale, and three items measuring interest in working with different media, on a five-point scale. This was followed by nine GSC tasks. Five tasks contained only Dimension 3 items, the other four tasks comprised both Dimensions 1–2 and Dimension 3 items. All in all, there were seven items for Dimension 1, five items for Dimension 2 and 11 items for Dimension 3. At the end, there was an open feedback field, as well as four statements (e.g., "The example countries were well chosen") that the students had to state their (dis)agreement to, on a five-point scale. A sample item can be seen in Fig. 4.5.

4.5.2 Dimensions of the Competency Model

Similarly to Q1, the three dimensions were first tested individually for one-dimensionality, with the help of a CFA in Mplus (Table 4.6) and a Rasch Analysis in Conquest. In the CFA, the Dimension 1 items fitted well to a one-dimensional model and also showed acceptable WMNSQ and *t*-values in the Rasch analysis. The Dimension 2 model did not converge in the CFA and thus had to be excluded from further analyses. For Dimension 3, the CFA showed that the 11 items had a bad model fit based on the CFI (comparative fit index), and an acceptable fit according to the RMSEA (root mean square error of approximation), but that the model fit

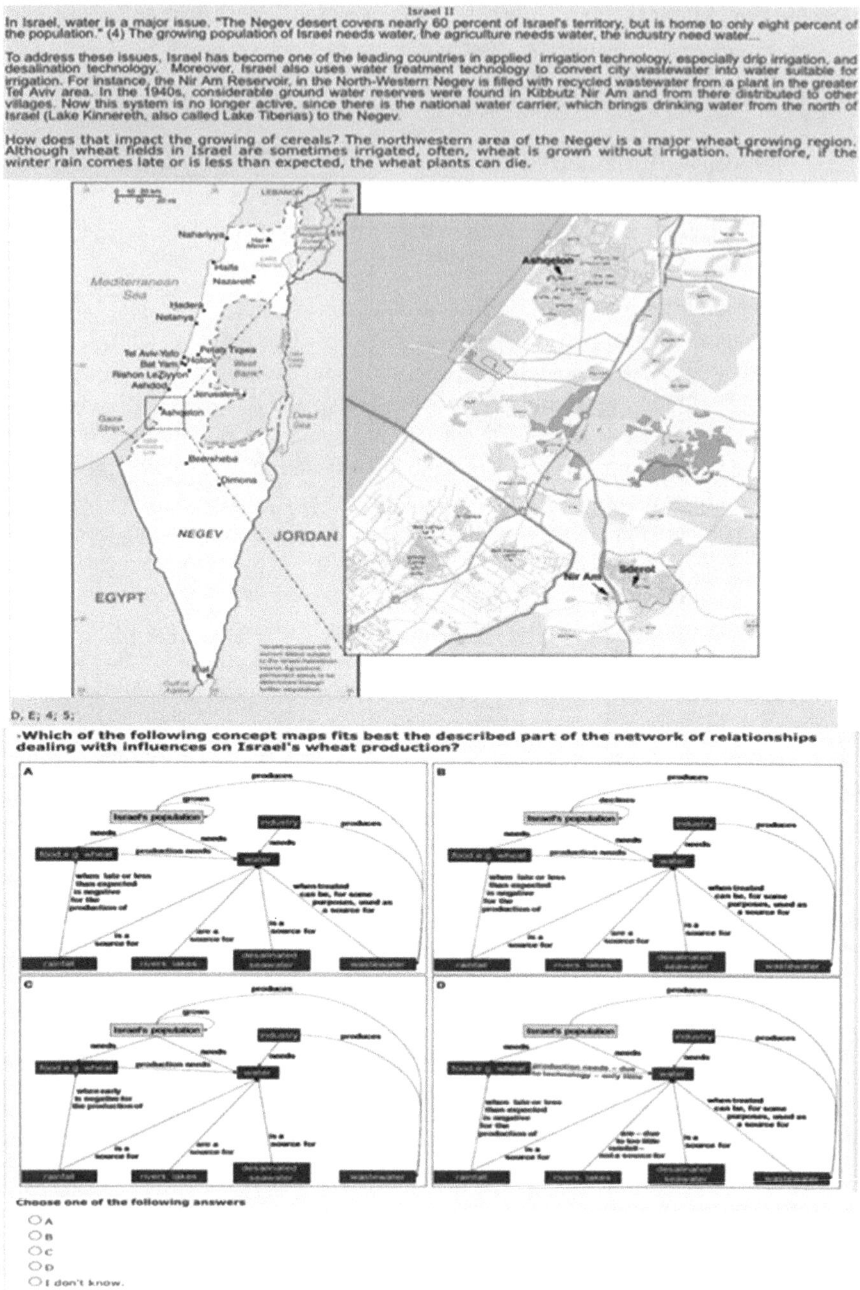

Fig. 4.5 Sample item from Q2: Item stem and one of the associated items (Dimension 1; English version)
Sources: images: (D) CIA World Factbook, (E) Open Street Map, text: (4) MFA: http://www.mfa.gov.il/MFA/InnovativeIsrael/Negev_high-tech_haven-Jan_2011.htm?DisplayMode=print

Table 4.6 Results of the separate tests for one-dimensionality for each dimension in Q2 (Mplus)

	Dimension 1: Comprehend and analyze systems	Dimension 2: Evaluate possibilities to act towards systems	Dimension 3: Spatial thinking
Number of items	7	5	11
Number of items without excluded items	7	–	6
χ^2	6.032		3.988
df	11		8
p	>0.10		>0.10
CFI	.99		.99
RMSEA	.00		.00
Conclusion	Items fit one-dimensional model well	Model did not converge; very low communalities ($h^2 > 0.02–0.07$)	Remaining items fit one-dimensional item well

could be greatly improved by excluding five items. The remaining items showed acceptable WMNSQ (weighted mean square) and *t*-values in the Rasch analysis.

Afterwards, a two- and a one-dimensional model were tested for the remaining Dimension 1 and 3 items. Both a one- and a two-dimensional model showed good fit values in the CFAs. The models did not differ significantly; thus, the one-dimensional model was preferred, due to parsimony. The Rasch Analysis in Conquest showed similar results (Table 4.7).

A possible reason for the differences from Q1 could be sample characteristics. In Q1, the sample had a slightly larger share of participants who had a very good GPA (grade point average) in the high school certificate (*Abitur*; Table 4.2). To test this hypothesis, the Q2 sample was split into a group with a GPA better than 2.5 (on a scale from 1 to 6, with 1 being the best and a 4 being considered a pass, $n = 173$) and a group with a GPA worse than 2.5 ($n = 151$).

The better than 2.5 GPA group did not show good model fit for both one- and two-dimensional models (Table 4.8). This seems to be caused by the items of Dimension 3 having very low communalities ($h^2 = 0.02–0.10$) and thus not constituting one factor. In contrast, the worse than 2.5 GPA group showed acceptable fit values for both models. The items of Dimension 3 constitute one factor ($h^2 = 0.10–0.76$). In the Rasch analysis, while for both groups the one-dimensional model was

Fig. 4.5 (continued) (5) http://www.ynetnews.com/articles/07340L-340392700.html, rest of the text based on: http://www.raymondcook.net/blog/index.php/2010/07/14/go-toisrael-drink-the-sea-israel-world-leader-on-desalination/, http://www.worldwatch.org/node/6544, http://tourguides0607.blogspot.com/2011/03/northern-negevtour.html, http://site.jnf.ca/projects/projectswater_reservoirs.html, http://www.jewishvirtuallibrary.org/jsource/judaica/ejud_0002_0015_0_14862.html, http://www.israelyoudidntknow.com/south-meansdesert/london-fires-negev-water/, http://site.jnf.ca/EDUCATIONSITE/jnf/negev3.html, http://mapsomething.com/demo/waterusage/usage.php, http://www.haaretz.com/news/low-rainfall-threatens-negev-wheat-and-golan-cattleranchers-1.207708

Table 4.7 Results of the tests for dimensionality (Dimensions 1 and 3) for the remaining items in Q2

Mplus	Two-dimensional model	One-dimensional model	χ^2 test of difference	
χ^2	21.644	21.392	χ^2	0.190
df	36	36	*df*	1
p	>0.10	>0.10	*p*	>0.10
CFI	.99	.99		
RMSEA	.00	.00		
Conclusion	One-dimensional to be preferred			
Conquest	Two-dimensional model	One-dimensional model	χ^2 test of difference	
Final deviance	3500.79	3502.75	χ^2	1.97
Number of estimated parameters	16	14	*df*	2
			p	0.374
Conclusion	One-dimensional to be preferred			

Table 4.8 Results of the tests for dimensionality (Dimensions 1 and 3) for the remaining items in Q2 by GPA higher (better) or lower (worse) than 2.5

Mplus	Two-dimensional model		One-dimensional model		χ^2 test of difference		
	High GPA	Low GPA	High GPA	Low GPA		High GPA	Low GPA
χ^2	35.360	18.810	39.065	18.475	χ^2	0.478	0.098
df	20	28	22	28	*df*	1	1
p	<0.05	>0.10	<0.05	>0.10	*p*	>0.10	>0.10
CFI	.38	.99	.31	.99			
RMSEA	.07	.00	.07	.00			
Conclusion	One-dimensional to be preferred						
Conquest	Two-dimensional model		One-dimensional model		χ^2 test of difference		
	High GPA	Low GPA	High GPA	Low GPA		High GPA	Low GPA
Final deviance	1763.79	1705.26	1766.40	1705.29	χ^2	2.61	0.03
Number of estimated parameters	16	16	14	14	*df*	2	2
					p	0.271	0.986
Conclusion	One-dimensional to be preferred						

to be preferred, there was a larger difference between the models for the better than 2.5 GPA group. Thus, while in both groups, the one-dimensional model had to be preferred, the results hint at some differences, especially with regard to Dimension 3. Therefore, the influence of GPA on competency structure should be further explored with a greater number of items for each spatial thinking skill.

Moreover, the sample also differed—to a much greater extent—with regard to the students' course of study (see Table 4.2). However, due to small cell sizes (e.g., for psychology students $n = 37$ in Q1 and $n = 58$ in Q2), separate models for psychology vs. geography education/geography students did not appear to be feasible.

4.5.3 Levels of the Competency Model

The GSC levels could only be examined on the basis of the remaining items of Dimensions 1 and 3. The item map, showing the difficulty of the items based on a one-dimensional Rasch model, can be seen in Fig. 4.6, which shows that the test was very easy for the sample.

For Dimension 1, similarly to Q1, levels could not be confirmed, because the Level 1 items were unexpectedly difficult. It is notable, however, that within the "N" item stem, dealing with New Zealand, the assumed levels were shown. Not every item stem had every level; thus, it cannot be confirmed whether there were systematic variations in difficulty between content areas or example countries.

For Dimension 3, an analysis of the raw data sum score of the remaining Level 3 items indicated the possibility of using the number of spatial thinking skills as a graduation. However, because of the exclusion of items, Level 3 could not be measured, with Level 1 being reached by 83.6 % of the respondents and Level 2 by 16.4 %. The item map (Fig. 4.6) shows differences in difficulty between the spatial thinking skills, pointing to future possibilities for a more qualitative graduation. However, a comparison with the item map from Q1 shows that item difficulty is not consistent, for instance, with hierarchy—the hardest spatial thinking item in Q1 and the easiest in Q2.

4.6 Discussion

The main aim of the studies was to explore the structure of GSC, especially with regard to the relationship between systemic and spatial thinking. The studies showed common results in part, but also differences.

4.6.1 Dimensions of GSC

Firstly, Dimension 2 could not be measured in the originally intended form of "acting towards systems", and had to be changed to "evaluating possibilities to act towards systems". Originally it had been planned to approximate the "acting" with MicroDYN items, which have proven useful in the assessment of interactive problem solving skills (see e.g., Greiff et al. 2013; Wüstenberg et al. 2012). However, the

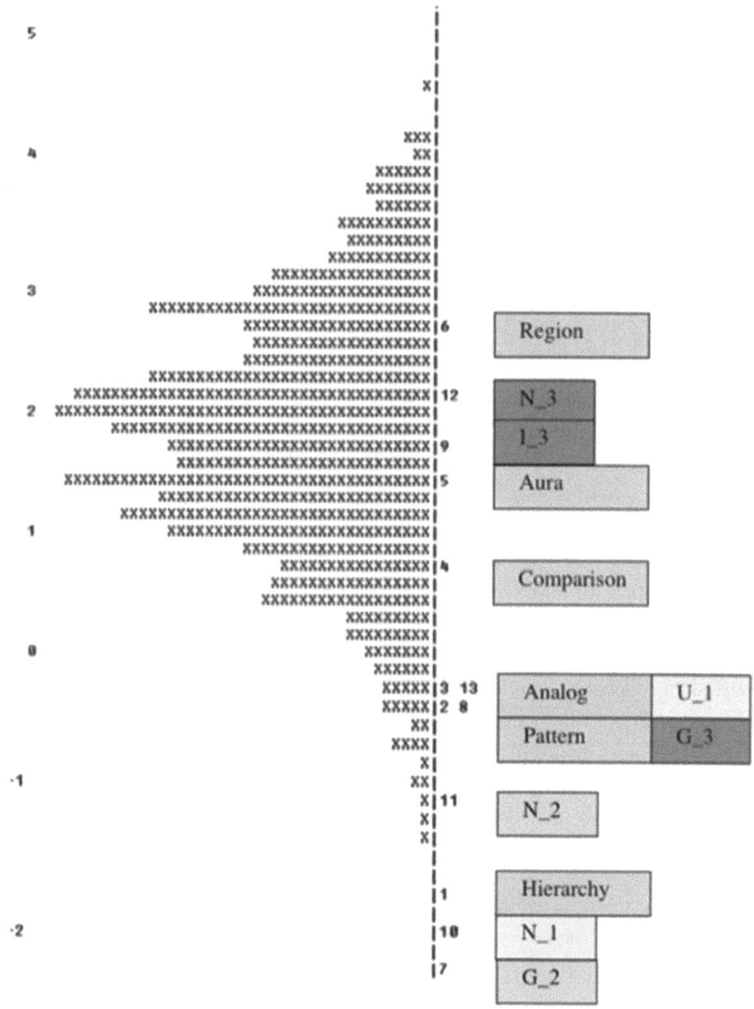

Fig. 4.6 Item map for Q2 without the excluded items
Dimension 1: the letter indicates the item stem, the number, the assumed level

CogLabs showed that MicroDYN items seem to be content-unspecific, making them not well suited to measuring geography-specific competencies. Even for systemic thinking as a general competency, however, there might be better-suited instruments than MicroDYN items, because systemic thinking means more than applying a VOTAT ("vary one thing at a time") strategy for exploration and drawing causal diagrams. For instance, the stock-flow failure reported by Sweeney and Sterman (2000) taps important issues in systems thinking that are not addressed by linear structural equation systems.

The revised Dimension 2 was not identifiable in both quantitative studies. This could be due to the small number of items or to the existing conception of this competency area. While learning to act adequately towards systems is a central part of geography education in Germany (e.g., DGfG 2010; Köck 1993), including competencies like being able to "[...] assess the natural and social spatial consequences of selected individual actions and think of alternatives" (DGfG 2007, p. 26), the studies showed some difficulties in measuring this dimension. Due to test time considerations, Dimension 2 should be removed from the competency model in further studies and rather treated separately, until a measurement scale for this dimension has been empirically validated, or the conception of that competency area is further developed.

Secondly, with regard to the other two dimensions, the studies showed differences. While Dimensions 1 and 3 fit a two-dimensional model in Q1, they fit both a two- and a one-dimensional model in Q2, leading to the preference of a one-dimensional model, due to parsimony. To further explore the reasons for these differences, several measures could be taken. Despite an item overhaul after Q1, several items for Dimension 3 had to be excluded in Q2. Further studies should employ a greater number of items for Dimension 3, including more than one item for each spatial thinking skill. This would lead to a longer test-time, however. Moreover, further analyses in Q2 hinted at a possible influence of GPA on competency structure, especially with regard to the fit of the Dimension 3 items. Consequently, a thinking-aloud study (CogLab) that comprised only spatial thinking items could be conducted with high and low GPA students, to investigate why for low GPA but not for high GPA students, the spatial thinking items constitute a homogenous factor. Additionally, the sample differed also with regard to other sample characteristics, such as the percentage of geography (higher in Q2), geography education (lower in Q2) and psychology students (lower in Q2). The items were designed to focus either on systemic thinking or on spatial thinking separately. However, in geographic inquiry, both are often interlinked, and thus might become more inseparable for students with a more extensive background in geography education. This could be further explored in expert-novice studies for instance. Furthermore, it might be helpful to have a third category of items that explicitly requires both spatial and systemic thinking skills.

Overall, the studies showed that in *geographic* contexts, systemic and spatial thinking are highly correlated or even inseparable. Thus, while studies focusing on just one of the two aspects *are* necessary for specific questions, they might only show a fragmented picture when it comes to understanding many geographic issues.

4.6.2 GSC Levels

Overall, the results of the levels are tentative till the structure of GSC is further explored. In general, Q1 was more difficult for the sample than was Q2, an effect possibly caused at least partly by the item formats used. Moreover, Q2 only used one broad topic area ("agriculture"), while in Q1, students had to switch between different topic areas.

In both quantitative studies, for Dimension 1, the remaining Level 2 items were consistently easier than the remaining Level 3 items. Level 1 items were shown to be more difficult than expected on the basis of the research literature (Ben-Zvi Assaraf and Orion 2005; Orion and Basis 2008). The reasons for this need to be explored. In general, there are recall items, for which students have to draw on their own pre-knowledge, or largely pre-knowledge-free tasks in which some or all information is given in the item stem. HEIGIS items belong to the second category. Thus, one avenue would be to compare both item types for the same topic and degree of complexity, to look at possible differences in level order. For recall tasks, it might be easiest to be able to name a concept as belonging to a sub-system (e.g., fertilizer has something to do with the topic "soil"), without remembering what exactly is the connection. In contrast, for item-stem-given information, to some degree participants might need to understand the information, before being able to decide whether a concept mentioned in the stem belongs to a sub-system or not. An alternative option would be to test one sample with both a translated version of the measurement instrument used by Ben-Zvi Assaraf and Orion (2005), and with the HEIGIS one. Another avenue could be, for instance, to have a substantial number of experts classify the items into the respective competency model components before the next study.

Additionally, new items and item formats could be tested and more control variables introduced, to explore potential effects of the kind of item, reading literacy or testwiseness. One promising item format seems to be multiple-select items, for which students have to check "right" or "wrong" for each choice (e.g., Pollmeier et al. 2011). This item format would ensure that students had to evaluate every single choice. It also could provide a closer link to pre-concepts, which is another option to improve the items.

For Dimension 3, quantitative graduation is one possibility. However, a more qualitative graduation would be preferable. In both studies, there is variation in difficulty between the items. However, as expected on the basis of Gersmehl and Gersmehl (2006), no general graduation can be observed. For instance, the spatial thinking skill "hierarchy" is very easy in Q2 but is among the most difficult spatial thinking skills in Q1. A greater number of items for each spatial thinking skill should be included, to find possible qualitative graduations and to test whether a one-dimensional scale comprising all spatial thinking skills is possible, as in both studies, some items had to be excluded. One possible graduation is complexity, as could be observed for the spatial thinking skill "condition" in Q1.

4.7 Conclusions

As outlined at the beginning, both systemic and spatial thinking are important aims of geographic education, but their relationship has not to any great extent yet been explicitly explored empirically. Hitherto, systemic and spatial thinking have often been studied separately (e.g., Battersby et al. 2006; Ben-Zvi Assaraf and Orion 2005; Lee 2005; Rempfler and Uphues 2012). The HEIGIS studies, however, show a close connection between systemic and spatial thinking when dealing with geographic systems. Consequently, while for some questions, focusing on either skill is necessary, both skills are needed in modeling GSC.

The studies also hint at some difficulties in measuring systemic and spatial thinking in geographic contexts. Thus, the model and associated items need to be further improved, to examine the relationship between both skills.

The HEIGIS studies were conducted predominantly with university students. The studies hinted at a potential influence of GPA on competency structure. A study by Orion and Basis (2008) showed an influence of grade on level order. In general, systemic thinking has been studied from kindergarten (see e.g., the project "Shaping the future" at the Heidelberg University of Education, http://www.rgeo.de/cms/p/pzukunft/) to postgraduate level. Ultimately, it would be helpful to have one model that can cover a person's whole learning history from beginner to expert, similar to what already exists in the area of foreign language learning (Council of Europe 2001). It should also comprise different interconnected versions, so that both a general competency overview and a more detailed picture for specific areas are possible within the same framework (see Viehrig 2015). This seems to be especially necessary in the light of current changes to the school system (e.g., the so-called *Gemeinschaftsschule* in Baden-Wurttemberg). Consequently, further studies should investigate the effect of grade level and GPA on both the structure and levels of geographic system competency to differentiate and improve the model. The HEIGIS studies showed that test time is a major constraining factor; this could be alleviated by using multi-matrix-designs for instance.

In summary, the project highlights the need for more research in this central area of geography education.

Acknowledgements This chapter is largely based on the final project report. The HEIGIS-project was funded by grants SI 877/6-1 and FU 173/13-1 from the German Research Foundation (DFG) in the Priority Program "Competence Models for Assessing Individual Learning Outcomes and Evaluating Educational Processes" (SPP 1293). Thanks also to the student research assistants, who played an important role, especially with regard to the data collection in the CogLabs. Thanks also to all experts who provided valuable advice during item generation for all studies. Of course, thanks also to all participants.

References

Battersby, S. E., Golledge, R. G., & Marsh, M. J. (2006). Incidental learning of geospatial concepts across grade levels: Map overlay. *Journal of Geography, 105*, 139–146. doi:10.1080/00221340608978679.

Bell, T. (2004). Komplexe Systeme und Strukturprinzipien der Selbstregulation: Konstruktion grafischer Darstellungen, Transfer und systemisches Denken [Complex systems and structural principles of self-regulation: construction of graphical displays, transfer, and systemic thinking]. *Zeitschrift für Didaktik der Naturwissenschaften, 10*, 183–204.

Ben-Zvi Assaraf, O., & Orion, N. (2005). Development of system thinking skills in the context of earth system education. *Journal of Research in Science Teaching, 42*, 518–560. doi:10.1002/tea.20061.

CoE (Council of Europe). (2001). Common European framework of reference for languages. http://www.coe.int. Accessed 22 Oct 2007.

DGfG (German Geographical Society). (2007). *Educational standards in geography for the intermediate school certificate*. Berlin: Author.

DGfG (German Geographical Society). (Ed.). (2010). *Bildungsstandards im Fach Geographie für den Mittleren Schulabschluss—mit Aufgabenbeispielen* [Educational standards in geography for the intermediate school certificate—with sample tasks]. Bonn: Selbstverlag Deutsche Gesellschaft für Geographie.

Funke, J. (1990). Systemmerkmale als Determinanten des Umgangs mit dynamischen Systemen [System features as determinants of behavior in dynamic task environments]. *Sprache & Kognition, 9*, 143–154.

Funke, J., & Greiff, S. (2017). Dynamic problem solving: Multiple-item testing based on minimal complex systems. In D. Leutner, J. Fleischer, J. Grünkorn, & E. Klieme (Eds.), *Competence assessment in education: Research, models and instruments* (pp. 427–443). Berlin: Springer.

Gersmehl, P. J., & Gersmehl, C. A. (2006). Wanted: A concise list of neurologically defensible and assessable spatial thinking skills. *Research in Geographic Education, 8*, 5–38.

Gersmehl, P. J., & Gersmehl, C. A. (2007). Spatial thinking by young children: Neurologic evidence for early development and "educability". *Journal of Geography, 106*, 181–191. doi:10.1080/00221340701809108.

Greiff, S. (2010). *Individualdiagnostik der komplexen Problemlösefähigkeit* [Individual diagnostics of complex problem solving skills]. Münster: Waxmann.

Greiff, S., & Funke, J. (2009). Measuring complex problem solving: The MicroDYN approach. In F. Scheuermann & J. Björnsson (Eds.), *The transition to computer-based assessment. New approaches to skills assessment and implications for large-scale testing* (pp. 157–163). Luxembourg: Office for Official Publications of the European Communities.

Greiff, S., Holt, D. V., & Funke, J. (2013). Perspectives on problem solving in educational assessment: Analytical, interactive, and collaborative problem solving. *Journal of Problem Solving, 5*(2), 71–91. doi:10.7771/1932-6246.1153.

Hammann, M., Phan, T. T. H., Ehmer, M., & Grimm, T. (2008). Assessing pupils' skills in experimentation. *Journal of Biological Education, 42*, 66–72. doi:10.1080/00219266.2008.9656113.

Kerski, J. J. (2013). Understanding our changing world through web-mapping based investigations. *J-Reading—Journal of Research and Didactics in Geography, 2*(2), 11–26. doi:10.4458/2379-02.

Klaus, D. (1985). Allgemeine Grundlagen des systemtheoretischen Ansatzes [General foundations of the systems theory approach]. *Geographie und Schule, 33*, 1–8.

Klieme, E., Hartig, J., & Wirth, J. (2005). Analytisches Problemlösen: Messansatz und Befunde zu Planungs- und Entscheidungsaufgaben [Analytical problem solving: measurement approach and results of planning and decision tasks]. In E. Klieme, D. Leutner, & J. Wirth (Eds.), *Problemlösekompetenz von Schülerinnen und Schülern* (pp. 37–54). Wiesbaden: VS.

Köck, H. (1993). Raumbezogene Schlüsselqualifikationen: Der fachimmanente Beitrag des Geographieunterrichts zum Lebensalltag des Einzelnen und Funktionieren der Gesellschaft [Space-related key qualifications: the subject-innate contribution of geographic education to the everyday life of individuals and functioning of society]. *Geographie und Schule, 84*, 14–22.

Lee, J. W. (2005). *Effect of GIS learning on spatial ability.* Doctoral dissertation, Texas A & M University, Texas. Retrieved from https://repository.tamu.edu/handle/1969.1/3896

Muthén, L. K., & Muthén, B. O. (2007). *MPlus user's guide*. Los Angeles: Author.

Orion, N., & Basis, T. (2008, March). *Characterization of high school students' system thinking skills in the context of earth systems*. Paper presented at the NARST annual conference, Baltimore.

Ossimitz, G. (1996). *Das Projekt "Entwicklung vernetzten Denkens": Erweiterter Endbericht* [The project "Development of networked thinking": Extended final report]. Klagenfurt: Universität Klagenfurt.

Ossimitz, G. (2000). *Entwicklung systemischen Denkens* [Development of systemic thinking]. Wien: Profil.

Pollmeier, J., Hardy, I., Koerber, S., & Möller, K. (2011). Lassen sich naturwissenschaftliche Lernstände im Grundschulalter mit schriftlichen Aufgaben valide erfassen [Can scientific achievements in primary school age be validly measured with written tasks]? *Zeitschrift für Pädagogik, 57*, 834–853.

Rempfler, A., & Uphues, R. (2010). Sozialökologisches Systemverständnis: Grundlage für die Modellierung von geographischer Systemkompetenz [Socio-ecological system understanding: foundation for the modeling of geographic system competence]. *Geographie und Ihre Didaktik, 38*, 205–217.

Rempfler, A., & Uphues, R. (2011). Systemkompetenz im Geographieunterricht: Die Entwicklung eines Kompetenzmodells [System competence in geographic education: The development of a competence model]. In C. Meyer, R. Henrÿ, & G. Stöber (Eds.), *Geographische Bildung. Kompetenzen in didaktischer Forschung und Schulpraxis* (pp. 36–48). Braunschweig: Westermann.

Rempfler, A., & Uphues, R. (2012). System competence in geography education. Development of competence models, diagnosing pupils' achievement. *European Journal of Geography, 3*(1), 6–22.

Rieß, W., & Mischo, C. (2008). Entwicklung und erste Validierung eines Fragebogens zur Erfassung des systemischen Denkens in nachhaltigkeitsrelevanten Kontexten [Development and first validation of a questionnaire to measure systemic thinking in sustainability-related contexts]. In I. Bormann & G. De Haan (Eds.), *Kompetenzen der Bildung für nachhaltige Entwicklung. Operationalisierung, Messung, Rahmenbedingungen, Befunde* (pp. 215–232). Wiesbaden: VS.

Smithson, P., Addison, K., & Atkinson, K. (2002). *Fundamentals of the physical environment*. London: Routledge.

Sommer, C. (2005). *Untersuchung der Systemkompetenz von Grundschülern im Bereich Biologie* [Examination of system competence of primary school students in the area of biology]. Doctoral dissertation. Retrieved from http://eldiss.uni-kiel.de/macau/receive/dissertation_diss_1652

Sweeney, L. B., & Sterman, J. D. (2000). Bathtub dynamics: initial results of a systems thinking inventory. *System Dynamics Review, 16*, 249–286. doi:10.1002/sdr.198.

Viehrig, K. (2015). *Exploring the effects of GIS use on students' achievement in geography*. Doctoral dissertation. Retrieved from http://opus.ph-heidelberg.de/frontdoor/index/index/docId/71

Viehrig, K., Greiff, S., Siegmund, A., & Funke, J. (2011). Geographische Kompetenzen fördern: Erfassung der Geographischen Systemkompetenz als Grundlage zur Bewertung der Kompetenzentwicklung [Fostering geographic competencies: Measurement of geographic system competence as foundation of evaluating the competence development]. In C. Meyer, R. Henrÿ, & G. Stöber (Eds.), *Geographische Bildung: Kompetenzen in didaktischer Forschung und Schulpraxis* (pp. 49–57). Braunschweig: Westermann.

Viehrig, K., Siegmund, A., Wüstenberg, S., Greiff, S., & Funke, J. (2012). Systemisches und räumliches Denken in der geographischen Bildung: Erste Ergebnisse zur Überprüfung eines Modells der Geographischen Systemkompetenz [Systemic and spatial thinking in geographic education: First results of testing a model of geographic system competence]. In A. Hüttermann, P. Kirchner, S. Schuler, & K. Drieling (Eds.), *Räumliche Orientierung: Räumliche Orientierung, Karten und Geoinformation im Unterricht* (pp. 95–102). Braunschweig: Westermann.

Wu, M. L., Adams, R. J., & Wilson, M. R. (2007). *ACER ConQuest version 2.0. Generalised item response modelling software*. Camberwell: ACER Press.

Wüstenberg, S., Greiff, S., & Funke, J. (2012). Complex problem solving—More than reasoning? *Intelligence, 40*, 1–14. doi:10.1016/j.intell.2011.11.003.

Chapter 5
An Extended Model of Literary Literacy

Christel Meier, Thorsten Roick, Sofie Henschel, Jörn Brüggemann, Volker Frederking, Adelheid Rieder, Volker Gerner, and Petra Stanat

Abstract Empirical findings on the question whether the competencies of understanding literary and non-literary (expository) texts are distinct, have been lacking for a long time. In our research we have made an attempt to resolve this issue. Our aim was to develop and evaluate a model of literary literacy, based on the theory of aesthetic semiotics, that includes a content-related and a form-related understanding of literary texts. We conducted several studies to test whether comprehending literary and expository texts represents partly distinct facets of reading literacy. This chapter presents an extended model of literary literacy that expands the range of competence facets of literary understanding. Our findings indicate that the competence of comprehending literary texts encompasses—in addition to content and form-related understanding—the ability to apply specific literary knowledge, to recognize foregrounded passages and to recognize emotions that are intended by the text.

Keywords Literary literacy • Reading literacy • Competence model • Aesthetic semiotics • Literature class

C. Meier (✉) • V. Frederking • A. Rieder • V. Gerner
Friedrich-Alexander-University of Erlangen-Nürnberg, Erlangen, Germany
e-mail: christel.meier@fau.de; Volker.Frederking@t-online.de; adelheid.rieder@gmx.de; VolkerGerner@gmx.de

T. Roick
Senate Department for Education, Youth and Science, SIBUZ Pankow, Berlin, Germany
e-mail: thorsten.roick@senbjw.berlin.de

S. Henschel • P. Stanat
Humboldt-Universität zu Berlin, Institute for Educational Quality Improvement (IQB), Berlin, Germany
e-mail: sofie.henschel@hu-berlin.de; petra.stanat@iqb.hu-berlin.de

J. Brüggemann
Carl von Ossietzky University of Oldenburg, Oldenburg, Germany
e-mail: joern.brueggemann@uni-oldenburg.de

D. Leutner et al. (eds.), *Competence Assessment in Education*, Methodology of Educational Measurement and Assessment, DOI 10.1007/978-3-319-50030-0_5

5.1 The Comprehension of Literary and Expository Texts

In current research on discourse comprehension it is a controversial issue whether the understanding of literary and expository texts represents distinct aspects of reading comprehension (e.g., Graesser et al. 1997; Meutsch 1987; Zwaan 1993). In contrast, concepts of literary education suggest that understanding literary texts requires additional (cognitive, motivational, and affective) processes that are less relevant for expository texts (e.g., Spinner 2006; Levine 2014).

Although all types of texts theoretically can be read as literary or non-literary, readers usually recognize a text as either more literary or non-literary based on text-internal factors, such as ambiguity, fictionality, content- and style-related features (Hoffstaedter 1986; van Peer 1986) or text-external factors (e.g., reading instructions; Meutsch 1987; Zwaan 1993). Both sources can affect the applied reading mode. Zwaan (1993), like Vipond and Hunt (1984), has shown that reading texts in a literary mode increases attention to linguistic features. Moreover, in contrast to an expository (*information-driven*) reading mode, the construction of a situational representation is delayed when reading a text in a literary mode. Such results are supported by psycholinguistic (Meutsch 1987; Zwaan 1993) and neurocognitive studies (e.g., Altmann et al. 2014) suggesting that the same levels of representation are involved in constructing a mental model (surface, propositional textbase, and situation model; Graesser et al. 1997) when reading texts in a literary or non-literary (expository) mode. However, the applied reading mode seems to trigger qualitatively and quantitatively different processing on these levels (e.g., more bottom-up or top-down processing, different types of elaboration; Meutsch 1987; Zwaan 1993). While previous research on literary reading comprehension has focused primarily on cognitive processes and products, research on a competence model and the internal structure of literary literacy is lacking.

5.2 Current Research on Literary Literacy and Further Directions

In our research project, we defined, assessed, and validated the competence of understanding literary texts, which we refer to as *literary literacy* (Frederking et al. 2012). The findings of our project provide empirical evidence for the theoretical assumption that understanding literary and expository texts entails partly distinct competences (Roick et al. 2013; Roick and Henschel 2015). The two-faceted view of reading comprehension was further supported by the identification of specific cognitive (Meier et al. 2012), motivational (Henschel et al. 2013; Henschel and Schaffner 2014), and affective factors (Henschel and Roick 2013) that contribute significantly more strongly to the comprehension of literary than of expository texts.

Although we were able to generate initial insights into the internal competence structure of literary literacy, some issues are still unsettled. Starting with an illustration of the two core facets of literary literacy on the basis of a literary text, we will describe these insights and unresolved issues below. Subsequently, we will introduce an expansion of our initial model and submit it to an empirical test.

5.2.1 *The Internal Structure of Literary Literacy*

> Mr. Keuner and the helpless boy
>
> Mr. Keuner asked a boy who was crying to himself why he was so unhappy. I had saved two dimes for the movies, said the lad, then a boy came and grabbed one from my hand, and he pointed at a boy who could be seen in some distance. Didn't you shout for help? asked Mr. Keuner. Yes I did, said the boy and sobbed a little harder. Didn't anyone hear you? Mr. Keuner went on asking, stroking him affectionately. No, sobbed the boy. Can't you shout any louder? asked Mr. Keuner. No, said the boy and looked at him with new hope. Because Mr. Keuner was smiling. Then hand over the other one as well, he said to the boy, took the last dime out of his hand and walked on unconcerned. (Brecht 1995, p. 19; translation by the authors).

Which aspects are typically required to understand a literary text shall be illustrated with Brecht's *Mr. Keuner and the helpless boy*. First of all, the "openness" of the work has to be considered when interpreting a literary text (Eco 1989). Brecht's text is a good example of this openness, which is particularly caused by the semantically irritating last sentence. Similarly to the boy, the reader is likely to expect that Mr. Keuner would help. Mr. Keuner, however, does the contrary: He takes the money and leaves. This unexpected turn could lead to multiple plausible semantic meanings: Should we feel sorry for the boy? Is the text an expression of social criticism? Or is the boy himself guilty because he does not shout loud enough? This openness is due not only to the content but also to formal aspects of the text, such as the structure (the unexpected turn) and the objective mode of narration. The third person narrator tells the story from an unbiased point of view and does not give any hints as to how it should be understood (Nutz 2002).

According to Eco, "describing and explaining for which formal reasons a given text produces a given response" goes beyond a mere content-related semantic interpretation. Eco calls this semiotic mode of reading "critical" and defines it as "a metalinguistic activity" (Eco 1990, p. 54f). A critical reader is interested in form-related aspects of the text, the so called "aesthetic idiolect" (Eco 1976, p. 272) and tries to understand how the structure and the narration mode of Brecht's text stimulate his semantic interpretation.

Referring to the specific requirements illustrated above, we theoretically derived two core facets of literary literacy from Eco's semiotic aesthetics (Frederking et al. 2012): Content-related *semantic literary literacy* is the ability to construct a coherent meaning of a literary text. Form-related *idiolectal literary literacy* refers to the ability to understand and analyze the function and effects of stylistic features (see Sect. 5.2 for item samples).

Although semantic and idiolectal literary literacy are strongly associated, empirical analyses support differentiation between the two facets as well as between semantic and idiolectal literary literacy on the one hand, and expository reading comprehension on the other hand (Frederking et al. 2012; Roick et al. 2013). The strong correlation between semantic and idiolectal literary literacy seems partly due to differences in expository reading comprehension, as shown in a nested factor model (Frederking et al. 2012), and the correlation varies as a function of school track. The less advanced the students were, the more clearly could the two facets of literary literacy be distinguished (Roick et al. 2013).

5.2.2 The Need for an Extended Model of Literary Literacy

Our model of literary literacy is in accordance with general assumptions of cognitive theories on reading comprehension. Consequently, we consider reading as a cognitive process with different levels of representation and inferences that are constrained by characteristics of text, reader, and context. However, our model differs on two points from most other models in reading comprehension research. First, it is explicitly derived from literary theory and includes two core facets of understanding literature that are usually not the subject of text comprehension research, nor are specifically assessed in large-scale assessments such as PISA (OECD 2009). Second, our model refers to key aspects of literary education that are also specified in the standards for German language learning (KMK 2004).

Despite this however, our initial model includes only two core facets of the comprehension aspects that are regarded as important in literary education. Spinner (2006) developed a detailed list of 11 aspects that are assumed to be relevant for teaching and learning in the field of literature. Some of them are covered by our initial competence model (understanding the plot, dealing with the openness of the work, understanding stylistic features). Others, however, are not yet included, such as the ability to apply specific literary knowledge (e.g., about genres or historical aspects) or to recognize striking linguistic features that in empirical studies of literature are usually referred to as "foregrounded passages" (Miall and Kuiken 1994). In addition, it is widely discussed whether cognitive processes related to emotional inferences might be important in understanding a literary text adequately (Frederking and Brüggemann 2012; Kneepkens and Zwaan 1994; Levine 2014; Mar et al. 2011). Other aspects, such as imagination, involvement, or perspective-taking, might represent necessary cognitive (and affective) prerequisites, rather than distinct structural facets of literary literacy. In expanding our initial two-faceted competence model, which is based on Eco's semiotics, we theoretically derived, assessed, and modeled three new comprehension facets, including the ability to recognize foregrounded passages, the ability to apply specific literary knowledge, and the ability to recognize emotions intended by the text.

The ability to recognize foregrounded passages is an important aim of literary education (KMK 2004; Spinner 2006). It requires the reader to scan the surface level of the text for striking linguistic patterns which then are selected and focused on for further interpretation (Hanauer 1999). Being aware of these features is regarded as an important precondition for higher-order processing (e.g., constructing elaborations, integrating specific knowledge) in order to develop a sophisticated interpretation of a literary text (Miall and Kuiken 1994). Eco points out that "artistic devices [...] seem to work exactly as self-focusing appeals [...] to attract the attention of a critical reader" (1990, p. 55). Empirical studies suggest that the ability to recognize foregrounded passages might be less dependent on expertise than the ability to interpret the meaning of a stylistic device (idiolectal literary literacy), but both seem to contribute positively to the comprehension process (Miall and Kuiken 1994). We therefore differentiate these two competence facets in our extended model of literary literacy.

The ability to apply specific literary knowledge is regarded as important for inference making in text comprehension. Usually the situation model integrates information given in the text with prior knowledge, to develop an advanced mental representation (Kintsch 1988). However, this ability is also considered to be crucial for detecting linguistic patterns on the surface level of literary texts (Hanauer 1999). The ability to apply specific literary knowledge, such as knowledge about different genres, historical contexts of literature, or technical terms for stylistic devices, is also mentioned in the educational standards (KMK 2004).

The relevance of specific literary knowledge to understanding a literary text was shown in a study by Meier et al. (2012), who found that students who were given specific literary knowledge in the task instruction (e.g., explanations of technical terms, such as "dialogue") performed significantly better than students who completed the task without additional explanations. The effects remained, even after controlling for several cognitive (e.g., general cognitive ability), motivational (e.g., reading motivation), and background characteristics (e.g., gender, school track). The results suggest that students were able to integrate the additional literary knowledge presented in the task instruction to derive a coherent meaning of the text. According to these findings, it seems worthwhile to disentangle task processing and the availability of specific literary knowledge. Therefore, the availability of specific literary knowledge was assessed by means of a separate test, while the required specific literary knowledge in the test of literary literacy was provided in the task instruction.

The *ability to recognize emotions intended by a literary text* refers to inferences about text-encoded emotions. On the one hand, emotions can be described or articulated as part of the plot of a literary text (Winko 2003). On the other hand, a literary text can "intend" to evoke a non-arbitrary spectrum of emotional reactions (Frederking and Brüggemann 2012). It is important to distinguish between emotions intended by the text and emotions actually evoked by a literary text. While the latter are emotional phenomena that accompany the reader before, during and after the comprehension process, intended emotions are not necessarily felt by the reader, but are cognitively demanding, since they have to be identified and integrated into the situational representation of the text. In the case of *Mr. Keuner and the helpless boy*, outrage, astonishment, or pity (for the boy) can be regarded as intended emotions, as these three emotions are plausible emotional reactions, according to the content and structure of Brecht's story (see Sect. 5.4.2.5 for further explanation).

5.3 Research Objectives

Our theoretical considerations point to five distinct aspects of literary literacy. They describe competence facets that we regard to be crucial for understanding a literary text. These facets should be empirically distinguishable from each other and—as previous findings suggest—also with respect to understanding expository texts. The purpose of the present study, therefore, was to examine the internal structure of reading literacy and to develop an extended and ecologically valid competence model that refers to the demands of literary education according to best practice recommendations (Spinner 2006) and educational standards for German language learning in secondary school (KMK 2004).

5.4 Method

5.4.1 Sample

A sample of 964 tenth grade students (50 % girls, mean age 16.71 years, $SD = 0.73$) participated in our study. The students attended 42 secondary classrooms in the upper track (German *Gymnasium*, 32 classes) and in the intermediate track (German *Realschule*, 10 classes) of the German school system. The sample was drawn from rural and urban areas in Bavaria. The number of classrooms in the upper track was higher because the students of the intermediate track had already passed their final exams when the assessments took place. Since participation was voluntary, students, or whole classes, dropped out after the exams.

The students completed tests of literary and expository reading comprehension. Information on school track and self-reported gender was also obtained and included as control variables in all analyses. The study had a cross-sectional design, with two testing sessions of 90 min each, which were conducted about seven days apart. Data were collected by trained research assistants in the summer of 2012.

5.4.2 Measures

In order to assess the five facets of literary literacy, items were constructed for each of the theoretically derived facets described above. A multi-stage approach was used in which items were developed and revised after a cognitive laboratory procedure and again after a pilot study before they were used in the main study. Determinants of item difficulty had been examined in a former study, which revealed that open-ended response tasks tend to be more difficult than closed-ended items (Meier et al. 2013). Overall, 61 % of the test items were presented in a closed-ended format.

The tasks were administered as eight testlets, consisting of a stimulus text and semantic (overall 41 items, 54 % closed-ended, $r_{tt} = .80$) as well as idiolectal items (overall 30 items, 60 % closed-ended, $r_{tt} = .78$), and questions assessing the ability to recognize emotions that are intended by the text (10 items, all closed-ended, $r_{tt} = .59$). To assess the availability of specific literary knowledge, a new test was developed (53 items, 66 % closed-ended, $r_{tt} = .84$). Students' ability to apply specific literary knowledge was connected to the test of literary literacy by administering two knowledge-based items in each of the eight testlets. The ability to recognize foregrounded passages (hereafter referred to as "foregrounding") was assessed with a newly developed test, consisting of 11 items (18 % closed-ended, $r_{tt} = .75$).

In addition, expository reading comprehension was assessed with six testlets (IQ 2009; IQB 2012). The six testlets comprised a total of 50 items (64 % closed-ended, $r_{tt} = .81$).

All measures were presented in a multi-matrix design: that is, every student answered only a subset of the 195 test items. In the first session, the test of literary literacy and a questionnaire were administered. In the second session, students completed the tests of expository reading comprehension, specific literary knowledge, and foregrounding. Open-ended tasks were initially scored independently by two trained masters students, in the fields of educational science and German studies respectively. Initial interrater reliability was, on average, $\kappa = .79$ ($SD = 0.03$, $\kappa_{min} = .75$, $\kappa_{max} = .83$). Ratings that diverged between the first two raters were subsequently recoded by a third trained rater.

The following item samples, which refer to the stimulus text *Mr. Keuner and the helpless boy*, illustrate the operationalization of the five dimensions of literary literacy.

5.4.2.1 Semantic Literary Literacy

Assessing *semantic literary literacy* involves different aspects. Items can, for example, focus on (several) plausible global meanings of a text as well as on the construction of local coherence, on the extraction of specific information, or on the ability to provide text-based evidence for one's interpretation, as illustrated below:

> Cite three pieces of textual evidence which make the reader think that the man will help the boy.

Seven passages of the text can be quoted here, including "stroking him affectionately", "with new hope", or "because Mr. Keuner was smiling". Three pieces of evidence resulted in full credit (two points), and two pieces of evidence in partial credit (one point).

5.4.2.2 Idiolectal Literary Literacy

Items assessing *idiolectal literary literacy* address phonetic, grammatical, syntactical, and structural elements, as well as stylistic devices. These items require students not only to recognize stylistic features of the text, but also to analyze their structure, in order to explain their function within the text or their effect on the reader. What is crucial here is to draw parallels between form-related and semantic aspects of the text. The cognitive procedures associated with those items are often demanding, because they require drawing inferences between abstract formal phenomena and semantic information (Meier et al. 2013). The following item example illustrates this:

> The helpless boy in contrast to Mr. Keuner is nameless. Explain the effect of this stylistic feature.

Possible right answers are: "the boy's fate seems more anonymous", "the boy is only an example for a certain kind of behaviour", and "one can identify better with the boy because it could be any boy". Examples of incorrect answers are that "Mr. Keuner does not know the boy's name" (which is not convincing, because Mr. Keuner does not tell the story), or stating that "the name of the boy is not important", without explaining why.

5.4.2.3 The Ability to Recognize Foregrounded Passages (Foregrounding)

Foregrounding was assessed with items that focus on all linguistic levels, such as phonemes and morphemes, as well as semantic stylistic devices such as metaphors or syntactical changes (e.g., from ellipses to complex hypotaxes; van Peer 1986). These items require students to focus on the linguistic patterns of a text. In contrast to knowledge-based tasks or genuine idiolectal tasks, students are neither expected to give an accurate technical term nor to describe the effect or function of the stylistic device. To identify a foregrounded passage by quoting it, or by describing the style of a text, is a typical task, as illustrated by the following item:

> Describe three characteristics of the language that is used in the text *Mr Keuner and the helpless boy* in your own words.

To solve this item, students have to recognize, for example, that the story is written in a very simple language as a dialogue, which—and this might be the most irritating fact—is not indicated by quotation marks.

5.4.2.4 Specific Literary Knowledge

Some of the items assessing the *ability to apply specific literary knowledge* according to the educational standards for German language learning (KMK 2004) pertain to common motifs (e.g., typical motifs in fairy tales), symbols (e.g., symbolic meanings of colors) or famous books or authors. Other knowledge-based items require students to detect and name stylistic devices, different literary genres, or narrative modes, as the following example demonstrates:

> How would you name the narrative mode that is used in *Mr. Keuner and the helpless boy*? Please state the exact technical term.

This item requires the students to provide a technical term such as "third person objective narration".

5.4.2.5 The Ability to Recognize Emotions Intended by a Literary Text

The ability to recognize emotions intended by a literary text was assessed solely with items using a forced-choice format (response format: *rather agree* vs. *disagree*). This is due to the fact that multiple meanings of a text might be plausible and that one text might trigger a whole set of emotions simultaneously. The ability to deal with ambiguity is necessary in deciding which emotions are textually intended. The following example demonstrates this type of item:

> Which different moods or emotions does the text want to evoke in the reader (regardless of what you are actually feeling right now)? Several emotions may be plausible. Please indicate with a tick if you rather agree or disagree.

The emotions "shame", "astonishment", "outrage" and "envy" were presented. The unexpected end of the text is surprising and quite clearly intends to cause astonishment or outrage. These two emotions had to be marked as plausible (*rather agree*) for full credit. In contrast, neither content-related nor stylistic-related features suggest that shame or envy may be textually intended (cf. Frederking et al. 2016).

5.4.3 Statistical Analyses

For scaling purposes, and to explore the internal structure of literary literacy, we applied two-parameter logistic models (2PL; see Yen and Fitzpatrick 2006) in conjunction with a Bayesian approach, with the MCMC method. By separating item difficulty and item discrimination, the 2PL model takes into account variation across items in the relationship between students' item performance and ability. Item discrimination parameters varied between −.04 and .59. Given these variations, it is appropriate to apply the 2PL model.

A Bayesian approach with the MCMC method was applied because maximum or weighted likelihood estimation becomes computationally unwieldy with data for 195 categorical items and up to six different facets of reading literacy. Moreover, Bayesian estimates can effectively address drift and unusual response patterns, and are more appropriate for smaller sample sizes (Rupp et al. 2004).

All analyses were conducted with Mplus 7.2 (Muthén and Muthén 1998–2012). We specified all constructs as latent variables and used categorical items as indicators. First, we estimated a six first-order factor model using the total number of 195 items to identify poorly fitting items. Seven items with small or negative discrimination (i.e., the lower limit of a 95 % confidence interval of item slope is at or below zero) were excluded from further analyses. In a second step, the remaining 188 items were used to estimate various first- and second-order factor models, including both gender and school track simultaneously as control variables. Higher-order factor models are more parsimonious than first-order factor models if it is theoretically sensible to assume higher-order factors.

Our baseline model is a two first-order factor model, proposing that item performances are due to literary literacy on the one hand and expository reading comprehension on the other hand. This two-faceted model of reading literacy is empirically well supported (e.g., Frederking et al. 2012; Roick and Henschel 2015). We compared this model with alternative plausible models in which we gradually expand the number of facets of literary literacy. Because we assume that the five theoretically derived facets describe the complex competence of understanding a literary text, it seems appropriate to estimate a second-order factor model of literary literacy with the facets originating from the higher-order factor.

Considerations related to the cognitive processes that pertain to different levels of mental text representation guided the order of our model extension. We started by distinguishing foregrounding, as this requires the reader to focus on the surface level of the text. Applying specifically literary knowledge should be primarily relevant with higher-order levels of the comprehension process (Graesser et al. 1997), and seems to be useful in developing a complex mental model when reading literary texts (Meier et al. 2012). In addition, specific knowledge might guide the detection of foregrounded passages at the surface level (Hanauer 1999). For this reason, specific knowledge was considered as another facet of our competence model. Since recognizing textually intended emotions requires the reader to reflect and identify which emotions might be intended, and to integrate them at the level of situational text representation, we distinguished this ability in a further model. In the final model, we additionally distinguished between the two core facets: semantic and idiolectal literary literacy. The models and their corresponding facets, as examined in our study, are summarized in Table 5.1. To capture the local dependence of test items on the availability of specific literary knowledge, recognizing textually intended emotions, semantic and idiolectal literary literacy—all of which were assessed within common testlets—all models included testlet factors (Huang and Wang 2013).

In evaluating alternative 2PL models, we used the Bayesian Information Criterion (BIC; Schwarz 1978), the Deviance Information Criterion (DIC; Spiegelhalter et al. 2002), and the Posterior Predictive p-value (PPP; Scheines et al. 1999). The PPP reflects the discrepancy between the replicated data of the model and the observed data. A PPP substantially above zero indicates a well-fitting model.

In addition to the BIC, the DIC can be used to compare two different models. Models with small BIC or DIC values should be preferred, whereas it has to be

Table 5.1 Description of the estimated factor models

Models	Factorial structure
Model A	(1) Expository reading comprehension
	(2) Literary literacy (including semantic and idiolectal literary literacy, recognizing textually intended emotions, specific literary knowledge, and foregrounding)
Model B	(1) Expository reading comprehension
	(2) Literary literacy with two facets:
	Facet I: Foregrounding
	Facet II: Residual factor including semantic and idiolectal literary literacy, recognizing textually intended emotions, and specific literary knowledge
Model C	(1) Expository reading comprehension
	(2) Literary literacy with three facets:
	Facet I: Foregrounding
	Facet II: Specific literary knowledge
	Facet III: Residual factor including semantic and idiolectal literary literacy, and recognizing textually intended emotions
Model D	(1) Expository reading comprehension
	(2) Literary literacy with four facets:
	Facet I: Foregrounding
	Facet II: Specific literary knowledge
	Facet III: Recognizing textually intended emotions
	Facet IV: Residual factor including semantic and idiolectal literary literacy
Model E	(1) Expository reading comprehension
	(2) Literary literacy with five facets:
	Facet I: Foregrounding
	Facet II: Specific literary knowledge
	Facet III: Recognizing textually intended emotions
	Facet IV: Semantic literary literacy
	Facet V: Idiolectal literary literacy

noted that the DIC under-penalizes complex models (Plummer 2008). According to Raftery (1995), differences in BIC scores of more than five units indicate *strong* evidence for differences in model appropriateness.

Missing data in test results is a practically unavoidable occurrence in educational research. Items that students failed to complete (4 % of the items were omitted or not reached) were coded 0 in our scaling process. Due to the applied multi-matrix design in our study, about 59 % of data were missing by design. The Bayes estimator in Mplus is capable of handling this and uses all available data for parameter estimation.

5.5 Results

Zero-order correlation coefficients among the variables are reported in Table 5.2. The literary facets that are assumed to be located on higher levels of the comprehension process (recognizing textual intended emotions, specific literary knowledge,

Table 5.2 Correlations among literary literacy facets, expository reading comprehension, gender, and school track

Variable	(1)	(2)	(3)	(4)	(5)	(6)	(7)
(1) Semantic literary literacy (SL)[a]							
(2) Idiolectal literary literacy (IL)[a]	.89*						
(3) Recognizing textually intended emotions (IE)[a]	.71*	.70*					
(4) Specific literary knowledge (LK)[a]	.72*	.72*	.53*				
(5) Foregrounding (FG)[a]	.66*	.68*	.54*	.72*			
(6) Expository reading comprehension (ER)[a]	.65*	.67*	.52*	.66*	.67*		
(7) Gender (GE, 1 = male)[b]	−.36*	−.33*	−.20*	−.24*	−.29*	−.22*	
(8) School track (ST, 1 = upper)[b]	.24*	.28*	.15*	.35*	.30*	.28*	.04

$N = 964$
$^{*}p < .01$
[a]Modeled as a latent variable
[b]Manifest control variable

semantic and idiolectal literary literacy) are somewhat more strongly correlated with each other than with foregrounding or expository reading comprehension.

Comparing the correlations between gender and school track shows that gender is slightly stronger associated with the ability to recognize textually intended emotions, as well as semantic and idiolectal literary literacy, than is school track. School track shows a stronger relationship to specific literary knowledge and expository reading comprehension than gender. To a certain extent these results support the sequence of models to be estimated and the consideration of gender and school track as control variables.

Table 5.3 contains information on the model fit of the five estimated 2PL models. According to the BIC, DIC, and PPP, all second-order factor models (Models B to E) fit the data better than the two first-order factor model (Model A). Comparing the Models B to E reveals an increasing improvement in model fit up to Model C. According to the BIC and PPP, Model D shows a slight decrease in model fit. This does not apply for the DIC of Model D, but it is known that the DIC tends to favour the more complex model (Plummer 2008). For Model E, in contrast, all fit measures point to a decrease in the goodness of fit.

Table 5.4 provides further information about our five models. In Model A, we find the lowest correlation between literary literacy and expository reading comprehension, as well as the lowest regression coefficients of both measures on gender and school track. But literary literacy is modeled as a heterogeneous construct without taking into account its different facets. Considering the multifaceted structure (Models B to E), all facets show substantial loadings on the second-order factor of literary literacy. In Models D and E, it is clearly evident that the ability to recognize textual intended emotions has the smallest loading on the second-order factor of

Table 5.3 Comparisons of the estimated models

Models[a]	BIC[b]	Δ BIC[c]	DIC[b]	Δ DIC[c]	PPP[d]	Δ PPP[c]
Model A	123,908		120,625		.10	
Model B	123,809	99	120,514	111	.14	.04
Model C	123,650	258	120,331	294	.17	.07
Model D	123,655	253	120,331	294	.16	.06
Model E	123,684	224	120,366	259	.14	.04

All models used Bayesian estimation with MCMC method. The analyses conducted controlled for gender and school track simultaneously

[a]See Table 5.1 for further descriptions

[b]Bayesian (BIC) resp. Deviance (DIC) Information Criteria were estimated defining items as continuous

[c]Difference score to Model A

[d]Posterior predictive p-value (PPP) was estimated, defining items as categorical. $N = 964$

literary literacy. Finally, in Model E, we found a significant decrease in model fit after differentiating between semantic and idiolectal literary literacy. One reason might be that both facets are highly correlated (see Table 5.2), as shown in previous studies (e.g., Frederking et al. 2012; Roick et al. 2013).

Overall, as shown in Table 5.3, Model C seems to fit the data best. The latent correlation between literary literacy as a second-order factor and expository reading comprehension of .76 (see Table 5.4), suggests that the competence of literary literacy, operationalized by three facets—the ability to recognize foregrounding passages, the ability to apply specific literary knowledge, and a common factor consisting of the ability to recognize textual intended emotions as well as semantic and idiolectal literary literacy—is well separable from expository reading comprehension. For the covariates included in our model, two typical results of research on general reading comprehension are evident: Girls, as well as students from upper secondary schools, reach higher performances in reading literacy for both literary and expository texts than do boys and students from intermediate secondary schools.

5.6 Discussion

The aim of this chapter was to propose a competence structure model that captures the abilities of secondary school students in understanding literary texts. Several results of our study are relevant for discourse comprehension research. Furthermore, a competence structure model of literary literacy with distinguishable facets may serve as a starting point for instructional research and for developing teaching approaches to fostering this competence.

Table 5.4 Parameters of the estimated models

Models[a]	$\Psi_{LL,ER}^{a,b}$	$\beta_{LL,FG}^{a,c}$	$\beta_{LL,LK}^{a,c}$	$\beta_{LL,IE}^{a,c}$	$\beta_{LL,SL}^{a,c}$	$\beta_{LL,IL}^{a,c}$	$\beta_{LL,RF}^{a,d}$	$\beta_{GE,LL}^{a,e}$	$\beta_{GE,ER}^{a,e}$	$\beta_{ST,LL}^{a,f}$	$\beta_{ST,ER}^{a,f}$
Model A	.62*	–	–	–	–	–	–	−.30*	−.21*	.34*	.27*
Model B	.79*	.86*	–	–	–	–	.76*	−.36*	−.23*	.41*	.28*
Model C	.76*	.85*	.83*	–	–	–	.79*	−.35*	−.22*	.39*	.29*
Model D	.75*	.84*	.82*	.66*	–	–	.82*	−.36*	−.23*	.38*	.28*
Model E	.74*	.83*	.82*	.67*	.86*	.89*	–	−.35*	−.22*	.37*	.29*

Abbreviations: *LL* Literary literacy, *ER* Expository reading comprehension, *FG* Foregrounding, *LK* Specific literary knowledge, *IE* Recognizing textually intended emotions, *SL* Semantic literary literacy, *IL* Idiolectal literary literacy, *RF* Residual factor, *GE* Gender, *ST* School track

All models used Bayesian estimation with the MCMC method. Four cases with missing gender information. $N = 960$

*$p < .01$

[a]See Table 5.1 for further descriptions of models

[b]Intercorrelation between literary literacy and expository reading comprehension

[c]Factor loadings of facets on literary literacy

[d]Factor loading of the residual facet with all remaining items on literary literacy

[e]Regression coefficient of gender (GE, 1 = male)

[f]Regression coefficient of school track (ST, 1 = upper track)

5.6.1 *The Structure of Literary Literacy*

According to our findings, the internal structure of literary literacy accounts for at least three main facets: First, the content- and form-related ability of understanding (including semantic and idiolectal literary literacy, and recognizing textually intended emotions); second, the ability to apply specific literary knowledge, and third, the ability to recognize foregrounded passages. Interestingly, we found substantial and very similar correlations between the availability of specific literary knowledge and semantic and idiolectal literary literacy, as well as foregrounding (see Table 5.2). This result suggests that specific literary knowledge can be crucial for both: drawing appropriate inferences while constructing the meaning of a literary text and detecting foregrounded passages in literary texts (Hanauer 1999).

Referring to the students' competence to understand literary texts at the end of secondary school, it seems not appropriate to differentiate between semantic and idiolectal literary literacy and the ability to recognize textually intended emotions. That does not necessarily contradict the assumptions of Eco's semiotic theory (Eco 1976), because both facets interact closely in the critical reading mode of advanced readers (Eco 1990). However, it remains unclear whether recognizing textually intended emotions should be considered as a distinct facet of literary literacy or not. Although the model fit indices did not clearly indicate this conclusion, the factor loadings (see Table 5.4) as well as the correlations with other facets of literary literacy (see Table 5.2) were comparatively low. Yet, the underlying cognitive and—perhaps—affective processes that are required to recognize and identify textually intended emotions are still unclear. This is surprising, because both emotional experiences during reading a literary text and their potential impact on comprehension are discussed and examined in discourse processing research (Kneepkens and Zwaan 1994; Mar et al. 2011). It is conceivable that consistency between recognizing textually intended emotions and evoked emotions in the reader would facilitate or moderate the understanding of a literary text. Further research is needed, to fully understand how the different facets of our model of literary literacy interact and to examine the validity of the proposed model and its relevance for research in discourse comprehension. For example, it could be possible that several facets show differential courses of development. Based on the theoretical assumptions, additional analyses are needed that take into account specific external criteria (individual, contextual, and institutional) that might contribute differentially to the proposed facets of literary literacy (see also Roick and Henschel 2015).

5.6.2 *Some Considerations on Teaching Literary Literacy*

Although the students' competence in literary literacy seems to consist of three main facets, it might be useful to apply a more complex model for teaching purposes, in order to address different, important aspects of understanding literary texts sufficiently.

First of all, our findings clearly indicate that the ability to apply specific literary knowledge might be relevant for differences in processing on various levels of the textual representation. Therefore, more efforts have to be made to develop methods of fostering specific literary knowledge. For instance, Hanauer (1999) points out that explicit as well as implicit methods (e.g., extensive reading) may contribute to the acquisition of literary knowledge and to an increase in the readers' sensitivity to literary patterns.

Second, being aware of striking stylistic features seems to be crucial for analyzing the meaning and function of aesthetic elements on higher-order levels of the comprehension process (idiolectal and semantic literary literacy). In addition to specific literary knowledge, emotional reactions might be relevant in recognizing stylistic features (Miall and Kuiken 1994), and they are important aspects of teaching literature (Spinner, 2006). Further research is needed, however, to examine which teaching methods are effective in raising students' abilities to identify foregrounded passages. In addition to teaching specific knowledge, exercises in poetry writing might improve competencies in this field (Zyngier et al. 2007).

Third, the ability to recognize textually intended emotions seems to be an area that should be examined more carefully. The good fit of Model C, in which this facet was included with content- and form-related demands, indicates that semantic and idiolectal literary literacy seem to be relevant in recognizing textually intended emotions, and vice versa. Thus, strategies for finding out which emotions a text most likely intends, based on its content and its form, may be important for comprehending the meaning of a text (Frederking and Brüggeman 2012). Furthermore, it seems especially worthwhile to address and reflect the feelings students experience while reading, as previous studies found positive effects of cognitive and affective activation on the complexity of literary interpretations (e.g., Levine 2014).

Further research is needed to examine the interdependence of the facets of literary literacy for teaching purposes, as well as to develop effective concepts that improve literature classes. These teaching applications need to satisfy two requirements: First, they have to be empirically evaluated, and second, they have to address, in particular, struggling readers at lower academic tracks, and boys (Henschel et al. 2016). Both groups seem to be highly disadvantaged, since girls and students from higher school tracks performed better in almost all facets of literary literacy (see Tables 5.2 and 5.4; see also Roick et al. 2013). This might be due to girls' higher interest in literary reading (e.g., Lehmann 1994), which seems to have positive effects on their performance in literary reading tasks. Differences between school tracks are also plausible, because literary literacy is less prominent in lower school tracks (e.g., Hertel et al. 2010). Ideally, an evidence based approach to fostering literary literacy should compensate for the disadvantages of boys and students at lower academic tracks, in the long term.

5.6.3 Limitations of the Study

Some limitations of our study should be noted when interpreting the results. First of all, we did not measure expository reading comprehension, as differentiated as literary literacy, because we focused on the understanding of literary texts. It is evident that knowledge-based processes play an important role in understanding expository texts also (e.g., Kintsch 1988). Likewise, metalinguistic reflection might be important when dealing with these texts. However, in our study we did not assess students' prior knowledge or specific metalinguistic reflections in response to expository texts.

Furthermore, it has to be noted that we only included students of intermediate and upper secondary school tracks at the end of compulsory schooling. Therefore, our findings are only valid for this subgroup of students, and further research is needed to investigate literary literacy and its facets in other student groups.

In sum, this paper has proposed the theoretical background, the assessment and the results of an extended model of literary literacy, with at least three facets that can be differentiated from expository reading competence. This model could serve as a starting point for the evidence-based development of an approach to teaching literary literacy in secondary school.

Acknowledgments The preparation of this chapter was supported by grant FR 2640/1-3 and RO 3960/1-3 from the German Research Foundation (DFG) in the Priority Program "Competence Models for Assessing Individual Learning Outcomes and Evaluating Educational Processes" (SPP 1293).

References

Altmann, U., Bohrn, I. C., Lubrich, O., Menninghaus, W., & Jacobs, A. M. (2014). Fact vs fiction: How paratextual information shapes our reading processes. *Social Cognitive and Affective Neuroscience, 9*, 22–29. doi:10.1093/scan/nss098.

Brecht, B. (1995). Herr Keuner und der hilflose Knabe [Mr. Keuner and the helpless boy] (1932). In B. Brecht, *Werke. V. 18: Prosa 3. Sammlungen und Dialoge* (p. 19). Berlin: Aufbau Suhrkamp.

Eco, U. (1976). *A theory of semiotics*. Bloomington: Indiana University Press.

Eco, U. (1989). *The open work*. Cambridge: Harvard University Press.

Eco, U. (1990). *The limits of interpretation*. Bloomington: Indiana University Press.

Frederking, V., & Brüggemann, J. (2012). Literarisch kodierte, intendierte bzw. evozierte Emotionen und literarästhetische Verstehenskompetenz: Theoretische Grundlagen einer empirischen Erforschung [Literary coded, intended, or evoked emotions and literary literacy: Theoretical background of some empirical research]. In D. Frickel, C. Kammler, & G. Rupp (Eds.), *Literaturdidaktik im Zeichen von Kompetenzorientierung und Empirie. Perspektiven und Probleme* (pp. 15–41). Freiburg: Fillibach.

Frederking, V., Henschel, S., Meier, C., Roick, T., Stanat, P., & Dickhäuser, O. (2012). Beyond functional aspects of reading literacy: Theoretical structure and empirical validity of literary literacy. *L1 – Educational Studies in Language and Literature, 12*, 35–58.

Frederking, V., Brüggemann, J., Albrecht, C., Henschel, S., & Gölitz, D. (2016). Emotionale Facetten literarischen Verstehens und ästhetischer Erfahrung. Empirische Befunde literaturdidaktischer Grundlagen- und Anwendungsforschung [Emotional facets of literary literacy and aesthetic experience. Empirical results of basic research and applied research in the pedagogy of literature]. In J. Brüggemann, M.-G. Dehrmann, & J. Standke (Eds.), *Literarizität. Herausforderungen für Literaturdidaktik und Literaturwissenschaft* (pp. 87–132). Baltmannsweiler: Schneider.

Graesser, A. C., Millis, K. K., & Zwaan, R. A. (1997). Discourse comprehension. *Annual Review of Psychology, 48*, 163–189. doi:10.1146/annurev.psych.48.1.163.

Hanauer, D. (1999). Attention and literary education: A model of literary knowledge development. *Language Awareness, 8*, 15–29. doi:10.1080/09658419908667114.

Henschel, S., & Roick, T. (2013). Zusammenhang zwischen Empathie und dem Verstehen literarischer Texte [The link between empathy and literary text comprehension]. *Zeitschrift für Entwicklungspsychologie und Pädagogische Psychologie, 45*, 103–113. doi:10.1026/0049-8637/a000084.

Henschel, S., & Schaffner, E. (2014). Differenzielle Zusammenhänge zwischen Komponenten der Lesemotivation und dem Verstehen literarischer bzw. expositorischer Texte [Differential relationships between components of reading motivation and comprehension of literary and expository texts]. *Psychologie in Erziehung und Unterricht, 16*, 112–126. doi:10.2378/peu2014.art10d.

Henschel, S., Roick, T., Brunner, M., & Stanat, P. (2013). Leseselbstkonzept und Textart: Lassen sich literarisches und faktuales Leseselbstkonzept trennen [Reading self-concept and text-type: Can literary and factual reading self-concept be differentiated]? *Zeitschrift für Pädagogische Psychologie, 27*, 181–191. doi:10.1024/1010-0652/a000103

Henschel, S., Meier, C., & Roick, T. (2016). Effects of two types of task instructions on literary text comprehension and motivational and affective factors. *Learning and Instruction, 44*, 11–21. doi:10.1016/j.learninstruc.2016.02.005

Hertel, S., Hochweber, J., Steinert, B., & Klieme, E. (2010). Schulische Rahmenbedingungen und Lerngelegenheiten im Deutschunterricht [Educational framework and learning opportunities in German lessons]. In E. Klieme, C. Artelt, J. Hartig, N. Jude, O. Köller, M. Prenzel, et al. (Eds.), *PISA 2009. Bilanz nach einem Jahrzehnt* (pp. 113–148). Münster: Waxmann.

Hoffstaedter, P. (1986). *Poetizität aus der Sicht des Lesers. Eine empirische Untersuchung der Rolle von Text-, Leser- und Kontexteigenschaften bei der poetischen Verarbeitung von Texten* [Poeticity from the reader's point of view. An empirical study on text, reader, and context in the poetical processing of texts]. Hamburg: Buske.

Huang, H.-Y., & Wang, W.-C. (2013). Higher order testlet response models for hierarchical latent traits and testlet-based items. *Educational and Psychological Measurement, 73*, 491–511. doi:10.1177/0013164412454431.

IQ (The Institute for Qualitiy Improvement) (2009). *Lese(verständnis)test 9 Hessen* [Reading comprehension test 9 Hessen]. Wiesbaden: Author.

IQB (The Institute for Educational Quality Improvement) (2012). *Vergleichsaufgaben Deutsch für Sekundarstufe I . Unveröffentlichtes Testmaterial* [Items for comparisons in German for secondary schools, unpublished test material]. Berlin: Author.

Kintsch, W. (1988). The role of knowledge in discourse comprehension: A construction-integration model. *Psychological Review, 95*, 163–182. doi:10.1037/0033-295X.95.2.163.

KMK (The Standing Conference of the Ministers of Education and Cultural Affairs of the Länder in the Federal Republic of Germany) (2004). *Bildungsstandards im Fach Deutsch für den Mittleren Schulabschluss: Beschluss vom 4.12.2003* [Educational Standards for German language learning in secondary-level schooling: Resolution approved by the Standing Conference on 4 December 2003]. München: Luchterhand.

Kneepkens, E. W., & Zwaan, R. A. (1994). Emotions and literary text comprehension. *Poetics, 23*, 125–138. doi:10.1016/0304-422X(94)00021-W.

Lehmann, R. H. (1994). Lesen Mädchen wirklich besser? Ergebnisse aus der internationalen IEA-Lesestudie [Do girls really read better? Results of the international IEA-reading study]. In

S. Richter & H. Brügelmann (Eds.), *Mädchen lernen ANDERS lernen Jungen: Geschlechtsspezifische Unterschiede beim Schriftspracherwerb* (pp. 99–109). Lengwil: Libelle.
Levine, S. (2014). Making interpretation visible with an affect-based strategy. *Reading Research Quarterly, 49*, 283–303. doi:10.1002/rrq.71.
Mar, R. A., Oatley, K., Djikic, M., & Mullin, J. (2011). Emotion and narrative fiction: Interactive influences before, during, and after reading. *Cognition and Emotion, 25*, 818–833. doi:10.1080/02699931.2010.515151.
Meier, C., Henschel, S., Roick, T., & Frederking, V. (2012). Literarästhetische Textverstehenskompetenz und fachliches Wissen. Möglichkeiten und Probleme domänenspezifischer Kompetenzforschung [Literary literacy and expert knowledge. Chances and problems of competence research in specific domains]. In I. Pieper & D. Wieser (Eds.), *Fachliches Wissen und literarisches Verstehen. Studien zu einer brisanten Relation* (pp. 237–258). Frankfurt: Lang.
Meier, C., Roick, T., & Henschel, S. (2013). Erfassung literarischen Textverstehens: Zu Faktoren der Aufgabenschwierigkeit bei der Konstruktion von Testaufgaben [Measuring literary literacy: Using factors of item difficulty in item construction]. In C. Rieckmann & J. Gahn (Eds.), *Poesie verstehen—Literatur unterrichten* (pp. 103–123). Baltmannsweiler: Schneider.
Meutsch, D. (1987). *Literatur verstehen* [Understanding Literature]. Braunschweig: Vieweg.
Miall, D. S., & Kuiken, D. (1994). Foregrounding, defamiliarization, and affect: Response to literary stories. *Poetics, 22*, 389–407. doi:10.1016/0304-422X(94)00011-5.
Muthén, L. K., & Muthén, B. O. (1998–2012). *Mplus user's guide* (7th edn.) Los Angeles: Author.
Nutz, M. (2002). Geschichten vom Herrn Keuner [Stories of Mr. Keuner]. In J. Knopf (Ed.), *Brecht Handbuch V.3: Prosa, Filme, Drehbücher* (pp. 129–155). Stuttgart: Metzler.
OECD (Organisation for Economic Cooperation and Development) (2009). *PISA 2009 Assessment framework. Key competencies in reading, mathematics and science.* Retrieved from http://www.oecd.org/pisa/pisaproducts/44455820.pdf. Accessed 21 Nov 2015.
Plummer, M. (2008). Penalized loss functions for Bayesian model comparison. *Biostatistics, 9*, 523–539. doi:10.1093/biostatistics/kxm049.
Raftery, A. E. (1995). Bayesian model selection in social research. *Sociological Methodology, 25*, 111–163.
Roick, T., & Henschel, S. (2015). Strategie zur Validierung von Kompetenzstrukturmodellen [A strategy to validate the structure of competence models]. In U. Riegel, I. Schubert, G. Siebert-Ott, & K. Macha (Eds.), *Kompetenzmodellierung und -forschung in den Fachdidaktiken* (pp. 11–28). Münster: Waxmann.
Roick, T., Frederking, V., Henschel, S., & Meier, C. (2013). Literarische Textverstehenskompetenz bei Schülerinnen und Schülern unterschiedlicher Schulformen [Literary literacy of students from different school tracks]. In C. Rosebrock & A. Bertschi-Kaufmann (Eds.), *Literalität erfassen: bildungspolitisch, kulturell, individuell* (pp. 69–84). Weinheim: Beltz.
Rupp, A. A., Dey, D. K., & Zumbo, B. D. (2004). To Bayes or not to Bayes, from whether to when: Applications of bayesian methodology to modeling. *Structural Equation Modeling, 11*, 424–451. doi:10.1207/s15328007sem1103_7.
Scheines, R., Hoijtink, H., & Boomsma, A. (1999). Bayesian estimation and testing of structural equation models. *Psychometrika, 64*, 37–52. doi:10.1007/BF02294318.
Schwarz, G. (1978). Estimating the dimension of a model. *The Annals of Statistics, 6*, 239–472. doi:10.1214/aos/1176344136.
Spiegelhalter, D. J., Best, N. G., Carlin, B. P., & van der Linde, A. (2002). Bayesian measures of model complexity and fit. *Journal of the Royal Statistical Society, 64*, 583–639. doi:10.1111/1467-9868.00353.
Spinner, K. H. (2006). Literarisches Lernen [Literary learning]. *Praxis Deutsch, 200*, 6–16.
van Peer, W. (1986). *Stylistics and psychology*. London: Croom Helm.

Vipond, D., & Hunt, R. A. (1984). Point-driven understanding: Pragmatic and cognitive dimensions of literary reading. *Poetics, 13*, 261–277.

Winko, S. (2003). *Kodierte Gefühle. Zu einer Poetik der Emotionen in lyrischen und poetologischen Texten um* 1900 [Coded emotions. On a poetics of emotions in lyrical and poetological texts around 1900]. Berlin: Schmidt.

Yen, W. M., & Fitzpatrick, A. R. (2006). Item response theory. In R. L. Brennan (Ed.), *Educational measurement* (4th ed., pp. 111–153). Westport: Praeger.

Zwaan, R. A. (1993). *Aspects of literary comprehension*. Amsterdam: Benjamins.

Zyngier, S., Fialho, O., & do Prado Rios, P. A. (2007). Revisiting literary awareness. In G. Watson & S. Zyngier (Eds.), *Literature and stylistics for language learners: Theory and practice* (pp. 194–209). New York: Palgrave Macmillan.

Chapter 6
Self-Regulated Learning with Expository Texts as a Competence: Competence Structure and Competence Training

Joachim Wirth, Melanie Schütte, Jessica Wixfort, and Detlev Leutner

Abstract Three studies are presented that take a look at self-regulated learning as a competence (assessed on the basis of achievement tests) rather than a self-reported learning experience (assessed on the basis of questionnaires). In the first step, in two correlational studies with $N = 559$ and $N = 795$ 9th graders, sub-competencies of self-regulated learning were identified that are predictive of successful learning with expository texts. In the second step, in an experimental study with $N = 647$ 9th graders, students were assessed with regard to these sub-competencies and were adaptively allocated to training programs that were designed to improve those two sub-competencies that had been shown to be weak in the assessment. The results are in line with a model that integrates component and process models of self-regulated learning. Specifically, it emerged that self-regulated learning as a competence can be broken down into sub-competencies that, in turn, can be taught, in order to improve students' overall learning achievement when learning with expository texts.

Keywords Self-regulated learning • Competence • Structure • Process • Training

6.1 Theoretical Background

The competence of self-regulated learning is regarded as a prerequisite of life-long learning (e.g., Commission of the European Community 2000). It enables learners to initiate, plan, control, and regulate their learning process, and it facilitates learning in multiple contexts and domains. Wirth and Leutner (2008) defined the competence of self-regulated learning as "a learner's competence to autonomously plan,

J. Wirth (✉) • M. Schütte • J. Wixfort
Ruhr-University Bochum, Bochum, Germany
e-mail: lehrlernforschung@rub.de; melanie.schuette@rub.de; jessica.wixfort@rub.de

D. Leutner
Faculty of Educational Sciences, Department of Instructional Psychology, University of Duisburg-Essen, Essen, Germany
e-mail: detlev.leutner@uni-due.de

D. Leutner et al. (eds.), *Competence Assessment in Education*, Methodology of Educational Measurement and Assessment, DOI 10.1007/978-3-319-50030-0_6

execute, and evaluate learning processes, which involves continuous decisions on cognitive, motivational, and behavioral aspects of the cyclic process of learning" (p. 103). However, the notion of "a learner's competence" does not mean that the competence of self-regulated learning is unidimensional. Researchers emphasize rather that learners need a whole set of competencies that are more or less domain- or task-specific, and that are needed within different phases of the learning process (Winne and Perry 2000; Wirth and Leutner 2008). Consequently, there is no single model of self-regulated learning competence that integrates all relevant competencies for all learning domains in all learning phases. Models differ concerning learning domains and concerning their focus on either the different competencies ("component models"; e.g., Boekaerts 1997; Schreiber 1998) or the different phases of self-regulated learning ("process models"; e.g., Winne and Hadwin 1998; Zimmerman 2000).

The purpose of our research was to develop and evaluate a model of self-regulated learning for the domain of learning with expository texts. Thus, our model is restricted to this specific domain. However, the core aspect of our model is that we aimed to overcome the distinction between competencies and phases (Winne and Perry 2000; Wirth and Leutner 2008). Instead, we wanted to develop an integrated model describing all relevant competencies and the structure of their relationships, as well as their occurrence and relevance in the different phases of a learning process (for a similar approach see Dresel et al. 2015). As a result, this model aims to integrate different kinds of models of self-regulated learning. Additionally, this model provides an integrated theoretical foundation for developing trainings in self-regulated learning that could in turn validate the integrated model.

In the current paper, we first describe our integrated model of self-regulated learning. Second, we report two studies analyzing the factorial structure of the different competencies described in the model. Third, we present data from a training study, which shows how the different competencies contribute to successful learning.

6.1.1 Integrated Model of Self-Regulated Learning

Our model integrates aspects of process models and also component models of self-regulated learning (Fig. 6.1). Process models (e.g., Pressley et al. 1987, 1989; Winne and Hadwin 1998; Zimmerman 2000) describe self-regulated learning in terms of phases or stages. Each phase is defined by the specific demands posed to learners within that phase. For example, in a first phase ("forethought phase"; Zimmerman 2000) learners need (among other considerations) to define their learning task. Based on this learning-task definition they have to set up one or more learning goals, and then have to plan how to achieve these learning goal(s). In the next, "performance phase" (Zimmerman 2000), learners need to execute their plan. In addition, while executing the plan, they need to observe themselves and their learning as neutrally as possible, and from a bird's-eye perspective. In the "self-reflection phase" (Zimmerman 2000), learners need to evaluate whether what they have

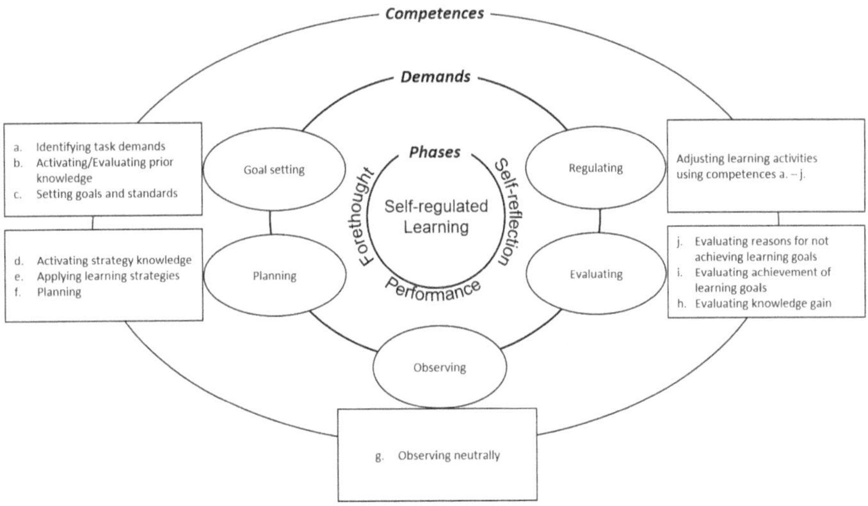

Fig. 6.1 Integrated model of self-regulated learning (Adapted from Schütte et al. 2010, 2012)

observed is in line with their learning goal(s) and plan. This evaluation can lead either to changes within any of the learning phases, or—if learners recognize that they have reached their goal(s)—to the end of the learning process.

Although process models describe the different phases in a linear manner, they all emphasize that the process of self-regulated learning is not a linear but a cyclic sequence of phases. Whenever learners end up with self-reflection, this is the starting point for a new cycle of self-regulation. For example, results of the self-reflection phase can lead to the need to change learning goal(s), which in turn can result in the need to adjust the learning plan, as well as the criteria used in the self-reflection phase. Winne and Hadwin (1998) even assume that learners do not always have to finish the whole cycle with a fixed sequence of phases, but can go back and forth whenever they realize that they need to change their learning activities to accomplish the different demands of self-regulated learning.

Of course, the different process models of self-regulated learning differ according to the number of phases they assume, the specific demands they assign to the different phases, and many other aspects. However, they share some common features: (a) All process models describe three kinds of phases. First, they include phases that prepare the actual learning activities. Second, they describe phases in which the actual learning activities are performed, and third, they emphasize phases of self-reflection. Therefore, we have included a planning phase, a performance phase, and a self-reflection phase (cf., Dresel et al. 2015; Zimmerman 2000) in our model of self-regulated learning (Fig. 6.1). (b) All process models describe self-regulated learning as a goal-directed process (Weinert 1982). Learners have to develop a plan to reach self-established learning goals, and they have to monitor whether the execution of their plan leads to the desired goal. Many researchers consider monitoring as one of the keys to successful self-regulated learning (e.g., Butler and Winne 1995). Monitoring consists of observing and evaluating the learning process, as well as regulating in the sense of adjusting learning activities so that learners reach their learning goal(s) (Schreiber 1998). Summing up, goal setting, planning, observing, evaluating, and regulating are demands on self-regulated learners that all process models address in one way or another. Therefore, we included these five demands in our model (Fig. 6.1). (c) All process models emphasize the cyclic nature of the process of self-regulated learning. The core assumption is that meeting the demands in one phase is dependent on the learner's success in meeting the demands of previous phases. For example, in order to plan their learning process successfully, learners need to have successfully set up their learning goals in advance. If learners come to realize that they have not sufficiently defined their learning goals, they need to go back and define their goals before they can again start with planning. Therefore, we arranged the different phases and demands in cycles, describing that the learners can go back and forth, and even if learners approach the end of the current learning process cycle, this end will be the starting point of the next learning process.

Process models describe phases and demands of self-regulated learning, but they usually fail in describing the competencies learners need to meet these demands. Competencies are usually a part of component models of self-regulated learning, and are often described in terms of strategy knowledge (e.g., Boekaerts 1997). Dresel et al. (2015) point out that component models have a broad understanding of knowledge that relates strategy knowledge to the task and the self, and that is not restricted to declarative knowledge. Additionally, they include procedural strategy knowledge (Anderson 1983), in the sense of being able to execute a specific strategy successfully, as well as conditional knowledge (Paris et al. 1983), which means that learners know under which situational and personal conditions a certain strategy is suitable to meet a specific demand. Describing competencies of self-regulated learning as knowledge in this broad sense highlights three key aspects of self-regulated learning competencies: (a) Both declarative and procedural strategy knowledge do not guarantee that learners really use their strategy knowledge in a specific learning situation. Several conditions (e.g., motivational problems) can prevent learners from using what they know and what they could do. This is in line with the common notion that competencies are dispositions rather than performances (Hartig et al. 2008). (b) Competencies of self-regulated learning include knowledge about personal characteristics (e.g., content-specific prior knowledge), task characteristics (e.g., structural features of a text that has to be read), and strategies (e.g., a concept-mapping strategy; Flavell 1979). (c) These competencies have to interact, in order to meet the demands of self-regulated learning.

We included a set of competencies in our model that enable learners to activate, apply, acquire, or evaluate their knowledge about personal characteristics, task characteristics, or strategies (Fig. 6.1). Each of the competencies relates to a demand (Wirth and Leutner 2008), which in turn links the competencies described in component models to the phases proposed by process models. During the forethought phase, learners need to set learning goal(s) and plan how to reach these goal(s). Goal setting requires that learners decide what they have to learn. It is therefore necessary that they are able to identify the task demands (e.g., task characteristics that make the task easy or hard to process) and to activate and evaluate their content-specific (prior) knowledge (e.g., to evaluate what they already know and what they do not know so far). Based on these evaluations, learners must be able to set learning goals and define standards to be used later in the self-reflection phase, when they need to be able to decide whether they have reached their learning goal(s) or not. Planning requires learners to be able to activate their declarative strategy knowledge and to evaluate whether they are able to execute the activated strategies successfully. Referring to the task demands and learning goals, learners then must have the competence to plan which strategy they want to apply, and when.

During the performance phase, learners execute the learning strategies. Thereby, they have to be able to keep track continuously and as objectively as possible of what they are doing, how they do it, and what they achieve by doing what they do (Schreiber 1998). During the self-reflection phase, learners have to evaluate their learning process. Therefore, they again have to be able to estimate their content-specific knowledge and to evaluate which knowledge they have gained by their learning activities. Furthermore, they need to be able to evaluate whether they have reached their learning goal(s) using the standards defined during goal setting. In the case of not achieving their goal(s), learners need to be able to analyze the reasons for non-achievement.

Regulating means that learners have to be able to adjust and modify their learning according to the results of their evaluation. These adjustments and modifications can be necessary for each of the phases, depending on which demand(s) the learners have not yet met. Thus, the competencies needed for regulating include all the competencies needed so far.

Figure 6.1 presents our integrated model of self-regulated learning. We derived the model by analyzing the core characteristics of process models and component models, with a specific focus on the demands defined by process models as links between competencies and phases. Based on these theoretical considerations, we now present three empirical studies investigating the structure of the so-defined competence of self-regulated learning, in the following sections.

6.2 Research Questions and Hypotheses

In Studies 1a and 1b, we explored the structure of self-regulated learning competence from a "component perspective". We were interested in how the different (sub-) competencies proposed by our model are related to each other. Therefore, we assessed the different competencies independently of each other, and ran explorative factor analyses. We assumed that the competencies would be positively correlated, but had no a priori hypotheses about the underlying competence structure.

In Study 2, we took a "process perspective". We investigated whether single competencies being fostered and improved by specific training would enhance the overall effect of competencies employed in later steps of the process of learning.

The study is based on two assumptions: (a) We assumed that the effect of a certain competence on learning outcomes would be dependent on the accomplishment of demands learners have to deal with in earlier steps of the learning process. That is, if learners, due to weak competencies, fail to accomplish earlier demands in a specific learning process, it can be expected that they will not be effective in applying their competencies in later demands of the same learning process. For example, the competence of planning can lead to an appropriate learning plan only if learners had earlier been able to set up appropriate learning goals. If they lack at least one of the competencies needed for setting up learning goals, they will not be able to develop a plan that leads to appropriate learning goals (and, thus, to the desired learning outcome) even if their competence in planning is high. (b) We assume that learners have individual strengths and weaknesses in respect of the different competencies. This means that the different (sub-) competencies may develop independently of each other, so that learners may be strong in some competencies but weak in others. Combining the two assumptions leads to the hypothesis that it should be sufficient to train an individual only in those competencies in which they are weak. In effect, all the (sub-) competencies of self-regulated learning should together deploy their full potential, which should, in turn, result in successful learning.

6.3 Studies 1a and 1b: A "Component Perspective" on the Structure of Self-Regulated Learning Competence

We investigated the structure of the competence of self-regulated learning. We were interested in how the (sub-) competencies proposed by our model correlate, and whether we could identify an underlying factorial structure. We had no a priori hypotheses about the factorial structure. However, at least two kinds of structures seemed to be reasonable: (a) One structure could emerge based on the demands of self-regulated learning. Within such a five-factorial structure, all competencies needed to accomplish one of the five demands would load on one common factor, representing the respective demand. For example, all competencies needed to set up goals would load on the factor "goal setting", whereas all competencies needed for planning would load on the factor "planning", and so forth. (b) Another structure could emerge based on the three kinds of knowledge: about task characteristics, personal characteristics, and learning strategies (Flavell 1979). Within such a three-factorial structure, all competencies needed to identify and use knowledge about the task, the learner, or the strategies, would load on common factors representing the respective kind of knowledge. Since we had no theoretical reason to prefer one of the described (or any other conceivable) factorial structures, we used an explorative approach to identify the structure of the competence of self-regulated learning.

In Study 1a, with a sample of $N = 559$ 9th graders, we assessed all competencies proposed by our model of self-regulated learning with expository texts (Fig. 6.1; Schütte 2012; Schütte et al. 2012). Concerning the competence of identifying task demands, we differentiated between the competencies of identifying text features

Table 6.1 Factor loadings (rotated solution) of Study 1a

Competencies	1	2
Evaluating task demands		
Text features increasing text difficulty	.047	**.429**
Text features decreasing text difficulty	−.193	**.522**
Activating/Evaluating prior knowledge		
Existing knowledge	**.426**	−.250
Knowledge gaps	**−.385**	.240
Setting goals and standards	.156	.159
Activating strategy knowledge	.038	**.588**
Applying learning strategies		
Text highlighting	.208	−.061
Concept mapping	.110	.205
Planning	−.002	.114
Evaluating knowledge gain		
Existing knowledge	**.636**	.227
Knowledge gaps	**−.643**	−.020
Evaluating achievement of learning goals		
Goals achieved	**.532**	.206
Goals not achieved	**−.637**	.082
Evaluating reasons for not achieving learning goals	−.201	**.441**

that either increase or decrease text difficulty. Similarly, we divided the competence of activating/evaluating (prior) knowledge into activating/evaluating existing knowledge or knowledge gaps. Regarding the competence of applying learning strategies, we chose the competencies that apply to strategies of text highlighting and concept mapping. Finally, the competence of evaluating the achievement of learning goals was assessed according to learning goals achieved or not achieved (see Schütte 2012 for details on test instruments, sample, and procedure).

We conducted an exploratory factor analysis (main component analysis, VARIMAX rotation) that proposed a two-factorial solution that accounted for 23.9 % of the variance (Table 6.1).

Competencies needed to activate and evaluate content-specific (prior) knowledge, as well as competencies needed for evaluating goal achievement, defined the first factor. We interpreted this first factor as competencies needed for activating and evaluating personal characteristics. The second factor built on the competencies of evaluating task demands, of activating strategy knowledge, and of evaluating reasons for not achieving goals. We interpreted this second factor as competencies needed for evaluating task characteristics. Note that our test of the competence of activating strategy knowledge assessed mainly conditional knowledge (Paris et al. 1983), where conditions are determined by task demands. In the same way, the test of the competence of evaluating reasons for not achieving goals had a focus on reasons attributed to the task (e.g., task difficulty).

The competencies of setting goals and standards, applying learning strategies and planning, did not clearly load on one of the two factors. Additionally, as regression analyses showed, the competencies of setting goals and standards, and planning, did not contribute to learning (Schütte 2012). The same is true for all competencies needed for evaluating (competencies h–j in Fig. 6.1). Thus, we were not able to identify a clear factorial structure in Study 1a. However, we found first hints that the competence structure of self-regulated learning might reflect Flavell's (1979) distinction of person, task, and strategy knowledge rather than the different demands.

In Study 1b, with N = 795 9th graders (Schütte and Wirth 2013), we again assessed the competencies of self-regulated learning. However, differently from Study 1a, we included neither the competence of setting goals and standards nor the competence of planning. We revised our test of the competence of applying learning strategies and added a third strategy (summarizing). Finally, we relinquished assessing the competencies needed for evaluating during the self-reflection phase, since they had proved to be non-predictive of learning outcomes in Study 1a.

Again we conducted an exploratory factor analysis (main component analysis, VARIMAX rotation), which proposed a three-factorial solution that accounted for 50.8 % of the variance (Table 6.2).

The three-factorial solution clearly supported Flavell's (1979) distinction between task characteristics (Factor 1), person characteristics (Factor 2), and learning strategies (Factor 3). By conducting a confirmatory factor analysis we modeled the relations between the three factors (Fig. 6.2; $\chi^2_{(17)} = 11.870$; $p = .808$; RMSEA = .000). We found a strong correlation between the competence of identifying task demands and that of activating and applying learning strategies. The competence of activating and evaluating (content-specific) knowledge was not related to other competencies.

The component perspective on the competence of self-regulated learning revealed that the underlying competence structure fitted best to Flavell's (1979) distinction of task characteristics, person characteristics, and learning strategies. We didn't find any hints that the different demands or the different phases may form

Table 6.2 Factor loadings (rotated solution) of Study 1b.

Competencies	1	2	3
Evaluating task demands			
Text features increasing text difficulty	**.868**	−.028	.008
Text features decreasing text difficulty	**.807**	−.020	.214
Activating/Evaluating knowledge			
Existing knowledge	.055	**−.715**	−.154
Knowledge gaps	.015	**.780**	−.069
Activating strategy knowledge	.203	-.126	**.482**
Applying learning strategies			
Text highlighting	.036	.025	**.616**
Concept mapping	.157	.036	**.580**
Summarizing	.037	.163	**.650**

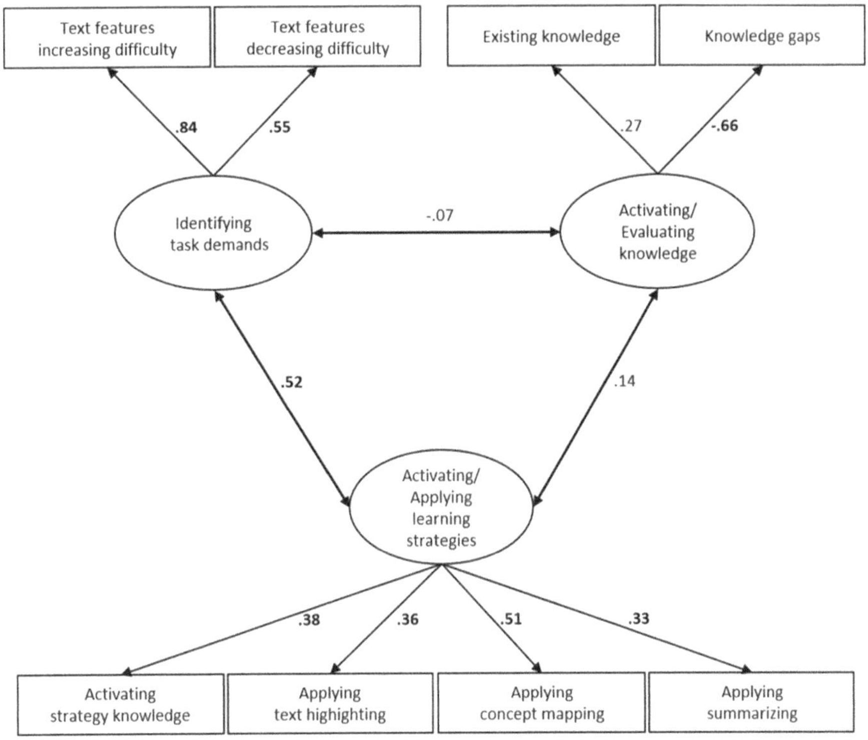

Fig. 6.2 Competence structure of self-regulated learning with expository texts (*bold text* = significant at $\alpha = .05$)

underlying factors. This result may be due to the cyclic nature of self-regulated learning: Learners often go back and forth, and do not work through the phases in a linear manner. Thus, the phases have less value for building an underlying competence structure.

Regression analyses, however, indicated that only some of the competencies proposed by our model (Fig. 6.1) proved to be relevant to learning. None of the competencies needed for self-reflection, nor the competence of setting goals and standards, nor the competence of planning, contributed to learning. From a theoretical point of view, this is surprising. However, from a methodological point of view, we assume that the competencies in question could not contribute to learning because our learning task was difficult for the learners, and learning time was short. Thus, in the specific learning task there was probably not enough time for careful goal setting and planning. The same is true for self-reflection. Additionally, we assume that we were not able to find effects of the competencies of self-reflection on learning because we had used only one learning task. Perhaps self-reflection would have had an effect on succeeding learning tasks. But due to time constraints we were not able to administer additional texts and tests to capture these possible effects.

6.4 Study 2: A "Process Perspective" on the Structure of Self-Regulated Learning Competence

Study 2 was designed as a training study. In this study, we investigated whether single competencies of self-regulated learning (SRL) after being fostered and improved by specific training, would enhance the overall effect on learning outcomes of SRL competencies needed in later steps of the process of learning. We assumed that it should be sufficient to train in only the few SRL competencies in which an individual learner is rather weak, so that, in effect, all the (sub-) competences of self-regulated learning can together deploy their full potential for successful learning.

We conducted the study with N = 647 9th graders. In a pre-test session we assessed their competencies of identifying task demands, of activating/evaluating knowledge, of activating strategy knowledge, and of applying the learning strategies of text highlighting, concept mapping, and summarizing (Table 6.2). We used tests that we had normalized in a preceding study, with N = 2215 9th graders from two German school types ("*Gymnasium*", as a higher track of secondary education and "*Gesamtschule*" as a lower track of secondary education). For all tests, separate norm references exist for both school types.

For each single student we identified those two competencies on which the student achieved the lowest norm reference scores. On the basis of these two competencies, we adaptively assigned two respective training modules to each student.

The training modules were administered as web-based trainings, as part of the students' homework assignments. Each of the two modules took 4 weeks. Whereas students had to work with the module at home, their teachers at school were responsible for ensuring that students really worked continuously with the modules.

After 8 weeks, we again assessed the students' competencies of identifying task demands, activating/evaluating knowledge, activating strategy knowledge, and applying the three learning strategies. Additionally, we gave students an expository text, and tested their respective content-specific prior knowledge. Students then had to study a text (in a completely self-regulated way) within 1 week as part of their homework assignments. After this week, students worked on a content-specific knowledge test on the information provided in the text.

As a first result, we had to deduce that only n = 146 students had worked sufficiently with the web-based training modules and had participated in all test sessions. Obviously, we had not been able to motivate all students (and teachers) to participate in the study conscientiously. However, in a first step, we analyzed whether working with one of the two training modules increased the respective SRL competence. We conducted repeated-measures analyses of variance with the norm reference scores on the respective competence tests before and after the training as a within-subject factor. For each module/competence, we compared students who were assigned to the module and worked with the module sufficiently, with those who refused to work with the module, as a between-subject factor. Additionally, we controlled for school type, since norm reference scores were assigned within school types. It turned out that most of our training modules increased the respective competence (Table 6.3). Only the modules fostering the SRL competencies of applying the text highlighting strategy and applying the concept mapping strategy, did not show any effect.

In a second step, we analyzed whether working with the modules not only increased the respective SRL competence but also enhanced overall self-regulated learning, leading to better learning outcomes when reading the expository text. For that reason, we compared the scores in the content-specific knowledge test between students who sufficiently processed no, one, or two modules of the two modules they had been allocated to. As an additional between-subject factor, we controlled for school type ("Gymnasium"/"Gesamtschule") in our analysis of variance (Fig. 6.3).

Table 6.3 Interaction of time (pre-test/post-test) and training module processing (yes/no) for each training module/competence; *p*-values one-tailed

Module/Competence	*F*	*df*	*p*	*d*
Identifying task demands	4.019	1,56	.025	0.54
Activating/Evaluating knowledge	6.546	1,66	.007	0.63
Activating strategy knowledge	3.881	1,100	.026	0.39
Applying text highlighting strategy	< 1	1,81		
Applying concept-mapping strategy	< 1	1,149		
Applying summarizing strategy	1.914	1,24	.090	0.57

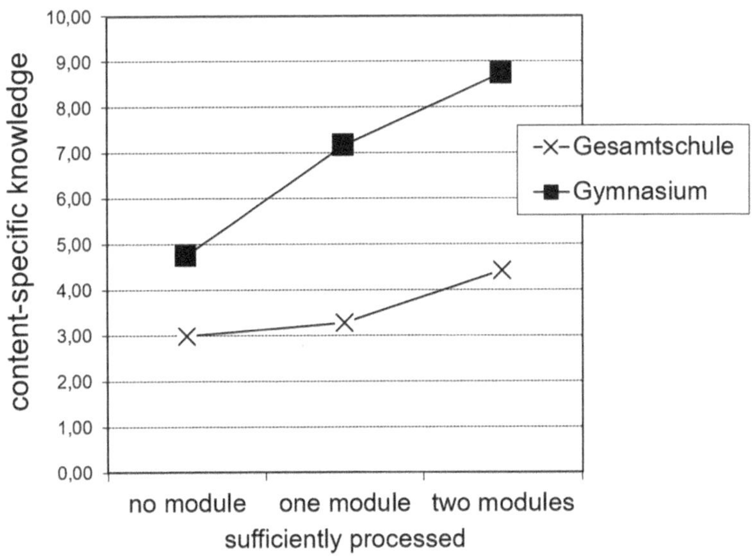

Fig. 6.3 Learning outcomes as a function of school type and number of sufficiently processed training modules. "Gymnasium" represents a higher, "Gesamtschule" a lower track of German secondary education

The results revealed a main effect for school type ($F_{(1,140)} = 44.66$; $p < .001$; $\eta^2 = .243$) and a main effect for number of modules sufficiently processed ($F_{(2,140)} = 4.92$; $p = .009$; $\eta^2 = .066$), but no interaction of the two factors ($F_{(2,140)} = 1.04$; $p = .358$). Thus, working on the training modules seriously improved students' learning outcomes, in what might be attributed to an increased overall competence of self-regulated learning with expository text—an effect that was independent of the specific type of school in which students were learning. We interpret this result as a first hint of the effectiveness of our adaptive training, where only weak SRL competencies were taught, rather than training in all self-regulated learning competencies. It seems that strengthening weak competencies helps learners to accomplish specific demands that are in turn a prerequisite for other (stronger) competencies: to unfold their learning potential in subsequent phases of the self-regulated learning process.

However, the results have to be interpreted carefully. Of course, the effects could be due to the large dropout rate in our sample. For example, it could be that very conscientious students worked with our training modules, while less-conscientious students refused to train in their competencies. If so, then the results presented in Fig. 6.3 could be attributable to the extent of conscientiousness, rather than to the number of modules sufficiently processed. However, since we were able to show that our training modules indeed increased the respective (sub-) competence of self-regulated learning (Table 6.3), it seems reasonable that the increase from no, to one, and two modules (Fig. 6.3) is responsible for the respective increases in learning outcomes.

6.5 Discussion

In three studies we investigated self-regulated learning as a competence, with a focus on those (sub-) competencies that are necessary for successful self-regulated learning. According to previous studies, and an integrated model of self-regulated learning (Schütte et al. 2010), the following (sub-) competencies enable students to meet the challenges of learning in a self-regulated way: In order to set their goals for learning, students have to be able to identify task demands, to activate and to evaluate their prior knowledge, and finally, to set goals and standards for their learning. In order to plan their learning, students have to be able to activate knowledge about learning strategies, to apply learning strategies and, finally, to plan the specific procedure in a given learning situation. While learning, students have to be able to observe their learning activities neutrally. In order to evaluate their learning, students have to be able to evaluate their knowledge gain, their achievement of learning goals, and reasons for not having achieved any learning goals. Finally, in order to regulate their learning, students have to be able to adjust their learning activities.

In Studies 1a and 1b, we explored the correlational structure of these (sub-) competencies from a "component perspective". The results indicate that competencies of activating and applying learning strategies can be differentiated from those of identifying task demands and activating and evaluating content-specific knowledge; this is in line with Flavell's (1979) distinction of learning strategies, task characteristics, and person characteristics.

In Study 2, we had a look at self-regulated learning from a "process perspective". The focus was on those sub-competencies that, in Studies 1a and 1b, turned out to be especially predictive of learning achievement. In a training study, we first assessed students on these sub-competencies and then adaptively trained them in relation to those two sub-competencies on which they were weak. The results indicate that this adaptive training in weak sub-competencies increased students' overall competence in self-regulated learning, as indicated by increased learning outcomes when learning with an expository text.

Of course, the present studies have limitations. First of all, the underlying model of self-regulated learning (Schütte et al. 2010) is restricted to the domain of learning with expository texts. This is due to the fact that the (sub-) competencies needed to meet the different demands differ between domains. For example, the learning strategies of text highlighting, concept mapping or summarizing are appropriate for learning with expository texts, but probably less helpful for learning how to drive a car. Thus, in line with Klieme and Leutner (2006), (sub-) competencies of self-regulated learning are domain-specific or even context-specific. However, on a more abstract level, the model can serve as a framework for the competence of self-regulated learning in almost all domains. The process of self-regulated learning includes phases of forethought, performance, and self-reflection that are independent of domain. The same is true for the demands of goal setting, planning, observing, evaluating, and regulating. Thus, only the competencies must be adapted to the specific domain.

A further limitation results from the use of Klieme and Leutner's (2006) definition of competence. They define competencies as context-specific cognitive dispositions that are acquired by learning and that are needed to successfully cope with certain situations or tasks in specific domains (p. 879). Thus, our model is limited to cognitive dispositions. This focus on cognitive dispositions excludes any non-cognitive aspects of competencies, such as for example, motivation. However, performance is low when motivation is low, even if the cognitive competence is high. Thus, we assume that our model would strongly benefit from including strategies of motivation regulation (Wolters 2003).

Taking these limitations into account, the present results have theoretical as well as practical implications. On the theoretical side, the results are in line with both component (e.g., Boekaerts 1997; Schreiber 1998) and process models (e.g., Winne and Hadwin 1998; Zimmerman 2000) of self-regulated learning, insofar as the underlying model (Schütte et al. 2010) integrates the two approaches to the study of self-regulated learning (Wirth and Leutner 2008). Note that in the present studies, we focused on self-regulated learning as a competence (that is composed of sub-competencies), rather than on self-regulated learning as a learning experience. Consequently, we developed a battery of achievement tests for assessing students' sub-competencies of self-regulated learning, rather than a questionnaire for assessing students' self-reported strategic learning behaviors (such as, e.g., the well-known

MSLQ; Pintrich et al. 1993). The results of our training study indicate that the sub-competencies of self-regulated learning can be regarded as links of a chain: If one of the links is weak, the whole chain will be weak. Or, in other words, if students are adaptively trained on those links of the chain that are weak, the whole chain will become stronger. This notion is completely in line with process theories of self-regulated learning which state that each step of a learning strategy has to be performed on a qualitatively high level in order to achieve high learning results (e.g., Leutner et al. 2007).

On the practical side, the results of the present studies indicate that self-regulated learning with expository texts is a multi-faceted competence that can be broken down into sub-competencies that are, to a varying degree, predictive of successful learning. The sub-competencies of self-regulated learning can be assessed, and weak sub-competencies can be taught adaptively, in order to improve students' learning outcomes when they are asked to learn from an expository text.

Acknowledgements The preparation of this chapter was supported by grant WI 2663/4-1, WI 2663/4-2 and WI 2663/4-3 from the German Research Foundation (DFG) in the Priority Program "Competence Models for Assessing Individual Learning Outcomes and Evaluating Educational Processes" (SPP 1293).

References

Anderson, J. (1983). *The architecture of cognition*. Cambridge, MA: Harvard University Press.

Boekaerts, M. (1997). Self-regulated learning: A new concept embraced by researchers, policy makers, educators, teachers, and students. *Learning and Instruction, 7*, 161–186.

Butler, D. L., & Winne, P. H. (1995). Feedback and self-regulated learning: A theoretical synthesis. *Review of Educational Research, 65*, 245–281. doi:10.1016/S0959-4752(96)00015-1.

Commission of the European Community. (2000). *A memorandum for life-long learning*. Brussels: Commission of the European Community.

Dresel, M., Schmitz, B., Schober, B., Spiel, S., Ziegler, A., Engelschalk, T., … Steuer, G. (2015). Competencies for successful self-regulated learning in higher education: Structural model and indications drawn from expert interviews. *Studies in Higher Education, 40*, 454–470. doi:10.1080/03075079.2015.1004236.

Flavell, J. H. (1979). Metacognition and cognitive monitoring. A new area of cognitive-developmental inquiry. *American Psychologist, 34*, 906–911. doi:10.1037/0003-066X.34.10.906.

Hartig, J., Klieme, E., & Leutner, D. (Eds.). (2008). *Assessment of competencies in educational contexts*. Göttingen: Hogrefe.

Klieme, E., & Leutner, D. (2006). Kompetenzmodelle zur Erfassung individueller Lernergebnisse und zur Bilanzierung von Bildungsprozessen: Beschreibung eines neu eingerichteten Schwerpunktprogramms der DFG. [Competence models for assessing individual learning outcomes and evaluating educational processes. Description of a new priority program of the German Research Foundation, DFG]. *Zeitschrift für Pädagogik, 52*, 876–903.

Leutner, D., Leopold, C., & den Elzen-Rump, V. (2007). Self-regulated learning with a text-highlighting strategy: A training experiment. *Journal of Psychology, 215*, 174–182. doi:10.1027/0044-3409.215.3.174.

Paris, S. G., Lipson, M. Y., & Wixson, K. K. (1983). Becoming a strategic reader. *Contemporary Educational Psychology, 8*, 293–316. doi:10.1016/0361-476X(83)90018-8.

Pintrich, P. R., Smith, D. A. F., Garcia, T., & McKeachie, W. J. (1993). Reliability and predictive validity of the motivated strategies for learning questionnaire (MSLQ). *Educational and Psychological Measurement, 53*, 801–813. doi:10.1177/0013164493053003024.

Pressley, M., Borkowski, J. G., & Schneider, W. (1987). Cognitive strategies: Good strategy users coordinate metacognition and knowledge. In R. Vasta & G. Whitehurst (Eds.), *Annals of child development* (Vol. 4, pp. 89–129). New York: JAI Press.

Pressley, M., Borkowski, J. G., & Schneider, W. (1989). Good information processing: What it is and how education can promote it. *International Journal of Educational Research, 13*, 857–867. doi:10.1016/0883-0355(89)90069-4.

Schreiber, B. (1998). *Selbstreguliertes Lernen* [Self-regulated learning]. Münster: Waxmann.

Schütte, M. (2012). *Selbstreguliertes Lernen aus Sachtexten: Modellierung und Erfassung der erforderlichen Teilkompetenzen* [Self-regulated learning with expository texts: Modeling and assessing of the required competences] (Doctoral dissertation). Retrieved from https://duepublico.uni-duisburg-essen.de/servlets/DerivateServlet/Derivate-30745/Diss_schuette.pdf

Schütte, M., & Wirth, J. (2013, August). *Self-regulated learning with expository texts: An exploratory structural analysis*. Paper presented at the EARLI biennial conference, Munich, Germany.

Schütte, M., Wirth, J., & Leutner, D. (2010). Selbstregulationskompetenz beim Lernen aus Sachtexten [Competence of self-regulated learning when learning with expository texts]. *Zeitschrift für Pädagogik, 56*, 249–257.

Schütte, M., Wirth, J., & Leutner, D. (2012). Lernstrategische Teilkompetenzen für das selbstregulierte Lernen aus Sachtexten [Strategic competences for self-regulated learning with expository texts]. *Psychologische Rundschau, 63*, 26–33. doi:10.1026/0033–3042/a000107.

Weinert, F. E. (1982). Selbstgesteuertes Lernen als Voraussetzung, Methode und Ziel des Unterrichts [Self-regulated learning as a pre-requisite, method, and goal of teaching]. *Unterrichtswissenschaft, 10*, 99–110.

Winne, P. H., & Hadwin, A. F. (1998). Studying as self-regulated learning. In D. J. Hacker, J. Dunlosky, & A. C. Graesser (Eds.), *Metacognition in educational theory and practice* (pp. 277–304). Hillsdale: Erlbaum.

Winne, P. H., & Perry, N. E. (2000). Measuring self-regulated learning. In M. Boekaerts, P. R. Pintrich, & M. Zeidner (Eds.), *Handbook of self-regulation* (pp. 531–566). San Diego: Academic.

Wirth, J., & Leutner, D. (2008). Self-regulated learning as a competence. Implications of theoretical models for assessment methods. *Zeitschrift für Psychologie/Journal of Psychology, 216*, 102–110. doi:10.1027/0044–3409.216.2.102.

Wolters, C. A. (2003). Regulation of motivation: Evaluating an underemphasized aspect of self-regulated learning. *Educational Psychologist, 38*, 189–205. doi:10.1207/S15326985EP3804_1.

Zimmerman, B. J. (2000). Attaining self-regulation: A social cognitive perspective. In M. Boekaerts, P. R. Pintrich, & M. Zeidner (Eds.), *Handbook of self-regulation* (pp. 13–39). San Diego: Academic.

Part II
Modeling and Assessing Teacher Competencies

Chapter 7
Investigating Pre-service Teachers' Professional Vision Within University-Based Teacher Education

Tina Seidel, Kathleen Stürmer, Manfred Prenzel, Gloria Jahn, and Stefanie Schäfer

Abstract The development of generic pedagogical competencies is regarded as a key element of university-based teacher education. In the Observe project, the professional vision of pre-service teachers is investigated as an indicator of the acquisition of applicable generic pedagogical knowledge with regard to important teaching and learning components. With the aim of bridging the research gap regarding the relationship between professional knowledge acquisition and professional practice, the structure of pre-service teachers' professional vision was modeled and then empirically tested using the Observer, a standardized yet contextualized instrument. Changes in the professional vision of pre-service teachers within university-based teacher education were measured, and approaches were developed to connect professional vision with teaching action in the classroom. In this chapter, we present a project overview and the most important findings of our research activities during the last 6 years.

Keywords Teacher competencies • Teacher education • Professional vision • Competence measurement

7.1 Introduction

The way teachers design and create learning opportunities in their classrooms strongly influences student learning (Darling-Hammond and Bransford 2005). Thus, defining and measuring the competencies that teachers require to create learning opportunities is particularly important in university-based teacher education

T. Seidel (✉) • M. Prenzel • G. Jahn • S. Schäfer
Technische Universität München, Munich, Germany
e-mail: tina.seidel@tum.de; manfred.prenzel@tum.de; gloria.jahn@tum.de; schaefer@zv.tum.de

K. Stürmer
University of Tübingen, Tübingen, Germany
e-mail: kathleen.stuermer@uni-tuebingen.de

D. Leutner et al. (eds.), *Competence Assessment in Education*, Methodology of Educational Measurement and Assessment, DOI 10.1007/978-3-319-50030-0_7

(Brouwer 2010; Cochran-Smith 2003; Koster et al. 2005). In this regard, generic pedagogical competencies, including several aspects, such as the knowledge of important teaching and learning components in classrooms, are stressed as important requisites (Kunter et al. 2013; Shulman 1987). Generic pedagogical knowledge is essential for creating learning environments across a wide variety of subjects (Voss et al. 2011) in a domain-general manner (Blomberg et al. 2011). In recent years, significant advances have been achieved in assessing the competencies of teachers by using standardized assessment of teachers declarative-conceptual knowledge (Baumert et al. 2010; Blömeke et al. 2006; Loewenberg and Cohen 1999 etc.). However, when it comes to targeting the transfer of knowledge about what constitutes effective teaching and learning, to teaching practice, context-dependent approaches and measures are required (Shavelson 2012). To bridge the gap regarding the relationship between professional knowledge and professional practice, those approaches have to focus on the assessment of integrated, flexible knowledge connected to multiple contexts of practice (Seidel et al. 2013).

Focusing on the investigation of generic pedagogical competencies, in the 6-year Observe project, we developed methodological constitutive approaches, which increase in their approximation to practice. Therefore, we draw on the concept of professional vision (Goodwin 1994) to investigate pre-service teachers' initial integrated knowledge acquisition processes. The concept describes the ability to use conceptual knowledge about teaching and learning to notice and interpret significant features of classroom situations (van Es and Sherin 2002). Taking the contextualized and situated nature of teacher knowledge into account (Borko 2004), pre-service teachers' professional vision represents how theory and practice are integrated into well-defined and differentiated knowledge structures (Seidel et al. 2013). Overcoming the traditional paper pencil tests in competence assessment, in this chapter we outline (1) how we modeled the structure of pre-service teachers' professional vision, and (2) how we tested it empirically by developing the standardized, yet contextualized instrument Observer. Regarding the formative assessments purpose of the instrument, we illustrate (3) findings of changes in pre-service teachers' professional vision within university-based teacher education, as measured by the Observer. Finally, we present (4) how we built a bridge from professional vision to teaching action by developing decomposed teaching events, in which pre-service teachers' teaching skills on generic pedagogical components were assessed and linked to their real teaching action in classroom.

7.2 Modeling the Structure of Professional Vision

Until now, teachers' professional vision has mainly been studied by using qualitative approaches (Santagata and Angelici 2010; van Es and Sherin 2002). These findings have provided a valid basis for describing the quality of teacher knowledge and learning. In order to investigate learning processes within university-based teacher education and to provide standardized instruments for formative assessment

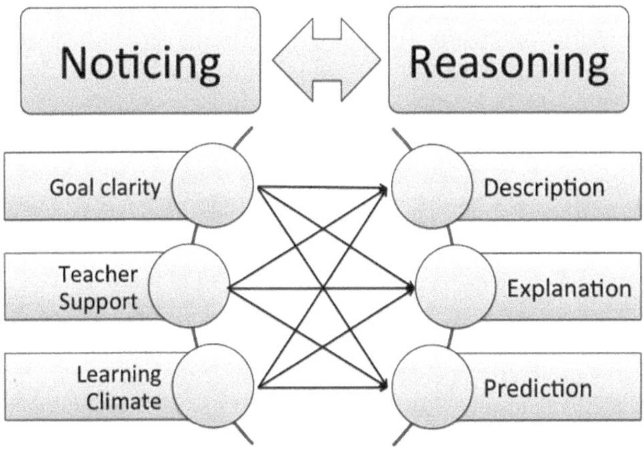

Fig. 7.1 The structure of reasoning, regarding noticed situations (Seidel and Stürmer 2014, p. 6)

purposes, we based our model of the structure of pre-service teachers' professional vision on the findings of the qualitative research.

This research highlights the key relevance of knowledge-based perceptual processes for teachers' professional vision (Goodwin 1994), a term that is used to describe the ability to notice and interpret relevant features of classroom events for student learning (Sherin 2007), as an important prerequisite for effective teaching practice (Grossman et al. 2009). Professional vision is informed by knowledge of what constitutes effective teaching and learning (Palmeri et al. 2004). It requires not only conceptual knowledge but also the ability to apply this knowledge to the observed situation (Seidel and Stürmer 2014). Research shows that the ability to make sense of an observed situation that is relevant for student learning, is related to teaching quality (Kersting et al., 2010). Regarding pre-service teachers' learning, the concept constitutes a promising approach for capturing knowledge acquisition that is relevant for future teaching practice (Wiens et al. 2013). Professional vision entails two interconnected knowledge-based subcomponents (see Fig. 7.1): (1) noticing, and (2) reasoning (van Es and Sherin 2008).

7.2.1 Noticing: Selective Attention to Important Classroom Events

Noticing involves identifying classroom situations that, from a professional perspective, are decisive in effective instructional practice (Seidel and Stürmer 2014). Pre-service teachers need to develop the ability to recognize the components of effective classroom teaching that support students' learning processes. In classroom teaching, numerous teaching and learning acts occur. Some are particularly important for student learning, others are not. In this vein, the situations to which pre-service teachers direct their attention while observing a classroom action serve as the first indicators of underlying knowledge (Sherin et al. 2011). When it comes to defining situations that are relevant for teaching and learning, different knowledge foci can be used that provide a frame for capturing pre-service teachers' application of knowledge. In our research, we focus on knowledge of the principles of teaching and learning as an aspect of generic pedagogical knowledge (Shulman 1987), which represents a basic component of initial university-based teacher education (Hammerness et al. 2002). Research on teaching effectiveness is based on knowledge about teaching and learning as an element of generic pedagogical knowledge. In this research, a number of teaching components have been repeatedly shown as relevant for students' learning (Fraser et al. 1987; Seidel and Shavelson 2007). We focus on three important components: goal clarity, teacher support and learning climate (Seidel and Stürmer 2014). The component of goal clarity (i.e., clarifying teaching and learning goals, structuring the lesson) is relevant in the cognitive and motivational aspects of student learning because students should activate their knowledge and be motivated to learn. Teacher support positively affects student learning, particularly in terms of motivational-affective aspects. Teachers' questions, as well as their reactions to student responses in the form of feedback, are the core elements of research in this area. The learning climate in a classroom is relevant for student learning because the climate provides the motivational and affective background in which learning takes place.

7.2.2 Reasoning: Interpretation of Important Classroom Events

The second subcomponent of professional vision describes teachers' reasoning about classroom events. This subcomponent captures the ability to process and interpret the situations noticed, based on knowledge of the principles of teaching and learning (Borko 2004; Sherin 2007; van Es and Sherin 2002). The ability to take a reasoned approach to noticed situations in the classroom provides insights into the quality of the pre-service teachers' mental representations of generic pedagogical knowledge (Borko et al. 2008). In conceptualizing teachers' reasoning, researchers distinguish among qualitatively different aspects (Berliner 2001; van Es and Sherin 2008), which we have termed as follows: (1) description, (2) explanation, and (3) prediction (Seidel and Stürmer 2014). *Description* reflects the ability to differentiate the relevant aspects of a noticed teaching and learning component (i.e., goal clarity: the teacher refers to what the students should learn), without making any additional judgments. *Explanation* refers to the ability to use conceptual knowledge about effective teaching to reason about a situation. This means classifying and accounting for the situations according to the terms and concepts of the teaching component involved. *Prediction* refers to the ability to predict the consequences of observed events in terms of student learning. It draws on broad knowledge about teaching and student learning, as well as their application to classroom practice.

Because knowledge-based reasoning is an indicator of the quality of the knowledge representation, we focus on assessing pre-service teachers' reasoning ability in regard to noticed teaching and learning components. Previous research has shown that pre-service teachers are capable of describing classroom situations. In contrast, their ability to explain and predict the consequences and outcomes of those situations lags behind that of experienced in-service teachers (Oser et al. 2010; Seidel and Prenzel 2007). However, little empirical research has systematically explored the interrelation of the three aspects of reasoning. For example, reasoning ability might be regarded as one-dimensional, so that the three aspects cannot clearly be separated; it might also be that the three aspects have to be seen as distinctive abilities but highly interrelated. Taking into account the higher-order knowledge application processes involved, and the results of previous studies (e.g., van Es and Sherin 2008), it also seems possible that explaining and predicting are so closely related that they can be treated as one aspect (i.e., as integration). Knowledge about the structure of reasoning, however, serves to advance the field, especially when it comes to designing learning environments in university-based teacher education. If the three aspects of reasoning are highly interrelated and represent distinctive dimensions of increasing difficulty, teacher educators could draw on this knowledge in order to structure and sequence courses on teaching and learning (Brouwer 2010).

7.3 Testing the Structure of Professional Vision

Based on the model derived from qualitative research, in the first 2 years of the project, the aim was to develop an instrument that would capture pre-service teachers' professional vision in a valid and reliable way (Seidel and Stürmer 2014). The use of video has been shown to be a suitable methodological approach to describing and investigating the phenomenon of professional vision, and has been applied to groups of teachers with diverse kinds of expertise, ranging from pre-service teachers in the early years of their university-based teacher education (van Es and Sherin 2002; Seidel and Stürmer 2014) to experienced in-service teachers (Borko et al. 2008; Kersting 2008). Video is typically used as item prompt to elicit the application of professional knowledge. Noticing and reasoning abilities are then assessed by open questions that are analyzed qualitatively. These approaches are prominent in professional vision research and have helped identify sub-processes and dimensions of professional vision. However, they are limited with regard to investigating larger samples. To test the structure of professional vision and to evaluate the developments of pre-service teachers over time, standardized measures that are suitable for formative assessment in the long term are helpful. They provide a valid and reliable indicator of the major achievement of objectives in teacher education programs (e.g., applicable and integrated knowledge about teaching and learning).

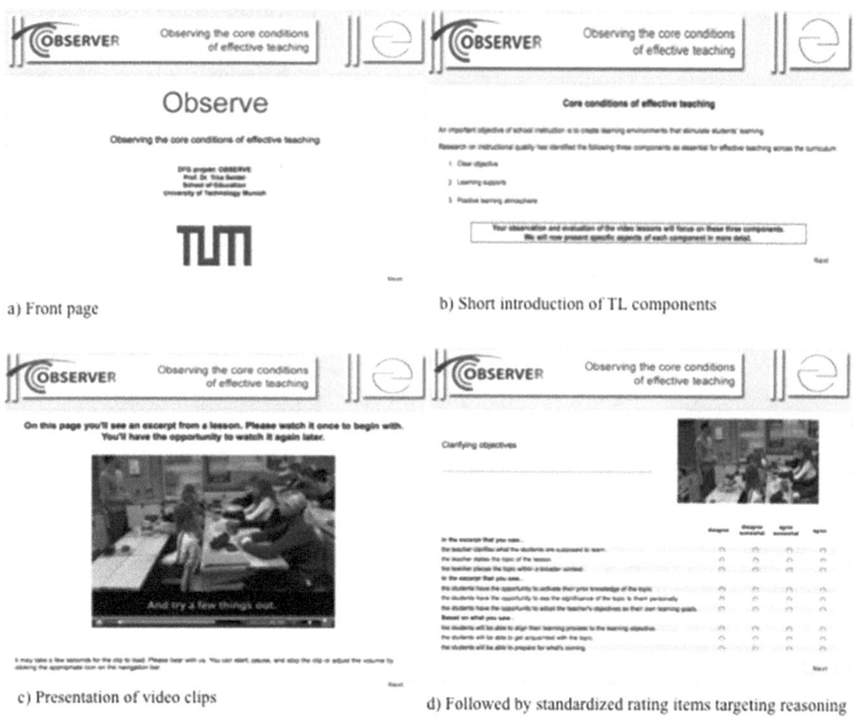

Fig. 7.2 The observer tool (Seidel and Stürmer 2014, p. 15)

7.3.1 The Assessment Tool Observer

In the project, the Observer instrument was developed as the first video-based measurement tool to assess pre-service teachers' professional vision in a standardized yet contextualized way (Seidel et al. 2010a), with videotaped classroom recordings being combined with rating items (see Fig. 7.2). Each video represents two teaching and learning components (e.g., teacher support and learning climate). The videos were selected on the basis of the following criteria: authenticity of the selected classroom situations, activation of teacher knowledge, and particular relevance for student learning. Based on the application of these criteria, twelve videos were selected. A pilot study with $N = 40$ pre-service teachers showed that all twelve videos were perceived as authentic and cognitively activating (Seidel et al. 2010b).

We also investigated the extent to which the twelve selected videos represent the three focused teaching and learning components (i.e., goal clarity, teacher support, and learning climate) and serve as "prompts" to elicit pre-service teachers' knowledge. In a study with $N = 119$ participants, two test versions were implemented, in which videos were systematically rotated and varied with respect to the subject shown and the teaching and learning components represented (Seidel and Stürmer 2014). The mean agreements between participants and the judgments of the research team were 66.9 % for goal clarity, 80.4 % for teacher support, and 75.8 % for learning climate. Consequently, the twelve videos can be regarded as valid examples of the three teaching and learning components.

The videos were embedded in rating items with a four-point Likert-scale ranging from 1 (*disagree*) to 4 (*agree*). Rating items were developed to target the three reasoning aspects equally: describe (e.g., the teacher clarifies what the students are supposed to learn); explain (e.g., the students have the opportunity to activate their prior knowledge of the topic); and predict (e.g., the students will be able to align their learning process to the learning objective). Using the rating items, the measurement of pre-service teachers' professional vision was compared to a measurement that used a qualitative approach with open questions (Schäfer and Seidel 2015). The positive correlation between the quantitative and qualitative approaches implies that the rating items do capture the process of professional vision adequately.

Because the research on teaching effectiveness does not provide right or wrong answers regarding the quality of videos, we used an expert norm as a reference. To establish this norm, three expert researchers—each with 100–400 h of experience in observing classroom situations—independently rated all developed rating items in connection with the selected videos (Seidel et al. 2010b). The data were recoded according to their agreement with the expert rating: 1 (*hit expert rating*) and 0 (*miss expert rating*). This strict recoding proved to be superior to a less strict version that takes tendency into account (Seidel and Stürmer 2014).

The Observer tool is presented as a series of HTML pages. It starts with general instructions and short introductions to the three teaching and learning components: goal clarity, teacher support and learning climate. Brief contextual information about the class is provided before each video is presented. Participants have the opportunity to watch the videos a second time before responding to the rating items. In order to limit the completion time and to reach a balanced ratio between the represented subjects and the teaching and learning components, we created a final version of the Observer tool, which comprised six videos showing secondary classroom instruction in physics, math, French, and history. In this form, the completion time of the instrument is about 90 min. In order to investigate learning processes within university-based teacher education and to use the tool for the purpose of formative assessment, we investigated whether the measurement was stable over time. Evidence for this re-test reliability can be provided (Seidel and Stürmer 2014). Furthermore, the Observer tool was processed under different conditions ("online" versus "on-site" processing and "voluntary" versus "compulsory" participation). Thus, we ensured that assessment of pre-service teachers' professional vision was not affected by different assessment conditions (Jahn et al. 2011). Regarding the assessment of generic pedagogical knowledge application, a third study shows no dependencies between the subject background of pre-service teachers (e.g., math) and the subject shown in the videos (Blomberg et al. 2011).

7.3.2 Interrelation Between the Three Reasoning Dimensions

In scrutinizing the assumptions of different models regarding the structure of professional vision, we conducted two scaling studies, the second of which was built on the results of the first. We followed the requirements of item response theory and used different Rasch models for scaling. We assumed that the ratings of the videos were indicators of the latent variable of professional vision. In a study with $N = 152$ pre-service teachers enrolled in a teacher education program at a German university, we tested a one-dimensional (reasoning as one overall ability) and a two-dimensional model (describe, and integrating explain and predict) against the theoretically postulated three-dimensional model (describe, explain, and predict; Seidel and Stürmer 2014). The three models were compared using scale indices, BICs (Bayesian Information Criterion), and Likelihood-Ratio-Tests. Additionally, bivariate (Pearson) latent correlations of personal ability scores among the three aspects, and the total score for reasoning, were calculated. All three models reliably assessed reasoning, but the three-dimensional model explained the most variance.

Moreover, the three-dimensional model fitted the data best (significant Likelihood-Ratio-Test and smallest BIC). However, bivariate latent correlations of the personal ability scores of pre-service teachers showed that the components describe, explain, and predict were interrelated and highly correlated with the overall reasoning score. Taking into account the heterogeneity of teacher education in Germany, we conducted a second scaling-up study to replicate the findings (Jahn et al. 2014). The sample used consisted of $N = 1029$ pre-service teachers from 16 German universities with different teacher education programs and teacher education tracks. The model comparisons and the bivariate latent correlations revealed results similar to those in the first scaling study. Moreover, the structure of reasoning proved to be comparable to that of pre-service teachers in different teacher education tracks (primary, secondary, and vocational education). Thus, the Observer tool provided a reliable and valid measure of pre-service teachers' professional vision and their sub-abilities of describing, explaining, and predicting classroom situations in university-based teacher education.

7.4 Investigating Changes in Professional Vision Within University-Based Teacher Education

Based on the results achieved in the first two project years, the second phase (Years 3 and 4) focused on using the Observer tool as a formative assessment measure. In this vein, the measure should be sensitive to changes in professional vision within university-based teacher education. For this reason, the following sections present studies focusing on the investigation of pre-service teachers' professional vision within formal and informal learning opportunities (OTL), which are pointed out as important sources for knowledge acquisition. Based on the findings we are able to discuss features of supportive OTL designs.

7.4.1 The Role of Formal and Informal OTL

Regarding pre-service teachers' formal learning, first findings indicated that university-based teacher education in general fostered a continuous and accumulative acquisition of conceptual professional knowledge (see Kleickmann et al. 2013). In this vein, in one study we investigated the relationship between important student capacities, such as interest in topics of teaching and learning, pre-experience in university courses on teaching and learning, and practical pre-experience and level of professional vision (Stürmer et al. 2014). It was shown that the number of university courses attended, on teaching and learning, and the level of interest in this field, were systematically related to higher levels of professional vision. In particular, these two factors were positively associated with the subscales explanation and prediction, which indicate higher order learning and knowledge integration.

In a second study, the Observer tool was used as a pre- and post-test measure to study changes in the professional vision of pre-service teachers during their participation in three courses on the subject of teaching and learning principles (Stürmer et al. 2013a). The three courses included (1) a very specific video-based course directly targeting effective teaching and learning components, (2) a course focusing on important principles of learning and learner characteristics connected to principles of teaching, and (3) a broad course on "hot topics in instruction", partly dealing with teaching and learning components, but accompanied by other topics, such as the relevance of homework or assessment. For all three courses, positive changes in professional vision were shown. Regarding the three subcomponents, differential effects occurred. The two content-specific courses on teaching and learning components showed the highest increases in explaining and predicting, and seem to support the integration of knowledge about teaching and learning components and student learning. The general course showed the highest increases in describing. The introduction of the teaching and learning components without broaching the issue of specific effects on student learning seems to advance more preservice teachers' ability to differentiate observed situations according to relevant components. These findings indicate that the Observer tool is sensitive to specific learning effects that might occur because of different course objectives and learning goals in university courses.

In addition to formal OTL, informal learning, such as practical experiences in teaching, is seen as essential in acquiring integrated knowledge structures. It has been argued that well-defined and integrated knowledge can only be developed when it is applied to practice through contextualized generalization over long periods of time (Darling-Hammond and Bransford 2005). Consequently, different forms of internship and praxis elements have been implemented in initial, university-based, teacher education programs (Bauer et al. 2012). Positive effects of practical experiences on pre-service teachers' reported self-efficacy and teaching skills have been demonstrated so far (Gröschner et al. 2013). In this context, a third project study (Stürmer et al. 2013b) examined the impact of practical experience (in form of a praxis semester) accompanied by video-based courses at university, on pre-service teachers' changes in professional vision. The findings revealed overall positive changes, with a special benefit for low entry-level students at the beginning of the semester. Because the students' practical experiences were guided by video-based courses at university, the study underlines the attempt to combine formal and informal OTL in order to foster the development of integrated knowledge in the domain of generic pedagogical knowledge.

7.4.2 The Design of Formal and Informal OTL

Research to date has strengthened the assumption that formal and informal OTL within university-based teacher education are sources of knowledge acquisition that constitute a baseline for initial professional development processes. Nevertheless, to support pre-service teachers in acquiring knowledge and applying it to real classroom situations, the constant monitoring of course instruction and activities is necessary for creating effective university-based OTLs (Hiebert et al. 2007). Research on the design of OTLs has outlined the advantage of videos as a learning tool that guides the acquisition, activation and application of pre-service teachers' knowledge in a meaningful way (Seago 2003). However, videos must be implemented with clear objectives in mind. Because relatively little research has empirically investigated the effect of different video-based designs, using different instructional strategies, on pre-service teachers' learning, Seidel et al. (2013) examined the impact of two instructional strategies (rule-example vs. example-rule) embedded in video-based courses, on pre-service teachers' learning. The results revealed that pre-service teachers who were taught by the rule-example strategy scored higher on reproducing declarative knowledge about relevant teaching and learning components and on professional vision, whereas pre-service teachers in the example-rule group scored higher on lesson planning, particularly in identifying possible occurring challenges in a situated way.

Furthermore, distinct differences in the capacities of pre-service teachers to reflect about teaching were shown (Blomberg et al. 2014). The rule-example approach facilitated reasoning abilities in observing videotaped classroom situations, whereas the example-rule teaching approach fostered pre-service teachers' long-term reflection skills about own learning in a learning journal. These findings underline the importance of choosing an appropriate instructional approach in the design of video-based formal OTLs, depending on specific learning goals (Blomberg et al. 2013, 2014). In addition, OTLs in teacher education should have clear learning goals, and they should take into account the heterogeneity of the target group (Stürmer et al. 2013a).

7.5 Building the Bridge from Professional Vision to Teaching Action

Despite advances in measuring pre-service teachers' theory-practice integrated generic pedagogical knowledge in a standardized yet contextualized way, one major question still has to be answered: How is the acquired knowledge linked to performance in teaching? Therefore, a central objective of the third phase of our project was to investigate the relationship between professional knowledge and professional action. Initial findings revealed a positive relation between in-service teachers' professional vision and their effectiveness, measured by student achievement (Kersting et al. 2010). Current research approaches investigate variations in teachers' professional knowledge in direct relation to variations in their teaching quality (Grossman et al. 2013; Kersting et al. 2012). Thereby, many contextual factors (e.g., students, school, and classroom) have to be taken into consideration in interpreting these findings.

In addition, this approach is limited with regard to the disposable teaching opportunities that enable the systematic and standardized assessment of teaching performance in initial teacher education. In comparison with other professional fields, in which simulations and performance assessments have been established in systematic ways (i.e., Shavelson 1991), teacher education greatly lags behind. Therefore, based on the Approximation-of-Practice (AoP) framework (Grossman et al. 2009), we developed standardized teaching events (M-teach events) to assess the teaching performance of pre-service teachers within university-based teacher education (Seidel et al. 2015). This framework provides a model for the integration of professional knowledge and professional practice (Grossman et al. 2009). It demonstrates that the acquisition of professional practice requires more than teaching practice in classrooms. Because classroom teaching is a highly complex, dynamic process, myriad factors must be considered in the initial experience of teaching.

Thus, the acquisition of professional practice is not characterized by simply increasing the quantity of classroom teaching practice but by building up a series of approximations to practice, which increase in complexity and allow for the systematic linking of elements of professional knowledge to corresponding elements in professional practice (Seidel et al. 2015). In order to assess the extent to which pre-service teachers had acquired teaching skills based on generic pedagogical knowledge, we provided "training" settings. Given the current state of the art, we characterize the settings as teaching events (Grossman et al. 2009). In contrast to traditional micro teaching approaches (Garvey 1978), such events do not focus on the training of teaching skills in a procedural manner. Instead, the events represent a "decomposed" component of practice (e.g., structuring a short teaching sequence) and allow the participants to experience the authentic nature of teaching (Shavelson 2012).

7.5.1 M-Teach Events as Assessment of Teaching Action

The designing of M-Teach events focused on the standardized assessment of pre-service teachers' actions, including planning, performing, and self-reflection with regard to structuring and supporting learning as relevant teaching and learning components. In order to provide events with reduced complexity, two forms in which pre-service teachers often have experience were developed: tutoring and the teaching of small groups (Bauer et al. 2012). In the tutoring situation, the preservice teachers were asked to teach one preservice teacher acting as a student (1:1), whereas in the small group situation, they were asked to teach four students (1:4). Both M-Teach events had a reduced instruction time of 20 min; 40 min were allotted for planning, and 10 min for reflection afterwards. To ensure that the pre-service teachers' prior knowledge was comparable and that the events could be implemented in a variety of teacher education programs, we decided to focus on two instructional topics: (1) teaching strategies for a tactical game (Monopoly); (2) finding the best ticket in Munich's public transport system.

The topics were generic in nature and unrelated to school subjects, but we assumed them to be relevant to pre-service teachers' personal lives. Because one aim was to assess the implementation of important teaching and learning components the pre-service teachers received a standardized instruction task, which encouraged them to focus on goal clarity and teacher support in their teaching. Furthermore, they received an introduction to the teaching event, and information regarding their learner group. Information was also provided on the available teaching material. In order to ensure authentic and comparable conditions for all pre-service teachers, the participants were simulated students. Therefore, we developed acting scripts based on student profiles, as identified in the IPN video study (Seidel 2006), which take into account differences in student characteristics with regard to cognitive and motivational-affective competencies. We adapted four different student profiles to the 1:4 M-Teach event, focusing on the two teaching topics: a *strong profile* (high pre-requisites with regard to cognitive abilities, prior knowledge, self-concept, and interest); an *underestimated profile* (high cognitive abilities and knowledge, low self-concept, intermediate level of interest); an *uninterested* profile (mixed cognitive abilities, low interest); and a *struggling profile* (low cognitive ability, knowledge, and self-concept).

The struggling profile was also used for the 1:1 M-Teach event, because it is the profile most often encountered in authentic tutoring situations. To ensure the fidelity of the events, as authentic teaching experiences (Shavelson 2012), we conducted a pilot study in which the pre-service teachers acted as teachers (8), as simulated learners (6), and as experts (6) who observed videotapes of the pre-service teachers

Table 7.1 Perceived authenticity depending on instruction topic and form of micro-teaching event

	Instruction	Acting script	Teaching situation
Topic			
Transport system	3.27 (0.71)	3.40 (0.66)	3.26 (0.70)
Tactical game	3.22 (0.44)	3.38 (0.50)	3.27 (0.51)
Format			
Tutor (1:1)	3.28 (0.75)	3.38 (0.88)	3.36 (0.53)
Small group (1:4)	3.39 (0.42)	3.38 (0.56)	3.30 (0.59)

Scale: '1' *totally disagree* to '4' *totally agree*; mean values (standard deviation in parentheses)

teaching in the M-Teach events. The experts had at least 5 years of experience in teacher education and the analysis of classroom instruction. The participants rated the authenticity of the instruction and the acting script (e.g., "I experienced the instruction as authentic"), as well as the authenticity of the M-Teach events (e.g., "The situation seemed to me like a real teaching situation"). The standardized instructions and acting scripts were generally rated as authentic. With regard to the M-Teach topic, no differences were found $t(14) = .06$, $p = .96$ $d = 0.29$ (see Table 7.1). With regard to the M-Teach form, the tutor situation was perceived as more authentic than the small group situations, which nevertheless showed a high level of authenticity $t(23) = 2.32$, $p = .03$, $d = 0.45$.

7.5.2 *Pre-service Teachers' Teaching Skills in M-Teach Events*

In order to assess the teaching actions of pre-service teachers, we conducted a study with a full cohort of $N = 89$ pre-service teachers who planned, performed, and reflected upon the M-Teach events (Seidel et al. 2015). The participants were randomly assigned to a combination of topic and form (tactical game/tutoring; tactical game/small group; public transport/tutoring; public transport/small group). After 2 weeks, they performed this task a second time and switched to a different combination of format and topic. We collected pre-service teachers' written instruction plans and self-reflections about their teaching. To record teaching skills, the performances of the pre-service teachers in M-Teach events were videotaped. Furthermore, to investigate whether the performance of important teaching and learning components in M-Teach events was valid for performance on teaching subject content in school classrooms, a subsample of $n = 23$ pre-service teachers was drawn from the main sample (i.e., pre-service teachers with low and high abilities in professional vision). High inference rating items were developed to code the videotaped M-Teach events, as well as the classroom teaching (Seidel et al. 2015).

Regarding teaching performance, the results showed that the performances of pre-service teachers were distributed from a mainly low/medium skill level to a high skill level in some students. This result indicates that pre-service teachers were partly able to show good practice in structuring and supporting learning within the M-Teach events. Furthermore, the results showed that the skills of pre-service teachers in supporting student learning were highly correlated with tutoring and small group teaching, as well as with teaching in a classroom (Seidel and Stürmer 2014). Structuring skills were also related to small group and classroom teaching, but less so to tutoring. Thus, the fact that the performance in the M-Teach events was highly and systematically related to classroom teaching performance is an important indication of the fidelity of these events (Shavelson 2012).

7.6 Conclusion and Outlook

Given the aim of bridging the research gap regarding the relationship between professional knowledge acquisition and learning for professional practice, the measure and investigation of pre-service teachers' professional vision is a promising and practical approach. Based on mainly qualitative descriptions, we modeled the structure of pre-service teachers' professional vision with regard to generic pedagogical aspects of teaching. By developing the contextualized yet standardized tool, Observer, we were able to measure professional vision reliably and provide evidence for the proposed structure. Furthermore, across different studies, the Observer proved to be a valid instrument that can be used for formative assessment in teacher education. The measurements achieved by using this tool showed that the professional vision of pre-service teachers can change positively within university-based teacher education, including formal and informal OTL. However, the abilities and capacities of pre-service teachers to acquire integrated knowledge were affected by individual prerequisites and instruction design principles. With the aim of building a bridge from professional vision to teaching action, we were successful in developing standardized teaching events. With regard to the use of the acquired teaching skills of pre-service teachers as indicators of the development of professional practice, the results of the first study indicate the validity of such events as authentic teaching experiences. The next steps in our research will take into account the teaching actions of pre-service teachers in relation to their acquired generic pedagogical knowledge.

Acknowledgements The preparation of this chapter was supported by grant WI 2663/4-1, WI 2663/4-2 and WI 2663/4-3 from the German Research Foundation (DFG) in the Priority Program "Competence Models for Assessing Individual Learning Outcomes and Evaluating Educational Processes" (SPP 1293).

References

Bauer, J., Diercks, U., Rösler, L., Möller, J., & Prenzel, M. (2012). Lehramtsstudium in Deutschland: Wie groß ist die strukturelle Vielfalt [Teacher education in Germany: How diverse is the structural variety]? *Unterrichtswissenschaft, 40*, 101–120. doi:09201202101.

Baumert, J., Kunter, M., Blum, W., Brunner, M., Voss, T., Jordan, A., ... Yi-Miau, T. (2010). Teachers' mathematical knowledge, cognitive activation in the classroom, and student progress. *American Educational Research Journal, 47*, 133–180. doi:10.3102/0002831209345157.

Berliner, D. C. (2001). Learning about and learning from expert teachers. *International Journal of Educational Research, 35*, 463–482. doi:10.1016/S0883-0355(02)00004-6.
Blomberg, G., Stürmer, K., & Seidel, T. (2011). How pre-service teachers observe teaching on video: Effects of viewers' teaching subjects and the subject of the video. *Teaching and Teacher Education, 27*, 1131–1140. doi:10.1016/j.tate.2011.04.008.
Blomberg, G., Renkl, A., Sherin, M. G., Borko, H., & Seidel, T. (2013). Five research-based heuristics for using video in preservice teacher education. *Journal of Educational Research Online, 5*(1), 90–114.
Blomberg, G., Sherin, M. G., Renkl, A., Glogger, I., & Seidel, T. (2014). Understanding video as a tool for teacher education: Investigating instructional strategies integrating video to promote reflection. *Instructional Science, 4*, 443–463. doi:10.1007/s11251-013-9281-6.
Blömeke, S., Kaiser, G., Lehmann, R., Felbich, A., & Müller, C. (2006). *Learning to teach mathematics: Teacher education and development study (TEDS-M)*. Berlin: Humboldt-Universität.
Borko, H. (2004). Professional development and teacher learning: Mapping the terrain. *Educational Researcher, 33*(8), 3–15. doi:10.3102/0013189x033008003.
Borko, H., Jacobs, J., Eiteljorg, E., & Pittman, M. E. (2008). Video as a tool for fostering productive discussions in mathematics professional development. *Teaching and Teacher Education, 24*, 417–436. doi:10.1016/j.tate.2006.11.012.
Brouwer, N. (2010). Determining long term effects of teacher education. In P. Peterson, E. Baker, & B. McGaw (Eds.), *International encyclopedia of education, 7* (pp. 503–510). Oxford: Elsevier.
Cochran-Smith, M. (2003). Assessing assessment in teacher education. *Journal of Teacher Education, 54*, 187–191. doi:10.1177/0022487103054003001.
Darling-Hammond, L., & Bransford, J. D. (Eds.). (2005). *Preparing teachers for a changing world: What teachers should learn and be able to do*. San Francisco: Jossey-Bass.
Fraser, B. J., Walberg, H. J., Welch, W. W., & Hattie, J. A. (1987). Syntheses of educational productivity research. *International Journal of Educational Research, 11*, 147–252. doi:10.1016/0883-0355(87)90035-8.
Garvey, B. (1978). Microteaching: Developing the concept for practical training. *British Journal of Educational Technology, 9*, 142–149.
Gröschner, A., Schmitt, C., & Seidel, T. (2013). Veränderung subjektiver Kompetenzeinschätzungen von Lehramtsstudierenden im Praxissemester [Changes in preservice teachers' subjective competence judgments within a practical internship]. *Zeitschrift für Pädagogische Psychologie, 27*, 77–86. doi:10.1024/1010–0652/a000090.
Grossman, P., Compton, C., Igra, D., Ronfeldt, M., Shahan, E., & Williamson, P. W. (2009). Teaching practice: A cross-professional perspective. *Teachers College Record, 111*, 2055–2100.
Grossman, P., Loeb, S., Cohen, J., & Wyckoff, J. (2013). Measure for measure: The relationship between measures of instructional practice in middle school English language arts and teachers' value-added scores. *American Journal of Education, 119*, 445–470. doi:10.3386/w16015.
Goodwin, C. (1994). Professional vision. *American Anthropologist, 96*, 606–633. doi:10.1525/aa.1994.96.3.02a00100.
Hammerness, K., Darling-Hammond, L., & Shulman, L. (2002). Toward expert thinking: How curriculum case writing prompts the development of theory-based professional knowledge in student teachers. *Teaching Education, 13*, 219–243. doi:10.1080/1047621022000007594.
Hiebert, J., Morris, A. K., Berk, D., & Jansen, A. (2007). Preparing teachers to learn from teaching. *Journal of Teacher Education, 58*, 47–61. doi:10.1177/0022487106295726.
Jahn, G., Prenzel, M., Stürmer, K., & Seidel, T. (2011). Varianten einer computergestützten Erhebung von Lehrerkompetenzen: Untersuchungen zu Anwendungen der Tools Observer [Computer-based assessment of preservice teachers' competencies]. *Unterrichtswissenschaft, 39*, 136–153.
Jahn, G., Stürmer, K., Seidel, T., & Prenzel, M. (2014). Professionelle Unterrichtswahrnehmung von Lehramtsstudierenden: Eine Scaling-up Studie des Observe-Projekts [Professional vision of pre-service teachers: A scaling-up study of the Observe project]. *Zeitschrift für Entwicklungspsychologie und Pädagogische Psychologie 46*, 171–180.

Kersting, N. (2008). Using video clips of mathematics classroom instruction as item prompts to measure teachers' knowledge of teaching mathematics. *Educational and Psychological Measurement, 68*, 845–861. doi:10.1177/0013164407313369.

Kersting, N., Givvin, K. B., Sotelo, F. L., & Stigler, J. W. (2010). Teachers' analyses of classroom video predict student learning of mathematics: Further explorations of a novel measure of teacher knowledge. *Journal of Teacher Education, 61*, 172–181. doi:10.1177/0022487109347875.

Kersting, N., Givvin, K. B., Thompson, B. J., Santagata, R., & Stigler, J. W. (2012). Measuring usable knowledge: Teachers' analyses of mathematics classroom videos predict teaching quality and student learning. *American Educational Research Journal, 49*, 568–589. doi:10.3102/0002831212437853.

Kleickmann, T., Richter, D., Kunter, M., Elsner, J., Besser, M., Krauss, S., & Baumert, J. (2013). Teachers' content knowledge and pedagogical content knowledge: The role of structural differences in teacher education. *Journal of Teacher Education, 64*, 90–106. doi:10.1177/0022487112460398.

Koster, B., Brekelmans, M., Korthagen, F., & Wubbels, T. (2005). Quality requirements for teacher educators. *Teaching and Teacher Education, 21*, 157–176. doi:10.1016/j.tate.2004.12.004.

Kunter, M., Baumert, J., Blum, W., Klusmann, U., Krauss, S., & Neubrand, M. (2013). *Cognitive activation in the mathematics classroom and professional competence of teachers: Results from the COACTIV Project*. New York: Springer.

Loewenberg Ball, D., & Cohen, D. K. (1999). Developing practice, developing practitioners toward a practice-based theory of professional education. In G. Sykes & L. Darling-Hammond (Eds.), *Teaching as the learning profession: Handbook of policy and practice* (pp. 3–32). San Francisco: Jossey Bass.

Oser, F., Heinzer, S., & Salzmann, P. (2010). Die Messung der Qualität von professionellen Kompetenzprofilen von Lehrpersonen mit Hilfe der Einschätzung von Filmvignetten. Chancen und Grenzen des advokatorischen Ansatzes [Measuring the quality of professional competence profiles in teachers]. *Unterrichtswissenschaft, 38*, 5–28.

Palmeri, T. J., Wong, A. C. N., & Gauthier, I. (2004). Computational approaches to the development of perceptual expertise. *Trends in Cognitive Sciences, 8*, 378–386. doi:10.1016/j.tics.2004.06.001.

Santagata, R., & Angelici, G. (2010). Studying the impact of the lesson analysis framework on preservice teachers' abilities to reflect on videos of classroom teaching. *Journal of Teacher Education, 61*, 339–349. doi:10.1177/0022487110369555.

Schäfer, S., & Seidel, T. (2015). Noticing and reasoning of teaching and learning components by pre-service teachers. *Journal of Educational Research Online, 7*, 34–58.

Seago, N. (2003). Using video as an object of inquiry: Mathematics teaching and learning. In J. Brophy (Ed.), *Using video in teacher education* (Vol. 10, pp. 259–285). EGP: Bradford.

Seidel, T. (2006). The role of student characteristics in studying micro teaching-learning environments. *Learning Environments Research, 9*, 253–271. doi:10.1007/s10984-006-9012-x.

Seidel, T., & Prenzel, M. (2007). Wie Lehrpersonen Unterricht wahrnehmen und einschätzen—Erfassung pädagogisch-psychologischer Kompetenzen bei Lehrpersonen mit Hilfe von Videosequenzen [The assessment of pedagogical psychological competencies in teachers]. *Zeitschrift für Erziehungswissenschaft*, Sonderheft *8*, 201–216. doi:10.1007/978-3-531-90865-6_12.

Seidel, T., & Shavelson, R. J. (2007). Teaching effectiveness research in the past decade: The role of theory and research design in disentangling meta-analysis results. *Review of Educational Research, 77*, 454–499. doi:10.3102/0034654307310317.

Seidel, T., & Stürmer, K. (2014). Modeling and measuring the structure of professional vision in preservice teachers. *American Educational Research Journal, 51*, 739–771. doi:10.3102/0002831214531321.

Seidel, T., Blomberg, G., & Stürmer, K. (2010a). "Observer": Validierung eines videobasierten Instruments zur Erfassung der professionellen Wahrnehmung von Unterricht ["Observer": Validation of a video-based instrument to assess the professional vision of pre-service teachers]. *Zeitschrift für Pädagogik*, Beiheft *56*, 296–306.

Seidel, T., Stürmer, K., & Blomberg, G. (2010b). Observer: Video-based tool to diagnose teachers' professional vision [Software]. Unpublished instrument. Retrieved from http://ww3.unipark.de/uc/observer_engl/demo/kv/
Seidel, T., Blomberg, G., & Renkl, A. (2013). Instructional strategies for using video in teacher education. *Teaching and Teacher Education, 34*, 56–65. doi:10.1016/j.tate.2013.03.004.
Seidel, T., Stürmer, K., Schäfer, S., & Jahn, G. (2015). How preservice teachers perform in teaching events regarding generic components of teaching. *Zeitschrift für Entwicklungspsychologie und Pädagogische Psychologie, 47*(2), 84–96. doi:10.1026/0049-8637/a000125.
Shavelson, R. J. (1991). *Performance assessment for the workplace*. Washington, DC: National Academy Press.
Shavelson, R. J. (2012). Assessing business-planning competence using the collegiate learning assessment as a prototype. *Empirical Research in Vocational Education and Training, 4*, 77–90.
Sherin, M. G. (2007). The development of teachers' professional vision in video clubs. In R. Goldman, R. Pea, B. Barron, & S. J. Derry (Eds.), *Video research in the learning sciences* (pp. 383–395). Mahwah: Lawrence Erlbaum.
Sherin, M. G., Jacobs, V. R., & Philipp, R. A. (Eds.). (2011). *Mathematics teacher noticing: Seeing through teachers' eyes*. New York: Routledge.
Shulman, L. S. (1987). Knowledge and teaching: Foundations of the new reform. *Harvard Educational Review, 57*, 1–22.
Stürmer, K., Könings, K. D., & Seidel, T. (2013a). Declarative knowledge and professional vision in teacher education: Effect of courses in teaching and learning. *British Journal of Educational Psychology, 83*, 467–483. doi:10.1111/j.2044-8279.2012.02075.x.
Stürmer, K., Seidel, T., & Schäfer, S. (2013b). Changes in professional vision in the context of practice. Preservice teachers' professional vision changes following practical experience: A video-based approach in university-based teacher education. *Gruppendynamik & Organisationsberatung, 44*, 339–355. doi:10.1007/s11612--013--0216--0.
Stürmer, K., Könings, K. D., & Seidel, T. (2014). Factors within university-based teacher education relating to preservice teachers' professional vision. *Vocations and Learning, 8*, 35–54. doi:10.1007/s12186-014-9122-z.
van Es, E., & Sherin, M. G. (2002). Learning to notice: Scaffolding new teachers' interpretations of classroom interactions. *Journal of Technology and Teacher Education, 10*, 571–596.
van Es, E., & Sherin, M. G. (2008). Mathematics teachers' "learning to notice" in the context of a video club. *Teaching and Teacher Education, 24*, 244–276. doi:10.1016/j.tate.2006.11.005.
Voss, T., Kunter, M., & Baumert, J. (2011). Assessing teacher candidates' general pedagogical and psychological knowledge: Test construction and validation. *Journal of Educational Psychology, 103*, 952–969. doi:10.1037/a0025125.
Wiens, P. D., Hessberg, K., LoCasale-Crouch, J., & DeCoster, J. (2013). Using standardized video-based assessment in a university teacher education program to examine preservice teachers' knowledge related to effective teaching. *Teacher and Teacher Education, 33*, 24–33. doi:10.1016/j.tate.2013.01.010.

Chapter 8
Teacher Knowledge Experiment: Conditions of the Development of Pedagogical Content Knowledge

Thilo Kleickmann, Steffen Tröbst, Aiso Heinze, Andrea Bernholt, Roland Rink, and Mareike Kunter

Abstract Pedagogical content knowledge (PCK)—that is, knowledge necessary to make subject matter accessible to students—is considered to be a key component of teacher competence. Thus, how teachers develop PCK is an important issue for educational research and practice. Our study aimed at investigating the conditions of development of PCK, and especially at testing competing assumptions about the role of prior content knowledge (CK) and prior pedagogical knowledge (PK) for PCK development. We targeted three assumptions: (1) CK and PK amalgamate, (2) CK is a necessary condition and facilitates PCK development, and (3) CK is a sufficient condition for teachers' PCK development. One hundred German pre-service elementary teachers participated in a randomized controlled trial. Participants' prior knowledge was manipulated through five courses, constituting three experimental conditions and two controls. In this chapter, we report on the conceptualization of the treatments, and provide a detailed analysis of our knowledge measures. We further give an overview of the initial, preliminary results of the experiment. The findings of our study may have important implications for the discussion of how PCK can best be fostered in teacher education.

Keywords Teachers' professional knowledge • Pedagogical content knowledge • Mathematics • Elementary school • Development

T. Kleickmann (✉) • S. Tröbst
Kiel University, Kiel, Germany
e-mail: kleickmann@paedagogik.uni-kiel.de; troebst@paedagogik.uni-kiel.de

A. Heinze • A. Bernholt
Leibniz Institute for Science and Mathematics Education (IPN), Kiel, Germany
e-mail: heinze@ipn.uni-kiel.de; abernholt@ipn.uni-kiel.de

R. Rink
Technische Universität Braunschweig, Braunschweig, Germany
e-mail: r.rink@tu-braunschweig.de

M. Kunter
Goethe University Frankfurt, Frankfurt/Main, Germany
e-mail: kunter@paed.psych.uni-frankfurt.de

D. Leutner et al. (eds.), *Competence Assessment in Education*, Methodology of Educational Measurement and Assessment, DOI 10.1007/978-3-319-50030-0_8

8.1 Introduction

Teachers substantially differ in their capability to foster student learning and progress (Nye et al. 2004). Consequently, extensive research has examined what features characterize competent teachers. These features comprise professional knowledge, beliefs, motivational orientations, and self-regulation. Professional knowledge, including content knowledge (CK), pedagogical content knowledge (PCK), and pedagogical knowledge (PK) are all considered important cognitive components of teacher competence (Baumert and Kunter 2013). Inspired by the work of Lee Shulman (1987), pedagogical content knowledge (PCK)—that is, knowledge needed to make concrete subject matter accessible to students—has become a promising construct that has been widely investigated (Depaepe et al. 2013). PCK is therefore "per definition" considered a core component of teacher competence, which has been substantiated in recent research on its impact on quality of instruction and student progress (Baumert et al. 2010; Hill et al. 2005; Sadler et al. 2013).

However, research has just started to investigate how and under which conditions teachers develop PCK (Friedrichsen et al. 2009). In the research literature, three assumptions prevail, concerning the role of prior PK and CK for the development of PCK: (1) CK and PK amalgamate, (2) CK is a necessary condition and facilitates PCK development, and (3) CK is a sufficient condition for teachers' PCK development. From these as yet unsatisfactorily tested assumptions, strong implications for teacher education arise. In this chapter, we first elaborate on these theoretical assumptions and then present detailed information about the experimental study we conducted to test these hypotheses. This study was situated in the domain of mathematics (fractions: concept and computations). As our project was funded in the third phase of the priority program (Leutner et al. 2017, in this volume), only preliminary results can be reported. However, we present detailed information on the construction of courses and the tests of PCK, CK, and PK used in this study.

8.1.1 The Construct of Pedagogical Content Knowledge

Besides CK and PK, PCK is considered to be a unique domain of teacher knowledge. Although conceptualizations of PCK differ, two components are included in most PCK conceptualizations: (1) Knowledge of student understanding and learning, and (2) knowledge of teaching in a concrete content domain (Depaepe et al. 2013). The fact that these categories refer to concrete subject matter distinguishes PCK from general PK about learners, learning and teaching.

A major issue in research on PCK is the proper assessment of this knowledge. Much research has relied on distal measures for teachers' PCK: for instance, coursework, certifications, or participation in professional development programs. However, in most studies, these measures were poor predictors of classroom practice or student learning (e.g., Kennedy et al. 2008). It was only recently that research made progress in the more direct assessment of PCK (Krauss et al. 2008; Hill et al. 2005; Sadler et al. 2013). These measures have allowed for further testing the assumption of PCK as a unique dimension of teacher knowledge. Several studies provided factor analytical evidence that PCK may indeed be considered a separate dimension in teachers' knowledge base for teaching (Blömeke et al. 2014; Hill et al. 2004; Krauss et al. 2008). Further, recent studies show that compared to CK, for instance, PCK possesses differential and unique properties concerning the prediction of classroom practice and student learning (Baumert et al. 2010; Sadler et al. 2013). From all these results, at least two PCK conceptualizations are called into question. First, some authors judged the concept of PCK to be redundant, contained within subject-matter knowledge (McEwan and Bull 1991). Second, in the integrative model of PCK (Gess-Newsome 1999), CK, PK and context knowledge constitute unique dimensions of teacher knowledge, and PCK must be formed from these resources in the concrete and situated act of teaching. In this conception, PCK is considered an elusive cognition. Gess-Newsome (1999) contrasts this model with the transformative model, in which PCK is conceptualized as a unique knowledge category. In the present study, we follow the idea of PCK as a unique dimension in teachers' professional knowledge.

8.1.2 Conditions for the Development of Pedagogical Content Knowledge: The Role of Prior Content Knowledge and Pedagogical Knowledge

Given the educational impact of PCK, the state of research on PCK development in pre- and in-service teachers is unsatisfactory (Depaepe et al. 2013; Schneider and Plasman 2011; Seymour and Lehrer 2006). Although research has started to investigate the conditions for PCK development, the factors fostering teachers' PCK construction remain obscure (Seymour and Lehrer 2006). In the literature, a major concern is the role of teachers' prior CK and PK as individual resources for the development of PCK (Magnusson et al. 1999; Schneider and Plasman 2011; Van Driel et al. 1998).

Again it was Shulman who substantially influenced the fundamental ideas on the formation of PCK. He claimed that PCK represents the "blending of content and pedagogy" into an amalgam he called PCK (1987, p. 8). Consequently, CK and PK were considered important individual resources for PCK development (Grossman 1990; Krauss et al. 2008; Magnusson et al. 1999). However, what is more important: Is it the amalgamation of PK and CK that constitutes PCK construction? Is the formation of PCK mainly based on teachers' CK resources? Or are there different routes or pathways to PCK development? These questions have broad implications for teacher education and professional development.

Amalgamation of CK and PK Concerning PCK as an amalgam of content and pedagogy, a subtle differentiation has to be made: Is it a description of the process of PCK development, or is it a description of the properties of PCK? Ball, Thames and Phelps, for instance, displayed examples of mathematical knowledge of teaching and content, one of their components of PCK. They summarized that in all these examples, PCK "is an amalgam, involving a particular mathematical idea or procedure and familiarity with pedagogical principles for teaching that particular content" (Ball et al. 2008, p. 402). In this sense, the term amalgam refers to a property of PCK, and the authors do not infer that PCK necessarily needs to be developed from PK and CK. By contrast, in their review of science teacher PCK, Schneider and Plasman state that in order to develop PCK "science teachers need an understanding of science, general pedagogy, and the context (students and schools) in which they are teaching" (2011, p. 534). From these individual resources PCK is constructed in a process of "amalgamation or transformation" (Schneider and Plasman 2011, p. 533). This notion of amalgamation—that is, the process of constructing PCK from PK and CK as individual resources—is widespread (e.g., Krauss et al. 2008; Schneider and Plasman 2011). As Gess-Newsome points out, the assumption that PCK develops through an amalgamation of CK and PK is also reflected in traditional patterns of pre-service teacher education, with spatial and temporal separation of subject matter and pedagogical issues (Gess-Newsome 1999).

CK as the Main Resource In the literature on teacher knowledge, there is some agreement that CK represents a main resource for PCK development (e.g., Depaepe et al. 2013; Friedrichsen et al. 2009; Krauss et al. 2008; Sadler et al. 2013). This assumption is often justified with the claim that it is CK that needs to be transformed into PCK (Shulman 1987). Further, this assumption is based on the observation that pre- and in-service teachers fail to develop proper PCK when CK is missing or deficient. Several qualitative studies have found that CK constraint the scope for PCK construction: Pre- and in-service teachers themselves often have misconceptions or fragmented content knowledge that limit, for example, their knowledge of student conceptions, or their knowledge of cognitively challenging learning situations (e.g., Friedrichsen et al. 2009; Van Driel et al. 1998).

Quantitative research also provides supportive evidence for the assumption that CK is a necessary or facilitating condition for PCK development (Hill et al. 2004; Krauss et al. 2008; Sadler et al. 2013). For instance, factor analyses of CK and PCK measures show that both constructs represent unique dimensions, but are often highly correlated (Krauss et al. 2008; Hill et al. 2004). In contrast, PK seems to be more loosely associated with PCK (Voss et al. 2011). Sadler and colleagues inspected constellations in teachers' levels of CK and PCK. In their sample of 181 secondary physics teachers, they found teachers with high CK and PCK, teachers with high CK and low PCK, but almost no teachers showing high PCK levels and low levels of CK. They inferred that CK must be a necessary condition of PCK development (Sadler et al. 2013).

CK may even be considered a sufficient condition of PCK development. On the one hand, there is some evidence that higher levels of CK are not necessarily linked with higher levels of PCK (Lee et al. 2007; Sadler et al. 2013; Schneider and Plasman 2011). However, on the other hand, studies with German mathematics teachers showed that teachers teaching at academic track schools (*Gymnasien*) exhibited consistently higher levels of PCK than teachers from nonacademic track schools (Baumert et al. 2010; Kleickmann et al. 2013). This result is contrary to expectations, as teachers from academic track schools received broader and deeper learning opportunities for CK, but less for PCK. Profound CK may therefore even represent a sufficient condition for PCK development. A good example of how this assumption is reflected in education is the university teaching system: University professors and lecturers are usually appointed on account of their presumed knowledge in their field of study, and it is assumed that they will be able to teach these topics thanks to their CK; explicit instruction in PCK is not deemed necessary. Another example is the practice of lateral entry into teaching. Lateral entry allows content specialists to obtain a teaching position in schools without previous participation in a teacher education program.

Multiple Pathways Some authors have assumed that there might be multiple pathways or routes to teachers' PCK development (Gess-Newsome 1999; Magnusson et al. 1999; Schneider and Plasman 2011). Gess-Newsome, for instance, has suggested that teachers' PCK construction may primarily be based on or facilitated by teachers' CK resources, but, when CK is deficient, teachers may rely on their PK (1999). This assumption was also proposed by Krauss et al. (2008). In a sample of biology and chemistry physics teachers, they found low levels of mathematical CK, but comparably high levels of PCK. The authors suggested that these teachers may have drawn on their general PK when constructing PCK. However, this notion is challenged by results from a quasi-experimental field study by Strawhecker (2005). She found that a method course for pre-service mathematics teachers addressing general PK did not substantially contribute to PCK development (Strawhecker 2005).

8.1.3 The Present Study

The present study was concerned with the role of prior PK and CK as individual resources for the development of teachers' PCK. In teacher education, the balancing of learning opportunities for CK, PK and PCK is a matter of great concern (Gess-Newsome 1999; Strawhecker 2005). Providing evidence on the role of prior CK and PK for the development of PCK is therefore an important issue for educational research, as it may inform this debate.

In previous research on the role of CK and PK for PCK development, three main assumptions may be differentiated: (1) teachers construct PCK from their prior CK and PK in a process of amalgamation, (2) CK is a necessary condition and facilitates PCK development, and (3) CK is sufficient for teachers' PCK development. Finally, some authors suggest that there might be multiple pathways to PCK development.

Up to now, these assumptions have mainly been based on case studies, with some of them including longitudinal designs and/or cross-sectional field studies. Quasi-experimental studies are rare and, as far as we know, no experimental studies have yet been conducted. Thus, causal inferences on the validity of the aforementioned assumptions are not yet warranted.

In the present study, we aimed to complement existing research by a randomized controlled trial on the role of prior CK and PK for pre-service mathematics teachers' PCK in the domain of fractions and computations with fractions. We thereby aimed at providing causal evidence on the validity of the aforementioned assumptions concerning the development of PCK. To this end, we experimentally manipulated pre-service teachers' CK, PK, and PCK and inspected effects on their PCK development. We chose the domain of fractions as it is well researched with regard to student conceptions and instructional strategies fostering student understanding.

The focus of this chapter is (1) to describe the treatments implemented to experimentally manipulate participants' professional knowledge, (2) to introduce our measures of PCK, CK, and PK, and (3) to present findings on the quality of our measures, as well as to provide a summary of preliminary results of tests of the three aforementioned assumptions.

8.2 Methods

Participants attended intensive two-day workshops featuring various combinations of lessons on CK, PCK and PK that are potentially relevant for teaching fractions and fractional arithmetic in sixth-grade mathematics. The experimental design featured three experimental and two control groups. Each experimental group was devised to represent one hypothesis about the development of PCK. The experimental group representing the amalgamation hypothesis received lessons on CK on the first day and lessons on PK on the second day (EG amalg). The experimental group representing the hypothesis that CK is a necessary condition and facilitates PCK development received lessons on CK on the first day and lessons on PCK on the second day (EG facil). The experimental group representing the hypothesis that CK is sufficient for the development of PCK received lessons on CK on both days (EG suffi). The control groups were further divided into a weak and a strong control group; participants in the weak control group received only instruction on PK (CG weak), while participants in the strong control group received only instruction on PCK (CG strong).

The experimental design contained four measurement occasions: a pretest at the beginning of the first workshop day, an intermediate test at the beginning of the second day, a posttest at the end of the second day and a follow-up test approximately 6 weeks after the workshops. The current chapter reports on the first three measurement occasions (see Fig. 8.1).

Relations between PCK, CK, and PK depend to a great extent on the definitions of these constructs. Knowledge of classroom management, for instance, which is

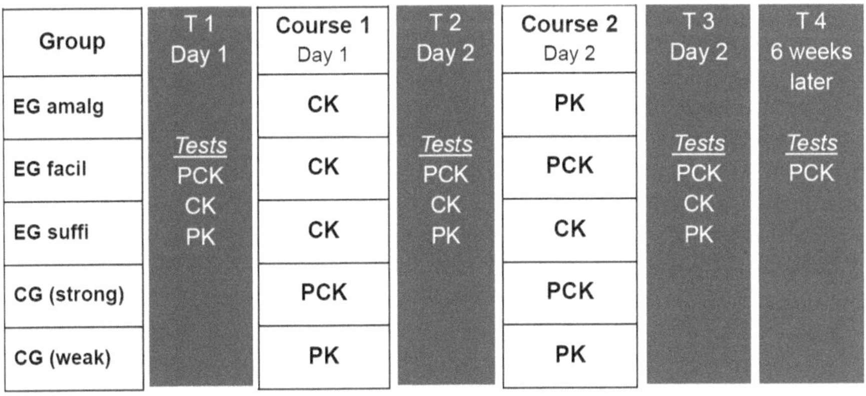

Fig. 8.1 Experimental design with groups, tests, and measurement occasions. Additional covariates not included

often included in PK definitions, should be more distal to PCK than general PK on student conceptions and conceptual change. In our study, we tried to closely attune tests and treatments on PCK, CK, and PK.

8.2.1 *Participants*

One hundred pre-service teachers who were enrolled in undergraduate programs that prepared them for teaching both at the elementary and at the lower secondary levels, participated in the study. Twelve participants were male. Participants' ages ranged from 19 to 46 years; most participants were in their early twenties ($M = 22.9$ years, $SD = 5.0$). Ninety-five percent were in the first year of their academic studies. Participants received a payment of 200 Euro. This payment was reduced to 160 Euro where participants missed the follow-up assessment. We recruited participants from universities in Potsdam and Berlin. We randomly assigned persons from the pool of 165 applicants seeking to participate in our study, to each of the five groups of our experimental design. This procedure resulted in moderately unequal group sizes, ranging from 16 participants for CG weak to 23 participants for EG suffi.

8.2.2 *Treatments*

The two-day workshops followed a common time schedule: Each day began with a testing session (120 min on the first and 60 min on the second day), followed by a half hour break. After this, two 105-min instruction blocks followed, divided by a one hour lunch break. The end of second day additionally included a half hour break and another testing session (90 min). In sum, the two-day workshops included seven hours of treatment in the respective domains, equaling four to five regular seminar sessions of 90 min. The treatments were conducted by an experienced lecturer in elementary mathematics education who, when teaching the courses, was unaware of the precise content of the tests on PCK, CK, and PK.

The implementation of the treatments followed instructional storyline provided by lesson plans and presentation slides. Participants were equipped with corresponding handouts. Naturally, we aimed for a constant level of participant activity and involvement across treatments. Thus, treatments were interspersed with various tasks for participants, ranging from short questions to role play. Treatment blocks concluded with writing assignments prompting participants to recapitulate the major contents of the respective treatment blocks. When participants asked for information not intended by the treatment at hand—for instance, when participants during a treatment on CK asked for information on PCK—these questions were left unanswered, with a cursory reference to the rationale of the study. However, after the follow-up test, all participants were provided with the complete course material. Preliminary versions of the treatments had been piloted with a total of 100 preservice teachers.

Both the treatment on PK and the treatment on CK, possessed specific overlap with the treatment on PCK, while they had no overlap with each other. For instance, the treatment on PK generically covered the hierarchy of enactive, iconic and symbolic representations. In contrast, the treatment on PCK introduced instructional representations for specific aspects of the area of fractions and fractional arithmetic, such as enactive and iconic representations for expanding and reducing fractions. The treatment on CK, finally, covered the topic of expanding and reducing fractions without reference to instructional representations.

In the experimental design, three of the five groups (EG suffi, CG weak and CG strong), featured repeated instruction in the same area of professional knowledge on both days of the workshops. In these groups, we devised a basic and an advanced course for each area of professional knowledge. Beyond repetition of some contents, advanced courses added further perspectives to basic courses, without extending the scope delimited by previous basic courses.

Treatment on Content Knowledge The basic course on CK started with conveying very simple facts, such as clarification of the terms numerator, vinculum and denominator. After that, the set of positive rational numbers was constructed from the set of natural numbers as equivalence classes of simple linear equations ($a = b \cdot x$, $a, b \in N$, $b \neq 0$). In this context, a fraction corresponded with the desirable solution of an equation that has no solution in the set of natural numbers. Accordingly, a “new” set of numbers was constructed that is closed under division. Moreover, the equivalence of fractions representing the same rational number was highlighted. The procedures of expanding and reducing were introduced as techniques for converting equivalent fractions into each other. This concluded the first block of the basic course. The second block of the basic course was reserved for defining and exercising arithmetic operations with fractions. This included addition, multiplication and division. Participants examined these operations with respect to the definition of fractions by linear equations. The aspect of closure was discussed in this context. Moreover, participants practiced the ordering of fractions. Here, participants discovered the density of rational numbers.

The advanced course was mostly a straightforward repetition of the basic course. In particular, the first block included constructing the set of positive rational numbers from the set of natural numbers, differentiating fractions and rational numbers, expanding and reducing fractions, as well as discussing the density and the cardinality of the set of positive rational numbers. Apart from repetition, the second block featured demonstrations of the validity of the commutative, distributive and associative laws for the set of rational numbers.

Treatment on Pedagogical Knowledge At the beginning of the basic course on PK, participants were introduced to the conception of classroom instruction as the provision of opportunities to learn; the teacher was presented as an influential orchestrator of these opportunities. Apart from that, the first block of the basic course covered general principles of learning. Participants were familiarized with the central role of student conceptions and learned about the idea of learning as conceptual change. The second block of the basic course was concerned with generic principles of teaching. Specifically, this covered tolerance for errors, the use of misunderstandings for learning, the provision of adequate scaffolding and the use of representations for fostering understanding.

The advanced course mirrored the arrangement of the basic course; the first block focused on learning, the second block on teaching. Beyond repetition, the first block expanded participants' capabilities with respect to the diagnosis of student conceptions, for example. Similarly, the second block concentrated on structuring content and reducing complexity of content as vehicles for facilitating understanding within a repetition of the basic principles of teaching.

Treatment on Pedagogical Content Knowledge The basic course on PCK began with a general introduction to the relevance of student conceptions and conceptual understanding for teaching mathematics. The following first block of the basic course was concerned primarily with conceptual aspects of fractions. For instance, participants were introduced to the part-whole and the operator concepts of fractions; they discussed advantages and disadvantages of these concepts with regard to several aspects of teaching fractions in elementary school. Furthermore, participants were provided with methods for explicating the density of rational numbers and the fact that a rational number can be represented by varying fractions. The second block covered the topic of teaching operations with fractions. Specifically, participants learned about strategies elementary school students might use for comparing fractions, and how to foster the flexible use of these strategies. Moreover, the second block presented information on typical errors with respect to the addition and division of fractions; participants were instructed how to introduce these operations to elementary school students—for instance, by the use of appropriate representations. The second block concluded with discussing the fundamental changes student conceptions have to undergo when transcending from the set of natural numbers to the realm of fractions.

The advanced course on PCK started with a repetition of the necessary fundamental changes in student conceptions in face of the introduction of fractions. The rest of the first block tapped teaching operations with fractions. This included multiplication and division as well as comparing fractions; participants were confronted with typical errors committed in elementary school and with different approaches for introducing these operations with fractions into the elementary school classrooms. The second block covered representations. This included enactive, iconic and symbolic representations for expanding and reducing fractions, for addition with fractions and for multiplication with fractions.

8.2.3 Measures

Test of Content Knowledge Measurement of participants' CK was based on an item pool of 27 items. For economy of assessment, the item design was incomplete. Participants completed 20, 19 and 24 items on pretest, intermediate test and posttest, respectively. A set of 11 anchor items appeared in all three assessments; 15 items were utilized on two measurement occasions, while one item was presented exclusively on a single measurement occasion. The item pool comprised 6 closed-response and 21 free-response items. The CK item pool covered the correspondence of fractions and linear equations, the conversion of fractions into decimals (and vice versa), the ordering and comparison of fractions, calculations with fractions (including word problems), and specific properties of the set of rational numbers (see Fig. 8.2 for a sample item).

Test of Pedagogical Knowledge Assessment of participants' PK was based on a pool of 40 items. In correspondence to the other measures of participants' knowledge, items were partially rotated across measurement occasions. Particularly, participants worked on 29, 27 and 34 items on pretest, intermediate test and posttest, respectively. There were 16 anchor items appearing in all three assessments. Of the other items, 16 items were presented twice and eight items were presented once. The item pool was divided in 11 closed-response and 29 free-response items.

The PK item pool covered the relevance of student conceptions and prior knowledge for subsequent learning, the basic principles of conceptual change, the handling of errors, the role of representations, scaffolding and various methods for fostering understanding. Naturally, this categorization of items was only tentative. It was possible, for instance, to solve some items on scaffolding with knowledge about representations (see Fig. 8.2 for a sample item).

Test of Pedagogical Content Knowledge Assessment of participants' PCK was based on a pool of 41 items. In part, items were rotated across measurement occasions. On pretest, intermediate test, posttest and follow-up test, participants completed 36, 29, 38 and 41 items, respectively. A set of 23 anchor items was used on all measurement occasions, whereas 17 items were presented twice. One item was

Sample Item Pedagogical Content Knowledge (PCK)

Draft an assignment that requests your students to illustrate expanding fractions with an enactive representation (through overt behavior) and an iconic representation (through a graphical depiction).

enactive

Sample Item Content Knowledge (CK)

How has the subtraction assignment $\frac{2}{3} - \frac{1}{4}$ to be rearranged in order to obtain a correct solution?

Sample Item Pedagogical Knowledge (PK)

Name **two** examples for enactive, iconic and symbolic representations, respectively. Please do not define the terms enactive, iconic and symbolic, instead try to name concrete examples related to teaching in elementary school.

enactive

Fig. 8.2 Sample items from the tests on PCK, CK, and PK

presented exclusively on the follow-up test. While 24 items had a closed response format, 17 items called for free responses.

The PCK item pool covered the use of enactive and iconic representations for facilitating understanding of fractions and operations with fractions, knowledge of typical errors and command of approaches for introducing the operations into the elementary school classroom, and knowledge about students' conceptual understanding of fractions. Obviously, items regularly touched on the aforementioned item characteristics simultaneously. So, the presented classification of items is only conjectural (see Fig. 8.2 for a sample item).

8.2.4 Baseline Equivalence and Treatment Implementation Checks

We checked whether our random assignment procedure resulted in baseline equivalence of the three experimental and two control groups with regard to their professional knowledge and with regard to covariates, such as motivational characteristics, epistemological beliefs, and beliefs on teaching mathematics. We found only minor and insignificant group differences in the PCK, CK, and PK pretest scores, as well as in the covariates, indicating that randomization was successful.

We further checked whether our PCK, CK, and PK courses succeeded in manipulating participants' professional knowledge as intended. An inspection of PCK, CK, and PK growth for each treatment day and each of the groups featured in our design, exhibited the desired significant gains in participants' professional knowledge. Moreover, we videotaped all courses in order to check whether only the intended knowledge domain was taught; these analyses are not yet completed.

8.3 Results

In this section, we present findings on the quality of our measures of PCK, CK, and PK, and then give a short summary of preliminary results on the tests of the three assumptions on PCK formation.

8.3.1 *Measurement of Pre-service Teachers' Knowledge*

Test of Content Knowledge For descriptive purposes—that is, to map item content on person ability—we submitted pre-service teachers' responses on the test of CK to a concurrent calibration of pretest, intermediate test, and posttest, according to the simple Rasch model. Item difficulties ranged from −3.26 logits to 2.60 logits. The easiest item called for the subtraction of a proper fraction from another proper fraction, whereas the most difficult item required the production of all fractions with a denominator of three between a given proper fraction and a given mixed numeral. On average, items aiming at calculations with fractions were comparatively easy ($M = -0.86$ logits) though, with a range from −3.26 logits to 0.83 logits, they varied considerably in difficulty ($SD = 1.72$ logits). Relative to this, items covering the conversion of fractions into decimals ($M = -0.34$ logits, $SD = 0.38$ logits) and items affording the comparison or ordering of fractions ($M = -0.34$ logits, $SD = 1.43$ logits) exhibited intermediate average item difficulties. Finally, items involving the expression of fractions as classes of equivalent eqs. ($M = 0.66$ logits, $SD = 0.32$ logits) and items asking for general properties of the set of rational numbers ($M = 1.21$ logits, $SD = 0.49$ logits) possessed the highest average difficulties of all items of the test of content knowledge. In addition, items featuring improper fractions or mixed numerals ($M = 0.01$ logits, $SD = 1.63$ logits) outstripped items presenting exclusively proper fractions ($M = -0.79$ logits, $SD = 1.14$ logits) in terms of average difficulty. Infit values varied between 0.83 and 1.26, indicating reasonable fit to the simple Rasch model.

For model identification, the distribution of item difficulties possessed a predefined mean of 0.00 logits ($SD = 1.33$). In comparison, the mean of the distribution of person ability for pretest equaled −0.65 logits ($SD = 1.11$). On the intermediate test, mean person ability was .19 logits ($SD = 1.38$). Finally, on the posttest, the mean person ability equaled 0.50 logits ($SD = 1.27$). In other words, on average, participants started the workshops with the ability to solve simple calculations with fractions, mastered the conversion of fractions into decimals, as well as the comparison and ordering of fractions in the intermediate test, and approached the ability to handle fractions in the form of equations at posttest. Cronbach's alphas were .80, .80 and .84 for pretest, intermediate test and posttest, respectively. The person separation reliability for the weighted likelihood estimates of ability obtained from the concurrent calibration of the three measurement occasions was .82.

Test of Pedagogical Knowledge A calibration following the simple Rasch model was performed on pre-service teachers' responses on the test of PK. A range of item difficulties from −5.06 logits to 3.23 logits was obtained. The easiest item requested participants to recognize mistakes in the classroom as opportunities to learn. The most difficult item asked for brief definitions of the notions of enactive, iconic and symbolic representations. The average difficulty of items focusing on learning (M = −0.06 logits, SD = 1.31 logits) did not differ considerably from the average difficulty of items centering on teaching (M = 0.07 logits, SD = 1.72 logits). Specifically, items concerned with the proper handling of mistakes in classroom instruction constituted a relatively easy set of items with a remarkable variation in difficulty (M = −1.58 logits, SD = 3.12 logits). In comparison, knowledge about the importance of student conceptions and prior knowledge for successful learning represented a more advanced step in proficiency on the test of PK (M = −0.56 logits, SD = 1.32 logits). Items probing participants' capabilities with respect to the concept of scaffolding, denoted even further advanced proficiency (M = 0.31 logits, SD = 1.09 logits). Finally, on average, command of the basic principles of conceptual change theory (M = 0.65 logits, SD = 0.96 logits) and of the notions of enactive, iconic and symbolic representations (M = 0.69 logits, SD = 1.70 logits) constituted the apex of proficiency in PK. Infit values ranged from 0.81–1.14, reflecting adequate fit to the simple Rasch model.

The distribution of item difficulties of the test of PK had a predefined mean of 0.00 logits (SD = 1.49). In relation to this, on the pretest the mean of the ability distribution was −1.59 logits (SD = 0.66). On the intermediate test, average person ability equaled −1.61 logits (SD = 0.78 logits). Eventually, on the posttest, the mean of the ability distribution amounted to −0.85 logits (SD = 0.85). In essence, on average, the test of PK was very difficult. Most participants mastered merely the easiest items of the test. In fact, only in eight cases did item difficulty fall below average person ability on posttest. Internal consistency, in terms of Cronbach's alphas, was .48, .68 and .78, for pretest, intermediate test and posttest, respectively. The person separation reliability of the weighted likelihood estimates of ability was .67.

Test of Pedagogical Content Knowledge Calibration according to the simple Rasch model based on pre-service teachers' responses on the test of PCK for the first three measurement occasions, yielded item difficulties that varied between −3.53 logits and 2.33 logits. The easiest item was concerned with the shortcomings of introducing fractions initially via equations. On the other hand, the most difficult item afforded participants the opportunity to provide an intuitively accessible explanation for the use of the reciprocal of a fraction in division involving fractions. On average, items aiming for knowledge about elementary school students' conceptual understanding of fractions per se, were comparatively easy to solve (M = −0.34 logits, SD = 1.48 logits). Items probing for participants' proficiency with regard to the use of representations for fostering understanding were somewhat more difficult (M = −0.09 logits, SD = 1.31 logits). Finally, items centering on the teaching of operations constituted the set of items with highest average difficulty (M = 0.42 logits, SD = 1.07 logits). However, disparities in mean difficulty between the three tentative groups of items tended to be moderate. Infit values varied between 0.89 and 1.09 indicating excellent fit to the simple Rasch model.

The distribution of item difficulties for the test of PCK was predefined with a mean of 0.00 logits (SD = 1.30). On the pretest, the mean of the ability distribution was −0.31 logits (SD = 0.61). On the intermediate test, the average person ability was −0.01 logits (SD = 0.68). Eventually, on the posttest, the mean of the ability distribution equaled 0.31 logits (SD = 0.73). This indicates a steady increase of participants' average ability with regard to pedagogical content knowledge, across the three measurement occasions, without floor or ceiling effects. Cronbach's alphas amounted to .61, .60, and .72, for pretest, intermediate test and posttest, respectively. The weighted likelihood estimates of person ability displayed a separation reliability of .68.

Exploration of Dimensionality and External Validity To assess the dimensionality of professional knowledge captured with our instruments, we submitted participants' responses on the three tests to a unidimensional, to two two-dimensional, and to a three-dimensional calibration, according to the simple Rasch model; in each case the measurement occasions of pretest, intermediate test and posttest were calibrated concurrently. In each of the two-dimensional calibrations, two domains of professional knowledge with partially overlapping content formed a single dimension: that is, CK and PCK, or PK and PCK, were combined. Subsequent likelihood ratio tests uncovered that the three-dimensional model possessed better relative model fit than did the unidimensional model, $\chi^2(5) = 746.98$, $p < .001$, the two-dimensional model featuring a combination of CK and PCK, $\chi^2(3) = 285.94$, $p < .001$, and the two-dimensional model featuring a combination of PK and PCK, $\chi^2(3) = 281.29$, $p < .001$. Latent correlations retrieved from the three-dimensional calibration, between the test of CK and the test of PCK, between the test of CK and the test of PK, and between the test of PK and the test of PCK, amounted to .61, .05 and .25, respectively. In sum, it appears completely justified to view the three tests as assessments of distinct dimensions of professional knowledge.

To explore the external validity of the tests of PCK, CK, and PK, we investigated correlations with participants' motivational characteristics, epistemological beliefs and beliefs about teaching. As expected the test of CK was significantly related to interest in math, math self-concept and the epistemological belief of math as a process. PCK was also significantly related to these math-specific measures, but to a smaller degree. However, it correlated to a higher degree than CK with a transmission belief about teaching math. PK was not significantly related to these math-specific measures.

8.3.2 Testing the Assumptions on PCK Development

In this section, we summarize the first findings of the experimental tests of the assumptions on PCK development. Please note that these are preliminary results that will need to be substantiated with more elaborative analyses (Troebst et al. in prep.). The control group, which exclusively received instruction on PK (CG weak) did not display significant PCK development either on the first or on the second day. The EG amalg group, which participated in lessons on CK on the first day and lessons on PK on the second day, yielded significantly larger PCK development than did CG weak. The EG suffi group, which was provided with lessons on CK on both days, also showed significantly larger PCK growth than did CG weak. EG facil, which featured lessons on CK on the first day and lessons on PCK on the second day, as well as CG strong, which participated in lessons on PCK on both days, demonstrated the largest PCK gains. Our design allowed further testing of the assumption that CK facilitates PCK development. Two groups, on one of the two treatment days, received exactly the same lessons on PCK, but differed in their prior CK: CG strong received the same lessons on PCK on their first day as did EG facil on their second day, after their participation in CK lessons on the first day. In our present, preliminary analyses, both groups exhibited the same gains in PCK in the course of their lessons on PCK.

8.4 Discussion

In the debate as to how to best prepare teachers, there are many speculations on the role of CK and PK in teacher education. However, these speculations are often not based on evidence. Our study is one of the first to address these questions in a randomized controlled trial (RCT). For the purpose of experimentally testing the aforementioned assumptions on PCK development, we designed courses for pre-service teachers that were aimed at manipulating teachers' prior professional knowledge. Further, we constructed tests to assess participants' PCK, CK, and PK. The courses and tests on CK and PK were closely attuned to those for PCK. Preliminary results indicate the high internal validity of our RCT. Our randomized assignment of participants to treatments resulted in baseline equivalence in our three measures of teacher knowledge. Moreover, treatment implementation checks revealed that participants' PCK, CK, and PK were manipulated through our courses as intended. Video-based analyses will allow us to further probe the intended implementation of our courses. As our courses on PCK, CK, and PK resembled those courses ordinarily implemented in university-based teacher education, we also consider the external validity to be high. Our block courses could quite readily have been part of regular teacher education programs.

Concerning the measurement of pre-service mathematics teachers' knowledge, our analyses yielded the following results. In the pretest, the tests of PCK, CK, and particularly PK, were comparably difficult for the participating pre-service teachers. Concerning PCK, tasks on teaching strategies and representations facilitating student understanding of fractions, appeared to be particularly difficult. With regard to CK, even some of the tasks on the computation of fractions were difficult for the pre-service teachers. However, all three tests proved to be sensitive with regard to our treatments. In the posttest, participants had substantially higher probabilities of solving the items. With regard to PCK, our main dependent variable, we observed a steady increase of participants' average ability across the three measurement occasions, without floor or ceiling effects.

Multidimensional Rasch Analyses supported the three-dimensional structure of pre-service mathematics teachers' professional knowledge. The three factors represented were PCK, CK, and PK. PCK and CK were more highly correlated than were PCK and PK whereas CK and PK were the least correlated. These findings support the notion of closely related subject matter knowledge: that is CK and PCK on the one hand, and general PK on the other hand (Ball et al. 2008; Shulman 1987). PK was substantially more weakly related to PCK than CK, although our PK test only included knowledge of learning and teaching that was closely attuned to the PCK construct. For this purpose, the PK test also featured knowledge of student conceptions, conceptual change theories, and teaching strategies to overcome student misconceptions, from a general perspective however. Correlations to external variables like interest in math and beliefs about the teaching of math provided evidence for external validity of our measures of teacher knowledge.

Preliminary tests of the three assumptions about PCK development pointed to the following results. Our control group, which received lessons on general PK only (CG weak), did not develop any PCK. As often assumed in the literature, we found—at least to a certain degree—evidence of an amalgamation of CK and PK. Further, CK seemed to be—also at least to a certain degree—sufficient for PCK development. However, two other routes to the development of PCK proved to be far more effective. The first route consists of explicitly addressing PCK: that is, knowledge of students, learning and teaching in concrete content domains (CG strong). The second route featured a combination of CK and PCK (EG facil). In all, these preliminary results indicated that there are different pathways to PCK development. The notion that CK and/or PK need to be transformed, seems to be not the only route to PCK construction. Actually, explicitly addressing the knowledge of students, learning and teaching in concrete content domains, whether with or without antecedent CK instruction, appeared to be the most effective pathway.

Evidence for the role of prior PK for the development of PCK appeared to be flimsy although our measures and treatments of PK and PCK were closely attuned. The control group receiving only PK instruction (CG weak) did not show any growth in PCK, and in the EG amalg we only detected comparably weak effects on PCK development. Moreover, the overall amalgamation effect was partly due to PCK development from CK only. These results call into question the role of general PK for the development of PCK. However, beyond the target of PCK development,

PK should be considered an important dimension of teacher knowledge: for instance, with regard to effective classroom management (Voss et al. 2014). Moreover, conditions that improve the transformation of PK into PCK, and the applicability of PK in classroom teaching, should be examined in future research. Our previous results show the advantages of teacher-specific versus polyvalent traditional teacher education, respectively. Fostering CK and PK separately, as realized in polyvalent or traditional teacher education (Gess-Newsome 1999) appeared to be comparably the least effective, in terms of PCK development. Other routes to PCK development, as realized in EG facil and CG strong, seem to be far more effective.

However, our study investigated the development of pre-service teachers' PCK in just one content area. Our results need therefore to be replicated in other subjects and with other groups of teachers: for instance, with secondary school teachers and with in-service teachers. Future studies could also consider the role of teaching experience in the process of PCK development and include measures of teachers' actions. In the present study, we embedded a lesson preparation task into the follow-up assessment. These data will be considered in a subsequent publication. Finally, whereas we inspected the effects of separate CK and PCK courses, an investigation of integrated CK and PCK instruction would also be worthwhile.

Acknowledgments The preparation of this chapter was supported by grant KL 2355/1-1 and KU 1939/5-1 from the German Research Foundation (DFG) in the Priority Program "Competence Models for Assessing Individual Learning Outcomes and Evaluating Educational Processes" (SPP 1293).

References

Ball, D. L., Thames, M., & Phelps, G. (2008). Content knowledge for teaching. What makes it special? *Journal of Teacher Education, 59*, 389–407. doi:10.1177/0022487108324554.

Baumert, J., & Kunter, M. (2013). The COACTIV model of teachers' professional competence. In M. Kunter, J. Baumert, W. Blum, U. Klusmann, S. Krauss, & M. Neubrand (Eds.), *Cognitive activation in the mathematics classroom and professional competence of teachers, Results from the COACTIV project* (pp. 25–48). New York: Springer.

Baumert, J., Kunter, M., Blum, W., Brunner, M., Voss, T., Jordan, A., … Tsai, Y.-M. (2010). Teachers' mathematical knowledge, cognitive activation in the classroom, and student progress. *American Educational Research Journal, 47*, 133–180. doi:10.3102/0002831209345157.

Blömeke, S., Houang, R. T., & Suhl, U. (2014). Diagnosing teacher knowledge by applying multidimensional item response theory and multiple-group models. In S. Blömeke & F.-J. Hsieh (Eds.), *International perspectives on teacher knowledge, beliefs and opportunities to learn. TEDS-M results* (pp. 483–501). Dordrecht: Springer.

Depaepe, F., Verschaffel, L., & Kelchtermans, G. (2013). Pedagogical content knowledge: A systematic review of the way in which the concept has pervaded mathematics educational research. *Teaching and Teacher Education, 34*, 12–25. doi:10.1016/j.tate.2013.03.001.

Friedrichsen, P. J., Abell, S. K., Pareja, E. M., Brown, P. L., Lankford, D. M., & Volkmann, M. J. (2009). Does teaching experience matter? Examining biology teachers' prior knowledge for teaching in an alternative certification program. *Journal of Research in Science Teaching, 46*, 357–383. doi:10.1002/tea.20283.

Gess-Newsome, J. (1999). Pedagogical content knowledge: An introduction and orientation. In J. Gess-Newsome & N. G. Lederman (Eds.), *Examining pedagogical content knowledge. The construct and its implications for science education* (pp. 3–17). Dordrecht: Kluwer.

Grossman, P. L. (1990). *The making of a teacher. Teacher knowledge and teacher education.* New York: Teachers College Press.

Hill, H. C., Schilling, S. G., & Ball, D. (2004). Developing measures of teachers' mathematics knowledge for teaching. *The Elementary School Journal, 105*, 11–30. doi:10.1086/428763.

Hill, H. C., Rowan, B., & Ball, D. (2005). Effects of teachers' mathematical knowledge for teaching on student achievement. *American Educational Research Journal, 42*, 371–406. doi:10.3102/00028312042002371.

Kennedy, M. M., Ahn, S., & Choi, J. (2008). The value added by teacher education. In M. Cochran-Smith, S. Feiman-Nemser, D. J. McIntyre, & K. E. Demers (Eds.), *Handbook of research on teacher education* (3rd ed., pp. 1249–1273). New York: Routledge.

Kleickmann, T., Richter, D., Kunter, M., Elsner, J., Besser, M., Krauss, S., & Baumert, J. (2013). Pedagogical content knowledge and content knowledge: The role of structural differences in teacher education. *Journal of Teacher Education, 64*, 90–106. doi:10.1177/0022487112460398.

Krauss, S., Baumert, J., & Blum, W. (2008a). Secondary mathematics teachers' pedagogical content knowledge and content knowledge: Validation of the COACTIV constructs. *The International Journal on Mathematics Education, 40*, 873–892. doi:10.1007/s11858-008-0141-9.

Krauss, S., Brunner, M., Kunter, M., Baumert, J., Blum, W., Neubrand, J., & Jordan, A. (2008b). Pedagogical content knowledge and content knowledge of secondary mathematics teachers. *Journal of Educational Psychology, 100*, 716–725. doi:10.1037/0022-0663.100.3.716.

Lee, E., Brown, M. N., Luft, J. A., & Roehrig, G. H. (2007). Assessing beginning secondary science teachers' PCK: Pilot year results. *School Science and Mathematics, 107*, 52–60. doi:10.1111/j.1949-8594.2007.tb17768.x.

Leutner, D., Fleischer, J., Grünkorn, J., & Klieme, E. (2017). Introduction. In D. Leutner, J. Fleischer, J. Grünkorn, & E. Klieme (Eds.), *Competence assessment in education: Research, models and instruments* (pp. 1–6). Berlin: Springer.

Magnusson, S., Krajcik, J., & Borko, H. (1999). Nature, sources and development of pedagogical content knowledge for science teaching. In J. Gess-Newsome & N. G. Lederman (Eds.), *Examining pedagogical content knowledge* (Vol. 6, pp. 95–132). Dordrecht: Kluwer.

McEwan, H., & Bull, B. (1991). The pedagogic nature of subject matter knowledge. *American Educational Research Journal, 28*, 316–334. doi:10.3102/00028312028002316.

Nye, B., Konstantopoulos, S., & Hedges, L. V. (2004). How large are teacher effects? *Educational Evaluation and Policy Analysis, 26*, 237–257. doi:10.3102/01623737026003237.

Sadler, P. M., Sonnert, G., Coyle, H. P., Cook-Smith, N., & Miller, J. L. (2013). The influence of teachers' knowledge on student learning in middle school physical science classrooms. *American Educational Research Journal, 50*, 1020–1049. doi:10.3102/0002831213477680.

Schneider, R., & Plasman, K. (2011). Science teacher learning progressions: A review of science teachers' pedagogical content knowledge development. *Review of Educational Research, 81*, 530–565. doi:10.3102/0034654311423382.

Seymour, J. R., & Lehrer, R. (2006). Tracing the evolution of pedagogical content knowledge as the development of interanimated discourses. *The Journal of the Learning Sciences, 15*, 549–582. doi:10.1207/s15327809jls1504_5.

Shulman, L. S. (1987). Knowledge and teaching: Foundations of the new reform. *Harvard Educational Review, 57*(1), 1–22.

Strawhecker, J. (2005). Preparing elementary teachers to teach mathematics: How field experiences impact pedagogical content knowledge. *Issues in the Undergraduate Mathematics Preparation of School Teachers, 4*, 1–12.

Troebst. S. et al. (in preparation). Teacher knowledge experiment: The relevance of content knowledge and pedagogical knowledge for the formation of pedagogical content knowledge.

Van Driel, J., Verloop, N., & De Vos, W. (1998). Developing science teachers' pedagogical content knowledge. *Journal of Research in Science Teaching, 35*, 673–695. doi:10.1002/(SICI)1098-2736(199808)35:6<673.

Voss, T., Kunter, M., & Baumert, J. (2011). Assessing teacher candidates' general pedagogical and psychological knowledge: Test construction and validation. *Journal of Educational Psychology, 103*, 952–969. doi:10.1037/a0025125.

Voss, T., Kunter, M., Seiz, J., Hoehne, V., & Baumert, J. (2014). Die Bedeutung des pädagogisch-psychologischen Wissens von angehenden Lehrkräften für die Unterrichtsqualität [The role of preservice teachers' pedagogical-psychological knowledge for quality of instruction]. *Zeitschrift für Pädagogik, 60*, 184–201.

Chapter 9
Teachers' School Tracking Decisions

Ines Böhmer, Cornelia Gräsel, Sabine Krolak-Schwerdt, Thomas Hörstermann, and Sabine Glock

Abstract Teachers' tracking decisions strongly influence students' future academic and professional careers, and are assumed to contribute to social inequalities in the German school system. Drawing on dual process models, we focused on the cognitive processes underlying teachers' tracking decisions and developed a two-component model of teachers' adaptive diagnostic competence. This model involves a cognitive component that refers to the ability to process information in either heuristic or rule-based ways in making a decision. The situation-specific component refers to the ability to switch flexibly between the different strategies, according to situational demands: case consistency and accountability for the decision. Teachers' expertise is a necessary precondition for both components. Employing student case vignettes that were developed and tested in two pre-studies, two (quasi) experiments supported the assumptions of the model: Teachers adapted their processing strategies according to the situational demands. Pre-service teachers, as novices, lacked this competency as yet. Therefore, we designed a training program to help pre-service teachers develop the ability to optimize their decision making. Preliminary results indicate that as the quality of pre-service teachers' tracking decisions improved, the influence of social background variables was reduced. The results may prove helpful for reducing the social inequalities that are intensified by biased tracking decisions.

Keywords School tracking • Dual process theories • Student case vignettes • Adaptive diagnostic competency model • Teacher education

---

I. Böhmer (✉) • C. Gräsel • S. Glock
University of Wuppertal, Wuppertal, Germany
e-mail: boehmer@uni-wuppertal.de; graesel@uni-wuppertal.de; glock@uni-wuppertal.de

S. Krolak-Schwerdt • T. Hörstermann
University of Luxembourg, Esch-sur-Alzette, Luxembourg
e-mail: sabine.krolak@uni.lu; thomas.hoerstermann@uni.lu

D. Leutner et al. (eds.), *Competence Assessment in Education*, Methodology of Educational Measurement and Assessment, DOI 10.1007/978-3-319-50030-0_9

9.1 Introduction

In the German school system, students begin their educational careers in primary school at about the age of six. After 4 or 6 years of primary school (depending on the state), teachers make important tracking decisions by recommending students to appropriate secondary school tracks. In general, there are different achievement-based hierarchical tracks. The explicit between-school tracking system (Maaz et al. 2008) is designed to produce homogenous ability groups as a way of providing adequate classroom instruction to students with different learning prerequisites. Each track involves different achievement requirements and learning environments, and thus offers different opportunities for students' future academic careers. Although flexibility for corrective changes between the tracks does exist in theory, changes—especially from lower to higher tracks, and therefore for better future opportunities—seldom occur in reality (Ditton 2013). In making the actual choice of a secondary school track, parents often follow teachers' tracking decisions, even when they are non-mandatory (e.g., Bos et al. 2004). Thus, teachers' tracking decisions play a pivotal role in students' future academic and professional careers. Hence, research on teachers' tracking decisions and possible sources of biases within those decisions, is vital. In this vein, several studies on teachers' tracking decisions have been conducted in different countries (e.g., Bos et al. 2004; Driessen 1993; Klapproth et al. 2012). Such studies have consistently shown that teachers' tracking decisions are primarily influenced by achievement-related information such as students' grades or working behavior. Yet, the school grades themselves may be influenced by achievement-unrelated variables, such as social background. Students from families with lower socio-economic status (SES) achieve lower grades even when they show the same standardized test results as high SES students (Maaz and Nagy 2009). In addition to this indirect effect, studies on teachers' tracking decisions have provided evidence that students' social backgrounds affect teachers' tracking decisions directly. This influence disadvantages low SES students, as they are more frequently recommended to the lowest school track, even after academic achievement is controlled for (e.g., Bos et al. 2004). Thus, direct and indirect influences of social background information on teachers' tracking decisions might contribute to social inequalities in the German tracking system.

In general, previous tracking studies have investigated the correlational relation between different students' or parents' characteristics on the one hand, and teachers' decisions on the other. Thereby, students' or parents' characteristics are usually measured by students' or parents' questionnaires or achievement tests, and analyzed for their ability to predict teachers' actual tracking decisions. Hence, the question of how teachers make their decisions has yet to be considered. Thus, the goal of the present research was to gain deeper insights into teachers' decision-making processes by (quasi) experimentally investigating the underlying cognitive processes. Drawing on dual process models of decision making (e.g., Ferreira et al. 2006; Fiske and Neuberg 1990) we developed an adaptive diagnostic competency model (ADCM) specifically with regard to school tracking decisions.

The model specifies how expert teachers process students' information to derive their tracking decisions. Thereby, we assumed that teachers are able to use different processing strategies and that they flexibly switch between these strategies depending on different situational demands, such as case consistency and accountability for the decision. To investigate tracking decision processes using the adaptive diagnostic competency model, we conducted two studies. Employing student case vignettes in these studies, two pre-studies analyzed whether the vignettes can be used to investigate real tracking decisions. We also developed a training program to help pre-service teachers practice adequate decision making. An evidence-based training that allows reflection and improving upon tracking decisions can, in turn, be implemented in pre-service teacher education, as well as in teacher training. This might be an important option for reducing social inequalities caused or intensified by biased tracking decisions made by teachers. The training program was evaluated in one further study.

9.2 Dual Process Models of Decision Making

In general, dual process models suggest that people can use different types of information processing strategies when they make decisions about people: controlled or automatic strategies. Controlled strategies such as information-integrative (Fiske and Neuberg 1990) or rule-based strategies (Ferreira et al. 2006) are effortful, systematic, and consciously accessible. People using information-integrative strategies tend to search all available information and integrate it into a decision as a whole (Fiske and Neuberg 1990). People applying rule-based strategies formulate an explicit rule about what kind of information is relevant for the decision. This rule determines what information people search for and integrate into their decision (Ferreira et al. 2006). By contrast, automatic strategies such as heuristic strategies require less cognitive effort (Ferreira et al. 2006). Only some of the available information, and often just one "good" piece of information, such as students' grades, is searched for and automatically processed using simplifying rules of thumb or social categories such as "No. 1 student in class" in making a decision (Fiske and Neuberg 1990).

Dual process models further suggest a flexible use of the different information processing strategies, depending on different context factors or situational demands. One context factor is information or case consistency: the extent to which person information is contradictory. Consistent information (i.e. no piece of information contradicts other pieces) results in more heuristic strategies, while inconsistent information (i.e., different pieces of information contradict each other) should lead to more rule-based or information-integrative strategies (Fiske and Neuberg 1990). Another context factor is the person's accountability for the decision. People who feel highly accountable for their decision employ more rule-based or integrative strategies, whereas people who feel less accountable rely on more heuristic strategies (e.g., Lerner and Tetlock 1999).

Besides these two context factors, the decision-makers' expertise is a necessary precondition for use of the different strategies (Böhmer et al. 2012; Findell 2007; van Ophuysen 2006). Due to their long-term experience in their professional domain, experts develop a rich and elaborated professional knowledge base that enables them to show adaptive decision making. They possess the ability to process information in different ways and can flexibly switch between the different processing strategies, depending on the contextual factors present in a particular situation (e.g., Krolak-Schwerdt et al. 2009, 2013; Showers and Cantor 1985). By contrast, novices have not yet developed this broad knowledge base and thus are not yet able to process the information in different ways. Hence, they do not show such situation-specific adaptive processing. Previous studies in the school context have shown that novices generally tend to use information-integrative processing strategies to assess students (Krolak-Schwerdt et al. 2009; Böhmer et al. 2012).

9.3 The Adaptive Diagnostic Competency Model (ADCM)

Drawing on the assumptions of dual process models, we developed a process-based model of teachers' diagnostic competencies specifically with regard to school tracking decisions. This model considers experienced teachers' ability to adapt their information processing strategies flexibly to situational demands, and thus involves cognitive and situation-specific components. The cognitive component refers to the ability to process information using different strategies, while the situation-specific component refers to the ability to switch flexibly between these strategies according to situational demands. For both components, teachers' expertise is a necessary prerequisite. The ability to process information and assess students in different ways is a necessary precondition for the ability to flexibly switch between such strategies – an ability that novices tend to lack. That teachers' competency is characterized by cognitive components, situational factors and acquisition through learning is also in line with the competency definition, stated in the priority program "models of competencies" (Klieme et al. 2008), in which the present research is embedded.

The ADCM assumes that teachers, due to their domain-specific knowledge of tracking-relevant information, mainly rely either on rule-based or on heuristic processing strategies for making their tracking decisions. The usage of both strategies depends on case consistency and accountability (Fig. 9.1). We further assumed that teachers rarely rely on information-integrative strategies because in this processing mode, all information, even irrelevant information, would be integrated into the decision.

Teachers rely on rule-based strategies when they follow the German tracking regulations. The official rules specify that tracking decisions should be based on achievement-related variables such as grades and working behavior, whereas social background information should not be taken into account (KMK 2015). Thus, using rule-based strategies should result in less-biased decisions. In particular, in highly accountable situations, or given inconsistent student information (e.g. both above-

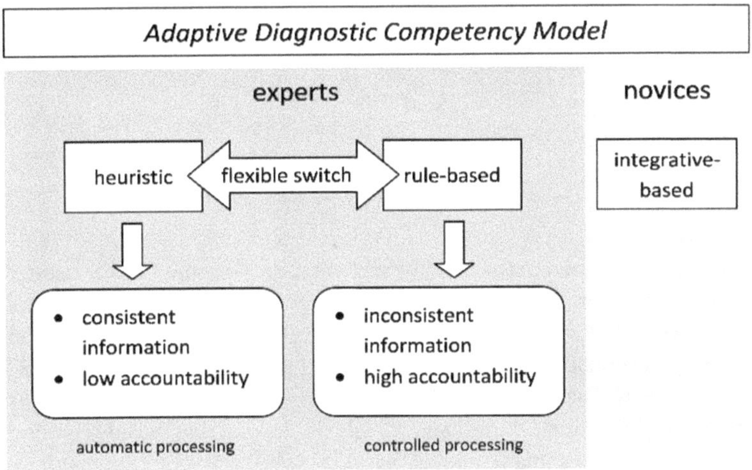

Fig. 9.1 Adaptive diagnostic competency model (ADCM)

and below-average grades in the main subjects), teachers should primarily follow rule-based strategies, in addition to grades, as the most important tracking information (Bos et al. 2004; Nölle et al. 2009), teachers should search for more achievement-related information and integrate it into their decision. By contrast, in less accountable situations, or given consistent information about a student (e.g., above-average grades in all main subjects), teachers can adapt their processing to heuristic strategies. For instance, teachers might make their decisions by relying on "one good reason", such as consistently above-average grades. Heuristic strategies might also lead to less-biased judgments when the one or the few pieces of information teachers rely on is adequate for the decision (Gigerenzer and Goldstein 1996).

However, when teachers rely on social background information instead of achievement-related information to make tracking decisions, thereby applying heuristic strategies, their decisions are biased, as they might reflect the students' social background. Hence, the application of heuristic strategies might be a moderator of social inequalities in tracking systems. In contrast to experts, we assumed, pre-service teachers tend to use more information-integrative strategies. Due to the fact that all information, even information irrelevant to a tracking decision, is integrated into the decision, this may also lead to biased decisions, as nondiagnostic information can dilute the power of relevant information (Nisbett et al. 1981).

9.4 Testing the ADCM

As empirical support for the ADCM, we conducted two studies. Study 1 investigated the ability to switch flexibly between the processing strategies according to the decision-makers' expertise and case consistency. Study 2 analyzed the influence of accountability on adaptive decision making. Since these studies employed student case vignettes, two pre-studies were conducted beforehand to develop and test the vignettes.

9.4.1 Student Case Vignettes (Pre-studies 1 and 2)

Pre-study 1 was designed to develop the student case vignettes. We investigated the kinds of student information teachers subjectively considered relevant for tracking, as teachers' points of view have been neglected in previous research (Nölle et al. 2009). In a half-standardized interview, we asked 52 German primary school teachers to freely mention student information that they considered diagnostically relevant for tracking decisions. A frequency analysis showed that, besides grades in the main subjects (German, mathematics, and sciences), 85 % of the teachers mentioned the development of students' achievement. Moreover, 85 % of the teachers mentioned information about students' working behavior, and 47 % referred to social behavior. Students' SES and immigrant background were not considered relevant. This inconsistency with previous research findings, which showed that family SES influenced teachers' tracking decisions (e.g., Bos et al. 2004), could stem from social desirability considerations (Nölle et al. 2009). From the teachers' perspective, parental support was found to play a vital role in tracking decisions, as 65 % of the teachers considered it to be relevant. The information that was considered relevant by at least 20 % of the teachers was categorized and included in the student case vignettes. Although teachers avoided explicitly citing social background information as being important in their tracking decisions, research on tracking decisions has provided evidence for the influence of such variables. Thus, we included information about students' background in the vignette as well. Beside demographic variables such as gender and age, the vignettes contained information about the students' grades, working and social behaviors, and social background (Fig. 9.2). Furthermore, information on the school track preferred by the parents was also included.

Pre-study 2 tested whether the student case vignettes we developed were useful for investigating teachers' actual tracking decisions. Only if the vignettes led to decision processes that were comparable to real tracking decisions should they be employed in further research. Hence, we examined whether teachers relied on the same student information with the same weighting, when making decisions about their actual students as they did about students described in the vignettes. Fifty-six German fourth grade teachers participated in the study. First, we provided them with templates of the student case vignettes (Fig. 9.2).

Teachers were asked to fill in the information about their real students in the templates and to indicate which secondary school track they had actually recommended for each of their students.

Second, we asked the same teachers to make tracking decisions for 24 fictitious students described in the vignettes. To construct the fictitious students, we filled in

uni.lu
UNIVERSITÉ DU LUXEMBOURG

School Tracking Decisions at the End of Elementary School

Teacher Questionnaire

IfB
Institut für Bildungsforschung in der School of Education Bergische Universität Wuppertal

Dear teachers,

Please complete the following questionnaire for the child whose code is **NAD01AH**.

Grades in the last mid-year report		**Gender of child** ☐ Female ☐ Male
Mathematics		**Age of child** ________ **years**
Sciences		**How long has the child been in this class?** Since ______ grade
German (total)		**How long have you known the child?** Since ______ grade

Please rate the following aspects of the child's working and social behavior. There are six scales with sentences describing the child's behavior at each end. Please use these scales to indicate which sentence better describes the child.

	1	2	3	4	5	
The child follows the instructional content with ***very little*** interest.	☐	☐	☐	☐	☐	The child follows the instructional content with a ***high level of*** interest.
The child works on ***almost no*** school tasks independently.	☐	☐	☐	☐	☐	The child works on ***almost all*** school tasks independently.
It is ***very difficult*** for the child to work in a sustained and diligent way.	☐	☐	☐	☐	☐	It is ***very easy*** for the child to work in a sustained and diligent way.
The child cooperates ***very poorly*** with his/her peers in group and partner assignments.	☐	☐	☐	☐	☐	The child cooperates ***very well*** with his/her peers in group and partner assignments.
The child is ***not very reliable*** in meeting his/her responsibilities.	☐	☐	☐	☐	☐	The child is ***very reliable*** in meeting his/her responsibilities.
It is ***very difficult*** for the child to concentrate.	☐	☐	☐	☐	☐	It is ***very easy*** for the child to concentrate.

Aspects of the social environment

	1	2	3	4	5	
The child's parents are ***almost never*** able to help the child with school problems.	☐	☐	☐	☐	☐	The child's parents are ***almost always*** able to help the child with school problems.

What is – to your knowledge – the parents' profession?

Mother's profession

Father's profession

Fig. 9.2 Student case vignette template (first side)

the student information derived from the first part of the study, into the templates of the student vignettes. To reflect differences between teachers' decision making for real and for the fictitious students described in the vignettes, we computed a hierarchical logistic multilevel analysis. After a Bonferoni correction, the analysis revealed no significant differences between the two decision settings (all $ps > .05$). The analysis showed similar influences of grades, working behavior, and parental support, independent of whether the tracking decisions were for real or fictitious students. In the two decision settings, grades in German in particular, exhibited a great influence on tracking decisions, *OR* (odds ratio) = 13.8. Students with higher German grades had about a 14 times higher chance of getting recommended to a higher track than students with average grades. Higher grades in Math, *OR* = 6.9, Science, *OR* = 6.4, and better working behavior, *OR* = 3.1, increased the chance of being recommended to a higher track and decreased the chance of being recommended to a lower track. In addition, the results showed that students with a higher level of parental support had a higher chance of a higher track recommendation even after grades were controlled for, *OR* = 2. Social background information such as immigrant background did not significantly alter the decisions in the two settings. These results support previous findings that demonstrated a large impact of achievement-related information on tracking decisions (e.g., Bos et al. 2004; Nölle et al. 2009). Furthermore, the available level of parental support seemed to influence teachers' tracking decisions. Because the two decision settings led to comparable decision processes, the student case vignettes were employed in the studies to test the assumptions of the competency model.

9.4.2 The ADCM: Case Consistency and Expertise (Study 1)

Study I was conducted to provide empirical support for the ADCM by investigating the information search processes using the computer-based mouselab method (Payne et al. 1993). As the use of heuristic or rule-based strategies determines—even in the early stages of the decision process—which information is attended to and is actively searched for (Fiske and Neuberg 1990), the information search process might provide deeper insights into the cognitive processes that underlie tracking decisions and the assumed components of the model. To investigate the two model components, and in particular the situation-specific component, according to case consistency, we presented two consistent and two inconsistent student case vignettes in this study. According to the assumption of teachers' adaptive competencies, we expected consistent student information to result in more heuristic processes, whereas inconsistent information should lead to more rule-based strategies. Since our model assumes that both components involve expertise, we asked 62 German primary school teachers as experts and 68 pre-service teachers as novices, to make tracking decisions for the four different vignettes. Participants were asked to search for the kinds of student information they required to make the decisions.

Thereby, the different pieces of information about the students were presented as uncoverable information fields on the computer screen.

By clicking on a field (e.g., school interest) with the computer mouse, participants could uncover the hidden information (e.g., the student follows school lessons with high interest). By clicking on the field again, participants could hide this information and continue their search. The presented fields referred to the categories grades, working- and social-behavior and social background (for a detailed description see Böhmer et al. 2012). To systematically vary case consistency, we presented the students' fourth year grades in the main subjects prior to teachers' information search. The consistent case vignettes described students whose achievement information was non-contradictory; students who were easy to recommend. The students had consistent grades (above vs. below average) in the main subjects and consistently excellent versus poor working behavior. The inconsistent students showed contradictory grades and working behavior. The information search frequency was used as a process indicator, as research has shown that confronting people with inconsistent cases leads to a higher search frequency, in contrast to a lower search frequency when information is consistent (Fiske et al. 1987).

The search frequency was submitted to a mixed 2 × 2 MANOVA with expertise as a between-subjects factor and case consistency as a within-subjects factor. The results also showed that pre-service teachers, as well as teachers, search for more information when confronted with inconsistent cases. But in contrast to teachers, pre-service teachers generally search for more, and somewhat different kinds of information. Both pre-service teachers and teachers mainly search for grades and information on students' working behavior as achievement-related information. But in contrast to teachers, pre-service teachers additionally tended to search for more irrelevant information, such as parental profession or immigrant background as social background information. This implies more information-integrative processing, whereby all available information, even if irrelevant, is searched for decision making.

Teachers' adaptive competency in switching between heuristic and rule-based strategies was indicated by the finding that teachers searched for more achievement-related information when confronted with inconsistent rather than consistent cases. This higher search frequency for achievement-related information suggests more rule-based strategies, as teachers mainly searched for all available diagnostically relevant information. The reductions in information search for consistent cases imply the use of more heuristic strategies. The findings support the assumption that teachers can switch between the different processing strategies according to case consistency. Further, the results show that teachers generally considered social background variables less, with the exception of parental support. Consistently with our previous findings, parental support proved to be important information teachers considered in their tracking decisions, particularly when the achievement information did not allow for a clear decision (i.e., in inconsistent student cases). With regard to students' equivalent opportunities, the influence of parental support in tracking decisions should be discussed critically. Figure 9.3 gives a summary of the main results of the separate ANOVAs for different information categories.

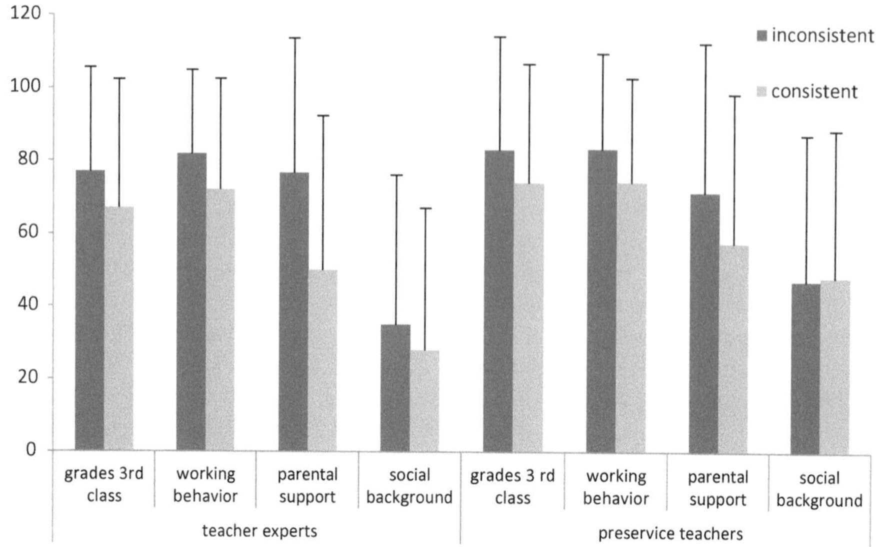

Fig. 9.3 Information search frequency for different information categories, depending on case consistency, in percentages (Data taken in part from Böhmer et al. 2012)

These findings support the two components of the model and additionally indicate that novices lack the ability to switch between heuristic and rule-based information processing strategies.

9.4.3 The ADCM: Case Consistency and Accountability (Study 2)

To provide further empirical support for the competency model, we investigated the influence of accountability, as another situation-specific component, on teachers' decision processes. Previous research has not examined the situational switch from rule-based to heuristic strategies in relation to accountability for the decision. As our findings provided evidence that case consistency is an important moderator of the use of information processing strategies, we also included case consistency in this study. We expected that high accountability would lead to rule-based strategies, independent of case consistency, whereas low accountability would lead to heuristic processing when the vignettes were consistent, and to rule-based processing when the vignettes were inconsistent (Krolak-Schwerdt et al. 2009).

We designed a computer-based experimental study to test these predictions. As we investigated 37 experienced teachers, we ensured that the participants possessed the competency to process information about students in both heuristic and rule-based ways. The teachers were asked to make tracking decisions for three consistent and three inconsistent vignettes (see Fig. 9.2). To manipulate accountability, different instructions sets were compiled. The high accountability instructions informed teachers that the decisions they were required to make were of high importance and that they were solely responsible. The other instructions asked teachers to give brief advice to a colleague concerning tracking decisions for some of the colleague's students (Krolak-Schwerdt et al. 2013). First, teachers worked under the high and afterwards under the low accountability instructions. Reading times for each vignette were recorded as a process indicator, as research has shown that rule-based processes are more time-consuming than heuristic processes (Sherman et al. 1998) and lead to increases in memory for person information (Glock et al. 2011). To analyze person memory as another process indicator, we asked the teachers to perform an error correction task. After teachers made tracking decisions for the vignettes, they were presented with the vignettes again. Thereby, errors were implemented into the vignettes and presented as a memory task by asking teachers to detect and correct the errors in the vignettes. Errors consisted of wrong information (e.g., the grades deviated from the grades presented in the original vignettes). As indicators of person memory, we used the error correction rate and the non-detected error rate and submitted them to a 2 × 2 repeated-measures ANOVA, with the factors being accountability and case consistency. The results provided further evidence for the situation-specific component of the model; teachers were able to switch their processing strategy in order to respond adequately to the different situational demands. Under high accountability, no differences in processing times and person memory occurred between consistent and inconsistent profiles, whereas under low accountability, consistent profiles led to faster reading times, a lower correct correction rate, and a higher non-detected error rate than inconsistent profiles (Fig. 9.4).

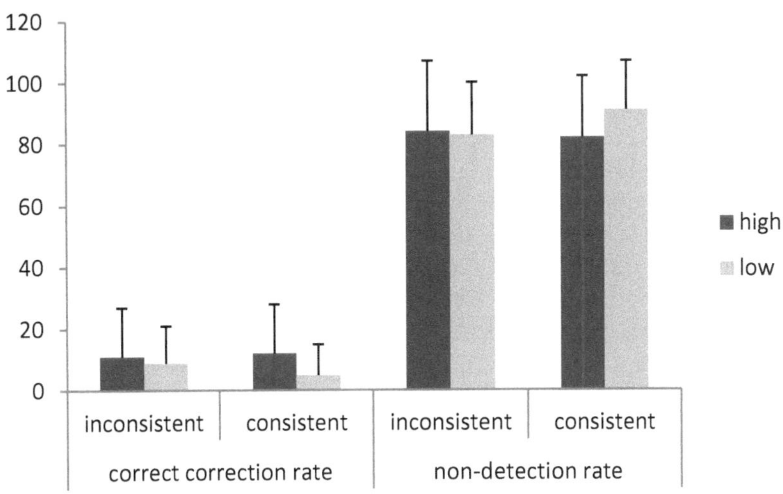

Fig. 9.4 Correct correction rate and nondetection rate in percentage, depending on case consistency and accountability

However, in order for flexible switching between processing strategies to occur, people are required to possess the ability to process information in either a heuristic or rule-based way. In contrast to experienced teachers, pre-service teachers have not yet developed this ability. Thus, fostering pre-service teachers to develop the cognitive component of the model seems important. We designed a training study to foster the ability to use different processing strategies, and thus to practice the cognitive component.

9.5 Training Study

The training study consisted of two main parts: (1) acquiring theoretical knowledge about tracking decisions and (2) training participants to optimize their tracking decisions based on case vignettes and feedback. Thirty-six pre-service teachers participated in a regular university course. They were asked to make tracking decisions for student case vignettes (see Fig. 9.2). These student cases were chosen out of the database of "real" students created during our pre-studies. Thus, the real teacher tracking decision for each student was known.

Part 1: To acquire theoretical knowledge about tracking decisions, the participants were introduced to the regulatory framework of the German tracking system and the importance of teachers' tracking decisions. The research findings on tracking were discussed critically. Moreover, participants were introduced to social cognitive theories of decision making and the implications for educational practice.

Part 2: To teach pre-service teachers to optimize their decisions, they first worked on 30 student case vignettes as baseline measures, and were asked to make tracking decisions for each student. Based on statistical prediction rules (Swets et al. 2000), the observed decision rule of each participant was estimated by analyzing the weighting of each piece of student information presented in the cases. Next, participants were asked to indicate their desired decision rule: that is, the extent to which they would take the different pieces of student information into account for their tracking decisions. Thus, the participants weighted the relevance of single pieces of information for their tracking decisions in percentages, from no to high relevance. In the training session afterwards, the participants worked on further case vignettes and received feedback for each of their tracking decisions, including the actual tracking decision made for these cases, and the probability with which a particular secondary school track decision corresponded to their desired rule. After working on the training vignettes, participants were given overall feedback on the correspondence between their desired and observed decision rule, as well as the teachers' rule. For the posttest measure, another 30 student cases were used. The control group worked on the student vignettes without receiving any theoretical instructions and no training.

First, we compared pre-service teachers' tracking decisions before and after the training session, with the experts' actual decisions. Results revealed that, compared with the baseline measure, the accordance of the pre-service teachers' and expert teachers' tracking decisions improved more in the training group. Second, we investigated how participants weighted the different pieces of student information in their tracking decisions before and after the training. Preliminary results showed that, after the training, participants weighted school grades and parental support more strongly, whereas the weights of immigrant background and parental educational level were reduced. Compared with the control group, participants in the training group relied more on achievement-related variables and parental support. Hence, the training was successful in that respect: pre-service teachers' decisions approximated to those of the experts and hence, the influence of immigrant background and parental educational level was reduced. This indicates that the cognitive component of the model, as a requirement of the situational component, can be taught.

9.6 Discussion

This research focused on teachers' tracking decisions, including their underlying cognitive processes. Drawing on dual process models (e.g., Ferreira et al. 2006; Fiske and Neuberg 1990), we specified different information processing strategies teachers might rely on when making their tracking decisions. Heuristic strategies are based on social categories or simple rules of thumb and exclusively selected pieces of information. Heuristic strategies can lead to adequate decisions if the selected information pieces are relevant. Applying heuristic strategies might also contribute to social inequalities when teachers rely on inadequate information, such as social background information. Rule-based strategies are more effortful and should result in less-biased decisions. By applying these strategies, teachers follow the official German regulations for making tracking decisions. The different strategies were included in our teachers' adaptive diagnostic competency model (ADCM), which involves a cognitive and a situation-specific component: Teachers as experts are able to process information using different strategies (cognitive component) and they flexibly switch between these strategies to make their decision, depending on case consistency and accountability (situational component). In the presented (quasi) experimental studies we found that teachers, in contrast to pre-service teachers, adapted their information search and processing to the situational demands of case consistency and accountability as they flexibly switched between more rule-based and more heuristic processing strategies. Teachers' expertise in switching between these strategies was indicated by the finding that inducing high accountability for the decision, in contrast to a lower accountability, led to higher processing effort. Teachers showed a more elaborate person memory, a higher error correction rate and a lower error non-detection rate.

In respect of information searching, teachers searched for more information when they were confronted with inconsistent student cases that were difficult to recommend, than with consistent cases. This generally higher search frequency for inconsistent cases implies rather rule-based strategies, as teachers search more for achievement-related information to make their decision. The reduced information search for consistent cases indicates more heuristic strategies. Furthermore, the results show that pre-service teachers generally search for more information than do teachers. Besides achievement-related information, they search for more irrelevant social background information, such as parental SES. This indicates that pre-service teachers rather used information-integrative strategies as they search through all information, even that which is irrelevant. Relying on such information might lead to the dilution effect (Nisbett et al. 1981), as irrelevant information dilutes the power of relevant information. Hence, it might contribute to biased tracking decisions.

Across all studies, besides school grades and working behavior, parental support turned out to be one important piece of information for teachers' tracking decisions, particularly, when the achievement information does not allow for a clear decision (i.e., for inconsistent student cases). The results indicate that teachers rather did not directly rely on social background information such as immigrant background or SES. Instead, they focused more on "indirect" information, such as parental support. Although parental support has an essential impact on students' future academic achievement (Jeynes 2005), one should keep in mind that relying on parental support is also an important factor that contributes to social inequalities, as it is positively related to a family's SES (e.g., Rumberger et al. 1990) and negatively related to immigrant background (Aldous 2006). Students for whom teachers have trouble making secondary school track decisions might be at higher risk of experiencing social inequalities, as teachers might rely more on parental support, with potential to thereby derive a socially biased decision.

Further studies should disentangle the influences that are actually derived from parental support from those that stem from SES. The separation of these variables might not only provide a deeper understanding of teachers' tracking decisions but could also shed light on social inequality.

Parental support includes different facets, and future research should focus on the facets that are the most important for teachers. Research has shown that checking student homework or attending school functions is not strongly related to the academic success of the students (Jeynes 2005). As in our research, parental support was not divided into facets, future research should investigate whether, for instance, financial support and emotional support might differentially affect teachers' tracking decisions. The question also arises whether teachers could validly assess the "real" level of parental support or whether they—perhaps by trend—use stereotypes to infer the level of parental support. This could be a further source of social disparities.

To foster pre-service teachers' expertise in making tracking decisions, we developed a training program that was based on acquiring theoretical knowledge and training in how to make an adequate tracking decision. In response to the feedback, participants could reflect on their own decision behavior and hence could adapt their behavior towards adequate decision making. The training program turned out to be effective, since pre-service teachers learned to generate and follow decision rules that were similar to the experts' rules. Therefore, the influence of social background variables on pre-service teachers' tracking decisions was reduced, and accordance with the experts' decisions was increased. However, we cannot draw stringent conclusions about whether the experts' decisions were adequate. Further research is needed to investigate the predictive validity of the tracking decisions experts made for real students described in the case vignettes. Thereby, it might prove valuable to find different indicators of correct tracking decisions. Besides indicators such as changes of track or repeating a class, an alternative indicator was formulated by comparing a student's achievement profile in school with typical profiles of students in different school tracks. Validating those profiles among experts, and investigating the predictive validity of the decisions based on the identified student profiles, supported the accuracy indicator (Glock et al. 2015). However, adequate tracking decisions might be indicated not only by achievement-related variables but also by socioemotional variables, such as school attitudes, classmate acceptance, or academic self-concept. To formulate such accuracy indicators might help to answer the question of whether the training program can also lead to more adequate tracking decisions.

The current research provides empirically based knowledge about the cognitive processes of primary school teachers in making tracking decisions. This knowledge can be used in pre-service teacher education and in the professionalization of teachers to reflect on and improve their tracking decisions. This might be an option for reducing social inequalities that are intensified by biased tracking decisions.

In addition, teachers' adaptive diagnostic competency plays a pivotal role, not only in school tracking decisions. Teachers also face different decision tasks and situational demands in their school environment, such as making adequate "micro decisions" during school lessons, to adapt classroom instructions in response to the students' actual performance level (Schrader and Helmke 2001). The ability to flexibly switch between different processing strategies enables teachers to deal with them. Further research based on the ADCM should investigate the teachers' diagnostic competency in different school-related decision tasks and therefore focus in particular on the situational component of diagnostic competency. In this vein, further studies focusing on decisions' accuracy in combination with decision processing, might provide more empirical knowledge about the adequacy of teachers' adaptive decision making, and might shed light on differences in the decisions' accuracy as it is affected by situational factors.

Acknowledgements The research reported in this chapter was funded by grants GR 1863/5-1, 5-2 and 5-3; KR 2162/4-1, 4-2 and 4-3 from the German Research Foundation (DFG) in the Priority Program "Competence Models for Assessing Individual Learning Outcomes and Evaluating Educational Processes" (SPP 1293) and grants INTER/DFG/09/01 and INTER/DFG/11/03 from the Fonds Nationale de la Recherche Luxembourg.

References

Aldous, J. (2006). Family, ethnicity, and immigrant youths' educational achievements. *Journal of Family Issues, 27*, 1633–1667. doi:10.1177/0192513X06292419.

Böhmer, I., Hörstermann, T., Krolak-Schwerdt, S., & Gräsel, C. (2012). Die Informationssuche bei der Erstellung der Übergangsempfehlung: die Rolle von Fallkonsistenz und Expertise

[Information search in making a transition recommendation]. *Unterrichtswissenschaft, 40*, 140–155.
Bos, W., Voss, A., Lankes, E.-M., Schwippert, K., Thiel, O., & Valtin, R. (2004). Schullaufbahnempfehlungen von Lehrkräften für Kinder am Ende der vierten Jahrgangsstufe [Teachers' tracking decisions at the end of primary school]. In W. Bos, E.-M. Lankes, M. Prenzel, K. Schwippert, R. Valtin, & G. Walther (Eds.), *IGLU:Einige Länder der Bundesrepublik Deutschland im nationalen und internationalen Vergleich* (pp. 191–228). Münster: Waxmann.
Ditton, H. (2013). Bildungsverläufe in der Sekundarstufe: Ergebnisse einer Längsschnittstudie zu Wechseln der Schulform und des Bildungszugangs [Educational careers in secondary education]. *Zeitschrift für Pädagogik, 59*, 887–911.
Driessen, G. W. J. M. (1993). Social or ethnic determinants of educational opportunities? Results from the evaluation of the education priority policy programme in the Netherlands. *Studies in Educational Evaluation, 19*, 265–280. doi:10.1016/S0191-491X(05)80010-0.
Ferreira, M. B., Garcia-Marques, L., Sherman, S. J., & Sherman, J. W. (2006). Automatic and controlled components of judgment and decision making. *Journal of Personality and Social Psychology, 91*, 797–813. doi:10.1037/0022-3514.91.5.797.
Findell, C. R. (2007). What differentiates expert teachers from others? *Journal of Education, 188*, 11–23.
Fiske, S. T., & Neuberg, S. L. (1990). A continuum of impression formation from category-based to individuating processes: Influences of information and motivation on attention and interpretation. In M. P. Zanna (Ed.), *Advances in experimental social psychology* (Vol. 23, pp. 1–74). New York: Academic Press.
Fiske, S. T., Neuberg, S. L., Beattie, A. E., & Milberg, S. J. (1987). Category-based and attribute-based reactions to others: Some informational conditions of stereotyping and individuating processes. *Journal of Experimental Social Psychology, 23*, 399–427. doi:10.1016/0022-1031(87)90038-2.
Gigerenzer, G., & Goldstein, D. G. (1996). Reasoning the fast and frugal way: Models of bounded rationality. *Psychological Review, 103*, 650–669. doi:10.1037/0033-295X.103.4.650.
Glock, S., Kneer, J., & Krolak-Schwerdt, S. (2011). Impression formation or prediction? Category fit and task influence forensic person memory. *Journal of Forensic Psychology Practice, 11*, 391–405. doi:10.1080/15228932.2011.588529.
Glock, S., Krolak-Schwerdt, S., & Pit-Ten Cate, I. (2015). Are school placement recommendations accurate? The effect of students' ethnicity on teachers' judgments and recognition memory. *European Journal of Psychology of Education, 30*, 169–188. doi:10.1007/s10212-014-0237-2.
Jeynes, W. H. (2005). A meta-analysis of the relation of parental involvement to urban elementary school student academic achievement. *Urban Education, 40*, 237–269.
Klapproth, F., Glock, S., Böhmer, M., Krolak-Schwerdt, S., & Martin, R. (2012). School placement decisions in Luxembourg: Do teachers meet the Education Ministry's standards? *The Literacy Information and Computer Education Journal, 1*, 765–771.
Klieme, E., Hartig, J., & Rauch, D. (2008). The concept of competence in educational contexts. In J. Hartig, E. Klieme, & D. Leutner (Eds.), *Assessment of competencies in educational contexts* (pp. 3–22). Göttingen: Hogrefe.
KMK (Standing Conference of the Ministers of Education and Cultural Affairs of the States in the Federal Republic of Germany). (Ed.). (2015). *Übergang von der Grundschule in Schulen des Sekundarbereichs I und Förderung, Beobachtung und Orientierung in den Jahrgangsstufen 5 und 6 (sog. Orientierungsstufe). Beschluss vom 19.02.2015* [Transition from primary to secondary schools. Resolution approved by the Standing Conference on 19 February 2015]. http://www.kmk.org/fileadmin/Dateien/veroeffentlichungen_beschluesse/2015/2015_02_19-Uebergang_Grundschule-SI-Orientierungsstufe.pdf. Accessed 23 Aug 2015.
Krolak-Schwerdt, S., Böhmer, M., & Gräsel, C. (2009). Verarbeitung von schülerbezogener Information als zielgeleiteter Prozess. Der Lehrer als "flexibler Denker" [Processing students' information as goal-oriented process]. *Zeitschrift für Pädagogische Psychologie, 23*, 175–186.

Krolak-Schwerdt, S., Böhmer, M., & Gräsel, C. (2013). The impact of accountability on teachers' assessments of student performance: A social cognitive analysis. *Social Psychology of Education, 16*, 215–239. doi:10.1007/s11218-013-9215-9.

Lerner, J. S., & Tetlock, P. E. (1999). Accounting for effects of accountability. *Psychological Bulletin, 125*, 255–275.

Maaz, K., & Nagy, G. (2009). Der Übergang von der Grundschule in die weiterführenden Schulen des Sekundarschulsystems: Definition, Spezifikation und Quantifizierung primärer und sekundärer Herkunftseffekte [The transition from elementary to secondary education in Germany]. *Zeitschrift für Erziehungswissenschaft, 12*, 153–182. doi:10.1007/978-3-531-92216-4_7.

Maaz, K., Trautwein, U., Lüdtke, O., & Baumert, J. (2008). Educational transitions and differential learning environments: How explicit between-school tracking contributes to social inequality in educational outcomes. *Child Development Perspectives, 2*, 99–106. doi:10.1111/j.1750-8606.2008.00048.x.

Nisbett, R. E., Zukier, H., & Lemley, R. E. (1981). The dilution effect: Nondiagnostic information weakens the implications of diagnostic information. *Cognitive Psychology, 13*, 248–277. doi:10.1016/0010-0285(81)90010-4.

Nölle, I., Hörstermann, T., Krolak-Schwerdt, S., & Gräsel, C. (2009). Relevante diagnostische Informationen bei der Übergangsempfehlung: Die Perspektive der Lehrkräfte [Diagnostic relevant information for school tracking decisions: Teachers' perspectives]. *Unterrichtswissenschaft, 37*, 294–310.

Payne, J. W., Bettman, J. R., & Johnson, E. J. (1993). *The adaptive decision maker*. Cambridge: Cambridge University Press.

Rumberger, R. W., Ghatak, R., Poulos, G., Ritter, P. L., & Dornbusch, S. M. (1990). Family influences on dropout behavior in one California high school. *Sociology of Education, 63*, 283–299. doi:10.2307/2112876.

Schrader, F.-W., & Helmke, A. (2001). Alltägliche Leistungsbeurteilung durch Lehrer [Teachers' assessment of school performance]. In F. E. Weinert (Ed.), *Leistungsmessungen in Schulen* (pp. 45–58). Weinheim: Beltz.

Sherman, J. W., Lee, A. Y., Bessenoff, G. R., & Frost, L. A. (1998). Stereotype efficiency reconsidered: Encoding flexibility under cognitive load. *Journal of Personality and Social Psychology, 75*, 589–606.

Showers, C., & Cantor, N. (1985). Social cognition: A look at motivated strategies. *Annual Review of Psychology, 36*, 275–305. doi:10.1146/annurev.ps.36.020185.001423.

Swets, J. A., Dawes, R. M., & Monahan, J. (2000). Better decisions through science. *Scientific American, 283*, 82–87.

Van Ophuysen, S. (2006). Vergleich diagnostischer Entscheidungen von Novizen und Experten am Beispiel der Schullaufbahnempfehlung [Comparison of diagnostic decisions between novices and experts: The example of school career recommendation]. *Zeitschrift für Entwicklungspsychologie und Pädagogische Psychologie, 38*, 154–161.

Chapter 10
Modeling, Measuring, and Training Teachers' Counseling and Diagnostic Competencies

Mara Gerich, Monika Trittel, Simone Bruder, Julia Klug, Silke Hertel, Regina Bruder, and Bernhard Schmitz

Abstract In their professional routines, teachers must perform highly complex and demanding tasks that require extensive counseling and diagnostic competence. There is a growing request for programs that foster these important teacher competencies in educational practice (e.g., German Society for Psychology, Psychologie in den Lehramtsstudiengängen: Ein Rahmencurriculum [Psychology in teacher education: A framework curriculum]. Retrieved from http://www.dgps.de/_download/2008/Psychologie_Lehramt_Curriculum.pdf, 2008) as well as a call for the theoretical modeling of competencies and approaches for their assessment in educational research (Koeppen et al., J Psychol 216:61–73, 2008). In the current research project we theoretically conceptualized and empirically validated specific models of teachers' counseling and diagnostic competence for the domain of student learning behavior, and constructed several instruments for their assessment. Subsequently, we developed specific training programs on counseling and diagnostics for prospective and in-service teachers based on the models, and evaluated them by means of the specified instruments. We describe the results of the research project in this chapter and discuss future prospects for educational research and teacher training.

Keywords Counseling competence • Diagnostic competence • Structural equation modeling • Teacher competencies • Training programs

---

M. Gerich (✉) • M. Trittel • R. Bruder • B. Schmitz
Technische Universität Darmstadt, Darmstadt, Germany
e-mail: gerich@zfl.tu-darmstadt.de; trittel@psychologie.tu-darmstadt.de; bruder@mathematik.tu-darmstadt.de; schmitz@psychologie.tu-darmstadt.de

S. Bruder
Paediatric Clinic Princess Margaret Darmstadt, Darmstadt, Germany
e-mail: simone.bruder79@gmail.com

J. Klug
University of Vienna, Vienna, Austria
e-mail: julia.klug@univie.ac.at

S. Hertel
University of Heidelberg, Heidelberg, Germany
e-mail: hertel@ibw.uni-heidelberg.de

D. Leutner et al. (eds.), *Competence Assessment in Education*, Methodology of Educational Measurement and Assessment, DOI 10.1007/978-3-319-50030-0_10

10.1 Introduction

Counseling students and their parents is specified as a central pedagogical task in government recommendations and standards for teacher education all over the world (e.g., NCTAF 1997; KMK 2004). Accordingly, counseling competence has been included in concepts of teachers' professional competencies (e.g., Baumert and Kunter 2006).

Against the background of international education studies (TIMSS, PISA) parent counseling concerning students' learning difficulties and strategies, especially, has become increasingly important. As research on parental involvement shows, parental support in doing homework and learning activities plays an important role in students' learning processes (Cox 2005). However, parents often feel insecure in supporting their children in homework and learning activities and, therefore, increasingly request guidance from teachers (Hoover-Dempsey et al. 2002). Within the context of counseling talks, teachers and parents can come together to jointly identify possible learning difficulties that need to be addressed and determine specific intervention strategies in the school and home contexts (Keys et al. 1998).

It is clear that teachers must be well educated in counseling in order to meet the high demands concerning the participation of parents in their children's academic development. This is becoming particularly important in light of the challenges associated with the increasing diversity of the parent and student population, in terms of family circumstances, socioeconomic status, cultural norms, academic abilities, and learning conditions (Boethel 2003).

Although the importance of counseling parents in supporting their children's educational progress has been noted in current research, there are still few studies that explicitly address the specific counseling skills that teachers must possess in order to be competent counselors. Thus, clear definitions and models of teachers' counseling competence are lacking. In fact, there is an explicit need for a detailed definition of teachers' counseling competence, as well as for the specification of individual competence dimensions on the basis of sophisticated psychometric models (e.g., Strasser and Gruber 2003). There is an absence of theoretical and empirical models, and also, suitable instruments for a reliable assessment of teachers' counseling competence are not available. Furthermore, counseling competence has not received sufficient consideration in the context of practical teacher education (Walker and Dotger 2012). As a consequence, teachers do not feel well prepared to meet job demands concerning cooperation with parents (Mandel 2006). This, in turn, leads to diminished willingness of teachers to offer counseling talks (Wild 2003), as well as decreased job satisfaction, increased occupational stress, and a greater risk of burnout (Pas et al. 2012). Consequently, improved integration of counseling in teacher preparation and continuing education is needed urgently.

Teachers' counseling competence is not unrelated to other competencies; in particular, it is enmeshed in the competence of assessing student learning (Klug et al. 2012), wherein adequate intervention becomes a possibility. The measurement of student learning achievement is, perhaps, the most prominent example of educational diagnostics. This primarily summative type of assessment suits the purpose of surveying the effectiveness of instruction units in achieving gains in school performance. Students' results on such measures determine their subsequent educational opportunities, for which teachers' adequate judgments are vital. According to Weinert (2001), diagnostic competence is one of the key competencies for teachers. Vogt and Rogalla (2009) have specified the meaning of teachers' diagnostic competence in creating effective instruction as follows: "Teachers are challenged to meet diverse learning needs and adapt their teaching to heterogeneous academic ability as well as multiple interests and motivations" (p. 1051). First and foremost, empirical educational research concerning the diagnostic competence of teachers addresses summative assessment; definitions of diagnostic competence vary but are typically operationalized as a teacher's ability to judge student achievement and/or task difficulties accurately. Here, accuracy is measured by correlating teachers' judgments with the results of standardized tests (Südkamp et al. 2012). Nevertheless, there is an increasing call to shift the focus from summative to formative diagnostics in order to facilitate didactic intervention (cf. Abs 2007). This means that accurate judgments of student achievement are important as ever, but that teachers' diagnostic actions should also include the assessment of learning processes. The aim is to foster students on an individual basis, support their learning, and adapt instruction to the divergent needs of students. A contemporary model of teachers' diagnostic competence must account for the specific qualities in educational action that these tasks necessitate. Indeed, such a model of teachers' diagnostic competence that focuses explicitly on student learning behavior, does not yet exist. Furthermore, appropriate domain-specific instruments for its assessment are lacking. Just as in the case of teachers' counseling competence, few early university and continuing teacher education programs include training in diagnostic competence in regard to student learning behavior.

10.2 Project Goals

Against this background of the absence of theoretical and psychometric models of teachers' counseling and diagnostic competencies, of appropriate approaches for their measurement, and the growing demand for programs to foster teachers' counseling and diagnostic competencies, the central goals of the current research project consisted in the development of: (1) domain-specific competence models of teachers' counseling and diagnostic competencies concerning student learning behavior,[1] (2) instruments for their assessment, and (3) comprehensive training programs to foster these important teacher competencies.

---

[1] Henceforth, we use the abbreviated terms 'counseling competence' and 'diagnostic competence'.

10.3 Modeling Teachers' Counseling and Diagnostic Competencies

The central purpose of the current research project was to develop detailed competence models for teachers' counseling and diagnostic competencies. As competencies are considered to be precisely defined in specific domains (Koeppen et al. 2008), the models were conceptualized for the domain of student learning behavior. In a first step, we identified theoretical components of teachers' counseling and diagnostic competencies in relation to learning behaviors, by summarizing the multiple demands identified in the current literature. In a second step, the hypothesized models were tested on the basis of empirical data, with the help of structural equation modeling.

Throughout the project period, we continually optimized the models in several studies, using different samples of prospective and in-service teachers (Bruder 2011; Bruder et al. 2010; Gerich et al. 2015; Klug 2011; Klug et al. 2013). Furthermore, we investigated the relationship between these two competence areas, of counseling and diagnosis.

10.3.1 Theoretical Background

Counseling Competence The identification of theoretical components of teacher's competence in counseling parents was based on a predecessor model established by Hertel (2009), as well as literature on counseling in general, counseling in schools, and short-term therapy (McLaughlin 1999; McLeod 2003; Reid 1990; Strasser and Gruber 2003; Schwarzer and Buchwald 2006; West and Cannon 1988). In a preliminary study with a sample of German grammar school teachers, these components were divided into four central dimensions (Bruder 2011).

The first dimension, *counseling skills*, includes the elementary counseling procedures of active listening and paraphrasing, which are known to signalize understanding and acceptance. Furthermore, this dimension implies the ability to structure a counseling talk, which has been identified in the literature as an important aspect of successful counseling. The second dimension, *diagnostic and pedagogical knowledge*, contains aspects that are necessary to finding appropriate and customized solutions for student learning difficulties. To do so, teachers must first clearly define the existing problem and search for possible causes. In order to successfully provide appropriate solutions or advice, teachers must possess knowledge of strategies regarding the support of children in their learning processes, and apply this knowledge with a particular goal orientation. The third dimension, *collaboration and perspective taking*, includes cooperative actions, perspective taking, and resource and solution orientation. These competencies suggest that counseling should be a cooperative act that encourages collaboration between teachers and parents. Beyond that, the teachers should hold a certain resource and solution orientation, in order to determine which student and/or parent competencies can be used to support the problem-solving process. Finally, the fourth dimension, *coping*, includes strategies for professionally coping with criticism from parents and appropriately dealing with difficult situations that may arise in the course of the counseling talk.

Given that this factorial structure had been confirmed on the sole basis of a sample of grammar school teachers, so far, the first aim of the main study was to test its validity for the entire population of primary and secondary school teachers.

As counseling is frequently conceptualized as a process in the literature (e.g., McLeod 2003; Strasser and Gruber 2003), we secondly sought to test an alternative model structure that provides more consideration to the counseling talk as a process comprising two central phases (e.g., Thiel 2003): (1) a diagnostic phase, including the analysis of the existing problem and the identification of possible explanatory factors; and (2) a problem-solving phase, comprising the development of appropriate solution strategies (for further theoretical remarks, see Gerich et al. 2015). On this basis, we reassigned the manifest variables related to Bruder's (2011) dimensions, "diagnostic and pedagogical knowledge" and "collaboration and perspective taking", to the two new dimensions *diagnostic-skills* and *problem-solving-skills*. Consequently, in the re-specified model the variables "problem definition", "search for possible causes", and "perspective taking" comprised the diagnostic skills dimension, whereas the variables "strategy application", "goal orientation", "solution and resource orientation", and "cooperative actions" formed the problem-solving skills dimension. For purposes of clarity, we renamed the counseling skills dimension *communication-skills* and the coping dimension *coping-skills*.

Diagnostic Competence We also identified theoretical components of diagnostic competence by summarizing the multiple demands mentioned in the literature (Abs 2007; Hattie and Timperley 2007; Helmke et al. 2004; Jäger 2007; van Ophuysen 2006; Strasser and Gruber 2003). On this basis we postulated a three-dimensional process model (Klug et al. 2013) as follows.

The first dimension consists of the *preactional phase*, in which the teacher sets the aim of the diagnosis, to watch the individual student's learning process and provide support based on the diagnosis. In this dimension, basic diagnostic skills (knowledge about methods for gathering information, psychological quality criteria of tests, and judgment formation) that the teacher possesses are activated. The second dimension of the model consists of the *actional phase*, in which the actual diagnostic action takes place. Most important in this phase is acting systematically to make a prediction about the student's development and possible underlying learning difficulties, as well as gathering information from different sources. The third and final dimension consists of the *postactional phase*, in which pedagogical actions that follow from the diagnosis are implemented in terms of giving feedback to the student and his or her parents, writing down plans for the student's advancement, and teaching self-regulated learning in class.

Because of the assumed cyclical nature of the model, the three dimensions were expected to influence each other. We also postulated a connection between the postactional phase in a diagnostic situation and the preactional phase in the consecutive diagnostic situation.

10.3.2 Method

The empirical validation of the proposed models of teachers' counseling and diagnostic competence was carried out as part of cross-sectional studies (Gerich et al. 2015; Klug et al. 2013) based on samples of $N = 357$ German in-service teachers (counseling competence) and $N = 293$ German prospective and in-service teachers (diagnostic competence).

For the measurement of teachers' counseling and diagnostic competence we used specific scenario tests that were also developed as part of the research project (for a detailed description of the scenario tests, see Sect. 10.4.1). We analyzed all data using a latent-variable approach with structural equation modeling.

10.3.3 Results

Counseling Competence To test the generalizability of the factorial structure of teachers' counseling competence observed in the preparatory study with grammar school teachers (Bruder 2011), to the broader population of teachers working in primary and secondary education, we conducted a confirmatory factor analysis (CFA) on the basis of the current sample, which resulted in an unsatisfactory model fit ($\chi^2(48) = 109.354$, $p < .001$; $\chi^2/df = 2.278$; CFI (comparative fit index) = .801; TLI (Tucker-Lewis index) = .727; RMSEA (root mean square error of approximation) = .060; SRMR (standardized root mean square residual) = .049). An additional CFA based on the re-specified process-oriented model structure revealed a very good fit to the empirical data ($\chi^2(44) = 48.417$, $p = .299$; $\chi^2/df = 1.100$; CFI = .986; TLI = .979; SRMR = .033; RMSEA = .071). Moreover, by means of comparative analyses, we demonstrated that the four-dimensional model fitted the data significantly better than a g-factor model.

In order to examine the existence of a second-order factor representing overall counseling competence, we conducted a second-order CFA, which revealed a very good model fit ($\chi^2(47) = 53.572$, $p = .237$; $\chi^2/df = 1.140$; CFI = .978; TLI = .969; RMSEA = .020; SRMR = .036; for detailed results see Gerich et al. 2015). Figure 10.1 depicts the final model of teachers' counseling competence.

Diagnostic Competence To test the factorial validity of the proposed three-dimensional model of teachers' diagnostic competence, we also conducted a confirmatory factor analysis. The results showed that the model fitted the data very well

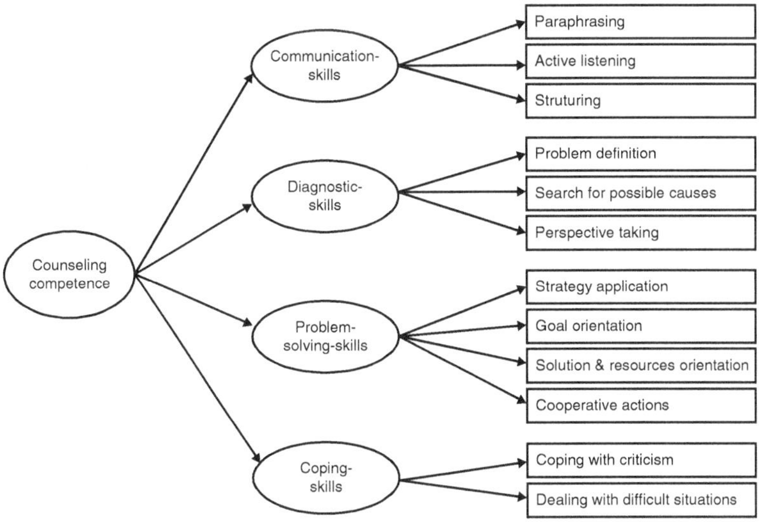

Fig. 10.1 Model of teachers' counseling competence (Gerich et al. 2015)

($\chi^2(36) = 47.704$, $p = .092$; $\chi^2/df = 1.325$; CFI = .954; RMSEA = .033; SRMR = .045). Comparative analyses also revealed that the three-dimensional model fitted the data significantly better than a g-factor structure and a two-factor structure. According to the model's proposed process structure, the dimensions are substantially inter-correlated (for detailed results, see Klug et al. 2013). Figure 10.2 displays the three-dimensional model of teachers' diagnostic competence.

10.3.4 Relationship Between Teachers' Counseling and Diagnostic Competence

In the context of developing and validating the outlined competence models, diagnostic skills have been shown to be an important dimension in the model of teachers' counseling competence, whereas counseling also plays an important role in the postactional phase of the process model of teachers' diagnostic competence. These results are in line with theoretical considerations, in which a relationship between these important teacher competencies is described. Particularly, the professional diagnosing of students' learning behavior is characterized as the essential basis for counseling parents concerning support for their children's learning processes (e.g., McLeod 2003). However, few approaches have empirically examined this postulated relationship, so far.

Thus, we aimed to investigate the correlative association of teachers' counseling and diagnostic competence, on the basis of a sample of $N = 293$ prospective and in-service teachers (Klug et al. 2012). Participants' diagnostic and counseling com-

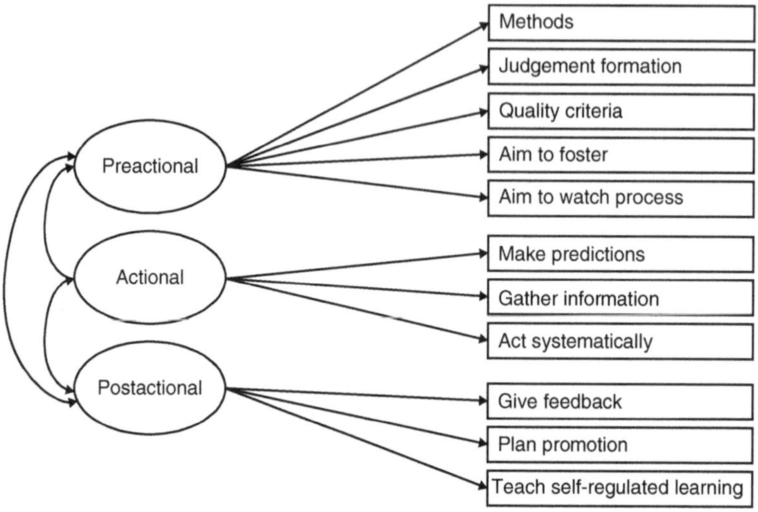

Fig. 10.2 Three-dimensional model of teachers' diagnostic competence (Klug et al. 2013)

petence were measured by means of specific scenario tests (see Sect. 10.4.1). We found a statistically significant correlation at the level of the overall scores for counseling and diagnostic competence ($r = .21$, $p < .01$). Consequently, our data demonstrate empirically that the postulated relationship between both competence areas does exist.

10.4 Measuring Teachers' Counseling and Diagnostic Competence

10.4.1 Scenario Tests

Empirical validation of the models outlined above was realized by means of specific scenario tests (one for each competence area). Scenario tests are considered to be an appropriate and effective method to measure competencies in a standardized manner that is context specific and closely related to behavior. Such tests have frequently been applied to assess competencies, even in the field of teacher education (e.g., Rivard et al. 2007).

Each scenario test contains a case study of a student with learning difficulties, followed by 12 open-ended questions relating to the information provided in the case study, which includes the contents of the competence models. Here, the scenario test for the assessment of teachers' counseling competence comprises questions concerning a potential counseling talk with the characterized student's mother, such as "How do you structure the counseling talk?" (structuring) or "What learning aids or changes can you think of that you would recommend to Kristina's mother?"

(strategy application). The questions presented in the scenario test for assessing teachers' diagnostic competence refer to general diagnostic proceedings in the case of student learning difficulties. For example, "If you want to assess Marco's learning and achievement, with what do you compare his performance level?" (aim to watch process) or "After you have detected the causes of Marco's learning difficulties, what do you do next?" (plan promotion).

In order to transform the qualitative statements to these open-ended questions into quantitative data, we developed detailed rating systems. The rating systems proved to be objective within the scope of our studies, as the calculation of inter-rater reliabilities for each question resulted in satisfactory intra-class-correlations between ICC = .72 and ICC = 1.00 for counseling (Gerich et al. 2015) and ICC = .67 and ICC = .95 for diagnostic competence (Klug et al. 2013).[2]

10.4.2 Situational Judgment Test

To assess teachers' counseling competence, we furthermore developed a situational judgment test (SJT; Bruder 2011; Bruder et al. 2011). In several studies, SJTs have been shown to have substantial criterion-related validities for the criterion of job performance (McDaniel et al. 2001). The SJT for measuring teachers' counseling competence consists of 13 items referring to the four dimensions. Each item describes a short realistic counseling situation in which a particular behavior is requested, followed by four multiple-choice answer options. The participant is asked to choose the best and worst possible activities. Item difficulties were calculated on a sample of 78 grammar school teachers and ranged from .20 to .80, except for items of structuring, problem definition, and searching for reasons. The middle item difficulty for the SJT was .70. In a comparative study with $N = 296$ prospective and in-service teachers, analyses on the basis of a short test form of the SJT (six items) resulted in a significant correlation of the measured overall score of the SJT with the overall score of the scenario test (Bruder et al. 2011).

10.4.3 Knowledge Tests and Self-Assessment Questionnaires

In addition to the scenario tests and the SJT, we developed instruments for the assessment of several variables related to teachers' counseling and diagnostic competence (see Bruder 2011; Klug 2011).

For this purpose, we firstly constructed specific multiple-choice knowledge tests for the measurement of teachers' theoretical knowledge of counseling and diagnostics. The knowledge test on counseling consists of a set of nine closed-ended ques-

[2] A detailed description of the situational judgment test (SJT) and the results of further analyses are published in Bruder (2011) and Bruder et al. (2011).

tions, each with several possible correct answers. For example: "Which advantages are associated with the technique of active listening? (1) The listener can make sure that he or she has accurately understood how the speaker is feeling. (2) It makes it easier for the listener to identify with the speaker. (3) The speaker feels understood. (4) It makes it easy to structure the conversation."The multiple-choice tests on knowledge of diagnostics consisted of eleven closed-ended questions. For example: "Which quality criteria should diagnostic information correspond to? (1) Accuracy, representativeness, independency. (2) Completeness, stability, economy. (3) Objectivity, validity, reliability. (4) Objectivity, valence, relevance." Participants were asked to choose the best answer or answers (the latter in cases where multiple answers were allowed. In such cases this was clearly marked next to the respective item). Item difficulties of the knowledge tests were between .35 and .89 for counseling and .33 and .82 for diagnostics, thus allowing for differentiation in a broad range of characteristics.

Secondly, we developed specific self-assessment questionnaires for both competence areas, measuring teacher's professional self-concept (counseling: 17 items, $\alpha = .87$; diagnosing: 12 items, $\alpha = .77$) and reflected experience (counseling: eight items, $\alpha = .75$; diagnosing: four items, $\alpha = .75$). The scales on professional self-concept comprise items on teachers' motivation, self-efficacy, and attitude towards counseling or diagnosing, respectively. For example, "I am motivated to look into reasons for the learning problems of my students." The professional self-concept for counseling scale additionally includes items on teachers' sense of self as a counselor. For example, "I believe that, as a teacher, part of my job is to counsel parents." The reflected experience scales comprise items on teachers' counseling or diagnosing experiences and their subsequent reflection. For example, "After finishing a counseling talk, I think about whether I am satisfied with my performance as a counselor." Participants were asked to respond to those items on a six-point rating scale, ranging from 1 (*I completely disagree*) to 6 (*I completely agree*).[3]

10.5 Training Teachers' Counseling and Diagnostic Competence

As several sources of teacher professionalization report inadequate consideration of counseling and diagnostic competencies in the context of early and continuing teacher education, we developed specific training programs for prospective and in-service teachers (Gerich et al. 2012; Klug 2011; Trittel et al. 2014). Here, the training programs developed and evaluated within the framework of the research project initially focused either on counseling or on diagnostic competence however, with the aim of creating a solid basis for the subsequent development of training programs that focus on both competence areas. Nevertheless, due to the outlined

[3] For a detailed description of the multiple-choice knowledge tests and the self-assessment questionnaires see Bruder (2011) and Klug (2011).

relationship between teachers' counseling and diagnostic competence, the training programs overlapped in certain contents. Within the framework of intervention studies, we investigated the effects of the training programs as well as several additional interventions on participants' counseling competence and diagnostic competence, respectively.

10.5.1 Training Program in Diagnostic Competence for In-Service Teachers

As part of the first intervention study within the current research project (Klug 2011), we studied the effects of participating in a training program on educational diagnostics and working on a standardized diary about teachers' diagnostic competence. The development of the training program was based on the three-dimensional process model (Klug et al. 2013) and, consequently, covered all the contents of the three phases of the diagnostic process. It consisted of three weekly sessions, with a high degree of activity and reflection. In order to ensure the transfer of the theoretically acquired knowledge to teachers' professional routines, participants worked on a specific diagnostically relevant case of one of their own students, describing each step in the diagnostic process, from setting the goal of the diagnostic process to the development of individual educational plans. After every session participants completed weekly homework assignments that encouraged them to revise and reflect further on the latest training content.

The standardized diary was intended to consolidate the transfer of the learned content by means of self-monitoring. It was likewise constructed with reference to the three phases of the process model, and contained questions on diagnostic action in teachers' professional routines. For example, "Today I explicitly cared about special judgment errors so that they do not bias my assessment" (judgment formation), or "Today, to judge my pupils' learning behavior adequately, I compared their current learning behavior with their earlier learning behavior" (aim to watch process).

$N = 47$ grammar school teachers voluntarily participated in the training program. Based on a longitudinal quasi-experimental design, we combined pre- and posttest assessment with time-series measures. The first experimental group completed the pretest, then received three weekly training sessions, and subsequently completed the posttest. The second experimental group additionally completed the standardized diary, starting one week before the first training session and finishing one week after the last training session. Control group participants completed the pretest and posttest and were offered the opportunity to enroll in a shortened training program afterwards. For the pre- and the post-test, we used the scenario test for the assessment of teachers' diagnostic competence, outlined in Sect. 10.4.1. The acquisition of time series data was realized by means of the standardized diary.

A multivariate one-way ANOVA showed that participation in the training program enhanced teachers' diagnostic skills in both the preactional ($F(2, 44) = 5.48$, $p < .01$, $\eta^2 = .199$) and the actional phases ($F(2, 44) = 6.37$, $p < .01$, $\eta^2 = .224$) of the diagnostic process, as both experimental groups showed significantly larger increases than the control group. Completing the diary had no additional intervention effect on the values of experimental group 2. However, time series analyses on the basis of the diary data showed significant linear trends for most of the assessed variables. In the course of the training program and the completion of the diary, teachers applied the learned strategies in class increasingly often.

10.5.2 Training Programs in Counseling and Diagnostic Competence for Prospective Teachers

As part of our longitudinal intervention studies, we furthermore aimed to investigate the effectiveness of specific training programs as well as additional feedback interventions on prospective teachers' counseling competence and diagnostic competence, respectively.[4]

Each study took place at a university in Germany in compulsory optional courses on educational psychology. A total of $N = 71$ prospective teachers participated in the study on counseling competence. The sample in the study on diagnostic competence consisted of $N = 73$ prospective teachers. In each study, there were two experimental groups and one control group. After completing a pretest, experimental groups one (training condition) and two (training and feedback condition) participated in a training program on either counseling or diagnostic competence. The control groups participated in an alternative compulsory course. Participants in each experimental group additionally received individual feedback on their competence development on two occasions during the course of the training period (after the pretest and the posttest). In order to test the long-term effects of the realized interventions, participants in the experimental groups completed a follow-up test eight weeks after the posttest. To assess participants' counseling competence and diagnostic competence, respectively, at all three measurement time points, we applied the scenario tests outlined in Sect. 10.4.1.[5]

The training program consisted of either 9 (counseling competence) or 10 (diagnostic competence) weekly sessions. The learning contents of the particular sessions were selected on the basis of the outlined competence models of Gerich et al. (2015) and Klug et al. (2013). The training programs were particularly characterized by their focus on the development of practical competencies with actual relevance for participants' future professional work. For that purpose, the training

[4] In the training study on diagnostic competence, we additionally examined the effects of working on a portfolio of educational diagnostics. Attention will be drawn here especially to the effects of the interventions training and feedback. A description of the portfolio can be found in Trittel et al. (in prep. a).

[5] In the study on counseling competence, we additionally implemented simulated parent-teacher conversations to assess prospective teachers' counseling competence. These were video recorded and rated by means of a detailed rating system. A specific description of the video-instrument, as well as the results gained from the simulated parent-teacher conversations, can be found in Gerich and Schmitz (submitted).

programs comprised large sequences of situated learning. By means of working on specific cases, participants were able to apply their new theoretical knowledge in practical situations, as well as to continually reflect on their own professional practice in realistic problem contexts. After every session, participants completed weekly homework assignments that encouraged them to revise and reflect further on the latest training content.

As feedback is known to have a positive impact on learning (Kluger and DeNisi 1996), we additionally aimed at testing its effects on the development of teachers' competencies in counseling and diagnostics. For this, participants in each experimental group received individual written feedback concerning their actual counseling or diagnostic competence, after the pretest and the posttest, on the basis of their individual measurement results. In special consideration of process-orientation, the feedback comprised information on participants' individual strengths and weaknesses as well as individual areas of improvement. This so-called formative feedback (cf. Shute 2008) was itemized according to the dimensions of the outlined competence models (Gerich et al. 2015; Klug et al. 2013). In order to investigate the short and long-term effects of participation in the training programs and feedback interventions, we performed mixed-model MANOVAs with the between-subjects factor group and within-subjects factor time (pretest, posttest, follow-up test).

Within the scope of the intervention study on counseling competence, the pre-post comparison by means of a mixed-model MANOVA, revealed a significant interaction effect of group and time ($F(2, 68) = 175.69, p < .001, \eta^2 = .84$). The two experimental groups showed a significantly greater improvement in counseling competence than did the control group, which did not demonstrate increases on any dependent variables during the training period. Furthermore, the participants who received individual feedback on their pretest results (experimental group 2) showed a significantly higher competence increase than those who only participated in the training program (experimental group 1). The post-follow-up comparison revealed no significant decrease in participants' counseling competence, thereby indicating the long-term stability of the intervention effects.

Mixed-model MANOVAs in the context of the intervention study on diagnostic competence also revealed a significant interaction of group and time in the development of participants' diagnostic competence from pretest to posttest ($F(2, 72) = 152.30, p = .001, \eta^2 = .81$), indicating an advantage for the experimental groups over the control group. The examination of long-term effects by means of the post-follow-up comparison revealed a significant interaction of group and time ($F(1, 46) = 32.86, p < .001, \eta^2 = .42$). In the space of time from the posttest to the follow-up test, experimental group 1 showed a decrease of measured diagnostic competence, whereas the experimental group 2, which received individual feedback on posttest results, showed an increase.[6]

Results of the intervention studies on the overall level of teachers' counseling and diagnostic competence are displayed in Fig. 10.3.

[6] A detailed description of the interventions and their effects on the particular competence dimensions can be found in Gerich et al. (under review) and Trittel et al. (in prep. b).

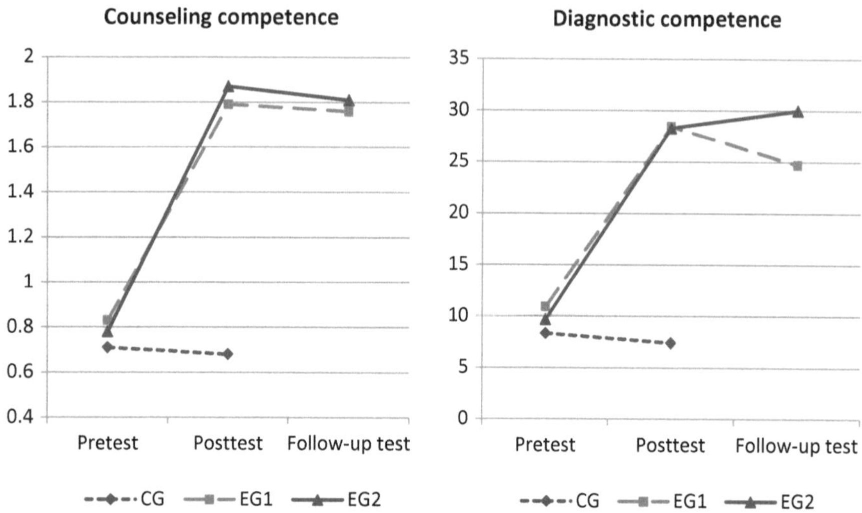

Fig. 10.3 Results of the intervention studies on the overall level of teachers' counseling and diagnostic competence (Gerich et al. under review; Trittel et al. in prep. b; *CG* control group, *EG1* experimental group 1, *EG2* experimental group 2)

10.6 Conclusions and Outlook

Over the course of the research project, we were able to establish a second-order four-dimensional model of teachers' counseling competence, as well as a three-dimensional process model of teachers' diagnostic competence, in the specific domain of students' learning behavior. With regard to further research, a central objective should be the development of a common model that emphasizes the interrelationship of both competence areas, as well as their particular dimensions. As our research on the relationship of teachers' diagnostic and counseling competence is based only on cross-sectional data, so far, further longitudinal studies should focus especially on the examination of causal relationships between both competence areas.

The scenario tests turned out to be objective and efficient strategies for the itemized measurement of teachers' practical counseling and diagnostic competencies, with simultaneous consideration of the required economy, especially in studies with large sample sizes. Using the scenario tests, we were able to obtain both an assessment of general competence and a detailed measurement, itemized according to the specific competence dimensions. Certainly, scenario tests are not able to measure actual behavior; however, for studies with large sample sizes, they are the method of choice (Hedlund et al. 2006). Especially in early teacher education, case scenarios prove to be beneficial for measuring competencies, given that observation in real practice contexts is not possible. Nevertheless, future research should focus on further improvement of the scenario tests. To do so, data obtained from the outlined scenario tests should first be compared to data obtained from other case scenarios measuring teachers' counseling and diagnostic competence. Then, with a view to validation in the field, data may be compared to video recordings of counseling talks or classroom observations of teachers' actual professional routines. This also applies to the outlined situational judgment test for measuring counseling competence.

The specified competence models and the instruments for their assessment provide a profound empirical basis for the targeting of contents and skills to be acquired during teacher education programs, as well as the differentiated and competence-based measurement of participating teachers' learning outcomes. The demonstrated appropriateness of the multi-dimensional models indicates that teacher training programs are not limited to a focus on the development of general counseling and diagnostic competencies, but may also be used for the advancement of specific subsidiary skills. On the other hand, the outlined instruments allow for assessment of the specific needs of individual and groups in terms of continuing education, as well as the designing of precisely tailored training programs and their systematic evaluation.

From this initial position, based on these models, we developed specific training programs on counseling and diagnostics for prospective and in-service teachers. Utilization of the specified instruments allowed for the comprehensive monitoring of participants' individual learning processes, as well as providing detailed individual feedback. Within the framework of our intervention studies, we were able to show that it is possible to enhance prospective and in-service teachers' counseling and diagnostic competence in the long term through training. Moreover, in our studies with prospective teachers, formative feedback additionally proved beneficial in the context of participants' competence development. As we only developed and evaluated interventions on either counseling or diagnostic competence over the course of the research project, the outlined training programs could serve as a blueprint for corresponding programs that focus on both competence areas. Given the currently insufficient consideration of counseling and diagnostic skills in the context of teacher education, appropriate curricula should become a fixed component in early teacher preparation as well as in continuing education.

Acknowledgments The preparation of this chapter was supported by grant SCHM 1538/5-3 from the German Research Foundation (DFG) in the Priority Program "Competence Models for Assessing Individual Learning Outcomes and Evaluating Educational Processes" (SPP 1293).

References

Abs, H. J. (2007). Überlegungen zur Modellierung diagnostischer Kompetenz bei Lehrerinnen und Lehrern [Deliberations on the modeling of teachers'diagnostic competence]. In M. Lüders & J. Wissinger (Eds.), *Forschung zur Lehrerbildung. Kompetenzentwicklung und Programmevaluation* (pp. 63–84). Münster: Waxmann.

Baumert, J., & Kunter, M. (2006). Stichwort: Professionelle Kompetenz von Lehrkräften [Keyword: Teachers' professional competence]. *Zeitschrift für Erziehungswissenschaft, 9*, 469–520. doi:10.1007/s11618-006-0165-2.

Boethel, M. (2003). *Diversity. School, family, & community connections: Annual synthesis 2003.* Austin: Southwest Educational Development Laboratory, National Center for Family and Community Schools.

Bruder, S. (2011). *Lernberatung in der Schule: Ein zentraler Bereich professionellen Lehrerhandelns* [Counseling in terms of learning strategies in school: A central aspect of teachers' professional action]. Doctoral dissertation, Technische Universität Darmstadt, Darmstadt, Germany. Retrieved from http://tuprints.ulb.tu-darmstadt.de/2432/

Bruder, S., Klug, J., Hertel, S., & Schmitz, B. (2010). Modellierung der Beratungskompetenz von Lehrkräften [Modeling teachers'counseling competence]. *Zeitschrift für Pädagogik, Beiheft, 56*, 274–285.

Bruder, S., Keller, S., Klug, J., & Schmitz, B. (2011). Ein Vergleich situativer Methoden zur Erfassung der Beratungskompetenz von Lehrkräften [Comparison of situational methods for assessing teachers' counseling competence]. *Unterrichtswissenschaft, 39*, 123–137.

Cox, D. D. (2005). Evidence-based interventions using home-school collaboration. *School Psychology Quarterly, 20*, 473–497. doi:10.1521/scpq.2005.20.4.473.

Gerich, M., & Schmitz, B. (submitted). Simulated parent-teacher talks. A behavior-related instrument for the assessment and improvement of prospective teachers' counseling competence. *Journal of Counseling Psychology.*

Gerich, M., Trittel, M., & Schmitz, B. (2012). Förderung der Beratungskompetenz von Lehrkräften durch Training, Feedback und Reflexion. Methoden handlungsorientierter Intervention und Evaluation [Promoting teachers' counseling competence by training, feedback, and reflection. Methods of action-oriented intervention and evaluation]. In M. Kobarg, C. Fischer, I. M. Dalehefte, F. Trepke, & M. Menk (Eds.), *Lehrerprofessionalisierung wissenschaftlich begleiten: Strategien und Methoden* (pp. 51–68). Münster: Waxmann.

Gerich, M., Bruder, S., Hertel, S., Trittel, M., & Schmitz, B. (2015). What skills and abilities are essential for counseling on learning difficulties and learning strategies? Modeling teachers' counseling competence in parent-teacher talks measured by means of a scenario test. *Zeitschrift für Entwicklungspsychologie und Pädagogische Psychologie, 47*, 62–71. doi:10.1026/0049-8637/a000127.

Gerich, M., Trittel, M., Schmitz, B. (under review). Improving pre-service teachers' counseling competence in parent-teacher talks. Effects of training and feedback. *Journal of Educational and Psychological Consultation.*

German Society for Psychology (DGPs). (Ed.). (2008). *Psychologie in den Lehramtsstudiengängen: Ein Rahmencurriculum* [Psychology in teacher education: A framework curriculum]. Retrieved from http://www.dgps.de/_download/2008/Psychologie_Lehramt_Curriculum.pdf

Hattie, J., & Timperley, H. (2007). The power of feedback. *Review of Educational Research, 77*, 81–112. doi:10.3102/003465430298487.

Hedlund, J., Witt, J. M., Nebel, K. L., Ashford, S. J., & Sternberg, R. J. (2006). Assessing practical intelligence in business school admissions: A supplement to the graduate management admission test. *Learning and Individual Differences, 16*, 101–127. doi:10.1016/j.lindif.2005.07.005.

Helmke, A., Hosenfeld, I., & Schrader, F.-W. (2004). Vergleichsarbeiten als Instrument zur Verbesserung der Diagnosekompetenz von Lehrkräften [Comparative tests as an instrument for the improvement of diagnostic competence of teachers]. In R. Arnold & C. Griese (Eds.), *Schulmanagement und Schulentwicklung* (pp. 119–144). Hohengehren: Schneider.

Hertel, S. (2009). *Beratungskompetenz von Lehrern. Kompetenzdiagnostik, Kompetenzförderung und Kompetenzmodellierung* [Teachers' counselling competence: diagnostic, advancement, modeling]. Münster: Waxmann.

Hoover-Dempsey, K. V., Walker, J. M. T., Jones, K. P., & Reed, R. P. (2002). Teachers involving parents (TIP): Results of an in-service teacher education program for enhancing parental involvement. *Teaching and Teacher Education, 18*, 843–867. doi:10.1016/S0742-051X(02)00047-1.

Jäger, R. S. (2007). *Beobachten, bewerten, fördern. Lehrbuch für die Aus-, Fort- und Weiterbildung* [Monitoring, evaluating, promoting. Textbook for education and training]. Landau: Empirische Pädagogik.

Keys, S. G., Bemak, F., Carpenter, S. L., & King-Sears, M. E. (1998). Collaborative consultant. A new role for counselors serving at-risk youths. *Journal of Counseling & Development, 76*, 123–133. doi:10.1002/j.1556-6676.1998.tb02385.x.

Klug, J. (2011). Modeling and training a new concept of teachers' diagnostic competence. Doctoral dissertation, Technische Universität Darmstadt, Darmstadt. Retrieved from http://tuprints.ulb.tu-darmstadt.de/2838/

Klug, J., Bruder, S., Keller, S., & Schmitz, B. (2012). Hängen Diagnostische Kompetenz und Beratungskompetenz von Lehrkräften zusammen? Eine korrelative Untersuchung [Do teachers' diagnostic competence and counseling competence correlate?]. *Psychologische Rundschau, 63*, 3–10. doi:10.1026/0033-3042/a000104.

Klug, J., Bruder, S., Kelava, A., Spiel, C., & Schmitz, B. (2013). Diagnostic competence of teachers. A process model that accounts for diagnosing learning behavior tested by means of a case scenario. *Teaching and Teacher Education, 30*, 38–46. doi:10.1016/j.tate.2012.10.004.

Kluger, A. N., & DeNisi, A. (1996). The effects of feedback interventions on performance. A historical review, a meta-analysis, and a preliminary feedback intervention theory. *Psychological Bulletin, 119*, 254–284. doi:10.1037/0033-2909.119.2.254.

KMK (Standing Conference of the Ministers of Education and Cultural Affairs of the States in the Federal Republic of Germany). (Ed.). (2004). *Standards für die Lehrerbildung: Bildungswissenschaften. Beschluss vom 16.12.2004.* [Standards for teacher education: Educational sciences. Resolution approved by the Standing Conference on 16 December 2004]. Retrieved from http://www.kmk.org/fileadmin/veroeffentlichungen_beschluesse/2004/2004_12_16-Standards-Lehrerbildung.pdf

Koeppen, K., Hartig, J., Klieme, E., & Leutner, D. (2008). Current issues in competence modeling and assessment. *Journal of Psychology, 216*, 61–73. doi:10.1027/0044-3409.216.2.61.

Mandel, S. (2006). What new teachers really need. *Educational Leadership, 63*(6), 66–69.

McDaniel, M. S., Morgeson, F. P., Finnegan, E. B., Campion, M. A., & Braverman, E. P. (2001). Use of situational judgment tests to predict job performance: a clarification of the literature. *Journal of Applied Psychology, 80*, 730–740. doi:10.1037/0021-9010.86.4.730.

McLaughlin, C. (1999). Counselling in schools: Looking back and looking forward. *British Journal of Guidance and Counselling, 27*, 13–22. doi:10.1080/03069889908259712.

McLeod, J. (2003). *An introduction to counselling*. Buckingham: Open University Press.

NCTAF (National Commission on Teaching and America's Future). (1997). *Doing what matters most. Investing in quality teaching*. New York: Author.

Pas, E. T., Bradshaw, C. P., & Hershfeldt, P. A. (2012). Teacher- and school-level predictors of teacher efficacy and burnout. Identifying potential areas for support. *Journal of School Psychology, 50*, 129–145. doi:10.1016/j.jsp.2011.07.003.

Reid, W. J. (1990). An integrative model for short-term treatment. In R. A. Wells & V. J. Giannetti (Eds.), *Handbook of the brief psychotherapies* (pp. 55–77). New York: Plenum Press.

Rivard, L. M., Missiuna, C., Hanna, S., & Wishart, L. (2007). Understanding teachers' perceptions of the motor difficulties of children with developmental coordination disorder (DCD). *British Journal of Educational Psychology, 77*, 633–648. doi:10.1348/000709906X159879.

Schwarzer, C., & Buchwald, P. (2006). Beratung in Familie, Schule und Beruf [Counseling in family, school, and profession]. In A. Krapp & B. Weidenmann (Eds.), *Pädagogische Psychologie: Ein Lehrbuch* (5th ed., pp. 575–612). Weinheim: Beltz.

Shute, V. (2008). Focus on formative feedback. *Review of Educational Research, 78*, 153–189. doi:10.3102/0034654307313795.

Strasser, J., & Gruber, H. (2003). Kompetenzerwerb in der Beratung. Eine kritische Analyse des Forschungsgegenstands [Competence acquisition in counseling. A critical review of research literature]. *Psychologie in Erziehung und Unterricht, 50*, 381–399.

Südkamp, A., Kaiser, J., & Möller, J. (2012). Accuracy of teachers' judgments of students' academic achievement: A meta-analysis. *Journal of Educational Psychology, 104*, 743–762. doi:10.1037/a0027627.

Thiel, H.-U. (2003). Phasen des Beratungsprozesses [Stages of the counseling process]. In C. Krause, B. Fittkau, R. Fuhr, & H.-U. Thiel (Eds.), *Pädagogische Beratung* (pp. 73–84). Paderborn: Schöningh.

Trittel, M., Gerich, M., & Schmitz, B. (2014). Training prospective teachers in educational diagnostics. In S. Krolak-Schwerdt, S. Glock, & M. Böhmer (Eds.), *Teachers'professional development. Assessment, training, and learning* (pp. 63–78). Rotterdam: Sense.

Trittel, M., Gerich, M., & Schmitz, B. (in preparation-a). Development of an educational diagnostics portfolio for prospective teachers.

Trittel, M., Gerich, M., & Schmitz, B. (in preparation-b). Fostering diagnostic competence of prospective teachers by training and feedback.

Van Ophuysen, S. (2006). Vergleich diagnostischer Entscheidungen von Novizen und Experten am Beispiel der Schullaufbahnempfehlung [Comparison of diagnostic decisions between novices and experts: The example of school career recommendation]. *Zeitschrift für Entwicklungspsychologie und Pädagogische Psychologie, 38*, 154–161. doi:10.1026/0049-8637.38.4.154.

Vogt, F., & Rogalla, M. (2009). Developing adaptive teaching competency through coaching. *Teaching and Teacher Education, 25*, 1051–1060. doi:10.1016/j.tate.2009.04.002.

Walker, J. M. T., & Dotger, B. H. (2012). Because wisdom can't be told. Using comparison of simulated parent-teacher conferences to assess teacher candidates' readiness for family-school partnership. *Journal of Teacher Education, 63*, 62–75. doi:10.1177/0022487111419300.

Weinert, F. E. (2001). Concept of competence: a conceptual clarification. In D. Rychen & L. Salganik (Eds.), *Defining and selecting key competencies* (pp. 45–65). Seattle: Hogrefe.

West, J. F., & Cannon, G. S. (1988). Essential collaborative consultation competencies for regular and special educators. *Journal of Learning Disabilities, 21*, 56–63. doi:10.1177/002221948802100111.

Wild, E. (2003). Lernen lernen: Wege einer Förderung der Bereitschaft und Fähigkeit zu selbstreguliertem Lernen [Learning how to learn: Ways of promoting willingness and ability for self-regulated learning]. *Unterrichtswissenschaft, 31*, 2–5.

Chapter 11
Development and Evaluation of a Competence Model for Teaching Integrative Processing of Texts and Pictures (BiTe)

Annika Ohle, Nele McElvany, Britta Oerke, Wolfgang Schnotz, Inga Wagner, Holger Horz, Mark Ullrich, and Jürgen Baumert

Abstract Teaching and learning from texts with integrated pictures are challenging tasks for teachers and students. Nevertheless, this kind of material is universal in secondary school as well as in elementary school and holds huge potential for student learning, if instruction and presentation are appropriate. The project "BiTe" investigates teachers' and students' competencies in secondary and elementary school. This chapter focuses on components of teachers' competence in the specific field of Picture-Text-Integration (PTI), embracing teachers' knowledge as well as their attitudes, motivation, and self-related cognitions. Also, teachers' judgment accuracy is investigated, as especially relevant for judging students' competencies and the level of difficulty of teaching materials. Regarding the outcomes of teachers' competencies, instructional quality and students' engagement are described.

Keywords Teacher competencies • Picture-text-material • Multi-media learning • Elementary and secondary school

---

A. Ohle (✉) • N. McElvany • B. Oerke
TU Dortmund University, Dortmund, Germany
e-mail: Annika.Ohle@tu-dortmund.de; Nele.McElvany@tu-dortmund.de; Britta.Oerke@tu-dortmund.de

W. Schnotz • I. Wagner
University of Koblenz-Landau, Landau, Germany
e-mail: schnotz@uni-landau.de; iwagner@zepf.uni-landau.de

H. Horz • M. Ullrich
Goethe University Frankfurt, Frankfurt/Main, Germany
e-mail: Horz@psych.uni-frankfurt.de; M.Ullrich@psych.uni-frankfurt.de

J. Baumert
Max Planck Institute for Human Development, Berlin, Germany
e-mail: sekbaumert@mpib-berlin.mpg.de

D. Leutner et al. (eds.), *Competence Assessment in Education*, Methodology of Educational Measurement and Assessment, DOI 10.1007/978-3-319-50030-0_11

11.1 The "BiTe-Project"

The German acronym "BiTe" stands for "*Bild-Text-Integration*" (Picture-Text-Integration); the aim of this project is to investigate teachers' and students' competencies in teaching and learning with multi-representational material—more precisely, material consisting of texts with instructional pictures. Within this project, teachers and students from secondary schools (funding phases 1 and 2) and elementary schools (funding phase 3) participated. The first funding phase was dedicated to the development of competence models and instruments for evaluating those models. The following chapter presents results from the first, second and third phase of funding, focusing on teacher competencies. Results regarding students' competencies are reported in Schnotz et al. (2017, in this volume).

11.2 Theoretical Background

11.2.1 Challenges of Picture-Text-Integration (PTI)

Multi-representational learning material is omnipresent in secondary and elementary school classrooms. Such material—as it is understood in this project—refers to material consisting of texts and instructional pictures, like diagrams, maps or similar illustrations (Mayer 2001). Whenever information is presented by different representations, the recipient needs to make use of different channels (here: verbal and pictorial) in order to extract information from both sources and to construct a mental model of the given information (Ayres and Sweller 2005; Schnotz and Bannert 2003). Although integrating information from pictures and texts is cognitively challenging for students, learning with this kind of material can be very effective when material is offered adequately (e.g., Ainsworth 2006). Information from different sources can work complementarily, but usually there is little redundancy between text and pictures in learning materials; for students, this increases the difficulty of integrating information from both sources.

11.2.2 Teachers' Competencies for Teaching the Integrative Processing of Pictures and Texts

Teachers play an essential role in student learning (e.g., Good, 1979; Hattie and Anderman, 2013), as they are responsible for offering high quality instruction. Models of classroom interactions between teachers and students describe teachers' competencies as a multi-dimensional construct including *professional knowledge*, *attitudes*, *motivation*, and self-related cognitions, such as *emotional distance*, *self-efficacy beliefs*, *self-regulation* or *self-reflection* (e.g., Kunter et al. 2013). There is empirical evidence that these dimensions are relevant for teachers' performance in the classroom and therefore also impact student learning (e.g., Hattie and Anderman 2013; Pajares 1992; Tschannen-Moran et al. 1998). It seems reasonable that these dimensions of teachers' competence are also relevant for teaching with texts and integrated pictures. Especially in cognitively demanding learning situations—such as the integrative processing of texts and pictures—teachers' *judgment accuracy* in respect of students' competencies and the difficulty of learning material (e.g., Vogt and Rogalla 2009) is essential for providing adequate learning and adaptive support for students.

It is widely assumed that teachers' competencies are gained during their education and further developed through experience (e.g., Blömeke 2011; Klassen and Chiu 2010). Furthermore, teachers' expertise in a certain domain can be fostered by teacher training (e.g., Lipowsky 2004).

11.2.3 Quality of Instruction

There is a consensus that quality of instruction is essential for student learning (e.g., Helmke 2009). Common models of classroom interaction describe instructional quality as a mediating factor between teachers' competencies and students' learning outcomes. It seems reasonable that those models can also be applied to describing teaching and learning with picture-text-material. Hence, teachers' competencies in PTI are regarded as an essential prerequisite for students' learning processes with this kind of material. In the literature a variety of descriptions for quality of instruction can be found, but in general, three basic dimensions can be distinguished (Klieme and Rakoczy 2008): Classroom management (e.g., prevention of disruptions) is the basis of successful learning processes, which include teaching and learning with picture-text-material. Cognitive activation (e.g., through challenging tasks) is a more content-related aspect of instructional quality and is probably especially relevant for learning with cognitively challenging PTI-material. A supportive and student-oriented environment (e.g., adaptive explanations) builds the third dimension of instructional quality. Adequate teacher explanations are supposed to be essential for learning with difficult material such as PTI-material. Aspects of instructional quality, which can be summarized in those three dimensions, are supposed to ensure fluent learning processes, cognitive challenges, and adequate teacher support for students.

11.3 Research Questions and Hypotheses

Based on the challenges of picture-text-integration (Sect. 11.2.1) as well as theoretical models and empirical evidence of teacher competencies (Sect. 11.2.2) and instructional quality (Sect. 11.2.3) four major research questions were derived for the area of picture-text-integration. These have regard to professional knowledge, attitudes, motivation, and self-related cognitions as dimensions of teacher competence (adapted for PTI):

(1) (a) What do teachers know about Picture-Text-Integration (PTI)?
(b) Can this knowledge be fostered by systematic intervention?
(2) What are teachers' attitudes, motivations, and self-related cognitions in the field of PTI and PTI-diagnostics?
(3) (a) How accurate are teachers' judgments with regard to student achievement and the difficulty of picture-text-material?
(b) Is the accuracy of teacher judgments related to their knowledge of PTI and the duration of contact between teacher and students?
(4) Are teachers' competencies in the field of PTI related to
(a) instructional quantity and quality, and
(b) students' engagement?

Since PTI is not an integral part of teacher education we expected to find rather low expertise in this field, while an interventional teacher training (Lipowsky 2004) should be suitable for fostering teachers' knowledge about PTI (Hypotheses 1a + b). It is expected that teachers' attitudes, motivation and self-related cognitions are distinct, but correlated components of teachers' PTI-competencies (Hypothesis 2). For teachers' accuracy of judgment, we presume secondary teachers to be more accurate, due to their education and the amount of PTI in secondary school books. Furthermore, positive relations between accuracy and teachers' knowledge and duration of contact to students are assumed (Hypotheses 3a + b). Based on general models of classroom interaction we presume positive relations between teachers' competencies in the field of PTI and instructional quality, as well as students' engagement (Hypotheses 4 a + b).

11.4 Methods

11.4.1 Sample and Study Design

Here, the overall samples and descriptive results from secondary and elementary school are presented; subsamples for specific analyses are described in the corresponding results section.

The *pilot study* in funding phase 1 took place in 2008 with $N = 48$ randomly drawn schools of all tracks in Rhineland-Palatinate, Germany. From each school one class from Grades 5, 6, 7, or 8 was drawn randomly, and that class' biology, geography, and German teachers were invited to participate in the study. The *main study* in funding phase 2 in secondary schools was a longitudinal study with a similar design. $N = 48$ classes from Grades 5 and 6 and their biology, geography, and German teachers, participated from 2009–2011. The science subjects were chosen because of the importance of PTI-material, in contrast to German as a subject, which mainly demands text-reading competence. Data was assessed in two cohorts on three measurement points in Grades 5–6–7, and 6–7–8 respectively. Parallel to this main study, a video-based *teacher training* on fostering PTI-knowledge was conducted, with N = 58 biology teachers providing different levels of in-depth knowledge about PTI.

Data collection in elementary school (funding phase 3) was similarly designed to the main study in secondary school. In a *longitudinal study* with two measurement points, data was collected in Grade 4 classes in two cohorts in Rhineland-Palatinate (2011–2012) and in North Rhine-Westphalia (2012–2013), Germany. Altogether, N = 78 classes and their science and German teachers participated (in Germany, natural and social science are taught in one comprehensive subject in elementary school). Again, these subjects were chosen because of the relevance of PTI-material.

11.4.2 Measures

Teacher Competencies Teacher competencies: *knowledge about picture-text-integration*, *attitudes*, *motivation*, and *self-related cognitions*, in (a) the general field of PTI and (b) specifically in diagnostics in PTI, were assessed with paper-pencil-instruments. Teachers' *knowledge about PTI* was assessed by 23 items about PTI-instruction, materials and necessary students' skills. Table 11.1 provides an overview

Table 11.1 Prompts and items of the PTI-knowledge scales

Prompt in secondary school	Prompt in elementary school	PTI-scales (Item examples)
Please mark the following suggestions with grades from 1 = *very good* to 6 = *insufficient* on how to instruct students to read texts with instructional pictures.	There are several options of guiding students to read texts with instructional pictures. Please think about your subjects practice and state how often the following approaches occur in your lessons.	*Instruction* (e.g., I recommend that students identify central concepts in text and picture)
Please mark the following suggestions with grades from 1 = *very good* to 6 = *insufficient* on how to simplify texts with instructional pictures for students.	There are several options of simplifying texts with instructional pictures. Please think about your subjects practice and state how often the following approaches occur in your lessons.	*Material* (e.g., I reduce the picture's complexity)
Please rate the relevance of students' skills for integrated reading of texts and pictures with grades from 1 = *very good* to 6 = *insufficient*.	There are several options for training student skills in reading texts with instructional pictures. Please think about your subjects practice and state how often the following approaches occur in your lessons.	*Student skills* (e.g., Relating information from two different sources)

of item examples and the corresponding prompts for secondary and elementary school teachers.

In secondary school teachers were asked to rate the adequacy of items, while teachers in elementary school had to report their instructional behavior, which is regarded as an indicator of professional knowledge. Based on comparisons of two items among each other, teachers were scored from 0–2 points: Teachers' relative estimation of adequacy between two items was (a) contrary to the expert rating (0 points), (b) not the reverse of the expert rating (the better option was not rated worse by teachers) (1 point), or c) equal to the expert rating (2 points). Teachers' total score was divided by the number of comparisons, resulting in a maximum score of 2 and a minimum of 0 points. The item comparisons for the whole test showed satisfying quality criteria for both school forms (Cronbach's $\alpha_{\text{secondary school}} = .79$; Cronbach's $\alpha_{\text{elementary school}} = .70$). Due to the different prompts in this test, the results are reported separately for both school levels. In the intervention study, teachers' *knowledge about PTI* was assessed by multiple-choice (MC) items consisting of 19 items about instructional pictures and the related reading and instruction processes, showing a reliability of Cronbach's Alpha $\alpha = .66$ in the pilot study (McElvany et al. 2009).

Teachers' *attitudes*, *motivation*, *emotional distance*, and *self-regulation* in the *field of text picture integration* were assessed by questionnaire items and a 4-step Likert scale, ranging from 1 = *I totally disagree* to 4 = *I totally agree*. All scales reached satisfying reliabilities. Table 11.2 provides an overview of descriptive statistics for $N = 339$ secondary and elementary school teachers ($M_{\text{age}} = 42.8$ years, $SD = 12.4$; 76.4 % female). In Table 11.3 intercorrelations are reported.

Accuracy of Judgments In order to estimate the accuracy of judgments, teachers filled in a questionnaire depicting items from a PTI-test that had been administered to the teachers' classes to assess students' PTI-competencies. Teachers were asked to rate students' competence, and item difficulty aspects. The following measures were used to describe teachers' accuracy of judgment (see McElvany et al. 2012):

- *Absolute judgment accuracy for individual items*: percentage of students, who solved each of the six items correctly (average difference between teachers' estimation and empirical solution rate);
- *Absolute judgment accuracy for overall test*: number of items solved correctly by class (difference between teachers' estimation and empirical solution rate);
- *Diagnostic sensitivity regarding item difficulty*: correlation between teachers' estimated difficulty ranking of six items and the empirical difficulty order;
- *Diagnostic sensitivity regarding student competence*: correlation between teachers' estimated ranking of seven (randomly drawn) students and the empirical competence order

Quantity and Quality of Instruction Instructional quantity and quality were assessed in a multi-perspective way: teacher and student questionnaires with 4-point Likert scales, ranging from 1 = *I totally disagree* to 4 = *I totally agree* in the case of instructional quantity, and assessing discussion time on a range from 1 = *never* to 6 = *very often*. The presented results in secondary school are based on teachers'

Table 11.2 Descriptive statistics for facets of teachers' competencies

Scale (item example)	No. of Items	Reliability Cronbachs' α	*M* (*SD*)
For picture-text-material (PTM) in general			
Attitudes towards the utility of PTM (Texts with integrated pictures support students' understanding.)	3	.67	3.37 (0.39)
Attitudes towards the importance of support (Fostering stud. PTM-competence is one of the most important tasks.)	5	.73	3.21 (0.46)
Attitudes towards the importance of practice (Reading and understanding of PTM has to be practiced repeatedly.)	4	.83	3.38 (0.48)
Attitudes towards strategy use (Stud. gain PTM-understanding especially when shown clear routines.)	4	.83	3.13 (0.52)
Attitudes towards independent learning (Teachers should encourage stud. For finding own PTM-interpretations.)	4	.78	3.51 (0.46)
Emotional distance towards PTM[a] (I feel insecure when I see pictures, "integrated" in texts, in schoolbooks.)	4	.84	3.52 (0.50)
Intrinsic motivation towards usage of PTM (I enjoy teaching with PTM.)	3	.86	3.32 (0.49)
Self-efficacy beliefs towards PTM (I am sure to be able to integrate PTI-material into lessons meaningfully.)	4	.78	3.27 (0.41)
Engagement in teaching with PTM (When a picture is integrated in a text, I ensure that all stud. Understand the picture and its relation to the text)	4	.85	3.18 (0.51)
Avoidance in teaching with PTM[a] (When a picture is integrated in a text, I avoid discussing the picture)	4	.70	3.43 (0.42)
For diagnostics for teaching with picture-text-material			
Attitudes towards the *importance of diagnostics* (It is important for teaching and learning processes, to meticulously analyze the difficulty of PTM for students in advance.)	4	.78	3.17 (0.49)
Motivation towards diagnostics (I enjoy estimating the adequacy of text-picture-material for my class.)	4	.82	2.74 (0.53)
Diagnostic self-efficacy beliefs (When teaching with PTM, I usually scrutinize the adequacy of text-picture-material that I selected for my class.)	4	.77	2.98 (0.38)
Self-reflection in diagnostics (I spend time on estimating the challenges of PTM during lesson prep.)	5	.83	3.21 (0.50)

Note: [a]Recoded scales; items are formulated negatively

Table 11.3 Intercorrelations of Teachers' competence facets

Measure	1.	2.	3.	4.	5.	6.	7.	8.	9.	10.	11.	12.	13.	14.	15.
1. Utility		.35**	.27**	.12*	.20**	.30**	.42**	.31**	.23**	.28**	.25**	.22**	.06	.07	.05
2. Support			.47**	.26**	.21**	.20**	.26**	.22**	.31**	.30**	.33**	.33**	.07	.16*	.03
3. Practice				.45**	.18*	.08	.20**	.22**	.30**	.27**	.20**	.19*	.08	.19**	.09
4. Strategy					.19**	−.01	.14*	.05	.31**	.12*	.36**	.18*	.08	.30**	−.05
5. Independence						.15**	.30**	.24**	.32**	.26**	.26**	.13	.05	.13	.03
6. Emo. distance							.36**	.39**	.23**	.40**	.28**	.14	.19*	.06	.17*
7. Motivation								.37**	.38**	.24**	.27**	.42**	.17*	.06	.13*
8. SEB: PTI									.38**	.30**	.30**	.28**	.34**	.27**	−.01
9. Engagement										.25**	.42**	.37**	.26**	.25**	.00
10. Avoidance											.29**	.16*	.03	−.05	.14*
11. D: Importance												.44**	.35**	.35**	−.01
12. D: Motivation													.32**	.34**	.01
13. D: SEB														.38**	.04
14. D: Reflection															−.09
15. Knowledge															

Note: Analyses are based on whole sample ($N = 339$). The "emotional distance" and "Avoidance" scales were recorded (see Table 11.3)
$^{*}p < .05$ two-tailed. $^{**}p < .01$, two-tailed

self-reported instructional quantity (*frequency of use of picture-text-material*; M = 4.15; SD = 0.77; α = .82) and quality (*teachers' engagement*; M = 3.23, SD = 0.48; α = .86) (McElvany et al. 2012). Furthermore, students' perception of teachers' instructional behavior was assessed: *classroom management* (M = 2.45; SD = 0.57; α = .96), *discussion time* (M = 3.11; SD = 0.39; α = .90), and *adaptive explanations* (M = 2.89; SD = 0.42; α = .91) (Schroeder et al. 2011).

In elementary school, students' perception of *classroom management* (5 items; α = .88), *challenging tasks* (5 items; α = .87), and *adaptive explanations* (5 items; α = .82) were utilized as indicators of instructional quality.

Students' Engagement Students' *engagement* was assessed with a newly developed scale of four items (α = .79; M = 2.34, SD = 0.73) covering students' general engagement in learning activities, including PTI. On a 4-point Likert scale (1 = *I totally disagree* to 4 = *I totally agree)* students rated statements such as "We are very enthusiastic when reading texts with integrated pictures in our biology classes" (Schroeder et al. 2011).

11.5 Results

11.5.1 Research Question (1): Knowledge About PTI

For the elementary and secondary school teachers the main study-test showed a difficulty of $M_{elementary\ school}$ = 0.93 (SD = 0.16) and $M_{secondary\ school}$ = 1.20 (SD = 0.18) indicating the potential for optimization of teachers' PTI-knowledge base. In a video-based teacher training in secondary school, teachers received different levels of in-depth knowledge about PTI: Group A received advanced detailed information about PTI, while group B was provided with broader orientation knowledge about PTI. Results from the MC test showed that teachers who received detailed in-depth information gained more knowledge of PTI than did teachers who received merely a broad overview of the topic (McElvany and Willems 2012).

11.5.2 Research Question (2): Teachers' Attitudes, Motivation, and Self-Related Cognitions Towards PTI and Diagnostics in PTI

Teachers from both school types were convinced that picture-text-material was valuable for their teaching, and that students need to practice integrative processing of texts and pictures (see Table 11.2). Compared to the utility of mere text-material (M = 3.6; SD = 0.43), teachers reported a slightly higher value (M = 3.7; SD = 0.39) for the utility of PTI ($t(333) = -1.94$, p = .05). They also reported few negative emotions regarding PTI and seldom felt insecure when teaching with picture-text-material. Teachers were motivated, showed positive self-efficacy beliefs, and did not tend to avoid discussing PTI in their lessons.

Regarding teachers' attitudes, motivation and self-related cognitions for diagnostics in the field of PTI, confirmatory factor analyses with item parcels revealed that the four aspects (see Table 11.2) were distinct but correlated constructs for the whole sample. The four-factor model showed satisfying model fit criteria: (χ^2 = 25.50, df = 14, p = .03; comparative fit index [CFI] = 0.97). Chi-square-difference tests revealed that the model fit of a hierarchical model (χ^2 = 26.60, df = 16, p = .05; CFI = 0.98) was not significantly better than the four-factor model, while the global-factor model (χ^2 = 164.54, df = 20, p < .001; CFI = 0.67) had a significant poorer model fit. Teachers also scored rather high on attitudes, motivation and self-related cognitions for diagnostics in the specific field of PTI.

11.5.3 Research Question (3a): Teachers' Accuracy of Judgment

Analyses from the second and third project phases provided a diverse picture of judgment accuracy of secondary and elementary school teachers. Since teachers from elementary school worked on different tasks than did secondary school teachers, the results are presented separately. The level of accuracy differed among the four measures, as illustrated in Table 11.4.

Table 11.4 Overview of teachers' judgment accuracy measures

		Secondary School (N = 116)	Elementary School (N = 133)
Measure	Definition	M (SD)	M (SD)
Absolute judgment accuracy (individual items)[a]	Difference between teachers' estimation and empirical solution rate	17 % (13 %)	19 % (9 %)
Absolute judgment accuracy (overall test)[b]		7 (6) tasks	8 (6) tasks
Diagnostic sensitivity (item difficulty)[c]	Correlation between teachers' estimation and empirical order	$\bar{r}$ = .50 (.31)	$\bar{r}$ = .79 (.25)
Diagnostic sensitivity (student competencies)[c]		$\bar{r}$ = .34 (.49)	$\bar{r}$ = .43

[a]Perfect judgment = 0 %
[b]Perfect judgment = 0 tasks
[c]Perfect judgment $\bar{r}$ = 1.00

11.5.4 Research Question (3b): Teachers' Accuracy of Judgment, Knowledge, and Duration of Contact

In secondary school, inconsistent relations were found between teachers' knowledge about PTI, the accuracy of their judgments regarding students' competencies, and the difficulty of picture-text-material (McElvany et al. 2009). Furthermore, whether the duration of teacher-student contact improved the judgment accuracy of teachers was tested. There was very little support in favor of teachers' correct judgment of students' overall test performance, or the ranking of students and test items (Oerke et al. 2015). The tendency towards a reduced overestimation of students' achievement in the total test by teachers with longer contact with the class (1.5 years) compared to teachers with shorter contact (0.5 years), was not statistically significant in cross-sectional comparisons and was only marginally significant in a longitudinal test. One reason for the non-significant outcomes was the high variance between teachers (for example: after 1.5 years of contact: $M = 0.0$ ($SD = 1.0$) overestimation of tasks in cross-sectional comparisons; $M = 0.2$ ($SD = 1.2$ overestimation of tasks in longitudinal comparisons). Not all teachers overestimated their students—about one third underestimated them. Another reason may be that teachers do not get the feedback needed to evaluate the correctness of their estimations. The evidence found for this was weak however, indicating a learning effect in teachers, concerning their ability to properly judge students' performance in specific tasks. It is yet to be analyzed how this learning effect can be used in further education.

11.5.5 Research Question (4a): Relations Between Teachers' Competencies and Instruction

Results from the second phase of the BiTe-project showed that secondary school teachers' *attitudes towards the importance of practice* and *self-efficacy beliefs* were positively related to their self-reported engagement ($\beta_{importance} = .34$; $p < .05$; $\beta_{self\text{-}efficacy} = .26$; $p < .05$). Teachers' self-reported use of picture-text-material was predicted primarily by their *intrinsic motivation* and negatively related to teachers' *attitudes towards strategy use* ($\beta_{motivation} = .23$; $p < .05$; $\beta_{strategy\ use} = -.23$; $p < .05$). These relations between constructs were independent from teachers' educational background (McElvany et al. 2012).

Multilevel results from elementary school are not yet available, but students perceived *classroom management* in PTI-lessons as quite good ($M = 2.65$; $SD = 0.81$) and considered PTI-*tasks* to be *rather challenging* ($M = 2.30$; $SD = 0.80$). They also reported that teachers' *adaptive explanations* were helpful ($M = 3.21$; $SD = 0.61$).

11.5.6 Research Question (4b): Relations Between Teachers' Competencies and Students' Competence and Engagement

Focusing on students' self-reported *engagement*, positive relations to teachers' attitudes towards strategy use ($\beta = .13$, $p = .05$) could be found for the secondary school sample. In contrast, teachers' attitude towards independent learning was negatively related to students' engagement ($\beta = .14$, $p = .05$). As multilevel analyses revealed, these relations were completely mediated by instructional quality measures: classroom management, discussion time, and adaptive explanations (Schroeder et al. 2011).

11.6 Discussion

Teaching the integrative processing of texts and pictures is an everyday task for teachers in secondary schools as well as in elementary schools. Describing teachers' competencies in the field of PTI (Research Questions 1 and 2), are aware of the importance of picture-text-material for their daily work, but they have a rather low level of knowledge about it, especially in elementary school.

Since learning with this kind of material is challenging for students, teachers need to possess certain skills and competencies to enable successful learning processes when teaching with PTI-material. Being able to accurately judge students' competencies and the difficulty of tasks is a prerequisite skill for adaptive teaching (Research Question 3a). Although teachers from elementary and secondary school rated different items, it is surprising that elementary school teachers judged their students' competencies more correctly than did their colleagues from secondary schools. Addressing our research questions for elementary and secondary school teachers separately, is the next step. Results from secondary school show that teachers with longer contact with the class show a tendency towards a reduced overestimation of students' achievement (Research question 3b).

Research questions 4a + b address the impact of teachers' competencies on teaching and learning processes. Results from both school levels provide some evidence that teachers' attitudes, motivation, and self-related cognitions are related to classroom activities. The negative relations between quantity of PTI and teachers' attitudes towards strategy use might be an indicator that teachers are aware of the complexity of PTI-material. Therefore, they might believe that they need to teach explicit strategies and be more careful in their use of PTI-material in their classrooms. On the other hand, teachers' attitudes towards strategy use are positively related to students' engagement when teachers show high classroom management skills and provide adaptive explanations; these results strengthen the importance of instructional quality.

Teaching and learning processes were assessed by teacher and student questionnaires, which might have provided biased views on classroom interactions. Therefore, a video-study was conducted in the third funding phase in elementary school, regarding surface- and deep-structure aspects of instructional quality, such as duration and structure of lessons, motivational quality, and cognitive activation. Further insights can be expected from analyzing these videos, informing us further on instructional quality and its relation to teacher competencies and student outcomes.

So far, results from the BiTe project provide some preliminary insights into teachers' competencies in the field of PTI and their relevance for teaching. As discussed earlier, research on teaching and learning with picture-text-material is rare, and the project provides results for both elementary and secondary school. Since working with picture-text-material is relevant for all school forms, the BiTe results can be regarded as good starting points for future research, such as a comparison between elementary and secondary school teachers. With regard to their different educational background and the differing judgment accuracy results, these analyses might further clarify the essentials of teaching and learning with PTI-material at different school levels.

Acknowledgments The preparation of this chapter was supported by grants to Jürgen Baumert (BA 1461/7-1, BA 1461/8-1), Wolfgang Schnotz (SCHN 665/3-1, SCHN 665/5-1) and Nele McElvany (MC 67/7-2), from the German Research Foundation (DFG) in the Priority Program "Competence Models for Assessing Individual Learning Outcomes and Evaluating Educational Processes" (SPP 1293).

References

Ainsworth, S. (2006). DeFT: A conceptual framework for considering learning with multiple representations. *Learning and Instruction, 16*, 183–198. doi:10.1016/j.learninstruc.2006.03.001.

Ayres, P., & Sweller, J. (2005). The split-attention principle in multimedia learning. In R. E. Mayer (Ed.), *The Cambridge handbook of multimedia learning* (pp. 135–146). Cambridge UK: Cambridge University Press.

Blömeke, S. (2011). Forschung zur Lehrerbildung im internationalen Vergleich [Research on teacher education in an international comparison]. In E. Terhart, H. Bennewitz, & M. Rothland (Eds.), *Handbuch der Forschung zum Lehrerberuf* (pp. 345–361). Münster: Waxmann.

Good, T. L. (1979). Teacher effectiveness in the elementary school. *Journal of Teacher Education, 30*(2), 52–64. doi:10.1177/002248717903000220.

Hattie, J., & Anderman, E. M. (2013). *International guide to student achievement. Educational psychology handbook series*. New York: Routledge.

Helmke, A. (2009). *Unterrichtsqualität und Lehrerprofessionalität: Diagnose, Evaluation und Verbesserung des Unterrichts [Quality of instruction and teacher professionalism: Diagnosis, evaluation and improvement of teaching]* (1st ed.). Seelze-Velber: Kallmeyer.

Klassen, R. M., & Chiu, M. M. (2010). Effects on teachers' self-efficacy and job satisfaction: Teacher gender, years of experience, and job stress. *Journal of Educational Psychology, 102*, 741–756.

Klieme, E., & Rakoczy, K. (2008). Empirische Unterrichtsforschung und Fachdidaktik. Outcome-orientierte Messung und Prozessqualität des Unterrichts [Empirical clasroom research and didactics. Outcome-oriented measurement and process quality of teaching]. *Zeitschrift für Pädagogik, 54*, 222–237.

Kunter, M., Klusmann, U., Baumert, J., Richter, D., Voss, T., & Hachfeld, A. (2013). Professional competence of teachers: Effects on instructional quality and student development. *Journal of Educational Psychology, 105*, 805–820. doi:10.1037/a0032583.

Lipowsky, F. (2004). Was macht Fortbildungen für Lehrkräfte erfolgreich [What makes teacher trainings successful]? *Die Deutsche Schule, 96*, 462–479.

Mayer, R. E. (2001). *Multimedia learning*. Cambridge, UK: Cambridge University Press.

McElvany, N., & Willems, A. S. (2012). Videobasiertes Fortbildungsmodul zur Bild-Text-Integration [Video-based teacher training for picture-text-integration]. *Schule NRW: Amtsblatt des Ministeriums für Schule und Weiterbildung, 64*, 68–71.

McElvany, N., Schroeder, S., Hachfeld, A., Baumert, J., Richter, T., Schnotz, W., et al. (2009). Diagnostische Fähigkeiten von Lehrkräften bei der Einschätzung von Schülerleistungen und Aufgabenschwierigkeiten bei Lernmedien mit instruktionalen Bildern [Teachers' diagnostic skills in estimating student achievement and task difficulty for learning material with instructional pictures]. *Zeitschrift für Pädagogische Psychologie, 23*, 223–235.

McElvany, N., Schroeder, S., Baumert, J., Schnotz, W., Horz, H., & Ullrich, M. (2012). Cognitively demanding learning materials with texts and instructional pictures: Teachers' diagnostic skills, pedagogical beliefs and motivation. *European Journal of Psychology of Education, 27*, 403–420. doi:10.1007/s10212-011-0078-1.

Oerke, B., McElvany, N., Ohle, A., Ullrich, M., & Horz, H. (2015). Verbessert sich die diagnostische Urteilsgenauigkeit von Lehrkräften bei längerem Kontakt mit der Klasse [Do teachers' diagnostic skills improve with increasing duration of teacher-student contact]? *Psychologie in Erziehung und Unterricht, 63*(1), 34.

Pajares, M. F. (1992). Teachers' beliefs and educational research: Cleaning up a messy construct. *Review of Educational Research, 62*, 307–332. doi:10.2307/1170741.

Schnotz, W., & Bannert, M. (2003). Construction and interference in learning from multiple representation. *Learning and Instruction, 13*, 141–156. doi:10.1016/S0959-4752(02)00017-8.

Schnotz, W., Wagner, I., Zhao, F., Ullrich, M., Horz, H., McElvany, N., et al. (2017). Development of dynamic usage of strategies for integrating text and picture information in secondary schools. In D. Leutner, J. Fleischer, J. Grünkorn, & E. Klieme (Eds.), *Competence assessment in education: Research, models and instruments* (pp. 303–313). Berlin: Springer.

Schroeder, S., Richter, T., McElvany, N., Hachfeld, A., Baumert, J., Schnotz, W., et al. (2011). Teachers' beliefs, instructional behaviors, and students' engagement in learning from texts with instructional pictures. *Learning and Instruction, 21*, 403–415. doi:10.1016/j.learninstruc.2010.06.001.

Tschannen-Moran, M., Woolfolk Hoy, A., & Hoy, W. K. (1998). Teacher efficacy: Its meaning and measure. *Review of Educational Research, 68*, 202–248. doi:10.3102/00346543068002202.

Vogt, F., & Rogalla, M. (2009). Developing adaptive teaching competency through coaching. *Teaching and Teacher Education, 25*, 1051–1060. doi:10.1016/j.tate.2009.04.002.

Part III
Modeling and Assessing Vocational Competencies and Adult Learning

Chapter 12
Multidimensional Competency Assessments and Structures in VET

Tobias Gschwendtner, Stephan Abele, Thomas Schmidt, and Reinhold Nickolaus

Abstract This chapter clarifies, for the occupations of car mechatronics and electronic technicians: (1) whether the conceptual competency dimensions *action-centered* and *not directly action-centered occupation-specific knowledge* have further sub-dimensions and if so, whether these sub-dimensions change during vocational training; (2) whether the conceptual competency dimensions *occupation-specific problem solving*, *action-centered* and *not directly action-centered occupation-specific knowledge* can be empirically validated; and (3) what can be held responsible for the sub-dimensions and their potential change over time? To answer these questions, we conducted three consecutive projects, embedding three longitudinal ($n = 880$) and two cross-sectional studies ($n = 911$). Confirmatory analyses confirm the conceptual competency structure but also show the existence of up to six sub-dimensions of *not directly action-centered knowledge* and up to three sub-dimensions of *action-centered knowledge*, depending on the occupation and the point of measurement in training. In both occupations, the competency structures rise progressively with time spent in training. Based on certain indications we assume that the multidimensional fluidity, for instance, is caused by increasing diversity and complexity of contents and actions in training, and diversity of learning environments at school and in the workshop. This chapter highlights the main findings, discussing the impact of the test instruments' characteristics on their capability to show dimensionality, and their satisfying psychometric properties.

Keywords Car mechatronics • Electronic technicians • Competency assessment • Competency structures

T. Gschwendtner (✉)
University of Education, Ludwigsburg, Germany
e-mail: gschwendtner@ph-ludwigsburg.de

S. Abele • T. Schmidt • R. Nickolaus
University of Stuttgart, Stuttgart, Germany
e-mail: abele@bwt.uni-stuttgart.de; schmidt@bwt.uni-stuttgart.de;
nickolaus@bwt.uni-stuttgart.de

D. Leutner et al. (eds.), *Competence Assessment in Education*, Methodology of Educational Measurement and Assessment, DOI 10.1007/978-3-319-50030-0_12

12.1 Introduction

This contribution summarizes the main theoretical issues, research questions, hypotheses and findings of three consecutive DFG projects that mostly focus on designing competency assessments, measuring professional competency and evaluating the interaction of the competency assessments´ characteristics and measurement outcomes (e.g., psychometric properties, competency structures and levels) within the field of Vocational Education and Training (VET); more precisely, with apprenticeships in car mechatronics and electronic technicians. In VET, the characteristics of professional competency assessments can vary not only as a function of the occupation under consideration and, with it, occupation-specific contents and actions, but also with the author's definition or theory of professional competency and its operationalization.

Various plausible cognitive and noncognitive sub-dimensions of professional competency (e.g., occupation-specific knowledge, occupation-specific problem solving (OPS), occupation-specific literacy and numeracy, occupational identity, metacognition, motivation, creativity) are described in the existing literature on the subject. Simplifying the various specific approaches into a dichotomy, sub-dimensions are assessed and modeled either holistically and inclusively (cf. Rauner et al. 2009) or in a more psychologically focused, rather reductionist perspective: assessed and modeled separately, while statistically validating the original definition/theory (cf. Nickolaus et al. 2013).

The characteristics of the assessments are most likely also influenced by the modality (and quality)—besides objective scientific procedures—of the construct's operationalization. Nickolaus et al. (2009) pointed out, that professional competency can be operationalized, for example, by paper-pencil tests, real-life or computer-simulated work samples, work life observations or self-assessments. In this regard, medial presentation (real life vs. simulation), or the gap between test content, test contextualization and real work life can result in differential validity of the tests or in capturing more facets of a multidimensional construct. Furthermore, different item formats of paper-pencil tests may also influence the item-difficulty descriptors, and therefore the descriptions of the competency-levels.

Having made these preliminary statements, we now turn to: (1) theoretical issues and operationalization, (2) research questions, (3) the research design of the three conducted studies, (4) findings and (5) a final summary and discussion.

12.2 Theoretical Issues and Operationalization

The core occupational constructs we examined in our studies, derived from empirical and theoretical work (cf. Achtenhagen and Winther 2009; Seeber and Lehmann 2011; Rosendahl and Straka 2011; Abele 2014), were (1) occupation-specific knowledge and (2) the application of this specific knowledge in the context of an occupation-specific action. In this regard, knowledge can be seen as the construct that serves, amongst others (e.g., motivation), more or less as a facilitator of coping with occupation-specific actions in a competent manner. In car mechatronics, the relevant occupation-specific actions are: trouble-shooting, repair, standard car service and installation of accessories (cf. Becker 2009), where trouble-shooting the cause of a malfunction, together with subsequently repairing it, can be labeled as problem solving. On the basis of Nickolaus et al. (2009) the primarily cognitive process of trouble-shooting can be seen as the success-critical component, in comparison with the primarily psychomotor activity of repairing. As a conclusion, we solely addressed the action of trouble-shooting in our studies concerning the second point mentioned above.

Using the CLARION model (cf. Sun 2002; Abele 2014), we conceptually differentiated occupation-specific knowledge according to its relationship to occupation-specific actions.[1] In this sense, we distinguished between two knowledge dimensions: action-centered occupation-specific knowledge (AK), and not directly action-centered occupation-specific knowledge (NAK). Both knowledge dimensions can be further differentiated conceptually by different means: for example, different contents and actions within different occupations, increasing complexity and diversity of actions and contents during time in training, or specific item content and/or item design, such as items covering declarative/procedural knowledge, mathematical knowledge, content links to secondary school curricula, or incorporating workshop-related or school-related knowledge.

We assume AK to be inherent when people are involved in occupation-specific actions. We refer to involvement when people perform an action themselves or when people closely observe an action performed by somebody else. AK can be identified by asking people questions related to the action, together with occupation-specific action involvement. These questions should cover the nature of an action by questioning: (1) the knowledge of relevant prospective action plans and (2) the knowledge of success-critical steps in the line of action (e.g., evaluating actions according to standards of craftsmanlike behavior and craftsmanlike results) and (3) the technological background knowledge underlying the action, alongside their involvement in an occupation-specific action.

In order to assess the AK of standard car service, we developed a computer-based assessment architecture. This assessment architecture demonstrates videos to the test taker that contain occupation-specific actions: more precisely, oil and tire changes, and checks of engine cooling and brake systems. These actions were authentically recorded in a real workshop, using real tools and cars, and covering the complete line of action, beginning with reading the work assignment, then executing the relevant action and signing the work assignment when the task is com-

[1] The occupation-specific actions in our studies covered trouble-shooting (both electronic technicians and car mechatronics), repair (car mechatronics) and standard car service (car mechatronics).

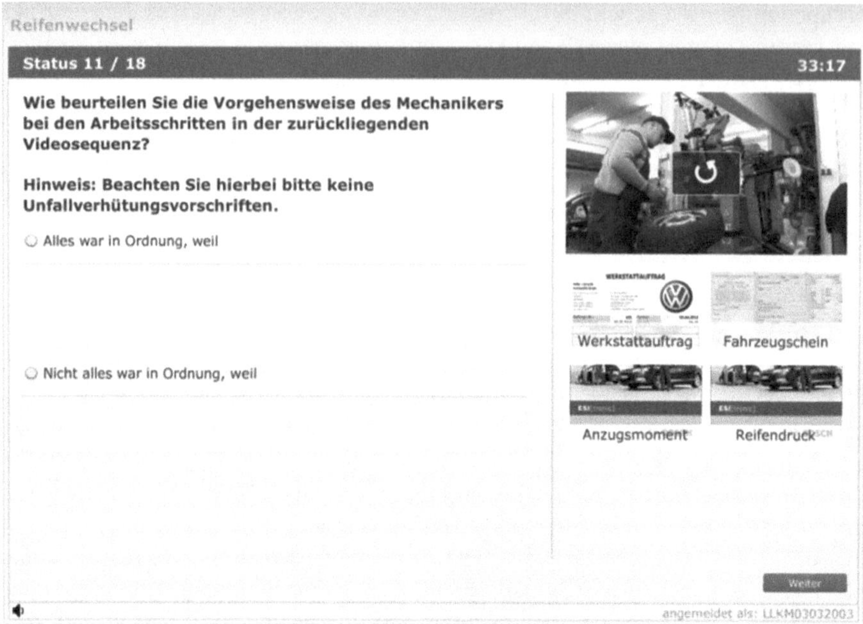

Fig. 12.1 Computer-based assessment architecture to assess AK

pleted. The videos show correct and incorrect actions[2] and are automatically stopped at default time points, giving room to pose action-centered questions (containing all three above-mentioned aspects of an action). Figure 12.1 shows the moment at which the test taker should retrospectively evaluate the quality of the success-critical steps of the line of action that was shown in the video prior to the question being put.

When the test taker gets the question, he is, by clicking on the specific pictures, allowed to re-watch the relevant scenes (top right corner in Fig. 12.1) plus use additional information as found in reality (e.g., information from the vehicle registration certificate or a computer expert system; to the right of center in Fig. 12.1), prior to answering the specific question. The test time is restricted not on the basis of the number of items, but on the basis of the complete actions (e.g., 35 min for the videos and questions about the oil change). The test time remaining and the question number relative to total items are shown to the test takers in an information bar (Fig. 12.1 at the top).

The AK of trouble-shooting was also assessed using a computer-based assessment architecture (below).

[2]Incorrect actions can be, for instance, forgetting to reassemble parts that were initially removed, tightening screws with the wrong tightening torque or pouring the wrong ratios or amounts of liquids into the car.

In contrast to AK, NAK has no direct link to involvement in occupation-specific actions. This type of knowledge can either be isolated technological facts and relationships that can be questioned with or without a context of action, or it can be visualized via items that try to capture the above-mentioned aspects of the nature of occupation-specific actions through written language, figures and graphics, that are translators of actions but not the action per se. In our studies, test instruments measuring NAK were mostly represented through an array of items covering a multitude of occupation-specific contents and actions. The use of this sort of assessment approach, in comparison to action-centered approaches or the action itself, is mainly driven by the idea that it is less costly, as there is no need for complex involvement links via computer-based architectures, and because eventually it does give a general overview of one's knowledge in a domain.

As stated above, OPS was operationalized solely as trouble-shooting. Trouble-shooting was assessed using either a computer-based assessment architecture or—in the case of a rather narrow curriculum in the first year of training—paper-pencil tests (for actions that are in reality also based on that format). The computer-based assessment architectures can be viewed in Gschwendtner et al. (2007) and Nickolaus et al. (2011) for the electronic technicians, and in Nickolaus et al. (2009) and Abele et al. (2014) for the car mechatronics. The paper-pencil tests are described in greater detail in Gschwendtner et al. (2010).

Whether, and to what extent, the conceptual perspective on (sub-) dimensionality, which was unfolded in this section, can empirically be confirmed, and what impact the point in time of training has on the potential change of (sub-) dimensionality are questions fundamental to establishing the validity of diagnostics within different occupations and training period points. This is addressed further on.

12.3 Research Questions

The following research questions cover all three consecutive projects and refer to both occupations, of car mechatronics and electronic technicians. The various hypotheses that are related to these questions are contextually embedded in the sections below. The research questions are *expressis verbis*:

1. Do the conceptual competency dimensions *not directly action-centered occupation-specific knowledge (NAK)* and *action-centered occupation-specific knowledge (AK)* have further sub-dimensions, and do the sub-dimensions, assuming their existence, change during vocational training?
2. Can the conceptual competency dimensions *occupation-specific problem solving (OPS)*, *NAK* and *AK* be empirically validated?
3. What can account for the sub-dimensions and their potential change over time?

It is important to note that the projects deal with many more issues, such as which endogenous variables explain the development of the occupation-specific competencies (cf. Nickolaus et al. 2012), and what competency levels can be derived from an item analysis (cf. Nickolaus et al. 2011).

12.4 Research Design

To answer these research questions, three consecutive studies were conducted in the state of Baden-Württemberg in Germany. The first research question was addressed using the partly cross-sectional and partly longitudinal data of all three studies. The cross-sectional component provided a basis for dimensional analyses, and the longitudinal component for analyses of dimensional change over time. The second research question was related to the first, with regard to a dimensional analysis, and used the cross-sectional data. The third research question was a rather interpretative amalgam of the findings of all three projects. Although all three studies can be arranged to answer these research questions, the measured variables differ, in fact, in number and format (e.g., item format) over the studies. In total, the measured variables were: NAK, AK, OPS, general mental ability (CFT 3 resp. CFT 20-R; cf. Weiß 1999; Weiß 2006) and dynamic problem solving (MicroDYN approach, cf. Greiff and Funke 2010). The test instruments assessing the studies´ core occupational constructs, which are partly described above, were developed in close cooperation with teachers, trainers and members of examination boards.

The research designs of the three studies are described in the following passages.

Study 1 (DFG Ni 606/3-1) was undertaken at the beginning of 2006 and ended in 2008. This study consisted of $N = 489$ apprentices attending the first year of 3.5-year vocational training course. Out of these 489 apprentices $n = 203$ attended the occupational track of electronic technicians (nine classes within six different schools) and $n = 286$ attended the occupational track of car mechatronics (11 classes within three schools). Two points of measurement (PoM) were realized: one at the beginning (1st PoM) and one at the end (2nd PoM) of the first-year's training.[3] The measured variables were NAK (1st and 2nd PoM) and OPS (2nd PoM).

Study 2 was executed between 2009 and 2011 and consisted of $N = 814$ apprentices attending the end of the third year of vocational training. The study was split into a longitudinal and a cross-sectional setting. The longitudinal setting consisted of a sample of $n = 77$ car mechatronics (nine classes) and $n = 96$ electronic technicians (eight classes). The longitudinal sample was recruited from those apprentices of Study 1 that were still in training at the time of assessment. The cross-sectional setting consisted of $n = 335$ car mechatronics (14 classes) and $n = 306$ electronic technicians (11 classes). One PoM for each setting was implemented in Study 2. The measured variables in the longitudinal sample (in addition to those already measured in Study 1) were NAK and OPS. The measured variables in the cross-sectional setting were NAK, OPS, dynamic problem solving and general mental ability.

[3] Effectively, five POM were implemented. To give the picture more clearly, the original five POM were condensed to two POM for this contribution, without simplifying the research design significantly.

Study 3 was conducted between 2011 and 2013. The study comprised only apprentices of the car mechatronics vocational track: in sum, $N = 488$. The study consisted also of a longitudinal ($n = 218$ apprentices, 12 classes, 8 schools) and a cross-sectional sample ($n = 270$ apprentices, 14 classes, 11 schools). The longitudinal sample was composed of apprentices attending the second year of training, while the cross-sectional sample was composed of apprentices attending the end of the third year of training. The study implemented one PoM in the cross-sectional setting and two POM in the longitudinal setting. In the latter, one PoM was located at the beginning and one at the end of the second year's training. The assessments for both samples contained tests measuring NAK, AK and OPS.

All data were collected within complete classes by members of the research staff only.

12.5 Hypotheses and Results

With regard to the first research question, we will start by looking at the empirical structures and their possible shift over time within NAK and successively integrate the other knowledge construct and research questions as well. Information about the third research question will be reported integratively.

12.5.1 Research Question 1: Competency Structures Within the Construct of Not Directly Action-Centered Occupation-Specific Knowledge: Dimensionality and Its Development

Starting in the first year of training in both occupations, we looked at two POM, one at the beginning and one at the end. The same regimen was set in the second year. In the third year only one PoM, at the year's end, was implemented.

We firstly deduced possible knowledge dimensions from different theoretical perspectives. Then we conducted confirmatory analyses (CA; confirmatory factor analysis, structure equation models, or multidimensional between-item Rasch models) and compared the deviances between competing models either with the Chi-square statistics and information criteria, or, depending on the study, with the model fit indices plus the latent correlations, to decide on dimensionality.

Competency Structures in the First Year of Training For the first year of training[4] (and partly more specifically at the first PoM) we hypothesized: (1) Items having content links to secondary school curricula, in comparison to items that are based on totally new occupational knowledge, can be solved with supplementary cognitive resources (e.g., mathematical knowledge). Therefore, these two different types of items are better represented by two dimensions rather than just one single dimension. (2) Items demanding declarative rather than procedural knowledge are solved on the basis of different cognitive resources (cf. Fortmüller 1996) and are better represented by a two-dimensional model. (3) Items stressing different technological macro contents rely on interindividual and intraindividual different learning experiences (both prior to and in the VET system) and are therefore dimensionally discriminable. The hypotheses each assume that a two-dimensional model fits the data better than a one-dimensional reference model. These assumptions were empirically tested. The CA showed that the acceptance of a one-dimensional model fitted the data significantly better at the second PoM than any other, potentially competing multidimensional model for both occupations (cf. Gschwendtner et al. 2010; see also the bibliographical reference for scale statistics). With regard to item content, the results imply that items having mathematical content cannot be discriminated against items that do not have mathematical content. The same circumstance accounts for items demanding either declarative knowledge or procedural knowledge, and for items stressing either mechanical or electrotechnical knowledge. On the other hand (car mechatronics), a two-dimensional model at the 1st PoM, consisting of different technological macro contents (mechanical and electrotechnical contents), was more convenient (ibid.). Interpreting the data, it is possible that interindividual different prior learning experiences (e.g., hobbies) were reflected in the two-dimensional solution at the first PoM and that the binding curricula streamlined interindividual and intraindividual cognitions at the second PoM in respect thereof (ibid.).[5]

---

[4] The test material at both POM in the first year of training was essentially identical, and oriented to the VET curricula for this first year. The step from secondary school to the VET system represents a curricular gap between the school systems for the pupils, whereby the curricula are primarily linked only by individual interests and their own learning experiences on the one hand, and by points of content (for the occupations of interest in this contribution) through science (e.g., electrotechnical phenomena) and mathematics on the other hand, which are often implicitly or explicitly embedded in technological contexts. This assessment constellation in the first year of training (1) made possible a valid knowledge test at the end of the first year (weaker at the beginning of the first year, in comparison) and (2) gave first theoretical cues for the probable dimensionality of the tests.

[5] The first year of training must be differentiated from the following years as it is the year where the "*Grundbildung*" takes place, which places different jobs under one occupational umbrella. In this year, the apprentices spend the vast bulk of their time at school (school classroom and school workshop). After that time, the situation is reversed, and the apprentices are socialized in very heterogeneous workshops. In this sense, learning in the first year of training takes place in a very controlled fashion, where the aim of education is to provide the apprentices with a broad array of basic occupational competencies. "Streamlining" should be understood in this context.

Competency Structures in the Second Year of Training The hypothesis for the beginning of the second year of training was that the competency structure of the end of the first year of training would stay constant (note however: the sample and the test instrument were changed), since learning opportunities and the time between the end of the first and the beginning of the second year (1.5 months of school holidays) were too limited. This hypothesis was tested only in the occupation of car mechatronics. We developed a test consisting of 71 items, mainly in a multiple choice format, that could be conceptually related to six dimensions. The dimensions can be distinguished through different technological contents and actions and are, namely: (1) motor; (2) engine management system; (3) lighting/energy supply/starter system; (4) transmission; (5) undercarriage and (6) standard car service.[6] To test the hypothesis (assuming a one-dimensional model is best to model the data), Schmidt et al. (2014) compared the one-dimensional model to different and (besides the hypothesis) also plausible multidimensional models. The competing multidimensional models were: (1) a content-driven five-dimensional model consisting of the above-mentioned conceptual dimensions (except for transmission) as a basis for all other multidimensional models; (2) a three-dimensional model based on the idea that some of the distinguished conceptual dimensions above can be aggregated at the level of technological macro structures (similar to Study 1: namely mechanical and electrotechnical contents) on the one hand. On the other hand, the authors believed that these structures can be separated from a workshop dimension.[7] The idea of a single workshop dimension arose (1) from the observation that apprentices are mostly confronted with these contents and actions at that specific time of training in the workshop and (2) that these workshop-related contents and actions may correlate with specific proficiencies. (3) Another multidimensional model was a content-driven and aggregated two-dimensional model negating the possibility of a specific workshop influence on dimensionality. The two dimensions were mechanical knowledge (consisting of motor, undercarriage and standard car service) and electrotechnical knowledge (consisting of the engine management system and lighting/energy supply/starter system). (4) The last multidimensional model was a two-dimensional model that accentuates the idea of a workshop dimension (consisting of undercarriage and standard car service) and negates the idea of technological macro contents by condensing the former two dimensions into one (consisting of motor, engine management system and lighting/energy supply/starter system).

Five separate CAs (one for each multidimensional setting and one for the one-dimensional reference model) were calculated. The deviances between these models were then compared using, besides the chi-square statistics, mainly the

[6] The test was basically identical at the two POM in the second year of training, and also the same for one of two studies focused on the end of the third year of training (further below). It is important to state that for curricular validity, the transmission dimension was only considered for analyses of the third year's data.

[7] The three dimensions were (1) mechanical knowledge (identical to the former motor dimension), (2) electrotechnical knowledge (identical to the former dimensions of engine management system and lighting/energy supply/starter system) and (3) workshop-related knowledge (identical to the former dimensions of undercarriage and standard car service).

information criteria AIC (Akaike information criterion), cAIC (conditional Akaike information criterion) and BIC (Bayesian information criterion) to decide on the most favorable model. Since all information criteria were numerically in favor of the last-described two-dimensional model (4), the hypothesis was rejected (cf. Schmidt et al. 2014), although in this result, the latent correlations between the two dimensions were relatively high (r = .89), which could eventually justify a one-dimensional solution (see Artelt and Schlagmüller 2004) also. The reliabilities of the two dimensions were in a relatively good range (EAP/PV = .81 and .84; WLE = .70 and.79; n_{items} = 24 and 30; ibid.).

Looking at the results more closely, although there was a discrepancy between the results at the PoM at the end of the first year of training (one-dimensional solution) and at the PoM at the beginning of the second year (more likely a two-dimensional solution), there was also a core similarity: At both POM, models consisting of dimensions that should represent technological macro contents (as was convenient at the beginning of the first year of training) were empirically denied and the items were forced to be allocated to one single dimension. The reason why a two-dimensional solution at the beginning of the second year seemed possible, can likely be seen in the vastly extended test (content-wise) in comparison to the first year test, with the potential to show more dimensionality, provided that there was something that could be measured. It can therefore be hypothesized that if the sample at the end of the first year of training had been assessed with the test materials of the second year, a similar two-dimensional structure could have also appeared.

For the end of the second and third year of training we mainly hypothesized: Increasing complexity and diversity (gradually more and different occupation-specific technological contents and actions plus different occupational realities and learning potentiality, primarily at workshop level but also at school level) over time leads to a progressive cognitive dimensional differentiation process that can be documented if the test actually represents the increasingly demanding contents and actions. As a result of this, a multidimensional solution should fit the data better than a one-dimensional one.

The methodical arrangement for analyses at the end of the second year resembles that of the beginning of the second year. The results showed that (the same situation as at the beginning of the second year) all information criteria numerically preferred the same two-dimensional model. Interestingly enough, the latent correlations between the two dimensions were even higher (r = .94). Schmidt et al. (2014) assumed that a one-dimensional solution was possible as well. Nevertheless, the authors argued for the two-dimensional solution. Having said that, the hypothesis that assumes rising dimensionality over time had to be rejected for the time interval from beginning to the end of the second year. The reliabilities of the two dimensions were in the same range as at the beginning of the second year (EAP/PV = .83 and .85; WLE = .71 and .78; n_{items} = 26 and 24) (ibid.).

Competency Structures in the Third Year of Training At the end of the third year of training, we constructed tests of three conceptual sub-dimensions for electronic technicians: (1) traditional electrical installation technology, (2) modern electrical installation technology and control engineering, (3) electrotechnical groundwork and six conceptual sub-dimensions for car mechatronics: the 5 dimensions mentioned above, plus the dimension of transmission (cf. Gschwendtner 2011; Nickolaus et al. 2011). The hypothesis assuming increasing dimensionality over time was empirically tested. For both occupations, the analyses showed that the assumption of a multidimensional model fits the data better than the competing one-dimensional model. Therefore, the hypothesis can be accepted for the time interval from the end of the second year to the end of the third year of training.

More precisely, a CA for the electronic technician data showed relatively low latent correlations between the three conceptual sub-dimensions, varying between $r = .24$ and $r = .57$ (Nickolaus et al. 2011, p. 86). Furthermore, the analysis showed that all three sub-dimensions can be represented psychometrically satisfyingly by a single latent factor (NAK). The reliabilities (EAP/PV) of the dimensions were mainly good (electrotechnical groundwork =.74 [6 items]; modern electrical installation technology and control engineering =.78 [14 items]) but also offered scope for improvement (traditional electrical installation technology =.54 [8 items]) (ibid.).

For the car mechatronics we conducted two studies to test the hypothesis assuming increasing dimensionality over time (Studies 2 and 3; Study 3 being a replication study of Study 2 with an altered test instrument).[8] The first study showed that the car mechatronics data was significantly better explained through either a five- or six-dimensional model in comparison to a one-dimensional model (cf. Gschwendtner 2011, p. 64 *et seq.*).[9] The latent correlations between the conceptual dimensions were higher (r between .32 and .87) than those in the electronic technician sample but low enough to further justify the CA results on the level reported above (ibid.). Abele et al. (2012) additionally showed that, by using a structural equation model, five dimensions (excluding transmission) represented a single latent factor (NAK) in a psychometrically satisfying fashion. The reliabilities (EAP/PV) of the dimensions were relatively weak: motor = .49 (30 items), engine management system = .44 (7 items), lighting/energy supply/starter system = .47 (12 items), transmission =.31 (4 items), undercarriage =.43 (7 items) and standard car service =.44 (16 items; cf. Gschwendtner 2011, p. 63). We interpret the relatively weak reliabilities as being caused by the sparse number of items per dimension, also in part by the low item discrimination (item load) and the problems in realizing high evaluation objectivity standards by coding the pupils´ answers in the frequently used open ended item formats. For the replication study (Study 3), we modified the test instrument by

[8] Study 3 used the same test instrument plus the items from the dimension transmission, which by this time was curricular-valid, in the second year of training.

[9] In this study we used three test booklets in a multi-matrix design. The results of the analyses differed between the test booklets used and oscillated between a five- and a six-dimensional model, depending on the booklet. The difference between the two models was that the five-dimensional model packed the two highest-correlated dimensions (and with regard to the electric/electronic content the most associated ones) into one single dimension. The two condensed dimensions were engine management system and lighting/energy supply/starter system (latent $r = .87$).

altering the items of Study 2 and generating more items per dimension, almost all items being in the multiple choice format.[10]

The replication study aimed to validate the results of Study 2 with a different sample of persons and items on the one hand, and to find out whether the relatively weak reliabilities could be increased with the modified test instrument, on the other. The methodical arrangement for the analyses was basically the same: assuming the existence of the identically tailored five or six dimensions in comparison to a one-dimensional reference model, plus the three- and the two-dimensional models (which have already been discussed in the analyses of the second year of training). In addition to this analysis structure, various CA were calculated and compared, in the same fashion as above. The authors identified two alternately preferred models, these being the three- or five-dimensional models (cf. Schmidt et al. 2014). The reliabilities of the dimensions in the three-dimensional model (EAP/PV = .79 and .85; WLE = .67 and .76) were largely good. The reliabilities of the dimensions in the five-dimensional model (EAP/PV = .67–.85; WLE = .40–.66) were considerably weaker for the fewer items per dimension (ibid.).

The data of the replication study supports the assumption that a progressive cognitive dimensional differentiation process can be documented over time.[11] Concerning the replication of the competency structure of Study 2, the fact that a multidimensional rather than a one-dimensional model exists can be replicated on the one hand, but accurate information on the number and underlying structure of the dimensions cannot be furnished, on the other hand. The improvements have clearly reduced the reliability problems of Study 2.

12.5.2 Research Question 1: Competency Structures Within the Construct of Action-Centered Occupation-Specific Knowledge: Dimensionality and Its Development

In this section, we describe and discuss the findings on the dimensionality of AK and its development. In consideration of dimensionality, we checked whether the advertised three conceptual components of action, ([1] knowledge of relevant prospective action plans, [2] knowledge of success-critical steps in the line of action and [3] technological background knowledge underlying the action) also appear to be present empirically. We analyzed this at two POM in the second year of training and at one PoM in the third year of training. Doing this in a chronological way,

[10] The response options of the multiple choice items of the altered items were generated using the most frequently used answers to the open ended items of Study 2.

[11] Both Schmidt et al. (2014) and Gschwendtner (2011) assumed that, besides specific class composition effects on the level of classes, the de facto realized curricula varies substantially over the time of apprenticeship by cross referencing substantial class-specific differences between the competency dimensions.

Table 12.1 Latent correlations of the three conceptual components of action at PoM[a]

	PoM 1		PoM 2		PoM 3	
	Action steps	Background	Action steps	Background	Action steps	Background
Action plans	.93	.94	.79	.81	.58	.71
Action steps		.92		.71		.73

PoM 1: point of measurement at the beginning of the second year of training, *PoM 2* point of measurement at the end of the second year of training, *PoM 3* point of measurement at the end of the third year of training. *Action plans*: knowledge of relevant prospective action plans, *action steps*, knowledge of success-critical steps in the line of action, *background*, technological background knowledge underlying the action
[a]cf. Schmidt et al. (2014)

we could also illustrate and try to theoretically explain possible dimensional development.[12] According to Ackerman's three-phase-theory and the CLARION model (cf. Ackerman 1992; Abele 2014), skill acquisition at an early stage (cognitive phase) is accompanied by a relatively high correlation[13] between the performance of specific actions and specific abilities.[14] This association falls in the process to the point of automaticity.[15]

We hypothesized that the correlations between standard car service actions and abilities that are directly or not directly associated with the actions fall with the progressive automaticity of the skills and with the time in training, respectively.

To simplify the picture somewhat, we reset our methodical arrangement for the analysis of dimensionality and its development solely by looking at the latent correlations, using the reference of Artelt and Schlagmüller (2004) to judge dimensionality.

Table 12.1 shows the latent correlations of the three conceptual components of action at all PoM (cf. Schmidt et al. 2014). According to the numerical levels of all intercorrelations on PoM 1 ($r \geq .92$), a single dimension is most likely to be assumed

[12] At this point, our analyses were solely based on two out of six assessed videos respectively action situations, namely oil and tire changes.

[13] Specific abilities in the context of our studies can be AK and/or NAK. The reason for the high association of these factors can be seen in the fact that, in order to perform a novel action as well as possible, you have to consciously reflect the action and activate appropriate knowledge that is directly or indirectly associated with the action.

[14] We assumed that our computer-based assessment architecture assessing AK was in itself a valid indicator of these specific actions. We operationalized specific abilities as being NAK. Another way to operationalize the two constructs of Ackerman's theory works by redefining the measured construct of AK: We assumed that the first two components of action are even closer to action than the third component of action. We further assumed that the first two components of action can be interpreted as specific actions by themselves and that the third component of action can be interpreted as specific abilities.

[15] Once automaticity is achieved, it is largely independent of consciousness resp. Cognition. We assumed that the standard car service actions (which were used to construct the test) are skills that become automatic gradually during the apprenticeship.

as adequate to describe the data at PoM 1. In contrast, the data at the other two PoM seem to show a progressively increasing multidimensionality over time, as the numerical levels of intercorrelations shrink almost consistently (and statistically significantly) over time. The data of Table 12.1 also shows, as the hypothesis assumed, that with progressive automaticity (time in training) the correlations between technological background knowledge and both facets of AK (knowledge of relevant prospective action plans and knowledge of success-critical steps in the line of action) decrease.[16]

Concerning dimensional development, the same picture appeared when AK as one single dimension[17] consisting of the two facets of knowledge, of relevant prospective action plans and knowledge of success-critical steps in the line of action was correlated with NAK at all PoM. The latent correlations decrease, beginning at PoM 1 (at the beginning of the second year: $r = .85$), again at PoM 2 (at the end of the second year: $r = .72$) and finally at PoM 3 (at the end of the third year: $r = .61$; ibid.). Following these two analyses, the hypothesis can be accepted.

12.5.3 Preliminary Analysis for Research Question 2: Construct of Occupation-Specific Problem Solving: Validity and Reliability

The assessment of OPS suffers not infrequently from: (1) a lack either of construct validity, of reliability, or both together (cf. Nickolaus et al. 2013), (2) a lack of analysis of internal structures and (3) of a deeper understanding of the process of problem solving actions (examples can be viewed in e.g., Gschwendtner et al. 2007; Achtenhagen and Winther 2009; Gschwendtner et al. 2009; Nickolaus et al. 2011; Abele et al. 2012).

Recent developments, mainly in the field of car mechatronics, have improved the situation considerably. We will describe these developments in this section.[18]

In the field of car mechatronics, we developed and validated (criterion-related) a computer-based assessment architecture that serves as the latest assessment tool today. By comparing the trouble-shooting of 257 apprentices on the computer and with a real car, we found that the computer-based assessment had a high validity measured by reality: trouble-shooting within the two different contexts was highly associated (latent $r = .94$; CA identified a one-dimensional solution as beneficial, in

[16] The reliabilities of the components of action are not satisfactory as yet; however, in the case of scaling the data at all PoM on a single dimension, the reliability becomes largely acceptable (EAP/PV = .59–.71; WLE =. 57–.72).

[17] Taking the one-dimensional solution was a rather pragmatic decision to reduce complexity. This does not totally reflect the empirical reality, as illustrated above.

[18] The paper-pencil based (car mechatronics) and the computer-based (electronic technicians) assessments will not be described and discussed in this chapter. We refer to Gschwendtner et al. (2010) for more insight.

comparison to a two-dimensional model); the two different contexts are therefore interchangeable (cf. Gschwendtner et al. 2009; Nickolaus et al. 2009).[19] The problems of this measurement architecture lay primarily in the overlong test time required to get sufficent information on the test takers, since test time is naturally a sparse asset: each complex problem (item) takes 30 min test time. The apprentices in the validity study had to solve eight complex problems altogether, within four hours. Sadly, the reliability was barely adequate (EAP/PV = .65).

Study 2 used an altered assessment platform[20] but reduced the test time to four complex problems per test taker. The reliability then fell to EAP/PV = .55 (Abele et al. 2012).[21] The approach to solving the test time/reliability problem was characterized through steps of development. The core objective was to find additional items (to the complex problems) that were short in time and that functioned psychometrically similarly to the complex problems (both in one dimension), thereby increase the total number of items and finally solving the reliability problem.[22]

The first approach was to create paper-pencil items that used visual media of the assessment platform and questioned the knowledge underlying the process of trouble-shooting. The items were given to the test takers prior to the complex problems, without them having a direct problem involvement. This approach led to somewhat insufficient results, because the latent correlations between the additional items and the complex problems were just .76 and .80 respectively, depending on the subsample in the validity study (cf. Gschwendtner et al. 2009). Rather than having assessed trouble-shooting with these items, we had probably assessed NAK. However, Nickolaus et al. (2011) presented a CA that showed an integration (with good model fit indices) of seven additional items to eight complex problems with the data of the electronic technicians, but reported a gain of just .08 points in the EAP/PV scale through integration.

The second approach was to shorten the complex problems; this can however induce validity problems (making the complex reality artificially less complex). This approach allowed some new complex items to be generated (15–25 min test time) by carefully looking at item parts that could be removed without losing the context. The third approach (cf. Abele et al. 2014) was to create items that were to be assessed in the same computer-based assessment architecture as the complex problems but that only addressed parts of a holistic trouble-shooting process, in respect of the parts of that competency underlying this process. In order to create items that captured success-critical steps in such a process, and items with variable

[19] The assessment architecture for the electronic technicians has just recently been validated: the results are in preparation.

[20] The complex problems were extended to 13 and the assessment platform was partly redesigned.

[21] The assessment platform used in the study to assess occupation-specific problem solving in the field of electronics could realize similar reliabilities (EAP/PV = .54), using eight complex problems (Nickolaus et al. 2011).

[22] The idea of using a test takers's log, in which we asked them to meticulously note their steps in trouble-shooting was not useful, in the sense that these steps could be modeled using a partial credit model.

difficulties at once, we used a rational reconstruction of a trouble-shooting process (cf. Abele et al. 2014) and a proficiency scale developed by Nickolaus et al. (2012) to develop seven short partial competency items (approx. 4.5 min per item test time). In order to test this set-up, $n = 275$ apprentices at the end of the third year of training were assessed (cf. Abele et al. 2014). Each test taker had to solve five of a total of six complex problems (youden-square-design) and seven short partial competency items.

Dimensionality was tested by comparing the goodness of fit indices and factor loadings of a two-dimensional model separating the items according to the upper condition, and a one-dimensional model consisting of all 13 items. The analyses showed that the short partial competency items can well be used to assess the same construct as complex problems (cf. Abele et al. 2014). There were obvious gains in reliability if the complex problems were scaled additionally using the short partial competency items: only the complex problems (SEM-reliability = .62), only the short partial competency items (SEM-reliability = .65) and the complex problems plus the short partial competency items (SEM-reliability = .75) (ibid.).

It is important to note that the short partial competency items were assessed after the test takers had solved all the complex problems. While this approach has potential to make some measurement process routine with the use of the computer-based assessment platform once the short partial competency items are arrived at, there is also a potential to discourage test-takers (first the complex tasks and afterwards the less complex tasks). Further research must show whether different short partial competency item placements—to the extent that they are compatible with the content and the test logic in its entirety—within the test regimen, have an effect on dimensionality and reliability.

12.5.4 Research Question 2: Competency Structures Between Different Constructs

In this section we briefly initiate the discussion of two questions: (1) are the competencies presented in detail in this contribution (NAK, AK and OPS) distinct dimensions? We mainly used the intercorrelations between the constructs to highlight some background aspects.[23] (2) Are the—from the theoretical perspective of the underlying mental processes—related constructs dynamic problem solving (cf. Greiff and Funke 2010) and general mental abilities more closely related to OPS than to occupation-specific knowledge?

Concerning the first question, the findings presented in Sect. 12.5.2 showed that NAK and AK, besides being clearly associated, seem to represent different constructs, and that this is true independent of the time in training. Furthermore, NAK and OPS are relatively highly associated with each other, but seem also to represent

[23] Once again, we relied on the references given by Artelt and Schlagmüller (2004, p. 171).

two different constructs, and, this being true, both are independent of the time in training and occupation. At the end of the first year of training Gschwendtner et al. (2010) reported a latent correlation of $r = .76$ (car mechatronics); Schmidt et al. (2014) reported latent correlations of $r = .81$ (car mechatronics: end of second year of training) and $r = .83$ (car mechatronics: end of the third year of training); Nickolaus et al. (2011) even reported a latent correlation of $r = .86$ (electronic technicians). As the results in Sect. 12.5.3 show, paper-pencil tests closely related to the problem tasks seem also to represent a construct other than problem solving—more precisely, presumably, the construct of NAK. In sum, the reported results can approve the first question, from a correlational point of view.[24] Further analyses integrating all occupational competencies in structural equation models should validate the findings more profoundly, for example, by additionally questioning if a single factor (which could be interpreted as a professional competency) explains the occupational dimensions adequately.

Concerning the second question, Abele et al. (2012) have shown that dynamic problem solving and general mental abilities are moderately associated with each other (car mechatronics: $r = .45$; electronic technicians: $r = .54$) and that the impact of these two constructs on OPS clearly are minor (only indirect effects in structure equation models) in comparison to the direct and prominent impact of NAK on OPS. The second question also can be confirmed.

12.6 Summary and Final Discussion

This chapter has demonstrated that professional competency is empirically a highly differentiated construct. The construct holds horizontal and vertical differentiation. On a *superordinate level*, knowledge and action can be differentiated, as the dimensional distinctness of different aspects of occupation-specific knowledge and trouble-shooting documents. On a *second level*, occupation-specific knowledge can be separated empirically into not directly action-centered knowledge and action-centered knowledge, in all likelihood the degree of involvement (mediated by the assessment format) in an occupation-specific action primarily making the difference. Although theoretical reconstructions of problem solving processes adapted to occupational actions do exist (cf. Abele et al. 2014), empirical data proving the internal structure of occupation-specific problem solving on a *second level* are sparse. More research has to follow on this issue. On a *third level*, both not directly action-centered occupation-specific knowledge and action-centered occupation-specific knowledge show further empirical differentiation, depending on the time in training and (for the former knowledge) the selected occupation. Time in training implies several moments. On the one hand, progressive intrapersonal diversity (contents and actions are getting more and more complex and diverse) and interpersonal

[24] The results for the relationship between the constructs of NAK and occupation-specific problem solving will be reported in another publication.

diversity (the learning environment workshops differentiate vastly in their learning potentiality and the learning environment classroom differentiates in consideration of the curriculum implemented) most likely causes progressive dimensional differentiation over time in training. The time of training is, in all probability, in many (not all) contents and actions (also varying interindividually) a correlate of the degree of skill acquisition (cf. Nickolaus et al. 2013). According to Ackerman (1992) we can show that multidimensionality becomes more likely in the process of automatization. On the other hand, we can also demonstrate that only assessments that capture the relevant diversity in its depth and breadth are capable of documenting this multidimensional fluidity.

The given multidimensionality challenges assessment enormously. Restricted test time generally conflicts with the degree of integration of all dimensions (and within a dimension) in a content-valid and reliable fashion. We have illustrated the successful development steps reducing concurrently test time and increasing reliability with the use of short partial competency items (cf. Abele et al. 2014), concerning the otherwise criterion-valid problem solving assessment architecture (cf. Gschwendtner et al. 2009). Likewise, we had some success in raising reliabilities in all sub-dimensions of the not directly action-centered occupation-specific knowledge test material (cf. Schmidt et al. 2014). Multidimensional fluidity also affects the question whether, and how, intrapersonal change can be modeled psychometrically satisfyingly, especially over the total time of training. Using at least a one-dimensional solution and a limited time span as an "assessment crutch" works with, for example, the assessment of action-centered occupation-specific knowledge in the second year of training (Schmidt et al. 2014).

Further research is indicated, related to the following issues at least: (1) we should systematically construct and validate research designs, assessment architectures (items) and psychometrical approaches, with the aim of getting even closer to assessing intrapersonal change. (2) We should further increase the reliability of the occupation-specific knowledge tests (while first steps towards an adaptive assessment architecture are presently being taken in the context of ASCOT).[25] (3) We should validate the measures of the architecture to assess action-centered occupation-specific knowledge in reality, referring to the validity study of problem solving. (4) Concerning problem solving, we should test the impact of varying the sequences of short partial competency items within the test regimen, on dimensionality and reliability. (5) Apart from assessment, we could use highly reliable test elements to assess the success of instructional programs within the occupations.

Acknowledgments This publication was funded by grants Ni 606/3-1, Ni 606/6-1 and Ni 606/8-1 from the German Research Foundation (DFG) in the Priority Program "Competence Models for Assessing Individual Learning Outcomes and Evaluating Educational Processes" (SPP 1293).

[25]ASCOT is the acronym for Technology-based Skills and Competencies in VET. ASCOT is a program funded by the Bundesministerium für Bildung und Forschung.

References

Abele, S. (2014). *Modellierung und Entwicklung berufsfachlicher Kompetenz in der gewerblich-technischen Ausbildung* [Modeling and development of occupation-specific competency in the technical education]. Stuttgart: Steiner.

Abele, S., Greiff, S., Gschwendtner, T., Wüstenberg, S., Nickolaus, R., Nitzschke, A., & Funke, J. (2012). Dynamische Problemlösekompetenz. Ein bedeutsamer Prädiktor von Problemlöseleistungen in technischen Anforderungskontexten [Dynamic problem solving. An important predictor of problem-solving performance in technical domains]? *Zeitschrift für Erziehungswissenschaft, 15*, 363–391. doi:10.1007/s11618-012-0277-9.

Abele, S., Walker, F., & Nickolaus, R. (2014). Zeitökonomische und reliable Diagnostik beruflicher Problemlösekompetenzen bei Auszubildenden zum Kfz-Mechatroniker [Time saving and reliable diagnostics of occupation-specific problem solving competency of car mechatronic apprentices]. *Zeitschrift für Pädagogische Psychologie, 28*, 167–179. doi:10.1024/1010-0652/a000138.

Achtenhagen, F., & Winther, E. (2009). *Konstruktvalidität von Simulationsaufgaben: Computergestützte Messung berufsfachlicher Kompetenz—am Beispiel der Ausbildung von Industriekaufleuten* [Construct validity of items within a simulation: Computer-based assessment of occupation-specific competency—Using the example of the apprenticeship of industrial clerks]. Göttingen: Georg August Universität.

Ackerman, P. L. (1992). Predicting individual differences in complex skill acquisition: dynamics of ability determinants. *Journal of Applied Psychology, 77*, 589–613.

Artelt, C., & Schlagmüller, M. (2004). Der Umgang mit literarischen Texten als Teilkompetenz im Lesen? Dimensionsanalysen und Ländervergleiche [Dealing with literary texts as partial competence in reading? Dimensional analyses and cross-national comparisons]. In U. Schiefele, C. Artelt, W. Schneider, & P. Stanat (Eds.), *Struktur, Entwicklung von Lesekompetenz. Vertiefende Analysen im Rahmen von PISA 2000* (pp. 169–196). Wiesbaden: VS.

Becker, M. (2009). Kompetenzmodell zur Erfassung beruflicher Kompetenz im Berufsfeld Fahrzeugtechnik [Competence model for measuring professional competency in the occupational field of car mechatronics]. In C. Fenzl, G. Spöttl, F. Howe, & M. Becker (Eds.), *Berufsarbeit von morgen in gewerblich-technischen Domänen* (pp. 239–245). Bielefeld: Bertelsmann.

Fortmüller, R. (1996). Wissenschaftsorientierung und Praxisbezug als komplementäre Prinzipien lernpsychologisch fundierter Lehr-Lern-Arrangements [Scientific orientation and practical relevance as complementary principles of learning-teaching arrangements based on the fundamentals of the psychology of learning]. In R. Fortmüller & J. Aff (Eds.), *Wissenschaftsorientierung und Praxisbezug in der Didaktik der Ökonomie* (pp. 372–400). Wien: Manz.

Greiff, S., & Funke, J. (2010). Systematische Erforschung komplexer Problemlösefähigkeit anhand minimal komplexer Systeme [Systematic investigation of complex problem solving competency on the basis of minimal complex systems]. *Zeitschrift für Pädagogik, Beiheft, 56*, 216–227.

Gschwendtner, T. (2011). Die Ausbildung zum Kraftfahrzeugmechatroniker im Längsschnitt. Analysen zur Struktur von Fachkompetenz am Ende der Ausbildung und Erklärung von Fachkompetenzentwicklungen über die Ausbildungszeit [The apprenticeship of car mechatronics in a longitudinal perspective. Analyses of occupation-specific competency structures at the end of vocational training and explanations of the development of occupation-specific competency during time in training]. *Zeitschrift für Berufs- und Wirtschaftspädagogik, Beiheft, 25*, 55–76.

Gschwendtner, T., Geißel, B., Nickolaus, R. (2007). Förderung und Entwicklung der Fehleranalysefähigkeit in der Grundstufe der elektrotechnischen Ausbildung [Fostering and development of trouble-shooting competency in the „Grundbildung“ of the electrotechnical apprenticeship]. *Berufs- und Wirtschaftspädagogik—online, 13*. Retrieved from http://www.bwpat.de.

Gschwendtner, T., Abele, S., & Nickolaus, R. (2009). Computersimulierte Arbeitsproben: Eine Validierungsstudie am Beispiel der Fehlerdiagnoseleistung von KFZ-Mechatronikern [Computer-simulated work samples: A statistical validation study using the example of trouble-shooting competency of car mechatronics]. *Zeitschrift für Berufs- und Wirtschaftspädagogik, 105*, 557–578.

Gschwendtner, T., Geißel, B., & Nickolaus, R. (2010). Modellierung beruflicher Fachkompetenz in der gewerblich-technischen Grundbildung [Modeling of occupation-specific competency in the first year of technical education]. *Zeitschrift für Pädagogik, Beiheft, 56*, 258–269.

Nickolaus, R., Gschwendtner, T., & Abele, S. (2009). *Die Validität von Simulationsaufgaben am Beispiel der Diagnosekompetenz von Kfz-Mechatronikern: Vorstudie zur Validität von Simulationsaufgaben im Rahmen eines VET-LSA [Validity of simulation-based items using the example of trouble-shooting competency of car mechatronics: Pilot study in the validity of simulation-based items within a VET-LSA framework].* .https://www.bmbf.de/files/Abschluss-Bericht_Druckfassung.pdf. Accessed 31 Mar 2014

Nickolaus, R., Geißel, B., Abele, S., & Nitzschke, A. (2011). Fachkompetenzmodellierung und Fachkompetenzentwicklung bei Elektronikern für Energie- und Gebäudetechnik im Verlauf der Ausbildung: Ausgewählte Ergebnisse einer Längsschnittstudie [Modeling and development of occupation-specific competency of electronic technicians during time in training: Selected findings of a longitudinal study]. *Zeitschrift für Berufs- und Wirtschaftspädagogik, Beiheft, 25*, 77–94.

Nickolaus, R., Abele, S., Gschwendtner, T., Nitzschke, A., & Greiff, S. (2012). Fachspezifische Problemlösefähigkeit als zentrale Kompetenzdimension beruflicher Handlungskompetenz: Modellierung, erreichte Niveaus und relevante Einflussfaktoren in der gewerblich-technischen Berufsausbildung [Occupation-specific problem solving competency as an essential competency dimension of professional competency: Models, achieved levels and relevant predictors in technical education]. *Zeitschrift für Berufs- und Wirtschaftspädagogik, 108*, 243–272.

Nickolaus, R., Gschwendtner, T., & Abele, S. (2013). Herausforderungen und Wege der Diagnose berufsfachlicher Kompetenzen in der gewerblich-technischen Berufsbildung [Challenges and paths of diagnostics of occupation-specific competency in the technical education]. *Zeitschrift für Berufs- und Wirtschaftspädagogik, Beiheft, 26*, 183–201.

Rauner, F., Haasler, B., Heinemann, L., & Grollmann, P. (2009). *Messen beruflicher Kompetenzen. Band 1: Grundlagen und Konzeption des KOMET-Projekts [Measuring occupational competencies. Volume 1: Background and concept of the KOMET project]* (2nd ed.). Berlin: LIT.

Rosendahl, J., & Straka, G. A. (2011). Kompetenzmodellierungen zur wirtschaftlichen Fachkompetenz angehender Bankkaufleute [Competency models of economic competency of prospective bankers]. *Zeitschrift für Berufs- und Wirtschaftspädagogik, 107*, 190–217.

Schmidt, T., Nickolaus, R., & Weber, W. (2014). Modellierung und Entwicklung des fachsystematischen und handlungsbezogenen Fachwissens von Kfz-Mechatronikern [Modeling and development of action-centered and not directly action-centered occupation-specific knowledge of car mechatronics]. *Zeitschrift für Berufs- und Wirtschaftspädagogik, 110*, 549–574.

Seeber, S., & Lehmann, R. (2011). Determinanten der Fachkompetenz in ausgewählten gewerblich-technischen Berufen [Determinants of occupation-specific competency in selected occupations of technical educational]. *Zeitschrift für Berufs- und Wirtschaftspädagogik, Beiheft, 25*, 95–111.

Sun, R. (2002). *Duality of the mind. A bottom-up approach toward cognition*. Mahwah: Erlbaum.

Weiß, R. H. (1999). *Grundintelligenztest CFT 3 Skala 3. Handanweisung für die Durchführung, Auswertung und Interpretation* [Culture fair intelligence test CFT 3, Scale 3. Manual.]. Göttingen: Hogrefe.

Weiß, R. H. (2006). *Grundintelligenztest Skala 2: CFT 20-R – Revision* [Culture fair intelligence test CFT 20-R, Scale 2]. Göttingen: Hogrefe.

Chapter 13
Professional Competencies of Building Trade Apprentices After Their First Year of Training

Kerstin Norwig, Cordula Petsch, and Reinhold Nickolaus

Abstract The study presented here (DFG Ni 606 7-1) focuses on the professional competencies of building trade apprentices after their first year of training. Its main objectives are (1) to examine the dimensional structure of the apprentices' professional competence and (2) to provide a description of their actual competencies by defining different competency levels. For this purpose, empirical data on 273 building trade apprentices (carpenters, tilers and plasterers) were collected. Confirmatory factor analyses and chi-square difference tests, corresponding to theoretical assumptions, show that a four-dimensional solution provides the best model fit—the four dimensions being technical drawing, basic technical mathematics, professional knowledge, and professional problem-solving. As was expected, all four dimensions show high latent correlations ($r > .71$). As previous studies have reported, the competency level of building trade apprentices is generally rather low. Major differences exist between apprentices of the different professions: on average, carpenters perform significantly better than do tilers or plasterers. A closer look at the competency levels in professional problem-solving reveals that almost two-thirds of the tilers and plasterers score at the lowest level (below level 1) and do not reach the curricular goals of the first year of training.

Keywords Professional competencies • Building trades • Competency model • Competency levels

13.1 Introduction

In the area of commercial or technical professions, competence models have mainly been developed for occupations in the electronic or metal working domain (for an overview see Nickolaus and Seeber 2013 and Gschwendtner et al. 2017, in this volume). Occupations in the building trade have—until now—not been in the focus

K. Norwig (✉) • C. Petsch • R. Nickolaus
University of Stuttgart, Stuttgart, Germany
e-mail: norwig@bwt.uni-stuttgart.de; petsch@bwt.uni-stuttgart.de; nickolaus@bwt.uni-stuttgart.de

D. Leutner et al. (eds.), *Competence Assessment in Education*, Methodology of Educational Measurement and Assessment, DOI 10.1007/978-3-319-50030-0_13

of competence modeling research. Studies in this sector have mainly dealt with pedagogical issues, such as the outcomes of different learning arrangements in carpenter apprentice classes in the second or third year of training (Wülker 2004; Bünning 2008). In addition, the tests that were employed in these studies encompass only a small range of topics from the overall curriculum. Therefore, no general information about the apprentices' professional competence can be drawn from these tests. Our own studies in the field of building trade occupations concentrated on improving the professional competence of low-achieving apprentices in their first year of training (Norwig et al. 2013; Petsch et al. 2014). Two successive intervention studies have evidenced that the training concept *BEST* (the acronym for *Berufsbezogenes Strategietraining*, or "professional strategy training") had a positive and significant impact on apprentices' competence development. However, other important questions—the construct's dimensionality, and the precise competencies that correspond to the apprentices' raw scores, for example—have not been focused on, and are as yet unanswered. Nevertheless, our studies provide ample basis for the present project as we gained from them valuable knowledge of (1) the curricular structure of the apprentices' first year of training, (2) the apprentices' average cognitive abilities and motivational state and (3) test-related aspects such as appropriate item format and item difficulty.

Research findings from other commercial or technical professions offer additional information (see, e.g., Abele et al. 2012; Gschwendtner 2008; Nickolaus et al. 2010, 2012; Rosendahl and Straka 2011; Seeber 2008; Winther and Achtenhagen 2009). In regard to the dimensional structure of professional competence in different domains,[1] the evidence mostly points to the distinction of two dimensions: (1) conceptual knowledge and (2) professional problem-solving. Even though a third dimension of manual abilities is theoretically plausible and might be of considerable relevance for occupational tasks in the building sector, research on this question is still warranted. Dimensionality analyses of several conceptual knowledge scales suggest the distinction of more factors or sub-dimensions, which would usually correspond to larger curricular or professional topics (see Gönnenwein et al. 2011; Gschwendtner 2011; Nickolaus et al. 2012). Until now, there has been no evidence for other sub-dimensions that have been conceptualized theoretically, such as a distinction between declarative or procedural knowledge, for example (Gschwendtner 2008; Gschwendtner et al. 2009).

Studies concerned with students' or apprentices' competency levels indicate great differences between curricular goals and the students' actual competency level (Gschwendtner 2008; Nickolaus et al. 2012). Similar findings were made by Wülker (2004) and Bünning (2008), who both reported comparably low achievement and high variance among carpenter apprentices. Factors that contribute to the difficulty of test items have been discussed in several studies, both from the technical (see Gschwendtner 2008; Nickolaus et al. 2008) and the commercial domains (see

[1]Most of the studies mentioned here concentrated on cognitive aspects of professional competence; effects of motivation or volition were usually not considered, or were analyzed separately, as suggested by Klieme and Leutner (2006).

Winther and Achtenhagen 2009). Post-hoc analyses indicate that matters such as complexity,[2] the interconnectedness of thoughts and knowledge, the level of cognitive skills needed for a task (according to Bloom's taxonomy), prerequisite knowledge, and the students' familiarity with the task, all play major roles in this respect (see Nickolaus 2014).

13.2 Aims and Objectives

Against the background of the current state of research (see Sect. 13.1), five aims were defined for the project here presented (DFG Ni 606 7–1): (1) to develop valid and reliable test instruments for assessing the professional competence of building trade apprentices at the end of their first training year, (2) to examine the dimensional structure of the construct, (3) to describe the apprentices' actual competencies on the basis of competency levels, (4) to develop an explanatory model of professional competence, and (5) to investigate the effects of occupation-related motivation on apprentices' professional competence. As it is not possible to elaborate on all aspects here, the focus of this article will be on the second and third issues only.

13.3 Vocational Training in the Building Trades

As many as 15 different occupations (e.g., bricklayer, carpenter, road builder, tiler, and plasterer) are officially registered for vocational training in the building trade sector in Germany (Bundesministerium der Justiz 1999). Apprenticeships in these occupations usually last three years: While the first year provides a general introduction to topics related to all building trades, the second and third years focus on training in one specific occupation. Accordingly, apprentices spend most of their time in vocational schools in the first year and receive intense in-company training in the following two years. In most regions of the state of Baden-Württemberg the first year of training is provided by full-time vocational schools (*einjährige Berufsfachschule Bautechnik*).[3] Following the idea of a shared knowledge basis for all building-related occupations, the curriculum of the first year covers a wide range of topics and is structured into six different so-called "learning fields" (*Lernfelder*). The first learning field gives a rough introduction to working on a construction site

[2] It has to be pointed out that the works cited here do not share a common concept of complexity. While some studies employ global ratings of complexity, other research approaches make use of indicators such as the number or interconnectedness of elements (see Nickolaus 2014).

[3] It is important to know that the students in these schools have already signed a pre-agreement for an apprenticeship with an employer or firm. It is part of this agreement that the apprentices attend one day per week (or several weeks per year) at the employer's workplace.

and is of similar importance to all apprentices alike. The following five learning fields correspond to one or several occupations, and cover themes such as paving, foundations and utility connections, bricklaying, casting reinforced concrete, timber constructions, tiling and plastering. In the curricular guidelines tasks in all six learning fields refer to authentic professional actions. Despite the wide scope of topics and the multitude of different tasks, these actions are generally based on three types of requirement: professional knowledge, technical drawing, and basic technical mathematics.[4] All three types of requirement may be separate, but commonly they are combined when dealing with more complex professional tasks.

13.4 Professional Competence of Building Trade Apprentices

Considering the wide scope of tasks and requirements, it appears plausible that the overall professional competence of building trade apprentices in their first year is multidimensional and encompasses a whole range of competencies. It is important to note that our research does not include manual competencies, as they are developed through practical experience in the workshop or at the workplace. Rather, the focus is on certain cognitive competencies. According to a current working definition of competencies in educational assessment, competencies are defined "as context-specific cognitive dispositions that are acquired by learning and are needed to successfully cope with certain situations or tasks in specific domains" (Klieme et al. 2008, p. 9). Against the background of pertinent research findings (see Sect. 13.1) and the curricular content and structure of the first year of training in the building trades (see Sect. 13.3), several alternative structural models of building-related professional competence can be hypothesized.

One possibility would be to distinguish six dimensions, representing the six aforementioned learning fields, all corresponding to different occupations and their respective areas of knowledge. However, given the results of our earlier studies (see Norwig et al. 2010; Petsch et al. 2014), which indicated that the apprentices' strengths and weaknesses were similar across learning fields but varied in respect of the different types of requirements (as described in Sect. 13.3), a model based on these basic requirements is favored instead. Taking into account not only the three basic types of requirements but also their combination leads to a model with the following four competencies or dimensions: (1) professional knowledge (PK), (2) technical drawing (TD), (3) basic technical mathematics (BTM), and (4) professional problem-solving (PPS).

PK refers to formal knowledge about facts and the underlying principles of building-related topics: for example, knowledge of construction principles, materials and methods. TD includes basic understanding of technical drawings and skills

[4]The importance of these basic requirements for building-related tasks is reflected not least in the fact that all three were taught as individual subjects before curricular reform introduced the learning fields in 1999 (see KMK 1999).

in basic drafting procedures, such as for example, reading drawings of floor plans, elevations or sections, dealing with scales, dimensions and symbols. BTM covers basic mathematics as it is typically used when solving building-related tasks: for example, basic arithmetic, conversion of measurement units, the "rule of three", calculation of percentages and basic geometry. PPS refers to the ability to solve professional tasks with higher complexity. These tasks usually combine requirements from the other three dimensions (PK, TD, and BTM) and call for the application of subject-specific cognitive strategies for their solution (see Petsch and Norwig 2012; Norwig et al. 2013). This would be the case when an apprentice is asked to calculate the amount of bricks needed to build a wall depicted in a technical drawing, for example.

Following these assumptions about the multidimensionality of the construct in question, a paper-and-pencil test was developed for each of the four dimensions. To ensure content validity of all four tests, the content of curricula, textbooks and workbooks was analyzed. On top of that, expert ratings on important tasks and requirements were collected. Items developed and evaluated in earlier studies (see Petsch et al. 2011; Norwig et al. 2012) were included where appropriate. All items were free-response items and were designed to vary in difficulty; the item difficulty of the PPS scale was varied with regard to certain task characteristics (see Sect. 13.6.2).

13.5 Research Design and Data Collection

The study was divided into two stages: In preparation for the main study, which took place in the school year 2012/13, two smaller pilot studies were carried out in June 2012. The major aim of both pilot studies was to test the adequacy of the test instruments that were to be applied in the main study. The results of both pilot studies were mostly satisfactory: All scales fitted the unidimensional[5] one-parameter partial credit model. Poorly fitting items[6] were either removed or altered for further use in the main study (for more detailed information on the pilot studies, see Nickolaus et al. 2013).

For the main study, cross-sectional data were collected at two points in time. The first round of measurements took place in October 2012: that is, at the beginning of the training year. Sixteen classes of full-time vocational schools for building trade apprentices, with a total of $N = 282$ students, participated in the study. About two

[5] Unidimensionality was evaluated in Conquest 2.0 (Wu et al. 2007) by comparing alternative unidimensional and multidimensional models. Model evaluation criteria included Akaike Information Criterion (AIC), Bayesian Information Criterion (BIC) and conditional Akaike Information Criterion (cAIC).

[6] Item fit was evaluated according to the following criteria: (1) correct order of threshold parameters, (2) appropriate item-total correlation ($\geq .3$), (3) appropriate weighted-t fit statistics (≤ 1.9), (4) homogeneity of parameter estimates between subsets of data ($r \geq .9$), and (5) differential item functioning (DIF) for apprentices of different occupations.

thirds of the students were carpenter apprentices (n = 196); the remainder being either tilers or plasterers (n = 86).[7] Tilers and plasterers are considered as one group here, as previous studies have shown that they are comparable in respect of their cognitive and sociodemographic background (see Norwig et al. 2013 and Petsch et al. 2014). In addition, both occupations are addressed in the same learning field (see Sect. 13.3). At the first point of measurement, three tests were conducted: a test of general cognitive abilities (CFT 20-R, Weiß 2006), a test of prior knowledge in the professional domain, and a test of basic numeracy skills. Additionally, sociodemographic data were collected in a short questionnaire.

The tests of apprentices' professional competence after their first year of training (see Sect. 13.4) were conducted in a second round of measurements in June 2013. With a sample size of N = 273, the number of participants was slightly lower than at the beginning of the main study. Closer analysis revealed that 31 apprentices were added to the initial sample. They had either missed the first test round or had started training at a later point in time. On the other hand, 40 participants did not show up for the final tests, or had dropped out of training altogether, which made a total study dropout rate of 14.2 %. As in our earlier studies, the number of study dropouts varied greatly between occupations: while only 8.7 % of the carpenter apprentices did not participate in the final test round, the proportion was more than a quarter among tilers and plasterers, and totaled 26.7 %.

Additionally, a questionnaire on the apprentices' learning motivation[8] in class was handed out at the termination of each learning field. This was to provide insight into their motivational development over the first training year, and to explore content-related differences in learning motivation.

13.6 Results

Before addressing the main results of the study, some findings of the first measurement are summarized. Altogether, they support the evidence from our earlier studies of the apprentices' sociodemographic background, their cognitive abilities, and prior knowledge in the domain of building and construction (see Norwig et al. 2010; Petsch et al. 2014). At a later point in time, most of the data presented in Sect. 13.6.1 will be incorporated into an explanatory model of professional competence.

---

[7]The sizes of the subsamples corresponded approximately to the distribution of apprentices in the respective occupations in the state of Baden-Württemberg (cf. Statistische Berichte Baden-Württemberg 2014). Mean differences, as reported in Sectns. 13.6.2 and 13.7, are not biased by unequal sample size.

[8]Following Prenzel et al. (1996), different types of motivation were distinguished in the questionnaire. Yet, due to time and space constraints, only the following four types were included: amotivation, extrinsic, identified, and interested motivation. Additionally, data was collected on a selection of social-contextual conditions, facilitating or forestalling positive motivational development: perceived difficulty, feeling of competence, perceived relevance, and teacher's feedback.

13.6.1 *Sociodemographic Factors, Cognitive Abilities and Apprentices' Performance at the Beginning of the First Training Year*

As can be seen in Table 13.1, the vast majority of apprentices in our sample (n = 282) were male. Taking into account that the carpenter, tiler, and plasterer occupations are usually dominated by men, this fact was certainly expected. There was a slight age difference between the two groups, with the tilers and plasterers being marginally older than the carpenters. This appears surprising, as almost 80 % of the tilers and plasterers attended only lower secondary school (*Hauptschule*), while about 40 % of the carpenter apprentices managed to graduate from the next higher type of secondary school (*Realschule*). It can be assumed, however, that the tilers' and plasterers' problems during their school careers, and their attempts to find an apprenticeship position, more than offset the shorter time spent in school. Major differences between the two groups also become apparent upon looking at the apprentices' mother tongues. Almost half of the tilers and plasterers grew up with a first language other than German, exceeding by far the 8 % of carpenters who shared the same experience. Another clear disadvantage was the tilers' and plasterers' average IQ of just 89.2 points, which was significantly lower than that of the carpenters (Cohen's $d = 0.61$, $p < .001$), whose score was almost nine points higher, and close to the population mean of 100 points. According to normative data, the difference between the two groups represents a move from the 44th to the 23rd percentile (see Weiß 2006). Even larger—at least when considering the effect size—were the differences between the two groups' basic numeracy skills[9] ($d = 0.95$, $p < .001$) and prior knowledge[10] ($d = 0.97$, $p < .001$). Accordingly, the item-person-maps of both tests indicate bimodal distribution.[11]

[9] The numeracy test scale consisted of 11 items. Test reliability (based on weighted likelihood estimates, WLE) was acceptable (.72). As the variance of the latent ability distribution was 2.59, the test differentiated well between the subjects. The average standard error of the WLE person parameter estimates was comparably high (0.84), due to the relatively small number of items for a wide range of ability.

[10] The test of prior knowledge included 16 items. WLE reliability was acceptable (.73); the variance of the latent ability distribution (1.23) indicated a good differentiation between subjects. The average standard error of the WLE person parameter estimates (0.62) pointed to a balanced distribution of persons' abilities and item difficulties.

[11] The fact that our sample consisted of two quite different groups became especially important during item scaling. Analyses of differential item functioning (DIF) were carried out for both test scales (basic numeracy skills and prior knowledge in the professional domain). Items that were differentially more difficult for one of the groups were deleted from the scales.

Table 13.1 Sociodemographic characteristics and test results at the beginning of the training year

Group	Gender [male] in %	Age *M* (*SD*)	Type of Secondary Education in %			Native Language [German] in %	IQ-Points *M* (*SD*)	Basic Numeracy *M* (*SD*)	Prior Knowledge *M* (*SD*)
			LSS	ISS	USS				
TL/P	100	18.2 (2.4)	78.4	19.6	2.0	54.9	89.2 (13.4)	−1.01 (1.50)	−0.76 (1.21)
C	98	17.1 (1.8)	55.0	40.9	4.1	92.0	97.8 (15.0)	0.45 (1.58)	0.35 (1.08)

TL/P tilers and plasterers, *C* carpenters, *M* mean, *SD* standard deviation, *LSS* Lower Secondary School (*Hauptschule*), *ISS* Intermediate Secondary School (*Realschule*), *USS* Upper Secondary School (*Gymnasium* or similar).

13.6.2 Professional Competence at the End of the First Training Year

The main focus of the study was on the apprentices' professional competence at the end of their first year of training. As stated in Sect. 13.2, several questions arise in this context. The following paragraphs deal with (a) the question of the dimensional structure of the construct and (b) the apprentices' actual level of competence, or—when talking about multidimensionality—competencies.[12]

Competence Structure Following our theoretical assumptions (see Sect. 13.4), a confirmatory factor analysis (CFA) was first conducted on a four-dimensional model.[13] The results of this analysis were then compared to a one-dimensional model.[14] While the four-dimensional solution assumes professional knowledge (PK), technical drawing (TD), basic technical mathematics (BTM), and professional problem-solving (PPS) to be distinct dimensions, the one-dimensional model proposes the combination of PK, TD, BTM, and PPS into one factor. Both models are theoretically plausible, as the abilities to master the different requirements are assumed to be different but nonetheless related.[15] This is because the concept of learning fields sets the focus on comparably realistic and complex tasks, which often combine several of the requirements that are distinguished in the model (see Sect. 13.3).

Figure 13.1 depicts the four-dimensional model and the corresponding model fit statistics. The correlations of the observed variables with the respective latent dimensions were all above .32, the average being .56 (average $SE = .08$). The chi-square test of model fit suggested that the specified model did not fit the data adequately ($p < .001$). However, this test of model fit is sensitive to sample size: that is, large samples ($N > 200$) often lead to statistically significant chi-square values. Therefore, other fit indices were deemed more appropriate here (see Finney and DiStefano 2006). Indicating marginal (comparative fit index, CFI and Tucker-Lewis index, TLI: see Bentler and Bonett 1980; Tucker and Lewis 1973; Hu and Bentler 1998) or close model fit (root mean square errow of approximation, RMSEA: see Yu 2002), they basically supported the assumed structure.[16] The results of the chi-

[12] Following Weinert (2001), "competence" is understood as a "system of abilities, proficiencies, or skills that are necessary or sufficient to reach a specific goal." (ibid., 45). The term "competencies" is used when referring to specific components of the respective system (see ibid.).

[13] Following the recommendations of Muthén and Muthén (2012) and Finney and DiStefano (2006), all analyses were run using Mplus's WLSMV estimator, as the research points to advantages over other estimators when dealing with ordered categorical data and few categories (<3).

[14] CFA and the chi-square difference test were carried out using Mplus 6.12 (Muthén and Muthén 2010).

[15] For reasons of space, other multi-dimensional solutions, which were either deemed implausible or were discounted due to low model fit, are not discussed and elaborated on here.

[16] According to Finney and DiStefano (2006), RMSEA and WRMR (weighted root mean square residual) appear to be the most promising fit indices with ordered categorical data and a low number of categories.

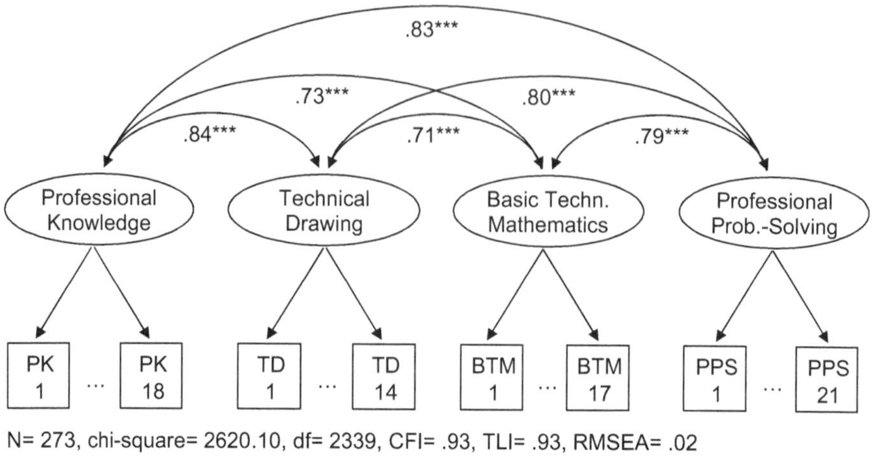

Fig. 13.1 Four-dimensional competence model (end of first training year)

square difference tests (Asparouhov and Muthén 2006) also supported the four-dimensional solution, as they fitted the data comparably better than did the one-dimensional model ($p < .001$).

The estimates of the correlations between the latent factors were all in the range of .71–.84 (see Fig. 13.1). Considering the fact that the curriculum is organized in terms of learning fields and focuses on authentic tasks, which often combine the different requirements, these results are not surprising. Additional interpretations may arise once the explanatory model has been built, as it will include other relevant variables (e.g., IQ).

Competency Levels In this article, in relation to the apprentices' competency levels, the focus is on professional problem-solving, as it is the most comprehensive of the four dimensions and is therefore deemed to be the most important aspect here. The definition of competency levels was carried out post-hoc, following the procedure described by Hartig (2007) and Hartig et al. (2012): In a first step, all items of the professional problem-solving scale[17] were closely analyzed with respect to certain task characteristics or features that were assumed to contribute to item difficulty. After that, each item was scored according to task characteristics by three expert raters (Kendall's $W > .80$, average = .90). In a last step, a linear regression model was used to predict empirical item difficulties as a linear function of item characteristics.[18] This allowed the specification of cut-off points or level thresholds

[17] The scale of professional problem-solving comprised 25 items. Scale reliability (WLE) and the variance of the latent ability distribution were acceptable (.71 and 0.98 respectively). The average standard error of the WLE person parameter estimates was 0.59: i.e., item difficulties were relatively evenly distributed over the ability range.

[18] Item difficulties were transformed to represent a 65 % chance of success in solving the task, instead of the 50 % that is configured in the Rasch standard setting.

on the continuous competency scale and formed the basis for describing the competency levels.

As was described in Sect. 13.4, professional problem-solving takes place when complex[19] professional tasks have to be solved. The difficulty of these tasks originates from several sources, some of which might be similar to those in other domains (see Sect. 13.1); others appear to be specific to tasks in the domain of building and construction. On the whole, the following 13 task characteristics were included in the analysis: (1) number of steps to solve the problem, (2) complexity as described by Kauertz et al. (2010)—that is: (2a) the number of task elements and (2b) the number of interconnections between these elements, (3) level of cognitive skills needed for the task (according to Bloom's taxonomy), (4) task is made up of interdependent steps, (5) curricular weight of the task content, (6) level of mathematical modeling needed, (7) number of different mathematical operations, (8) operations include different units of measurement, (9) task is illustrated in a figure or drawing, (10) amount of distracting information presented in the figure or drawing, (11) number of distractors presented in the task, (12) number of subject-specific terms that have to be known to solve the problem, and (13) amount of help provided in the construction chart book.

The first step required checking whether the different task characteristics had the expected impact on task difficulty. This means that for each characteristic it was checked whether the average task difficulty actually rose when the characteristic was present. Characteristics that did not meet this assumption were excluded from further analyses. In a next step, several regression analyses were performed. Item characteristics corresponding to negative or very small ($\beta < .02$) regression coefficients, or showing instances of high multicollinearity (VIF > 5) were successively excluded from the regression model. The six remaining item characteristics explained a total of 62 % (corrected R-square) of the total variance; the resulting regression equation reads as follows:

$$y = -.30 + .50\,x_1 + .48\,x_2 + .47\,x_3 + .38\,x_4 + .28\,x_5 + .18\,x_6.$$

According to this analysis, tasks become more difficult when:

- no graphic illustration of the problem is provided (x_1),
- the number of interconnections between task elements is more than five (x_2),
- the number of steps needed to solve the problem is also more than five (x_3),
- work-related real-world information has to be transformed into a mathematical model (x_4),
- the task has low weight in the curriculum, as it appears only in one of the six learning fields, for example (x_5), and
- the task requires deep understanding of two or more subject-specific terms (x_6).

[19] Complex means here a combination of requirements from the three dimensions PK, TD, and BTM.

Based on these six task characteristics, four hierarchical competency levels were defined[20]:

- Level A ($x_1 \ldots x_6 = 0$): Apprentices can solve problems that (1) are not only described in a text but are additionally illustrated in a figure or drawing, (2) have less than five interconnections between task elements, (3) require less than five steps to reach a solution, (4) do not require mathematical modeling of a given real-life work situation, (5) are given great importance in the curriculum, and (6) include only one subject-specific term.
- Level B ($x_1 = 1, x_2 = 1, x_3 \ldots x_6 = 0$): Apprentices can solve problems that (1) have to be visualized mentally, (2) require the connection of five or more task elements, (3) require less than five steps to reach a solution, (4) do not require mathematical modeling of a given real-life work situation, (5) are given great importance in the curriculum, and (6) include only one subject-specific term (see Fig. 13.2 for a depiction of a task representing this level).
- Level C ($x_1 \ldots x_3 = 1, x_4 = 0, x_5 = 0, x_6 = 1$): Apprentices can solve problems that (1) have to be visualized mentally, (2) require the connection of five or more task elements, (3) require five or more steps to reach a solution, (4) do not require mathematical modeling of a given real-life work situation, (5) are given great importance in the curriculum, and (6) include at least two subject-specific terms.
- Level D ($x_1 \ldots x_6 = 1$): Apprentices can solve problems that (1) have to be visualized mentally, (2) require the connection of five or more task elements, (3) require five or more steps to reach a solution, (4) require mathematical modeling of a given real-life work situation, (5) are given low importance in the curriculum, and (6) include at least two subject-specific terms.

Apprentices below level A have very low probability of success even when trying to solve some of the easier tasks in the test—that is, those tasks corresponding to level A.

Table 13.2 gives an overview of the levels just described and shows their location relative to the logit scale. Additionally, the percentages of apprentices scoring on the respective levels are presented. As can be seen, the overall results were quite alarming, as only about 30 % of the whole group reached a level higher than A. Another 30 % of the apprentices were on this lowest level. While they could be expected to master the easiest tasks—with none of the six characteristics present—the remaining 42.1 %, achieving below level A, were likely to fail even these.

A closer look at the results of the two occupational groups (carpenters and tilers or plasterers) revealed great differences, as was expected against the background of our earlier findings (see Petsch et al. 2011 and Nickolaus et al. 2013), and the results from the first point of measurement (see Sect. 13.6.1). The observed mean difference between the two groups amounted to 0.74 logits (carpenters: $M = 0.18$, $SD = 1.05$; tilers and plasterers $M = -0.56$, $SD = 1.23$), resembling a medium to high

[20] The number of items corresponding to the competency levels is as follows: $N_{\text{Level A}} = 9$, $N_{\text{Level B}} = 9$, $N_{\text{Level C}} = 7$. Two items correspond to the segment below level A. No item and very few apprentices are located on level D, which is reported here to reflect the high curricular expectations.

A wall with a surface area of 12.48 m² is to be constructed of bricks (size 2DF). The wall thickness is planned to be 24 cm. Your task is to calculate the number of bricks needed to build the wall.

Hint: *You need to check your construction chart book for solving this task!*
(Check ***construction material, bricks****in the index)*

In total [**bricks**] are needed.

Fig. 13.2 Exemplary task of level B (construction of a brick wall)

Table 13.2 Competency levels (professional problem-solving)

Logit scale	Levels	Task characteristics	All apprentices %	Carpenters %	Tilers/ plasterers %
	Level D	+ task has low curricular weight + mathematical modeling is required	2.6	3.5	-
1.99	Level C	+ number of subject-specific terms ≥ 2 + number of steps to solve the task ≥ 5	8.2	8.8	6.3
1.33	Level B	+ connection of ≥ 5 task elements + mental visualization is needed	17.6	21.2	7.9
0.68	Level A	none	29.6	31.8	23.8
-0.30	Below Level A		42.1	34.7	61.9

effect ($d = 0.65$, $p < .001$). Accordingly, the distribution on the respective levels differed between the two groups (see Table 13.2): While about a third of the carpenters reached level B or higher, only around 14 % of the tilers and plasterers showed similar achievements, and none of the latter were found on level D. Another third of the carpenters scored on level A; the remaining 35 % did not even reach this level. Level A was only reached by slightly more than 20 % of the tilers and plasterers. More than 60 % of this group scored below this lowest level, which means the majority of this group had serious problems in solving the most common and easiest professional problems presented in school.

Overall, the results are far from satisfying, especially when taking into account the high curricular goals and the fact that the test items tend to be shorter and less complex than tasks that are posed in the textbooks or in real-world work situations. Intensive and comprehensive supportive measures are certainly required, in the light of these results. As mentioned in Sect. 13.1, the training concept *BEST* is an approach that has proven successful in this respect (see Petsch et al. 2014; Norwig et al. 2013, e.g.). Its focus is on improving the apprentices' professional problem-solving competencies by training in the use of general metacognitive and subject-specific cognitive strategies. The training material is based on real-world construction scenarios and allows—and encourages—the learners to develop at their individual pace. As these strategies also require the application of professional knowledge, basic technical mathematics and technical drawing skills, these competencies are likewise supported during training.

13.7 Additional Findings and Prospects

The paper presented here provides a model not only of the dimensional structure of professional competence after the first year of building trade apprenticeship, but also of the apprentices' proficiency level in regard to their professional problem-solving competencies. Analogous models for other competencies, such as professional knowledge, technical drawing or basic technical mathematics, are yet to be completed. Overall, the initial findings suggest similar results: mean differences between carpenters and tilers or plasterers were significant (based on WLE estimates of person parameters) and partly exceeded the effect measured for professional problem-solving (professional knowledge: $d = 1.17$, $p < .001$; technical drawing: $d = 0.93$, $p < .001$; basic technical mathematics: $d = 0.62$, $p < .001$).[21] When relating the groups' average scores on the logit scale to the respective items at this level, training needs in all three competency areas became apparent. Competency models with a precise description of the different levels will help to specify these needs and may support further training efforts.

Analyses of the motivational data provide interesting insights into the apprentices' motivational development during their first year of training.[22] As was expected, motivation varied across the learning fields and depended greatly on the focal topic. The carpenter apprentices' motivation, for example, reached its positive peak on

[21] The three scales (PK, TD, and BTM) consisted of 23, 19, and 19 items respectively. Scale reliabilities (based on WLE) were all satisfactory (≥.75). The variance of the latent ability distribution was the highest for BTM (1.71) and the lowest for TD (1.01); for PK the variance amounted to 1.25. The average standard error of the WLE person parameter estimates was similar for PK and TD (0.58 and 0.59 respectively). The higher average standard error for BTM (0.64) is a result of the higher variance and hints at a more unbalanced distribution of item difficulties and persons' abilities.

[22] Due to space constraints, it is not possible to present the findings on the apprentices' motivational development in detail here. Another paper will discuss related issues.

three of the four motivation types (i.e., lowest amotivation and highest identified and interested motivation) in learning field five, which focuses on timber constructions (see Sect. 13.3). Accordingly, motivation was lower in the other learning fields. Similar but less distinct tendencies were apparent concerning the tilers and plasterers' motivational development, save for the fact that their motivational peak corresponded to learning field six, which deals with content related to tiling and plastering. Findings on motivational conditions underline these results, as perceived relevance was the only factor that showed corresponding trends; conditions such as a feeling of competence or perceived difficulty remained quite stable over time.

An explanatory model will allow more precise statements about the relation between motivational, cognitive and sociodemographic factors and their influence on the apprentices' professional competence. This knowledge, in turn, will provide valuable information to all those who are committed to the apprentices' learning. The necessity of supporting the apprentices during their training has been pointed out repeatedly. It can only be speculated that some of these problems will continue to exist during the following two years of training. However, this is just one of the questions to be tackled in the next project (Ni 606 7-2), which will focus on the carpenters' professional competencies after three years of training—that is, at the end of their apprenticeship.

Acknowledgments The preparation of this chapter was supported by grant Ni 606 7-1 from the German Research Foundation (DFG) in the Priority Program "Competence Models for Assessing Individual Learning Outcomes and Evaluating Educational Processes" (SPP 1293).

References

Abele, S., Greiff, S., Gschwendtner, T., Wüstenberg, S., Nickolaus, R., Nitzschke, A., & Funke, J. (2012). Dynamische Problemlösekompetenz [Dynamic problem-solving]. *Zeitschrift für Erziehungswissenschaft, 15*, 363–391. doi:10.1007/s11618-012-0277-9.

Asparouhov, T., & Muthén, B. O. (2006). *Robust chi square difference testing with mean and variance adjusted test statistics*. Retrieved from http://www.statmodel.com/download/webnotes/webnote10.pdf

Bentler, P. M., & Bonett, D. G. (1980). Significance tests and goodness of fit in the analysis of covariance structures. *Psychological Bulletin, 88*, 588–606. doi:10.1037/0033-2909.88.3.588.

Bünning, F. (2008). *Experimentierendes Lernen in der Bau- und Holztechnik. Entwicklung eines fachdidaktisch begründeten Experimentalkonzepts als Grundlage für die Realisierung eines handlungsorientierten Unterrichts für die Berufsfelder der Bau- und Holztechnik* [Experimental learning in classes of woodwork and building trade apprentices] (Habilitation thesis, Otto-von-Guericke-Universität Magdeburg, Magdeburg, Germany). Retrieved from edoc2.bibliothek.uni-halle.de/hs/download/pdf/1414?originalFilename=true

Bundesministerium der Justiz. (1999). *Bundesgesetzblatt Jahrgang 1999 Teil I Nr. 28. Verordnung über die Berufsausbildung in der Bauwirtschaft, vom 02.06.1999* [Federal regulation on vocational education in the building trades, dated 02 June 1999]. Retrieved from http://www2.bibb.de/tools/aab/ao/bauwirtschaft_1999.pdf

Finney, S. J., & DiStefano, C. (2006). Non-normal and categorical data in structural equation modeling. In G. R. Hancock & R. O. Mueller (Eds.), *Structural equation modeling: A second course* (pp. 269–314). Greenwich: IAP.

Gönnenwein, A., Nitzschke, A., & Schnitzler, A. (2011). Fachkompetenzerfassung in der gewerblichen Ausbildung am Beispiel des Ausbildungsberufs Mechatroniker,-in. Entwicklung psychometrischer Fachtests [Assessment of professional competencies in technical education (mechatronics technicians)]. *Berufsbildung in Wissenschaft und Praxis, 5*, 14–18.

Gschwendtner, T. (2008). Raschbasierte Modellierung berufsfachlicher Kompetenz in der Grundbildung von KraftfahrzeugmechatronikerInnen [Rasch modelling of professional competence of car mechatronics apprentices in their first year of training]. In K. Breuer, T. Deißinger, & D. Münk (Eds.), *Probleme und Perspektiven der Berufs- und Wirtschaftspädagogik aus nationaler und internationaler Sicht* (pp. 21–30). Opladen: Budrich.

Gschwendtner, T. (2011). Die Ausbildung zum Kraftfahrzeugmechatroniker im Längsschnitt. Analysen zur Struktur von Fachkompetenz am Ende der Ausbildung und Erklärung von Fachkompetenzentwicklungen über die Ausbildungszeit [Longitudinal study on the structure and development of professional competence of car mechatronics apprentices]. *Zeitschrift für Berufs- und Wirtschaftspädagogik, Beiheft, 25*, 55–76.

Gschwendtner, T., Abele, S., & Nickolaus, R. (2009). Computersimulierte Arbeitsproben: Eine Validierungsstudie am Beispiel der Fehlerdiagnoseleistung von KFZ-Mechatronikern [Validity study on interactive computer-based simulations for assessing car mechatronics' trouble shooting skills]. *Zeitschrift für Berufs- und Wirtschaftspädagogik, 105*, 557–578.

Gschwendtner, T., Abele, S., Schmidt, T., & Nickolaus, R. (2017). Multidimensional competency assessments and structures in VET. In D. Leutner, J. Fleischer, J. Grünkorn, & E. Klieme (Eds.), *Competence assessment in education: Research, models and instruments* (pp. 183–202). Berlin: Springer.

Hartig, J. (2007). Skalierung und Definition von Kompetenzniveaus [Proficiency scaling and definition of competence levels]. In B. Beck & E. Klieme (Eds.), *Sprachliche Kompetenzen. Konzepte und Messung* (pp. 83–99). Weinheim: Beltz.

Hartig, J., Frey, A., Nold, G., & Klieme, E. (2012). An application of explanatory item response modeling for model-based proficiency scaling. *Educational and Psychological Measurement, 72*, 665–686. doi:10.1177/0013164411430707.

Hu, L., & Bentler, P. M. (1998). Fit indices in covariance structure analysis: Sensitivity to underparameterized model misspecification. *Psychological Methods, 3*, 424–453.

Kauertz, A., Fischer, H. E., Mayer, J., Sumfleth, E., & Walpuski, M. (2010). Standardbezogene Kompetenzmodellierung in den Naturwissenschaften der Sekundarstufe I [Modeling competence according to standards for science education in secondary schools]. *Zeitschrift für Didaktik der Naturwissenschaften, 16*, 135–153.

Klieme, E., & Leutner, D. (2006). Kompetenzmodelle zur Erfassung individueller Lernergebnisse und zur Bilanzierung von Bildungsprozessen. Beschreibung eines neu eingerichteten Schwerpunktprogramms der DFG [Competence models for assessing individual learning outcomes and evaluating educational processes. Description of a new DFG priority program]. *Zeitschrift für Pädagogik, 52*, 876–903.

Klieme, E., Hartig, J., & Rauch, D. (2008). The concept of competence in educational contexts. In J. Hartig, E. Klieme, & D. Leutner (Eds.), *Assessment of competencies in educational contexts* (pp. 3–22). Göttingen: Hogrefe.

KMK (Standing Conference of the Ministers of Education and Cultural Affairs of the States in the Federal Republic of Germany). (Ed.). (1999). *Rahmenlehrpläne für die Berufsausbildung in der Bauwirtschaft. Beschluss vom 5.2. 1999* [Framework for the national curriculum for vocational education in the building trades. Resolution approved by the Standing Conference on 05 February 1999]. Retrieved from http://www.kmk.org/fileadmin/pdf/Bildung/BeruflicheBildung/rlp/Zimmerer.pdf

Muthén, L. K., & Muthén, B. O. (2010). *Mplus computer software*. Los Angeles: Author.

Muthén, L. K., & Muthén, B. O. (2012). *Mplus—Statistical analysis with latent variables: User's guide.* (7th edn.). Los Angeles: Author. Retrieved from http://www.statmodel.com/download/usersguide/Mplus%20user%20guide%20Ver_7_r6_wb.pdf

Nickolaus, R. (2014). Schwierigkeitsbestimmende Merkmale von Aufgaben und deren didaktische Relevanz [Task characteristics and their didactical relevance]. In U. Braukmann, B. Dilger & H.-H. Kremer (Eds.), Wirtschaftspädagogische Handlungsfelder: Festschrift für Peter F. E. Sloane zum 60. Geburtstag (pp. 285–304). Detmold: Eusl.

Nickolaus, R., & Seeber, S. (2013). Berufliche Kompetenzen: Modellierungen und diagnostische Verfahren [Modeling and measuring professional competencies]. In A. Frey, U. Lissmann, & B. Schwarz (Eds.), *Handbuch Berufspädagogische Diagnostik* (pp. 166–195). Weinheim: Beltz.

Nickolaus, R., Gschwendtner, T., & Geißel, B. (2008). Entwicklung und Modellierung beruflicher Fachkompetenz in der gewerblich-technischen Grundbildung [Development of professional competencies in technical vocational education and first approaches to a model of competence]. *Zeitschrift für Berufs- und Wirtschaftspädagogik, 104*, 48–73.

Nickolaus, R., Rosendahl, J., Gschwendtner, T., Geißel, B., & Straka, G. A. (2010). Erklärungsmodelle zur Kompetenz- und Motivationsentwicklung bei Bankkaufleuten, Kfz-Mechatronikern und Elektronikern [Explanatory models for the development of competencies and motivation of bank clerks, car mechatronics and electronics technician apprentices]. *Zeitschrift für Berufs- und Wirtschaftspädagogik, Beiheft, 23*, 73–87.

Nickolaus, R., Abele, S., Gschwendtner, T., Nitzschke, A., & Greiff, S. (2012). Fachspezifische Problemlösefähigkeit in gewerblich-technischen Ausbildungsberufen: Modellierung, erreichte Niveaus und relevante Einflussfaktoren [Competence structures, competence levels and important predictors of professional problem-solving skills in technical vocational education]. *Zeitschrift für Berufs- und Wirtschaftspädagogik, 108*, 243–272.

Nickolaus, R., Petsch, C., & Norwig, K. (2013). Berufsfachliche Kompetenzen am Ende der Grundbildung in bautechnischen Berufen [Professional competencies of building trade apprentices at the end of their first year of training]. *Zeitschrift für Berufs- und Wirtschaftspädagogik, 109*, 538–555.

Norwig, K., Petsch, C., & Nickolaus, R. (2010). Förderung lernschwacher Auszubildender: Effekte des berufsbezogenen Strategietrainings (BEST) auf die Entwicklung der bautechnischen Fachkompetenz [Professional strategy training for improving professional competencies of low-achieving apprentices in the building trades]. *Zeitschrift für Berufs- und Wirtschaftspädagogik, 106*, 220–239.

Norwig, K., Petsch, C., & Nickolaus, R. (2012). Den Übergang in die Berufsausbildung sichern — Fördertraining in der einjährigen Berufsfachschule Bautechnik [Supporting transition to dual vocational education: A training program for building trade apprentices in full-time vocational schools]. In A. Bojanowski & M. Eckert (Eds.), *Black Box Übergangsystem* (pp. 227–238). Münster: Waxmann.

Norwig, K., Petsch, C., & Nickolaus, R. (2013). Improving the professional competence of low-achieving apprentices: How to use diagnostics for successful training. In K. Beck & O. Zlatkin-Troitschanskaia (Eds.), *From diagnostics to learning success: Proceedings in vocational education and training* (pp. 169–182). Rotterdam: Sense.

Petsch, C., Norwig, K., & Nickolaus, R. (2011). (Wie) Können Auszubildende aus Fehlern lernen? Eine empirische Interventionsstudie in der Grundstufe Bautechnik [How to learn from mistakes? Results from an intervention study with building trade apprentices]. *Zeitschrift für Berufs- und Wirtschaftspädagogik, Beiheft, 25*, 129–146.

Petsch, C., & Norwig, K. (2012). *Berufsbezogenes Strategietraining BEST. Grundlagen und unterrichtliche Umsetzung* [BEST: Professional strategy training. Concept and implementation]. Stuttgart: Landesinstitut für Schulentwicklung.

Petsch, C., Norwig, K., & Nickolaus, R. (2014). Kompetenzförderung leistungsschwächerer Jugendlicher in der beruflichen Bildung: Förderansätze und ihre Effekte [Improving professional competence of low-achieving apprentices: Training programs and their effects]. *Zeitschrift für Erziehungswissenschaft, 17*, 81–101. doi:10.1007/s11618-013-0457-2.

Prenzel, M., Kristen, A., Dengler, P., Ettle, R., & Beer, T. (1996). Selbstbestimmt motiviertes und interessiertes Lernen in der kaufmännischen Erstausbildung [Self-determined and interest-driven learning in commercial vocational education]. *Zeitschrift für Berufs- und Wirtschaftspädagogik, Beiheft, 13*, 108–127. doi:10.1007/978-3-663-10645-6_2.

Rosendahl, J., & Straka, G. A. (2011). Kompetenzmodellierungen zur wirtschaftlichen Fachkompetenz angehender Bankkaufleute [Modeling professional competence of future bank clerks]. *Zeitschrift für Berufs- und Wirtschaftspädagogik, 107*, 190–217.

Seeber, S. (2008). Ansätze zur Modellierung beruflicher Fachkompetenz in kaufmännischen Ausbildungsberufen [Proposals for modeling professional competence in commercial vocational education]. *Zeitschrift für Berufs- und Wirtschaftspädagogik, 104*, 74–97.

Statistische Berichte Baden-Württemberg. (2014). *Unterricht und Bildung: Auszubildende in Baden-Württemberg 2013* [Teaching and education: Statistics on vocational education in Baden-Württemberg 2013]. Retrieved from https://www.statistik-bw.de/Veroeffentl/Statistische_Berichte/3241_13001.pdf

Tucker, L. R., & Lewis, C. (1973). A reliability coefficient for maximum likelihood factor analysis. *Psychometrika, 38*(1), 1–10. doi:10.1007/BF02291170.

Weinert, F. E. (2001). Concept of competence: A conceptual clarification. In D. S. Rychen & L. H. Salganik (Eds.), *Defining and selecting key competencies* (pp. 45–65). Seattle: Hogrefe & Huber Publishers.

Weiß, R. H. (2006). *CFT 20-R: Grundintelligenztest Skala 2—Revision* [Culture fair intelligence test, revised version]. Göttingen: Hogrefe.

Winther, E., & Achtenhagen, F. (2009). Skalen und Stufen kaufmännischer Kompetenz [Scales and levels of commercial professional competence]. *Zeitschrift für Berufs- und Wirtschaftspädagogik, 105*(4), 521–556.

Wu, M. L., Adams, R. J., & Wilson, M. R. (2007). *ACER ConQuest version 2.0. Generalised item response modelling software*. Camberwell: ACER Press.

Wülker, W. (2004). *Differenzielle Effekte von Unterrichtskonzeptionsformen in der gewerblichen Erstausbildung in Zimmererklassen: Eine empirische Studie* [Concepts of teaching and their effects on learning. An empirical study in classes of carpenter apprentices]. Aachen: Shaker.

Yu, C.-Y. (2002). *Evaluating cutoff criteria of model fit indices for latent variable models with binary and continuous outcomes*. Doctoral dissertation, University of California, Los Angeles. Retrieved from http://www.statmodel.com/download/Yudissertation.pdf

Chapter 14
Assessing Tomorrow's Potential: A Competence Measuring Approach in Vocational Education and Training

Viola Katharina Klotz and Esther Winther

Abstract Adequate measurement of action competence remains a central target of vocational education and training research; adequate measurement approaches in the vocational domain clearly are a prerequisite for accountable systems to authorize access to professional activities, as well as for future large-scale assessments. For the German Chamber of Commerce and Industry, competence assessments in the area of business and commerce rely mainly on final examinations that attempt to measure not just knowledge but also action competence. To evaluate and improve a test instrument, this chapter considers two questions: (1) how valid and reliable was the original test-format, and (2) how valid and reliable are the corresponding assessment results of a recently developed prototype? The study relies on statistical procedures (e.g., IRT scaling), applied empirically to a sample of 1768 final examinations of industrial managers in the original format, and to 479 industrial managers taking a prototype new format. The advanced prototype version appears as a more valid and accurate instrument to capture action competence. We conclude that several practical steps can be undertaken to improve current assessment practices in the area of business and commerce.

Keywords Vocational competence • Action competence • Assessment • Validity • Test reliability

V.K. Klotz (✉)
University of Mannheim, Mannheim, Germany
e-mail: viola.klotz@bwl.uni-mannheim.de

E. Winther
German Institute for Adult Education – Leibniz Centre for Lifelong Learning (DIE), Bonn, Germany
e-mail: winther@die-bonn.de

D. Leutner et al. (eds.), *Competence Assessment in Education*, Methodology of Educational Measurement and Assessment, DOI 10.1007/978-3-319-50030-0_14

14.1 Background

14.1.1 *Prospects and Demand for Adequate Competence Assessments in Vocational Education*

Explicit or implicit measures of vocational competence are relevant to many facets of vocational education and training (VET), and thus constitute an ever-growing research field. They pertain to national educational factors, such as the relevant information and instruments for managing the quality of the vocational educational systems and developing adequate support programs, but increasingly, they also appear in international policy agendas (e.g., BMBF 2008). That is, international comparisons and the acknowledgement of qualifications, as well as the encouragement of lifelong, informal learning, require adequate measurement concepts and innovative evaluation methods. To meet these multiple expectations, two major conditions must be fulfilled a priori (Klotz and Winther 2012).

First, we require empirically confirmable competence models that encompass conceptual operationalizations of competencies but also reveal a well-postulated theoretical structure that captures their empirical structure. From a scientific perspective, researchers seek empirical results related to the "true" structure of professional competencies. From a political point of view, knowledge about the structure and comparability of competencies is required to achieve large-scale assessments of VET, such as across Europe. In this context, compulsory education likely refers to a common curriculum of basic competencies, such as literacy or numeracy, but the structure of competencies within VET is more varied in content and therefore tends to be more complex. Thus, VET content is heterogeneous not only between countries but also across different professions within nations (Baethge et al. 2009) and even in specific workplaces (Billett 2006). This abundant variation creates an ongoing dilemma in respect of the need to construct generally valid competence tests. Uncertainty about the structure of competencies also undermines international comparisons and the development of binding international agreements for consistent competence standards. Some (albeit scarce) empirical research into the appropriate structure or model of competence suggests a content-based classification, such that item content exerts a characteristic influence on the structure. Other studies assume dimensionality, based on different cognitive processing heuristics, which may determine response behaviors (Nickolaus 2011; Nickolaus et al. 2008; Rosendahl and Straka 2011; Seeber 2008; Winther and Achtenhagen 2009).

A second necessary condition pertains to the reliability of the test results—that is, the certainty with which we can classify students according to a chosen test instrument. Neglecting these conditions poses serious risks, because people can easily be misclassified on the basis of their test results, and such classification errors can have severe consequences for their future professional advancement—for example, in terms of admission requirements.

With this study, we seek to evaluate both necessary conditions with respect to the current testing efforts on the original final examinations—which were examined in a former study (Klotz and Winther 2012; Winther and Klotz 2013)—but also on a newly developed assessment prototype within the research project "Competence-oriented assessments in VET and professional development". Specifically, we first describe how the German VET system currently operationalizes and measures competencies in the economic domain. Empirical results obtained from a sample of 1768 final examinations of industrial managers[1] reveal the extent to which current German assessment instruments in the area of business and commerce are qualified, in terms of their validity and reliability, to measure and classify students' economic action competence. We then describe our design criteria for a new prototype-version of final industrial examinations, and test this instrument on the empirical basis of 479 industrial managers. This study, in accordance with the SPP's broader research program, therefore seeks to develop valid and reliable competence models and thereby to improve current assessment practices. The results offer guidelines for the design of the final examinations for industrial managers and possibly for assessment in the broader vocational sector of business and commerce.

14.1.2 The Original Conceptualization of Final Examinations in the Area of Business and Commerce

Action competence offers a constitutive element of the German vocational system, and has been a significant topic of scientific and political discourse since the early 1980s, particularly in relation to the didactic implications of action regulation theory (Hacker 1986; Kuhl 1994; Volpert 1983). In the mid-1990s, the Standing Conference of the Ministers of Education and Cultural Affairs (*Kultusministerkonferenz*) formally adopted the concept of action competence as a central target. Specifically, by law, students must be instructed in a way that enables them to *plan*, *execute*, and *monitor* an entire action process in a working environment. This concept appears largely heuristic, but still must form the foundation for any test construction (BBIG 2005; §5). In practice, these assessments come from the German Chamber of Commerce and Industry (GCCI) and comprise both oral and written components. The oral component consists of a presentation and then a related expert discussion; it accounts for 30 % of the assessment. The written component comprises practical tasks pertaining to economics and social studies (10 %), as well as commercial management and control (20 %). The last part of the examination contains situational tasks that take the form of case studies related to business processes. This last, business processes section, represents the most important assessment area, in terms of processing time (180 min) and weighting (40 % of the final grade). For this reason, this study focuses on this assessment component.

According to the GCCI (2009), the design of the business processes test component is intended to require test takers to model processes, undertake complex tasks,

[1]The data were acquired from six offices of the German Chamber of Commerce and Industry: Luneburg, Hanover, Frankfurt on Main, Munich, Saarland, and Nuremberg.

analyze business processes, and solve problems in an outcome- and customer-oriented way. To implement these goals, the test designers operationalized action competence as three mutually exclusive process dimensions: planning, executing, and monitoring (GCCI 2009). Thus again, the business processes section seems particularly suitable for our empirical analysis of the structure of action competence.

If these process dimensions actually characterize a test situation, their solutions should require different sets of cognitive abilities in the test taker. This possibility was tested within an analysis of the structural validity of the original final examinations (Klotz and Winther 2012; Winther and Klotz 2013) on the empirical basis of $N = 1768$ industrial mangers. As a result, the structure of the assessment did not follow this postulated process-oriented operationalization, but instead appeared to be organized according to the four content domains of the assessment: *marketing and distribution*, *acquisition*, *human resource management (HRM)*, and *goods and services*. Such an alternative content-related model of competence measurement appears in some other vocational assessments (Nickolaus 2011; Rosendahl and Straka 2011; Seeber 2008). However, in the case of the final examinations of industrial managers, this solution appears disputable. The items depicting one dimension are often in close neighborhood and/or characterized by a common initial situation. The empirical solution of a content-related structure (root mean square error of approximation, RMSEA: .041; comparative fit index, CFI: .957; Tucker-Lewis index, TLI: .965) therefore does not necessarily represent cognitive structures, but might also be the mere consequence of the previous curriculum of commercial schools—which was officially abolished in 1996, and replaced by cross-disciplinary learning fields that sought to foster greater action competence by introducing the idea of process-orientation—or possibly even a relict of test sequence.

Besides the aspect of structural validity, we found infringements of the assessment's content validity in terms of content weighting (Winther 2011; Winther and Klotz 2013). As a final examination, the assessment should validly represent the commercial curriculum of industrial managers, which in turn should be based largely on real assignments in the workplace. With regard to content validity, a predominant part of the curriculum is dedicated to the *goods and services* domain (47 % of the curriculum and about one-third of practical training), and yet the proportion of content related to that topic in the original test was rather small (21 %). In particular, tasks related to modeling the processes of value creation and quantifiable production management are underrepresented, whereas the *marketing and distribution* content area appears overrepresented (38 % of the test), in relation both to percentage of the curriculum (26.7 %) and to practical relevance (25 %; see also Table 14.1).

In addition to these aspects of validity, the reliability of the original assessment was examined (Klotz and Winther 2012; see Fig. 14.1).

The information function for the test reaches its maximum for persons with an approximately average competence level. That is, near this area, it is possible to estimate, very precisely, test takers' true level of expertise (information = 7.4; reliability = .88). Further away from this maximum however, the test's estimation

Table 14.1 Weighting of content

Content area	Prototype weighting (%)	Original test's weighting (%)	Curricular content weighting (%)	Practical learning (/25 months)
Marketing and distribution	25	38.00	26.67	5–7 months
Acquisition	18.33	20.00	13.33	5–7 months
Human resources	15	21.00	13.33	2–6 months
Goods and services	41.66	21.00	46.67	6–10 months

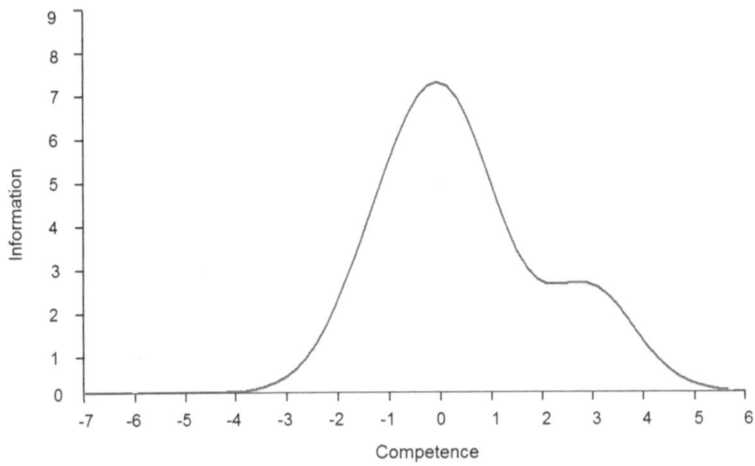

Fig. 14.1 Information curve for the original test

precision decreases rapidly. Students of relatively high ability, who are located in the positive space, reveal a lower albeit still sufficient information value. In contrast, students with strongly below-average expertise are estimated with an information value tending to zero. The test provides many measurement items related to an average ability level, along with some items to measure high ability levels, but features few easy items, designed to measure low levels of expertise. Therefore, the GCCI final examination lacks power to effectively differentiate test takers of low versus very low ability. However, this fact does not necessarily cause problems. Some tests are constructed explicitly to differentiate students precisely at a specific, crucial point. That is, we need to consider the specific purpose of any particular test instrument to assess its reliability. The primary purpose of the final examinations is to regulate access to the industrial management profession, such that test takers are separated simply into those who pass the test, and thus receive certification to enter the professional community, and those who do not.

Annually, approximately 95 % of test takers pass the test, based on a norm-oriented test decision,[2] so the most important separation point must fall far below an average competence level. Yet the amount of test information available in this range tends toward zero. This lack of reliability in final examinations not only infringes on statistical test standards but also has severe implications for the professional development and life of a vast number of students. Considering that about 12,000 apprentices take this final examination[3] yearly, 600 test decisions, regulating access to the apprentice's targeted profession, are taken with low certainty and are therefore possibly false.

In summary, evaluation of the validity and reliability of the original assessment reveals that the test entails not the intended process-oriented structure but rather, a subject-specific content structure that reflects a previous, officially abolished teaching structure and curriculum. This makes it quite surprising that this conceptualization still dominates in the test. The empirical results pertaining to the structure of vocational competence are consistent with studies in other vocational areas that similarly suggest the high relevance of subject-related domains in the structuring of professional competence measures (e.g., Nickolaus et al. 2008; Seeber 2008). However, this approach seems unsatisfactory for measuring competence acquired in VET. In particular, on the basis of constructivist theory (Gijbels et al. 2006), a theory-based assessment design must capture students' skills in thinking and reasoning effectively, and in solving complex problems autonomously.

In terms of the test's reliability, it should be acknowledged, that the original test format yielded good reliability values for an average competence value. However, the items do not demonstrate reliability in their ability to show up rather low competence values. The low reliability in this crucial area limits accurate identification of failures. Therefore, some examinees may—possibly wrongly—be denied certain positions within the professional community and within society as a whole. The reliability of the GCCI test instrument thus could be improved in this crucial competence area.

14.1.3 Assessment Model for Commercial Vocations

In order to improve the current examination we designed a new foundational conceptualization of the assessment, following the subsequent construct, design standards and concrete implementation steps (Winther and Klotz 2013):

1. *Construct Definition: A Domain Model*: The design of an evidence-based assessment is always initiated by a theoretical model of a given construct (Mislevy and Haertel 2006; Wilson 2005). We adopted the modeling approach of Gelman and Greeno (1989), who suggest that "failure due to the absence of knowledge of a

[2] Acquired from GCCI statistics for Munich and Upper Bavaria.

[3] Acquired from GCCI statistics for Chemnitz.

principle should be distinguished from failure due to the lack of the domain-relevant knowledge" (p. 141). We believe that such a competence model, comprising both general competencies in the economic domain (domain-related) and specific competence components (domain-specific) at a first stage, better depicts the development and nature of commercial competence. We modeled items for both competence dimensions, focusing on work requirements in specific occupations, but with a varying degree of generalizability (Winther and Achtenhagen 2008; Winther and Achtenhagen 2009; Winther 2010). We further assumed, in line with findings in general education, the existence of a verbal and a numerical component of domain-related competence (e.g., National Educational Psychological Service–NEPS). From a didactic as well as from an empirical point of view, verbal and numerical domain-related components (numeracy, literacy) influence the formation of domain-specific vocational competence (e.g., Nickolaus and Norwig 2009; Lehmann and Seeber 2007). Such a separation might also prevail for domain-specific competence, as the commercial curricula entail both verbal and numerical abilities. Therefore, the two dimensions of domain-linked and domain-specific competence might, at a second stage, subdivide into a verbal and a numerical component respectively. These two considerations generate a four-dimensional structure consisting of domain-related economic literacy, domain-related economic numeracy, domain-specific verbal competence and domain-specific numerical competence, such as is depicted in Fig. 14.2.

From a developmental perspective, however, we assume that at the end of the vocational training the domain-specific and the domain-related dimensions could

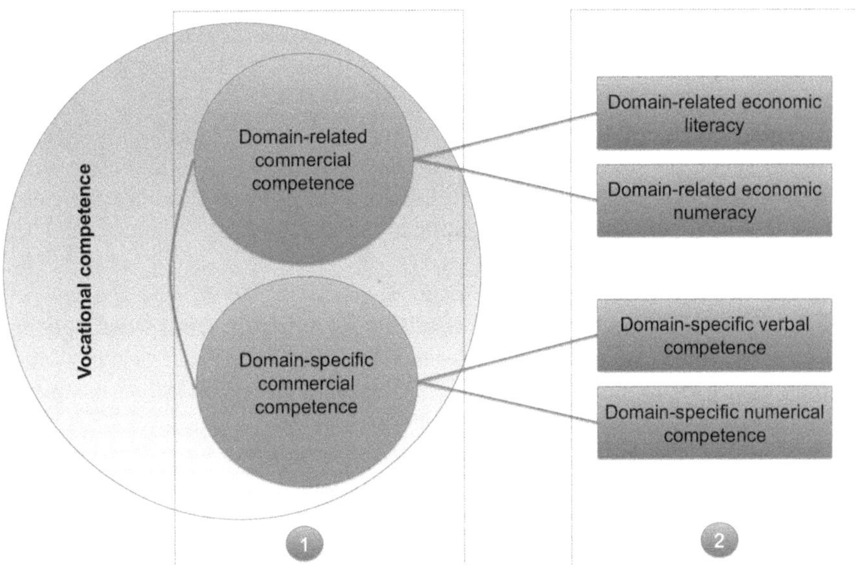

Fig. 14.2 Domain model of commercial competence

integrate into one dimension as the result of knowledge integration (Piaget 1971; Bransford et al. 1999). Knowledge integration should occur as the process of incorporating new information (domain-specific knowledge) into a body of existing knowledge (domain-related knowledge).

2. *Increasing Curricular Content Validity*: Within this general model of competence in the commercial domain, a crucial step within the item construction process was filling this model with concrete curricular-valid contents, focusing on work requirements in the specific occupational context of industrial managers. Here we designed, in accordance with our curricula analysis, more items pertaining to the *acquisition* and *goods and services* content areas, in order to better depict the vocational curriculum in terms of content weighting.
3. *Offering Sufficiently Complex Test Situations*: Recent commentary (e.g., Schmidt 2000; Winther 2010) suggests that the current test practices fail to give students sufficient room or potential to apply their knowledge to solve complex problems in a working context. We therefore, referring to the theoretical framework of Greeno et al. (1984), modeled items on three cognitive levels within our item design process:

   - Conceptual competence corresponds to factual knowledge as knowledge of facts and structures, which can be transmitted into action schemata;
   - Procedural competence subsumes the application of knowledge: that is, how to operate with facts, structures, knowledge nets and their corresponding elements;
   - Interpretative competence focuses on an interpretation of results and on decision processes.

   Forming a vertical competence structure based on a cognitive construct map (Wilson 2005) to test different competence qualities was also intended to increase the interpretability of the IRT (item response theory) test scores (i.e., criterion-based assessment).
4. *Securing Adequate Vocational Authenticity*: Test tasks for vocational education are authentic if they model real-life situations (Shavelson and Seminara 1968; Achtenhagen and Weber 2003). We therefore designed a model company as a test setting on the basis of a real company, and within this company modeled realistic work situations and work tasks.
5. *Implementing the Concept of Process-Orientation Within Test-Design*: We implemented the concept of process-orientation (Hacker 1986) by stimulating company operations across departments and their specific economic interrelations. In our design, learners had to analyze certain problems across departments and to integrate preceding information on the operating work process. That is, they could not—with regard to information management—exclude the informational context given for the other items, within the operating process. For example, with regard to our sample sequence of an operating process, given in Appendix, learners had to anticipate that the cheapest sub-contractor for the acquisition department would not meet the goods and services department's production deadline. Also, the apprentices had to deduce information from foregoing

client-relation events. For example, if an offer had already expired at its acceptance date, no binding contract would be in place.

6. *Raising the Test's Reliability*: To appropriately assign learners into grade-categories, and to achieve greater accuracy at the most crucial separation point of the test, at a low competence level, we designed some rather difficult items and also some items targeting a low competence level.

By incorporating these guiding principles into the final examination, we aimed to render the assessment instrument more valid and reliable and to move it beyond the current focus on component skills and discrete bits of knowledge, to encompass theoretically sound aspects of student achievement (Pellegrino et al. 2001) and of vocational competence as a coherent and transgressional concept. Furthermore, such a test structure might offer more information about the level of competence students actually acquire, and concrete starting points for developing support measures to improve their learning process, as well as a more detailed view of the development of the apprentices' competence.

14.2 Method

14.2.1 Sample

We implemented the above guiding principles within 30 tasks for a new prototype final examination for industrial managers. The test took 125 min, including reading test instructions (10 min) and completing a context survey (10 min). Sample tasks of our instrument can be found in Appendix. We determined the tests' validity and reliability on an empirical basis of $N = 479$ industrial managers who were assessed in March, April, October and November 2013 at four German vocational schools.[4] The sample consisted of 55 % women and 45 % men. The test takers were on average 21 years old.

14.2.2 Examination of Validity

Our evaluation of the validity criterion comprises two facets. First, it describes the operationalization of a theoretical concept, together with its potential subdimensions and observable indicators, to determine whether the focal approach offers a good notion of measurement in relation to the latent trait. It therefore entails the translation of the latent trait into contents, and then the contents into reasonable measurement items, and in this sense, it refers to *content validity* (Mislevy 2007). But even if an abstract concept is carefully operationalized, including all theoretical

[4] Munich, Hanover, Bielefeld and Paderborn.

aspects and a reasonable item design, it remains possible that the theoretical concept simply does not exist in the real world—or at least not in the way assumed by the researcher. Second, to address the potential gap between theory and observed reality, validity assessments entail testing *construct validity* to determine if the postulated theoretical structures arise from empirical test results (Embretson 1983; Mislevy 2007).

In order to ensure this first aspect of content validity, we first operationalized the vocational curriculum into content areas, then further into individual learning contents and, on the basis of this operationalization, developed test tasks. We then gave our developed test tasks to $N = 24$ vocational experts (10 industrial teachers and 14 industrial staff managers) in order to ensure that our situated item setting, as well as the content of the developed items, modeled real-life, authentic situations (Achtenhagen and Weber 2003; Shavelson 2008). The experts had to rate on a five-point Likert scale whether the test tasks referred to realistic work assignments carried out in the occupational practice, and on what level of cognitive complexity they resided. These expert ratings formed an integral part of our test design: If the external criterion of authenticity in terms of workplace relevance was evaluated as low for an item, such items were withdrawn from the assessment.

Because competence, as measured by final examinations, seemingly constitutes a multidimensional concept, the confirmation of its structure requires a multidimensional modeling approach. To analyze construct validity, we used multidimensional item response theory (MIRT). We implemented this approach in Mplus (Muthén and Muthén 2010) and used 1PL Rasch modeling.

14.2.3 Examination of Reliability

The term "reliability" describes the replicability and thus the accuracy with which each item measures its intended trait (Kiplinger 2008). According to Fischer (1974), item precision can be depicted by item information curves (or functions), which indicate the range over the measurement construct in which the item discriminates best among individuals. The inverse of the squared standard measurement error is equivalent to item information with respect to the latent trait (in our case, vocational competence). If the information is expansive, it is possible to identify a test taker whose true ability is at that level, with reasonable precision. For this analysis, we again applied an IRT standard. An important characteristic of IRT models is that they describe reliability in terms of measurement precision as a continuous function that is conditional on the values of the measured construct. It is therefore possible to model the test's reliability for each individual value of competence for every test taker (Hambleton and Russell 1993).

14.3 Results

14.3.1 Results for the Test's Validity

Our final weighting of test content was determined by relating the developed items back to the content domains of the vocational curriculum. We show the content weighting of each content area relative to all items of the test instrument, in Table 14.1.

Regarding the test's authenticity, in terms of the workplace relevance of the developed tasks, the items of the instrument achieved an average expert rating of workplace relevance four from five, indicating a "rather high" level of workplace authenticity. In terms of complexity, 38 % of the tasks were rated on a conceptual competence level, another 38 % on a procedural level and 24 % on an interpretative competence level.

After an analysis of the instrument's items, 2 tasks from 30 had to be removed, due to low separation ability, so that the instrument then comprised 28 tasks (7 for domain-related literacy, 11 for verbal domain-specific tasks, 7 for numeric domain-specific tasks and 3 for domain-related numeracy). In order to examine the construct validity of the prototype-version, we implemented, besides our theoretically assumed model (Model 6, depicted in Fig. 14.2, and here the second model stage), all alternative models (five possible combinations of lower dimensionality) and calculated the respective relative and absolute fit indices (see Table 14.2).

As the result of a relative consideration (Chi-Square difference testing), the theoretically-assumed four-dimensional structure fitted the data significantly better than the lower dimensional models. In terms of absolute fit, this model assumed a domain-related economic literacy component, a domain-related economic numeracy component, a domain-specific verbal competence component and a domain-specific numerical competence component, in which strong global model fit (RMSEA: .041; CFI: .931; TLI: .954) inhered. The four resulting dimensions correlate moderately to highly (Table 14.3).

Table 14.2 Relative and absolute fit indices of the postulated and alternative models

			Relative fit indices			Absolute fit indices		
Model	Parameter	*df*	AIC	BIC	χ^2	RMSEA	CFI	TLI
1	45	–	17,831	17,861	549,042	.075	.779	.848
2	47	2	17,805	17,836	493,386	.069	.810	.869
3	47	2	17,771	17,802	436,166	.063	.842	.892
4	50	3	17,761	17,795	452,960	.065	.832	.885
5	50	3	17,637	17,671	319,141	.048	.908	.938
6	54	4	17,591	17,627	277,329	.041	.931	.954

df degrees of freedom, *AIC* Akaike information criterion, *BIC* Bayes information criterion, χ^2 Chi-Square, *RMSEA* root mean square error of approximation, *CFI* comparative fit index, *TLI* Tucker-Lewis index

Table 14.3 Correlations, variance (σ^2) and reliability (based on EAP/PVs and WLEs) for model 6

Model 6	1.	2.	3.	4.	σ^2	EAP/PV	WLE
1. Domain-related literacy	1				0.92	.74	.47
2. Domain-specific verbal	.78***	1			1.01	.78	.67
3. Domain-specific numerical	.76***	.71***	1		0.96	.71	.50
4. Domain-related numeracy	.34***	.37***	.50***	1	1.29	.71	.45

EAP/PV reliability based on expected a posteriori scores, *WLE* reliability based on weighted likelihood estimates, ***$p < .001$

Taking a closer look, the dimensions correlated strongly among the degree of specificity and verbal versus numerical access. It is further noteworthy that the domain-specific components correlate more strongly than do the domain-related components.

14.3.2 Results for the Test's Reliability

The test's overall WLE (weighted likelihood estimates) reliability was .826. However, due to only 28 items being used in the final instrument, given the restricted test time for the final examination, the values for the four-dimensional model were not sufficient to accurately depict each test taker on all of the four scales, as can be seen in Table 14.3. Only the EAP/PV (expected a posteriori scores) scale reliability, as a value of internal scale coherence, yielded sufficient values for all four scales. Using the IRT standard, we then computed the amount of information for each ability level for the developed prototype test, in order to compare it with that on the original GCCI test instrument. Here we used the one-dimensional model—not only because we had to, in order to make a comparison between the original and the prototype version—but also because we found it appropriate to enable us to make statements about how precisely students can be distinguished from one another through the use of this instrument, in respect of their final grading. This final test decision has to be made for the instrument as a whole. The resulting information function was generally increased in height and spread, and was characterized by an overall flatter gradient compared to the original test's function (see Fig. 14.3).

The information function for the prototype test reaches its maximum for persons with an approximately −.05 competence value on the logit scale. That is, at this point, test takers' true level of expertise is estimated with high precision (reliability = .89). However, for this competence area the original instrument seemed just as good (reliability = .88). For students with relatively high ability (2 on the logit scale) the test still revealed a good informative value (reliability = .78). Even for the best student, with a value of 5.8 on the logit scale, the reliability still amounted to .50, compared to zero for the original test. For students with a rather low competence level (−2 on the logit scale) their competence value was estimated with a reliability of .86 (compared to a reliability of .69 for the original instrument). And even for a

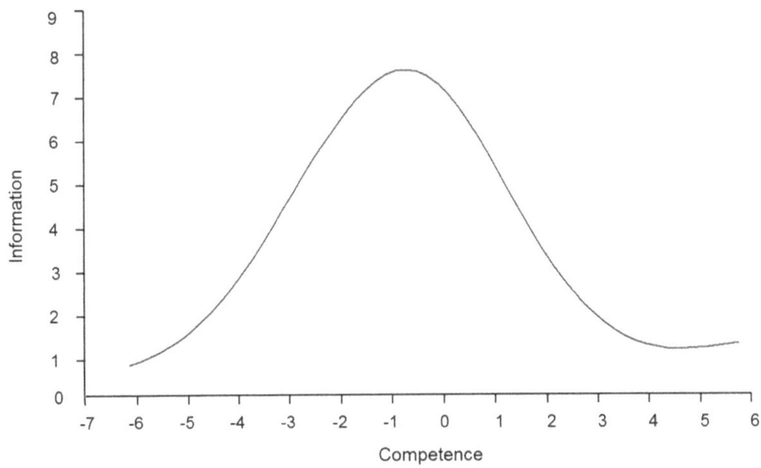

Fig. 14.3 Information curve for the prototype test

very low competence value, constituting the crucial separation area of passing or failing the test, at about a logit of −4, a reasonable reliability value of .69 was obtained, compared to a value of zero in the original test format.

14.4 Discussion

Regarding validity, we examined two concepts: (1) the translation of the latent trait into contents, as well as the resulting contents into reasonable measurement items *(content validity)*, and (2) the potential gap between the assumed theoretical content structure and observed reality *(construct validity)*. Regarding content validity, we adapted the test assembly in such a way that the final weighting of the test content now related more adequately to the amount of content weight within the vocational curriculum, compared to the original version. Further, a more salient distribution of the test items over the taxonomy of cognitive complexity was implemented within the test design and then confirmed by expert ratings. Finally, the expert ratings also functioned as a critical counterpoint within the assessment design. Within the test assembly process ("assembly model"; Mislevy and Riconscente 2005) the rating of workplace authenticity formed a crucial criterion for the final item selection; that is, that only items with an above average rating were taken into the final test. The final degree of authenticity of the instrument in terms of workplace relevance is satisfactory, but possibly could be further improved by a second round of item modeling and expert selection.

Regarding construct validity, the comparison of relative model fit, as well as Chi-Square difference testing, suggests a four-dimensional structure, comprising a domain-related economic literacy component, a domain-related economic numeracy component, a domain-specific verbal competence component and a domain-specific numerical competence component. The correlations between the resulting dimensions suggest that the structures are sufficiently divergent in terms of discriminant validity (see Table 14.3). However, in terms of an absolute model fit, a model suggesting a three-dimensional structure consisting of a domain-specific component, a numeracy and a literacy component, such as that suggested by Winther (2010) already attains a sufficient global model fit (RMSEA: .048; CFI: .908; TLI: .938). This is due to the higher correlation of numerical and verbal aspects for domain-specific competence ($r = .71$; $p < .001$) than for domain-related competence ($r = .34$; $p < .001$). It seems that, with an increasing degree of vocational specificity, the importance of the distinction of numerical versus verbal access decreases appreciably, supporting the idea of the integration of numerical and verbal knowledge aspects in specific vocational abilities.

However, the integration of domain-related and domain-specific competence at the end of the vocational training, in the sense of a total integration into one dimension, like that suggested by Winther (2010), cannot be found within our data. It is imaginable that this integration takes place at a later developmental stage, with an increasing degree of vocational experience and routine. Or we may have to acknowledge that there is no absolute integration of domain-related and domain-specific competence dimensions, and that the two competence dimensions are indeed related (correlation of domain-specific and domain-related competence within a two-dimensional model: $r = .77$; $p < .001$) but remain separate dimensions in terms of dimensionality over the vocational trajectory.

Regarding the test's reliability, we designed the assessment instrument explicitly in regard to the specific purpose of the final examinations. That is, first of all, to differentiate students precisely at the most crucial point of separation, of passing or failing the test and therefore being granted or denied access to the vocational community as a full member. Second, to allow for a signaling function for future employers in the vocational final assessment, in terms of a dependable grading (Weiß 2011). We therefore designed more items targeting a low competence level and also some more difficult items, in order to also differentiate precisely for a progressed level of competence.

The obtained information curve suggests that the prototype examination is capable of a precise measurement of an around average ability—similarly to the original instrument. It also effectively differentiates test takers of low versus very low ability and test takers with high versus very high ability, and therefore measures precisely along the logit scale and visibly adds significant value, compared to the original instrument. However, this only applies to the test instrument as a whole. Accuracy at an individual diagnostic level was not reached for each of the four dimensions separately. We conclude therefore that the desired function of the new prototype examination of classifying students, can be administered with an adequate degree of certainty only for a one-dimensional model and not for the postulated four-dimensional structure, within restricted test times.

14.5 Conclusions

Our research endeavor focusing explicitly on the improvement of current assessment practice, illustrates that the identification of theoretically sound and empirically confirmable structures and reliability is not intended as a question of statistical test esthetics, but is a necessary prerequisite of school policy and assessment as they move towards an evidence-based practice (Slavin 2002), in turn optimizing educational processes and educational decisions (Koeppen et al. 2008).

First, evaluation of the validity of the original final examinations, provided by a former study within our research project, reveals that the criteria of content validity were not completely adhered to. Furthermore, the analyzed GCCI assessment entailed not the intended, process-oriented structure but rather a content-related structure. Finally, with regard to the accuracy with which the final examination distinguishes and classifies students, the test did not provide enough items to measure below-average competence levels accurately.

In order to improve the final examination of commercial competence for industrial clerks, we designed a new foundational conceptualization of the assessment, following the idea of an evidence-based assessment design, including a careful construct operationalization, a reviewed item design process and an extensive empirical checkup on the obtained data, in order to draw inferences about students' knowledge and skills (Mislevy and Riconscente 2005). Our results suggest that the developed prototype version of the final examinations can capture students' skills in thinking and reasoning effectively and in solving complex problems (Pellegrino et al. 2001) in a more valid and also precise way: The items are adequate in terms of their content (curricular validity, complexity, authenticity) and in terms of their intended structural validity (construct validity). The instrument furthermore demonstrates reliability in its ability to differentiate adequately among students and to assign them to classes with a sufficient degree of certainty, as a prerequisite for fair opportunities to attain certain positions within the professional community and within society as a whole.

Acknowledgments The preparation of this chapter was supported by grant "Competence-oriented assessments in VET and professional development" (Winther, 2009-2014; Wi 3597/1-1; 1-2) from the German Research Foundation (DFG) in the Priority Program "Competence Models for Assessing Individual Learning Outcomes and Evaluating Educational Processes" (SPP 1293).

Appendix

Ceraforma Keramik AG

Since its foundation in 1982, Ceraforma Keramik AG has developed into an expanding and globally active industrial enterprise, having their head office in Aachen, Germany. The company is involved in the production of ceramic goods, such as china and porcelain for tableware and vases or sanitary ware.

In the past, the management of Ceraforma Keramik realized that the four divisions: procurement logistics, production, human resource management as well as marketing and sales, were operating too independently of each other, which caused disturbances in the performance process and led to customer complaints. In response to these problems, so-called *horizontal teams* were established, consisting of work members from different company divisions.

You have been employed with Ceraforma Keramik in such a horizontal team since the beginning of this year. Here, the allocated customer orders are being handled in all business processes, ranging from the receipt of orders to the settlement of accounts. Ms. Kenk, the team leader, Mr. Friebel and Ms. Hoffmann, the new trainee, are your colleagues in the horizontal team.

Business Process 1

Situation
Your team just received a new customer enquiry. Your colleague, Mr. Friebel, shows you the following e-mail, which arrived on 30 March 20… at 10:17.

An… 'info@ceraforma.de';
Cc…
Bcc…
Betreff: Waschbecken der Reihe "Swing"

Dear Sir/Madam,

Whilst seeking manufacturers of ceramic goods, we have come across your company, which has attracted our attention.

We are DIY retailers and our head office is in Hannover. We are looking for a supplier for sanitary ceramics and are especially interested in the washbasin in your design series „Swing".

We would appreciate receiving your corresponding quotation for 2,400 pieces, your soonest delivery date and terms of delivery at your earliest convenience.

Sincerely yours,

Karl Schwiene´
Head of Procurement

Bauhannes GmbH
Junkersstraße 8
30179 Hannover
eMail: karl.schwienert@bauhannes.de
Tel.: +49 (0)511-123321
Fax: +49 (0)511-456654
Mobil: +49 (0)176-123654

Amtsgericht Hannover, HRB 1234, Geschäftsführer:
Dr. Konrad Kluge, Aufsichtsratsvorsitz: Emanuel Windig
Umsatzst.-Id: DE123456789

1.1 Since there have not yet been any business relations with the Bauhannes Ltd. company, you are requested by Mr. Friebel to gather detailed information on the financial standing of the potential customer.

Which two kinds of information would you gather to assess the risk and which two outside sources would you contact?

1.4 After repeated negotiations the company Ceraforma accepts the order from the DIY Bauhannes at the price stipulated by Mr. Schwienert. Receipt of confirmation of the order by email is on Friday, 6 April 20... You have been informed that there is no suffient quantity of quartz crystal on stock to execute the order. You are therefore required to order 25 tons of new quartz crystals. You then contact various suppliers by mail and you receive the emails below from Mineral Seifert AG from Aachen, and Tam-Quarz Ltd. from South Africa:

An: horizontalteam3@ceraforma.de
Kopie:
Blindkopie:
Betreff: Unser Angebot für Sie

Lieber Herr Friebel,

wir freuen uns, dass wir Sie wieder einmal von unseren Produkten und Leistungen überzeugen konnten.

Aufgrund unser langjährigen Geschäftsbeziehungen, können wir Ihnen zu Ihrer Anfrage folgende Konditionen anbieten:

Produkt	reiner Quarz, Bergkristall, weiß
Preis/Menge:	500,00 EUR/t inkl. MwSt.
Zahlungsbedingungen:	10 Tage 3 % Skonto; 60 Tage netto Kasse
Bezugskosten:	100,00 EUR pauschal/Lieferung
Lieferzeit	3 Werktage ab Bestellungseingang
Angebot ist gültig:	bis zum 15.04.20..

Wir würde uns freuen, wenn Sie sich erneut für unsere Produkte und unseren Service entscheiden würden.

Einen schönen Tag noch und freundliche Grüße

Jörg Schewe
Vertrieb
Mineral Geifert AG Aachen

An: horizontalteam3@ceraforma.de
Kopie:
Blindkopie:
Betreff: RE: Angebotsanfrage

Dear Sir/ Madam,

In reply to your enquiry dated xy.20.. we are pleased to make the following offer:

- white mountain quartz crystal: € 450.00/ ton
- minimum order quantity: 10 tons
- shipping charges: € 13.00/ 100kg

Since this is your first order, we allow a quantity discount of 3% per ton for orders exceeding 30 tons.

This offer is valid until April 15, 20.. Please consider that transportation by ship might takes up to a month.

We look forward to hearing from you soon!

Sincerely, (alternative: Yours sincerely/ Kind regards)

J. Stones
Tam-Quarz, South Africa
Mail: stones@tam.za

Please compare both offers and give reasons for which offer you would decide. When making your decision you should consider also possible risks and social and ecological issues, besides financial aspects. Also bear in mind that Ceraforma have sufficient liquid funds and that discounts granted can be fully exploited.

References

Achtenhagen, F., & Weber, S. (2003). "Authentizität" in der Gestaltung beruflicher Lernumgebung ["Authenticity" in the design of vocational learning environments]. In A. Bredow, R. Dobischat, & J. Rottmann (Eds.), *Berufs- und Wirtschaftspädagogik von A-Z. Grundlagen, Kernfragen und Perspektiven: Festschrift für Günter Kutscha* (pp. 185–199). Baltmannsweiler: Schneider.

Baethge, M., Arends, L., & Winther, E. (2009). International large-scale assessment on vocational and occupational education and training. In F. Oser, U. Renold, E. G. John, E. Winther, & S. Weber (Eds.), *VET boost: Towards a theory of professional competences: Essays in honor of Frank Achtenhagen* (pp. 3–24). Rotterdam: Sense.

BBIG (Berufsbildungsgesetz) 1. (2005, April). Retrieved from http://www.gesetze-im-internet.de/bundesrecht/bbig_2005/gesamt.pdf.

Billett, S. (2006). *Work, change and workers*. Dordrecht: Springer.

BMBF (Bundesministerium für Bildung und Forschung). (2008). *Framework programme for the promotion of empirical educational research*. Bonn: Author.

Bransford, J. D., Brown, A. L., & Cooking, R. R. (1999). *How people learn: Brain, mind, experience, and school*. New York: National Academy of Sciences.

Embretson, S. E. (1983). Construct validity: Construct representation versus nomothetic span. *Psychological Bulletin, 93*, 179–197. doi:10.1037/0033-2909.93.1.179.

Fischer, G. H. (1974). *Einführung in die Theorie psychologischer Tests* [An introduction to the theory of psychological tests]. Bern: Huber.

GCCI (German Chamber of Commerce and Industry), & Aufgabenstelle für käufmännische Abschluss- und Zwischenprüfungen (AKA). (Eds.). (2009). *Prüfungskatalog für die IHK-Abschlussprüfungen* [Test catalog for the GCCI's final examinations]. Nürnberg: AKA.

Gelman, R., & Greeno, J. G. (1989). On the nature of competence: Principles for understanding in a domain. In L. B. Resnick (Ed.), *Knowing and learning: Essays in honor of Robert Glaser* (pp. 125–186). Hillsdale: Erlbaum.

Gijbels, D., Van De Watering, G., Dochy, F., & Van Den Bossche, P. (2006). New learning environments and constructivism: The students' perspective. *Instructional Science, 34*, 213–226. doi:10.1007/s11251-005-3347-z.

Greeno, J. G., Riley, M. S., & Gelman, R. (1984). Conceptual competence and children's counting. *Cognitive Psychology, 16*, 94–143. doi:10.1016/0010-0285(84)90005-7.

Hacker, W. (1986). *Arbeitspsychologie. Psychische Regulation von Arbeitstätigkeiten* [Action-regulation-theory. Psychological regulation of occupational actions]. Bern: Huber.

Hambleton, R. K., & Russell, W. J. (1993). Comparison of classical test theory and item response theory and their applications to test development. *Educational Measurement, 12*(3), 38–47. doi:10.1111/j.1745-3992.1993.tb00543.x.

Kiplinger, L. (2008). Reliability of large scale assessment and accountability systems. In K. E. Ryan & L. A. Shepard (Eds.), *The future of test-based educational accountability* (pp. 93–113). New York: Routledge.

Klotz, V. K., & Winther, E. (2012). Kompetenzmessung in der kaufmännischen Berufsausbildung: Zwischen Prozessorientierung und Fachbezug [Competence measurement in commercial vocational training: Between processual and content-related perspectives]. *Bwp@ Berufs- und Wirtschaftspädagogik —Online, 22.*

Koeppen, K., Hartig, J., Klieme, E., & Leutner, D. (2008). Current issues in competence modeling and assessment. *Journal of Psychology, 216*(2), 61–73.

Kuhl, J. (1994). A theory of action and state orientation. In J. Kuhl & J. Beckmann (Eds.), *Volition and personality: Action vs. state orientation* (pp. 97–129). Seattle: Hogrefe.

Lehmann, R., & Seeber, S. (Eds.). (2007). *ULME III. Untersuchung von Leistungen, Motivation und Einstellungen der Schülerinnen und Schüler in den Abschlussklassen der Berufsschulen* [ULME III. Examination of performance, motivation and attitudes of students at the end of their vocational training]. Hamburg: HIBB.

Mislevy, R. J. (2007). Validity by design. *Educational Researcher, 36*, 463–469. doi:10.3102/0013189X07311660.

Mislevy, R. J., & Haertel, G. D. (2006). Implications of evidence-centered design for educational testing. *Educational Measurement, 25*(4), 6–20. doi:10.1111/j.1745-3992.2006.00075.x.

Mislevy, R. J., & Riconscente, M. (2005). *Evidence-centered assessment design: Layers, structures, and terminology* (PADI Technical report 9). Menlo Park: SRI International.

Muthén, L. K., & Muthén, B. O. (2010). *Mplus user's guide* (6th ed.). Los Angeles: Author.

Nickolaus, R. (2011). Die Erfassung fachlicher Kompetenz und ihrer Entwicklungen in der beruflichen Bildung: Forschungsstand und Perspektiven [Assessing professional expertise and its development: Current state of research and future perspectives]. In O. Zlatkin-Troitschanskaia (Ed.), *Stationen empirischer Bildungsforschung: Traditionslinien und Perspektiven* (pp. 331–351). Wiesbaden: Springer.

Nickolaus, R., & Norwig, K. (2009). Mathematische Kompetenzen von Auszubildenden und ihre Relevanz für die Entwicklung der Fachkompetenz: Ein Überblick zum Forschungsstand [Mathematical competences of apprentices and their relevance for the development of vocational expertise: An overview regarding the current state of research]. In A. Heinze & M. Grüßing (Eds.), *Mathematiklernen vom Kindergarten bis zum Studium. Kontinuität und Kohärenz als Herausforderung für den Mathematikunterricht* (pp. 204–216). Münster: Waxmann.

Nickolaus, R., Gschwendter, T., & Geißel, B. (2008). Modellierung und Entwicklung beruflicher Fachkompetenz in der gewerblich-technischen Erstausbildung [Assessing vocational expertise and its development over commercial-technical initial trainings]. *Zeitschrift für Berufs-und Wirtschaftspädagogik, 104*, 48–73.

Pellegrino, J. W., Chudowsky, N., & Glaser, R. (2001). *Knowing what students know: The science and design of educational assessment*. Washington, DC: National Academy Press.

Piaget, J. (1971). *Biology and knowledge; an essay on the relations between organic regulations and cognitive processes*. Chicago: University of Chicago Press.

Rosendahl, J., & Straka, G. A. (2011). Kompetenzmodellierungen zur wirtschaftlichen Fachkompetenz angehender Bankkaufleute [Modeling commercial expertise of beginning bankers]. *Zeitschrift für Berufs- und Wirtschaftspädagogik, 107*, 190–217.

Schmidt, J. U. (2000). Prüfungen auf dem Prüfstand: Betriebe beurteilen die Aussagekraft von Prüfungen [Examining final examinations: Firms evaluate the explanatory power of final examinations]. *Berufsbildung in Wissenschaft und Praxis, 29*(5), 27–31.

Seeber, S. (2008). Ansätze zur Modellierung beruflicher Fachkompetenz in kaufmännischen Ausbildungsberufen [Approaches for the modeling of vocational expertise in commercial vocations]. *Zeitschrift für Berufs- und Wirtschaftspädagogik, 104*, 74–97.

Shavelson, R. J. (2008). Reflections on quantitative reasoning: An assessment perspective. In B. L. Madison & L. A. Steen (Eds.), *Calculation vs. context: Quantitative literacy and its implications for teacher education* (pp. 27–47). Washington, DC: MAA.

Shavelson, R. J., & Seminara, J. L. (1968). Effect of lunar gravity on man's performance of basic maintenance tasks. *Journal of Applied Psychology, 52*, 177–183.

Slavin, R. E. (2002). Evidence-based education policies: Transforming educational practice and research. *Educational Researcher, 31*(7), 15–21. doi:10.3102/0013189X031007015.

Volpert, W. (1983). *Handlungsstrukturanalyse als Beitrag zur Qualifikationsforschung* [Analysis of the structure of actions as a contribution to qualification research]. Köln: Pahl-Rugenstein.

Weiß, R. (2011). Prüfungen in der beruflichen Bildung: Ein vernachlässigter Forschungsgegenstand [Examinations in vocational education: A neglected field of research]. In E. Severing & R. Weiß (Eds.), *Prüfungen und Zertifizierung in der beruflichen Bildung: Anforderungen–Instrumente–Forschungsbedarf* (pp. 37–52). Bielefeld: Bertelsmann.

Wilson, M. (2005). *Constructing measures: An item response modeling approach*. Mahwah: Erlbaum.

Winther, E. (2010). *Kompetenzmessung in der beruflichen Bildung* [Competence measurement in vocational education]. Bielefeld: Bertelsmann.

Winther, E. (2011). Kompetenzorientierte Assessments in der beruflichen Bildung: Am Beispiel der Ausbildung von Industriekaufleuten [Competence-oriented assessments in vocational education]. *Zeitschrift für Berufs- und Wirtschaftspädagogik, 107*, 33–54. doi:10.1186/1877-6345-5-2.

Winther, E., & Achtenhagen, F. (2008). Kompetenzstrukturmodell für die kaufmännische Bildung. Adaptierbare Forschungslinien und theoretische Ausgestaltung [A structural competence model for commercial education]. *Zeitschrift für Berufs- und Wirtschaftspädagogik, 104*, 511–538.

Winther, E., & Achtenhagen, F. (2009). Measurement of vocational competencies—A contribution to an international large-scale assessment on vocational education and training. *Empirical Research in Vocational Education and Training, 1*, 88–106.

Winther, E., & Klotz, V. K. (2013). Measurement of vocational competences: An analysis of the structure and reliability of current assessment practices in economic domains. *Empirical Research in Vocational Education & Training, 5*(2), 1–12. doi:10.1186/1877-6345-5-2.

Part IV
Competency Development: Modeling of Change and Training of Competencies

Chapter 15
The Development of Students' Physics Competence in Middle School

Susanne Weßnigk, Knut Neumann, Tobias Viering, David Hadinek, and Hans E. Fischer

Abstract The German National Education Standards (NES) for biology, chemistry and physics define the level of competence students are expected to have developed in these subjects by the end of middle school. In order to help students meet these goals, models are needed that describe how students develop competence in the respective subjects. This chapter details our efforts in developing such a model for physics. More specifically, we focused on how students develop an understanding of energy — a concept central to physics. Based on a model derived from previous research, a set of 118 energy tasks were authored and utilized to investigate students' progression in understanding the concept of energy in (1) a cross-sectional study with students from Grades 6, 8, and 10 of middle school, and (2) a longitudinal study following students from Grade 6 through middle school. The results indicate that students progress in understanding energy by successively developing an understanding of four key ideas about energy. Results from the longitudinal study suggest moreover that students' progression depends on the (school) curriculum. These results provide important information for further improving the teaching and learning of energy in middle school physics.

Keywords Student competence • Competence development • Learning progression • Energy

---

S. Weßnigk (✉)
Institut für Didaktik der Mathematik und Physik, Leibniz Universität Hannover, Hannover, Germany
e-mail: wessnigk@idmp.uni-hannover.de

K. Neumann • D. Hadinek
Leibniz Institute for Science and Mathematics Education (IPN), Kiel, Germany
e-mail: neumann@ipn.uni-kiel.de; hadinek@ipn.uni-kiel.de

T. Viering
Ulrich-von-Hutten-Gymnasium, Schlüchtern, Germany
e-mail: tobias@viering.biz

H.E. Fischer
University of Duisburg-Essen, Essen, Germany
e-mail: hans.fischer@uni-due.de

D. Leutner et al. (eds.), *Competence Assessment in Education*, Methodology of Educational Measurement and Assessment, DOI 10.1007/978-3-319-50030-0_15

15.1 Introduction

In response to ever-accelerating scientific progress, expectations of what students should learn about science in school have changed (National Research Council [NRC] 2012). Instead of accumulating vast amounts of knowledge about science, students are now expected to develop competence in science (Organisation for Economic Co-operation and Development [OECD] 2001). That is, students are expected to develop a deep understanding of core science concepts and to be able to use this understanding to solve problems across multiple contexts (e.g., NRC 2012; KMK 2005). In order to help students advance toward competence in science, models describing ideal pathways of student learning from one grade to the next, and over multiple grades, are needed (Duschl et al. 2011). These models could then serve as a foundation for examining students' progression toward competence in science as a function of the current curriculum, and for designing improved curricula to better support students in developing competence in science in the future.

In this chapter, we report on our efforts to create a model of how students develop competence in physics. More specifically, we are proposing and validating a model of how students—as a function of middle school physics instruction—develop understanding of the concept of energy, and the ability to use this understanding to solve physics problems across multiple contexts.

15.2 Theoretical Background

Energy is a core idea in physics (NRC 2012). It has been the key to solving some of the most important physics problems in the past, and will be the key to many others in the future. However, energy is also a key to phenomena in other domains of science, as well as to major social issues such as the energy crisis (Driver and Millar 1986). In order to be able to solve physics-related problems across a variety of contexts, from physics, science and their everyday life — and thus develop competence in physics — students need to develop a deep understanding of the concept of energy.

15.2.1 Students' Understanding of Energy

Students' understanding of the concept of energy has been subject to many studies at different age levels and different levels of schooling (for an overview see Doménech et al. 2007 or Chen et al. 2014). Studies of students' understanding prior to instruction about energy have provided ample evidence that at this level, students' understanding is mainly determined by non-normative ideas (e.g., Duit 1981; Stead 1980; Solomon 1983; Trumper 1990, 1993; for a summary see Watts 1983).

Students in the first year of secondary education (i.e., at an age of about 10–11 years) were, for example, found to associate energy mainly with living things (e.g., Stead 1980; Solomon 1983; Trumper 1993). And although students in later years (i.e., at an age of about 12–16 years) associated energy also with non-living things, their understanding was still restricted to scientifically inappropriate ideas, such as the idea of energy as some kind of (universal) fuel required to keep machines running, or more generally, the idea of energy as the cause of events (e.g., Solomon 1983; Trumper 1993).

Studies exploring students' understanding after energy instruction (e.g., Duit 1981; Solomon 1983; Trumper 1990), have suggested that these non-normative ideas are relatively persistent. However, these studies have also shown that after instruction, students exhibit a somewhat more scientific understanding of energy and that this understanding includes ideas about energy forms, energy transfer and transformation, energy degradation, and energy conservation (e.g., Boyes and Stanisstreet 1990; Duit 1981; Trumper 1990, 1991). Only at the end of secondary education, however, were students (and only the most able students) found to have an understanding of energy that included the idea of energy conservation (Duit 1981; see also Boyes and Stanisstreet 1990; Driver and Warrington 1985).

15.2.2 Students' Learning About Energy

Based on their review of the extensive research on students' understanding of energy, Driver et al. (1994) proposed that students' ideal progression in understanding energy is marked by students (successively) developing understanding of the following ideas: (1) personal energeticness, (2) the energeticness of other living things, (3) nonliving things spontaneously being able to do things, (4) the energeticness of some nonliving things that possess energy, storage of energy in elastic materials, gravitational potential energy, (5) energy transformation and transfer, (6) energy conservation, and (7) energy degradation. Taking Driver, Squires, Rushworth, and Wood-Robinson's (1994) work as a point of departure, Liu and McKeough (2005) investigated students' progression in understanding the concept of energy from elementary to high school. The results suggested that students progress in understanding energy from (non-normative) ideas developed from everyday experiences, such as the idea of energy as an activity, by successively developing understanding of the following key (scientific) ideas: (1) energy forms and sources, (2) energy transfer and transformations, (3) energy degradation, and (4) energy conservation (Liu and McKeough 2005). These findings were subsequently corroborated by several other researchers (e.g., Dawson-Tunik 2006; Lee and Liu 2010; Nordine et al. 2010). However, while these findings inform us about how students progress in developing an understanding of energy as a whole, they provide little information on how students develop understanding of the individual (key) ideas. That is, how students who have mastered an understanding of one key idea develop an understanding of the next.

In the past, science education researchers have successfully used the complexity of students' knowledge base to describe different qualities in students' understanding of science as a whole, of individual domains of science and even scientific concepts (e.g., Bernholt and Parchmann 2011; Geller et al. 2014; Kauertz and Fischer 2006; Liu et al. 2008; see also Bransford et al. 2000). Liu et al. (2008), for example, have provided evidence that the level of knowledge integration students exhibit (i.e., the number of [scientific] ideas students can link to each other) provides a sound framework for describing students' understanding of science. Kauertz and Fischer (2006) have successfully demonstrated that the difficulty of physics items depends on the complexity of the knowledge required to solve the item. Similar findings have been presented for the domain of chemistry (Bernholt and Parchmann 2011). Geller et al. (2014) have utilized the framework developed by Kauertz and Fischer (2006) to measure students' learning about electricity. And Stevens et al. (2010) have built on the idea of the complexity of students' knowledge to describe different levels of understanding the concept of matter. Most importantly, however, the complexity of students' knowledge base has been used to explain why understanding energy conservation (which requires the integration of many scientific ideas) is more difficult than understanding energy forms (which requires fewer ideas to be linked; Lee and Liu 2010), and to measure students' learning about energy as a function of instruction (Nordine et al. 2010). All this research builds on the idea that students develop understanding of a particular idea, topic or domain by (1) acquiring new knowledge elements and (2) establishing links between these new knowledge elements and previously acquired knowledge elements. This suggests that students develop understanding of the individual key ideas by acquiring knowledge elements (facts), establishing links between these elements (mappings), and qualifying the links between the elements (relations) — up to the point where students have developed a well-connected knowledge base about the respective idea (cf. Bransford et al. 2000).

15.3 Research Questions

In our research we aimed to develop and validate a model of how students develop understanding of the concept of energy as a result of middle school physics instruction. Based on our review of previous research we hypothesized that students' progress in their understanding of energy by successively developing understanding of four key ideas about energy: (1) energy forms and sources, (2) understanding energy transfer and transformation, (3) understanding energy degradation, and (4) understanding energy conservation. We hypothesized moreover, that students develop understanding of the individual key ideas by developing an increasingly complex knowledge about them. Building on the above synthesis of different frameworks of knowledge complexity that have been used in science education in the past, we distinguished between four levels of knowledge complexity: (a) facts, (b) mappings, (c) relations and (d) conceptual understanding. This resulted in a model of how

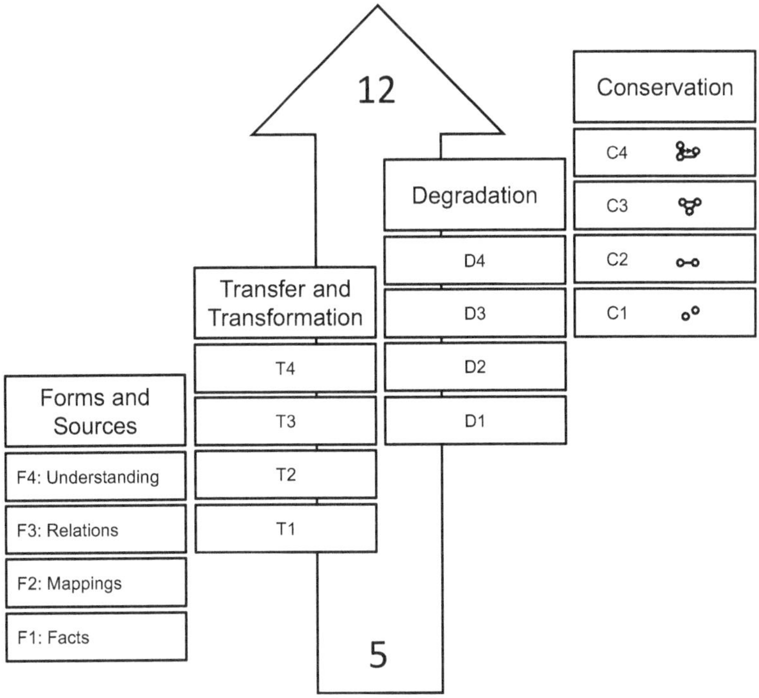

Fig. 15.1 Hypothesized model of students' progression in understanding the concept of energy

students develop understanding of energy, with an associated total of 16 levels of understanding (Fig. 15.1). Note that some overlap was to be expected between the levels (for details see Neumann et al. 2013).

According to our model we expect that students first develop an understanding of energy forms and sources from the everyday conceptions with which they enter formal instruction. Students do so by learning (F1) about energy-related phenomena (facts), (F2) that energy relates to these phenomena (mappings), (F3) how energy relates to these phenomena (relations), in order to finally understand (F4) how energy manifests itself differently in the different phenomena (conceptual understanding). This understanding will serve as a basis for students' learning (T1) about energy transformation and transfer processes (facts), (T2) that these processes involve different forms or different places (mappings), (T3) how in a given process the different forms are transformed into each other, or how they are transferred from one place to another, to finally understand (T4) how every phenomenon involves energy changing its form or place of appearance. This process continues for energy degradation (D1–D4) and conservation (C1–C4). Overlap is expected between levels F3–F4 and T1–T2, T3–T4 and D1–D2 as well as D3–D4 and C1–C4.

As guidance for our efforts to obtain evidence for the validity of the hypothesized model and to investigate students' progression in understanding the concept of energy we formulated the following research questions:

1. To what extent does the hypothesized model describe students' progression in understanding the concept of energy?
2. How do students progress in their understanding of the concept of energy as a function of middle school physics instruction?

15.4 Project Design

In our project we addressed these two research questions in two successive phases (Fig. 15.2). In the first phase, we developed a test instrument to assess students' understanding of energy, based on the hypothesized model. We conducted a series of studies to ensure the psychometric quality of the instrument. Then, we utilized this instrument to investigate students' progression in understanding energy in a cross-sectional study with students from middle school. In the second phase we conducted a longitudinal study, in which we repeatedly tested students throughout middle school, to identify (school) curriculum-specific trajectories in students' progression in understanding energy. We also carried out a series of supplemental studies to further refine our model. All studies were carried out at *Gymnasien* (i.e., schools of the highest school track) in the states North Rhine-Westphalia, Schleswig-Holstein and Hamburg, Germany. This choice of states and of school track offered middle school curricula with a particular emphasis on the concept of energy. That is, energy was taught in each or every other grade of middle school (i.e., Grades 5/6, 7/8 and 9/10) and typically, students from different schools would have received similar amounts of energy teaching at the end of Grades 6, 8 and 10.

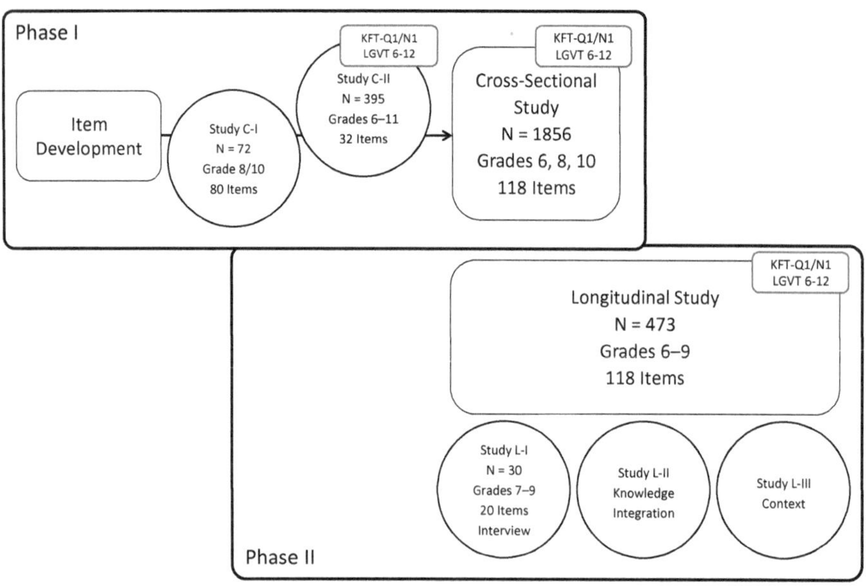

Fig. 15.2 Design of the project

15.5 Phase 1: The Cross-Sectional Study

15.5.1 Method

The first phase of the project started with the operationalization of the model by test items in order to create a new instrument, the Energy Concept Assessment (ECA), suitable for measuring students' development in understanding the concept of energy. To ensure sufficient fit with the hypothesized model, items were authored following a rigorous process specified by an item-authoring manual. The first step in this process was to identify a scenario involving a scientific phenomenon or technical process (e.g., a stone being dropped or an aircraft taking off). In the second step the energy story underlying this scenario was written down (see also Papadouris and Constantinou 2014). Based on the energy story, in the third step, multiple-choice items were created that required conceptual understanding of each of the four key ideas. In a fourth step, less complex items were created by successively adding more complex cues to the item (for details of the authoring process and the technical manual including all items, see Neumann et al. 2013).

Following the described procedure, a first set of items was authored. Sixty-four of these items were piloted with a voluntary sample of $N = 72$ students from Grades 8 and 10 (at the approximate ages of 14 and 16 years respectively). Each item was administered together with an item quality questionnaire that included questions on wording issues, text complexity, or item difficulty (American Association for the Advancement of Science [AAAS] 2007). Based on the information from this study, the existing items were refined and new items were developed. In a second study a set of 40 items in two booklets of 20 items (with an overlap of 8 items) each, was administered to $N = 395$ students from Grades 7 to 11 (at approximate ages of 11–17 years). Participants also filled in a cognitive ability test (Heller and Perleth 2000) and a reading ability test (Schneider et al. 2007). Again, the findings were used to further refine existing items and develop new, improved items (Neumann et al. 2010; Viering et al. 2010). Altogether, a set of 272 items was authored, of which 120 were chosen to be included in the cross-sectional study. The items were selected on the basis of expert judgements of the following criteria: (1) model representation, (2) equal distribution of items across the four key ideas and four levels of complexity, (3) local stochastic independence, (4) overall item quality. Items were distributed across 12 blocks (B1…B12) of 10 items each. From these blocks 12 test booklets were composed, where each booklet would contain 2 blocks and 2 adjacent booklets would share a common block (B1–B2, B2–B3, … B12–B1; for details on item development and booklet composition see Neumann et al. 2013).

The ECA was then administered to $N = 1856$ students from Grades 6, 8 and 10 (at approximate ages of 12, 14, and 16 years) in Gymnasiums in North Rhine-Westphalia, in order to obtain information about the extent to which the instrument can measure the development of students' understanding of energy. Since both cognitive abilities and reading abilities were shown to have particular influence on students' performance on test instruments such as the ECA (for cognitive abilities e.g., Helmke and Weinert 1997; for reading abilities e.g., Leutner et al. 2004; see also Viering et al. 2010), students were also administered a cognitive ability and a reading ability test. To assess students' cognitive abilities, two subscales of a cognitive ability test were utilized (Heller and Perleth 2000): a non-verbal/figural (KFTN) and a quantitative scale (KFTQ). To measure students' reading abilities we utilized an instrument developed by Schneider et al. (2007) that measures reading speed (RS) and reading comprehension (RC).

15.5.2 Results

The main aim of the cross-sectional study was to investigate the extent to which the hypothesized model presents a valid model of how students develop understanding of the concept of energy (Research Question 1). In order to do so, in the first step of our analysis, we used Rasch analysis to examine the extent to which (1) the items represent the continuum of students' understanding of energy (i.e., the latent trait) and (2) students progress along this continuum as hypothesized in our model. Based on our model we expected that students would first develop an understanding of energy forms by building an increasingly complex knowledge base about this idea, then develop an understanding of energy transfer and transformation, energy degradation and, finally, energy conservation. That is, we assumed the items to define a one-dimensional trait and the key ideas to represent stages of understanding with respect to this trait. However, it may also be that the key ideas represent individual entities, of which students develop understanding independently. As a consequence we began our analysis by exploring the assumption of a one-dimensional trait against a four-dimensional trait. We were unable, however, to obtain interpretable results for the latter, as for different estimation parameters, the solution reaching convergence never exhibited the highest likelihood. Results of the one-dimensional analysis revealed a remarkably good fit of the data to the (one-dimensional) Rasch model. Of 118 items (2 of the 120 items had to be excluded from the analysis, due to scoring issues), only 16 items exhibited a sub-standard model fit. Most of these items were excluded, due to low discrimination. We used the final set of 102 items to obtain Warm's Mean Weighted Likelihood (WLE) estimates as person ability measures (WLE reliability = .61).

Utilizing the item difficulty parameters we obtained from this analysis, we investigated item difficulty measures as a function of the key idea and the complexity, and the person ability measures as a function of grade. Based on our model we expected items related to more elaborate key ideas (e.g., energy conservation) to be more difficult than items related to less elaborate conceptions (e.g., energy forms), and for each key idea we expected items requiring a more complex understanding of the idea to be more difficult than items that required factual knowledge only. Analyzing the effect of the key idea on item difficulty, we indeed found the key idea to have a significant influence: $F(3, 98) = 12.58$, $p < 0.001$, $\eta^2 = 0.28$. More specifically, we found item difficulty to increase for more elaborate key ideas, $\tau = 0.39$, $p < 0.001$.

Regarding the effect of the complexity on item difficulty, our analysis revealed no effect, $F(3, 86) = 0.93$, $p = .43$. Also, no interaction effect of key idea and complexity on item difficulty was found, $F(9, 86) = 0.39$, $p = .94$. Finally, we utilized person ability parameters obtained from Rasch analysis to examine whether students of higher grades would exhibit higher abilities than would students from lower grades; and indeed, students' person ability parameters were found to increase with grade: $F(2, 1853) = 161.29$, $p < 0.001$, $\eta^2 = 0.15$, $\tau = .29$, $p < .001$. Based on these findings we concluded that the following sequence of key ideas marks (overlapping) stages of students' understanding of energy: (1) energy forms, (2) energy transformations, (3) energy degradation, and (4) energy conservation. And we concluded that students across middle school progress in their understanding of energy along this sequence. We could not confirm, however, that students develop understanding of the individual key ideas by developing an increasingly complex knowledge base about them (for details, see Neumann et al. 2013).

In the second step of our analysis, we included measures of students' cognitive and reading abilities in our analysis, using a background model (e.g., Carstensen et al. 2007). In doing so we aimed to clarify the influence of (the development of) cognitive and reading abilities over energy instruction on students' performance on the ECA. Data from the cognitive ability tests were prepared using multidimensional Rasch analysis, with each of the two subscales (KFTN: nonverbal, KFTQ: quantitative) reflecting different dimensions. The respective WLE estimates were included in our analysis. For reading speed (RS) and reading comprehension (RC) scores calculated on the basis of the manual (Schneider et al. 2007) were used. All four covariates were z-standardized. Students' grades were incorporated through two dummy variables (Grade 6: G1 = 0, G2 = 0; Grade 8: G1 = 1, G2 = 0; Grade 10: G1 = 1, G2 = 1). Finally, variables reflecting interaction effects between cognitive abilities and grade, as well as reading abilities and grade, were included with the background model (e.g., g1*kftn, g2*kftn). Table 15.1 shows the regression coefficients obtained (for details see Weßnigk and Neumann 2015).

According to Table 15.1 the influence of the reading speed (RS) on students' performance is nearly negligible. Reading comprehension (RC) has some impact: if the RC score increases by about one standard deviation, students' ability parameter increases by 0.150 logits. In comparison to the quantitative cognitive abilities (KFTQ), the influence of non-verbal, figural cognitive abilities (KFTN) seems limited, given the increase in students' ability parameter of 0.173 logits per standard deviation of the KFTQ parameter, compared to an increase of 0.045 logits for the KFTN parameter. Thus, the impact of KFTQ is comparable to the impact of RC. With respect to the influence of energy instruction on students' understanding, an increase of 0.175 logits can be observed in students' ability parameter from Grade 6 to Grade 8, and an increase of 0.344 logits from Grade 8 to 10. This was expected, as the curriculum students were taught with a stronger emphasis on energy in Grades 9 and 10, compared to Grades 7 and 8. The comparable increase in students' ability parameter from Grades 6 to 8, and for one standard deviation in KFTQ and RC, as well as the larger increase in students' ability parameter from Grade 8 to Grade 10, indicate a particular non-negligible influence of energy instruction.

Table 15.1 Regression coefficients for each of the four covariates and the dummy-coded grades in the background model analysis

Intercept	KFTN	KFTQ	RS	RC	G1	G2
−.904	0.045	0.173	−0.006	0.150	0.175	0.344

KFTN cognitive ability nonverbal, *KFTQ* cognitive ability quantitative, *RS* reading speed, *RC* reading comprehension; G1 and G2 are so-called dummy variables that allow for examining students' growth from Grades 6 to 8 and Grades 8 to 10, independently of each other (Grade 6: G1 = 0, G2 = 0; Grade 8: G1 = 1, G2 = 0; Grade 10: G1 = 1, G2 = 1)

This confirms that the ECA can validly assess students' progression in understanding energy, and at the same time suggests a particular influence of the curriculum on students' progression.

15.6 Phase 2: Longitudinal Study

15.6.1 Method

In the longitudinal study we aimed to examine students' progression as a function of (school specific) instruction. For this purpose, we followed a subsample of students from the cross-sectional study, the students from Grade 6, through middle school: that is, we repeatedly tested these students, who were tested at the end of Grade 6 in the cross-sectional study, at the end of Grades 7, 8, and 9.[1] In order to do so, grade-specific test booklets were composed on the basis of the information on the items obtained in the cross-sectional study. In each grade students received one out of three test booklets, each with 20 items specifically selected to match students' abilities in this grade. Each booklet contained a less difficult and a more difficult block of items. Again, two adjacent booklets shared one common block of items. Test booklets for higher grades included the more difficult block of items from the test booklets composed for the preceding grade, as well as a newly composed, still more difficult block. In addition to the test booklet on energy, students were again administered a cognitive ability test (Heller and Perleth 2000) and a reading ability test (Schneider et al. 2007). From a total of $N = 655$ students that had taken part in Grade 6 in the cross-sectional study, a subset of $n = 473$ students participated in this study. As a result of panel mortality, however, complete data sets were obtained for only $n = 283$ students.

In parallel to the longitudinal study, a series of three supplemental studies were planned and carried out in the states of Schleswig-Holstein and Hamburg, Germany. The first study, an interview study, was designed to explore the missing effect of complexity on item difficulty. A structured interview protocol was developed to

[1] Students were not tested in Grade 10, as these students were the first to complete the newly introduced 8-year Gymnasium and had, after Grade 9, received the same amount of teaching on the concept of energy as had students of Grade 10 in the cross-sectional study.

measure the complexity of students' knowledge about the four key ideas (Wille 2011; Weßnigk and Neumann 2014). The interview protocol was based on the same scenarios utilized in the ECA. Essentially, students were provided with a scenario and asked to tell the energy story of the scenario. Students were then specifically asked about the involved energy forms, the energy transformation or transfer processes occurring, as well as energy degradation and conservation. However, the pilot studies revealed that students were struggling with the open-ended format and had difficulties with telling the energy story. Even when specifically asked about the individual key ideas, students did not exhibit much knowledge (Weßnigk and Neumann 2014). As a consequence the interview protocol was refined, to the effect that students are still presented with different scenarios as used in the ECA, but now the students receive cards depicting energy forms and processes of energy transformation and transfer. The energy form cards were offered in different sizes to reflect different amounts of energy. Students were asked to model the scenarios by creating an energy transfer or transformation chain, respectively. Then the same protocol as above, asking students about forms and sources, transfer and transformation, degradation and conservation, was employed (Lindner 2014). A study with $N = 30$ students from Grades 7 to 9 using this procedure has just been completed.

In addition to the interview study, one study investigating the effect of item context on item difficulty and another study exploring the potential for assessing the complexity of students' knowledge using two-tier items, were planned (cf. Lee and Liu 2010). The study exploring the effect of item context (more specifically the disciplinary context of the items) on item difficulty has been completed, in cooperation with the departments of biology and chemistry education at the Leibniz-Institute for Science and Mathematics Education (IPN). The data are presently being analyzed. Regarding the study exploring the potential of using two-tier items to assess the complexity of students' knowledge about each of the four key ideas of energy, a pilot study has been successfully completed (Hadinek 2013). However, the results indicated insufficient internal consistency for the first (closed) tier ($\alpha = .48$). Since the internal consistency of the second (open) tier was found to be sufficient ($\alpha = .71$), we are currently exploring the use of open items together with a category system to score the complexity of knowledge exhibited by students in their answers to these items.

15.6.2 Results

The main aim of the longitudinal study was to examine if and how students' progression in understanding the concept of energy depends on different curricula. To do so we repeatedly tested $N = 473$ in Grades 6, 7, 8 and 9 of middle school. Again, we used Rasch analysis to analyze the obtained data. In the analysis, the data from the four measurement points were treated as if it were data from four different students. Thus, for each student we obtained up to four WLE person ability estimates, one for each measurement point the student took part in.

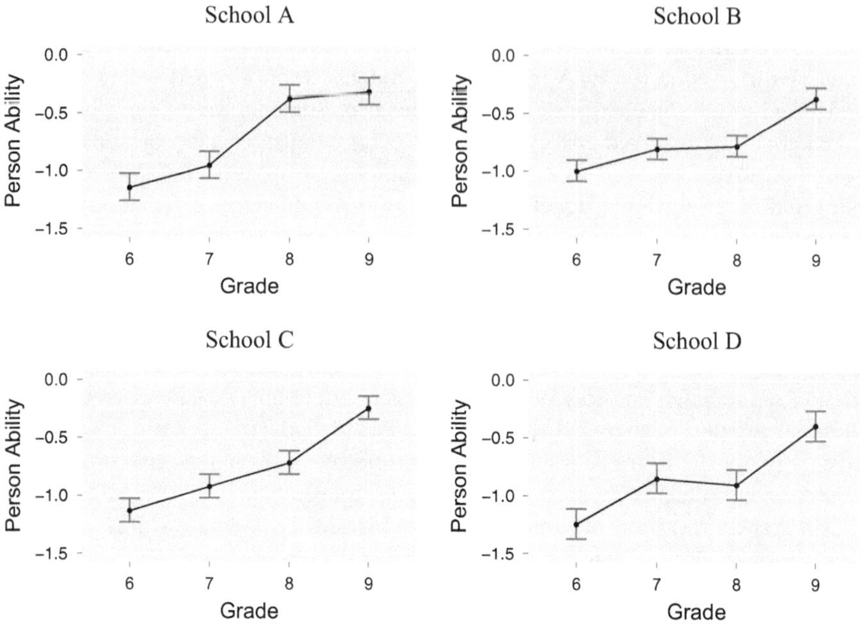

Fig. 15.3 Students' progression in understanding energy as a function of instruction

Before investigating students' ability, we examined whether the items utilized in this study defined the trait in the same way as did the items utilized in the cross-sectional study. That is, we investigated item difficulty as a function of key idea and complexity. Again, the key idea was found to have a considerable effect on item difficulty, $F(3, 114) = 7.87$, $p < .001$, $\tau = 0.31$, $p < .001$, whereas no effect could be observed for item complexity, $F(3, 114) = .72$, $p = .55$. Thus, again, we find the key ideas mark (overlapping) stages of students' understanding of energy, whereas we have to concede that again the complexity of the items did not present a suitable way to measure students' understanding of the individual key ideas.

Following the analysis of how well the items represented the trait or the hypothesized model, respectively, we investigated students' progression in understanding energy using Repeated Measures Analysis of Variances (RM-ANOVA). The results indicate that students' ability increases over time, $F(3, 846) = 73.78$, $p < 0.001$, $\eta^2 = 0.12$; that is, students progress towards a more sophisticated understanding of energy over middle school.

Figure 15.3 shows our findings for four sample schools. Clearly, students from these schools (on average) exhibit different trajectories with respect to their progression in understanding energy. Students from schools A and C exhibit an (on average) relatively continuous progression. Students from schools B and D, on the contrary, show a more stage-like progression pattern, with a noticeable (and significant) increase in their understanding of energy from the end of Grade 6 to the end of Grade 7, $t(273.55) = -3.22$, $p < .01$, and from the end of Grade 8 to the end of

Grade 9, $t(261.83) = -4.28$, $p < .001$ — yet students from these schools show no progression from the end of Grade 7 to the end of Grade 8, $t(273.42) = 0.03$, $p = .97$. Preliminary analysis of the schools' curricula suggests that this is a result of no energy instruction in Grade 8 in schools B and D, whereas students in schools A and C received energy instruction in every grade. One interesting finding in this context was that students in school B, according to the school curriculum for physics, should have not received teaching on energy in Grade 7. However, the school's curriculum for chemistry revealed that in chemistry students received a considerable amount of teaching on energy in Grade 7 (in particular, on phase changes and on energy related to chemical reactions). These findings indicate that the (school-specific) curriculum has a particular influence on students' progression in understanding the concept of energy (Fig. 15.3).

15.7 Summary and Outlook

The main aim of this project was to develop and validate a model of how students develop understanding of the concept of energy. In two successive phases we carried out two major studies, a cross-sectional and a longitudinal study, with students from middle school; these were each supplemented by a series of smaller studies. As a part of the cross-sectional phase we have, in a rigorous design process, developed a new instrument, the energy concept assessment (ECA). We have utilized this instrument to provide evidence that the model we derived from the literature is indeed (mostly) suitable to describe students' progression in understanding energy.

More specifically, we found that students progress in their understanding of energy by successively developing an understanding of four key ideas about energy: (1) energy forms, (2) energy transformation, (3) energy degradation, (4) energy conservation (cf. Neumann et al. 2013). These findings are in line with the findings from previous studies on students' learning about energy (Liu and McKeough 2005; Lee and Liu 2010; Nordine et al. 2010; Herrmann-Abell and DeBoer 2014). In addition, as a part of the cross-sectional phase, we were able to provide evidence about the validity of the ECA and its suitability to track students' progression, by showing that the amount of energy learning (measured by grade) has a larger effect on the difference in students' performance than covariates such as cognitive abilities or reading abilities.

Despite these achievements, we also had to acknowledge that we were not able to confirm that students develop an understanding of the individual key ideas by developing an increasingly complex knowledge of them. However, a recent re-analysis of the data indicates that while students do not develop an understanding of the key ideas by learning about them individually, instead they learn about energy by developing increasingly more connections between the four key ideas (Nagy and Neumann 2013). This is in line with the findings of Lee and Liu (2010). In the longitudinal phase we were able to confirm our findings from the cross-sectional phase.

We could also show that — in general — students' progression in understanding the concept of energy depends on the school's curriculum. Our data also suggest, however, that issues typically debated in the context of school curricula, such as whether physics should be taught every year instead of every other year, have little influence on students' progression (in understanding energy). Instead, our findings suggest that the interplay of the curricula in different subjects plays a much bigger role, and that more attention may need to be paid to the coherence of energy instruction across different disciplines if we want students to develop understanding of energy as a cross-cutting concept (see NRC 2012).

Acknowledgments The preparation of this chapter was supported by grant NE-1368/2-1/2/3 from the German Research Foundation (DFG) in the Priority Program "Competence Models for Assessing Individual Learning Outcomes and Evaluating Educational Processes" (SPP 1293).

References

AAAS (American Association for the Advancement of Science). (2007). Getting assessment right. *2061 Today, 17*(1), 2–7.

Bernholt, S., & Parchmann, I. (2011). Assessing the complexity of students' knowledge in chemistry. *Chemistry Education Research and Practice, 12*, 167–173. doi:10.1039/c1rp90021h.

Boyes, E., & Stanisstreet, M. (1990). Misunderstandings of "law" and "conservation": A study of pupils' meanings for these terms. *School Science Review, 72*(258), 51–57.

Bransford, J. D., Brown, A. L., & Cocking, R. R. (2000). *How people learn: Brain, mind, experience and school*. Washington, DC: National Academy Press.

Carstensen, C. H., Frey, A., Walter, O., & Knoll, S. (2007). Technische Grundlagen des dritten internationalen Vergleichs [Technical foundations of the third international comparison]. In M. Prenzel, C. Artelt, J. Baumert, W. Blum, M. Hammann, E. Klieme, & R. Pekrun (Eds.), *PISA 2006. Die Ergebnisse der dritten internationalen Vergleichsstudie* (pp. 367–390). Münster: Waxmann.

Chen, B., Eisenkraft, A., Fortus, D., Krajcik, J., Neumann, K., Nordine, J., & Scheff, A. (Eds.). (2014). *Teaching and learning of energy in K-12 education*. New York: Springer.

Dawson-Tunik, T. L. (2006). Stage-like patterns in the development of conceptions of energy. In X. Liu & W. J. Boone (Eds.), *Applications of Rasch measurement in science education* (pp. 111–136). Maple Grove: JAM Press.

Doménech, J. L., Gil-Pérez, D., Gras-Martí, A., Guisasola, J., Martínez-Torregrosa, J., Salinas, J., … Vilches, A. (2007). Teaching of energy issues: A debate proposal for a global reorientation. *Science & Education, 16*, 43–64. doi:10.1007/s11191-005-5036-3.

Driver, R., & Millar, R. (Eds.). (1986). *Energy matters: Proceedings of an invited conference: teaching about energy within the secondary science curriculum*. Leeds: University of Leeds, Centre for Studies in Science and Mathematics Education.

Driver, R., & Warrington, L. (1985). Students' use of the principle of energy conservation in problem situations. *Physics Education, 20*, 171–176. doi:10.1088/0031-9120/20/4/308.

Driver, R., Squires, D., Rushworth, P., & Wood-Robinson, V. (1994). *Making sense of secondary science: Supporting materials for teachers*. London: Routledge.

Duit, R. (1981). Understanding energy as a conserved quantity. *European Journal of Science Education, 3*, 291–301. doi:10.1080/0140528810030306.

Duschl, R., Maneg, S., & Sezen, A. (2011). Learning progression and teaching sequences: A review and analysis. *Studies in Science Education, 47*, 123–182. doi:10.1080/03057267.2011.604476.

Geller, G., Neumann, K., Boone, W. J., & Fischer, H. E. (2014). What makes the Finnish different in science? Assessing and comparing students' science learning in three countries. *International Journal of Science Education, 36*, 3042–3066. doi:10.1080/09500693.2014.950185.

Hadinek, D. (2013). *Entwicklung eines Two-Tier-Tests zur Erfassung des Verständnisses von 'Energie'* [Developing a two-tier-test for assessing students' understanding of energy]. Unpublished master's thesis, University of Kiel, Kiel, Germany.

Heller, K. A., & Perleth, C. (2000). *Kognitiver Fähigkeitstest für 4. bis 12. Klassen* [Cognitive ability test for Grades 4–12], Revision (KFT 4–12+R). Göttingen: Beltz.

Helmke, A., & Weinert, F. E. (1997). Bedingungsfaktoren schulischer Leistungen [Conditional factors of student achievement]. In F. E. Weinert (Ed.), *Enzyklopädie der Psychologie* (Vol. 3, pp. 71–176). Göttingen: Hogrefe.

Herrmann-Abell, C., & DeBoer, G. (2014). Developing and using distractor-driven multiple-choice assessments aligned to ideas about energy forms, transformation, transfer, and conservation. In R. F. Chen, A. Eisenkraft, D. Fortus, J. Krajcik, K. Neumann, J. Nordine, & A. Scheff (Eds.), *Teaching and learning of energy in K-12 education* (pp. 103–134). Heidelberg: Springer.

Kauertz, A., & Fischer, H. E. (2006). Assessing students' level of knowledge and analysing the reasons for learning difficulties in physics by Rasch analysis. In X. Liu & W. J. Boone (Eds.), *Applications of Rasch measurement in science education* (pp. 212–246). Maple Grove: JAM Press.

KMK (Standing Conference of the Ministers of Education and Cultural Affairs of the States in the Federal Republic of Germany). (Ed.). (2005). *Bildungsstandards im Fach Physik für den Mittleren Schulabschluss: Beschluss vom 16.12.2004* [Educational standards for middle school physics: Resolution approved by the Standing conference on 16 December 2004]. München: Luchterhand.

Lee, H.-S., & Liu, O. L. (2010). Assessing learning progression of energy concepts across middle school grades: The knowledge integration perspective. *Science Education, 94*, 665–688. doi:10.1002/sce.20382.

Leutner, D., Klieme, E., Meyer, K., & Wirth, J. (2004). Problemlösen [Problem solving]. In PISA-Konsortium Deutschland (Eds.), *PISA 2003: Der Bildungsstand der Jugendlichen in Deutschland: Ergebnisse des zweiten internationalen Vergleichs* (pp. 147–175). Münster: Waxmann.

Lindner, K. (2014). *Erfassung des Verständnisses von Energie im Rahmen einer Interviewstudie* [Assessing the understanding of energy through an interview study]. Unpublished master's thesis, University of Kiel, Kiel, Germany.

Liu, X., & McKeough, A. (2005). Developmental growth in students' concept of energy: An analysis of selected items from the TIMSS database. *Journal of Research in Science Teaching, 42*, 493–517. doi:10.1002/tea.20060.

Liu, O. L., Lee, H.-S., Hofstetter, C., & Linn, M. (2008). Assessing knowledge integration in science: Construct, measures, and evidence. *Educational Assessment, 13*, 33–55. doi:10.1080/10627190801968224.

Nagy, G., & Neumann, K. (2013, April). *How middle school students learn about energy.* Paper presented at the NARST conference, Puerto Rico, USA.

Neumann, K., Viering, T., & Fischer, H. E. (2010). Die Entwicklung physikalischer Kompetenz am Beispiel des Energiekonzepts [The development of physics competence in the example of the concept of energy]. *Zeitschrift für Didaktik der Naturwissenschaften, 17*, 285–298.

Neumann, K., Viering, T., Boone, W., & Fischer, H. E. (2013). Towards a learning progression of energy. *Journal of Research in Science Teaching, 50*, 162–188.

Nordine, J., Krajcik, J., & Fortus, D. (2010). Transforming energy instruction in middle school to support integrated understanding and future learning. *Science Education, 95*, 670–699. doi:10.1002/sce.20423.

NRC (National Research Council). (2012). *A framework for K-12 science education: Practices, crosscutting concepts, and core ideas*. Washington, DC: National Academies Press.
OECD (Organisation for Economic Co-operation and Development). (2001). *Knowledge and skills for life: First results from PISA 2000*. Paris: Author.
Papadouris, N., & Constantinou, C. (2014). Distinctive features and underlying rationale of a philosophically-informed approach for energy teaching. In R. Chen, A. Eisenkraft, D. Fortus, J. Krajcik, K. Neumann, J. Nordine, & A. Scheff (Eds.), *The teaching and learning of energy in K-12 education* (pp. 207–222). New York: Springer.
Schneider, W., Schlagmüller, M., & Ennemoser, M. (2007). *Lesegeschwindigkeits- und Verständnistest für die Klassen 6–12 (LGVT 6–12)* [Reading speed and reading comprehension test for Grades 6–12]. Göttingen: Hogrefe.
Solomon, J. (1983). Messy, contradictory and obstinately persistent: A study of children's out-of-school ideas about energy. *School Science Review, 65*(231), 225–230.
Stead, B. (1980). *Energy: A working paper on the learning in science project* (Working paper no. 17). Hamilton: University of Waikato.
Stevens, S. Y., Delgado, C., & Krajcik, J. S. (2010). Developing a hypothetical multi-dimensional learning progression for the nature of matter. *Journal of Research in Science Teaching, 47*, 687–715. doi:10.1002/tea.20324.
Trumper, R. (1990). Being constructive: An alternative approach to the teaching of the energy concept: Part one. *International Journal of Science Education, 12*, 343–354. doi:10.1080/0950069900120402.
Trumper, R. (1991). Being constructive: An alternative approach to the teaching of the energy concept: Part two. *International Journal of Science Education, 13*, 1–10. doi:10.1080/0950069910130101.
Trumper, R. (1993). Children's energy concepts: A cross-age study. *International Journal of Science Education, 15*, 139–148. doi:10.1080/0950069930150203.
Viering, T., Fischer, H. E., & Neumann, K. (2010). Die Entwicklung physikalischer Kompetenz in der Sekundarstufe I [The development of physics comptence at lower secondary level]. *Zeitschrift für Pädagogik, Beiheft, 56*, 92–103.
Watts, M. (1983). Some alternative views of energy. *Physics Education, 18*, 213–217. doi:10.1088/0031-9120/18/5/307.
Weßnigk, S., & Neumann, K. (2014). Erweiterung eines Kompetenzentwicklungstests zum Energieverständnis [Extending a competence development test for students' understanding of energy]. In S. Bernholt (Ed.), *Naturwissenschaftliche Bildung zwischen Science- und Fachunterricht: Gesellschaft für Didaktik der Chemie und Physik, Jahrestagung in München 2013* (pp. 375–377). Kiel: IPN.
Weßnigk, S., & Neumann, K. (2015). Understanding Energy – An exploration of the relationship between measures of students' understanding of energy, general cognitive abilities and schooling. *Science Education Review Letters (SERL), 2015*, 7–15.
Wille, S. (2011). *Entwicklung eines Verfahrens zur Validierung eines Kompetenzentwicklungstests für den Bereich Energie* [Development of a procedure for validating a competence development test for the concept of energy]. Unpublished master's thesis, University of Kiel, Kiel, Germany.

Chapter 16
Modeling and Fostering Decision-Making Competencies Regarding Challenging Issues of Sustainable Development

Susanne Bögeholz, Sabina Eggert, Carolin Ziese, and Marcus Hasselhorn

Abstract A model of decision-making competence for secondary school students was developed and validated within the project "Decision-Making Competence Regarding Challenging Issues of Sustainable Development". The model rests on three pillars: Education for Sustainable Development, decision-making theory, and educational competence modeling. Three dimensions of decision-making competence were identified: (1) "Understanding values and norms" in the context of Sustainable Development (SD), (2) "Developing solutions", and (3) "Evaluating solutions" for SD problems. The two last-mentioned dimensions stem from decision-making theory, and were adapted to educational purposes. Related measurement instruments were developed according to Wilson's developmental cycle, using a between-item-multidimensionality approach. The test development procedures and results are described for the dimension "Developing solutions". Moreover, we started with an experimental validation of a theory of socioscientific decision making. More specifically, we used training-induced strategies to realize experimental variation to differentiate empirically between two decision-making dimensions and problem solving. The results of a pilot study addressing the validation of "Developing solutions" and "Evaluating solutions", vis-à-vis problem solving, are reported and discussed. We close with considerations of future research, to realign the boundaries of our research program.

Keywords Socioscientific decision making • Sustainable Development • Competence modeling • Problem solving • Experimental validation

---

S. Bögeholz (✉) • S. Eggert • C. Ziese
Georg-August-Universität Göttingen, Göttingen, Germany
e-mail: sboegeh@gwdg.de; seggert1@gwdg.de; cziese@gwdg.de

M. Hasselhorn
German Institute for International Educational Research (DIPF), Frankfurt/Main, Germany
e-mail: hasselhorn@dipf.de

D. Leutner et al. (eds.), *Competence Assessment in Education*, Methodology of Educational Measurement and Assessment, DOI 10.1007/978-3-319-50030-0_16

16.1 Introduction

Worldwide biodiversity loss and climate change are challenging problems with respect to Sustainable Development (SD). These problems are tightly linked to political, economic, and societal concerns (Oulton et al. 2004). In the field of science education they are subsumed under the term socioscientific issues (e.g., Sadler et al. 2007). Typically, these issues are factually and ethically complex, ill-structured, subject to ongoing inquiry, and they lack an optimal solution (Bögeholz and Barkmann 2005; Ratcliffe and Grace 2003; Sadler et al. 2007). Rather, multiple solutions exist, all of which have their drawbacks. With respect to solving SD problems, decision-making competence is crucial to promote "technically and economically viable, environmentally sound, and morally just solutions" (Bögeholz et al. 2014, p. 237), and to foster student literacy as citizens (Ratcliffe and Grace 2003; Sadler et al. 2007).

Working with SD problems in the science classroom poses high processing demands on students (Eggert et al. 2013). Students do not only have to rely on a profound (scientific) knowledge base but also have to engage in various information search, argumentation, reasoning, and decision-making processes (Eggert et al. 2013; Jiménez-Aleixandre and Pereiro-Muñoz 2002; Ratcliffe and Grace 2003).

Socioscientific decision making was implemented in German science curricula (e.g., KMK 2005) as one reaction to German students' mediocre results in the PISA (Programme for International Student Assessment) studies. As one consequence, German educational authorities emphasized competence-oriented teaching (KMK 2005). In a similar vein, the priority program "Competence Models" was launched to overcome the lack of empirical support for basic assumptions of the competence approach.

According to Weinert (2001), the concept of competence is strongly linked to problem solving. It takes into account a "sufficient degree of complexity […] to meet demands and tasks", and includes "cognitive and (in many cases) motivational, ethical, volitional, and/or social components" (Weinert 2001, p. 62) in solving problems successfully. Referring to this definition, Klieme et al. (2008, p. 9) emphasize the cognitive facet and define competencies "as context-specific cognitive dispositions that are acquired by learning and needed to successfully cope with certain situations or tasks in specific domains". This definition was adopted for the present research on decision-making competencies with regard to the challenging issues of SD.

16.2 A Competence Model for Decision Making with Respect to Sustainable Development

Research on socioscientific reasoning and decision making as well as on argumentation in the area of science education draws on different theoretical models such as Toulmin's argumentation model (Toulmin 1958), Kuhn's developmental model of

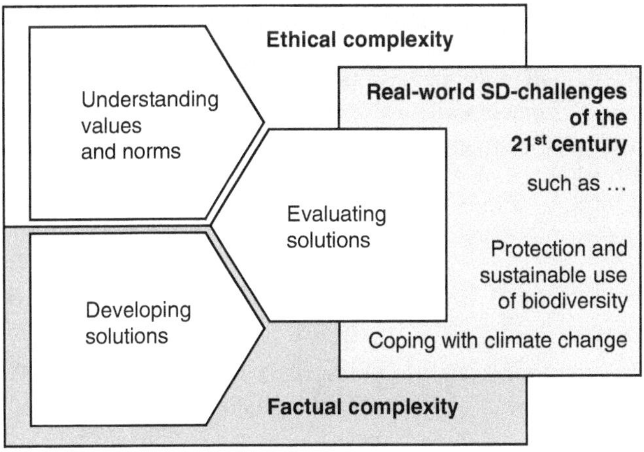

Fig. 16.1 Competence model for decision making with respect to challenging issues of Sustainable Development (SD)

critical thinking (Kuhn 1999), and models from descriptive decision theory (e.g., Betsch and Haberstroh 2005). All models highlight the need to compare and evaluate available options (i.e., solutions) by developing pro- and contra-arguments, and weighing these arguments or decision criteria in order to reach informed decisions (e.g., Eggert and Bögeholz 2010; Jiménez-Aleixandre and Pereiro-Muñoz 2002; Papadouris 2012; Ratcliffe and Grace 2003; Sadler et al. 2007). Being able to reach informed decisions is emphasized as a core competence in Education for Sustainable Development (ESD) as well as in citizenship education (Bögeholz and Barkmann 2005; Sadler et al. 2007). The competence model used in the present project is based on SD-related research as well as on a meta-model from descriptive decision theory (see Betsch and Haberstroh 2005; Bögeholz et al. 2014), and was adapted for educational purposes (Eggert and Bögeholz 2006; Bögeholz 2011). The model comprises three dimensions (see Fig. 16.1).

"Understanding values and norms": While working with SD problems, students need to consider and reflect on crucial normative guidelines, such as basic need orientation, intergenerational justice, international justice and simultaneous consideration of ecological, economic, and social objectives. This requires an understanding of the necessity of fulfilling human needs through a sustainable use of natural resources, and that satisfying needs in a sustainable manner eventually contributes to human well-being (MA 2005; cf. Bögeholz et al. 2014).

"Developing solutions": Students need to be able to comprehend and to describe multifaceted and complex SD problems, and to develop possible sustainable solutions. This implies taking into account various stakeholder perspectives with different ecological, economic, and social objectives. In addition, this dimension also includes the ability to reflect on developed solutions and the evidence that these solutions are based on (e.g., Gausmann et al. 2010).

"Evaluating solutions": Students need to be able to compare and evaluate multiple possible solutions to a SD problem. This includes the ability to develop pro- and contra-arguments, and to weigh these arguments by making use of trade-offs and/or cut-offs to reach informed decisions. In addition, the dimension comprises the ability to reflect on and to monitor decision-making processes (Bernholt et al. 2012; Eggert and Bögeholz 2010; Eggert et al. 2010).

16.3 Measurement Instruments and Competence Modeling

All measurement instruments were developed on the basis of Wilson's developmental cycle (Wilson 2005), using a between-item-multidimensionality approach (Wu et al. 2007). With respect to the measurement instrument for "Evaluating solutions", the procedure and results are described in Eggert and Bögeholz (2010, 2014). In this Sec. 16.3., we focus on the measurement instrument for "Developing solutions". Both measures are used in Sec. 16.4. as dependent variables in a training study designed to examine the relationship between decision making and problem solving.

With respect to "Developing solutions", we assumed that the postulated unidimensionality could be empirically supported. Second, we assumed that items representing the description of a problem situation would be easiest, while items representing the development of solutions to SD problems should be of medium item difficulty. Finally, items representing a reflection of presented solutions were assumed to have the highest difficulty.

16.3.1 "Developing Solutions": Development of the Measurement Instrument

16.3.1.1 Sample

678 students were analyzed in two subsamples of eighth to ninth graders and tenth to twelfth graders. The subsample of eighth to ninth graders consisted of 319 students (157 females, 162 males; mean age: 14.32, $SD = 0.68$), and the subsample of tenth to twelfth graders consisted of 359 students (187 females, 172 males; mean age: 16.76, $SD = 0.90$). All students attended the German *Gymnasium*, which is the academic track that prepares students for studies in higher education.

16.3.1.2 Measures: Tasks and Items

To measure student competencies with respect to the dimension "Developing solutions", a questionnaire with open-ended as well as multiple-choice items was developed. Based on an extensive literature and curriculum review, preliminary test tasks and items were developed, pre-piloted using think-aloud protocols, and optimized. Several complementary quantitative studies followed.

The contexts used in the questionnaire were overfishing of tuna in the South Pacific ("Tuna task"), soy production in the Paraguayan rainforest ("Soy task"), and the collection of hoodia plants in Africa for pharmaceuticals ("Hoodia task"). All these contexts are typical SD problems, also described as socio-ecological dilemmas (e.g., Ernst 1997).

With respect to the Soy task, for example, there is a growing worldwide demand for soy in meat production (economic aspect). This demand is met by installing more and more soy plantations in rainforest areas. As a consequence, rainforest areas decrease (ecological aspect). However, several social groups, such as local people, who depend on the rainforest as a resource (social aspect 1), are affected by rainforest conversion. Instead, soy plantation workers earn their living on the plantations (social aspect 2). Consequently, the soy industry influences the living conditions of the local farmers. In the long run, all involved social groups suffer from exploitation of the rainforest. In addition, institutions like governments and NGOs, but also consumers, play an important role in relation to such dilemmas.

With respect to the Tuna task and the Soy task, students were asked to describe the problem situation first, and then to develop a sustainable solution to the problem. With respect to the Hoodia task, students were given potential solutions to the SD problem, asked to reflect on these solutions in terms of their sustainability (Evaluate in Table 16.1), and to give suggestions for improvement (Improve in Table 16.1) to these solutions.

Student responses to the open-ended questions were analyzed with respect to the interrelated aspects of the socio-ecological dilemma (economic, ecological, and social aspects; see description above) as well as the institutions and consumers that influence the SD problem or may facilitate sustainable solutions (see Table 16.1).

In sum, eight items were used to analyze student answers to the description of the Tuna task and the Soy task (items 1–8 and 16–23). Seven items were used to analyze student answers on the development of solutions to each of these problems (items 9–15 and 24–30). Finally, for eighth to ninth graders, six items were used to analyze student answers to the Hoodia task with respect to the evaluation of Project A (items 31–36). For the older students (tenth to twelfth graders), the Hoodia task "Improve project B" was additionally used to depict student competencies at the upper end of the competency scale (items 37–42 added to items 31–36).

16.3.1.3 Instrument Functioning

Preliminary analyses showed that it is more appropriate to analyze eighth to ninth graders and tenth to twelfth graders separately, as several items exhibited medium to large differential item functioning (DIF) with respect to these two subsamples. Specifically, several items got disproportionally easier among the tenth to twelfth graders. Thus, in the following analyses, we analyzed both subsamples separately, using the unidimensional Rasch model (Rasch 1960). Item fit values as well as

Table 16.1 Tasks, items and item estimates for "Developing solutions" for eighth–ninth graders and tenth–twelfth graders, and their reliability indices

			Eighth to ninth graders	Tenth to twelfth graders
	Item no.	Item descriptions	Item estimates	Item estimates
Tuna describe problem/Soy describe problem	1/16	Ecological-economic relation [R1]	−1.19/−1.69	−1.37/−2.17
	2/17	Social1-ecological relation [R2]	−2.85/−1.13	−3.47/−1.73
	3/18	Social1-social2 relation [R3]	−2.62/0.32	−3.02/0.36
	4/19	Social2-economic relation [R4]	−0.96/0.60	−1.21/0.28
	5/20	Social1-economic relation [R5]	−1.26/−0.92	−1.29/−1.44
	6/21	Social2-ecological relation [R6]	−2.50/0.11	−3.38/0.08
	7/22	Role of institutions [I1]	−0.44/0.21	−0.72/0.14
	8/23	Role of consumers [C2]	−0.22/−1.56	−0.17/−1.66
Tuna develop solution/Soy develop solution	9/24	Ecological-economic relation [R1]	1.43/0.34	0.90/0.45
	10/25	Social1-ecological relation [R2]	−0.41/0.55	−0.26/0.53
	11/26	Social1-social2 relation [R3]	−0.06/1.76	−0.02/1.59
	12/27	Social2-economic relation [R4]	1.76/2.38	1.42/1.98
	13/28	Social1-economic relation [R5]	1.87/1.56	1.26/1.38
	14/29	Social2-ecological relation [R6]	−0.62/1.20	−0.68/1.08
	15/30	Role of institutions [I1]	−1.99/−0.15	−2.70/−0.09
Hoodia reflect (Evaluate) project A	31	Ecological-economic relation [R1]	2.14	2.19
	32	Social1-ecological relation [R2]	−0.08	−0.79
	33	Social1-social2 relation [R3]	−0.08	−0.59
	34	Social2-economic relation [R4]	2.30	2.31
	35	Social1-economic relation [R5]	1.71	1.74
	36	Social2-ecological relation [R6]	0.50	−0.02

(continued)

Table 16.1 (continued)

			Eighth to ninth graders	Tenth to twelfth graders
	Item no.	Item descriptions	Item estimates	Item estimates
Hoodia reflect (Improve) project B	37	Ecological-economic relation [R1]	–	2.44
	38	Social1-ecological relation [R2]	–	0.02
	39	Social1-social2 relation [R3]	–	0.25
	40	Social2-economic relation [R4]	–	2.78
	41	Social1-economic relation [R5]	–	2.61
	42	Social2-ecological relation [R6]	–	0.99
	Reliability indices			
	Item separation reliability		.99	.99
	WLE-Person separation reliability		.83	.87
	EAP/PV reliability		.75	.74
	Cronbach's alpha		.82	.85

traditional item discrimination values were analyzed. Items with discrimination values lower than .20 and weighted mean square (WMNSQ) values that were not within the range of 0.75 and 1.33 were eliminated (Wilson 2005). After deletion of non-functioning items, the final measurement instrument for eighth to ninth graders consisted of 36 items, and the instrument for tenth to twelfth graders consisted of 42 items respectively. Table 16.1 provides an overview of all final items, their item estimates and reliability indices, with respect to both subsamples.

16.3.2 Modeling of "Developing Solutions"

To investigate our assumptions with respect to a possible progression of item difficulty by task complexity, we classified the items into three different categories: "describing" (1), "developing" (2), and "reflecting" (3). With respect to eighth to ninth graders, average item difficulty for all "describing" items was −.96 logits, while item difficulty for all "developing" items was considerably higher (.53 logits). Average item difficulty for all "reflecting" items was highest, with 1.08 logits. An analysis of variance (ANOVA) of item difficulty, grouping items by item complexity, supports this assumption ($f(2, 33) = 8.69$, $p = .001$, $\eta 2 = .35$). Post hoc Tukey tests revealed that "reflecting" items and "developing" items were harder than "describing" items ($p < .01$), while no significant difference could be found between "developing" items and "reflecting" items.

With respect to tenth to twelfth graders, average item difficulty for all "describing" items was −1.24 logits; for all "developing" items it was higher at .31 logits. Average item difficulty for all "reflecting" items was highest at 1.16 logits. In accordance with our assumptions, an ANOVA was again statistically significant ($f(2, 39) = 11.65$, $p < .001$, $\eta 2 = .38$). Post hoc Tukey tests revealed that again "describing" items were easiest ($p < .01$), while the difference between "developing" items and "reflecting" items was again not significant. The Wright map for tenth to twelfth graders is depicted in Fig. 16.2.

In addition, we analyzed the influence of the different contexts on item difficulty. An ANOVA showed no significant differences between the Tuna task and the Soy task.

Analyzing the validity of the dimension "Developing solutions" for both groups, we found no relations with reading speed and reading comprehension ($p > .05$) or with different subject grades. Finally, no relation was found with strategy knowledge for solving problems (for measurement instrument see Scherer 2012).

Fig. 16.2 Wright map for "Developing solutions" for tenth to twelfth graders (*R* relation, *I* institutions, *C* consumers, *x* 2.2 cases)

16.3.3 Discussion

The purpose in this phase of the priority program was to develop new measurement instruments that could be used for analyzing student decision-making competencies with respect to complex issues of sustainable development. Analysis of item fit statistics as well as analysis of traditional item indices revealed that the instrument fits the requirements of the Rasch model. DIF analysis also showed that analyses should be conducted separately for eighth–ninth, and for tenth–twelfth graders. In addition, some items should be used specifically for measuring student competencies at the upper end of the competency continuum. In addition, we were able to show that the developed items can successfully differentiate between different cognitive processes (describing, developing, and reflecting).

Moreover, we could show that "Developing solutions", as part of socioscientific decision making, differs from reading comprehension, and from strategy knowledge in solving problems. This is quite important, as all items used in the measurement instrument ask students to read an information booklet on SD problems, to perform the tasks given, and to find solutions to SD problems.

16.4 Experimental Validation: A Comparison of Socioscientific Decision Making with Analytical Problem Solving

In the following we introduce a training-based experimental validation approach (cf. Mummendey and Grau 2008, p. 106) for the decision making part of our theoretical contribution. We argue that analytical problem solving is a good candidate for validation purposes, for studying decision making within an intervention study.

Even though decision making and problem solving are concepts from different theoretical research branches (Betsch and Haberstroh 2005; Pólya 1945; cf. Leutner et al. 2004), both refer to processes that deal with complex real-world problems. These processes include identifying the (decision-making) problem, identifying relevant information, developing solutions (solution paths), selecting solutions (solution strategies), solving the problem, and reflecting on the solution (Eggert and Bögeholz 2006; OECD 2004, p. 16).

However, decision making and problem solving differ from each other in some aspects. Problem-solving tasks primarily require one correct solution, even if, theoretically speaking, there should be different solution paths. In contrast, decision making focuses on argumentation and reasoning while taking a decision; consequently, there might be several legitimate decisions.

Problem solving as conceptualized in PISA 2003 covers the "overall capability to solve problems in real-life situations beyond the specific context of school subject areas" (OECD 2004, p. 16). In contrast, the relationships between "Developing solutions", "Evaluating solutions", and problem solving are not yet completely understood. Moreover, analytical problem solving seems to be a good candidate for validating the new concept of socioscientific decision making because of its structural similarity. In analytical problem-solving tasks, all information is given simultaneously or can be inferred, and individual competence is measured via paper-pencil tests. Both features are parallel to the assessment of decision making (e.g., Eggert and Bögeholz 2010). This allows us to concentrate on comparison of the two constructs, instead of dealing with changing conditions during problem solving, and divergent computer-based assessment, which are features of dynamic problem solving (cf. Leutner et al. 2004).

16.4.1 Objectives and Research Design

The purpose of the validation study was to analyze whether "context-specific" decision making—with its two dimensions—can be empirically differentiated from problem solving as a "cross-curricular" competence (cf. OECD 2004). We conducted a pre-posttest control group training study. The design included three training groups, each of which focused on specific processes of decision making or problem solving: Training Group 1 was trained in "Developing solutions" (TG1), Training Group 2 in "Evaluating solutions" (TG2), and Training Group 3 in "Problem solving" (TG3). In addition, a control group (CG) was tested, in which students attended regular biology courses without any explicit training in decision making or problem solving. However, the CG studied the same content as TG1, TG2, and TG3 (see below). The following hypotheses (dependent variables mentioned in first place) were derived:

- *"Developing solutions":* Students of Training Group 1, "Developing solutions", outperform students of all other groups (TG1 > TG2, TG3, CG).
- *"Evaluating solutions":* Students of Training Group 2, "Evaluating solutions", outperform students of the remaining groups (TG2 > TG1, TG3, CG).
- *"Problem solving":* Students of the "Problem solving" group (TG3) outperform students of the remaining groups (TG3 > TG1, TG2, CG).

16.4.2 Methods

In the pre- and posttest, paper-and-pencil tests for "Developing solutions" (see Sect. 16.3.1.2.), "Evaluating solutions" (cf. Eggert et al. 2010), and "Problem solving" (cf. OECD 2004) were used. Testing time for the pretests was 120 minutes, and for the posttests 90 minutes.

16.4.2.1 Participating Students and Teachers

Participants included four eighth grade classes from one high school in North Rhine-Westphalia, Germany (63 females and 54 males; mean age: 13.59, *SD* = 0.62). The study was conducted from January to March 2014, and supported by the school's vice-director. Three biology teachers participating in the study had no specific prior training in socioscientific decision making or problem solving.

All three teachers received introductory one-to-one coaching with respect to their specific treatment condition. The teaching units for TG1, TG2, and TG3 were developed by the researchers. The teaching approach, the materials and the methods of the corresponding teaching unit were discussed during the coaching sessions.

Teacher A (4 years teaching experience) taught TG1 (*n* = 28 students) and TG3 (*n* = 26). This teacher had a weak commitment to the study, was challenged in having to teach two different training groups, and underestimated student abilities with respect to the content of the teaching units. In addition, he was more used to teacher-centered instruction and had a more transmissive orientation towards teaching and learning. He spent the least amount of time in preparing for and reflecting on his teaching.

Teacher B (33 years teaching experience; vice-director) taught TG2 (*n* = 28), while teacher C (8 years teaching experience) taught in the control group and, thus, followed his own teaching approach (CG; *n* = 28). Teacher C used materials provided by the researchers but was free to restructure it, searched with enthusiasm for additional information, and developed the material to his own needs. Teachers B and C were highly committed to our study; they were self-confident and showed high identification with their teaching units.

All lessons were documented by a researcher who wrote a chronological protocol (Böhmann and Schäfer-Munro 2008). Observations revealed that students in the TG3 and the CG were interested in the teaching units and actively participated in the course. In contrast, students of the TG1 and the TG2 were more heterogeneous in terms of interest and motivation to participate.

16.4.2.2 Trainings and Learning Material

All trainings (TG1–3) and the regular CG instructions comprised 6 teaching units of 45 miuntes each, and taught in 90 minutes double periods. In the first two double periods students worked on palm oil production in Indonesian rainforest areas. In the final double period they worked on cotton production in Uzbekistan, and its consequences for the drying Aral Sea (see Table 16.2). All four conditions used cooperative learning methods such as gallery walk, jigsaw puzzle, fishbowl, and pair/team discussions. The three treatment conditions only differed with respect to the teaching of specific strategies for socioscientific decision making and problem solving.

Students in TG1 ("Developing solutions") focused on the analytical and comprehensive description of the SD problems, as well as development of solutions and

Table 16.2 Unit objectives for the three training groups of the experimental validation study (90 minutes: a double period)

		"Developing solutions"	"Evaluating solutions"	"Problem solving"
		Students	Students	Students
Palm oil production	90 min.	… understand the problem of palm oil production and their role as consumers by discovering palm oil substances in everyday products	… understand the problem in its factual complexity by considering the ecological, economic, and social aspects	…explore the SD problem associated with palm oil from Indonesia
		… apply an analytical framework to understand and describe the factual complexity of the problem as well as possible solutions	… apply a decision matrix to collect and collate necessary information for three given, real-world solutions	… understand the provided analytical problem-solving framework and perform step 1: "read and understand" to cope with the factual complexity
	90 min.	… develop solutions to the problem that integrate different stakeholder perspectives	… use the decision matrix to evaluate the three given solutions and their underlying value considerations, applying different decision-making strategies	… use problem-solving strategies to develop solutions by considering different stakeholder perspectives and perform steps 2-5: develop a plan, choose a plan, apply it and evaluate the solutions
		… use the analytical framework to reflect on the developed solutions and on one specific given real-world solution	… use the decision matrix to identify and reflect on the factual and ethical complexity in their own decision processes and decision processes of others	… perform the problem- solving steps to reflect on their own solution from a certain stakeholder perspective and on given solutions
Cotton production (Transfer)	90 min.	… use the analytical framework to develop solutions to the problem, acknowledging the factual complexity	… use the decision matrix to evaluate solutions to the problem, acknowledging the factual and ethical complexity	… use the steps of the analytical problem-solving framework to develop solutions to the problem

reflection on solutions. To help students understand the complex relations between the different ecological, economic and social aspects of the SD issue, the teacher used a specific analytical framework (see Bögeholz 2011; Gausmann et al. 2010; Ostermeyer et al. 2012; see Table 16.2).

Students in TG2 concentrated on the comparison of different, equally legitimate solutions to solve the presented SD problems. This also included the development of pro- and contra-arguments and the weighing of arguments or decision criteria in order to reach informed decisions. To help students compare the different possible options and their criteria in a systematic manner, a decision matrix was used. This decision matrix was also used to make value decisions transparent, and therefore allowed for discussing, reflecting on, and respecting different (legitimate) solutions and decision-making processes (e.g., Bögeholz 2006; Eggert and Bögeholz 2006; see Table 16.2).

TG3 worked on the presented SD problems by following the problem-solving steps (Buchwald et al. 2017, in this volume; see Table 16.2). While the students worked on the problem-solving steps "developing problem solving ideas" and "choosing a problem solving plan", they got to know a set of six problem-solving strategies (see Blum et al. 2006, p. 39), namely: principle of analogy, principle of decomposition, principle of illustration, working forward, working backward, and systematic trying. Our training builds on experiences from Buchwald et al. 2017, in this volume).

16.4.2.3 Measures

Socioscientific decision making and analytical problem solving were assessed as dependent variables. With respect to socioscientific decision making, both measures were used in an abridged version. The pretest for "Developing solutions" consisted of three tasks: (1) Rattan from Indonesia (see Eggert et al. 2013), (2) Oil and gas extraction in Siberia ("describing" and "developing" items), and (3) Shrimps from South-East Asia ("reflecting" items; cf. Eggert et al. 2013; Table 16.3). The final scale included 24 items ($\alpha = .75$). With respect to "developing" solutions, the scoring procedure was altered (comparing Table 16.3 with Table 16.1). Within the new scoring each single aspect (see [A] in Table 16.3) was scored instead of related aspects (see [R] in Table 16.1). The new scoring better aligns with student responses, due to the degree of item complexity. Compared to our measure in Table 16.1, we presented only one project per reflection task, and we reduced the number of items as a consequence of limited testing time.

The corresponding posttest integrated the Rattan and Soy tasks (see Table 16.1) with "describing" items, and "developing" items, as well as the Hoodia task (see Table 16.1) with "reflecting" items. The final scale included 24 items ($\alpha = .74$). All items for "describing" the SD problems, "developing" solutions and "reflecting" solutions were dichotomous.

The pretest for "Evaluating solutions" again comprised three different tasks: (1) the problem of cabbage white butterfly larvae in vegetable gardens, (2) a problem-

Table 16.3 Abridged measure of "Developing solutions"

		Item descriptions	Item no. Pre- and posttest
Rattan/Oil and gas (t1); Rattan/Soy (t2)	Describe problem	Ecological-economic relation [R1]	1/10
		Social1-ecological relation [R2]	2/11
		Social1-social2 relation [R3]	3/12
		Social2-economic relation [R4]	4/13
		Social1-economic relation [R5]	5/14
		Social2-ecological relation [R6]	6/15
	Develop solution	Economical aspect [A1]	–/16
		Ecological aspect [A2]	7/17
		Social2 aspect [A3]	8/18
		Social1 aspect [A4]	–/19
		Institution aspect [I2]	9/20
Shrimps (t1); Hoodia (t2)	Reflect project A	Ecological-economic relation [R1]	21
		Social1-ecological relation [R2]	22
		Social1-economic relation [R5]	23
		Social2-ecological relation [R6]	24

atic neophyte for riverbanks (both decision tasks), and (3) a reflection task on the means of transportation for holidays. The final scale included 11 items ($\alpha = .78$). In the posttest, we used the Neophyte task again and varied the other tasks ("overfishing of codfish", and a consumer choice task; cf. Eggert et al. 2010). The final scale included 11 items ($\alpha = .88$).

To assess analytical problem solving we applied items from PISA 2003. Thereby, we used a selected set of items and the corresponding scoring guide provided by a collaborating working group (Buchwald et al. 2017, in this volume). Specifically, we analyzed problem solving via a scale of three dichotomous items (cinema 1, watergate, design) as well as three trichotomous items (train, holiday camp, vacation). For the pretest ($\alpha = .51$) and posttest ($\alpha = .52$) we used the identical problem-solving tasks.

For all three measures, half of the items were double coded (Cohen's Kappa: .93–.99). As expected, validation analyses revealed very weak to weak correlations between "Developing solutions" and "Problem solving" ($r = .31$, $p < .01$), between "Evaluating solutions" and "Problem solving" ($r = .27$, $p < .01$) and also between "Developing solutions" and "Evaluating solutions" ($r = .20$, $p < .05$).

16.4.3 Results of the Pilot Study

As a first step, we conducted one-way ANOVAs to check for possible group differences on the pretest scores. Post hoc Tukey tests showed significant differences between the four treatment conditions with respect to all three dependent variables: “Developing solutions”, “Evaluating solutions”, and “Problem solving”. The training group “Evaluating solutions” (TG2) always displayed the lowest test performances (except for the measure on “Problem solving”), and differed from the Control Group in always having the best test performances ($p < .05$).

As a consequence of the identified pretest differences, we conducted multiple regression analyses using the pretest scores (prior knowledge) and the treatment conditions as independent variables. Concerning treatment conditions, contrasts were coded. The mean and standard deviations of the dependent variables by time and treatment are displayed in Table 16.4.

“Developing solutions” at posttest were predicted by prior knowledge as well as by both contrasts (see Table 16.5). The final statistical model accounts for 30 % of the variance with prior knowledge accounting for 14 %, the second contrast variable for 6 %, and the third contrast variable for 10 %. Remarkably, the third contrast reveals a negative relationship with posttest learning outcomes, that is TG3 outperforms TG1.

For “Evaluating solutions”, prior knowledge and the first contrast variable predict students’ learning outcomes in the posttest (see Table 16.5). The final statistical model accounts for 40 % of the variance, with prior knowledge accounting for

32 % and the contrast variable accounting for 8 %. The analyses reveal that the CG shows better posttest performances than the training groups.

Table 16.4 Mean scores and standard deviations for “Developing solutions”, “Evaluating solutions”, and “Problem solving” by time and treatment (TG: training group; CG: control group)

		TG1	TG2	TG3	CG
“Developing solutions”					
Pretest	*M* (*SD*)	13.95 (4.47)	10.52 (5.57)	13.00 (4.65)	15.81 (4.30)
Posttest	*M* (*SD*)	12.81 (5.39)	11.04 (5.24)	17.22 (4.03)	14.93 (3.52)
“Evaluating solutions”					
Pretest	*M* (*SD*)	12.10 (3.89)	9.72 (4.23)	14.04 (3.65)	14.11 (2.33)
Posttest	*M* (*SD*)	7.00 (5.29)	5.52 (4.94)	10.16 (5.60)	12.74 (3.05)
“Problem solving”					
Pretest	*M* (*SD*)	3.81 (1.75)	3.93 (1.69)	4.22 (2.17)	5.89 (1.93)
Posttest	*M* (*SD*)	3.81 (2.25)	3.59 (2.48)	4.87 (2.16)	6.11 (1.83)

Table 16.5 Multiple regression predicting posttest performance on "Developing solutions" and "Evaluating solutions" by prior knowledge and treatment

"Developing solutions"			
	B	*SE*	β
Step 1			
Prior knowledge (pretest score)	0.37	.09	.37***
Step 2			
Prior knowledge (pretest score)	0.31	.09	.31**
Contrast 2 (TG1, TG3 vs. TG2)	1.06	.39	.26**
Step 3			
Prior knowledge (pretest score)	0.33	.09	.33***
Contrast 2 (TG1, TG3 vs. TG2)	1.01	.36	.25**
Contrast 3 (TG1 vs. TG3)	−2.36	.65	−.31***
Note: $R^2 = .14$ for Step 1, $\Delta R^2 = .06$ for Step 2, $\Delta R^2 = .10$ for Step 3, ** $p < .01$, *** $p < .001$			
"Evaluating solutions"			
	B	SE	β
Step 1			
Prior knowledge (pretest score)	0.79	.12	.57***
Step 2			
Prior knowledge (pretest scores)	0.69	.11	.50***
Contrast 1 (TG2, TG1, TG3 vs. CG)	−0.91	.25	−.30***
Note: $R^2 = .32$ for Step 1, $\Delta R^2 = .08$ for Step 2, *** $p < .001$			

In addition, "Problem solving" was revealed to be exclusively predicted by prior knowledge, which accounts for 33 % of the variance (Prior knowledge [pretest score]: $B = 0.66$, $SE = .10$, $\beta = .57$, $p < .001$). Thus, the investigated contrast variables did not contribute to explaining the variance of the posttest scores.

16.4.4 Discussion

The aims of this pilot study were (1) to further improve the training procedures, (2) to further develop abridged measures, and (3) to initiate a training-based experimental validation of our approach in conceptualizing socioscientific decision making. A number of crucial factors have to be taken into account:

Educational and experimental setting: Even though the school administration showed an extraordinary commitment, our study was affected by the perils of field research. Specifically, our study was influenced, for example, by differences in teacher enthusiasm, different amounts of time spent in preparing teaching, and reflecting on the lessons taught. Working with just one school eased project management demands and tended to ensure a socially more homogeneous student population. Teachers were recruited by the school administration in a top-down approach. The school administration created special timetables so that all classes had an intervention of three double periods. However, the latter had the side effect that TG1 had to sacrifice their physical education lessons for the posttest, and a considerable decline in interest for TG1 was documented in the chronological protocols. With respect to the main study, we will follow a more bottom-up approach for recruiting teachers.

Measures: All SD problems addressed in the measurement instruments differ from the SD problems addressed in the treatments. The instruments applied for decision making were used in abridged versions. The abridged version of "Developing solutions" still covers all crucial features of our competence dimension. With respect to the abridged version of "Evaluating solutions", here again, all core characteristics of the competence dimension are considered in the measure (cf. Eggert and Bögeholz 2010). In sum, the reliabilities of our decision-making measures are promising and we succeeded in having widely varying pre- and posttest measures. However, it still remains a challenge (1) to model "Developing solutions" with polytomous items, and (2) to analyze the pre- and posttest design with IRT (cf. procedure in Eggert et al. 2010 for "Evaluating solutions").

Training outcomes: With respect to the dependent variable "Developing solutions", students of TG3 benefited from the well-designed teaching material with challenging tasks as well as from the participative teaching methods (e.g., fishbowl). In contrast, TG1—even though they had the same teacher—did benefit less. This might at least partly be due to the fact that the students had to cope with the disappointment that they missed their physical education lessons in favor of the posttest. With respect to "Evaluating solutions", the students of the CG performed best. The latter can partly be traced back to the enthusiasm of teacher C (cf. Kunter 2011). Teacher C used a constructivist approach of teaching, which might have produced higher levels of motivation and performance among the students of the CG compared to the students of the training groups. This can be explained by research on teacher beliefs and their impact on learning outcomes (constructivist beliefs > transmissive beliefs see Voss et al. 2011, p. 250). Teacher beliefs might change with teaching experience over the career span, for example, a portion of experienced teachers overcame their teacher-centered metaphors and proceeded with student-centered metaphors (Alger 2009). The three teachers in our pilot study varied strongly in their teaching experiences (4–33 years). In the main study, the (average) teacher experience of the different treatment groups will be more balanced.

Beyond these explanations, more general phenomena might also have influenced the results: The acquisition of complex strategies is accompanied by a stage of so-called inefficient utilization ("*Nutzungsineffizienz*"; see Hasselhorn and Gold 2013, p. 100). If students are confronted with a new, complex strategy, a hugh additional strain is placed on their working memory. As a result, learning outcomes may be worse after a training than before. Lower achievement at posttest measures can also be traced back to a "motivational valley", and can be overcome by strategy automating (Hasselhorn and Gold 2013, pp. 100, 101). The latter may finally result in higher learning outcomes in time-delayed measuring.

In sum, we could successfully advance the training procedures as well as their corresponding measures. We are in a good position now to optimize the realization of our main study. Even though we did not obtain much support for the hypotheses, the results can be plausibly explained by the circumstances, while validation of our theoretical contribution still remains a challenging endeavor.

16.5 Conclusions and Outlook

Though our research program on decision making regarding SD issues is far from being finalized, we provide several measures that stem from the Göttingen competence model. All in all, they allow for the adequate assessment of student competencies with respect to socioscientific decision making (Eggert et al. 2010, 2013; Gresch et al. 2013; Sakschewski et al. 2014). In addition, our approach has already inspired other working groups within the research community (Böttcher and Meisert 2013; Heitmann 2012; Hostenbach et al. 2011; Papadouris 2012).

To finish our experimental validation approach, we are currently conducting our main study, which includes six classes for each of the three training groups and the control group. The participating schools were recruited from four German federal states, and the composition of the treatment conditions (e.g., with respect to teacher experiences, teacher beliefs, teacher enthusiasm, student motivation, students social backgrounds) was as balanced as possible. To better cope with any potential "motivational valley" in acquiring complex strategies, we are carrying out the post-test of the main study six to eight weeks after the trainings.

The present contribution refers to an instructional approach to test whether the theoretical assumptions of the socioscientific decision-making theory addressed in our project are valid. The approach has been used in several fields of psychological research in order to test assumptions whether specific processes or strategies are responsible for the quality of specific individual behavior. It is the idea of the instructional approach to manipulate the relevant strategies and see whether the instruction has an effect on the target behavior. To be clear, although our project started to validate the socioscientific decision-making theory by means of an instructional approach, much further research seems to be necessary in order to come to a final assessment of the validity of the theory.

Beyond the above-mentioned open questions related to the validity of the theory, upcoming research on student competencies should go mainly into three directions: First of all, the model should be elaborated in more detail, since the evaluation of SD-problem solutions additionally requires considering quantitative impacts. Here, decision making profits from the use of simplified methods of economic validation, such as cost benefit analysis, cost effective analysis or profitability analysis. Thus, mathematical-economic modeling will complement the current research. A promising fourth competence dimension, "Evaluating solutions quantitatively-economically", is described in Bögeholz et al. (2014) as well as in Bögeholz and Barkmann (2014).

Second, the developed measures on "Evaluating solutions" of decision-making competence have been successfully applied to analyzing gains in learning outcomes in a pre- and posttest study via IRT-modeling (Eggert et al. 2010). For the current main study aiming at experimental validation, the abridged measure for "Developing solutions" has to be further strengthened so that decision making can be modeled with IRT in at least two measurement points, for both assessed decision-making dimensions. Besides having sensitive measures for decision making in intervention studies, we aim to further develop our measures for longitudinal studies with IRT-modeling, as well as for computer-based adaptive testing in the long run.

Third, our previous research has addressed the cognitive components of decision making. For the future, studies to foster decision making and studies on competence development should consider motivational factors. Studies on decision making with respect to biodiversity challenges should also integrate measures of interest in biodiversity issues. Because motivational factors impact learning outcomes (cf. Weinert 2001; cf. Rotgans and Schmidt 2011), linking research on motivation and cognitive competence is of practical relevance for real-world learning settings.

Beside these recent and future endeavors regarding student competencies, we aim at modeling and fostering teacher PCK for teaching socioscientific decision making. The latter benefits from the knowledge gained in the priority program—that is, knowledge on student decision-making competencies and on strategies to improve them.

In sum, our competence research on SD issues is a promising approach not only for ESD, but also for science teaching, and for citizenship education (e.g., Sadler et al. 2007; Eggert et al. 2013; Sakschewski et al. 2014; Bögeholz et al. 2014).

Acknowledgments The preparation of this chapter was supported by grant BO 1730/3-3 from the German Research Foundation (DFG) in the Priority Program "Competence Models for Assessing Individual Learning Outcomes and Evaluating Educational Processes" (SPP 1293).

We thank J. Hartig, D. Leutner, J. Rost and R. Watermann for methodological discussions as well as M. Möhlhenrich, F. Ostermeyer, and S. Teschner for contributing to the competence model.

References

Alger, C. L. (2009). Secondary teachers' conceptual metaphors of teaching and learning: Changes over the career span. *Teaching and Teacher Education, 25*, 743–751. doi:10.1016/j.tate.2008.10.004.

Bernholt, S., Eggert, S., & Kulgemeyer, C. (2012). Capturing the diversity of students' competences in the science classroom: Differences and commonalities of three complementary approaches. In S. Bernholt, K. Neumann, & P. Nentwig (Eds.), *Making it tangible: Learning outcomes in science education* (pp. 173–199). Münster: Waxmann.

Betsch, T., & Haberstroh, S. (Eds.). (2005). *The routines of decision making*. Mahwah: Erlbaum.

Blum, W., Drüke-Noe, C., Hartung, R., & Köller, O. (2006). Bildungsstandards Mathematik: Konkret. In *Sekundarstufe I: Aufgabenbeispiele, Unterrichtsanregungen, Fortbildungsideen [German educational standards in mathematics for lower secondary degree: Tasks, teaching suggestions, thoughts with respect to further education]*. Berlin: Cornelsen Scriptor.

Bögeholz, S. (2006). Explizit Bewerten und Urteilen: Beispielkontext Streuobstwiese [Explicit reasoning and decision making: The topic of orchards]. *Praxis der Naturwissenschaften, Biologie in der Schule, 55*, 17–24.

Bögeholz, S. (2011). Bewertungskompetenz im Kontext nachhaltiger Entwicklung: Ein Forschungsprogramm [Reasoning and decision-making competence in the context of sustainable development: A research program]. In D. Höttecke (Ed.), *Naturwissenschaftliche Bildung als Beitrag zur Gestaltung partizipativer Demokratie* (pp. 32–46). Münster: LIT.

Bögeholz, S., & Barkmann, J. (2005). Rational choice and beyond: Handlungsorientierende Kompetenzen für den Umgang mit faktischer und ethischer Komplexität [Rational choice and beyond: Action-oriented competencies for dealing with factual and ethical complexity]. In R. Klee, A. Sandmann, & H. Vogt (Eds.), *Lehr- und Lernforschung in der Biologiedidaktik* (pp. 211–224). Innsbruck: Studien-Verlag.

Bögeholz, S., & Barkmann, J. (2014). "… to help make decisions": A challenge to science education research in the 21st century. In I. Eilks, S. Markic, & B. Ralle (Eds.), *Science education research and education for sustainable development* (pp. 25–35). Aachen: Shaker.

Bögeholz, S., Böhm, M., Eggert, S., & Barkmann, J. (2014). Education for sustainable development in German science education: Past-Present-Future. *EURASIA Journal of Mathematics, Science & Technology Education, 10*, 219–236. doi:10.12973/eurasia.2014.1079a.

Böhmann, M., & Schäfer-Munro, R. (2008). *Kursbuch Schulpraktikum: Unterrichtspraxis und didaktisches Grundwissen [Course book teaching internship. Teaching practice and basic didactical knowledge]* (2nd ed.). Weinheim: Beltz.

Böttcher, F., & Meisert, A. (2013). Effects of direct and indirect instruction on fostering decision-making competence in socioscientific issues. *Science Education, 43*, 479–506. doi:10.1007/s11165-011-9271-0.

Buchwald, F., Fleischer, J., Rumann, S., Wirth, J., & Leutner, D. (2017). Training in components of problem-solving competence: An experimental study of aspects of the cognitive potential exploitation hypothesis. In D. Leutner, J. Fleischer, J. Grünkorn, & E. Klieme (Eds.), *Competence assessment in education: Research, models and instruments* (pp. 315–331). Berlin: Springer.

Eggert, S., & Bögeholz, S. (2006). Göttinger Modell der Bewertungskompetenz: Teilkompetenz "Bewerten, Entscheiden und Reflektieren" für Gestaltungsaufgaben nachhaltiger Entwicklung [Göttingen model for socioscientific decision making—Subdimension: "Evaluating solutions" for tasks concerning sustainable development]. *Zeitschrift für Didaktik der Naturwissenschaften, 12*, 177–199.

Eggert, S., & Bögeholz, S. (2010). Students' use of decision-making strategies with regard to socioscientific issues: An application of the Rasch partial credit model. *Science Education, 94*, 230–258. doi:10.1002/sce.20358.

Eggert, S., & Bögeholz, S. (2014). Entwicklung eines Testinstruments zur Messung von Schülerkompetenzen [Development of a measurement instrument for student competencies]. In D. Krüger, I. Parchmann, & H. Schecker (Eds.), *Methoden in der naturwissenschaftsdidaktischen Forschung* (pp. 371–384). Berlin: Springer.

Eggert, S., Bögeholz, S., Watermann, R., & Hasselhorn, M. (2010). Förderung von Bewertungskompetenz im Biologieunterricht durch zusätzliche metakognitive Strukturierungshilfen beim kooperativen Lernen: Ein Beispiel für Veränderungsmessung [The effects of metacognitive instruction on students' socioscientific decision making: An exemplary procedure for measurement of change]. *Zeitschrift für Didaktik der Naturwissenschaften, 16*, 299–314.

Eggert, S., Ostermeyer, F., Hasselhorn, M., & Bögeholz, S. (2013). Socioscientific decision making in the science classroom: The effect of embedded metacognitive instructions on students' learning outcomes. *Education Research International*. doi:0.1155/2012/309894.

Ernst, A. (1997). *Ökologisch-soziale Dilemmata [Socio-ecological dilemmas]*. Weinheim: PVU.

Gausmann, E., Eggert, S., Hasselhorn, M., Watermann, R., & Bögeholz, S. (2010). Wie verarbeiten Schülerinnen und Schüler Sachinformationen in Problem- und Entscheidungssituationen nachhaltiger Entwicklung [How do students process information in problem and decision-making situations]? *Zeitschrift für Pädagogik, Beiheft, 56*, 204–215.

Gresch, H., Hasselhorn, M., & Bögeholz, S. (2013). Training in decision-making strategies: An approach to enhance students' competence to deal with socio-scientific issues. *International Journal of Science Education, 35*, 2587–2607. doi:10.1080/09500693.2011.617789.

Hasselhorn, M., & Gold, A. (2013). *Pädagogische Psychologie: Erfolgreiches Lernen und Lehren [Pedagogical psychology: Successful learning and teaching]*. Stuttgart: Kohlhammer.

Heitmann, P. (2012). *Bewertungskompetenz im Rahmen naturwissenschaftlicher Problemlöseprozesse: Modellierung und Diagnose der Kompetenzen Bewertung und analytisches Problemlösen für das Fach Chemie* [Decision making in the context of problem solving regarding natural sciences: Modeling and diagnosis of decision-making and analytical problem-solving competencies with respect to chemistry]. Berlin: Logos.

Hostenbach, J., Fischer, H. E., Kauertz, A., Mayer, J., Sumfleth, E., & Walpuski, M. (2011). Modellierung der Bewertungskompetenz in den Naturwissenschaften zur Evaluation der nationalen Bildungsstandards [Modeling the evaluation and judgement of competence in science to evaluate national educational standards]. *Zeitschrift für Didaktik der Naturwissenschaften, 17*, 261–288.

Jiménez-Aleixandre, M.-P., & Pereiro-Muñoz, C. (2002). Knowledge producers or knowledge consumers? Argumentation and decision making about environmental management. *International Journal of Science Education, 24*, 1171–1190. doi:10.1080/09500690210134857.

Klieme, E., Hartig, J., & Rauch, D. (2008). The concept of competence in educational contexts. In J. Hartig, E. Klieme, & D. Leutner (Eds.), *Assessment of competencies in educational contexts* (pp. 3–22). Göttingen: Hogrefe.

KMK (Standing Conference of the Ministers of Education and Cultural Affairs of the States in the Federal Republic of Germany). (Ed.). (2005). *Bildungsstandards im Fach Biologie für den mittleren Schulabschluss (Jahrgangsstufe 10): Beschluss vom 16.12.2004* [German educational standards in biology for the lower secondary degree (Grade 10): Resolution approved by the standing conference on 16 December 2004]. München: Luchterhand.

Kuhn, D. (1999). A developmental model of critical thinking. *Educational Researcher, 28*, 16–25. doi:10.3102/0013189X028002016.

Kunter, M. (2011). Motivation als Teil der professionellen Kompetenz: Forschungsbefunde zum Enthusiasmus von Lehrkräften [Motivation as part of professional competence: Research results regarding enthusiasm of teachers]. In M. Kunter, J. Baumert, W. Blum, U. Klusmann, S. Krauss, & M. Neubrand (Eds.), *Professionelle Kompetenz von Lehrkräften: Ergebnisse des Forschungsprogramms COACTIV* (pp. 259–275). Münster: Waxmann.

Leutner, D., Klieme, E., Meyer, K., & Wirth, J. (2004). Problemlösen [Problem solving.]. In P. I. S. A.-K. Deutschland (Ed.), *PISA 2003. Der Bildungsstand der Jugendlichen in Deutschland — Ergebnisse des zweiten internationalen Vergleichs* (pp. 147–175). Münster: Waxmann.

MA (Millennium Ecosystem Assessment). (Ed.). (2005). *Ecosystems and human well-being: A framework for assessment*. http://www.maweb.org. Accessed 10 Oct 2014.

Mummendey, H. D., & Grau, I. (2008). *Die Fragebogenmethode [Method: Questionnaires]* (5th ed.). Göttingen: Hogrefe.

OECD (Organisation for Economic Co-operation and Development). (2004). *Problem solving for tomorrow's world: First measures of cross-curricular competencies from PISA 2003*. Paris: Author.

Ostermeyer, F., Eggert, S., & Bögeholz, S. (2012). Rein pflanzlich, dennoch schädlich [Exclusively vegetable, however dangerous]? *Unterricht Biologie, 36*(377/378), 43–50.

Oulton, C., Dillon, J., & Grace, M. M. (2004). Reconceptualizing the teaching of controversial issues. *International Journal of Science Education, 26*, 411–423. doi:10.1080/0950069032000072746.

Papadouris, N. (2012). Optimization as a reasoning strategy for dealing with socioscientific decision-making situations. *Science Education, 96*, 600–630. doi:10.1002/sce.21016.

Pólya, G. (1945). *How to solve it: A new aspect of mathematical method.* Princeton: University Press.

Ratcliffe, M., & Grace, M. (2003). *Science education for citizenship: Teaching socio-scientific issues.* Maidenhead: Oxford University Press.

Rasch, G. (1960). *Probabilistic models for some intelligence and attainment tests.* Copenhagen: Danmarks Padagogiske Institut.

Rotgans, J. I., & Schmidt, H. G. (2011). Situational interest and academic achievement in the active-learning classroom. *Learning and Instruction, 21*, 58–67. doi:10.1016/j.learninstruc.2009.11.001.

Sadler, T., Barab, S., & Scott, B. (2007). What do students gain by engaging in socio-scientific inquiry? *Research in Science Education, 37*, 371–391. doi:10.1007/s11165-011-9260-3.

Sakschewski, M., Eggert, S., Schneider, S., & Bögeholz, S. (2014). Students' socioscientific reasoning and decision making on energy-related issues: Development of a measurement instrument. *International Journal of Science Education, 36*, 2291–2313. doi:10.1080/09500693.2014.920550.

Scherer, R. (2012). *Analyse der Struktur, Messinvarianz und Ausprägung komplexer Problemlösekompetenz im Fach Chemie [Analyzing the structure, measurement invariance, and performance of complex problem-solving competency in chemistry].* Berlin: Logos.

Toulmin, S. (1958). *The uses of argument.* Cambridge: Cambridge University Press.

Voss, T., Kleickmann, T., Kunter, M., & Hachfeld, A. (2011). Überzeugungen von Mathematiklehrkräften [Beliefs of mathematics teachers]. In M. Kunter, J. Baumert, W. Blum, U. Klusmann, S. Krauss, & M. Neubrand (Eds.), *Professionelle Kompetenz von Lehrkräften: Ergebnisse des Forschungsprogramms COACTIV* (pp. 235–257). Münster: Waxmann.

Weinert, F. E. (2001). Concept of competence: A conceptual clarification. In D. S. Rychen & L. H. Salganik (Eds.), *Defining and selecting key competencies* (pp. 45–65). Seattle: Hogrefe.

Wilson, M. (2005). *Constructing measures: An item response modeling approach.* Mahwah: Erlbaum.

Wu, M. L., Adams, R. J., Wilson, M. R., & Haldane, S. A. (2007). *Acer conquest version 2.0.* Victoria: Acer.

Chapter 17
Metacognitive Knowledge in Secondary School Students: Assessment, Structure, and Developmental Change

Wolfgang Schneider, Klaus Lingel, Cordula Artelt, and Nora Neuenhaus

Abstract The construct of metacognitive knowledge—that is knowledge on cognitive processes, was established as a determinant of cognitive development in the 1970s. Early research focused on the domain of memory development in pre- and primary school children. While research activities on metacognition have diversified over time, some core issues in the assessment, structure, and development of metacognitive knowledge still remain unresolved:

(1) How can metacognitive knowledge be assessed? (2) How does metacognitive knowledge develop in secondary school? (3) Is metacognitive knowledge domain-specific or domain-general? (4) To what extent are developmental changes in metacognitive knowledge and achievement interrelated?

We addressed these research questions within our longitudinal research project on the development of knowledge components. Our database included 928 German students who were tested on six measurement points (from Grades 5 to 9). The focus of the longitudinal study was on the assessment of metacognitive knowledge, as well as achievement in mathematics, reading comprehension, English as a foreign language, and the changes in these variables over time. In this chapter, the main results on these four research questions are presented, after a brief description of the historical research background. The results of the last assessment period are given special emphasis.

Keywords Metacognitive knowledge • Domain-specific knowledge • Longitudinal study • Reading skills • Mathematics • English as a foreign language

W. Schneider (✉) • K. Lingel
University of Würzburg, Würzburg, Germany
e-mail: schneider@psychologie.uni-wuerzburg.de; lingel@uni-wuerzburg.de

C. Artelt • N. Neuenhaus
University of Bamberg, Bamberg, Germany
e-mail: cordula.artelt@uni-bamberg.de; nora.neuenhaus@uni-bamberg.de

D. Leutner et al. (eds.), *Competence Assessment in Education*, Methodology of Educational Measurement and Assessment, DOI 10.1007/978-3-319-50030-0_17

17.1 Theoretical Background

Research on metacognitive development was initiated in the early 1970s by Ann Brown, John Flavell, and their colleagues (for reviews, see Brown et al. 1983; Flavell et al. 2002). At the very beginning, this research focused on knowledge about memory, which was coined "metamemory" by Flavell (1971). Later on, the concept was also applied to studies investigating children's comprehension, communication, and problem-solving skills (Flavell 2000; Schneider and Pressley 1997). The term "metacognition" has usually been defined broadly as "any knowledge or cognitive activity that takes as its object, or regulates, any aspect of any cognitive enterprise" (Flavell et al. 2002, p. 150). According to this conceptualization, metacognition refers to people's knowledge about their own information-processing skills, the nature of cognitive tasks, and strategies for coping with such tasks. Moreover, it also includes executive skills related to the monitoring and self-regulation of one's own cognitive activities.

Most recent models of metacognition differentiate between declarative and procedural components of metacognition. This basic distinction, already apparent in Flavell and Wellman's (1977) taxonomy of metamemory, seems widely accepted in the developmental and educational literature (cf. Alexander et al. 1995; Kuhn 2000; Schneider 2010; Veenman et al. 2006). Nonetheless, it has also been argued that these two aspects of metacognition complicate its definition (see Joyner and Kurtz-Costes 1997). That is to say, while the two components are closely related, they are also fundamentally different in nature. Whereas the declarative knowledge component is primarily verbalizable, stable, and late-developing, the procedural knowledge component is not necessarily verbalizable, is rather unstable, relatively age-independent, and dependent on the specific task or situation. Thus, although there are substantial relations between the procedural (actual regulation) and declarative aspects (knowledge base) of metacognition, both from an analytical point of view and on the basis of research findings on the development of these components, it seems worthwhile to distinguish between the two (see also Hacker et al. 2009; Schneider 2015; Schneider and Artelt 2010; Schraw and Moshman 1995).

In our research project, the focus was on the exploration of (declarative) metacognitive strategy knowledge. As to the differentiation between components of declarative metacognitive knowledge, Paris and Byrnes (1989, see also Brown 1978) distinguished between *declarative strategy knowledge* ("knowing that"), *procedural strategy knowledge* ("knowing how"), and *conditional strategy knowledge* ("knowing when"). All three knowledge components are necessary, in order to apply strategies effectively. Taking into account Borkowski's metamemory model (Borkowski et al. 1988), it also seems worthwhile to look at students' knowledge about the usefulness of a certain strategy in relation to other strategies: that is, their *relational strategy knowledge*. Relational strategy knowledge is particularly important when individuals have a repertoire of strategies at their disposal and have to decide which is most adequate. Aspects of conditional and relational strategy knowledge were considered to be central components of the metacognitive knowledge measure used in our research project, EWIKO (Entwicklung metakognitiven Wissens und bereichsspezifischen Vorwissens bei Schülern der Sekundarstufe: development of metacognitive knowledge and domain-specific knowledge in secondary school students; see details below).

There is general agreement that, in the early stages of knowledge acquisition, specific aspects of declarative and procedural metacognitive knowledge influence performance across tasks and settings, and that the likelihood of transfer from one setting to another is quite low. A wealth of evidence for the domain specificity of metacognitive acquisition processes has led to the conclusion that metacognitive skills must be taught in context (Jacobs and Paris 1987). Furthermore, it is believed that repeated application and practice of metacognitive strategies enables learners to apply these strategies in diverse settings and domains in later stages of development. Metacognition and self-regulated learning thus are often considered domain-general constructs that transfer or generalize across domains.

A question repeatedly discussed in the relevant literature concerns the extent to which metacognitive knowledge is domain-specific. That is, does it vary within the same person as a function of the domain under investigation, such as reading, mathematics, or foreign language learning? Is there empirical evidence that it tends to become more general—that is, comparable for the same person across different domains, with increasing age? The development of metacognitive knowledge has often been proposed to be context-dependent and domain-specific at an early stage, and assumed to generalize throughout elementary school (e.g., Schneider 2008).

Given that there is not much empirical evidence on this issue for secondary school students, this research question was of particular interest in the present study. It was assumed that students at the beginning of secondary school (fifth graders in the German school system) are at an early stage of generalizing domain knowledge in reading, mathematics, or foreign language learning, which makes it likely that metacognitive knowledge can be identified as domain-specific during this early period of secondary school. Given that metacognitive knowledge develops not only within particular subject domains but also during regular school-based activities such as homework, exam preparation, etc., we assumed that the impact of domain transcending general metacognitive knowledge should increase over time. The expectation was that interrelations among the three domain-specific knowledge components should increase over time, thus indicating the increasing importance of domain-general knowledge.

Another important issue is how to characterize the development of declarative metacognitive knowledge and its relationship to memory behavior and (academic) performance. On the one hand, the empirical evidence suggests that declarative metacognitive knowledge increases substantially over the elementary school years. From early adolescence on, it is relatively stable, in the sense that individual differences do not change much over time. On the other hand, the procedural component of metacognition seems more "situated" and thus more unstable, since the actual regulation of learning depends on the learners' familiarity with the task, as well as on their motivation and emotions. Individuals need to regulate their thoughts about which strategy they are using and adjust its use to the situation in which it is being applied. Given that the selection and application of strategies during learning depends not only on metacognitive knowledge but also on individual goals, standards, situational affordances, text difficulty, task demands, and so forth (Campione and Armbruster 1985; see also Winne and Hadwin 1998), it cannot be assumed that strategies will be applied whenever possible. However, an individual who uses a particular strategy intelligently ought to have some metacognitive knowledge of that strategy. In other words, there is a correlation between metacognitive knowledge and the effective use of strategies, which should also affect memory performance. Although metacognitive knowledge is assumed to be a necessary condition, it may not be sufficient for reflective and strategic learning or for academic achievement, because other factors such as IQ, domain knowledge, and memory capacity (working memory) also play a role.

17.1.1 Methodological Issues Regarding the Assessment of Declarative Metacognitive Knowledge

Before we deal with these issues in more detail, we briefly discuss a methodological problem that has concerned developmental research on declarative metacognition for quite a while, and which has to be solved before substantive issues can be tackled in a meaningful way.

Most evidence for the impact of declarative metacognitive knowledge on learning and achievement is provided by studies using assessment procedures such as open interviews, or concurrent measures such as observation and think-aloud analysis (see Schneider and Pressley 1997, for a review). Standardized assessments (and especially paper-and-pencil instruments) that are also used to assess metacognition often fail to provide empirical evidence for a positive correlation between (metacognitive) learning strategies and achievement (Lind and Sandmann 2003; Muis et al. 2007). According to Artelt (2000), potential explanations for such low correlations can be described as follows: First, most of the classic inventories for assessing metacognition and strategy knowledge are constructed in such a manner that students have to judge the frequency of their strategy use (e.g., Pintrich et al. 1993; Schraw and Dennison 1994). Thus, these instruments draw primarily on students' recognition of strategies (i.e., their long-term memory) and not so much on their declarative metacognitive knowledge (Leopold and Leutner 2002). Second, such frequency judgments are not well suited for younger age groups, because they are cognitively demanding and require high degrees of abstract thinking, as well as the ability to objectively generalize over past behaviors—which in turn is likely to be influenced by social desirability and memory bias (Schraw 2000). Third, the instruments are incapable of assessing metacognitive knowledge independent of strategy usage. From a theoretical perspective this is problematic, because a potential gap between competence and performance might distort the metacognitive knowledge pupils possess when it is assessed through frequency judgments of strategy usage. Consequently, the quality of metacognitive knowledge remains subject to speculation.

To avoid such problems, more sophisticated measures of metacognition have to be used with older children and adolescents. Schlagmüller and Schneider (2007) came up with a standardized measure of metacognitive knowledge on reading that was based on a revised test instrument developed for PISA 2000 (see Artelt et al. 2001). The same approach, and some of the material, was later used as part of the international assessment in the PISA 2009 study (see Artelt et al. 2010). This instrument taps adolescents' knowledge of strategies that are relevant during reading and for comprehension, as well as for recall of text information. For each of up to six scenarios, students have to evaluate the quality and usefulness of five different strategies available for reaching the intended learning or memory goal. The rank order of strategies obtained for each scenario is then compared with an optimal rank order provided by experts in the field of text processing. The correspondence between the two rankings is expressed in a metacognition score, indicating the degree to which students are aware of the best ways to store and remember text information.

We decided to develop similar measures of metacognitive knowledge for our EWIKO study by asking students explicitly to judge the appropriateness and (relative to other strategies) the quality of specific strategies for a given learning situation (Artelt et al. 2009). Within the assessment of metacognitive knowledge, we thus concentrate on students' correct, veridical knowledge, implying that high scores on the knowledge measure do, in fact, indicate that an individual possesses adequate strategy knowledge.

17.1.2 Design of the EWIKO Study

Our initial sample consisted of 928 German fifth graders (450 female, 478 male) from 44 classrooms representing three different educational tracks (271 high, 377 intermediate, and 280 low)[1] who voluntarily participated in a class-wise administered paper-and-pencil assessment. There were six assessments during the course of the longitudinal study, starting at the beginning of Grade 5 and ending in Grade 9. The group-based tests took place in the classroom during schooling hours. At each measurement point, testing time took about three school lessons (45 min. each) replacing the regular class teaching for this period. During the 135 min test sessions, each participant filled in domain-specific metacognitive knowledge tests, the achievement tests, and additional scales assessing cognitive abilities and motivational variables (see below). All tests were administered by two research assistants specially trained to instruct the participants and to lead them through the session. The classroom teacher was also present to ensure discipline among students.

Fig. 17.1 gives an overview of the time schedule concerning the presentation of metacognitive knowledge and achievement tests

[1] It should be noted that the elementary school period in the German school system finishes at the end of Grade 4. From Grade 5 on, students are allocated to three educational tracks: high = academic, intermediate, and low = vocational, mainly based on achievement scores in primary school.

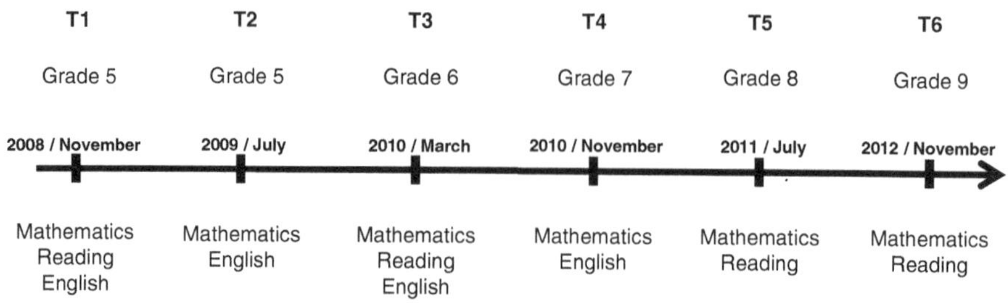

Fig. 17.1 Overview of the EWIKO design, showing how students were observed over a 4-year period between Grades 5 and 9 (time intervals between the adjacent measurement points being 8 months in Grades 5, 6, and 7, and 16 months in Grade 8 and 9, respectively)
T = Measurement point. Measurements included metacognitive knowledge and achievement in the corresponding domains

It should be noted that organizational problems caused us to expand the test intervals between T5 and T6. As expected, not all of the initial 928 students stayed with the longitudinal study. Missing data were generated for different reasons, for instance, due to student mobility (change of school), illness on the day of testing, and other reasons. Missing data rates varied between 38 % and 10 % (measurement points 6 and 2, respectively). Only 39 % of the students participated at all six measurement points. Post-hoc analyses revealed that the drop-out observed over the course of the project was systematic, indicating that more students with lower scores in achievement tests left the study (Lingel 2014; Lingel et al. 2014b). Thus, a missing pattern completely at random cannot be assumed (Little and Rubin 2002). To avoid biases in the results, we used regression-based strategies to impute the missing data (Neuenhaus 2011; Artelt et al. 2012; Lingel et al. 2014b).

17.1.3 Test Instruments

Assessment of Metacognitive Knowledge Due to organizational constraints, not all test instruments were applied at any given measurement occasion. Metacognitive knowledge in math was assessed at all six measurement points: that is, at intervals of about 8 months (T1–T5) and 16 months (T5–T6). Metacognitive knowledge in reading was assessed at intervals of 16 months from Grade 5 to Grade 9: that is, at T1, T3, T5, und T6. Metacognitive knowledge in English as a foreign language (EFL) was assessed at intervals of 8 months on four measurement occasions, from the beginning of Grade 5 until the beginning of Grade 7 (T1–T4).

The metacognitive knowledge tests were constructed to assess conditional and relational metacognitive knowledge in a situated way. The domain-specific tests were constructed to assess the metacognitive knowledge (MK) required for learning and achievement in the respective domains of mathematics, reading, and EFL (MK-mathematics; MK-reading; MK-EFL), in such a way that they provided

Scenario: "You have to understand and memorize a text. Give a grade to each of the following strategies. Better strategies should be given better grades. If you think that two or more strategies are of equal value, the same grades should be given to all of these strategies."

		Grade					
		1	2	3	4	5	6
A	I concentrate on the parts of the text that are easy to understand.						
B	I quickly read through the text twice.						
C	After reading the text, I discuss its content with other people.						
D	I underline important parts of the text.						
E	I summarize the text in my own words.						

Fig. 17.2 Example of a metacognition scenario in the domain of reading
Note. The grade scale of the German school system used was 1 = *best grade*, 6 = *worst grade*

domain-typical learning situations in combination with a list of strategies of varying appropriateness (for a more detailed description of construction principles and examples of metacognitive tests tapping reading and mathematics see Artelt et al. 2010; Lingel et al. 2014b; Schlagmüller and Schneider 2007).

Scenario-based testing procedures were developed according to the principles used with the Index of Reading Awareness ("IRA", Jacobs and Paris 1987).

In all tests, the students had to judge the relative effectiveness of strategies in a given situation (scenario) and in relation to other strategies. For an example concerning metacognitive knowledge related to reading, see Fig. 17.2. Scenarios in EFL concerned, among others, strategies related to vocabulary learning, and those for mathematics dealt, for example, with problem-solving activities in the context of a difficult math task (see also Artelt et al. 2009; Artelt and Schneider 2015).

Each test consisted of five tasks, beginning with a description of a typical learning scenario and followed by a list of efficient and less efficient strategies. Students had to judge the appropriateness of the strategies with respect to the scenario and in relation to the other strategies. An expert survey was conducted in all domains to ensure content validity of the tests and to provide an objective criterion for the efficiency of strategies (Neuenhaus 2011; Lingel 2014). In a pilot study, 311 students answered the test for reading, 361 students worked on the test for EFL, and 393 students worked on the metacognitive test concerning math. The main purpose was to evaluate the age appropriateness and reliability of the metacognitive knowledge tests (Lingel et al. 2010). Overall, the measures were found to be of sufficient reliability and validity, with reliability scores ranging from $\alpha = .69$ (MK-EFL, T1) to $\alpha = .85$ (MK-mathematics, T4 and T6) and a median $\alpha = .83$. The test assessing metacognitive knowledge in mathematics constructed for Grades 5 und 6 has been published recently (MAESTRA 5–6+; Mathematisches Strategiewissen für 5. und 6. Klassen; mathematical strategy knowledge for Grades 5 and 6; Lingel et al. 2014a). It should be noted that different test versions were used at different occasions, using anchor-procedures founded on Item Response Theory to establish common scales for the various tests (Embretson and Reise 2000; for more details see Lingel 2014).

The number of anchor items between tests on adjacent measurement occasions ranged between 69 and 100 %.

Achievement To assess achievement in the domains of mathematics, reading, and English as a foreign language (EFL), tests were developed in accordance with the current curricula for Grades 5–8, and were piloted to ensure appropriateness for the given sample. To assess reading comprehension, a multiple-choice reading test was used that was developed for the longitudinal assessments within the BiKS project (e.g., Pfost et al. 2013). The test comprised three different texts at each measurement occasion. The texts contained between 225 and 552 words each and were accompanied by 7–12 multiple-choice items. Within 20 min, 28 items were administered in Grade 5 (T1) and 30 items in Grade 9 (T6). To ensure measurement of change in reading achievement across time, the items on both measurement occasions were vertically scaled using a unidimensional Rasch model based on anchor items that were applied repeatedly (see Embretson and Reise 2000). The internal consistency of the reading test was $\alpha = .75$ in Grade 5. The corresponding scores for reading in Grade 9 averaged around $\alpha = .82$.

Achievement in EFL was assessed using a self-developed English version of a stumble-word speed test. The test consisted of 35 sentences. Each sentence builds one item in such a way that it contains a word that doesn't belong there. Under time restrictions, students were asked to correct as many sentences as possible. In Grade 5 (T1) they were given 3 min to cross out the stumble words in all 35 sentences. In Grade 7 (T4) they were given 2 min to cross out the stumble words. The amount of correct responses per minute was used as an indicator of achievement in this domain. The test reliability was $r_{tt} = .82$ in Grade 5 and $r_{tt} = .91$ in Grade 7.

Achievement in mathematics was assessed using tests that primarily covered students' competencies in arithmetic and algebra. Precautions were taken to ensure that the content areas were represented in the curricula of all educational tracks. The tests were successively adapted to the increasing achievement level of the sample. Moreover, items of subsequent tests were vertically scaled using Rasch modeling based on anchor items, to allow for measurement of change. Again, anchor-item linking founded on Item Response Theory was used to establish common scales for the various tests. The tests comprised 30–33 items and proved generally reliable and valid. The internal consistencies (alphas) were .83, .85, and .90 for Grades 5 (T1), 7 (T4), and 9 (T6), respectively.

In addition to the assessment of metacognitive knowledge and achievement in the three domains, several cognitive and non-cognitive variables were considered in the longitudinal study, with the goal of further explaining individual differences in developmental trends.

Cognitive Abilities The age-group appropriate subscales "verbal" and "non-verbal analogies" of the "Kognitiver Fähigkeitstest für 4. bis 12. Klassen (KFT 4–12+R)" (test of cognitive ability) developed by Heller and Perleth (2000) were chosen as indicators of general cognitive abilities. These measures of fluid intelligence were provided at the first measurement point. Moreover, a traditional memory span task (forward and backward) was presented to assess students' basic memory capacity.

Motivational Variables Students' self-concept in the domains of reading, mathematics, and EFL, as well as their interest in these domains, was assessed by using brief scales. Similarly, students' learning goal orientation, as well as their performance goal orientation, was assessed with a brief (4-item) scale.

Finally, to consider the impact of socio-economic status, parents' occupational status was also assessed.

17.2 Overview of Major Results

17.2.1 Development of Metacognitive Knowledge: Sources of Interindividual Differences

As noted above, several studies on various aspects of cognitive development also observed metacognitive knowledge development as a by-product (Schneider and Lockl 2008). However, studies with a focus on the development of metacognition and that used comprehensive approaches to explain interindividual differences in this development, and to explore their potential causes, are still very scarce.

Overall, the longitudinal EWIKO findings show a substantial growth in different kinds of metacognitive knowledge over the observed period (Neuenhaus 2011; Artelt et al. 2012; Lingel 2014). The respective means and standard deviations are given in Table 17.1. Growth rates observed within the first 24 months of secondary school (T1–T4) ranged between $d = 0.51$ (EFL) and $d = 0.72$ (mathematics; see Artelt et al. 2012; Lingel 2014). During the 16-month period between T1 and T3, metacognitive knowledge in the domain of reading increased substantially and with roughly comparable speed ($d = 0.37$). This development did not last long, however. In the last 16 months of the study (T5–T6), growth rates decreased in general, ranging between $d = 0.10$ (mathematics) and $d = 0.12$ (reading).

A well-known source of interindividual differences is school track. The allocation of students to school tracks creates differential learning environments, and is often found to result in differential developmental processes in cognitive characteristics (e.g., Becker et al. 2012). In fact, the differences in metacognitive knowledge observed among the three school tracks, both at the beginning and at the end of secondary school, were substantial (cf. Artelt et al. 2012; Lingel 2014; Lingel et al. 2010; Neuenhaus et al. 2013).

As indicated by the effect sizes for metacognitive knowledge in the domains of mathematics, reading, and EFL in Table 17.2, developmental changes differ as a function of school track and domain. That is, for the domain of mathematics, the differences between the high and intermediate tracks increased over time, whereas the differences between the intermediate and low tracks decreased. Overall, the findings thus indicate that developmental changes in the intermediate track were less pronounced than in the high and low tracks. For the domain of reading, however, the differences between the three tracks remained more or less constant over

Table 17.1 Means (*M*) and standard deviations (*SD*) of metacognitive knowledge in the overall sample and as a function of school track

		T1		T4		T6	
		M	*SD*	*M*	*SD*	*M*	*SD*
MK-mathematics	All	100.0	10.00	107.21	11.51	109.64	10.81
	High	103.95	9.58	112.69	11.46	115.16	11.65
	Interm.	100.96	954	107.14	10.44	109.03	9.06
	Low	94.89	8.80	101.99	10.41	105.11	9.70
MK-reading	All	100.00	10.00	n.a.	n.a.	105.99	12.60
	High	104.32	9.93	n.a.	n.a.	110.61	13.73
	Interm.	100.50	9.05	n.a.	n.a.	106.68	11.04
	Low	95.16	9.15	n.a.	n.a.	100.59	11.33
MK-EFL	All	100.00	10.00	105.13	11.84	n. a.	n. a.
	High	103.30	9.64	110.87	11.94	n. a.	n. a.
	Interm.	100.97	9.21	105.99	10.65	n. a.	n. a.
	Low	95.50	9.75	98.41	9.78	n. a.	n. a.

Table 17.2 Differences between school tracks as effect sizes (*d*) for measurement points 1, 4, and 6

	T1		T4		T6	
	High vs. interm.	Interm. vs. low	High vs. interm.	Interm. vs. low	High vs. interm.	Interm. vs. low
MK-mathematics	*d*=0.30	*d*=0.61	*d*=0.48	*d*=0.45	*d*=0.57	*d*=0.36
MK-reading	*d*=0.38	*d*=0.53	n.a.	n.a.	*d*=0.37	*d*=0.48
MK-EFL	*d*=0.23	*d*=0.55	*d*=0.41	*d*=0.64	n.a.	n.a.

T1 = Measurement Point 1; *T4* = Measurement Point 4; *T6* = Measurement Point 6; *MK* = metacognitive knowledge; *all* = whole sample; *high* = academic track; *interm.* = intermediate track; *low* = low track; *n.a.* = test not administered

time, thus indicating that developmental change rates in this domain are not associated with track or achievement level. In the domain of EFL, however, the differences between all three tracks increased in the observed period of time. Thus, the initial differences seemed to accumulate over time. It should be noted that the same instruments were used to assess developmental changes in English over time, whereas in the case of mathematics and reading, items of subsequent tests were vertically scaled using Rasch modeling based on anchor items, to allow for assessment of change (see above).

Somehow similar results were found for students' gender. At the beginning of the observational period (T1), only slight differences were found in favor of girls (d = 0.06 for the domains of mathematics and EFL; d = 0.17 for the reading domain). During the course of secondary school, these differences increased, regardless of domain (T4: d = 0.38 for the domain of EFL, d = 0.29 for the mathematics domain, and d = 0.50 for the domain of reading at T6). These findings indicate that girls acquire more metacognitive knowledge than boys during the first years of secondary school, particularly in language-related domains.

More fine-grained analyses for the domain of mathematics showed that the effects of tracking and gender persisted after controlling for cognitive characteristics such as intelligence, working memory capacity, and for motivational characteristics such as academic self-concept and interest, as well as for socio-economic background (Lingel 2014).

The EWIKO design also permitted an examination of the influence of student-level characteristics on metacognitive knowledge growth. Lingel (2014) used cognitive, motivational, and socio-economic characteristics to predict interindividual differences at the beginning of Grade 5 and in intraindividual changes over time. Among the cognitive variables, fluid intelligence predicted interindividual differences in metacognitive knowledge at the beginning and during the course of secondary school. Motivational characteristics such as interest and self-concept, however, did not influence intraindividual development in metacognitive knowledge. In contrast, students' socio-economic background showed a stable influence on the developmental pattern, in the sense that higher socio-economic status (SES) was related to a more positive developmental level.

An interesting and somewhat unexpected finding was that metacognitive knowledge development was found to be more pronounced for female students, regardless of domain. In reading, gender differences at the first measurement point were already significant (see Neuenhaus et al. 2016). In comparison, there were no initial differences between girls and boys for EFL, which may be due to the fact that EFL was a novel domain for all students. There were also no gender differences in initial metacognitive knowledge concerning mathematics (Lingel 2014). Interestingly, girls acquired metacognitive knowledge at a faster rate in all three domains of interest during the following measurement points. However, the gender differences identified for metacognitive knowledge were not always accompanied by corresponding differences in achievement. For instance, whereas girls in the EWIKO study in general outperformed boys in the domains of reading and EFL, showing significantly better performance on the achievement tests, a discrepancy was found in the domain of mathematics: Here, girls—as compared to boys—showed a higher level of metacognitive knowledge but performed more poorly on the mathematics achievement tests (cf. Lingel 2014).

17.2.2 Domain-Specificity—A Transitional Period of Metacognitive Development?

As noted above, metacognitive knowledge has often been proposed to be context-dependent and domain-specific during an early stage of development, whereas is it supposed to generalize throughout primary school. Such a transition was particularly proposed by the Good Strategy User model (Pressley et al. 1989) which assumes a task-specific acquisition of knowledge about a given strategy. The application of the strategy generates declarative knowledge on the properties of the strategy as well as on differences and similarities with other strategies. An inductive integration of task- and domain-specific strategy knowledge leads to a more and more generalized metacognitive knowledge. Accordingly, a successive domain-general structure of metacognitive knowledge should emerge.

To test the validity of this assumption, we compared the dimensional structure of metacognitive knowledge at the beginning of secondary school (T1) with the dimensional structure at the middle (T4) and also at the end of secondary school (T6). More specifically, two comparisons concerned the dimensional structure of metacognitive knowledge related to mathematics and reading (T1 and T6), whereas another comparison focused on metacognitive knowledge related to mathematics and EFL (T1 and T4). These analyses extend the research of Neuenhaus et al. (2011) which focused on the first measurement point (T1).

First, metacognitive knowledge on mathematics and reading was analyzed by comparing a unidimensional, domain-general structure with a two-dimensional, domain-specific structure at the beginning of Grade 5. Neuenhaus et al. (2011) found clear support for a domain-specific two-factor solution. A two-factor solution with two separate factors describing metacognitive knowledge for mathematics and reading, fitted the data better than a single-factor solution with a common factor (Δ BIC = 696). Both factors were moderately correlated ($r = .51$). Further analyses using the EWIKO data assessed at the end of secondary school (Grade 9, T6) showed a comparable factor solution. Again, the two factor-solution fitted the data better than the one-factor solution (Δ BIC = 585). Compared to the earlier findings, both factors showed a slightly increased correlation of $r = .58$. These findings seem to indicate that metacognitive knowledge in the domains of mathematics and reading may integrate into a more general knowledge structure as a function of time. However, the increase in correlations was not significant ($p = .08$).

Due to the specifics of the study design, it was impossible to carry out identical longitudinal analyses for all three domains (see Fig. 17.1). To validate the above finding in a second step, we included metacognitive knowledge in the domain of EFL in the analyses, and compared two models of metacognitive knowledge in the domains of mathematics and EFL as well as change in their dimensional structure between measurement points 1 and 4 (Neuenhaus et al. 2016). At the beginning of Grade 5 (T1), a two-dimensional model of metacognitive knowledge fitted the data better than a one-dimensional, domain-general model (Δ BIC = 399). Both resulting factors were substantially correlated ($r = .49$). Two years later, at Grade 7 (T4), the analyses again confirmed a two-dimensional structure (Δ BIC = 701). The slight decrease in intercorrelations between factors (.49 at T1 versus .45 at T4) did not prove to be significant. In any case, however, this finding does not support the assumption that metacognitive knowledge tends to be more general with increasing age.

One major conclusion from these findings is that metacognitive knowledge shows a clear-cut domain-specific structure even at the end of secondary school. Thus, the domain-specificity of metacognitive knowledge does not seem to be a short-term, transitional state restricted to the early school period.

17.2.3 Interrelations Between Metacognitive Knowledge and Achievement

One final issue concerned the question whether the relationship between metacognitive knowledge and achievement would change over time. To answer this question, synchronous correlations between the metacognitive knowledge components and achievement in the various domains were calculated. Overall, the correlational findings indicate increases over time: In mathematics, synchronous correlations between metacognitive knowledge and achievement increased from $r = .31$ (T1) to $r = .42$ (T6). The same pattern was observed in EFL and reading: correlations increased from $r = .22$ (T1) to $r = .29$ (T4) in EFL, and from $r = .29$ (T1) to $r = .39$ (T6) in reading.

Correlational analyses do not inform about cause-effect relationships. Lingel et al. (2014b) aimed at assessing the effects of metacognitive knowledge on subsequent performance, and proved a predictive effect of metacognitive knowledge on mathematics achievement. In this study, three common shortcomings of correlational studies dealing with knowledge-performance relationships were considered: (1) predictor and criterion were chronologically ordered, (2) prior knowledge, as the most prominent predictor of achievement was ruled out by being included in the prediction equation, and (3) confounding variables such as intelligence, motivation, and socio-economic status were controlled for. Under these restrictive conditions, metacognitive knowledge explained about 1 % of mathematics achievement change. That is, a rather small but still unique contribution of metacognitive knowledge to the development of achievement is documented. Although one may ask whether the comparably small contribution of metacognitive knowledge to the explanation of changes in mathematics development is practically important, one should note that estimates of unique contributions typically underestimate the true effect, and that metacognition still explained variance in achievement changes after the impact of several other important factors had been controlled.

The nature of the relation of metacognitive knowledge and achievement is conceived as bi-directional. Artelt et al. (2012) and Neuenhaus (2011) confirmed this theoretical assumption for reading, as well as for EFL. Using cross-lagged models, metacognitive knowledge (T1) predicted achievement in the respective domain (T3) substantially: $\beta = .42$ for reading, $\beta = .56$ for EFL. Moreover, metacognitive knowledge in both domains showed a moderate to low stability ($\beta = .36$ for reading and $\beta = .28$ for EFL). When controlling for these autoregressive effects, the cross-lagged effects of metacognitive knowledge on achievement remained significant ($\beta = .13$ for reading and $\beta = .17$ for EFL) as did the effects of achievement on metacognitive knowledge ($\beta = .17$ for reading and $\beta = .18$ for EFL). These findings support the assumption of a bi-directional developmental process.

17.3 Discussion

Taken together, the findings of the EWIKO study summarized above indicate that metacognitive knowledge develops substantially during the course of secondary school. The growth processes in mathematics and reading assessed between Grades 5 and 9 were found to be negatively accelerated, indicating that more metacognitive knowledge is acquired at the beginning of secondary school than thereafter. The initial level of metacognitive knowledge already varied as a function of school track, with students from the higher track showing higher levels of metacognitive knowledge. Whereas the overall developmental trend in observed metacognitive knowledge was similar across domains, the differences between the tracks seem to be domain-specific. That is, these differences seemed to be stable and invariant in the domain of reading, to increase in the domain of English as a foreign language, and to be inconsistent (i.e., partly growing and partly shrinking) in the domain of mathematics.

Our results indicate that most assumptions regarding the developmental and differential trajectories for educational track and gender were confirmed. Significant differences in metacognitive knowledge by the beginning of secondary education are likely to be due to individual difference variables such as domain knowledge, cognitive ability, and motivation, given that all students shared the same learning environment until then. With the allocation of students into three educational tracks by the beginning of Grade 5, differences in learning standards, class composition features, and instructional practices become increasingly important. Such differences seem to affect the development of metacognitive knowledge, regardless of domain.

Our findings regarding gender differences in metacognitive knowledge and achievement are generally interesting. Gender differences at the entrance level of secondary school were significant only for reading and not for the two other domains. The homogeneous base level of metacognitive knowledge in EFL may point to the importance of domain-specific experience for the development of metacognitive knowledge. As noted above, EFL is a novel domain for students at the beginning of Grade 5, while they are well familiar with the domain of reading, in which significant base-level advantages in metacognitive knowledge for girls were found. But how to explain the non-significant differences in entrance levels of metacognitive knowledge for the domain of mathematics? Given that boys outperformed girls on the achievement level, this finding points to a specific advantage of girls on the knowledge component that does not however materialize in performance. This assumption is also supported by the inspection of growth curves in metacognitive knowledge. Over time, girls developed significantly more metacognitive knowledge, regardless of the domain under consideration. Although the difference in metacognitive knowledge in favor of girls increased as a function of time, this pattern was not paralleled by achievement gains in mathematics. The findings for the domain of mathematics seem special, supporting the pattern of findings reported by Carr and Jessup (1997) for elementary school students. Clearly more research is needed to explain the gender-related metacognition-performance dissociation in the domain of mathematics.

Our study also contributes to the discussion about the domain-specificity of metacognitive knowledge. Throughout the developmental period under investigation, we found little evidence for the assumption of the increasingly general character of metacognitive knowledge (Pressley et al. 1989): metacognitive knowledge does not seem to generalize across domains, but it continues to show a strong domain-specific structure at the end of secondary school. Thus, the domain-specificity of metacognitive knowledge does not seem to be a short-term, transitional state restricted to the early school period. However, it needs to be kept in mind that we used assessments that focused on domain-typical strategies as indicators of knowledge in that domain, and that the test for a tendency towards the more general nature of these knowledge components was based only on tests of the dimensionality of these findings. There may however be knowledge components that do in fact transfer or generalize, but that are not yet tapped by our domain-specific assessments.

In sum, the findings of the EWIKO study replicate well-established findings in the literature, but also provide new insights, in that several domains were considered simultaneously. In accord with the existing literature, it could be shown that metacognitive knowledge is an important predictor of achievement in secondary school students. There was also evidence for a bi-directional relationship between metacognitive and cognitive development (Flavell and Wellman 1977). Here, the assumption is that the use of cognitive strategies improves the quality of metacognitive knowledge, and that improvement in metacognitive knowledge leads to a more sophisticated use of problem-solving strategies. Although the present research clearly indicates the importance of declarative (verbalizable) metacognitive knowledge for the development of performance in various domains, the design of the EWIKO study did not include aspects of procedural metacognitive knowledge: that is, the impact of monitoring and self-regulation skills that theoretically should facilitate this developmental process (Pressley et al. 1989). Thus, further research should focus on more fine-grained analyses exploring the interchange between declarative and procedural metacognitive knowledge in improving performance levels in different achievement domains.

Acknowledgments The preparation of this chapter was supported by grant SCHN 315/36 and AR 310/8 from the German Research Foundation (DFG) in the Priority Program "Competence Models for Assessing Individual Learning Outcomes and Evaluating Educational Processes" (SPP 1293).

References

Alexander, J. M., Carr, M., & Schwanenflugel, P. (1995). Development of metacognition in gifted children: Directions for future research. *Developmental Review, 15*, 1–37. doi:10.1006/drev.1995.1001.

Artelt, C. (2000). *Strategisches Lernen* [Strategic learning]. Münster: Waxmann.

Artelt, C., & Schneider, W. (2015). Cross-country generalizability of the role of metacognitive knowledge for students' strategy use and reading competence. *Teachers College Record, 117* (online publication).

Artelt, C., Schiefele, U., & Schneider, W. (2001). Predictors of reading literacy. *European Journal of Psychology of Education, 16*, 363–383. doi:10.1007/BF03173188.

Artelt, C., Beinicke, A., Schlagmüller, M., & Schneider, W. (2009). Diagnose von Strategiewissen beim Textverstehen [Diagnosis of strategy knowledge about text comprehension]. *Zeitschrift für Entwicklungspsychologie und Pädagogische Psychologie, 41*, 96–103.

Artelt, C., Naumann, J., & Schneider, W. (2010). Lesemotivation und Lernstrategien [Motivation for reading and learning strategies]. In E. Klieme, C. Artelt, J. Hartig, N. Jude, O. Köller, M. Prenzel, et al. (Eds.), *PISA 2009. Bilanz nach einem Jahrzehnt* (pp. 73–112). Münster: Waxmann.

Artelt, C., Neuenhaus, N., Lingel, K., & Schneider, W. (2012). Entwicklung und wechselseitige Effekte von metakognitiven und bereichsspezifischen Wissenskomponenten in der Sekundarstufe [Development of metacognitive and domain-specific knowledge and their mutual effects in secondary school]. *Psychologische Rundschau, 63*, 18–25. doi:10.1026/0033-3042/a000106.

Becker, M., Lüdtke, O., Trautwein, U., Köller, O., & Baumert, J. (2012). The differential effects of school tracking on psychometric intelligence: Do academic-track schools make students smarter? *Journal of Educational Psychology, 104*, 682–699. doi:10.1037/a0027608.

Borkowski, J. G., Milstead, M., & Hale, C. (1988). Components of children's metamemory: Implications for strategy generalization. In F. E. Weinert & M. Perlmutter (Eds.), *Memory development: Universal changes and individual differences* (pp. 73–100). Hillsdale: Erlbaum.

Brown, A. L. (1978). Knowing when, where and how to remember: A problem of metacognition. In R. Glaser (Ed.), *Advances in instructional psychology* (pp. 77–165). New York: Halsted.

Brown, A. L., Bransford, J. D., Ferrara, R. A., & Campione, J. C. (1983). Learning, remembering, and understanding. In J. H. Flavell & M. E. Markman (Eds.), *Handbook of child psychology, Vol. 3: Cognitive development* (pp. 77–166). New York: Wiley.

Campione, J. C., & Armbruster, B. B. (1985). Acquiring information from texts: An analysis of four approaches. Thinking and learning skills. In J. W. Segal, S. F. Chipman, & R. Glaser (Eds.), *Thinking and learning skills* (pp. 317–359). Hillsdale: Erlbaum.

Carr, M., & Jessup, D. L. (1997). Gender differences in first-grade mathematics strategy use: Social and metacognitive influences. *Journal of Educational Psychology, 89*, 318–328. doi:10.1037/0022-0663.89.2.318.

Embretson, S. E., & Reise, S. P. (2000). *Item response theory for psychologists*. New York: Psychology Press.

Flavell, J. H. (1971). First discussant's comments: What is memory development the development of? *Human Development, 14*, 272–278. doi:10.1159/000271221.

Flavell, J. H. (2000). Development of children's knowledge about the mental world. *International Journal of Behavioral Development, 24*, 15–23. doi:10.1080/016502500383421.

Flavell, J. H., & Wellman, H. M. (1977). Metamemory. In R. V. Kail & W. Hagen (Eds.), *Perspectives on the development of memory and cognition* (pp. 3–33). Hillsdale: Erlbaum.

Flavell, J. H., Miller, P. H., & Miller, S. A. (2002). *Cognitive development* (4th ed.). Upper Saddle River: Prentice Hall.

Hacker, D. J., Dunlosky, J., & Graesser, A. C. (2009). *Handbook of metacognition in education*. New York: Routledge.

Heller, K., & Perleth, C. (2000). *Kognitiver Fähigkeitstest für 4. bis 12. Klassen* [Cognitive ability test for Grades 4–12], *Revision (KFT 4–12+R)*. Göttingen: Beltz.

Jacobs, J. E., & Paris, S. G. (1987). Children's metacognition about reading: Issues in definition, measurement, and instruction. *Educational Psychologist, 22*, 255–278. doi:10.1207/s15326985ep2203&4_4.

Joyner, M., & Kurtz-Costes, B. E. (1997). Metamemory development. In N. Cowan (Ed.), *The development of memory in childhood* (pp. 275–300). Hove: Psychology Press.

Kuhn, D. (2000). The theory of mind, metacognition and reasoning: A life-span perspective. In P. Mitchell & K. J. Riggs (Eds.), *Children's reasoning and the mind* (pp. 301–326). Hove: Psychology Press.

Leopold, C., & Leutner, D. (2002). Der Einsatz von Lernstrategien in einer konkreten Lernsituation bei Schülern unterschiedlicher Jahrgangsstufen [The use of learning strategies in a specific learning situation by students of different grade levels]. *Zeitschrift für Pädagogik, Beiheft, 45*, 240–258.

Lind, G., & Sandmann, A. (2003). Lernstrategien und Domänenwissen [Learning strategies and knowledge about domains]. *Zeitschrift für Psychologie, 211*, 171–192. doi:10.1026//0044-3409.211.4.171.

Lingel, K. (2014). *Metakognitives Wissen Mathematik: Entwicklung und Zusammenhang mit der Mathematikleistung in der Sekundarstufe I.* [Metacognitive knowledge about mathematics: Its development and its relation to math performance in secondary school] (Doctoral dissertation, Julius-Maximilians-Universität Würzburg, Würzburg). Retrieved from https://opus.bibliothek.uni-wuerzburg.de/frontdoor/index/index/docId/7280. Accessed 13 Jan 2016.

Lingel, K., Neuenhaus, N., Artelt, C., & Schneider, W. (2010). Metakognitives Wissen in der Sekundarstufe: Konstruktion und Evaluation domänenspezifischer Messverfahren [Metacognitive knowledge in secondary school: On the construction and evaluation of domain-specific measurement instruments]. *Zeitschrift für Pädagogik, Beiheft, 56*, 228–238.

Lingel, K., Götz, L., Artelt, C., & Schneider, W. (2014a). *Mathematisches Strategiewissen für 5. und 6. Klassen* [Test of mathematics-related strategy knowledge for Grades 5 and 6; MAESTRA 5–6+]. Göttingen: Hogrefe.

Lingel, K., Neuenhaus, N., Artelt, C., & Schneider, W. (2014b). Der Einfluss des metakognitiven Wissens auf die Entwicklung der Mathematikleistung am Beginn der Sekundarstufe I [Effects of metacognitive knowledge on the development of math achievement at the beginning of secondary school]. *Journal für Mathematik-Didaktik, 35*, 49–77. doi:10.1007/s13138-013-0061-2.

Little, R. J. A., & Rubin, D. B. (2002). *Statistical analysis with missing data.* Hoboken: Wiley.

Muis, K. R., Winne, P. H., & Jamieson-Noel, D. (2007). Using a multitrait-multimethod analysis to examine conceptual similarities of three self-regulated learning inventories. *British Journal of Educational Psychology, 77*, 177–195. doi:10.1348/000709905X90876.

Neuenhaus, N. (2011). *Metakognition und Leistung: Eine Längsschnittuntersuchung in den Bereichen Lesen und Englisch bei Schülerinnen und Schülern der fünften und sechsten Jahrgangsstufe* [Metacognition and achievements: A longitudinal study assessing reading and English language development in fifth and sixth grade students] (Doctoral dissertation, Otto-Friedrich-Universität Bamberg, Bamberg, Germany. Retrieved from https://opus4.kobv.de/opus4-bamberg/files/327/DissNeuenhausseA2.pdf. Accessed 13 Jan 2016.

Neuenhaus, N., Artelt, C., Lingel, K., & Schneider, W. (2011). Fifth graders metacognitive knowledge: General or domain specific? *European Journal of Psychology of Education, 26*, 163–178. doi:10.1007/s10212-010-0040-7.

Neuenhaus, N., Artelt, C., & Schneider, W. (2016) *Lernstrategiewissen im Bereich Englisch: Entwicklung und erste Validierung eines Tests für Schülerinnen und Schüler der frühen Sekundarstufe* [Learning strategies in the subject of English: Development and first validation of a test for secondary school students]. *Diagnostica*. doi:10.1026/0012-1924/a000171.

Neuenhaus, N., Artelt, C., & Schneider, W. (2013, April). *The development of metacognitive knowledge among secondary-level students from Grade 5 to Grade 9: Do gender and educational track matter?* Paper presented at the annual meeting of AERA, San Francisco.

Paris, S. G., & Byrnes, J. P. (1989). The constructivist approach to self-regulation and learning in the classroom. In B. J. Zimmerman & D. H. Schunk (Eds.), *Self-regulated learning and academic achievement: Theory, research and practice* (pp. 169–200). New York: Springer.

Pfost, M., Artelt, C., & Weinert, S. (Eds.). (2013). *The development of reading literacy from early childhood to adolescence: Empirical findings from the Bamberg BiKS Longitudinal Studies.* Bamberg: University of Bamberg Press.

Pintrich, P. R., Smith, D. A., Garcia, T., & McKeachie, W. J. (1993). Reliability and predictive validity of the Motivated Strategies for Learning Questionnaire (MSLQ). *Educational and Psychological Measurement, 53*, 801–813. doi:10.1177/0013164493053003024.
Pressley, M., Borkowski, J. G., & Schneider, W. (1989). Good information processing: What it is and how education can promote it. *International Journal of Educational Research, 13*, 857–867. doi:10.1016/0883-0355(89)90069-4.
Schlagmüller, M., & Schneider, W. (2007). *WLST-12. Würzburger Lesestrategie Wissenstest für die Klassen 7 bis 12 [Würzburg reading strategy knowledge test for Grades 7–12]*. Göttingen: Hogrefe.
Schneider, W. (2008). The development of metacognitive knowledge in children and adolescents: Major trends and implications for education. *Mind, Brain, and Education, 2*, 114–121. doi:10.1111/j.1751-228X.2008.00041.x.
Schneider, W. (2010). Memory development in childhood and adolescence. In U. Goswami (Ed.), *The Blackwell handbook of cognitive development* (pp. 347–376). London: Blackwell.
Schneider, W. (2015). *Memory development from early childhood through emerging adulthood*. New York: Springer.
Schneider, W., & Artelt, C. (2010). Metacognition and mathematics education. *ZDM Mathematics Education, 42*, 149–161. doi:10.1007/s11858-010-0240-2.
Schneider, W., & Lockl, K. (2008). Procedural metacognition in children: Evidence for developmental trends. In J. Dunlosky & B. Bjork (Eds.), *A handbook of memory and metacognition* (pp. 391–409). Mahwah: Erlbaum.
Schneider, W., & Pressley, M. (1997). *Memory development between two and twenty*. Mahwah: Erlbaum.
Schraw, G. (2000). Assessing metacognition: Implications for the Buros Symposium. In G. Schraw & J. C. Impara (Eds.), *Issues in the measurement of metacognition* (pp. 297–322). Lincoln: Buros Institute of Mental Measurements.
Schraw, G., & Dennison, R. S. (1994). Assessing metacognitive awareness. *Contemporary Educational Psychology, 19*, 460–475. doi:10.1006/ceps.1994.1033.
Schraw, G., & Moshman, D. (1995). Metacognitive theories. *Educational Psychology Review, 7*, 351–371. doi:10.1007/BF02212307.
Veenman, M. V. J., van Hout-Wolters, B. H. A. M., & Afflerbach, P. (2006). Metacognition and learning: Conceptual and methodological considerations. *Metacognition and Learning, 1*, 3–14. doi:10.1007/s11409-006-6893-0.
Winne, P. H., & Hadwin, A. F. (1998). Studying as self-regulated learning. In D. J. Hacker, J. Dunlosky, & A. C. Graesser (Eds.), *Metacognition in educational theory and practice* (pp. 277–304). Mahwah: Erlbaum.

Chapter 18
Development of Dynamic Usage of Strategies for Integrating Text and Picture Information in Secondary Schools

Wolfgang Schnotz, Inga Wagner, Fang Zhao, Mark Ullrich, Holger Horz, Nele McElvany, Annika Ohle, and Jürgen Baumert

Abstract Students are frequently required to integrate text and picture information into coherent knowledge structures. This raises the questions of how students deal with texts and how they deal with graphics when they try to integrate the two sources of information, and whether there are differences between students from different school types and grades. Forty students from Grades 5 and 8, from higher and lower tiers of the German school system, were asked to process and integrate text and pictures in order to answer items from different hierarchy-levels of a text-picture integration taxonomy. Students' eye movements were recorded and analyzed. Results suggest a fundamental asymmetry between the functions of text and pictures, associated with different processing strategies. Texts are more likely to be used according to a coherence-formation strategy, whereas pictures are more likely to be used on demand as visual cognitive tools according to an information selection strategy. Students from different tiers of schooling revealed different adaptability with regard to the requirements of combining text and graphic information.

Keywords Mental model construction • Processing strategies • Textbooks

---

W. Schnotz (✉) • I. Wagner
University of Koblenz-Landau, Landau, Germany
e-mail: schnotz@uni-landau.de; wagneri@uni-landau.de

F. Zhao
University of Hagen, Hagen, Germany
e-mail: fang.zhao@fernuni-hagen.de

M. Ullrich • H. Horz
Goethe University Frankfurt, Frankfurt/Main, Germany
e-mail: M.Ullrich@psych.uni-frankfurt.de; Horz@psych.uni-frankfurt.de

N. McElvany • A. Ohle
TU Dortmund University, Dortmund, Germany
e-mail: Nele.McElvany@tu-dortmund.de; Annika.Ohle@tu-dortmund.de

J. Baumert
Max Planck Institute for Human Development, Berlin, Germany
e-mail: sekbaumert@mpib-berlin.mpg.de

D. Leutner et al. (eds.), *Competence Assessment in Education*, Methodology of Educational Measurement and Assessment, DOI 10.1007/978-3-319-50030-0_18

18.1 Texts Combined with Instructional Pictures

Learning materials usually include both written text and instructional pictures—this latter including schematic diagrams, maps, and graphs. Students are expected to integrate verbal and pictorial information in constructing mental representations of the learning content (Ainsworth 1999; Schnotz 2005). Abundant research has demonstrated that students generally learn better from text with pictures than from text alone (Levie and Lentz 1982; Mayer 2009). However, many students underestimate the informational value of pictures (Mokros and Tinker 1987; Weidenmann 1989). Schnotz et al. (2010) found that nearly half of the total variance of text-graphic integrating performance of Grade 5 to Grade 8 students could be explained by school type, whereas one fourth of the total variance could be explained by grade. The competency of integrating texts and pictures seems to be a by-product of schooling, rather than the result of systematic teaching.

To attain a better understanding of these competencies, we investigated in which way and to what extent students' working with texts differs from their working with pictures. For this purpose, we recorded the learners' eye-movements and analysed the temporal distribution of their visual and cognitive attention on different kinds of information while they answered items of varying complexity that required integration of verbal and pictorial information.

18.2 Theoretical Background

18.2.1 Taxonomies of Text-Picture-Integration

According to Schnotz and Bannert (2003), integrating verbal and pictorial information requires mapping between corresponding elements in the text and the picture. This mapping can occur at the level of surface structures and at the level of semantic deep structures. Surface structure mapping includes connecting verbal elements (words) and graphical elements (lines and shapes) based on cohesive devices such as common color coding, common numbers, common symbols, or common labels. Semantic deep structure mapping means connecting conceptual structures and structural characteristics of the mental model.

Regarding structure mapping between text and pictures, a distinction can be made in terms of the complexity of the structures to be mapped (Wainer 1992), which results in different integration levels: Level A (extraction and mapping of single information), Level B (extraction and mapping of simple relations), and Level C (extraction and mapping of complex relations). In an illustrated biology text about the legs of insects, an example of a Level A item would be "What is the name of the end part of an insect's leg?" An example of a Level B item would be "Does the leg for swimming have a shorter thigh than the leg for jumping?"

An example of a Level C item would be "Does the leg for running have a longer bar than the leg for swimming, but a shorter bar than the leg for jumping?"

As complex structures include more simple structures, and the latter are embedded into the former, a hierarchy of structure mapping emerges, wherein the embedded structures at lower levels are prerequisites for the embedding structures at higher levels. The hierarchy can serve as a taxonomy of text-picture integration tasks, wherein the levels of the taxonomy represent structure mappings of increasing complexity form a sequence of logical preconditions within each unit.

18.2.2 Strategies for Integrative Processing of Text and Pictures

Research has shown that pre-posed questions can result in highly selective processing at the expense of a global understanding of texts; this indicates an inherent conflict between a task-specific information-selection strategy and a global coherence-formation strategy (Kintsch 1998; Rickards and Denner 1978). When students use a task-specific information-selection strategy, they focus primarily on solving the task and selecting the required verbal and pictorial information from the text and the graphics. Items at Level A require less information than do items at Level B, which in turn requires less information than items at Level C. Thus, students using this strategy should have shorter reading times and graphic observation times for A-items than for B-items. By the same token, reading and graphic observation times for B-items should be shorter than for C-items. When students use a global coherence-formation strategy, they first read the whole text and observe the accompanying graphic, in order to understand the subject matter before dealing with specific questions. They engage in a non-task-specific initial construction of a coherent mental model. Accordingly, their text reading times and graphic observation times in answering the first item should on average be higher than for the following items. Even if the first item is at a lower level in the taxonomy, students would invest more time in reading the text and observing the graphic than for higher level items that might follow, and which would then require only a few mental model updates (if any).

18.3 Research Questions and Hypotheses

The present investigation aimed at analyzing how students deal with texts and pictures when they try to integrate the two sources of information in answering questions. More specifically, we tried to analyze whether and to what extent students adopt a task-specific information-selection strategy or a global coherence-formation strategy. Furthermore, we were interested in inter-individual differences between students from different school types and grades. We hypothesized an asymmetry between text processing and picture processing. On the one hand, pictures provide a more direct way to construct mental models than texts. Texts, on the other hand, guide the reader's conceptual analysis by a description of the subject matter, leading to a coherent semantic network, which in turn contributes to further elaborating the mental model. Accordingly, we assumed on the one hand that texts are more likely than pictures to be used for a coherence-formation strategy. On the other hand, we assumed that pictures are more likely than texts to be used for a task-specific information-selection strategy.

When students choose a task-specific information-selection strategy, the time invested in an information source (text or graphic) in answering an item at Level A should be shorter than for an item at Level B, which in turn should be shorter than for an item at Level C. Thus, predictions of a task-specific information-selection strategy are as follows: Time on Source (item A) < Time on Source (item B) < Time on Source (Item C). When students choose a global coherence-formation strategy, the time invested in an information source (text or graphic) will be highest for the first item and should be lower for the following items, because only updates have to be made for any remaining coherence gaps. Accordingly, one would expect a continuous decrease of time from the first item (Level A) via the second item (Level B) to the third item (Level C). Thus, predictions based on a global coherence-formation strategy are represented as follows: Time on Source (item A) > Time on Source (item B) > Time on Source (Item C).

18.4 Method

In order to test these hypotheses, we presented sets of text-graphic combinations to students from different grades and from different tiers of schooling. For each set, items from three different taxonomy levels were presented in a fixed sequence: The first item was from taxonomy Level A, the second item was from taxonomy Level B, and the third item was from taxonomy Level C. In order to measure the time invested in the texts and the pictures in answering the presented items, we analysed students' eye-movements with an EyeLink II system from SR Research in single lab sessions. Although the validity of the so-called eye-mind assumption has been questioned frequently, there is evidence that eye movements can provide useful information about cognitive processes (Holmquist et al. 2011).

Material The combinations of texts and pictures used in the following experiment were taken from a test for measuring text-graphic integration skills of students in a large-scale assessment study (Schnotz et al. 2010). Two hundred and eighty-eight test items had been presented via multiple matrix design to 1060 students from Grade 5 to Grade 8. The items had been analysed, on the basis of item-response theory, with a one-parametric logistic model (Rasch model) including DIF (differential item functioning) analyses for gender, grade, and school tier. Furthermore, the items had undergone a rational task analysis (Schnotz et al. 2011). Due to the high effort required by eye-tracking studies both from the participant and the experimenter, we selected only four units for the experiment, two units in biology and the other two in geography, according to the following criteria: The units should include a diversity of visualizations, including realistic schematic drawings, maps, and graphs, and they should vary in difficulty. For each unit, we selected three out of the six items: one item from taxonomy Level A, one item from Level B, and one item from Level C. The items had to be Rasch-homogenous (Eggen 2004) and stochastically independent (Zenisky et al. 2002). The selected text-graphic units and their average difficulties were: the social behavior of apes (text and pie graphs; $\beta = -1.10$), states of Australia (text and map; $\beta = -0.09$), the respiratory system (text and schematic drawing, $\beta = 1.30$), and the production of chocolate (text and schematic drawing, $\beta = 1.80$). The average beta value on the Rasch scale was −0.13 for items from taxonomy Level A, 0.61 for items from Level B, and 0.84 for items from Level C. The average number of text-graphic mappings according to the rational task analysis was 1.25 for items from taxonomy Level A, 1.50 for items from Level B, and 3.00 for items from Level C.

Participants 40 students, 20 from Grade 5 and 20 from Grade 8, participated in the study. Ten of the fifth graders and ten of the eighth graders were students from the higher tier of the German school system (*Gymnasium*). The other half of the fifth graders and the eighth graders were students from the lower tier of the German school system (*Hauptschule*). Fifth graders had an average age of 10.7 years ($SD = 0.58$) and eighth graders had an average age of 13.9 years ($SD = 0.66$). Twenty-four students were male, 16 were female.

Procedure The study was performed in individual sessions with computer-based presentation of the material. Participants were first instructed how to operate the system, with the help of a game pad. Then, the units were presented in a fixed order according to difficulty, as noted above. Within each unit, the text and the graphic were presented simultaneously on the screen, first in combination with an item from taxonomy Level A, then with an item from Level B, and finally, an item from Level C. Students' eye-movements were registered with an EyeLink II system from SR Research, which allows participants to move their head relatively freely. After successful calibration, students worked self-paced, answering the items with the help of a game pad. After they entered their answer for an item, the next item appeared automatically. Turning pages backwards was not possible. With four students, successful calibration was not possible. This reduced the number of participants for further analysis to 36 students. The display of each text-graphic unit with each item was subdivided into three areas of interest: the text area, the graphic area, and the item area. For each item and for each text-graphic unit, the total fixation time was determined separately for the text, for the graphic, and for the corresponding item. These times were averaged separately for the A-phase, for the B-phase, and for the C-phase across the units.

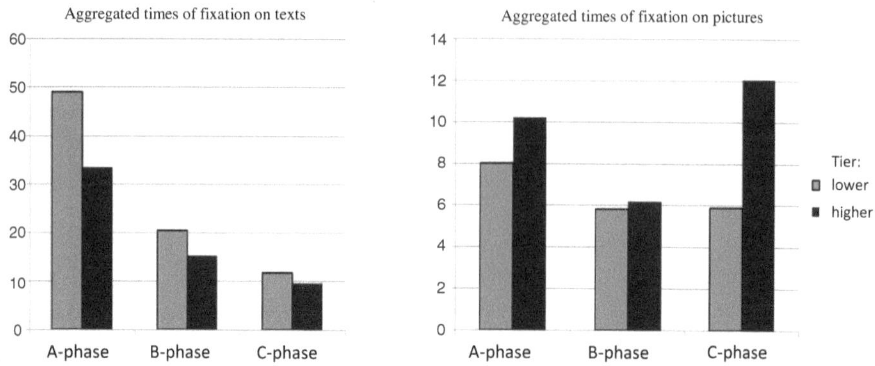

Fig. 18.1 Mean aggregated times (in seconds) of fixation on text areas (*left panel*) and on picture areas (*right panel*) invested by students from the lower tier (Hauptschule, *light*) and by students from the higher tier (Gymnasium, *dark*) in answering Item A, Item B, and Item C

18.5 Results

18.5.1 Reading and Observation Times

ANOVAs—2×2(×3)—were computed with the between-factors school type (higher tier/lower tier) and grade (5/8), and the within-factor phase (A/B/C), for the averaged total fixation times of the text areas and of the graphic areas. Total fixation times invested by students from higher tier schools (Gymnasium) and students from lower tier schools (Hauptschule) into texts during the phases A, B, and C averaged across all units are shown graphically in Fig. 18.1 (left panel). Reading times decreased dramatically from answering Item A to answering item B, and then further decreased from answering Item B to answering Item C. For the contrast between phases A and B, we found a highly significant effect of phase, $F(1, 32) = 78.48$; $p < .001$; $\eta^2 = .71$. For the contrast between phases B and C, we also found a highly significant effect of phase ($F(1, 32) = 47.11$; $p < .001$; $\eta^2 = .60$), whereas the interaction between phase and school type was not significant here. Finally, there was a marginally significant effect of school type ($F(1, 32) = 3.46$; $p = .072$; $\eta^2 = .10$), which means that students from the lower tier (Hauptschule) needed more time to answer the items than did students from the higher tier (Gymnasium). No significant main or interaction effect was found for grade.

Total fixation times invested by students into pictures during the phases A, B, and C, averaged across all units, are shown graphically in Fig. 18.1 (right panel). Observation times decreased from answering items A to answering items B, both for students from the higher tier and for students from the lower tier. Afterwards, observation times for pictures increased again, from answering Items B to answering C, but only for students from the higher tier, whereas for students from the lower tier, observation times remained at a low level in answering items in Levels B and C both. For the contrast between phases A and B, we found a highly significant effect of phase ($F(1, 32) = 18.66$; $p < .001$; $\eta^2 = .37$), but no significant interaction between phase and school type. For the contrast between phases B and C, we also found a highly significant effect of phase ($F(1, 32) = 15.94$; $p < .001$; $\eta^2 = .33$) as well as a significant interaction between phase and school type ($F(1, 32) = 15.31$; $p < .001$; $\eta^2 = .32$). Finally, there was a significant effect of school type ($F(1, 32) = 7.00$; $p = .013$; $\eta^2 = .18$), whereas no significant main or interaction effect was found for grade.

18.5.2 Transitions Between Texts, Pictures, and Items

Furthermore, we analysed the number of eye-movement transitions (saccades) between the text area, the picture area, and the item area within each of the three phases A, B, and C. For each phase, the total number of transitions between the text area, the picture area, and the item area was set to 100 %. We found significant differences between the phases regarding the proportion of text-picture transitions, text-item transitions, and picture-item transitions relative to the total number of transitions within the respective phase. The percentages of the different kinds of transition within each phase are shown in Fig. 18.2. The percentage of text-picture transitions decreased from phase A via phase B to phase C, whereas the percentage of picture-item transitions increased. The share of text-item transitions remained at a relatively low phase.

The ANOVA for the proportion of text-picture transitions revealed a significant effect of *phase*, $F(2, 64) = 18.66$, $p < .001$, $\eta^2 = .37$. This effect was due to the continuous decrease of the text-picture transition percentages from phases A via B to C. As for the text-item transitions, the ANOVA showed a significant effect of *phase*, $F(2, 64) = 4.74$, $p = .012$, $\eta^2 = .13$, as well as a significant interaction *phase x school*, $F(2, 64) = 5.36$, $p = .007$, $\eta^2 = .14$. Higher tier students had temporarily increased their text-item transition percentages from phase A to phase B, followed by a decrease to phase C, whereas the transitions of lower tier students were nearly constant. Finally, the ANOVA for the picture-item transitions revealed a significant effect of *phase*. This mirrors the continuous increase in the percentage of picture-item transitions from phase A via phase B to phase C: $F(2, 64) = 26.07$, $p < .001$, $\eta^2 = .45$.

18.6 Discussion

The present study is based on a relatively small sample of students and a limited number of text-picture combinations with corresponding items; this *per se* gives rise to cautious interpretation. Nevertheless, in consonance with our hypotheses, we found considerable effect sizes resulting in significant differences. Our findings

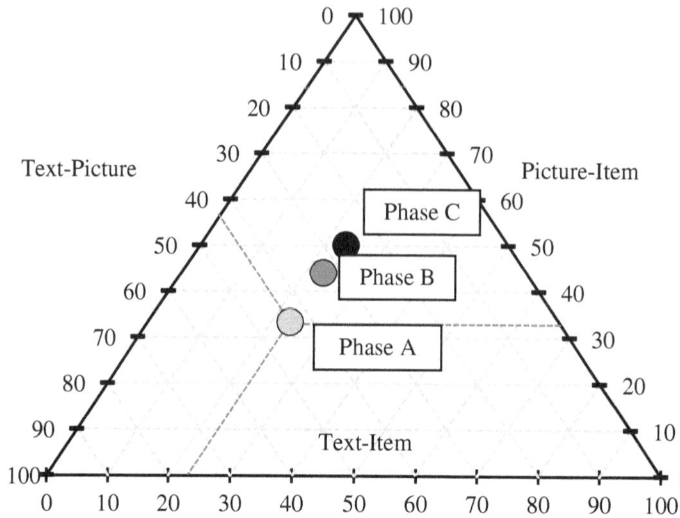

Fig. 18.2 Students' average percentages of transitions between texts, pictures, and items during the item-answering phases A, B, and C (In a triangular diagram, each point represents a combination of three variables, which add up to a constant value (in this case 100 %). The coordinates for each axis are tilted by 30°)

suggest a fundamental asymmetry between text and picture processing (cf. McNamara 2007). Texts are obviously used primarily according to a global coherence formation strategy. Students seem to engage first in a process of intensive coherence formation, which results in an initial mental model construction. Accordingly, they invest a high amount of time into the text. After this initial model construction, they seem to use the text only for mental model-updates if needed, and invest less time for the following items, even if these items are considerably more demanding.

As for the usage of pictures, the findings suggest the usage of a global coherence formation strategy initially, and a task-specific information selection strategy later. Students seem to use pictures as scaffolds (i.e., aids for coherence formation) for their initial mental model construction, although time for picture usage is shorter than time for text usage. After the initial mental model construction, those with higher learning prerequisites (i.e., students from higher tier schools) seem to adapt their processing to the difficulty of the task at hand, as they invest more time in graphic processing when items become more difficult. On the other hand, students with lower learning prerequisites (i.e., students from lower tier schools) do not use pictures more intensively when items become more difficult.

The asymmetry between text and picture processing manifests itself also in the eye-movement transitions between text, picture, and items. At the beginning of processing text-picture units, a high percentage of transitions between the text and the picture can be found; this indicates a high number of cross-referential connections between verbal and pictorial information. Then, the percentage of transitions between the text and the picture decreases from phase to phase, and is lowest when the most difficult item is to be answered. The opposite pattern can be found with the percentage of transitions between the picture and the item. This percentage is lowest in the first phase, obviously when initial mental model construction takes place. Then, the percentage of transitions between the picture and the item increases from phase to phase, and is highest when the most difficult item is to be answered. At the beginning of processing a text-picture unit, the picture is strongly associated with the text, in terms of conjoint processing (cf. Kulhavy et al. 1993). Afterwards, the picture is more and more used as an easily accessible external representation, according to the specific requirements of the item at hand.

As for students from the higher tier, text and pictures seem to serve different functions and are therefore used according to different strategies. Texts are more likely than pictures to be used according to a coherence-formation strategy: Texts guide the reader's conceptual analysis by a description of the subject matter, resulting in a coherent semantic network and mental model, regardless of the difficulty of the item at hand. Pictures are more likely than texts to be used according to a task-specific information selection strategy. Pictures serve as scaffolds for initial mental model construction, but are afterwards used on demand as easily accessible external representations for item-specific mental model updates.

As for students from the lower tier, the situation is somewhat different. Texts are also more likely to be used by these learners according to a coherence-formation strategy. They obviously have more difficulties with word recognition and lexical access, which is indicated by their average fixation times. However, they nevertheless invest a high amount of time into the text during the first phase of initial mental model construction, although the item to be answered is relatively easy. Afterwards, they invest much less time into the text, even when the following items are more demanding. Pictures seem also to serve for lower tier students as scaffolds for initial mental model construction. Contrary to higher tier students, however, the lower tier students do not use pictures more intensively afterwards when items become more difficult.

In summary, higher tier and lower tier students do not essentially differ in terms of their usage of text, but they do differ in terms of their usage of pictures. As higher tier students outperformed lower tier students in regard to successful answering of items requiring text-picture integration (Schnotz et al. 2010), these strategy differences are also to be expected in regard to successful and unsuccessful item answering. A previous investigation revealed a slight improvement of item performance with grade. However, the strategy differences between the usage of text and the usage of pictures seem not to differ essentially between grades.

We can only speculate at this point about the reasons why lower tier students do not adapt their processing of pictures to the demands of the items. One possible explanation would be that they are less meta-cognitively sensitive to item difficulty. Students with higher meta-cognitive skills are possibly better in recognizing the demands of an item and the usefulness of an accompanying graphic (Flavell and Wellmann 1977; Hartman 2001). Another reason for the lack of adaptation would be that they do not know how to deal with pictures, either because they do not possess the required graphic processing strategies or because they do not know when to apply which strategy (Hasselhorn 1996). These issues need further research.

Acknowledgements This research has been performed as part of the project "Development and Evaluation of competence models of integrative processing of text and pictures" (Entwicklung und Überprüfung von Kompetenzmodellen zur integrativen Verarbeitung von Texten und Bildern, BITE) supported by grants from the German Research Foundation (DFG), awarded to Jürgen Baumert, Wolfgang Schnotz, Holger Horz, and Nele McElvany (BA 1461/7-1, BA 1461/8-1, SCHN 665/3-1, SCHN 665/6-1, SCHN 665/6-2 and MC 67/7-2) within the Priority Program "Competence Models for Assessing Individual Learning Outcomes and Evaluating Educational Processes" (SPP 1293). The authors thank Dr. Thorsten Rasch for his support in implementing the experimental environment used in this chapter.

References

Ainsworth, S. (1999). The functions of multiple representations. *Computers & Education, 33*, 131–152. doi:10.1016/S0360-1315(99)00029-9.

Eggen, T. J. H. M. (2004). *Contributions to the theory of practice of computerized adaptive testing*. Enschede: University of Twente.

Flavell, J. H., & Wellman, H. M. (1977). Metamemory. In R. V. Kail & J. W. Hagen (Eds.), *Perspectives on the development of memory and cognition* (pp. 3–33). Hillsdale: Erlbaum.

Hartman, H. J. (2001). *Metacognition in learning and instruction: Theory, research and practice*. Dordrecht: Kluwer.

Hasselhorn, M. (1996). *Kategoriales Organisieren bei Kindern: Zur Entwicklung einer Gedächtnisstrategie [Category organization with children: On the development of a memory strategy]*. Göttingen: Hogrefe.

Holmquist, K., Nyström, M., Andersson, R., Dewhurst, R., Jarodzka, H., & Van de Weijer, J. (2011). *Eye tracking: A comprehension guide to methods and measures*. Oxford: Oxford University Press.

Kintsch, W. (1998). *Comprehension: A paradigm for cognition*. New York: Cambridge University Press.

Kulhavy, R. W., Stock, W. A., & Kealy, W. A. (1993). How geographic maps increase recall of instructional text. *Educational Technology, Research and Development, 41*(4), 47–62. doi:10.1007/BF02297511.

Levie, H. W., & Lentz, R. (1982). Effects of text illustration: A review of research. *Educational Communication and Technology Journal, 30*, 195–232. doi:10.1007/BF02765184.

Mayer, R. E. (2009). *Multimedia learning* (2nd ed.). New York: Cambridge University Press.

McNamara, D. S. (Ed.). (2007). *Reading comprehension strategies: Theories, interventions, and technologies*. Mahwah: Erlbaum.

Mokros, J. R., & Tinker, R. F. (1987). The impact of microcomputer based labs on children's ability to interpret graphs. *Journal of Research in Science Teaching, 24*, 369–383. doi:10.1002/tea.3660240408.

Rickards, J. P., & Denner, P. R. (1978). Inserted questions as aids to reading text. *Instructional Science, 7*, 313–346. doi:10.1007/BF00120936.

Schnotz, W. (2005). An integrated model of text and picture comprehension. In R. E. Mayer (Ed.), *The Cambridge handbook of multimedia learning* (pp. 49–69). New York: Cambridge University Press.

Schnotz, W., & Bannert, M. (2003). Construction and interference in learning from multiple representations. *Learning and Instruction, 13*, 141–156. doi:10.1016/S0959-4752(02)00017-8.

Schnotz, W., Horz, H., McElvany, N., Schroeder, S., Ullrich, M., Baumert, J., et al. (2010). Das BITE-Projekt: Integrative Verarbeitung von Bildern und Texten in der Sekundarstufe I [The BITE-project: Integrative processing of pictures and texts in secondary school I]. *Zeitschrift für Pädagogik, Beiheft, 56*, 143–153.

Schnotz, W., Ullrich, M., Hochpöchler, U., Horz, H., McElvany, N., Schroeder, S., & Baumert, J. (2011). What makes text-picture integration difficult? A structural and procedural analysis of textbook requirements. *Ricerche di Psicologia, 1*, 103–135. doi:10.3758/s13428-014-0528-1.

Wainer, H. (1992). Understanding graphs and tables. *Educational Researcher, 21*(1), 14–23. doi:10.3102/0013189X021001014.

Weidenmann, B. (1989). When good pictures fail: An information-processing approach to the effects of illustrations. In H. Mandl & J. R. Levin (Eds.), *Knowledge acquisition from text and pictures* (pp. 157–170). Amsterdam: North-Holland.

Zenisky, A. L., Hambleton, R. K., & Sireci, S. G. (2002). Identification and evaluation of local item dependencies in the medical college admissions test. *Journal of Educational Measurement, 39*, 291–301. doi:10.1111/j.1745-3984.2002.tb01144.x.

Chapter 19
Training in Components of Problem-Solving Competence: An Experimental Study of Aspects of the Cognitive Potential Exploitation Hypothesis

Florian Buchwald, Jens Fleischer, Stefan Rumann, Joachim Wirth, and Detlev Leutner

Abstract In this chapter, two studies are presented that investigate aspects of the cognitive potential exploitation hypothesis. This hypothesis states that students in Germany have cognitive potentials they do not use when solving subject-specific problems but that they do use when solving cross-curricular problems. This theory has been used to explain how students in Germany achieved relatively well on cross-curricular problem solving but relatively weakly on mathematical problem solving in the Programme for International Student Assessment (PISA) 2003. Our main research question in this chapter is: Can specific aspects of cross-curricular problem-solving competence (that is, conditional knowledge, procedural knowledge, and planning skills) be taught, and if so, would training in this area also transfer to mathematical problem solving? We investigated this question in a computer-based training experiment and a field-experimental training study. The results showed only limited effects in the laboratory experiment, although an interaction effect of treatment and prior problem-solving competence in the field-experiment indicated positive effects of training as well as a transfer to mathematical problem-solving for low-achieving problem-solvers. The results are discussed from a theoretical and a pedagogical perspective.

Keywords Analytical problem solving • Mathematical problem solving • Training • Transfer

F. Buchwald (✉) • S. Rumann
University of Duisburg-Essen, Essen, Germany
e-mail: florian.buchwald@uni-due.de; stefan.rumann@uni-due.de

J. Fleischer • D. Leutner
Faculty of Educational Sciences, Department of Instructional Psychology, University of Duisburg-Essen, Essen, Germany
e-mail: jens.fleischer@uni-due.de; detlev.leutner@uni-due.de

J. Wirth
Ruhr-University Bochum, Bochum, Germany
e-mail: joachim.wirth@rub.de

D. Leutner et al. (eds.), *Competence Assessment in Education*, Methodology of Educational Measurement and Assessment, DOI 10.1007/978-3-319-50030-0_19

19.1 Introduction

Today, life-long learning seems to be essential, in order to keep up with the rapidly changing demands of modern society. Therefore, general competencies with a broad scope, such as problem solving (Klieme 2004), become more and more important. The development of problem solving as a *subject-specific* competence is a crucial goal addressed in the educational standards of various subject areas (e.g., Blum et al. 2006; AAAS 1993; NCTM 2000). However, problem solving is seen not only as a subject-specific competence, but also as a *cross-curricular* competence: that is, an important prerequisite for successful future learning in school and beyond (OECD 2004b, 2013; cf. also Levy and Murnane 2005). Considering the crucial importance of problem solving, both as a subject-specific and as a cross-curricular competence, it has become a focus in large-scale assessments like the *Programme for International Student Assessment* (PISA; e.g., OECD 2004b, 2013).

The starting point for this chapter were the results from PISA 2003, showing that students in Germany achieved only average results in mathematics, science, and reading, while their results in problem solving were above the OECD average. According to the OECD report on problem solving in PISA 2003, this discrepancy has been interpreted in terms of a *cognitive potential exploitation hypothesis*, which suggests that students in Germany possess generic skills or cognitive potentials that might not be fully exploited in subject-specific instruction at school (OECD 2004b; cf. also Leutner et al. 2004). While the present chapter focuses on cross-curricular problem solving and mathematical problem-solving competence, the cognitive potential exploitation hypothesis also assumes unused cognitive potentials in science education (Rumann et al. 2010).

On the basis of the results of PISA 2003, and further theoretical and empirical arguments, outlined below, two studies aiming at investigating aspects of the cognitive potential exploitation hypothesis are presented. In a laboratory experiment and in a field experiment, problem solving (components) were taught, and the subsequent effects on mathematical problem solving (components) were investigated.[1]

19.2 Theoretical Framework

Research on problem solving has a long tradition in the comparatively young history of psychology. Its roots lie in research conducted in Gestalt psychology and the psychology of thinking in the first half of the twentieth century (e.g., Duncker 1935; Wertheimer 1945; for an overview, cf. Mayer 1992).

A problem consists of a problem situation (initial state), a more or less well-defined goal state, and a solution method that is not immediately apparent to the problem solver (e.g., Mayer 1992) because of a barrier between the initial state and

[1] Parts of this chapter are based on Fleischer et al. (in preparation) and Buchwald (2015).

the desired goal state (Dörner 1976). The solution of problems requires logically deriving and processing information in order to successfully solve the problem. Compared to a simple exercise or task, a problem is a non-routine situation for which no standard solution methods are readily at hand for the problem solver (Mayer and Wittrock 2006). Problem solving can thus be defined as "goal-oriented thought and action in situations for which no routinized procedures are available" (Klieme et al. 2001, p. 185, our translation).

The international part of the PISA 2003 problem solving test consisted of *analytical* problems (e.g., finding the best route on a subway map in terms of time traveled and costs; OECD 2004b). Analytical problems can be distinguished from *dynamic* problems (e.g., a computer simulation of a virtual chemical laboratory where products have to be produced by combining specific chemical substances; Greiff et al. 2012). In analytic problem solving, all information needed to solve the problem is explicitly stated in the problem description or can be inferred from it or from prior knowledge; analytical problem solving can thus be seen as the reasoned application of existing knowledge (OECD 2004b). In dynamic problem solving, in contrast, most of the information required to solve the problem has to be generated in an explorative interaction with the problem situation ("learning by doing"; Wirth and Klieme 2003). In this chapter we focus on analytical problem-solving competence, given that the cognitive potential exploitation hypothesis directly addresses this type of problem solving (for research on dynamic problem solving see Funke and Greiff 2017, in this volume).

19.2.1 Problem Solving in PISA 2003: The Cognitive Potential Exploitation Hypothesis

Since PISA 2003 (OECD 2003, 2004b), research on problem-solving competence in the context of school and educational systems has received growing attention. In PISA 2003, cross-curricular problem-solving competence is defined as

> an individual's capacity to use cognitive processes to confront and resolve real, cross-disciplinary situations where the solution path is not immediately obvious and where the literacy domains or curricular areas that might be applicable are not within a single domain of mathematics, science or reading. (OECD 2003, p. 156).

The definition of the domain of mathematics is based on the concept of literacy (OECD 2003, p. 26):

> Mathematical literacy is an individual's capacity to identify and understand the role that mathematics plays in the world, to make well-founded judgements and to use and engage with mathematics in ways that meet the needs of that individual's life as constructive, concerned and reflective citizen.

The PISA 2003 problem solving test showed unexpected results for Germany (Leutner et al. 2004; OECD 2004b): While students in Germany only reached average results in mathematics ($M = 503$, $SD = 103$), science ($M = 502$, $SD = 111$) and reading ($M = 491$, $SD = 109$), their results in problem solving ($M = 513$, $SD = 95$) were above average compared to the OECD metric, which sets the mean to 500 and the standard deviation to 100. This difference between students' problem-solving competence and their subject-specific competencies, for example in mathematics, is especially pronounced in Germany. Among all 29 participating countries, only Hungary and Japan showed greater differences in favor of problem solving (OECD 2004b). This large difference is especially surprising because of the high latent correlation of $r = .89$ of problem solving and mathematical competence in the international 2003 PISA sample (OECD 2005).

According to the OECD (2004b, p. 56; cf. also Leutner et al. 2004), this discrepancy can be interpreted in terms of a cognitive potential exploitation hypothesis: The test of cross-curricular problem-solving competence reveals students' "generic skills that may not be fully exploited by the mathematics curriculum". Within Germany, this unused potential seems to be especially pronounced for lower achievers (Leutner et al. 2004, 2005).

There are some arguments for this hypothesis: First, there are the conceptual similarities in terms of the theoretical process steps involved in successfully solving cross-curricular as well as mathematical problems (understanding the problem and the constraints, building a mental representation, devising and carrying out the plan to solve the problem, looking back; cf. Pólya 1945; cf. the mathematical modeling cycle). Second, the cognitive resources demanded in both domains are very similar (low demands for reading and science, high demands for reasoning; OECD 2003, cf. also Fleischer et al. in preparation).

Third, results from the German PISA 2003 repeated-measures study support the cognitive potential exploitation hypothesis with two arguments (cf. Leutner et al. 2006, for details): First, a path analysis of the longitudinal data, controlling for mathematical competence in Grade 9, showed that future mathematical competence in Grade 10 can be better predicted by analytical problem-solving competence ($R^2 = .49$) than by intelligence ($R^2 = .41$). Second, a communality analysis, decomposing the variance of mathematical competence in Grade 10 into portions that are uniquely and commonly accounted for by initial mathematical competence and problem-solving competence (and intelligence) was conducted. It showed that the variance portion commonly accounted for by analytical problem solving and initial mathematics ($R^2 = .127$) is larger than the variance portion commonly accounted for by intelligence and initial mathematics ($R^2 = .042$). Additionally, the variance portions uniquely accounted for by both intelligence ($R^2 = .006$) and problem solving ($R^2 = .005$) are near zero. These findings indicate that problem-solving competence and mathematical competence consist of several partly overlapping components that contribute differently to the acquisition of future mathematical competence.

19.2.2 Components of Problem-Solving Competence

Theoretically, several components of problem-solving competence can be distinguished: For example, knowledge of concepts, procedural knowledge, conditional knowledge, general problem solving strategies, and self-regulatory skills such as planning, monitoring and evaluation. We briefly describe the planning, procedural knowledge and conditional knowledge components, which are the focus of our study.

Planning, as an aspect of general problem solving competence (Davidson et al. 1994), is considered to be of crucial importance in school, work and everyday settings (Dreher and Oerter 1987; Lezak 1995). Planning can be defined as "any hierarchical process in the organism that can control the order in which a sequence of operations is to be performed" (Miller et al. 1960, p. 16). Planning is one of the first steps in models of mathematical problem solving (e.g., Pólya 1945). *Procedural knowledge*, "knowing how", can be defined as the knowledge of operators to change the problem state and the ability to realize a cognitive operation (Süß 1996). In the context of the PISA problem solving test procedural knowledge is important in respect of dealing with unfamiliar tables or figures (such as flow-charts). *Conditional knowledge* ("knowing when and why"; Paris et al. 1983) incorporates the circumstances of the usage of operators and is related to strategy knowledge. Strategy knowledge is important in situations where more than one option is available, as in the case of problem solving. Therefore, general problem solving strategies such as schema-driven or search-based strategies (Gick 1986) and metacognitive heuristics (Bruder 2002; Pólya 1945), which can be part of broader strategic approach (de Jong and Ferguson-Hessler 1996), are regarded as important components of problem solving as well. For more detailed taxonomies of knowledge and aspects of problem solving see, for example, Alexander et al. (1991) and Stacey (2005).

The relevance of these components for the PISA 2003 problem solving scale is empirically supported by an item demand analysis (Fleischer et al. 2010) that identified planning, procedural knowledge, and conditional knowledge as important components of both cross-curricular and mathematical problem-solving competence. Furthermore, problem solving items have turned out to be more demanding than mathematics items in respect of systematic and strategic approaches, and also in relation to dealing with constraints and procedural knowledge. Mathematics items, on the other hand, have turned out to be more formalized and to require, of course, more mathematical content knowledge.

To sum up, there is evidence for a strong overlap between cross-curricular and mathematical problem-solving competence in both theoretical and empirical frames. In this chapter we focus mainly on the common components of planning, procedural knowledge and conditional knowledge.

19.3 Research Questions

Analytical problem-solving competence, as it was assessed in PISA 2003, consists of different components that, to some extent, require different cognitive abilities. Training in a selection of these components should have an effect on analytical problem-solving competence in general. In accordance with the cognitive potential exploitation hypothesis, and on the basis of the assumption that both cross-curricular and subject-specific problem-solving competencies share the same principal components, training in components of analytical problem-solving competence should also have transfer effects on components of mathematical problem-solving competence and therefore, on mathematical problem-solving competence in general. Against this background, we investigate the following main research questions: Can specific components of problem-solving competence be trained, and does such training transfer to mathematical problem solving? These two main questions are split up into three specific research questions:

- Is it possible to train students in how to apply several important components of analytical problem-solving competence (conditional knowledge, procedural knowledge, and planning) in experimental settings (treatment check)?
- Does such training improve analytical problem-solving competence in general (near transfer)?
- Does transfer from analytical to mathematical problem solving occur (far transfer)?

19.4 Study I

In a first experimental training study, three components of analytical problem-solving competence—procedural knowledge, conditional knowledge, and planning—were taught.

We expected the experimental group to outperform a control group in all three components taught (conditional knowledge, procedural knowledge, and planning; treatment check) and on the global problem solving scale (near transfer). We further expected a positive transfer of the training to mathematical components (conditional knowledge, procedural knowledge, and planning) as well as on the global mathematics test (far transfer).

19.4.1 Methods

In a between-subjects design, a sample of 142 ninth grade students (44 % female; mean age = 15.04, *SD* = 0.84) from high and low tracks of secondary schools was randomly assigned to one of two experimental conditions.

In the experimental group, computer-based multimedia training in cross-curricular problem solving was used, with a focus on the components of procedural knowledge, conditional knowledge, and planning (cf. Fleischer et al. 2010). The training was mainly task-based and took 45 min. Students received feedback (knowledge of result) on each task and were given a second chance to solve the items; in the case of two wrong responses to an item, they were given the solution.

Students in the control group worked on a software tutorial without any mathematical tasks, in an online geometry package.

Randomization was done computer-based within each class. Due to time limitations, only a posttest was administered; there was no pretest.

The posttest (90 min) was composed of three parts:

1. four scales of analytical problem solving: procedural knowledge (Cronbach's $\alpha = .87$), conditional knowledge (Cronbach's $\alpha = .86$), planning (Cronbach's $\alpha = .96$), problem-solving competence (items from the PISA 2003 problem solving test; OECD 2004b; Cronbach's $\alpha = .65$),
2. four scales of mathematical problem solving: procedural knowledge (Cronbach's $\alpha = .80$), conditional knowledge (Cronbach's $\alpha = .82$), planning (Cronbach's $\alpha = .97$), mathematical problem-solving competence (items from the PISA 2003 mathematics test; OECD 2004a; Cronbach's $\alpha = .73$),
3. a scale of figural reasoning (Heller and Perleth 2000) as an indicator of intelligence as covariate.

19.4.2 Results

Due to the fact that participants were self-paced in the training phase and in the first part of the posttest, the control group spent less time on training and more time on the first part of the posttest than did the experimental group—although pre-studies regarding time on task had indicated equal durations for the experimental and control group treatments. Consequently, the first part of the posttest (the scales on analytical problem solving) was analyzed by means of an efficiency measure (performance [score] per time [min]). MANCOVAs, controlling for school track and intelligence, with follow-up-ANCOVAs, showed that the experimental group outperformed the control group on planning ($\eta^2 = .073$), conditional knowledge ($\eta^2 = .200$), and procedural knowledge ($\eta^2 = .020$), indicating a positive treatment check. The experimental group outperformed the control group on the global problem solving scale ($\eta^2 = .026$) as well, which indicates near transfer. Far transfer on the mathematical scales, however, was not found (multivariate $p = .953$, $\eta^2 = .005$). There was no interaction effect between group membership and school track ($F < 1$).

19.4.3 Discussion

In terms of *efficiency*, positive effects of the problem solving training on the trained components (treatment check) and on problem-solving competence in general (near transfer) were found in this first experimental training study. Thus, there is evidence that the trained components (i.e., procedural knowledge, conditional knowledge, and planning) are indeed relevant to analytical problem solving. However, no transfer of the training to the mathematical scales (i.e., far transfer) was found. Considering these results, the question arises as to whether the PISA 2003 test scales are sensitive enough to detect short-term training effects. Thus, in Study II we implemented an extended problem-solving training with a longitudinal design, additional transfer cues and prompts to enhance transfer to mathematics.

19.5 Study II

Study II focuses on an extended field-experimental training program in a school setting, including—as compared to Study I—more time for training, a broader variety of analytic problem solving tasks, and metacognitive support. The training aimed at fostering the joint components of problem solving and mathematical competence (i.e., planning, conditional knowledge, and procedural knowledge). In this study, we selected planning to be tested as a means of treatment check. We expected the experimental group to outperform the control group on a planning test (treatment check) and on a global problem solving test (near transfer). We further expected a positive transfer of the training on a global mathematics test (far transfer).

19.5.1 Methods

One hundred and seventy three students from six classes (Grade 9) of a German comprehensive school participated in the study (60 % female; mean age = 14.79, *SD* = 0.68) as part of their regular school lessons. The students in each class were randomly assigned to either the experimental or control group and were trained in separate class rooms for a weekly training session of 90 min. Including pretest, holidays, and posttest, the training period lasted 15 weeks (cf. Table 19.1).

The experimental group (EG) received broad training in problem solving with a focus on planning, procedural knowledge, conditional knowledge, and metacognitive heuristics (Table 19.1; cf. Buchwald 2015, for details). Due to the limited test time, only planning competence was tested.

Planning skills were taught through Planning Competence Training (PCT; Arling and Spijkers 2013; cf. also Arling 2006). In order to conduct the PCT in the school

Table 19.1 Procedure in Study II

Week	Experimental group	Control group
1	Introduction and demographic questionnaire	Introduction and demographic questionnaire
2	No sessions (holidays)	No sessions (holidays)
3	Pretest: cross-curricular and mathematical problem solving	Pretest: cross-curricular and mathematical problem solving
4	Pretest: planning	Pretest: planning
5–6	*Planning competence training*	*Rhetorical training*
7	Posttest: planning	Posttest: planning
8–9	No sessions (holidays)	No sessions (holidays)
10–14	*Problem solving training*	*Rhetorical training*
15	Posttest: cross-curricular and mathematical problem solving	Posttest: cross-curricular and mathematical problem solving

setting, the original training was modified in two ways:[2] First, students completed the training in teamwork (groups of two), not individually. Second, the training phase, consisting of two planning sessions with scheduling problems (i.e., planning a tour with many constraints in terms of dates and money), was complemented with additional reflection exercises (e.g., thinking about transfer of the in-tray working process to other activities).

After the PCT was finished, a variety of cross-curricular problem solving tasks were used for further problem solving training (e.g., the water jug problem, the missionaries and cannibals problem, Sudoku, dropping an egg without breaking it). The focus was again on planning, complemented by the use of heuristics (e.g., working forward or using tables and drawings; cf. Blum et al. 2006) and metacognitive questions (Bruder 2002; King 1991) that are also important for mathematical problem solving. Conditional knowledge was trained by judging, arguing for, and discussing options and solution methods.

The control group (CG; a wait control group) received rhetoric exercises (body language exercises, exercises against stage fright, learning how to use presentation software) in areas that are important in and outside school settings.

The pretest and posttest of cross-curricular problem-solving competence consisted of items from PISA 2003 (OECD 2004b). The pretest and posttest of mathematical problem-solving competence used items from PISA 2003 (OECD 2004a) and from a German test of mathematics in Grade 9 (a state-wide administered large-scale assessment of mathematics in North Rhine-Westphalia; Leutner et al. 2007). All items were administered in a balanced incomplete test design, with rotation of domains and item clusters. Consequently, each student worked on a test booklet consisting of 16–19 items per time point. Because no student worked on the same items on pre- and posttest occasions, memory effects are excluded.

[2] We thank Dr. Viktoria Arling for her cooperation.

19.5.1.1 Data Analysis

The pre- and posttest data for cross-curricular and mathematical problem solving were scaled per domain by concurrent calibration (Kolen and Brennan 2014) with the R package TAM (Kiefer et al. 2014), in order to establish a common metric for each domain. The following results are based on weighted likelihood estimates (WLE; Warm 1989). Please note that the results are preliminary; further analyses with treatment of missing data (e.g., multiple imputation; Graham 2012) are not yet available.

The descriptive pretest results for problem solving (EAP reliability = .48, variance = 0.71) show that the EG scored lower (M = 0.03, SD = 1.26) than the CG (M = 0.55, SD = 0.93). The descriptive posttest results for problem solving (EAP reliability = .49, variance = 0.92) show similar results for EG (M = 0.08, SD = 1.17) and CG (M = 0.06, SD = 1.35). The correlation between pre- and posttest is .62.

The descriptive pretest results for mathematics (EAP reliability = .58, variance = 1.30) show similar results for EG (M = 0.20, SD = 1.10) and CG (M = 0.14, SD = 1.32). The descriptive posttest results for mathematics (EAP reliability = .54, variance = 1.12) show similar results for EG (M = 0.03, SD = 1.05) and CG (M = 0.15, SD = 1.39) as well. The correlation between pre- and posttest is .80.

19.5.2 Results

19.5.2.1 Planning

As a treatment-check for the planning component of the training, the posttest of the PCT (Arling and Spijkers 2013) was conducted in Week 7 (Table 19.1). The results show, as expected, that the experimental group outperformed the control group (Cohen's d = 0.45; Buchwald 2015).

19.5.2.2 Problem Solving

To investigate global training effects in terms of near transfer, a linear model with group membership and problem solving at the pretest (T1) as predictors, and problem solving at the posttest (T2) as criterion, was calculated. The model[3] explained 16.3 % of the variance, with problem solving at T1 (f^2 = .37) and the interaction of problem solving at T1 and group membership (f^2 = .22) being significant effects. Thus, the results indicate an aptitude treatment interaction (ATI). A look at the corresponding effect plot (Fig. 19.1) reveals that the training shows near transfer for

[3] This and the following model were calculated using a sequential partitioning of variance approach: that is, introducing the predictors in the following order: (1) achievement at T1, (2) group membership, and (3) achievement at T1 x group membership.

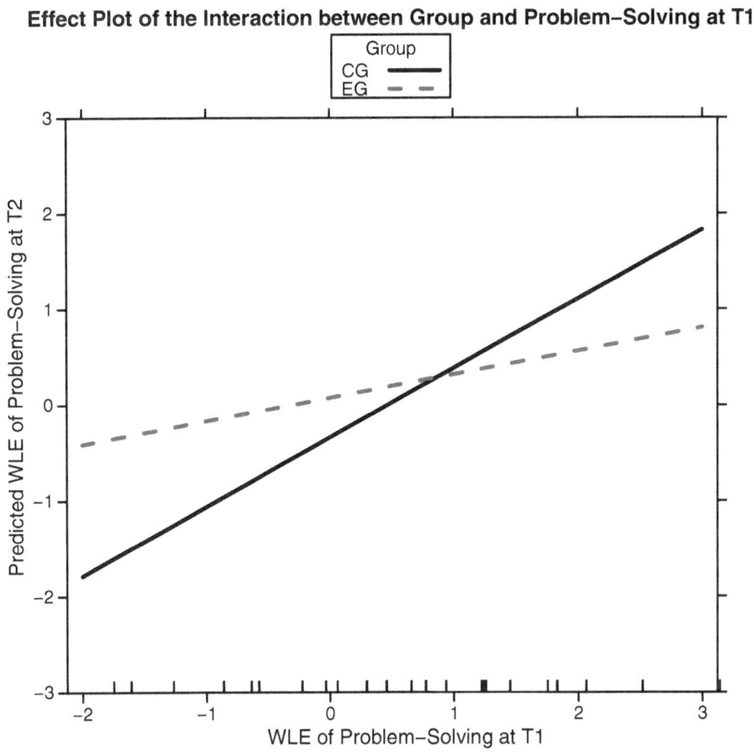

Fig. 19.1 Interaction (group * problem solving at the pretest [T1]) in the prediction of problem solving in the posttest (T2). *CG* = Control Group, *EG* = Experimental Group. The figure was generated with the R package *effects* (Fox 2003)

students with low problem solving competence at T1, but not for students with high problem-solving competence at T1.

19.5.2.3 Mathematics

To investigate global training effects in terms of far transfer, a linear model was calculated with group membership, problem solving at T1, and mathematics at T1 as predictors, and mathematics at T2 as criterion. The model explained 29.5 % of the variance with mathematics at T1 ($f^2 = .55$), problem solving at T1 ($f^2 = .21$), and the interaction of problem solving at T1 and group membership ($f^2 = .23$) as significant effects. Thus, the results indicate an aptitude treatment interaction (ATI) as well. A look at the corresponding effect plot (Fig. 19.2) reveals that the training shows far transfer for students with low problem-solving competence at T1 but not for students with high problem-solving competence at T1.

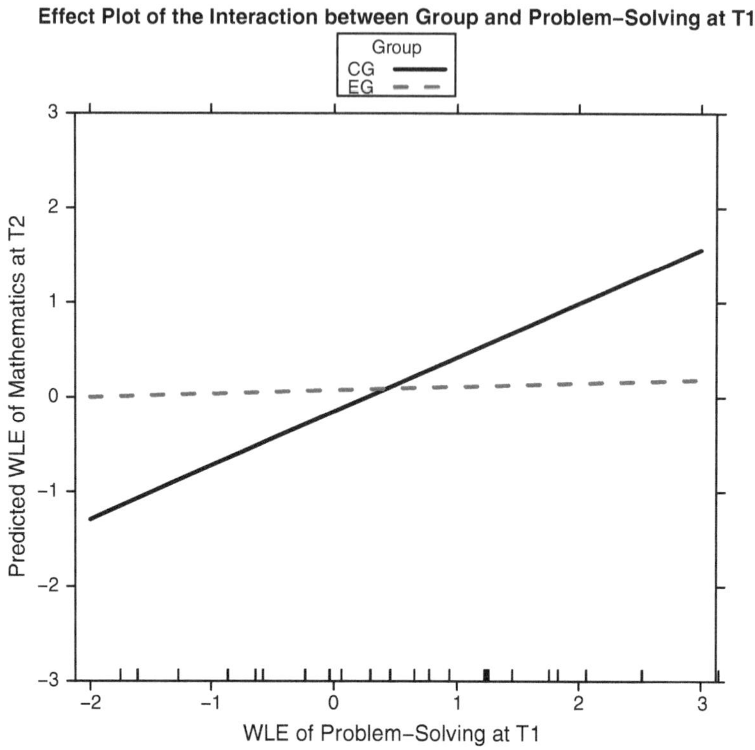

Fig. 19.2 Interaction (group * problem solving at the pretest [T1]) in the prediction of Mathematics in the posttest (T2). *CG* = Control Group, *EG* = Experimental Group. The figure was generated with the R package *effects* (Fox 2003).

19.5.3 Discussion

The results of Study II show a successful treatment-check for planning: that is, the planning component of the training program was effective. Other components of problem-solving competence (e.g., conditional knowledge) were part of the training, but for time reasons were not tested; these should be included in future studies.

For problem solving (near transfer) as well as mathematics (far transfer), an interaction of treatment and prior achievement in problem solving was found. These ATI (Aptitude Treatment Interaction) patterns of results indicate that, in terms of near and far transfer, the problem solving training is effective for students with low but not for students with high initial problem-solving competence, and also indicate a compensatory training effect with medium effect sizes. That the training is not helpful for high-achieving problem solvers might be due to motivational factors ("Why should I practice something I already know?") or to interference effects (new procedures and strategies might interfere with pre-existing highly automated procedures and strategies).

19.6 General Discussion

Problem solving is one of the most demanding human activities. Therefore, learning to solve problems is a long-lasting endeavor that has to take care of a "triple alliance" of cognition, metacognition, and motivation (Short and Weissberg-Benchell 1989). Following the results of PISA 2003, the present chapter aimed at testing some aspects of the cognitive potential exploitation hypothesis. This hypothesis states that students in Germany have unused cognitive potentials available that might not be fully exploited in subject-specific instruction at school—for example, in mathematics instruction.

In two experimental studies we aimed at fostering mathematical problem-solving competence by training in cross-curricular problem-solving competence. The expectation was that training in the core components of problem-solving competence (i.e., planning, procedural and conditional knowledge, and metacognition-components) that are needed both in cross-curricular and in subject-specific problem solving) should transfer to mathematical competence. In a laboratory experiment (Study I) no effects, in terms of far transfer to mathematics, were found. However, the results of a field experiment (Study II), based on an extensive long-term training program, show some evidence for the cognitive potential exploitation hypothesis: For low-achieving problem solvers the training fostered both problem-solving competence (near transfer) and mathematical competence (far transfer).

Analyzing potential effects from cross-curricular problem-solving competence to mathematical competence in experimental settings was an important step in the investigation of the cognitive potential hypothesis. Further training studies will need to focus on samples with unused cognitive potentials in order to test whether a higher exploitation of cognitive potentials could be achieved.

19.6.1 Limitations and Future Research

The Role of Content Knowledge This chapter focused on common components of cross-curricular and mathematical problem solving. Therefore, the role of domain-specific content knowledge in mathematics was somewhat neglected in our studies. An alternative approach to investigating the cognitive potential exploitation hypothesis is to focus on the difference between the domains: i.e., on the mathematical content knowledge.

Participants Concerning the results and their interpretation, one has to keep in mind that Study II was conducted at only one German comprehensive school in an urban area, as part of the regular school lessons in Grade 9. Thus, participation in the training was obligatory, which is ecologically valid for school settings, but could have had motivational effects. For test the generalizability of the results, further research is needed in other school settings (e.g., studies with other kinds of schools and in other grades, participation on a voluntary basis).

Adaptive Assessment and Training Following the ATI effect found in Study II, future research could use a more adaptive training, or identify students who require this kind of intervention. Finding evidence of effects from cross-curricular problem solving to the mathematical domain is an important step in investigating the cognitive potential exploitation hypothesis. Further studies on this hypothesis should concentrate on possible effects for students with high unused cognitive potentials. In order to select students with unused cognitive potential in the meaning of the cognitive potential exploitation hypothesis there is the need for individual assessment of this potential. This would require a more economical test with a higher reliability than the one used in our study. Adaptive testing (van der Linden and Glas 2000) could be a solution to this issue.

Problem-Solving Competence and Science Although this chapter has dealt only with cross-curricular problem solving and mathematics competence, the cognitive potential exploitation hypothesis also assumes unused cognitive potentials for science learning. This is targeted in ongoing research with a specific focus on chemistry education (Rumann et al. 2010, RU 1437/4–3).

Problem solving in PISA 2012 Nine years after PISA 2003, problem solving was assessed again, in PISA 2012. The results of PISA 2012 indicated that students in Germany perform above the OECD average in both problem solving and in mathematics. Furthermore, mathematical competence is a little higher than expected on the basis of the problem-solving competence test (OECD 2014). Since the test focus changed from analytical or static problem solving in PISA 2003 to complex or dynamic problem solving in PISA 2012, it is not yet clear, however, whether the improvement from 2003 to 2012 can be interpreted as the result of the better exploitation of the cognitive potentials of students in Germany. Further theoretical analysis and empirical research on this question is needed.

Acknowledgments The preparation of this chapter was supported by grants DL 645/12–2, DL 645/12–3 and RU 1437/4–3 from the German Research Foundation (DFG) in the Priority Program "Competence Models for Assessing Individual Learning Outcomes and Evaluating Educational Processes" (SPP 1293). Thanks to Dr. Viktoria Arling for her provision of Planning Competence Training. We would like to thank our student research assistants and trainers (Derya Bayar, Helene Becker, Kirsten Breuer, Jennifer Chmielnik, Jan. Dworatzek, Christian Führer, Jana Goertzen, Anne Hommen, Michael Kalkowski, Julia Kobbe, Kinga Oblonczyk, Ralf Ricken, Sönke Schröder, Romina Skupin, Jana Wächter, Sabrina Windhövel, Kristina Wolferts) and all participating schools and students. We thank Julia Kobbe, Derya Bayar and Kirsten Breuer for proofreading.

References

AAAS (American Association for the Advancement of Science). (1993). *Benchmarks for science literacy*. New York: Oxford University Press.

Alexander, P. A., Schallert, D. L., & Hare, V. C. (1991). Coming to terms: How researchers in learning and literacy talk about knowledge. *Review of Educational Research, 61*, 315–343.

Arling, V. (2006). *Entwicklung und Validierung eines Verfahrens zur Erfassung von Planungskompetenz in der beruflichen Rehabilitation: Der "Tour-Planer" [Development and validation of an assessment instrument of planning competence in vocational rehabilitation].* Berlin: Logos.

Arling, V., & Spijkers, W. (2013). Konzeption und Erprobung eines Konzepts zum Training von Planungskompetenz im Kontext der beruflichen Rehabilitation [Training of planning competence in vocational rehabilitation]. *bwp@ Spezial 6, HT 2013. Fachtagung, 05*, 1–12.

Blum, W., Drüke-Noe, C., Hartung, R., & Köller, O. (2006). *Bildungsstandards Mathematik: Konkret. Sekundarstufe I: Aufgabenbeispiele, Unterrichtsanregungen, Fortbildungsideen [German educational standards in mathematics for lower secondary degree: Tasks, teaching suggestions, thoughts with respect to further education].* Berlin: Cornelsen Scriptor.

Bruder, R. (2002). Lernen, geeignete Fragen zu stellen: Heuristik im Unterricht [Learning to ask suitable questions: Heuristics in the classroom]. *Mathematik Lehren, 115*, 4–9.

Buchwald, F. (2015). *Analytisches Problemlösen: Labor- und feldexperimentelle Untersuchungen von Aspekten der kognitiven Potenzialausschöpfungshypothese* [Analytical problem solving: Laboratory and field experimental studies on aspects of the cognitive potential exploitation hypothesis] (Doctoral dissertation, Universität Duisburg-Essen, Essen, Germany).

Davidson, J. E., Deuser, R., & Sternberg, R. J. (1994). The role of metacognition in problem solving. In J. Metcalfe & A. P. Shimamura (Eds.), *Metacognition: Knowing about knowing* (pp. 207–226). Cambridge, MA: MIT Press.

De Jong, T., & Ferguson-Hessler, M. G. M. (1996). Types and qualities of knowledge. *Educational Psychologist, 31*, 105–113. doi:10.1207/s15326985ep3102_2.

Dörner, D. (1976). *Problemlösen als Informationsverarbeitung [Problem solving as information processing].* Stuttgart: Kohlhammer.

Dreher, M., & Oerter, R. (1987). Action planning competencies during adolescence and early adulthood. In S. L. Friedman, E. K. Scholnick, & R. R. Cocking (Eds.), *Blueprints for thinking: The role of planning in cognitive development* (pp. 321–355). Cambridge: Cambridge University Press.

Duncker, K. (1935). *The psychology of productive thinking.* Berlin: Springer.

Fleischer, J., Wirth, J., Rumann, S., & Leutner, D. (2010). Strukturen fächerübergreifender und fachlicher Problemlösekompetenz. Analyse von Aufgabenprofilen: Projekt Problemlösen [Structures of cross-curricular and subject-related problem-solving competence. Analysis of task profiles: Project problem solving]. *Zeitschrift für Pädagogik, Beiheft, 56*, 239–248.

Fleischer, J., Buchwald, F., Wirth, J., Rumann, S., Leutner, D. (in preparation). Analytical problem solving: Potentials and manifestations. In B. Csapó, J. Funke, & A. Schleicher (Eds.), *The nature of problem solving.* Paris: OECD.

Funke, J., & Greiff, S. (2017). Dynamic problem solving: Multiple-item testing based on minimally complex systems. In D. Leutner, J. Fleischer, J. Grünkorn, & E. Klieme (Eds.), *Competence assessment in education: Research, models and instruments* (pp. 427–443). Berlin: Springer.

Fox, J. (2003). Effect displays in R for generalised linear models. *Journal of Statistical Software, 8*(15), 1–27.

Gick, M. L. (1986). Problem-solving strategies. *Educational Psychologist, 21*, 99–120. doi:10.1080/00461520.1986.9653026.

Graham, J. W. (2012). *Missing data: Analysis and design. Statistics for social and behavioral sciences.* New York: Springer.

Greiff, S., Wüstenberg, S., & Funke, J. (2012). Dynamic problem solving: A new assessment perspective. *Applied Psychological Measurement, 36*, 189–213. doi:10.1177/0146621612439620.

Heller, K. A., & Perleth, C. (2000). *Kognitiver Fähigkeitstest (KFT 4-12+R) [Cognitive ability test]* (3rd ed.). Göttingen: Beltz.

Kiefer, T., Robitzsch, A., & Wu, M. L. (2014). *TAM: Test analysis modules. R package version 1.0-2.1.* Retrieved from http://CRAN.R-project.org/package=TAM

King, A. (1991). Effects of training in strategic questioning on children's problem-solving performance. *Journal of Educational Psychology, 83*, 307–317. doi:10.1037/0022-0663.83.3.307.
Klieme, E. (2004). Assessment of cross-curricular problem-solving competencies. In J. H. Moskowitz & M. Stephens (Eds.), *Comparing learning outcomes. International assessments and education policy* (pp. 81–107). London: Routledge.
Klieme, E., Funke, J., Leutner, D., Reimann, P., & Wirth, J. (2001). Problemlösen als fächerübergreifende Kompetenz: Konzeption und erste Resultate aus einer Schulleistungsstudie [Problem solving as cross-curricular competence? Concepts and first results from an educational assessment]. *Zeitschrift für Pädagogik, 47*, 179–200.
Kolen, M. J., & Brennan, R. L. (2014). *Test equating: Methods and practices* (3rd ed.). New York: Springer.
Leutner, D., Klieme, E., Meyer, K., & Wirth, J. (2004). Problemlösen [Problem solving]. In PISA-Konsortium Deutschland (Eds.), *PISA 2003. Der Bildungsstand der Jugendlichen in Deutschland: Ergebnisse des zweiten internationalen Vergleichs* (pp. 147–175). Münster: Waxmann.
Leutner, D., Klieme, E., Meyer, K., & Wirth, J. (2005). Die Problemlösekompetenz in den Ländern der Bundesrepublik Deutschland [Problem-solving competence in the federal states of the federal republic of Germany]. In M. Prenzel et al. (Eds.), *PISA 2003. Der zweite Vergleich der Länder in Deutschland: Was wissen und können Jugendliche?* (pp. 125–146). Münster: Waxmann.
Leutner, D., Fleischer, J., & Wirth, J. (2006). Problemlösekompetenz als Prädiktor für zukünftige Kompetenz in Mathematik und in den Naturwissenschaften [Problem-solving competence as a predictor of future competencies in mathematics and science]. In PISA-Konsortium Deutschland (Ed.), *PISA 2003. Untersuchungen zur Kompetenzentwicklung im Verlauf eines Schuljahres* (pp. 119–137). Münster: Waxmann.
Leutner, D., Fleischer, J., Spoden, C., & Wirth, J. (2007). Landesweite Lernstandserhebungen zwischen Bildungsmonitoring und Individualdiagnostik [State-wide standardized assessments of learning between educational monitoring and individual diagnostics]. *Zeitschrift für Erziehungswissenschaft, Sonderheft, 8*, 149–167. doi:10.1007/978-3-531-90865-6_9.
Levy, F., & Murnane, R. J. (2005). *The new division of labor: How computers are creating the next job market*. Princeton: Princeton University Press.
Lezak, M. D. (1995). *Neuropsychological assessment* (3rd ed.). New York: Oxford University Press.
Mayer, R. E. (1992). *Thinking, problem solving, cognition* (2nd ed.). New York: Freeman.
Mayer, R. E., & Wittrock, M. C. (2006). Problem solving. In P. A. Alexander & P. H. Winne (Eds.), *Handbook of educational psychology* (pp. 287–303). Mahwah: Erlbaum.
Miller, G. A., Galanter, E., & Pribram, K. H. (1960). *Plans and the structure of behavior*. London: Holt, Rinehart and Winston.
NCTM (National Council of Teachers of Mathematics). (2000). *Principles and standards for school mathematics*. Reston: NCTM.
OECD (Organisation for Economic Co-operation and Development). (2003). *The PISA 2003 assessment framework: Mathematics, reading, science and problem solving knowledge and skills*. Paris: Author.
OECD (Organisation for Economic Co-operation and Development). (2004a). *Learning for tomorrow's world: First results from PISA 2003*. Paris: Author.
OECD (Organisation for Economic Co-operation and Development). (2004b). *Problem solving for tomorrow's world: First measures of cross-curricular competencies from PISA 2003*. Paris: Author.
OECD (Organisation for Economic Co-operation and Development). (2005). *PISA 2003. Technical report*. Paris: Author.
OECD (Organisation for Economic Co-operation and Development). (2013). *PISA 2012 assessment and analytical framework: Mathematics, reading, science, problem solving and financial literacy*. Paris: Author. doi:10.1787/9789264190511-en.

OECD (Organisation for Economic Co-operation and Development). (2014). *PISA 2012 Results: Creative problem solving: Students' skills in tackling real-life problems (Volume V)*. Paris: Author. doi:10.1787/9789264208070-en.

Paris, S. G., Lipson, M. Y., & Wixson, K. K. (1983). Becoming a strategic reader. *Contemporary Educational Psychology, 8*, 293–316. doi:10.1016/0361-476X(83)90018-8.

Pólya, G. (1945). *How to solve it: A new aspect of mathematical method*. Princeton: University Press.

Rumann, S., Fleischer, J., Stawitz, H., Wirth, J., & Leutner, D. (2010). Vergleich von Profilen der Naturwissenschafts- und Problemlöse-Aufgaben der PISA 2003-Studie [Comparison of profiles of science and problem solving tasks in PISA 2003]. *Zeitschrift für Didaktik der Naturwissenschaften, 16*, 315–327.

Short, E. J., & Weissberg-Benchell, J. A. (1989). The triple alliance for learning: Cognition, metacognition, and motivation. In C. B. McCormick, G. Miller, & M. Pressley (Eds.), *Cognitive strategy research: From basic research to educational application* (pp. 33–63). New York: Springer.

Stacey, K. (2005). The place of problem solving in contemporary mathematics curriculum documents. *Journal of Mathematical Behavior, 24*, 341–350. doi:10.1016/j.jmathb.2005.09.004.

Süß, H. M. (1996). *Intelligenz, Wissen und Problemlösen [Intelligence, knowledge and problem solving]*. Göttingen: Hogrefe.

van der Linden, W. J., & Glas, C. A. (Eds.). (2000). *Computerized adaptive testing: Theory and practice*. New York: Springer.

Warm, T. A. (1989). Weighted likelihood estimation of ability in item response theory. *Psychometrika, 54*, 427–450. doi:10.1007/BF02294627.

Wertheimer, M. (1945). *Productive thinking*. New York: Harper & Row.

Wirth, J., & Klieme, E. (2003). Computer-based assessment of problem solving competence. *Assessment in Education, 10*, 329–345. doi:10.1080/0969594032000148172.

Chapter 20
An Intensive Longitudinal Study of the Development of Student Achievement over Two Years (LUISE)

Gizem Hülür, Fidan Gasimova, Alexander Robitzsch, and Oliver Wilhelm

Abstract Educational researchers have long been interested in quantifying the amount of change in student achievement as a result of schooling. In this paper, we present an intensive longitudinal study of student achievement and cognitive ability over a time span of two academic years, from the beginning of ninth grade until the end of tenth. One hundred and twelve students participated in the intensive longitudinal study, which consisted of 44 testing sessions. A control group of 113 students participated only in the pretest and posttest. We provide descriptive results for the trajectories of German language and mathematics achievement in different domains and report comparisons between the study and control groups. Taken together, our findings reveal that student achievement increased over the course of two academic years, with effect sizes amounting to about 60–80 % of a full standard deviation unit for German achievement, and to about two thirds to a full standard deviation unit for mathematics achievement. Furthermore, the findings did not reveal any evidence for higher increases in student achievement for the study group. We conclude that intensive longitudinal studies allow for examining change in student achievement over shorter time spans without confounding the findings with learning effects related to retest and discuss open questions for future research.

Keywords Student achievement • Longitudinal • Language achievement • Mathematics • Secondary school

G. Hülür (✉)
University of Zurich, Zurich, Switzerland
e-mail: gizem.hueluer@uzh.ch

F. Gasimova • O. Wilhelm
Ulm University, Ulm, Baden-Wuerttemberg, Germany
e-mail: fidan.gasimova@uni-ulm.de; oliver.wilhelm@uni-ulm.de

A. Robitzsch
Leibniz Institute for Science and Mathematics Education (IPN), Kiel, Germany
e-mail: robitzsch@ipn.uni-kiel.de

D. Leutner et al. (eds.), *Competence Assessment in Education*, Methodology of Educational Measurement and Assessment, DOI 10.1007/978-3-319-50030-0_20

20.1 Introduction

Educational researchers have long been interested in quantifying the amount of change in student achievement as a result of schooling. In this study we concentrate on change in student achievement in ninth graders over the course of two academic years. We conducted an intensive-longitudinal study that encompassed 44 testing sessions (including pretest and posttest), where measures of student achievement, working memory, learning behaviours, and personality were administered (Längsschnittliche Untersuchung individueller schulischer Entwicklungsprozesse [Longitudinal Study of Individual Academic Development]; LUISE). In the present chapter we focus on student achievement in German and mathematics and provide an overview of our research questions, a detailed description of the intensive-longitudinal study and descriptive findings on change in student achievement in German and mathematics. Previous research suggests that student achievements in languages and mathematics are not one-dimensional constructs, but are instead characterized by multiple dimensions. To characterize change in these subject areas it is especially important to consider multidimensionality. In Sects. 20.2, 20.3, and 20.4, we give an overview of studies examining the factor structure of student achievement in foreign and native languages and mathematics. Then we summarize previous research on changes in student achievement, with the aim of quantifying the amount of change that can be expected over the course of the school years examined in the present study. This is followed by a summary of studies that have examined the structure of change in student achievement, and associations of achievement with cognitive ability.

In the intensive-longitudinal project, we follow a number of intertwined research questions on the development of student achievement. Our first set of research questions revolves around the characterization of change across the various domains of German and mathematics achievement. Our research questions specifically focus on the dimensionality of change in these domains. For example, will change in mathematics achievement be characterized by a single factor or by multiple factors? If there are multiple factors, how closely associated are they with each other? Is there an association between change in German achievement and change in mathematics achievement? Second, we aim to examine the role of cognitive ability for the development of student achievement. For example, can pretest fluid and crystallized intelligence predict changes in student achievement in the next 2 years? Furthermore, we are interested in synchronous associations between student achievement and working memory, which were also measured at each of the measurement points of the intensive-longitudinal study. Our third research question revolves around the role of non-cognitive factors in predicting changes in student achievement. Learning behaviours and personality traits, such as the Big Five, or typical intellectual engagement, are among the non-cognitive factors examined in our study.

20.2 Student Achievement in Languages

Standardized tests for language achievement measure many components of language competency. Earlier psychometric models of language achievement (Oller 1976), which primarily focused on foreign language achievement, proposed a comprehensive language competency. These theories were superseded by multidimensional models of language competency, leading to a more diverse assessment of language achievement in foreign and native languages (Jude et al. 2008). Language achievement typically can be divided into auditory versus written (e.g., listening versus reading comprehension) and productive versus receptive (e.g., writing versus audio-visual comprehension) achievement (Bremerich-Vos and Böhme 2009). This was also found in the DESI study (Deutsch Englisch Schülerleistungen International [German English Student Achievement International]; Beck and Klieme 2007), which assessed German and English language skills in a large sample of German ninth graders. In DESI, language achievement was assessed with a focus on written language. Language achievement in German (the native language) showed a multidimensional structure on the individual level, with correlated factors for seven competencies (vocabulary, reading, argumentation, awareness, orthography, pragmatics of text production, and systematics of text production), with small-to-moderate correlations ranging from $r = .15$ to $r = .36$ (Jude et al. 2008). At the classroom level, again, the above-described two-factor structure was found, with two hierarchical factors for reflection/reception and production. These two factors were very highly correlated ($r = .98$); however, the two-factor model fitted the data better than did a single-factor model. Foreign language achievement in English, as assessed in DESI, showed essentially the same factor structure as native language achievement in German.

Other studies focusing on foreign language achievement reported similar patterns of findings, with small differences in the number and interpretation of factors. Shin (2005) investigated the interindividual structure of performance in the Test of English as a Foreign Language (TOEFL) and in the Speaking Proficiency in English Assessment Kit (SPEAK). The data showed a factor model with a higher-order structure, with a higher-order general factor and three lower-order factors, representing listening, written language, and speaking achievement. In a large study of foreign language achievement, Sang et al. (1986) assessed the English performance of 14,000 German seventh graders. They established a three-factor structural model, with factors in elementary (pronunciation, spelling, and lexicon), complex (grammar, reading comprehension), and communicative (listening comprehension, interaction) skills. The factor intercorrelations ranged from $r = .60$ to $r = .84$ (Sang et al. 1986). Taken together, these previous studies reveal that student achievement in native and foreign language shows a multi-factor structure.

20.3 Student Achievement in Mathematics

In studies of student achievement, mathematics achievement is typically operationalized by tests based on school curriculum, or by tests based on the concept of mathematical literacy. Mathematical literacy comprises basic competencies that should facilitate the solving of everyday problems (OECD 1999). As a result, major studies of student achievement use different operationalizations of student achievement. For example, the TIMSS mathematics test (Trends in International Mathematics and Science Study: Baumert et al. 2000) was based on a cross-national core curriculum, but also embraced the concept of mathematical literacy. The PISA (Programme of International Student Achievement; OECD1999) mathematics test assessed mathematical literacy exclusively. For tests of student achievement in mathematics, it was shown that different content or operative areas of mathematical achievement tests were highly correlated (Brunner 2006). For example, in the TIMSS study, which assessed mathematics achievement of German eleventh to thirteenth graders, different mathematical content areas (e.g., geometry, equations, functions) as well as different operative areas (e.g., problem solving, routine procedures, complex procedures), showed high intercorrelations (ranging from $r = .77$ to $r = .81$ and ranging from $r = .82$ and $r = .87$, respectively; Klieme 2000). High intercorrelations between different mathematical domains have also been found in the NAEP (National Assessment of Educational Progress) study that is a nationally representative study of US American students' performance in various subject areas. Muthén et al. (1997) analyzed data from the NAEP study for the year 1992 for Grades 8 and 12. They found intercorrelations ranging from $r = .84$ to $r = .99$ (Grade 8) and from $r = .95$ to $r = 1.00$ (Grade 12) between five mathematical content areas (numbers and operations, measurement, geometry, data analysis and statistics, algebra). Taken together, these studies suggest that mathematics achievement can be conceptualized as multidimensional, albeit with highly interrelated factors.

20.4 Changes in Student Achievement in Mathematics and Native Language

Educational researchers have long been interested in quantifying the amount of change in student performance that typically occurs over the course of a school year. In their influential work, Cahan and Cohen (1989) investigated the effects of age and schooling on verbal and mathematic test scores. Using cross-sectional data, they used the regression discontinuity approach to examine the effects of age (scaled in months) and schooling. This allowed Cahan and Cohen (1989) to separate the effects of schooling from the effects of age, which are associated with maturation. The effect of 1 year of age on verbal test scores was associated with effect sizes ranging from $d = 0.05$ to $d = 0.18$ on different verbal subtests and with effect sizes ranging from $d = 0.15$ to $d = 0.16$ on the two mathematical subtests. The effect of

1 year of schooling was stronger than the age effects for verbal and mathematical subtests, with effect sizes ranging from $d = 0.23$ to $d = 0.41$ for 1 year of schooling on the verbal subtests, and effect sizes ranging from $d = 0.26$ to $d = 0.50$ for 1 year of schooling on the two mathematical subtests.

As we have previously addressed elsewhere (Hülür et al. 2011b), longitudinal studies of student achievement have allowed for quantifying gains in student achievement over time in students who pursued different tracks in the German school system. For example, in a study by Retelsdorf and Möller (2008), longitudinal mean comparisons of German language achievement over a period of 18 months in *Sekundarstufe I* (Grades 5–10 in most German federal states, level 2 according to International Standard Classification of Education; OECD 1999) showed an increase in reading comprehension of $d = 0.59$ for students attending *Realschule* (typically preparing for vocational education), and $d = 0.82$ for students attending *Gymnasium* (typically preparing for university). Studies based on large representative samples showed similar findings for mathematics achievement. In the TIMSS study, longitudinal mean comparisons of mathematics achievement from the end of seventh grade until the end of eighth grade showed, for a general factor of TIMSS items, an increase of $d = 0.60$ for students attending Realschule and $d = 0.79$ for students attending Gymnasium (Becker et al. 2006). In the supplementary study within PISA 2003 (PISA-I-Plus), German students show an increase of $d = 0.35$ in mathematics achievement from Grade 8 to Grade 9 (Ehmke et al. 2006). The difference in findings between the PISA and the TIMSS study might be attributed to differences in the operationalization of mathematics achievement: As addressed in the above subsection on student achievement in mathematics, mathematics achievement was operationalized as mathematics literacy in the PISA study, while the TIMSS mathematics test was based both on a concept of mathematics literacy and on a cross-national core curriculum.

Previous research further showed that the rate of change in student achievement is not the same across different school grades (as previously summarized in Hülür et al. 2011b). For example, Bloom et al. (2008) reported the mean effect size for the annual performance increase for seven standardized reading tests. The annual increase in reading performance decreased from $d = 1.52$ in the first grade to $d = 0.06$ in the twelfth grade. In the present study, we examined changes in student achievement in ninth and tenth grades. For the school years 9 and 10, Bloom et al. (2008) reported effects of $d = 0.24$ and $d = 0.19$ respectively for annual increase in reading performance. The annual increase in mathematics performance in six standardized tests also decreased from 1st ($d = 1.14$) to twelfth grade ($d = 0.01$). For the school years 9 and 10, Bloom et al. (2008) reported effect sizes of $d = 0.22$ and $d = 0.25$ respectively per academic year for mathematics performance.

The development of student achievement has been viewed as a cumulative development over a long time: Students with higher initial performance levels improve faster than do other students. This phenomenon of increasing interindividual differences has been called the "Matthew effect" or the "fan-spread pattern" (Cook and Campbell 1979; Walberg and Tsai 1983). These findings were replicated in some studies of reading comprehension (e.g., Bast and Reitsma 1998; Compton 2003;

Grimm 2008), whereas other studies reported a decrease of interindividual differences (e.g., Aunola et al. 2002). Also, a previous study showed that reading comprehension showed weaker associations with intelligence in higher grades (as previously addressed in Hülür et al. 2011b): The intercorrelations between the two domains were higher in Grades 1–4 than in Grades 5–8 and continued to decrease in Grades 9–12 (Ferrer et al. 2007). This finding is in line with theoretical notions of cognitive differentiation (see Hülür et al. 2011a), according to which the ability structure becomes more differentiated with weakly interrelated factors with increasing age during childhood and adolescence. Similar findings have been reported for mathematics achievement (as discussed in Hülür et al. 2011b). For example, Muthén and Khoo (1998) investigated mathematics achievement in two cohorts followed from seventh to twelfth grade, and found that the students' initial status was positively correlated with their growth rate (.51 in boys and .37 in girls). Regarding the relationship between cognitive abilities and mathematics achievement, a study by Rescorla and Rosenthal (2004) showed that the initial status of students' cognitive abilities was related to the initial status of student achievement, but not to its growth rate. However, this non-significant result might be due to the low statistical power of growth curve models to detect correlated change (Hertzog et al. 2008).

Although intensive-longitudinal studies are viewed as a viable tool for studying cognitive development (e.g., Siegler and Svetina 2006), analyses of change in terms of intensive-longitudinal data on academic achievement in native language and mathematics are rare, with a few notable exceptions (e.g., Strathmann and Klauer 2010; Strathmann et al. 2010). Intensive-longitudinal studies offer a promising route to study learning processes (for discussion, see Schmitz 2006). For example, the availability of a large number of observations per participant allows for describing individual learning trajectories, and the role of time-varying correlates in explaining individual differences in these learning trajectories. Also, intensive-longitudinal data on student achievement in different subject areas (e.g., German and mathematics) would allow for examining whether student achievement in different subject areas shows synchronous associations.

20.5 The Present Study

The goal in this present chapter is to provide a detailed description of the measurement of student achievement in a 2-year intensive-longitudinal study and to present descriptive analyses of change in student achievement in German language and mathematics in different domains from ninth to tenth grade. The following sections highlight important design characteristics of the study, the various student achievement tests administered, and descriptive information on change in student achievement in the various domains.

20.5.1 *Method*

20.5.1.1 Procedure and Participants

As part of our recruitment procedure, we contacted schools that were located in districts near our lab space, where the test sessions took place. The teachers were asked to distribute two sets of flyers to their ninth grade students (one for the students themselves and one for their parents), including a description of our study and contact information. Our study included two groups: a study group of students who participated in the intensive-longitudinal assessment, and a control group of students who only participated at pretest and posttest. For administrative reasons, students who registered to participate first were assigned to the study group, and the remaining students on the waiting list became part of the control group. In order to reach a sufficient sample size for the control group, further schools were contacted with the same procedure.

The students who took part in the intensive-longitudinal assessment participated approximately every 14 days in a 2 h testing session over a period of two academic years, resulting in a maximum of 44 measurement points per participant, including the pretest and the posttest. The tests were administered in groups of up to 12 students. For their participation in the study, the students received a payment of €40 at the end of every 5th testing session and at the end of the study. After the first half and at the end of the study the students received a bonus payment of €50. The testing sessions were conducted according to a manual, by research assistants who were undergraduate or graduate students of psychology or related disciplines.

The control group was tested only at pretest and at posttest. The students in the control group received €20 each for their participation in the pretest and €30 each for their participation in the posttest. The pretest and the posttest made up four testing sessions in total, with each session lasting about 2 h.

The sample initially included 196 ninth graders (107 girls, 54.6 %; age: $M = 14.7$, $SD = .70$). The students attended different secondary school tracks: 117 students (59.7 %) attended Gymnasium; 50 students (25.5 %) attended Realschule, and 29 students (14.8 %) attended *Gesamtschule*. Students attending *Hauptschule* were not recruited for the study, as they would leave school after ninth grade and would not be able to participate in the second year of the study. The present chapter is based on a sample of 112 ninth graders (72 girls, 64.3 %) who completed the 2-year longitudinal assessment. 76 students of the present sample (67.9 %) attended Gymnasium; 23 students (20.5 %) attended Realschule, and 13 students (11.6 %) attended Gesamtschule. The mean age at the beginning of the study was 14.7 years ($SD = 0.72$).

The control group initially consisted of 137 students (75 girls, 54.7 %, age: $M = 14.2$, $SD = .79$). The students in the control group also attended different school tracks: 104 students (75.9 %) attended Gymnasium, two students attended Realschule (1.5 %) and 31 students (22.6 %) attended Gesamtschule. One hundred and thirteen students from the control group (65 girls, 57.5 %) participated both in the pretest and the posttest. The present chapter is based on this remaining sample.

Ninety-two students in the present sample (81.4 %) attended Gymnasium, and 21 students (18.6 %) attended Gesamtschule. The mean age at the beginning of the study was 14.2 years ($SD = 0.71$).

20.5.1.2 Measures

At each measurement point, the following instruments were administered: (1) a 20 min achievement test in German, (2) a 20 min achievement test in mathematics, (3) two working memory measurements, consisting of three tasks each, with each task lasting about 9 mins, (4) a questionnaire on school-related behaviour and events, and (5) varying self-report measures of personality.

In the pretest and the posttest, a socio-demographic questionnaire was administered, as well as measures of fluid and crystallized intelligence. Students also completed a working memory measurement consisting of three working memory tasks as well as two student achievement tests of German language (covering the domains of reading and listening comprehension) and mathematics (covering the domains of number and functional relation) at pretest and at posttest. Of each test administered in the pretest and the posttest, two parallel versions were used. In order to evaluate training effects, the students were randomly assigned to one of the two parallel versions in the pretest, and completed the other version in the posttest.

Details relevant to the measurement of student achievement are given in Table 20.1 and in the following paragraphs.

Because a large number of student achievement tests were needed in the present study, we used nearly all of the instruments that were available at that time in the item pool of the Institute for Educational Progress (IQB) at the Humboldt University in Berlin. These items measure German and mathematics performance according to the national educational standards (*Bildungsstandards*; KMK 2005). All answers were rated according to the rating instructions used in the norming study of the educational standards, and scored using item parameters from a nationally representative norming study as fixed values in a one-dimensional Rasch model. The items were put together in 20-min tests, using the same test composition as in the norming study. Each student was administered the same test only once during the course of the study. The weighted likelihood estimates for person parameters (WLE; Warm 1989) were used as individual scores at each time point. We note that standard deviations of WLE scores may be overestimated, due to variance in the measurement error. Other measures used in the longitudinal study are described elsewhere (Hülür et al. 2011b, c).

20.5.1.2.1 German Achievement Tests

The educational standards outline four competence areas for the subject German in Sekundarstufe I: (1) speaking and listening, (2) writing, (3) reading, (4) language and language use. The operationalization of the educational standards includes tests from the following areas: reading comprehension, listening comprehension, language reflection, orthography, writing, and C-tests. The following item formats are used:

Table 20.1 Tests of German and mathematics achievement

Measurement point	German ach. test	Reliability Ger.	Mathematics ach. test	Reliability math.
Pretest1			1	.55
Pretest2	R/LC	.75/.66	4	.56
1	O	.92	1	.71
2	LR	.64	2	.60
3	R	.58	3	.75
4	LR	.71	4	.57
5	R	.64	5	.66
6	LC	.76	1	.76
7	C-Test	.91	2	.64
8	O	.88	4	.58
9	LR	.79	3	.62
10	R	.86	5	.52
11	W	single item	1	.34
12	LC	.39	2	.53
13	LR	.85	5	.54
14	R	.69	3	.72
15	LR	.82	4	.66
16	R	.68	2	.36
17	W	single item	4	.69
18	LC	.80	3	.68
19	LR	.00	5	.46
20	R	.75	1	.54
21	O	.92	2	.40
22	C-Test	.89	4	.60
23	W	single item	3	.64
24	LC	.79	5	.62
25	LR	.63	1	.67
26	R	.72	2	.47
27	LR	.82	1	.68
28	R	.76	4	.66
29	LR	.68	3	.70
30	LC	.71	5	.66
31	C-Test	.89	2	.47
32	LR	.72	1	.71
33	R	.64	4	.71
34	LR	.80	1	.66
35	LC	.62	4	.66
36	C-Test	.90	2	.69
37	LR	.74	4	.60
38	R	.51	3	.65
39	LC	.79	4	.60

(continued)

Table 20.1 (continued)

Measurement point	German ach. test	Reliability Ger.	Mathematics ach. test	Reliability math.
40	O	.80	5	.60
Posttest1			1	.60
Posttest2	R/LC	.73/.55	4	.67

Study group: n = 196 at pretest and n = 112 at posttest. Control group: n = 137 at pretest and n = 113 at posttest. *O* = Orthography, *LR* = Language Reflection, *R* = Reading Comprehension, *W* = Writing, *LC* = Listening Comprehension, *C-Test* = C-Test, *1* = Number, *2* = Measurement, *3* = Space and Form, *4* = Functional Relation, *5* = Data and Probability

(1) multiple-choice (with four alternatives), (2) true-false items, (3) matching items, (4) sorting items, (5) cloze-texts, (6) short-answer items, (7) essay items. The item format is confounded with the competence area; for example, writing is always assessed through essay items. In the norm population of ninth graders, reading comprehension had a mean of $M = -0.45$ logits and a standard deviation of $SD = 0.98$ logits. Among ninth grade students working toward an MSA (*Mittlerer Schulabschluss*, middle school degree) or to an *Abitur* (degree qualifying for university education; as the students in our sample did); listening comprehension ($M = -0.09$, $SD = 0.64$), language reflection ($M = -0.14$, $SD = 1.09$), orthography ($M = -0.06$; $SD = 0.99$), and writing ($M = -0.16$; $SD = 0.77$) were at similar average levels (Schipolowski et al. 2010). These descriptive statistics can be used to compare the performance of students in the present study to the national norming sample.

20.5.1.2.2 Mathematics Achievement Tests

The mathematics items were constructed on the basis of OECD studies (Adams and Wu 2002), for five overarching ideas, six general mathematical competencies, and three performance areas. Each test assesses mathematics achievement according to one of the five overarching ideas: (1) number, (2) measurement, (3) space and form, (4) functional relation, and (5) data and probability. Each item within a test represents one of the three performance areas, and assesses one or more of the six mathematical competencies. Among ninth graders working towards an MSA or a higher degree, mathematics achievement had an average level of $M = 0.00$ logits and a standard deviation of $SD = 1.00$ logit (A. Roppelt, personal communication, March 22, 2011).

20.5.2 Results

20.5.2.1 German Achievement

Figure 20.1 shows the mean performance in tests of German achievement over 40 measurement points in the domains of reading comprehension (Panel A), listening comprehension (Panel B), language reflection (Panel C), orthography (Panel D), writing (Panel E), and C-Tests (Panel F). At measurement point 19, the language reflection test showed a reliability of .00 (see Table 20.1) and the score on this measurement occasion can be identified as an outlier in Panel C of Fig. 20.1.

Figure 20.2 shows comparisons of the performance at pretest and at posttest for the study group and the control group. Approximate standard errors of the means were obtained by dividing the sample standard deviation by the square root of the sample size (see Algina et al. 2005). Standard errors were calculated under the assumption of independent sampling of students. In respect of Fig. 20.1, it is apparent that students in the study group tended to perform better at later measurement occasions, indicating increases in German achievement over the course of ninth and tenth grades. As can be seen in Fig. 20.2, the amount of increase in German achievement over the course of two academic years was similar for students in the study group and in the control group. This suggests that participation in the intensive-longitudinal study did not improve student achievement in German language. An examination of effect sizes in each group led to similar conclusions. Effect sizes were calculated by taking the difference between the posttest and pretest scores and dividing that difference score by the initial standard deviation at pretest, separately for each group (see Schmiedek et al. 2010). For reading comprehension, students in the study group showed an increase of $d = 0.82$ ($M_{pre} = -0.13$; $SD_{pre} = 1.37$; $M_{post} = 0.99$; $SD_{post} = 1.45$). Students in the control group showed a similar increase in reading comprehension ($d = 0.86$; $M_{pre} = 0.43$; $SD_{pre} = 1.13$; $M_{post} = 1.40$; $SD_{post} = 1.27$). In the domain of listening comprehension, students in the study group showed an increase of $d = 0.63$ ($M_{pre} = -0.37$; $SD_{pre} = 0.90$; $M_{post} = 0.20$; $SD_{post} = 0.77$). Again, students in the control group showed a similar increase in listening comprehension ($d = 0.66$; $M_{pre} = -0.06$; $SD_{pre} = 0.74$; $M_{post} = 0.43$; $SD_{post} = 0.74$). Taken together, these findings suggest that German achievement improved by approximately 60 to 80 % of a full standard deviation unit across Grades 9 and 10.

Next, we examined within-domain correlations in the different domains of German achievement displayed in Fig. 20.1: that is, the correlations among WLE scores at different measurement occasions for tests of the same domain. The within-domain correlations were moderate to high for reading comprehension (ranging from $r = .41$ to $r = .73$), listening comprehension (ranging from $r = .38$ to $r = .68$), language reflection (ranging from $r = .42$ to $r = .75$), and orthography (ranging from $r = .63$ to $r = .81$). For writing, the within-domain correlations were moderate, ranging from $r = .31$ to $r = .48$. For C-tests, within-domain correlations were high, ranging from $r = .79$ to $r = .84$. At pretest and posttest, the across-domain correlations between reading comprehension and listening comprehension were of moderate magnitude ($r = .59$ at pretest and $r = .58$ at posttest).

20.5.2.2 Mathematics Achievement

The mean performance in various domains of mathematics achievement over 40 measurement points is shown in Fig. 20.3 for the domains of number (Panel A), measurement (Panel B), space and form (Panel C), functional relation (Panel D), and data and probability (Panel E).

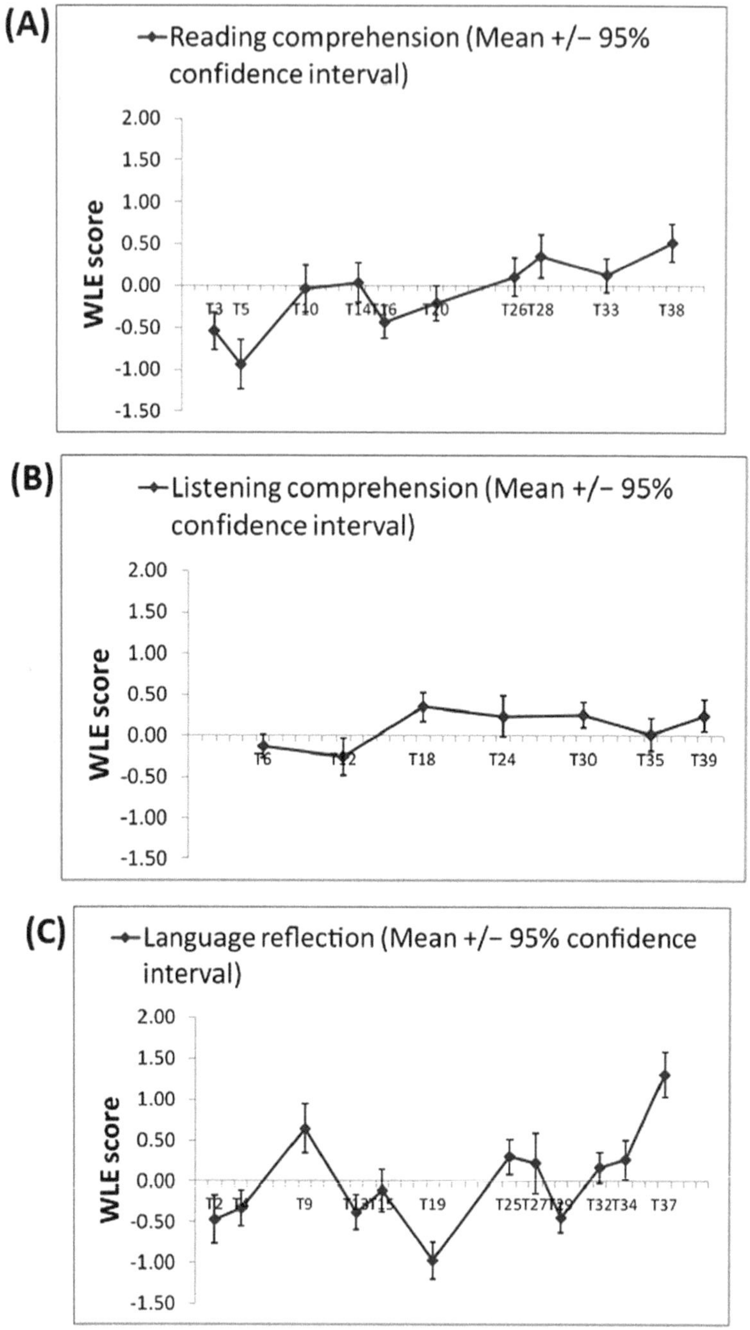

Fig. 20.1 Trajectories of German achievement in different domains across the 40 measurement occasions of the longitudinal study

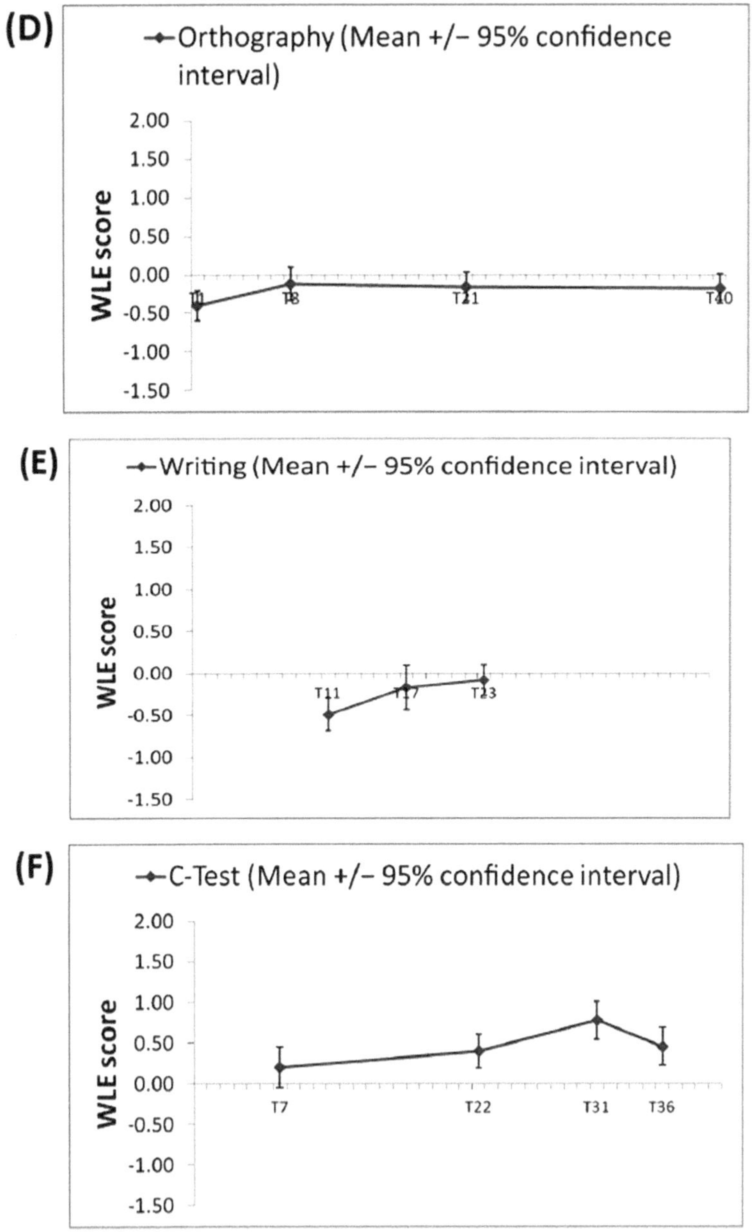

Fig. 20.1 (continued)

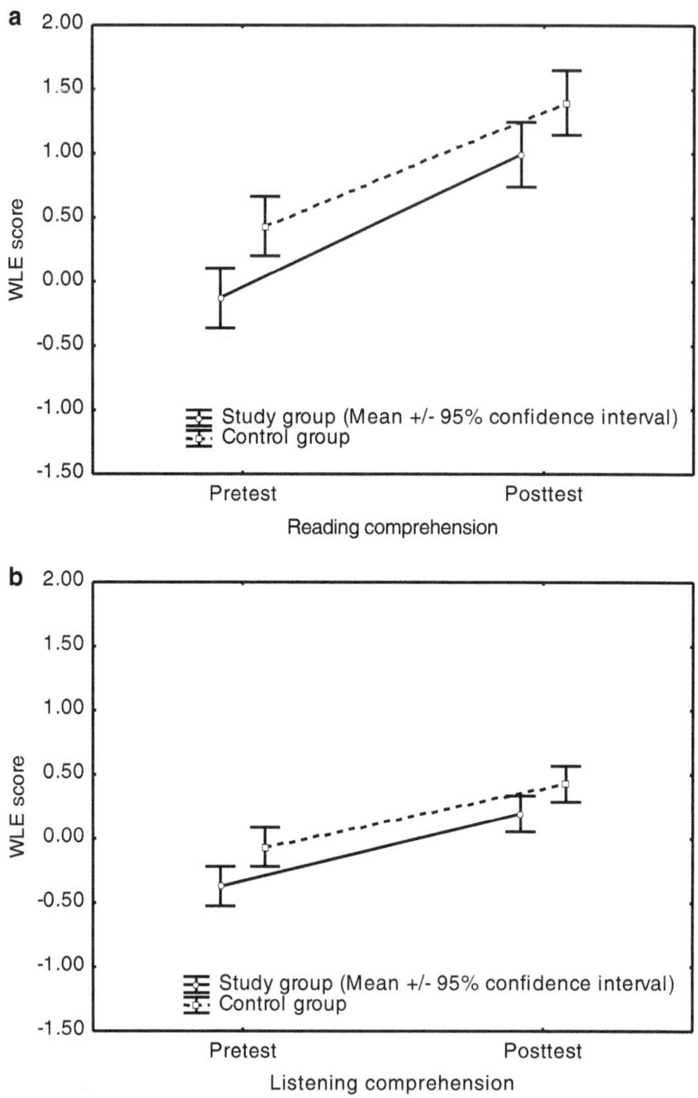

Fig. 20.2 German achievement of the study and control groups at pretest and posttest

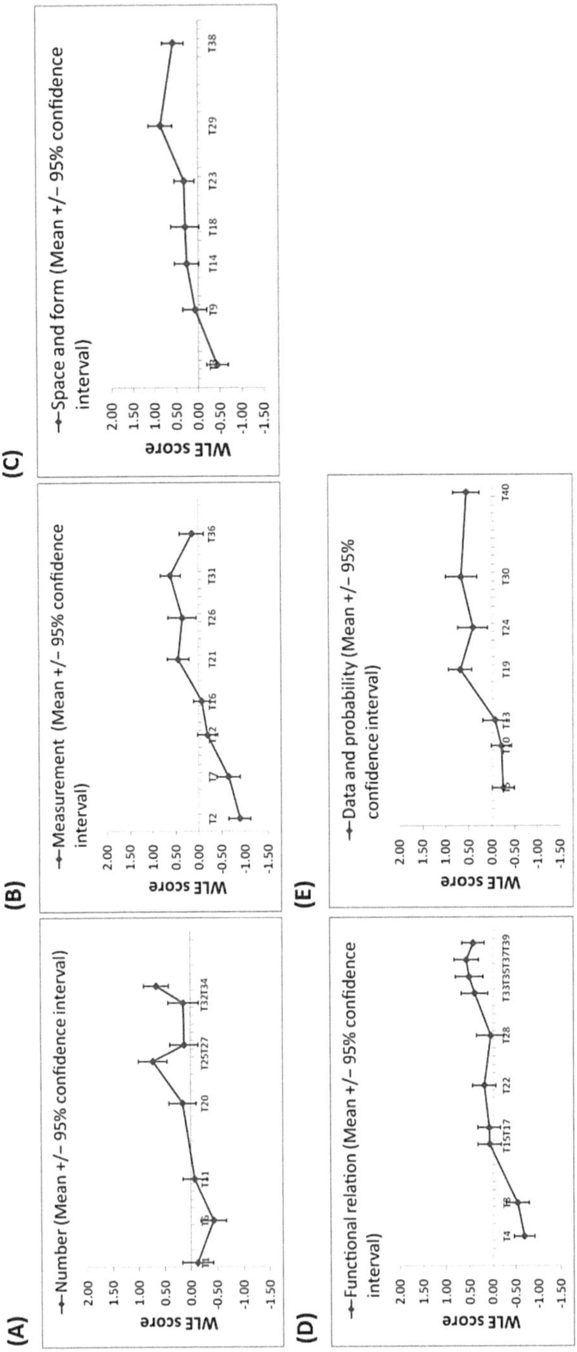

Fig. 20.3 Trajectories of mathematics achievement in different domains across the 40 measurement occasions of the longitudinal study

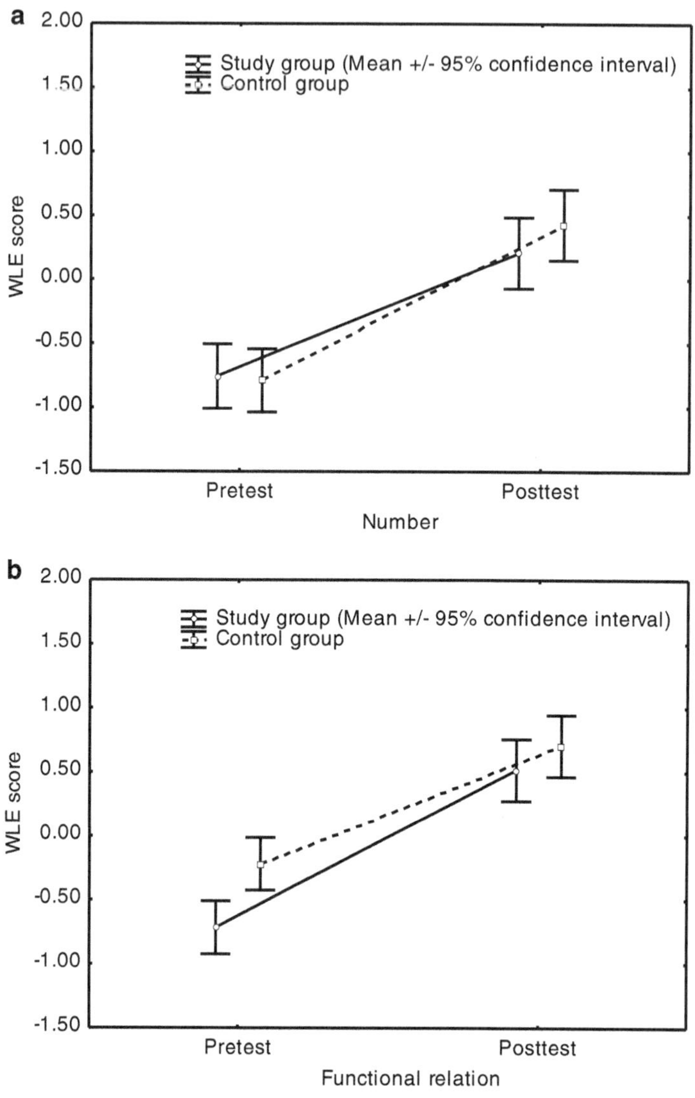

Fig. 20.4 Mathematics achievement of the study and control groups at pretest and posttest

Mean levels of performance at pretest and at posttest for the study group and the control group are displayed in Fig. 20.4. As can be seen in Fig. 20.4, students in the study group showed higher levels of performance at later measurement occasions, indicating that their mathematics achievement increased over the course of two academic years, from beginning of the ninth grade until the end of the tenth grade. As is evident in Fig. 20.4, the findings did not reveal any hint that students in the study group showed greater improvements in mathematics achievements. On the contrary, the findings suggest that students in the control group showed even larger improvements in the number domain. This could be due to the higher percentage of students attending Gymnasium (the school track that typically prepares student for a university education) in the control group. These findings suggest that participation in the intensive-longitudinal study did not improve student achievement in mathematics. Similar conclusions can be reached by examining the effect sizes for improvement in mathematics achievement for the study and control groups. In the number domain, students in the study group showed an increase of $d = 0.66$ ($M_{pre} = -0.77$; $SD_{pre} = 1.49$; $M_{post} = 0.21$; $SD_{post} = 1.51$). Students in the control group showed an even larger increase in the number domain ($d = 1.05$; $M_{pre} = -0.79$; $SD_{pre} = 1.16$; $M_{post} = 0.43$; $SD_{post} = 1.47$). Students in the study group showed an increase of $d = 1.04$ in the domain of functional relation ($M_{pre} = -0.72$; $SD_{pre} = 1.19$; $M_{post} = 0.52$; $SD_{post} = 1.38$). Students in the control group showed a similar increase in the domain of functional relation ($d = 0.90$; $M_{pre} = -0.22$; $SD_{pre} = 1.02$; $M_{post} = 0.70$; $SD_{post} = 1.21$). Taken together, these findings suggest that mathematics achievement improved by approximately two thirds to a full standard deviation unit across the two academic school years, from the beginning of ninth grade until the end of tenth grade.

Among the WLE scores displayed in Fig. 20.1, the within-domain correlations were moderate to high, and similar across the five domains (ranging from $r = .42$ to $r = .73$ for number, from $r = .43$ to $r = .61$ for measurement, from $r = .54$ to $r = .73$ for space and form, from $r = .48$ to $r = .75$ for functional relation, and from $r = .35$ to $r = .66$ for data and probability). At pretest and posttest, across-domain correlations between number and functional relation were of moderate magnitude ($r = .53$ at pretest and $r = .61$ at posttest).

20.6 Summary and Discussion

The aim of this chapter was to present an intensive-longitudinal study of student achievement and cognitive abilities, and to provide descriptive findings on the development of student achievement in German language and mathematics across two academic years, from ninth to tenth grade. One hundred and twelve students who initially attended ninth grade, and who were from different school tracks in the German school system, participated in the study and completed 44 assessments, including four pretest and posttest sessions over two academic years. A control group of 113 students participated only in the pretest and the posttest. Our findings showed that student achievement increased over the course of two academic years, with effect sizes amounting to about 60–80 % of a full standard deviation unit for German achievement, and effect sizes amounting to about two thirds to a full standard deviation unit for mathematics achievement. Furthermore, our findings did not reveal any evidence that the increase in student achievement was higher in the study group. This finding is in line with our previous report (Hülür et al. 2011b) on a subsample of Gymnasium students. In this previous study, we examined changes in student achievement and school grades from pretest to posttest in the study and control groups. The latent change score model showed complete measurement invariance for the study and control groups, and our findings revealed that students whose standardized test performance improved from pretest to posttest also showed improvements in their respective school grades. Taken together, these results suggest that findings from future studies using the intensive-longitudinal data can be interpreted without concern for confounding learning effects related to retest. Another common concern is that repeated administration of test materials might lead to improvement in test-taking skills, in turn improving student performance. Independent of such test-taking skills, it may also be expected that assessment of learning might operate as a confounding factor by increasing students' involvement with test materials, leading to learning effects. Our study did not indicate any evidence for improved test-taking skills or learning effects through increased involvement with test materials.

In closing, we note several limitations of our study. To begin with, we used item parameters from a nationally representative norming study as fixed values in one-dimensional Rasch models, in order to achieve scores in the same metric across all measurement occasions. However, this procedure did not always result in optimal estimates. For example, as can be seen in Figs. 20.1 and 20.3, mean performance levels showed high fluctuations for some domains. In order to investigate the variability of mean performance over 40 measurement points, several methods can be implemented to examine the linking error, such as analysis of differential item functioning, exclusion of items with extreme difficulties, examination of the role of school track in the norming study, of possible position and context effects in the norming study, and jackknifing procedures. In the jackknifing method, a sequence of analyses is performed, where in each case a single item is removed from the analysis. On the basis of these results, the standard error of the mean performance can be estimated (Monseur and Berezner 2007). To smoothe unexpected fluctuations in the mean curves, a compromise estimator could be defined that does not treat all item parameters as previously known and fixed. Using this approach, a functional form of the mean curve can be posed, and item parameters at time points with high fluctuations will effectively be left out in defining the mean curve (Michaelides 2010). More research is needed to derive better linking procedures for longitudinal studies. Also, the number of assessments, as well as the time intervals between assessments varied across the domains of student achievement assessed in the present study (see Table 20.1), because a similar number of measures was not available for each content domain.

Second, given that our study was quite time- and resource-intensive, a relatively small number of students participated. Our participants were a select sample of high achieving students—given that they attended the upper two tracks of the three-tier educational system in Germany. In this sample, we were able to demonstrate the practicality of intensive-longitudinal designs in studying student achievement. Future research should examine trajectories of student achievement over shorter time spans, in larger and more heterogeneous samples. Another limitation of our sample was that the students were not randomly assigned to study and control groups. Also, 42.9 % of the participants in the initial sample of the study group, and 17.5 % of the participants in the initial sample of the control group, respectively, left the study during the intensive-longitudinal phase, or did not take part in the posttest. The higher percentage of drop-outs in the study group could be explained by the particularly challenging design of the intensive longitudinal assessment, which required commitment over the course of two school years. It is important to note that students dropping out of the study prior to posttest belonged to groups that were underrepresented at the beginning of the study (e.g., boys, non-Gymnasium students). From this we conclude that in studies including volunteering students, sample selection could be a concern equally important to selective drop-out. Thus, future studies should seek practical solutions to motivate students from these underrepresented groups to participate in such studies and to maintain their participation.

Third, our study encompassed assessment of student achievement over 2 years with a time span of approximately 2 weeks between each assessment. School-related events, such as exams or the holiday schedule, are likely to be important factors explaining fluctuations in students' performance. Future studies with integrated micro- and macro-longitudinal designs that included more closely spaced assessments around those events would allow for (1) quantifying the amount of change in performance due to these events, and (2) assessing how students' behavior during these time periods relates to their trajectories in achievement. We conclude that intensive longitudinal data on student achievement, as presented in this chapter, provides many possibilities for examining antecedents, correlates, and consequences of student achievement.

Acknowledgments This research was supported by the Institute for Educational Progress (IQB), Humboldt University, Berlin, Germany, and by a grant from the German Research Foundation (DFG), awarded to Oliver Wilhelm and Alexander Robitzsch (WI 2667/7-1) in the Priority Program "Competence Models for Assessing Individual Learning Outcomes and Evaluating Educational Processes" (SPP 1293). Gizem Hülür and Fidan Gasimova were predoctoral fellows of the International Max Planck Research School: "The Life Course: Evolutionary and Ontogenetic Dynamics (LIFE)".

References

Adams, R., & Wu, M. (2002). *PISA 2000 Technical Report*. Paris: OECD.

Algina, J., Keselman, H. J., & Penfield, R. D. (2005). Effect sizes and their intervals: The two-level repeated measures case. *Educational and Psychological Measurement, 65*, 241–258. doi:10.1177/0013164404268675.

Aunola, K., Leskinen, E., Onatsu-Arvilommi, T., & Nurmi, J.-E. (2002). Three methods for studying developmental change: A case of reading skills and self-concept. *British Journal of Educational Psychology, 72*, 343–364. doi:10.1348/000709902320634447.

Bast, J., & Reitsma, P. (1998). Analyzing the development of individual differences in terms of Matthew effects in reading: Results from a Dutch longitudinal study. *Developmental Psychology, 34*, 1373–1399. doi:10.1037/0022-0663.97.3.299.

Baumert, J., Bos, W., Lehmann, R. (Eds.). (2000). *TIMSS/III. Dritte Internationale Mathematik- und Naturwissenschaftsstudie: Mathematische und naturwissenschaftliche Bildung am Ende der Schullaufbahn* [Third International Mathematics and Science Study: Mathematical and scientific literacy at the end of the school career]. *Band 1: Mathematische und naturwissenschaftliche Grundbildung am Ende der Pflichtschulzeit.* Opladen: Leske + Budrich.

Beck, B., & Klieme, K. (Eds.). (2007). *Sprachliche Kompetenzen, Konzepte und Messung: DESI-Studie (Deutsch Englisch Schülerleistungen International) [Language competencies, concepts and measurements: DESI-Study (German English student performance international)].* Weinheim: Beltz.

Becker, M., Lüdtke, O., Trautwein, U., & Baumert, J. (2006). Leistungszuwachs in Mathematik: Evidenz für einen Schereneffekt im mehrgliedrigen Schulsystem [Growth in mathematics achievement: Evidence for a scissor effect in a three-tracked school system]? *Zeitschrift für Pädagogische Psychologie, 20*, 233–242. doi:10.1024/1010-0652.20.4.233.

Bloom, H., Hill, C., Rebeck Black, A., Lipsey, M. (2008). Performance trajectories and performance gaps as achievement effect-size benchmarks for educational interventions. Retrieved from *MDRC Working Papers on Research Methodology.* http://www.mdrc.org/sites/default/files/full_473.pdf.

Bremerich-Vos, A., & Böhme, K. (2009). Lesekompetenzdiagnostik: Die Entwicklung eines Kompetenzstufenmodells für den Bereich Lesen [Assessment of reading competence]. In A. Bremerich-Vos, D. Granzer, & O. Köller (Eds.), *Bildungsstandards Deutsch und Mathematik* (pp. 219–249). Weinheim: Beltz.

Brunner, M. (2006). *Mathematische Schülerleistung: Struktur, Schulformunterschiede und Validität* [Student achievement in mathematics: Structure, school type differences and validity] (Doctoral dissertation, Humboldt-Universität Berlin, Berlin). Retrieved from http://edoc.hu-berlin.de/dissertationen/brunner-martin-2006-02-08/PDF/brunner.pdf.

Cahan, S., & Cohen, N. (1989). Age versus schooling effects on intelligence development. *Child Development, 60*, 1239–1249. doi:10.1111/j.1467-8624.1989.tb03554.x.

Compton, D. L. (2003). Modeling the relationship between growth in rapid naming speed and growth in decoding skill in first-grade children. *Journal of Educational Psychology, 95*, 225–239. doi:10.1037/0022-0663.95.2.225.

Cook, T. D., & Campbell, D. T. (1979). *Quasi-experimentation: Design and analysis issues for field settings.* Chicago: Rand McNally.

Ehmke, T., Blum, W., Neubrand, M., Jordan, A., & Ulfig, F. (2006). Wie verändert sich die mathematische Kompetenz von der neunten zur zehnten Klassenstufe [How does mathematical competence change from ninth until tenth grade]? In P. I. S. A.-K. Deutschland (Ed.), *PISA 2003. Untersuchungen zur Kompetenzentwicklung im Verlauf eines Schuljahres* (pp. 63–85). Münster: Waxmann.

Ferrer, E., McArdle, J. J., Shaywitz, B. A., Holahan, J. N., Marchione, K., & Shaywitz, S. E. (2007). Longitudinal models of developmental dynamics between reading and cognition from childhood to adolescence. *Developmental Psychology, 43*, 1460–1473. doi:10.1037/0012-1649.43.6.1460.

Grimm, K. J. (2008). Longitudinal associations between reading and mathematics. *Developmental Neuropsychology, 33*, 410–426. doi:10.1080/87565640801982486.

Hertzog, C., von Oertzen, T., Ghisletta, P., & Lindenberger, U. (2008). Evaluating the power of latent growth curve models to detect individual differences in change. *Structural Equation Modeling, 15*, 541–563. doi:10.1080/10705510802338983.

Hülür, G., Wilhelm, O., & Robitzsch, A. (2011a). Intelligence differentiation in early childhood. *Journal of Individual Differences, 32*, 170–179. doi:10.1027/1614-0001/a000049.

Hülür, G., Wilhelm, O., & Robitzsch, A. (2011b). Multivariate Veränderungsmodelle für Schulnoten und Schülerleistungen in Deutsch und Mathematik [Multivariate change models for student achievement and school grades in German and mathematics]. *Zeitschrift für Entwicklungspsychologie und Pädagogische Psychologie, 43*, 173–185. doi:10.1026/0049-8637/a000051.

Hülür, G., Wilhelm, O., & Schipolowski, S. (2011c). Prediction of self-reported knowledge with over-claiming, fluid and crystallized intelligence and typical intellectual engagement. *Learning and Individual Differences, 21*, 742–746. doi:10.1016/j.lindif.2011.09.006.

Jude, N., Klieme, E., Eichler, W., Lehmann, R., Nold, G., Schröder, K., et al. (2008). Strukturen sprachlicher Kompetenzen [Structure of language competencies]. In DESI-Konsortium (Ed.), *Unterricht und Kompetenzerwerb in Deutsch und Englisch* (pp. 191–201). Beltz: Weinheim.

Klieme, E. (2000). Fachleistungen im voruniversitären Mathematik- und Physikunterricht: Theoretische Grundlagen, Kompetenzstufen und Unterrichtsschwerpunkte [Academic performance in pre-university mathematics and physics: Theoretical foundations, competence levels, and core themes of instruction]. In J. Baumert, W. Bos, & R. Lehmann (Eds.), *TIMSS/III. Dritte Internationale Mathematik- und Naturwissenschaftsstudie—Mathematische und naturwissenschaftliche Bildung am Ende der Schullaufbahn: Band 2. Mathematische und physikalische Kompetenzen am Ende der gymnasialen Oberstufe* (pp. 57–128). Opladen: Leske + Budrich.

KMK (Standing Conference of the Ministers of Education and Cultural Affairs of the States in the Federal Republic of Germany). (Ed.). (2005). *Bildungsstandards der Kultusministerkonferenz, Erläuterungen zur Konzeption und Entwicklung. Beschluss vom 16.12.2004* [Educational standards, conception and development: Resolution approved by the Standing Conference on 16 December 2004]. Neuwied: Luchterhand.

Michaelides, M. P. (2010). A review of the effects on IRT item parameter estimates with a focus on misbehaving common items in test equating. *Frontiers in Quantitative Psychology and Measurement, 1*(167). doi:10.3389/fpsyg.2010.00167.

Monseur, C., & Berezner, A. (2007). The computation of equating errors in international surveys in education. *Journal of Applied Measurement, 8*, 323–335.

Muthén, B. O., & Khoo, S. T. (1998). Longitudinal studies of achievement growth using latent variable modeling. *Learning and Individual Differences, 10*, 73–101. doi:10.1016/S1041-6080(99)80135-6.

Muthén, B. O., Khoo, S.-T., & Goff, G. N. (1997). *Multidimensional description of subgroup differences in mathematics achievement data from the 1992 National Assessment of Educational Progress*. Los Angeles: CRESST/University of California.

OECD (Organisation for Economic Co-operation and Development). (1999). *Measuring student knowledge and skills: A new framework for assessment*. Paris: Author.

Oller, J. W. (1976). Evidence for a general language proficiency factor: An expectancy grammar. *Die Neueren Sprachen, 75*, 165–174.

Rescorla, L., & Rosenthal, A. S. (2004). Growth in standardized ability and achievement test scores from third to tenth grade. *Journal of Educational Psychology, 96*, 85–96.

Retelsdorf, J., & Möller, J. (2008). Entwicklungen von Lesekompetenz und Lesemotivation: Schereneffekte in der Sekundarstufe [Developments in reading literacy and reading motivation: Achievement gaps in secondary school]? *Zeitschrift für Entwicklungspsychologie und Pädagogische Psychologie, 40*, 179–188. doi:10.1026/0049-8637.40.4.179.

Sang, F., Schmitz, B., Vollmer, H. J., Baumert, J., & Roeder, P. M. (1986). Models of second language competence: A structural equation approach. *Language Testing, 3*, 54–79. doi:10.1177/026553228600300103.

Schipolowski, S., Böhme, K., Neumann, D., Vock, M., Pant, H. A. (2010). *Bereitstellung eines pilotierten und normierten Aufgabenpools für kompetenzbasierte Vergleichsarbeiten im Fach Deutsch in der 8. Jahrgangsstufe im Schuljahr 2009/2010* [Provision of a piloted and standardized item pool for competence-based assessments in German]. (Technical Report). Berlin: IQB.

Schmiedek, F., Lövdén, M., & Lindenberger, U. (2010). Hundred days of cognitive training enhance broad cognitive abilities in adulthood: Findings from the COGITO study. *Frontiers in Aging Neuroscience, 2*(27). doi:10.3389/fnagi.2010.00027.

Schmitz, B. (2006). Advantages of studying processes in educational research. *Learning and Instruction, 16*, 433–449. doi:10.1016/j.learninstruc.2006.09.004.

Shin, S.-K. (2005). Did they take the same test? Examinee language proficiency and the structure of language tests. *Language Testing, 22*, 31–57. doi:10.1191/0265532205lt296oa.

Siegler, R. S., & Svetina, M. (2006). What leads children to adopt new strategies? A microgenetic/cross sectional study of class inclusion. *Child Development, 77*, 997–1015. doi:10.1111/j.1467-8624.2006.00915.x.

Strathmann, A., & Klauer, K. J. (2010). Lernverlaufsdiagnostik: Ein Ansatz zur längerfristigen Lernfortschrittsmessung [Measurement of learning trajectories: An approach to long-term measurement of learning progress]. *Zeitschrift für Entwicklungspsychologie und Pädagogische Psychologie, 42*, 111–122.

Strathmann, A., Klauer, K. J., & Greisbach, M. (2010). Lernverlaufsdiagnostik. Dargestellt am Beispiel der Rechtschreibkompetenz in der Grundschule [Measurement of learning trajectories. The development of writing competency in primary school]. *Empirische Sonderpädagogik, 2*, 64–77.

Walberg, H., & Tsai, S. (1983). Matthew effects in education. *American Educational Research Journal, 20*, 359–373. doi:10.3102/00028312020003359.

Warm, T. A. (1989). Weighted likelihood estimation of ability in item response theory. *Psychometrika, 54*, 427–445. doi:10.1007/BF02294627.

Part V
Innovations in Psychometric Models and Computer-Based Assessment

Chapter 21
Multidimensional Structures of Competencies: Focusing on Text Comprehension in English as a Foreign Language

Johannes Hartig and Claudia Harsch

Abstract The project "Modeling competencies with multidimensional item-response-theory models" examined different psychometric models for student performance in English as a foreign language. On the basis of the results of re-analyses of data from completed large scale assessments, a new test of reading and listening comprehension was constructed. The items within this test use the same text material both for reading and for listening tasks, thus allowing a closer examination of the relations between abilities required for the comprehension of both written and spoken texts. Furthermore, item characteristics (e.g., cognitive demands and response format) were systematically varied, allowing us to disentangle the effects of these characteristics on item difficulty and dimensional structure. This chapter presents results on the properties of the newly developed test: Both reading and listening comprehension can be reliably measured (rel = .91 for reading and .86 for listening). Abilities for both sub-domains prove to be highly correlated yet empirically distinguishable, with a latent correlation of .84. Despite the listening items being more difficult, in terms of absolute correct answers, the difficulties of the same items in the reading and listening versions are highly correlated (r = .84). Implications of the results for measuring language competencies in educational contexts are discussed.

Keywords English as a foreign language • Multidimensional IRT • Item difficulties

J. Hartig (✉)
German Institute for International Educational Research (DIPF), Frankfurt/Main, Germany
e-mail: hartig@dipf.de

C. Harsch
University of Bremen, Bremen, Germany
e-mail: harsch@uni-bremen.de

D. Leutner et al. (eds.), *Competence Assessment in Education*, Methodology of Educational Measurement and Assessment, DOI 10.1007/978-3-319-50030-0_21

21.1 Introduction

The project "Modeling competencies with multidimensional item-response-theory models" (MIRT) examined different psychometric models for measuring receptive skills in English as a foreign language. The text comprehension process is characterized by a set of complex interacting factors that contribute to test item difficulty. Modeling item difficulty for tests targeting receptive skills is a recurrent theme in language testing research, since predicting item difficulty allows for reporting test results in an understandable way, improves item writer guidelines, and facilitates validation studies (e.g., Embretson 1998; Freedle and Kostin 1993; Grotjahn 2000; Lumley et al. 2012). Despite much research on which characteristics can best predict item difficulty, no study has yet reported a systematic examination of item difficulty-determining characteristics (IDCs) across the two receptive domains of listening and reading. Hence, a new test for reading and listening comprehension was constructed, operationalizing selected IDCs on the basis of the results of previous studies. In this test, both the reading and listening tasks are based on the same text material and make use of the same items, thus allowing for a closer examination of the relationship between the abilities required for the comprehension of both written and spoken texts. Furthermore, since the difficulty-determining characteristics were systematically varied across both domains, analyzing the test data allows for disentangling the effects of these characteristics on item difficulty and dimensional structure.

We first outline the test construction before presenting the results of the properties of the newly developed test and details of the multidimensional IRT analyses. Finally, we discuss implications of the results for the measurement of language competencies in educational contexts.

21.2 Test Development

The test reported here, aimed at ninth graders in the two higher school tracks of the triadic German school system, was in line with two national large-scale assessment studies that had been the focus of prior research which informed the current project: the DESI study (Beck and Klieme 2007; DESI-Konsortium 2008) and tests to evaluate the National Educational Standards (Rupp et al. 2008; Harsch et al. 2010).

21.2.1 Item Characteristics

In the re-analyses of the receptive tests of these two large-scale assessments, we examined IDCs that were reported in the literature to have effects on item difficulty; we employed human ratings and corpus analyses (Hartmann 2008; Hartig et al.

2009; Höhler 2012). For the test development reported here, we selected the following four IDCs, which had shown the highest explanatory power in the re-analyses: Linguistic demands of the input, speed of delivery (listening only), cognitive operations (i.e., comprehension processes) and item format. With regard to the linguistic demands of the input, we employed the Common European Framework of Reference (CEFR; Council of Europe 2001) in order to specify the level of proficiency required for a test taker to process the input successfully. The CEFR is the reference point for educational standards in Germany, and the receptive tasks in DESI have also been aligned to it, so that the CEFR offers a common point of reference between the three assessment studies. For the tests reported here, the four IDCs were defined in the item writer guidelines as follows:

1. The texts/inputs are to be placed at one of the following three difficulty levels, which should be accessible for learners situated at CEFR-levels A2, B1, B2 (e.g., Leucht et al. 2012). The following aspects are characteristic for each of the three targeted *text levels*:
   - A2: short texts; concrete and familiar topics; highly frequent vocabulary; basic grammatical phenomena, simple sentences; clear text structure;
   - B1: texts of medium length with accessible topics; some topic-specific but still frequent vocabulary; frequent linguistic structures with some complex patterns; uncomplicated text structure;
   - B2: longer and more complex texts, topics can be more abstract; less frequent and partly specialized vocabulary; grammatical structures can be complex and less frequent; text structure complex but with clear signaling.
2. For the listening input, we aimed at two variations of the *speech rate* for each of the targeted levels A2, B1 and B2, in order to systematically examine the effects of speed and articulation (e.g., Solmecke 2000). Here, some adjustment with audio editing software was allowed, as long as the input still sounded natural to a native speaker.
   - Slow, clearly articulated standard speech; slight accent acceptable as long as it is clearly articulated and familiar;
   - Normal to fast speech rate, with less clear articulation; familiar accents and dialects.
3. The items should operationalize one of the following five *cognitive operations* (e.g., Alderson et al. 2006; Nold and Rossa 2007) that define the construct of the test; they refer to the processes that are considered necessary in order to solve an item and find the answer in the text. The first four operations are assumed to be of ascending difficulty, in line with the cognitive process model suggested by Khalifa and Weir (2009), while the fifth—reading/listening for gist—is anticipated not to follow this order but to constitute a "sub-skill" of its own; one aim of the MIRT project is to examine such multidimensionality.
   - Recognition of explicit verbatim information in the text, also called scanning.

Table 21.1 Matrix of IDCs with numbers of items constructed for each combination of characteristics

		Text level					
		Accessible for A2		Accessible for B1		Accessible for B2	
		Speed		**Speed**		**Speed**	
		slow	fast	slow	fast	slow	fast
Cognitive Operation	**Response Format**	*Task 1*	*Task 2*	*Task 3*	*Task 4*	*Task 5*	*Task 6*
Recognition	MC	2	2	3	2	2	2
	SAQ	2	2	1	3	2	2
Simple retrieval	MC	1	2	2	3	3	2
	SAQ	**0**	1	3	1	3	3
Careful reading/ listng.	MC	4	**0**	1	**0**	1	3
	SAQ	1	**0**	1	2	1	1
Complex inferences	MC	1	1	1	1	1	1
	SAQ	1	1	1	2	1	**0**
Gist	MC	1	0	0	1	1	0
	SAQ	0	1	1	0	0	1

MC multiple choice, *SAQ* short open answer. Figures in bold mark combinations that could not be operationalized as intended

- Simple retrieval of information that is explicitly stated in the text, but paraphrased in the item; this involves searching for information or understanding simple paraphrases.
- Careful reading/listening in order to understand main ideas and relevant supporting information, which can be stated explicitly or implicitly in the text; if the information or idea is implied in the text, it is relatively simple to retrieve.
- Complex Inferences, using background knowledge, evaluating information not completely provided in in the text, such as identifying an author's stance or a narrator's appeal.
- Reading/listening in order to understand the gist.

4. We distinguished two *response formats* (e.g., Gorin et al. 2002; Shohamy 1984), in relation to the hypothesis that open answers are more difficult than multiple choice items; the MIRT project also aimed at examining whether the format constitutes a dimension of its own across the two domains of reading and listening.

   - MC items with four options;
   - Short answer questions (SAQ) that require a maximum of ten words (spelling and grammar not taken into consideration if answer is identifiably correct).

IDCs are usually correlated across test items, as test developers tend to manipulate several characteristics simultaneously (e.g., complexity of the stimulus as well as the response format) in order to construct items at a specific level of difficulty. An important aim of the test construction in the MIRT project was to disentangle effects of different IDCs. Therefore, IDC levels were systematically balanced across test items. Table 21.1 illustrates the test design and how the four IDCs were to be operationalized in test items. Each cell in the matrix was intended to be operationalized by at least one item; the figures in Table 21.1 show the actual number of items finally developed, with the figures in bold highlighting cells that could not be operationalized as intended; we explain the reasons below. The aim of varying IDCs independently of each other was achieved; the correlations of IDCs across items were all close to zero ($r < .10$).

21.2.2 Item Development

Three teachers who had previously been trained in test development were recruited to develop the tests and operationalize the matrix; a fourth trained teacher, a native speaker of English, was recruited to give feedback and check for linguistic appropriateness. The development started with selecting suitable authentic input that was available in both audio and written form on the internet. First, the listening items were constructed; here, a process called "mapping" (Sarig 1989) was employed wherein all three teachers would listen to the input several times: firstly to note the gist, then to scan/listen selectively to the input for relevant specific information, and lastly to listen carefully for main ideas, supporting details and implicit information. The results of this mapping were then compared and a consensus was reached. This process yielded the outcomes of the different targeted cognitive operations, on the basis of which the test questions could be constructed. This is one way to aim for construct-valid test items. It has to be conceded that, due to the aim of systematically balancing the selected IDCs, some items may seem contrived; the teachers did, however, strive to develop meaningful questions. Certain combinations of IDCs were harder to realize than others. In particular, higher cognitive operations were more difficult to combine with multiple choice responses and with less-demanding text levels. Nevertheless, the developers succeeded in constructing items with almost all desired combinations of IDCs; only a few combinations were not realized at all (see Table 21.1).

In the next step, the native speaker and the project team gave feedback on the tasks, which were then revised accordingly. This was followed by a pilot study conducted by the item developers in their classes, separately for listening and reading. We had a total of 12 classes and 150 students per item.

On the basis of the item analyses (based on classical test theory) of the pilot studies, the items were either excluded or revised. This resulted in six listening/reading tasks with a total of 82 items operationalizing the four IDCs, as outlined in the matrix in Table 21.1 above. While we originally aimed to fill each cell in the matrix with one item, it turned out that not all cells could meaningfully be filled with an item (e.g., some texts did not lend themselves to high inferencing; there is only one gist of a text, so we could not ask two gist questions per text), while other cells could be operationalized with more than one item. Each item was rated with regard to the mentioned IDCs by the item-writers; they also rated the CEFR-level that a test taker should minimally have reached in order to successfully solve the item.

21.2.3 Validation of Item Characteristics

The ratings of text level and cognitive operations were validated in a separate step by two trained students (one undergraduate student in educational science and one masters student in teaching English as a foreign language), with a view to examining the reliability of the test items and the validity with which they operationalized the matrix. The intraclass correlation coefficients (ICCs) for a two-way random effects model ($ICC_{A,k}$), indicating the degree of absolute agreement for average measures, were calculated to examine inter-rater agreement (Shrout and Fleiss 1979). With respect to cognitive operations, agreement turned out to be good between raters (ICC = .80), as well as between raters and item developers (ICC = .86 for rater 1 and ICC = .77 for rater 2). For text level, however, agreement was perfect between item developers and rater 1, but low between rater 2 and the other ratings (ICC = .44). Overall, we would conclude that these results indicate a satisfactory level at which characteristics can be used to specify input and items. However, further research is needed here to confirm these indicative first results.

21.3 Test and Item Analysis

21.3.1 Sample and Data Collection

The newly developed tasks for reading and listening comprehension were presented to a sample of German ninth graders. 102 classes from the two higher school tracks of the German school system were recruited within the Rhine-Main area, resulting in a sample of $N = 2370$ students. Testing took about 90 mins. A matrix design was used to administer the tasks, with all students within one classroom answering the same booklet. Each booklet contained three listening and three reading tasks; the order of tasks was balanced across booklets. Every combination of tasks was realized at least once within the booklets, except for reading and listening tasks based on the same text. Each task was answered by about 50 % of the total sample, resulting in more than 1000 valid responses for each item.

21.3.2 Unidimensional Test and Item Analysis

In a first step, responses to reading and listening items were analyzed separately with unidimensional item response models. The analyses were conducted with the *TAM* package (Kiefer et al. 2014) within the R environment (R Development Core Team 2014) and with Mplus 7.11 (Muthén and Muthén 2012). For both domains, unidimensional Rasch models were analyzed. Additional analyses with the package *mirt* (Chalmers 2012) were conducted to examine local item dependencies within the unidimensional models.

The infit (weighted mean square) item fit statistic, item-score correlations and a graphical inspection of expected vs. observed scores were used to identify badly-fitting test items. On the basis of these criteria, ten reading items (12 %) and eight listening items (10 %) were dropped. For the resulting selection of items, the range of the infit was 0.79–1.24 for reading and 0.85–1.19 for listening. Three items were dropped in their reading and also in their listening version, while seven items were only discarded in their reading version, and five only in their listening version. EAP reliabilities for the two scales of the retained items were .91 for reading and .86 for listening. Overall, the results indicate that the development of the new reading and listening tests was successful in terms of yielding highly reliable scales and losing only a small number of items in the analysis and selection process.

21.3.3 Item Difficulties Across Domains

Item difficulties of reading and listening items were compared on the basis of 67 items that had been retained in the reading as well as the listening version. With an average of 46 % correct responses for reading and 36 % for listening, reading items turned out to be easier than listening items for our sample. This difference is statistically significant ($t = 6.72$; $df = 66$; $p < .001$) and corresponds to a large effect (Cohen's $d = 0.82$).

Despite this pronounced difference in overall difficulty level, item difficulties turned out to be highly related across domains. The correlation between item difficulties is $r = .80$ between percent correct responses and $r = .84$ between item difficulty parameters from the unidimensional Rasch models. Figure 21.1 displays the relations between the percentage of correct responses across items in both domains.

21.3.4 Local Dependencies

To have a preliminary look at possible multidimensionality within the scales for reading and listening comprehension, the Q3 statistic proposed by Yen (1984) was calculated for both scales using the *mirt* package (Chalmers 2012). This Q3 statistic is the correlation of residuals from a given IRT model—in our case, the Rasch model—and positive values indicate local dependencies between test items. Only very few dependencies were higher than the commonly used cutoff value of Q3 > .2 (Chen and Thissen 1997). For reading, seven item pairs (0.3 %) had Q3 values above .2; for listening, ten item pairs (0.4 %) had values above the cutoff. An inspection of the highest dependencies revealed mostly local phenomena; for example, pairs of neighboring items referring to the same text passage. The mean of the Q3 values was slightly negative (−.04 for reading and −.03 for listening), which is to be expected when local independence holds (Yen 1984). Overall, the screening for local item dependence yielded no indications of systematic multidimensionality not accounted for by the unidimensional Rasch models.

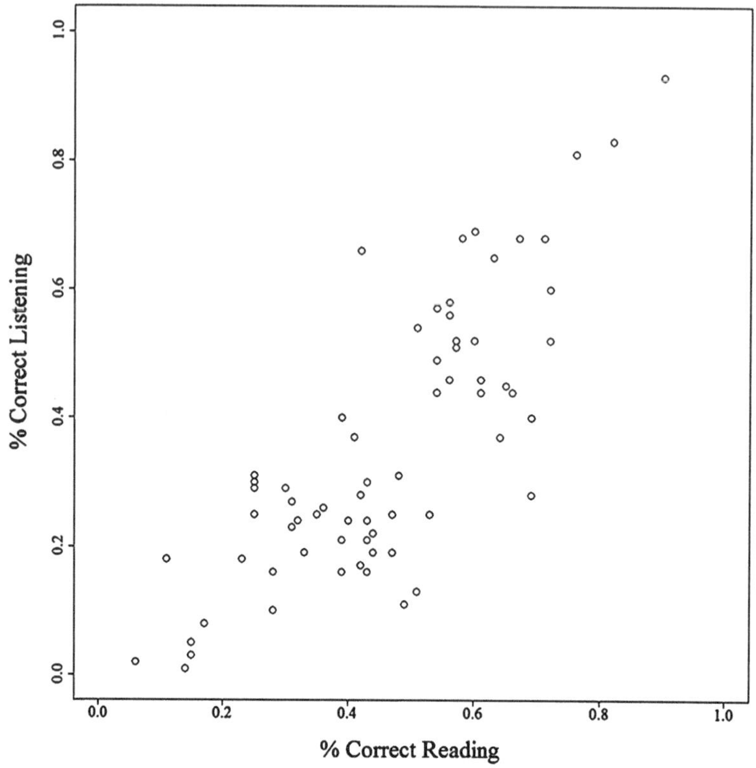

Fig. 21.1 Scatter plot of item difficulties (% correct responses) for 67 test items in their reading and in their listening versions

21.3.5 Multidimensional Analysis

A multidimensional Rasch model was used to estimate the relation between reading and listening comprehension. To ensure that differences between the abilities measured for both domains were not affected by item selection, only the 67 items retained in both versions were used for this analysis. The resulting latent correlation between reading and listening comprehension was .84, indicating that both receptive domains were strongly related yet empirically distinguishable. The separability of both domains is also supported by the fact that the two-dimensional model (137 free parameters) fits significantly better than a unidimensional model (136 free parameters, allowing for different item discriminations of reading and listening items) across both domains ($\text{LogLikelihood}_{1D} = -76{,}096$; $\text{LogLikelihood}_{2D} = -75{,}592$; BIC [Bayesian information criterion]$_{1D}$ = 153,249; BIC_{2D} = 152,248; AIC [Akaike information criterion]$_{1D}$ = 152,465; AIC_{2D} = 151,458; $\Delta\chi^2 = 2236.5$; $df = 1$; $p < .001$).

21.4 Discussion

21.4.1 Research Perspectives

The process of item construction used in the MIRT project aimed at balancing combinations of IDCs, resulting in IDCs being independent from each other across items. This may have resulted in somewhat "artificial" test items, as the item developers were forced to realize combinations of ICDs that would probably not occur in typical construction processes in educational evaluation studies without restrictions to item characteristics. Against the background of this possible limitation, it is all the more noteworthy that the test development turned out to be very successful. Only a few items had to be excluded from the test, and the resulting scales had very satisfying reliabilities. The newly constructed test items can be used for future research on receptive skills in English as a foreign language in a wide range of contexts. The reliabilities in our study were achieved with about 40 mins. of testing time per domain, meaning testing times of about 20 mins. would still result in reliability levels acceptable for research purposes (.75 for reading and .85 for listening, according to the Spearman-Brown prophecy formula; Brown 1910; Spearman 1910). An application of the tests that may prove particularly interesting is for studying reading and listening comprehension simultaneously, as they provide measures for both domains that are parallel with respect to item content. It has to be noted, however, that due to the parallel item content, the two dimensions assessed with the newly constructed test are probably more similar than they would be if assessed by separate tests using more authentic stimuli for everyday reading and listening situations. Our test is more likely to assess a two-dimensional ability of understanding text presented in different modes, rather than assessing distinct reading and listening competencies required in different contexts.

The fact that item characteristics were systematically balanced across items will allow a closer examination of the effects of these characteristics. This is particularly interesting with respect to item difficulties, as we selected characteristics that are known to have effects on item difficulty. Although local item dependencies don't indicate systematic multidimensionality within the scales, it could also be interesting to examine the effects of item characteristics on dimensionality, using confirmatory models. For example, closed versus open response formats have been shown to affect the dimensionality of language tests (e.g., Rauch and Hartig 2010; Wainer and Thissen 1993). Another angle worth analyzing is whether the above-outlined different cognitive operations, particularly the operation of understanding the main idea (gist), form separate dimensions within reading and listening skills, as this could inform diagnostic testing approaches.

21.4.2 Implications for Educational Contexts

As noted above, the tests developed are promising instruments for research purposes. They may, however, also be useful in applied contexts: for example, testing receptive language skills in classroom settings. Apart from the possible use of the tests developed within the project, the results that can be attained with the data already collected have general educational implications.

Our results indicate that reading and listening comprehension are distinguishable (although highly related) constructs, even when assessed with strictly parallel item content. This implies that both skills need separate attention in language classes; one is not necessarily be developed when the other is promoted. The item difficulties show that for the German ninth graders in our study, understanding spoken texts is the more difficult challenge than reading; this is in line with findings from the DESI study (Nold and Rossa 2008; Nold et al. 2008).

A deeper understanding of receptive language skills is important for testing as well as for teaching foreign languages. An examination of the empirical effects of IDCs on item difficulties could be useful for construct validation (construct representation; see Embretson 1983; Hartig and Frey 2012). If the effects of IDCs can be shown empirically, the assessed construct can be described in terms of the specific demands represented by the item characteristics. For instance, it can be tested whether reading comprehension in English as a foreign language is to be characterized by mastering specific cognitive operations and/or by mastering more difficult texts. For the reporting of test results, IDCs can be used to construct and describe proficiency levels for criterion-referenced feedback (Harsch and Hartig 2011; Hartig et al. 2012). When new test items are to be constructed, knowledge of the effects of IDCs can be drawn on to develop items targeted at specific difficulty levels.

Finally, an aim of ongoing work (e.g., Harsch and Hartig 2015) is to improve the link between scores from standardized language tests and the CEFR levels. These levels are more and more frequently used for criterion-referenced score interpretation, yet it is often not transparent how the link between test scores and CEFR levels is established. If certain combinations of IDCs can be aligned to certain CEFR levels; this would provide the basis for a transparent alignment between item content, test scores, and the CEFR.

Acknowledgments The preparation of this chapter was supported by grant HA5050/2-3 from the German Research Foundation (DFG) in the Priority Program "Competence Models for Assessing Individual Learning Outcomes and Evaluating Educational Processes" (SPP 1293).

References

Alderson, J. C., Figueras, N., Kuijper, H., Nold, G., Takala, S., & Tardieu, C. (2006). Analysing tests of reading and listening in relation to the common European framework of reference: The experience of the Dutch CEFR construct project. *Language Assessment Quarterly, 3*, 3–30. doi:10.1207/s15434311laq0301_2.

Beck, B., & Klieme, E. (Eds.). (2007). *Sprachliche Kompetenzen, Konzepte und Messung: DESI-Studie (Deutsch Englisch Schülerleistungen International). [Language competencies, concepts and measurements: DESI-Study (German English student performance international)]*. Weinheim: Beltz.

Brown, W. (1910). Some experimental results in the correlation of mental abilities. *British Journal of Psychology, 3*, 296–322. doi:10.1111/j.2044-8295.1910.tb00207.x.

Chalmers, R. P. (2012). mirt: A multidimensional item response theory package for the R environment. *Journal of Statistical Software, 48*(6). Retrieved from http://www.jstatsoft.org/article/view/v048i06/v48i06.pdf

Chen, W. H., & Thissen, D. (1997). Local dependence indexes for item pairs using item response theory. *Journal of Educational and Behavioral Statistics, 22*, 265–289. doi:10.2307/1165285.

Council of Europe. (2001). *The common European framework of reference for languages: Learning, teaching, assessment*. Cambridge, UK: Cambridge University Press.

DESI-Konsortium (Ed.). (2008). *Unterricht und Kompetenzerwerb in Deutsch und Englisch. [Instruction and competence development in the school subjects German and English]*. Weinheim: Beltz.

Embretson, S. E. (1983). Construct validity: Construct representation versus nomothetic span. *Psychological Bulletin, 93*, 179–197. doi:10.1037/0033-2909.93.1.179.

Embretson, S. E. (1998). A cognitive design system approach to generating valid tests: Application to abstract reasoning. *Psychological Methods, 3*, 380–396. doi:10.1037/1082-989X.3.3.380.

Freedle, R., & Kostin, I. (1993). The prediction of TOEFL reading item difficulty: Implications for construct validity. *Language Testing, 10*, 133–170. doi:10.1177/026553229301000203.

Gorin, J., Embretson, S., Sheehan, K. (2002, April). *Cognitive and psychometric modeling of text-based reading comprehension GRE-V items*. Paper presented at the meeting of NCME, New Orleans.

Grotjahn, R. (2000). Determinanten der Schwierigkeit von Leseverstehensaufgaben. [Difficulty determining characteristics of reading tests]. In S. Bolton (Ed.), *TESTDAF: Grundlagen für die Entwicklung eines neuen Sprachtests* (pp. 7–56). München: Goethe-Institut.

Harsch, C., & Hartig, J. (2011). Modellbasierte Definition von fremdsprachlichen Kompetenzniveaus am Beispiel der Bildungsstandards Englisch [Model-based definitions of competence levels in the case of the German educational standards]. *Zeitschrift für Interkulturelle Fremdsprachenforschung, 16*, 6–17.

Harsch, C., & Hartig, J. (2015). What are we aligning tests to when we report test alignment to the CEFR? *Language Assessment Quarterly, 12*, 333–362. doi:10.1080/15434303.2015.1092545.

Harsch, C., Pant, H. A., & Köller, O. (Eds.). (2010). *Calibrating standards-based assessment tasks for English as a first foreign language: Standard-setting procedures in Germany*. Münster: Waxmann.

Hartig, J., & Frey, A. (2012). Konstruktvalidierung und Skalenbeschreibung in der Kompetenzdiagnostik durch die Vorhersage von Aufgabenschwierigkeiten [Using the prediction of item difficulties for construct validation and model-based proficiency scaling]. *Psychologische Rundschau, 63*, 43–49. doi:0.1026/0033-3042/a000109.

Hartig, J., Harsch, C., Höhler, J. (2009, July). *Explanatory models for item difficulties in reading and listening comprehension*. Paper presented at the international meeting of the IMPS, Cambridge, UK.

Hartig, J., Frey, A., Nold, G., & Klieme, E. (2012). An application of explanatory item response modeling for model-based proficiency scaling. *Educational and Psychological Measurement, 72*, 665–686. doi:10.1177/0013164411430707.

Hartmann, C. (2008). *Schwierigkeitserklärende Merkmale von Englisch-Leseverstehensaufgaben* [The difficulty-determining characteristics of reading tests]. (Unpublished diploma thesis.) Humboldt-University Berlin, Berlin.

Höhler, J. (2012). *Niveau- und Strukturmodelle zur Darstellung von Schülerkompetenzen* [Level and structural models for students' competencies]. (Doctoral dissertation, Goethe University Frankfurt, Frankfurt.)

Khalifa, H., & Weir, C. J. (2009). *Examining Reading*. Cambridge, UK: Cambridge University Press.

Kiefer, T., Robitzsch, A., Wu, M. (2014). *TAM: Test Analysis Modules. R package version 1.0-2.* Retrieved from http://CRAN.R-project.org/package=TAM.

Leucht, M., Harsch, C., Pant, H. A., & Köller, O. (2012). Steuerung zukünftiger Aufgabenentwicklung durch Vorhersage der Schwierigkeiten eines Tests für die erste Fremdsprache Englisch durch Dutch Grid Merkmale [Guiding future task development for tests for English as a foreign language by predicting item difficulty employing the Dutch Grid]. *Diagnostica, 58*, 31–44. doi:10.1026/0012-1924/a000063.

Lumley, T., Routitsky, A., Mendelovits, J., Ramalingam, D. (2012). *A framework for predicting item difficulty in reading tests*. Retrieved from http://research.acer.edu.au/pisa/5

Muthén, L. K., & Muthén, B. O. (2012). *Mplus User's Guide* (7 ed.). Los Angeles: Author.

Nold, G., & Rossa, H. (2007). Hörverstehen. Leseverstehen [Listening and reading comprehension]. In B. Beck & E. Klieme (Eds.), *Sprachliche Kompetenzen: Konzepte und Messung. DESI-Ergebnisse Band 1* (pp. 178–211). Weinheim: Beltz.

Nold, G., & Rossa, H. (2008). Hörverstehen Englisch. [Listening comprehension in English]. In DESI-Konsortium (Ed.), *Unterricht und Kompetenzerwerb in Deutsch und Englisch: Ergebnisse der DESI-Studie* (pp. 120–129). Weinheim: Beltz.

Nold, G., Rossa, H., & Chatzivassiliadou, K. (2008). Leseverstehen Englisch. [Reading comprehension in English]. In DESI-Konsortium (Ed.), *Unterricht und Kompetenzerwerb in Deutsch und Englisch: Ergebnisse der DESI-Studie* (pp. 130–138). Weinheim: Beltz.

R Development Core Team. (2014). *R: A language and environment for statistical computing*. Vienna: R Foundation for Statistical Computing. Retrieved from http://www.R-project.org/

Rauch, D., & Hartig, J. (2010). Multiple-choice versus open-ended response formats of reading test items: A two-dimensional IRT analysis. *Psychological Test and Assessment Modeling, 52*, 354–379.

Rupp, A. A., Vock, M., Harsch, C., & Köller, O. (2008). *Developing standards-based assessment tasks for English as a first foreign language: Context, processes, and outcomes in Germany*. Münster: Waxmann.

Sarig, G. (1989). Testing meaning construction: can we do it fairly? *Language Testing, 6*, 77–94. doi:10.1177/026553228900600107.

Shohamy, E. (1984). Does the testing method make a difference? The case of reading comprehension. *Language Testing, 1*, 147–170. doi:10.1177/026553228400100203.

Shrout, P. E., & Fleiss, J. L. (1979). Intraclass correlations: uses in assessing rater reliability. *Psychological Bulletin, 86*, 420–428. doi:10.1037/0033-2909.86.2.420.

Solmecke, G. (2000). Faktoren der Schwierigkeit von Hörtests [Factors determining difficulty in listening tests]. In S. Bolton (Ed.), *TESTDAF: Grundlagen für die Entwicklung eines neuen Sprachtests* (pp. 57–76). München: Goethe-Institut.

Spearman, C. C. (1910). Correlation calculated from faulty data. *British Journal of Psychology, 3*, 271–295. doi:10.1111/j.2044-8295.1910.tb00206.x.

Wainer, H., & Thissen, D. (1993). Combining multiple-choice and constructed-response test scores: Toward a Marxist theory of test construction. *Applied Measurement in Education, 6*, 103–118. doi:10.1207/s15324818ame0602_1.

Yen, W. (1984). Effects of local item dependence on the fit and equating performance of the three parameter logistic model. *Applied Psychological Measurement, 8*, 125–145. doi:10.1177/014662168400800201.

Chapter 22
Multidimensional Adaptive Measurement of Competencies

Andreas Frey, Ulf Kroehne, Nicki-Nils Seitz, and Sebastian Born

Abstract Even though multidimensional adaptive testing (MAT) is advantageous in the measurement of complex competencies, operational applications are still rare. In an attempt to change this situation, this chapter presents four recent developments that foster the applicability of MAT. First, in a simulation study, we show that multiple constraints can be accounted for in MAT without a loss of measurement precision, by using the multidimensional maximum priority index method. Second, the results from another simulation study show that the high efficiency of MAT is mainly due to the fact that MAT considers prior information in the final ability estimation, and not to the fact that MAT uses prior information for item selection. Third, the multidimensional adaptive testing environment is presented. This software can be used to assemble, configure, and apply multidimensional adaptive tests. Last, the application of the software is illustrated for unidimensional and multidimensional adaptive tests. The application of MAT is especially recommended for large-scale assessments of student achievement.

Keywords Computerized adaptive testing • Item response theory • Multidimensional adaptive testing • Testing • Educational measurement

A. Frey (✉)
Friedrich Schiller University Jena, Jena, Germany

Centre for Educational Measurement (CEMO), University of Oslo, Oslo, Norway
e-mail: andreas.frey@cemo.uio.no

U. Kroehne
German Institute for International Educational Research (DIPF), Frankfurt/Main, Germany
e-mail: kroehne@dipf.de

N.-N. Seitz • S. Born
Friedrich Schiller University Jena, Jena, Germany
e-mail: nicki.nils@googlemail.com; sebastian.born@uni-jena.de

D. Leutner et al. (eds.), *Competence Assessment in Education*, Methodology of Educational Measurement and Assessment, DOI 10.1007/978-3-319-50030-0_22

22.1 Problem

The measurement of student competencies is a key element of modern output-oriented educational systems. On the basis of measured student competencies, the effectiveness of different aspects of educational systems is evaluated and sometimes far-ranging decisions are made. Given the high importance of student competence assessment, the instruments used for this purpose need to be theoretically accurate and psychometrically sound. However, it is difficult to meet both requirements simultaneously, since the theoretical frameworks underlying competence constructs are often complex. This means that, from a theoretical point of view, competence constructs can seldom be described by just one single aspect or—more technically—by just one latent variable. Much more often, competence constructs are specified as complex structures that include several interrelated components. The theoretical framework for mathematical literacy of the Programme for International Student Assessment (PISA), for example, differentiates between 14 components; three mathematical processes, seven fundamental mathematical capabilities, and four mathematical content categories (OECD 2013). Although it would be desirable to measure such a theoretical framework in its full complexity and to report precise scores for all components, this would inevitably necessitate very long testing sessions if conventional test instruments were used. As a consequence, in operational tests, competence constructs are often measured with severely reduced complexity in order to reach an acceptable testing time. Frequently, differentiated multidimensional theoretical frameworks are boiled down to one single dimension by the test instrument and/or the psychometric model used for scaling. This is problematic, because the resulting unidimensional test scores used for reporting cannot validly be interpreted with regard to the underlying theoretical framework.

Multidimensional adaptive testing (MAT; e.g., Frey and Seitz 2009; Segall 2010) offers a solution to this problem. MAT can achieve a much better fit between the theoretical underpinnings of complex competence constructs, test content and testing time, than testing with conventional, non-adaptive instruments can. This is possible for two reasons. First, in MAT, complex psychometric models can be used as measurement models. This makes it possible to include assumptions about the theoretical structure of a construct in the test instrument. Consequently, the resulting test scores can be interpreted unambiguously with regard to the theoretical framework. Second, very high measurement efficiency can be achieved with MAT. Thus, even complex constructs can be measured in a reasonable amount of time.

As psychometric models, multidimensional item response theory (MIRT; e.g., Reckase 2009) models are used in MAT. A general form for a MIRT model is the multidimensional three-parameter logistic model (M3PL). This model specifies the probability of a person $j = 1, \ldots, N$ correctly answering item i ($U_{ij} = 1$) as a logistic function of P latent abilities, $\boldsymbol{\theta}_j = (\theta_{j1}, \ldots, \theta_{jP})$ and a set of item parameters $\mathbf{a}_i$, b_i, and c_i:

$$P\left(U_{ij}=1|\boldsymbol{\theta}_j,\mathbf{a}_i,b_i,c_i\right)=c_i+\left(1-c_i\right)\frac{\exp\left(\mathbf{a}_i'\left(\boldsymbol{\theta}_j-b_i\mathbf{1}\right)\right)}{1+\exp\left(\mathbf{a}_i'\left(\boldsymbol{\theta}_j-b_i\mathbf{1}\right)\right)}. \tag{22.1}$$

The loading of item i on the different dimensions is represented by the $1 \times P$ item discrimination vector $\mathbf{a}_i^{'}$. The difficulty of item i is given by b_i. This parameter is multiplied with the $P \times 1$ -vector 1, which is filled with ones in order to use the same item difficulty for all dimensions. The pseudo-guessing parameter c_i can be regarded as a lower asymptote introduced to model item-specific random guessing. Different model structures can be incorporated into the M3PL by specifying the item discrimination vector $\mathbf{a}_i$ accordingly. Additionally, more simple models can be derived from Eq. 22.1 by imposing restrictions. If, for example, for all items of a test, exactly one element of the vector $\mathbf{a}_i^{'}$ is equal to one and all other elements are equal to zero, and $c_i = 0$, the multidimensional Rasch model results. However, even though the M3PL and the models that can be derived from it are frequently used in MAT, more complex MIRT models can also be applied (e.g., Frey et al. 2016; Mikolajetz and Frey 2016; Segall 2001).

The high measurement efficiency of computerized adaptive testing in general (uni- and multidimensional) is achieved by using information gained from the responses a participant has given to previous items. This information can be used to optimize the selection of the item that will be presented next (Frey 2012). In MAT, additional gains in measurement efficiency can be made by drawing on prior information about the multidimensional distribution of the measured dimensions. Segall (1996) suggested utilizing the $P \times P$ matrix $\mathbf{\Phi}$, including the variances of the measured dimensions and their covariances, to enhance ability estimation and item selection. As item selection criterion, Segall proposed selecting the candidate item i^* from the item pool (except the t already presented items) for presentation that maximizes the determinant of the matrix $\mathbf{W}_{t+i^*}$:

$$\left|\mathbf{W}_{t+i^*}\right| = \left|\mathbf{I}\left(\boldsymbol{\theta},\hat{\boldsymbol{\theta}}_j\right) + \mathbf{I}\left(\boldsymbol{\theta},u_{i^*}\right) + \mathbf{\Phi}^{-1}\right|. \tag{22.2}$$

The matrix $\mathbf{W}_{t+i^*}$ is derived by summing up the information matrix of the previously administered items, $\mathbf{I}\left(\boldsymbol{\theta},\hat{\boldsymbol{\theta}}_j\right)$, the information matrix of a response u_{i^*} to item i^*, $\mathbf{I}\left(\boldsymbol{\theta},u_{i^*}\right)$, and the inverse of the variance-covariance matrix $\mathbf{\Phi}$. The candidate item with the maximum value of Eq. 22.2 provides the largest decrement in the volume of the credibility ellipsoid around the current estimation of the latent ability vector $\hat{\boldsymbol{\theta}}_j$. In other words, the item is selected that makes the estimate $\hat{\boldsymbol{\theta}}_j$ more precise (see Yao 2014 for additional MAT item selection methods).

Using this strategy leads to a substantial gain in measurement efficiency compared to that achieved by conventional non-adaptive testing and a sequence of unidimensional adaptive tests (Frey and Seitz 2010; Segall 1996; Wang and Chen 2004). In their simulation study, Frey and Seitz (2010) found the measurement efficiency of MAT to be 3.5 times higher than in conventional testing, for highly correlated dimensions. Furthermore, MAT also proved to be very powerful under realistic test conditions. Making use of the operational item pool used in the PISA assessments from 2000 to 2006, and taking the typical restrictions of the study into account (link items, open items, testlets), the gain in measurement efficiency compared to conventional testing was still about 40 % (Frey and Seitz 2011). This increase in measurement efficiency can be used to report all ten of PISA's subdimensions (3 reading, 4 mathematics, 3 science) with sufficient reliability instead of reporting subdimensions for science only, as in PISA 2006 (Frey et al. 2013).

However, despite the salient advantages of MAT observed in simulation studies, empirical applications are still rare. This might be due to (1) a lack of uncomplicated methods to account for several constraints in the item selection process, (2) a lack of clarity about what exactly causes the high measurement efficiency of MAT, and (3) the absence of appropriate MAT software. In order to solve these problems, this chapter has four objectives:

1. To introduce an uncomplicated method that accounts for multiple constraints in MAT.
2. To clarify which proportions of the high measurement efficiency of MAT are due to item selection and which to ability estimation, respectively.
3. To present computer software that can be used to configure multidimensional adaptive tests, run pre-operational simulation studies, and administer multidimensional adaptive tests.
4. To describe the first steps towards the implementation of an operational multidimensional adaptive test.

The remaining text is organized into four sections, each of which is devoted to one of the four objectives. The chapter then closes with a conclusion and an outlook for the future of MAT.

22.2 Consideration of Multiple Constraints in MAT

In empirical applications of MAT, test specifications need to be managed. Test specifications are rules for the assembly of tests, and are generally expressed as constraints (Stocking and Swanson 1993). Especially in operational testing programs, it is often necessary for different test forms to be comparable with regard to a predefined set of test specifications. This requirement can be met by forcing the item selection algorithm of an adaptive test, to combine the rationale of maximizing statistical optimality with a strategy to fulfill the imposed constraints. Besides several other approaches to unidimensional computerized adaptive testing (UCAT; c.f. van der Linden 2005 for an overview), for MAT, the shadow test approach (Veldkamp and van der Linden 2002) is a frequently discussed and very flexible method. However, its implementation requires considerable knowledge of linear programming, is computationally intensive, and requires solver software. As an alternative to the shadow test approach, an uncomplicated method for dealing with multiple constraints in MAT is described in the following section, and the results from a simulation study evaluating its effectiveness will be presented.

22.2.1 Multidimensional Maximum Priority Index

The multidimensional maximum priority index (MMPI; Frey et al. 2011) is the multidimensional generalization of the maximum priority index method proposed by Cheng and Chang (2009). The MMPI is based on a $I \times K$ constraint relevance matrix **C**, where I is the number of items in the pool and K is the total number of constraints. The elements of **C** are $c_{ik} = 1$ if an item i is relevant for the constraint k and $c_{ik} = 0$ otherwise. The total number of constraints K is given by (a) the number of *constraint types* such as content area or answer key, and (b) the *levels* of these constraint types, such as mathematics, science, and reading, or key a, key b, key c, and key d as correct answers. Taking this example, for a test with three content areas and four answer keys, the total number of constraints would be seven.

During the item selection process, two major steps are taken: Firstly, the priority index (PI) for every eligible candidate item i^* in the item pool is calculated, and secondly, the item with the highest PI is selected. The PI for candidate item i^* can be computed with:

$$\mathrm{PI}_{i^*} = \left|\mathbf{W}_{t+i^*}\right| \prod_{K}^{k=1} (f_k)^{c_{i^*k}} \tag{22.3}$$

where $\left|\mathrm{W}_{t+i^*}\right|$ is the item selection criterion from Eq. 22.2 and f_k represents a scaled *quota left*. Suppose that T_k items for a constraint k are presented to each participant and that t_k items with this constraint have been administered so far, then f_k is given by:

$$f_k = \frac{(T_k - t_k)}{T_k}. \tag{22.4}$$

Thus, f_k quantifies how severely an item is needed at the present stage of the test. By multiplying the item selection criterion $\left|\mathbf{W}_{t+i^*}\right|$ with f_k, the MMPI offers a solution that combines aspects of maximizing measurement precision and managing test specifications in MAT.

22.2.2 Research Objective

To date, the MMPI has been proved to be capable of managing content constraints effectively without jeopardizing measurement precision (Born and Frey 2016). However, it is not yet known whether the MMPI can be used effectively to account for a larger number of constraints, and how much measurement precision would be affected by doing this. To provide this missing information, selected results from a comprehensive simulation study (Born and Frey 2013) are presented next.

22.2.3 Method

The simulation study was based on a full factorial design with two independent variables (IVs). In all conditions, three latent ability dimensions were considered. The first IV, *Constraint Management* (None, MMPI), compares item selection based solely on the criterion of statistical optimality with item selection using the MMPI approach. With the second IV, *Constraints* (5, 7, 9, 11), the total number of constraints was varied. In each cell of the design, 1,000 simulees were analyzed with 200 replications in regard to three dependent variables (DVs). The first two DVs were the percentage of constraint violations (*%Viol*) and the average number of violations (*#Viol*). Both DVs were used to evaluate the extent to which the constraints were fulfilled. *%Viol* was calculated by the ratio of the number of simulees per replication, with at least one constraint violation to the number of all simulees, multiplied by 100. *#Viol* is the average of constraint violations per replication. The third DV was the average mean squared error ($\overline{MSE}$) of the ability estimates across all *P* dimensions, computed by:

$$\overline{MSE} = \frac{1}{P \cdot N} \sum_{l=1}^{P} \sum_{j=1}^{N} \left(\hat{\theta}_{lj} - \theta_{lj} \right)^2 . \tag{22.5}$$

Thus, low values for the $\overline{MSE}$ denote high accuracy in the ability estimates.

22.2.4 Procedure

For the simulation study, 432 items (144 per dimension) associated with five constraint types were generated. One of the constraint types was the number of items presented per dimension, expressed by three constraints. The other four constraint types were additional constraint types representing any kind of item property (e.g., item format, answer key), each expressed by two constraints. Hence, in total, there were up to 11 constraints. Every item was relevant for one dimension and for four constraints. All in all, there were 48 constraint combinations (nine items per combination). The item difficulty parameters b_i were drawn from a uniform distribution, ranging from −3 to 3, $b_i \sim U(-3, 3)$. To ensure that the item difficulty distributions did not differ between the constraint combinations, item difficulties were generated separately for every combination.

The ability parameters were drawn from a multivariate normal distribution, $\boldsymbol{\theta} \sim MVN(\boldsymbol{\mu}, \boldsymbol{\Phi})$ with $\boldsymbol{\mu} = (0, 0, 0)$ and

$$\Phi = \begin{pmatrix} 1.00 & 0.85 & 0.85 \\ 0.85 & 1.00 & 0.85 \\ 0.85 & 0.85 & 1.00 \end{pmatrix}. \tag{22.6}$$

The high latent correlations of .85 between the three dimensions resemble the correlations typically found in large-scale assessments such as PISA.

The generated item and ability parameters were used to draw binary responses based on the multidimensional Rasch model. The simulations were carried out with SAS® 9.3, with a fixed test length of 60 items. In all conditions, the ability vector $\boldsymbol{\theta}_j$ was estimated by the multidimensional Bayes modal estimator (BME) using the true variance-covariance matrix $\boldsymbol{\Phi}$ from Eq. 22.6 as prior.

22.2.5 Results

The results of the simulation study are shown in Table 22.1. Under the condition of no constraint management, the observed percentages and the absolute numbers of violations were quite high. The MMPI met all imposed constraints in all conditions perfectly and thus was able to account for up to 11 constraints effectively. In regard to measurement precision, the results for no constraint management and the MMPI are virtually identical. Hence, in the present case, no "price" was paid for accounting for multiple constraints with the MMPI.

22.2.6 Discussion

We have introduced the MMPI as an uncomplicated method for dealing with multiple constraints in MAT, and evaluated it in a simulation study. The MMPI fulfilled the imposed constraints perfectly without a decrease in measurement precision. Nevertheless, the findings are restricted to test specifications in which the formulated constraints can be accounted for by the item pool, as in the present study. In practice, this is quite realistic because item pools are likely to be constructed in such a way that they can—in principle—meet the desired test specifications. In conclusion, the MMPI is a very promising uncomplicated method for the management of multiple constraints.

Table 22.1 Percentage of violations (%Viol), average number of violations (#Viol) and average mean squared error ($\overline{MSE}$) for all research conditions

Constraint Management	No. of Constraints	*%Viol*	*SE*	*#Viol*	*SE*	$\overline{MSE}$	*SE*
None	5	85.39	0.01	2.40	0.04	0.126	0.006
	7	96.80	0.01	3.99	0.05	0.126	0.006
	9	99.48	0.00	5.69	0.06	0.125	0.006
	11	99.96	0.00	7.71	0.06	0.125	0.005
MMPI	5	0.00	0.00	0.00	0.00	0.125	0.006
	7	0.00	0.00	0.00	0.00	0.126	0.006
	9	0.00	0.00	0.00	0.00	0.125	0.006
	11	0.00	0.00	0.00	0.00	0.125	0.006

22.3 Using Prior Information for Item Selection and Ability Estimation

MAT has considerably higher measurement efficiency than conventional non-adaptive tests or multiple unidimensional computerized adaptive tests (M-UCAT). Nevertheless, the relative contributions of the specific aspects of MAT that cause its high efficiency are not yet known. Two aspects of MAT can have a systematic impact on measurement efficiency. The first is *item selection*. In MAT, the item to be presented next is selected from an item pool covering several dimensions, instead of only one dimension, as in UCAT, making item selection more flexible. The second aspect of MAT likely to foster its measurement efficiency is *ability estimation*. When several dimensions are measured in MAT, multidimensional estimation (MEST) can be augmented by using the variance-covariance structure stored in $\mathbf{\Phi}$ as prior information for the derivation of Bayesian ability estimates, like the BME (Segall 1996). This information is not used for unidimensional estimation (UEST).

22.3.1 Research Questions

For the further development of MAT, it is important to understand which aspect of the method is responsible for its high measurement efficiency. This knowledge could be used, for example, to optimize the specification of adaptive test settings. In searching for this knowledge, the present study strives to answer the following three research questions:

1. How much efficiency can be gained by using multidimensional item selection in MAT instead of unidimensional item selection in M-UCAT?
2. How much efficiency can be gained by using Bayesian multidimensional ability estimation instead of Bayesian unidimensional ability estimation?
3. What is more important for the high measurement efficiency of MAT: item selection or ability estimation?

22.3.2 Method

Materials, Participants, and Design The research questions were examined with a simulation study based on the item pool characteristics of three operational, unidimensional dichotomously scored adaptive tests. These tests measure student competencies in reading (65 items), mathematics (105 items), and science (94 items), and were developed in the research project "Adaptive measurement of general competencies" (MaK-adapt; see "Empirical Application" section for project details).

The responses of $N = 1{,}632$ students were used to estimate item parameters of a three-dimensional Rasch model with between-item multidimensionality. Variances for mathematics (0.97), science (0.78), and reading (0.75), as well as latent correlations between mathematics and science (.83), mathematics and reading (.80), and science and reading (.77), were estimated from the same data.

The study was based on a fully crossed two-factorial design, with the IVs *Item Selection* (unidimensional, multidimensional) and *Final Ability Estimation* (UEST, MEST). Unidimensional item selection was conducted by sequentially presenting three unidimensional adaptive tests. Hence, M-UCAT was used in this condition with unidimensional provisional ability estimation. Multidimensional item selection was conducted by applying MAT with multidimensional provisional ability estimation. For both the unidimensional and the multidimensional item selection, Eq. 22.2 was used as item selection criterion.

Regarding the IV Final Ability Estimation, the BME was used for UEST and MEST. In the UEST condition, the final ability was estimated separately for each of the three dimensions, with the respective means and variances as priors. In the MEST condition, the final ability vectors were estimated simultaneously for all three dimensions, using the three-dimensional mean vector and the full empirical variance-covariance matrix as prior.

The research questions were examined by comparing the mean squared error (*MSE*) between the test conditions. Comparing the *MSE* between two conditions makes it possible to consider the relative efficiency (*RE*). According to de la Torre and Patz (2005), the *RE* is calculated as the ratio of the *MSE* of a baseline method to the *MSE* of a target condition. A value greater than 1.0 indicates that the target method is more efficient than the baseline method.

Procedure True abilities for a sample of 1,000 simulated test takers were drawn from a multivariate normal distribution with means of zero and variances, and correlations according to the prior. In all conditions, testing was terminated after 30 items. Ten items were presented per dimension for each M-UCAT, and the MMPI method was used to present comparable numbers of items for the three dimensions for MAT. 1,000 replications were simulated.

22.3.3 Results

Two different *RE*s were computed for each dimension: The *RE* for the comparison of unidimensional item selection (= baseline) vs. multidimensional item selection is related to the IV Item Selection (Research Question 1). The *RE* of UEST (= baseline) vs. MEST corresponds to the IV Final Ability Estimation (Research Question 2). The direct comparison of the two sets of *RE* values provides insights into the relative importance of item selection and final ability estimation, in relation to measurement efficiency (Research Question 3).

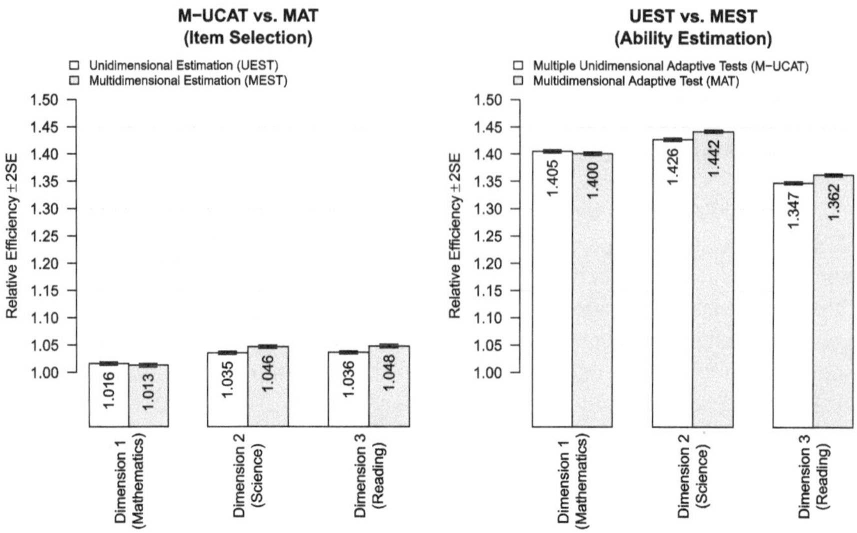

Fig. 22.1 Relative efficiencies of the independent variables item selection and ability estimation

The results displaying the relative gain in *MSE* when moving from unidimensional item selection to multidimensional item selection, are shown in the left part of Fig. 22.1. The relatively small values of 1.013–1.048 indicate that, by using multidimensional instead of unidimensional item selection, the average precision of the ability estimates was increased by 1.3–4.5 %. For reading and science, the *RE* of MEST was significantly higher than for UEST. For mathematics, no significant difference in *RE* was observed.

The relative decrease in *MSE* when using MEST instead of UEST is presented in the right part of Fig. 22.1. With *RE* values between 1.347 and 1.442, the effect of ability estimation is considerably larger than the effect of item selection: that is, the average precision of the ability estimates was increased by about 34.7–44.2 % by applying multidimensional instead of unidimensional final ability estimation. For reading and science, the *RE* values were significantly higher for multidimensional item selection (MAT) than for unidimensional item selection (M-UCAT). No significant differences were observed for mathematics. Overall, a comparison of the left and right parts of Fig. 22.1 reveals that the increased efficiency of MAT is obviously due mainly to the incorporation of multidimensionality into the final ability estimation (UEST vs. MEST), whereas the use of prior information for item selection, in conjunction with selecting items from a larger, multidimensional item pool (M-UCAT vs. MAT), is less important.

22.3.4 *Discussion*

The observed *RE*s were dimension-specific. This highlights the importance of pre-operational simulation studies that use the specific item pool to be used in a particular uni- or multidimensional adaptive test. The present study only focused on the *RE*; unremarkable results related to other dependent measures such as bias are not reported.

Based on the finding that the multidimensional ability estimation is especially relevant to the high measurement efficiency of MAT, specific modifications can be considered in order to adapt MAT to specific practical needs (Kroehne and Partchev 2010). One possible modification, MAT without an intermix of items from different dimensions, is described by Kroehne et al. (2014).

22.4 The Multidimensional Adaptive Testing Environment (MATE)

Given that about 20 years have passed since the first publications (Segall 1996; Luecht 1996), MAT is now coming of age. Various reasons for the application of MAT are described in the literature, such as increased measurement efficiency compared to UCAT and conventional testing (Frey and Seitz 2009), the possibility of estimating subdimensions with higher precision (Frey et al. 2013; Mikolajetz and Frey 2016), or improved facet scores (Makransky et al. 2013). However, the number of operational multidimensional adaptive tests is still very small.

One possible reason for the lack of applications, despite the very good performance of MAT in simulation studies, might be the absence of easy-to-use MAT software for pre-operational simulation studies and operational test administration.

To fill this gap, and to promote the application of MAT in empirical research, the *Multidimensional Adaptive Testing Environment* (MATE; Kroehne and Frey 2011) was developed within the research project "Multidimensional Assessment of Competencies" (MAT) under the priority program "Models of Competencies for Assessment of Individual Learning Outcomes and the Evaluation of Educational Processes" (SPP 1293), funded by the German Research Foundation (DFG). The programming was accomplished by the Technology-Based Assessment Unit (TBA) at the German Institute for International Educational Research. The software can also be used to perform flexible pre-operational simulation studies.

22.4.1 *Computerization of Items*

MATE can be used for items with a multiple choice response format (radio-buttons, check boxes) and for items with text input. The software allows for the importing of graphical material (image files or files in XPS format) to computerize items. Specific color markers and an optional control file can be used for a fully automated import of item banks.

Items can consist of one or multiple pages. Pages are assigned to so-called *entities*: that is, to chunks, which can be selected by an adaptive item selection algorithm. Buttons for forward and backward navigation between pages within entities can be added to the pages, to make items with multiple pages and unit structures possible.

22.4.2 Assignment of Item Parameters

Responses can be used either for logging only, or to be linked to one or multiple measured dimensions with an IRT model. MATE is appropriate for adaptive testing with dichotomously scored items scaled with a uni- or multidimensional IRT model (see Eq. 22.1). As a minimum, item difficulties and the assignments of the items to one of the dimensions of the test are necessary. Discrimination parameters for within-item or between-item multidimensionality and guessing parameters are optional. In addition, each response can be assigned to an integer number representing a content area (as a prerequisite for content management). Responses can also be assigned to item families; these families cannot be administered together within a single test. If pages are defined and responses are assigned to item parameters, operational testing and pre-operational simulations are possible.

22.4.3 Configuration of Tests and Test Batteries

Different test types can be administered and simulated with MATE: fixed forms (necessary for linear testing and calibration designs with multiple booklets), random selection of entities (for instance, to benchmark against adaptive testing), and UCAT, or MAT, depending on the properties of the item pool. Tests are organized into test batteries, allowing flexible combinations of adaptive tests, instructions and fixed test forms. User accounts can be generated or imported into MATE, and test administration can be resumed when interrupted.

In tests with IRT parameters, MLE and BME, as described by Segall (1996), can be used for ability estimation. The determinant of the posterior information matrix is evaluated for item selection in UCAT or MAT. The randomesque procedure (Kingsbury and Zara 1989) can be used for exposure control. The MMPI is implemented for content management. Test termination for adaptive tests can be defined by any combination of the following criteria: (1) overall number of entities, (2) number of entities in a particular dimension, (3) standard error in a particular dimension, and (4) testing time (not in simulation studies).

22.4.4 Pre-operational Simulation Studies

When IRT parameters are inserted or read into MATE, pre-operational simulations can be conducted to study the performance of a defined test. Typical research questions for pre-operational simulations include the comparison of different test specifications with respect to the resulting standard error, the mean squared error, the bias (conditional on theta), and the reliability of the test. Furthermore, pre-operational simulations can be used to study test specifications for different target populations. To run a pre-operational simulation study for a specific target population, true ability parameters can be drawn from one or multiple multivariate normal distributions or from one or multiple uniform distributions. To analyze the properties of an adaptive test with equal precision for selected points in the (multidimensional) ability space, alternatively, true ability parameters can be generated as replications, with true ability values corresponding to equidistant grid points. MATE makes it possible to export the generated true ability parameters, as well as to import existing values. Simulees can be assigned to groups, so that mixed ability distributions can be studied. Responses are automatically generated, randomly drawn from the probability computed from the specified IRT model using the (multidimensional) ability value of a simulee. To make it possible to simulate non-fitting IRT models, simulations with MATE can also be conducted with imported item-level responses, instead of with true ability values. The different dependent measures computed automatically for each cycle are summarized in Table 22.2.

Table 22.2 Dependent measures computed by MATE for each cycle of a simulation

Dependent Measure	Formula
Average Standard Error	$SE(\hat{\theta}_l)=\frac{1}{N}\sum_{j=1}^{N}\left(SE(\hat{\theta}_{jl})\right)$
Bias	$\text{Bias}(\hat{\theta}_l)=\frac{1}{N}\sum_{j=1}^{N}\left(\hat{\theta}_{jl}-\theta_{jl}\right)$
Approximated reliability as one minus the squared average standard error	$Rel(\hat{\theta}_l)=1-SE(\hat{\theta}_l)^2$
Root Mean Squared Error	$\text{RMSEA}(\hat{\theta}_l)=\sqrt{\frac{1}{N}\sum_{j=1}^{N}\left(\hat{\theta}_{jl}-\theta_{jl}\right)^2}$
Squared correlation between true and estimated ability	$Rel(\hat{\theta}_l)=cor(\hat{\theta}_l,\theta_l)^2$

All formulas given for $l = 1, \ldots, P$ dimensions and $j = 1, \ldots, N$ simulees

Plots representing the relationship between (1) true and estimated ability per dimension, (2) true or estimated ability and estimated standard error of ability, and (3) true or estimated ability and test length, are provided as graphical output.

Additional graphical information is given to summarize the item pool utilization and to visualize the change in the dependent measures during the testing process (with one point for each administered item). Additional simulation results are presented as text output. Multiple simulations can be conducted and stored within MATE under different settings; detailed results (including results for each simulee, results for each item, and the item level data) can be exported for further statistical analysis. Detailed descriptions of all input and output formats, as well as examples for the generated plots, are given in the user manual (Kroehne and Frey 2013).

22.4.5 Graphical User Interface, System Requirements, Availability and Manual

MATE is a Windows-based application with a user-friendly graphical interface that consists of five views: Pages, Entities, Tests, Test Taker, and Simulation. All of the main features of the program can be accessed by a point-and-click interface. No additional statistical software is necessary to work with MATE. However, the software runs on Microsoft Windows-based operating systems only, and requires an installed .NET framework 4.0 (or higher). MATE can be obtained free of charge for research and teaching purposes; a copy of the manual is included in the software package.

22.5 Empirical Application

The creation of MATE was an important step towards making an operational use of MAT possible in many test settings. Several time-intensive and demanding implementations are now directly available from a point-and-click interface. Thus, test developers do not need to program statistical routines for themselves, but can directly use MATE to computerize items, configure adaptive algorithms, run preoperational simulation studies, and deploy adaptive tests.

The first empirical application of MATE was realized in the research project MaK-adapt (Ziegler et al. 2016). MaK-adapt is one of six joint projects of the research initiative "Technology-based assessment of skills and competencies in VET" (ASCOT) funded by the German Federal Ministry of Education and Research. In the MaK-adapt project, computerized adaptive tests measuring student competencies in reading, mathematics, and science were developed and used by the other five ASCOT joint projects. Because some of the joint projects do not need data for all three domains to answer their specific research questions, three unidimensional adaptive tests were constructed.

Some of the items used in the three tests were written anew, but most were taken from existing large-scale assessments of student achievement (e.g., PISA, TIMSS, German Educational Standards for Mathematics). As item types, multiple choice, complex multiple choice, and short answer items were used. All items can be scored automatically by MATE. The initial item pool of 337 items (reading: 73 items; mathematics: 133 items; science: 131 items) was computerized and administered with MATE.

The items were given to a sample of $N = 1{,}632$ students in a calibration study in the year 2012. Since it would have taken too long for individual students to respond to all of the items, a balanced incomplete booklet design (e.g., Frey et al. 2009) was used to distribute the items to the students. The gathered responses were scaled separately for each domain with the unidimensional 1PL. This model is a special case of the M3PL in Eq. 22.1 with $\boldsymbol{\theta}_j = \theta_j$, $c_i = 0$, and $\mathbf{a}_i = a_i = 1$ for all items $i = 1, \ldots, I$. After item deletions were made due to poor model fit and differential item functioning (cf. Spoden et al. 2015), the item pools for reading, mathematics, and science amounted to 65, 105, and 94 items, respectively.

Based on the item pools, for each of the three domains, single unidimensional adaptive tests were configured using MATE. Several configurations were compared to each other in pre-operational simulation studies. In the final configuration, the first item was selected randomly from a set of ten items, with the highest information under the assumption of an average ability level. The one item with the highest information, given the examinee's provisional ability estimate (BME) was selected as the next item. This can be seen as a special case of Eq. 22.2, with $\boldsymbol{\theta} = \theta$ and $\boldsymbol{\Phi}$ only containing the variance of θ. In order to present comparable numbers of items for the different content areas within the domain, the MPI was used. The test was terminated after a pre-specified number of items were presented. This number could also be chosen by other ASCOT joint projects; this would enable them to find the balance between test length and measurement precision that best fits individual study objectives.

Figure 22.2 shows the expected reliability of the adaptive test for mathematics as a function of the number of presented items derived from a pre-operational simulation study with MATE ($N = 10{,}000$). The reliability was calculated with the squared correlation between the true and the estimated ability. It ascends rapidly and reaches a value of .76 after only 15 items. The results for the other two domains are similar. Note that, for a selection of 15 items with medium difficulty with respect to the target population, the expected reliability is .74. However, using items with medium difficulty brings at least two disadvantages, compared to UCAT. First, relatively few items are used, leading to the problem that an adequate construct coverage cannot be reached. Second, the statistical uncertainty of the ability estimates ($SE(\theta)$) is very small for participants in the middle of the scale only, but increases greatly towards the extremes of the scale. Hence, only students around the scale mean can be measured precisely, while the estimates for the others are very imprecise. The same problem accounts for group statistics such as means, variances, correlations, or others, for groups of students with very low or very high average ability. Thus, presenting a selection of items with medium difficulty would not be advantageous for most purposes, in comparison to CAT.

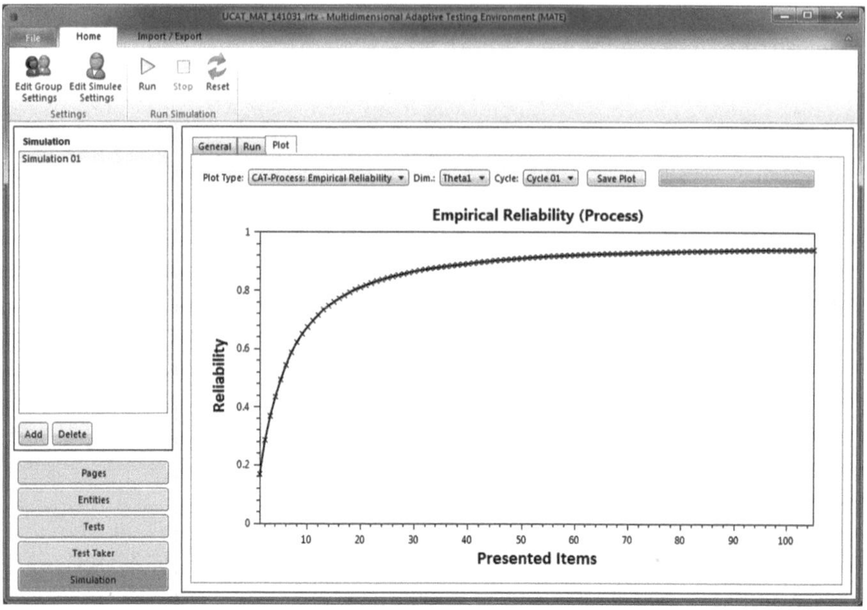

Fig. 22.2 Graphical output of MATE showing the reliability for the adaptive mathematics test as a function of number of presented items

In the ASCOT initiative, several thousand students had been tested with the MaK-adapt tests.

Going one step further, the three unidimensional adaptive tests were combined in a multidimensional adaptive test. Here, the MMPI was used to present comparable numbers of items per content domain. By moving from UCAT to MAT, an additional increase in measurement efficiency could be achieved. If, for example, a reliability of at least .75 is aimed at for all three domains, MAT will need a total number of 30 items while the three unidimensional adaptive tests would require 18 + 15 + 18 = 51. The three-dimensional adaptive test was recently trialed in an empirical study.

In summary, three unidimensional adaptive tests and a three-dimensional adaptive test were successfully set up, optimized based on pre-operational simulation studies, and delivered, in different studies in large-scale assessment contexts using the MATE.

22.6 Conclusion

MAT provides better solutions than conventional tests for a theoretically sound measurement of complex competence constructs. The main advantages of MAT are the possibility of directly including assumptions about the theoretical structure of the construct at stake into the test instrument, and its very high measurement efficiency. In the present chapter, four recent developments that foster the applicability of MAT have been presented.

First, a simulation study showed that multiple constraints can be accounted for in MAT by using the MMPI. If the item pools used fulfill the imposed constraints, no loss in measurement precision has to be expected. Since the MMPI method is very easy to implement and is computationally undemanding, we propose its use for MAT.

Second, the major reason for the very high measurement efficiency of MAT has now been pinpointed. The results of the second simulation study underline the fact that MAT's high efficiency is mainly due to its use of prior information in the derivation of Bayesian ability estimates in the final scaling. The gains achieved by using the same prior information for selecting items from a multidimensional item pool are considerably smaller. Thus, sequentially presenting multiple unidimensional adaptive tests will result in nearly the same measurement efficiency as MAT, as long as prior information is used for the final scaling. To the best of our knowledge, this is a new insight, as previous research has failed to disentangle the effects of using prior information for item selection, from using prior information for ability estimation. As a result, the high measurement efficiency has been attributed to MAT in general up until now.

Third, another important step was accomplished by making MATE available. With this computer program, the first platform to cover the workflow from item computerization, over test configuration and pre-operational simulation studies to operational testing, has been made freely available for research and teaching purposes. Thus, programming is no longer required to set up a multidimensional adaptive test; this makes the approach more readily accessible to a large range of researchers.

Finally, we have briefly illustrated how MATE can be used to set up unidimensional and multidimensional adaptive tests with the MMPI.

Even though the most important aspects of MAT have been developed and examined in past years, making MAT a very accessible approach, some research questions remain open. One such question, for example, is whether MAT's mixed presentation of items stemming from different content domains has psychological or psychometric effects. Additionally, methods to maintain a MAT system across several assessments are not yet fully developed, and need further attention in the future. However, in summary, the advantages of MAT for many situations are relatively striking. Therefore, we hope that this chapter will also provide an impulse for test developers and administrations to consider MAT as an efficient, modern, and appropriate way to measure complex competencies. Of course, aspects connected with computer-based assessments in general need to be considered when deciding whether the use of MAT is advantageous or not (see Frey and Hartig 2013 for a discussion). We believe that MAT has particularly good potential for large-scale assessments, as the outcomes gained from the high measurement efficiency of MAT are great, compared to the amount of work required for the test development in such studies.

Acknowledgments The preparation of this chapter was supported by grants FR 2552/2-3 and KR 3994/1-3 from the German Research Foundation (DFG) in the Priority Program "Models of Competence for Assessing Individual Learning Outcomes and Evaluating Educational Processes" (SPP 1293) and by grant 01DB1104 (MaK-adapt) from the German Federal Ministry of Education and Research (BMBF) within the initiative "Innovative skills and competence assessment to support vocational education and training (ASCOT)".

References

Born, S., & Frey, A. (2013, September). *Auswirkung schwierigkeitsbestimmender Strukturmerkmale auf die Aufgabenauswahl beim multidimensionalen adaptiven Testen* [Effects of difficulty-dependent item attributes on item selection in multidimensional adaptive testing]. Paper presented at the meeting of the Fachgruppe Methoden & Evaluation of the German Psychological Association (DGPs), Klagenfurt, Austria.

Born, S., & Frey, A. (2016). Heuristic constraint management methods in multidimensional adaptive testing. *Educational and Psychological Measurement.* Advance online publication. doi:10.1177/0013164416643744.

Cheng, Y., & Chang, H.-H. (2009). The maximum priority index method for severely constrained item selection in computerized adaptive testing. *British Journal of Mathematical and Statistical Psychology, 63*, 369–383. doi:10.1348/000711008X304376.

de la Torre, J., & Patz, R. J. (2005). Making the most of what we have: A practical application of multidimensional item response theory in test scoring. *Journal of Educational and Behavioral Statistics, 30*, 295–311. doi:10.3102/10769986030003295.

Frey, A. (2012). Adaptives Testen [Adaptive testing]. In H. Moosbrugger & A. Kelava (Eds.), *Testtheorie und Fragebogenkonstruktion* (2nd ed., pp. 261–278). Berlin: Springer.

Frey, A., & Seitz, N. N. (2009). Multidimensional adaptive testing in educational and psychological measurement: Current state and future challenges. *Studies in Educational Evaluation, 35*, 89–94. doi:10.1016/j.stueduc.2009.10.007.

Frey, A., & Seitz, N. N. (2010). Multidimensionale adaptive Kompetenzdiagnostik: Ergebnisse zur Messeffizienz [Multidimensional adaptive testing of competencies: Results regarding measurement efficiency]. *Zeitschrift für Pädagogik, Beiheft, 56*, 40–51.

Frey, A., & Seitz, N. N. (2011). Hypothetical use of multidimensional adaptive testing for the assessment of student achievement in PISA. *Educational and Psychological Measurement, 71*, 503–522. doi:10.1177/0013164410381521.

Frey, A., & Hartig, J. (2013). Wann sollten computerbasierte Verfahren zur Messung von Kompetenzen Anstelle von Papier- und Bleistift-basierten Verfahren eingesetzt werden [In which settings should computer-based tests be used instead of paper and pencil-based tests]? *Zeitschrift für Erziehungswissenschaft, 16*, 53–57. doi:10.1007/s11618-013-0385-1.

Frey, A., Hartig, J., & Rupp, A. (2009). Booklet designs in large-scale assessments of student achievement: Theory and practice. *Educational Measurement: Issues and Practice, 28*, 39–53. doi:10.1111/j.1745-3992.2009.00154.x.

Frey, A., Cheng, Y., Seitz, N. N. (2011, April). *Content balancing with the maximum priority index method in multidimensional adaptive testing*. Paper presented at the meeting of the NCME, New Orleans.

Frey, A., Seitz, N. N., & Kroehne, U. (2013). Reporting differentiated literacy results in PISA by using multidimensional adaptive testing. In M. Prenzel, M. Kobarg, K. Schöps, & S. Rönnebeck (Eds.), *Research on PISA* (pp. 103–120). Dordrecht: Springer.

Frey, A., Seitz, N. N., & Brandt, S. (2016). Testlet-based multidimensional adaptive testing. *Frontiers in Psychology*, *7*, 1-14. http://dx.doi.org/10.3389/fpsyg.2016.01758

Kingsbury, G., & Zara, A. (1989). Procedures for selecting items for computerized adaptive tests. *Applied Psychological Measurement,* 2, 359–375. doi:10.1207/s15324818ame0204_6.

Kroehne, U., & Partchev, I. (2010, June). *Benefits of multidimensional adaptive testing from a practical point of view*. Paper presented at the IACAT conference, Arnheim.

Kroehne, U., & Frey, A. (2011, October). *Multidimensional adaptive testing environment (MATE): Software for the implementation of computerized adaptive tests*. Paper presented at the IACAT conference, Pacific Grove.

Kroehne, U., & Frey, A. (2013). *Multidimensional adaptive testing environment (MATE) manual*. Frankfurt: German Institute for International Educational Research.

Kroehne, U., Goldhammer, F., & Partchev, I. (2014). Constrained multidimensional adaptive testing without intermixing items from different dimensions. *Psychological Test and Assessment Modeling, 56*, 348–367.

Luecht, R. M. (1996). Multidimensional computerized adaptive testing in a certification or licensure context. *Applied Psychological Measurement, 20*, 389–404. doi:10.1177/014662169602000406.

Makransky, G., Mortensen, E. L., & Glas, C. A. W. (2013). Improving personality facet scores with multidimensional computer adaptive testing: An illustration with the NEO PI-R. *Assessment, 20*, 3–13. doi:10.1177/1073191112437756.

Mikolajetz, A., & Frey, A. (2016). Differentiated assessment of mathematical competence with multidimensional adaptive testing. *Psychological Test and Assessment Modeling, 58*(4), 617–639.

OECD (Organisation for Economic Co-operation and Development) (2013). *PISA 2012 assessment and analytical framework: Mathematics, reading, science, problem solving and financial literacy*. Paris: Author.

Reckase, M. D. (2009). *Multidimensional item response theory*. Dordrecht: Springer.

Segall, D. O. (1996). Multidimensional adaptive testing. *Psychometrika, 61*, 331–354. doi:10.1007/BF02294343.

Segall, D. O. (2001). General ability measurement: An application of multidimensional item response theory. *Psychometrika, 66*, 79–97. doi:10.1007/BF02295734.

Segall, D. O. (2010). Principles of multidimensional adaptive testing. In: W. J. van der Linden und C. A. W. Glas (Eds.), *Elements of adaptive testing* (pp. 57–75). New York: Springer.

Spoden, C., Frey, A., Bernhardt, R., Seeber, S., Balkenhol, A., & Ziegler, B. (2015). Differenzielle Domänen- und Itemeffekte zwischen Ausbildungsberufen bei der Erfassung allgemeiner schulischer Kompetenzen von Berufsschülerinnen und Berufsschülern [Differential domain- and item functioning in tests measuring general competencies of students attenting vocational schools]. *Zeitschrift für Berufs- und Wirtschaftspädagogik, 111*, 168–188.

Stocking, M. L., & Swanson, L. (1993). A method for severely constrained item selection in adaptive testing. *Applied Psychological Measurement, 17*, 277–292. doi:10.1177/014662169301700308.

van der Linden, W. J. (2005). A comparison of item-selection methods for adaptive tests with content constraints. *Journal of Educational Measurement, 42*, 283–302. doi:10.1111/j.1745-3984.2005.00015.x.

Veldkamp, B. P., & van der Linden, W. J. (2002). Multidimensional adaptive testing with constraints on test content. *Psychometrika, 67*, 575–588. doi:10.1007/BF02295132.

Wang, W.-C., & Chen, P.-H. (2004). Implementation and measurement efficiency of multidimensional computerized adaptive testing. *Applied Psychological Measurement, 28*, 450–480. doi:10.1177/0146621604265938.

Yao, L. (2014). Multidimensional CAT item selection methods for domain scores and composite scores with item exposure control and content constraints. *Journal of Educational Measurement, 51*, 18–38. doi:10.1111/jedm.12032.

Ziegler, B., Frey, A., Seeber, S., Balkenhol, A., & Bernhardt, R. (2016). Adaptive Messung allgemeiner Kompetenzen (MaK-adapt) [Adaptive measurement of general competencies (MaK-adapt)]. In K. Beck, M. Landenberger, & O. F. (Eds.), *Technologiebasierte Kompetenzmessung in der beruflichen Bildung. Ergebnisse aus der BMBF-Förderinitiative ASCOT* (pp. 33–54). Bielefeld: wbv.

Chapter 23
Development, Validation, and Application of a Competence Model for Mathematical Problem Solving by Using and Translating Representations of Functions

Timo Leuders, Regina Bruder, Ulf Kroehne, Dominik Naccarella, Renate Nitsch, Jan Henning-Kahmann, Augustin Kelava, and Markus Wirtz

Abstract In mathematics education, the student's ability to translate between different representations of functions is regarded as a key competence for mastering situations that can be described by mathematical functions. Students are supposed to interpret common representations like numerical tables (N), function graphs (G), verbally or pictorially represented situations (S), and algebraic expressions (A). In a multi-step project (1) a theoretical competence model was constructed by identifying key processes and key dimensions and corresponding item pools, (2) different psychometric models assuming theory-based concurrent competence structures were tested empirically, and (3) finally, a computerized adaptive assessment tool was developed and applied in school practice.

Keywords Competence model • Mathematical representations • Computerized adaptive testing

---

T. Leuders (✉) • D. Naccarella • J. Henning-Kahmann • M. Wirtz
University of Education, Freiburg, Germany
e-mail: leuders@ph-freiburg.de; dominik.naccarella@ph-freiburg.de; jan.henning@ph-freiburg.de; wirtz@ph-freiburg.de

R. Bruder • R. Nitsch
Technische Universität Darmstadt, Darmstadt, Germany
e-mail: bruder@mathematik.tu-darmstadt.de; nitsch@mathematik.tu-darmstadt.de

U. Kroehne
German Institute for International Educational Research (DIPF), Frankfurt/Main, Germany
e-mail: kroehne@dipf.de

A. Kelava
Eberhard Karls Universität Tübingen, Tübingen, Germany
e-mail: augustin.kelava@uni-tuebingen.de

D. Leutner et al. (eds.), *Competence Assessment in Education*, Methodology of Educational Measurement and Assessment, DOI 10.1007/978-3-319-50030-0_23

23.1 Introduction

Assessing students' achievement is a key task in education and a prerequisite for designing and adapting instructional settings, for giving feedback on learning, and for making adequate placement decisions. Since teachers' judgments of students' achievements vary in accuracy (Südkamp et al. 2012) there is a demand for subsidiary instruments to assess students' achievement.

Typically, educational goals for different subjects are described as *competencies*: that is, complex abilities that are defined with respect to specific situations (Weinert 2001; Hartig et al. 2008). Through the last decade of international assessment efforts in Germany, a consensual comprehensive framework of mathematical competencies has been developed (OECD 1999; Niss 2003) that defines the curricular norm in all German federal states (KMK 2003). Accordingly, any assessment instrument intended for use in practice should adopt the competence perspective (the alignment principle of assessment).

Further, several compulsory, statewide assessment systems have been developed and implemented. These instruments allow for the summative measurement and comparison of the mathematics achievement of whole classes with respect to the competence goals at the end of certain grades. However, such assessments provide no adequate basis for individual diagnostics or for adaptive teaching. Instruments intended to enable the formative assessment of competencies should exhibit certain characteristics (cf. Pellegrino et al. 2001): They should yield information for immediate use in instructional decision making (Ketterlin-Geller and Yovanoff 2009; "embedded assessment", cf. Wilson and Sloane 2000). Furthermore, they should be based on theoretically sound and empirically tested competence models ("diagnostic assessment"; cf. Rupp et al. 2010). To fulfill these criteria, competence models are needed that (1) are sufficiently content-specific and focused on small competence areas aligned with the curriculum, (2) reflect the state of research with respect to students' knowledge, conceptions, and misconceptions in this area, and (3) can be practically and efficiently used in everyday teaching. These criteria refer in a broad sense to the diverse validity aspects of the assessment instrument, including content, cognitive, structural, and especially consequential, validity (Messick 1995; Leuders 2014).

Although these criteria are well understood in principle, until now, only very few competence models and assessment instruments have been developed (e.g., Wilson 2005; Elia et al. 2008, Lee and Corter 2011), and in very few domains. This is partly due to the enormous effort entailed in the multi-step and multi-discipline approach that is necessary to generate adequate competence models and assessment instruments (Pellegrino et al. 2001, Klieme and Leutner 2006), requiring the cooperation of educational psychologists, psychometricians and subject-specific educational researchers.

In this chapter the process and the main results of a 6 year project cycle promoted by the German Research Foundation (DFG; Klieme and Leuter 2006) are summarized. This project cycle aimed at developing a sound assessment approach in mathematics education that is in accordance with the framework suggested by the program's initiators (ibid.; cf. Leutner et al. 2017, in this volume):

1. Constructing a theoretical competence model for the competence area "functional thinking", incorporating the specific characteristics of certain situations
2. Adopting psychometric models that are in accordance with the theoretical constructs and that capture the structure and interindividual variance of student competencies
3. Developing procedures to measure competencies according to the chosen theoretical and psychometric models—from initial empirical validation within a paper-and-pencil scenario, to the development and implementation of a computer-based adaptive test
4. Evaluating the utility and consequential validity of model-based competence assessment in teaching practice.

In this chapter we present the crucial considerations entailed by this process, summarize the main results and discuss alternatives to and the limitations of the decisions made during our research.

23.2 Construction of a Theoretical Framework Model

The construction of alternative theoretical models took place in a multi-step process, integrating (1) overarching normative competence models, (2) diverse theories on student thinking in the selected competence area, and (3) evidence on students' competencies from subject-specific educational research.

Initially, a competence area was identified that (1) was highly relevant with respect to the curriculum (being reflected in educational standards and established textbooks), and (2) for which a sufficient body of research exists. Furthermore, the competence area was not supposed to be defined by curricular content (such as "linear functions"), but should—in line with the situational definition of competence—refer to a typical recurring situation requiring specific processes of problem solving in secondary mathematics education. The area selected can be described as follows: *Students are expected to understand situations involving the functional interdependence of two variables, to build adequate mental models and with these, to solve problems concerning values, types of dependence and global structure* (Vollrath 1989; Leinhardt et al. 1990). The process of dealing with such situations can be characterised by the use of four typical representations of functions, and translations between them (Swan 1985; see also Fig. 23.2): these representations of functions are *numerical tables (N), function graphs/diagrams (G), situations (S), described pictorially or verbally,* and *algebraic expressions (A),* such as $10x+5$.

The competence delineated by this type of situation can be located within the overarching competence model of educational standards in mathematics (KMK 2003)

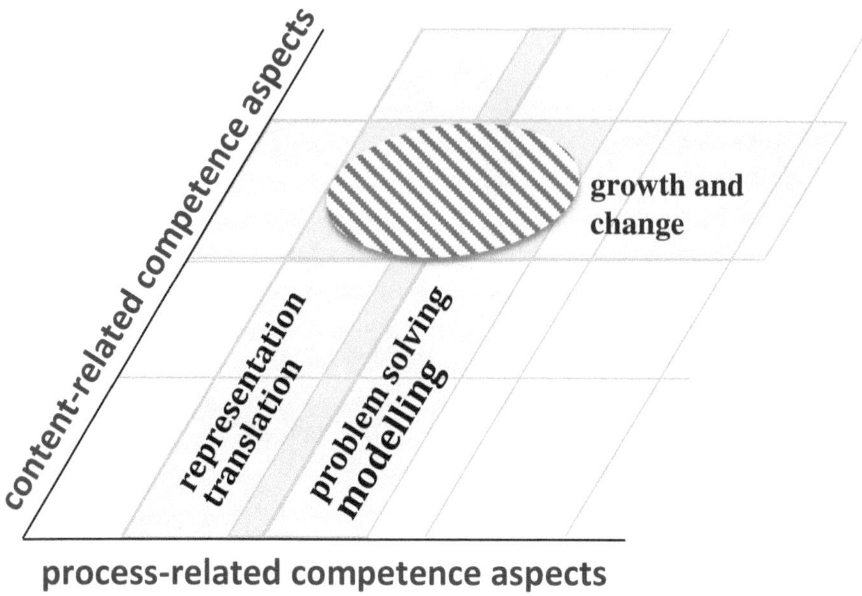

Fig. 23.1 The location of the competence area within an overarching model of mathematical competence

as two "cells" at the intersection of process-related competencies like "using representations" and "problem solving and modeling" on the one hand, and content-related competencies relating to "growth and change described by mathematical functions" on the other hand (see Fig. 23.1).

To achieve a structured, cognitively valid theoretical competence model in this area one can draw on a broad set of theories: One could differentiate between the use of single values, covariance phenomena and global types of functions (cf. Vollrath 1989), or one could refer to different processes of cognitive action (such as identifying, creating, etc.; cf. Bruder and Brückner 1989, or alternatively Anderson and Krathwohl 2001). Instead, we considered a different aspect to be more salient for the problem solving processes in this competence area: the use of the four representations, and the process of translating between them. This approach reflects the broad literature on the specific conceptions, procedures, and difficulties of students in using representations (Leinhardt et al. 1990; Lesh et al. 1987). It seemed appropriate to empirically identify and define competence sub-areas (or subdimensions) that reflect well-defined mental processes for which considerable interindividual differences could be expected. Our first step was to attain a rather general competence model, differentiating processing within four representations (see Fig. 23.2): *numerical tables (N), function graphs (G), verbally or pictorially represented situations (S)* and *algebraic expressions (A)*, and translations between them (such as S↔A, S↔N, S↔G, N↔G, N↔A, G↔A).

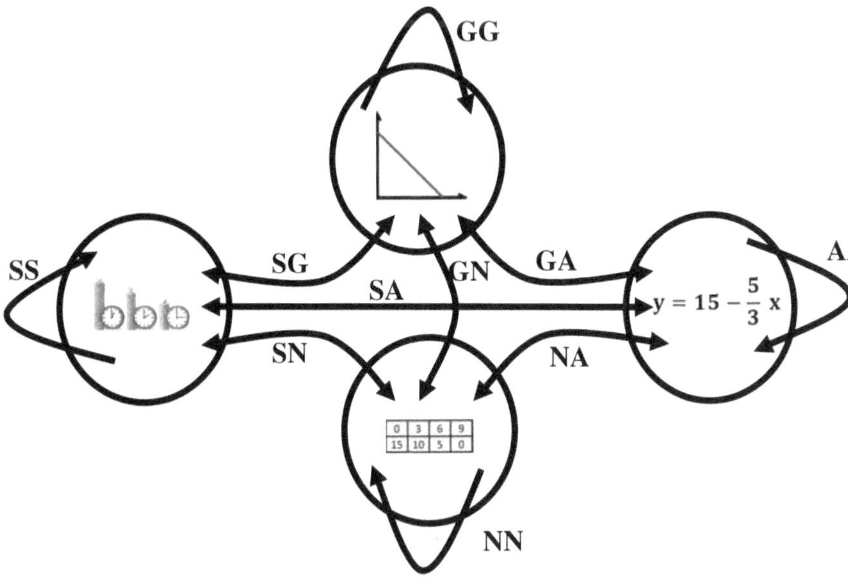

Fig. 23.2 Representations and translation processes during problem solving with functions: The framework model

23.3 Development and Empirical Validation of Psychometric Models

23.3.1 Basic Model: Representations and Translations Between and Within Situational, Numerical, and Graphical Representation

The overall structure shown in Fig. 23.2 is far too complex to be investigated empirically with a single test instrument. However, for our purposes it can be reduced to sub-models, in several ways. In different, partial projects we focussed on two to five relevant subdimensions.

During the process of test construction (Bayrhuber et al. 2010) it became evident that it was not possible to distinguish between different directions of translation between two representations: Although in most tasks, one could try to define the direction of translation between representations by identifying the initial representation and the goal representation, students can frequently change direction and test their translation by going back and forth between initial and intermediate representations. Therefore, the directional quality of representational change was omitted in all models.

For the first attempt at empirical corroboration (Bayrhuber et al. 2010), further restrictions were imposed on constructing a sub-model, to secure the feasibility of the assessment and the model evaluation. Of the four representations, algebraic representation (A) was omitted entirely, since this would have implied an increase of potential dimensions from six to ten, an additional set of items, and a far larger student population from Grades 7 to 10. Furthermore, we also abstained from constructing the dimension that describes translation processes between graphical and numerical representations, as the corresponding items were mostly of a technical nature. The resulting sub-model consisted of the following postulated dimensions:

- **Dimension GG**: Processing information within a graphical representation without any situational context (e.g., displacing graphs, reading information)
- **Dimension SG**: Translating between a situation and a graph (e.g., interpreting features of the graph, drawing graphs for situations explained in texts)
- **Dimension NN**: Processing information within a numerical representation without any situational context (e.g., finding special values in tables)
- **Dimension SN**: Translating between a situation and a value table (e.g., interpreting features values, completing tables from information in a text).

The 80 items were developed by drawing on typical examples from textbooks (thereby ascertaining curricular validity). Think-aloud interviews were conducted with $N = 27$ students, to validate the item content and to optimize the item pool. The items were distributed in a multi-matrix-design over seven testlets, and administered in seven different tests with varying testlet sequences to 872 students: 471 (54 %) female and 399 (46 %) male; 2 unknown. The students came from 37 classes of Grades 7 and 8 in Baden-Württemberg and Hessen (Germany). We exclusively tested students from *Gymnasien* (top-streamed secondary schools) to avoid language problems and school-type specific peculiarities.

The analysis was conducted with a multidimensional random coefficients multinomial logit model (MRCMLM, Adams et al. 1997). By comparing the four dimensional model with nested one and two dimensional models, we could show that the four dimensional model with the postulated dimensions fitted the data best (for the statistical analysis cf. Bayrhuber et al. 2010).

In a further analysis, a latent class analysis (LCA) was conducted with the four dimensional competence profiles of the students. Our model assumed that students can be assigned to qualitative profile types, and allowed for choosing specific training programs for each of the classes (Hartig 2007). Classification of the students into six clusters was found to describe the competence profiles best. In fact, some of the clusters contained students with specific strengths and weaknesses in using numerical or graphical representations (for details see Bayrhuber et al. 2010). However, it remained an open question whether these clusters would remain stable in further tests.

23.3.2 Extension: Inclusion of Algebraic Representation/ Cognitive Action

In order to examine the competence structure in higher grades (9 and 10), an extended version of the competence structure model was developed and adapted to the curricular content of Grades 9 and 10. Therefore, we (1) added items with content appropriate to the curricular level, (2) additionally considered the algebraic representation (A), and (3) restricted the model to translations between *different representations*, as translations within one representation (such as GG) no longer play an essential role in the grades considered. For the same reason, we also excluded the translation from situational description to numerical (SN). These assumptions led to a five-dimensional model wherein the various dimensions were formed by the following translations:

- **Dimension GA:** Translation between graph and algebraic equation
- **Dimension GN:** Translation between graph and numerical table
- **Dimension GS:** Translation between graph and situational description
- **Dimension NA:** Translation between numerical table and algebraic equation
- **Dimension SA:** Translation between situational description and algebraic equation.

To validate the choice of such a competence structure model, alternative models with different dimensions were considered. In a one-dimensional model the students' translation skills were assumed to be one single construct of skills and competencies. Hence, a single dimension contains all translations. Additionally, four different 2-dimensional models were considered in which one form of representation was considered to be the main factor: For example, in a two-dimensional model, one dimension consisted of all translations, including the algebraic representations (GA, NA, SA) and the other dimension contained the translations other than algebraic representation (GN, GS). The theoretical assumption underpinning these two-dimensional models was that the mathematics curriculum often focuses on specific forms of representation, while underrepresenting others (Leinhardt et al. 1990).

Drawing on the results of a pilot study, in the main study, tasks were optimized or created anew. The resulting 120 tasks were divided into four different assessment booklets in the form of a multi-matrix design (Gonzalez and Rutkowski 2010); a test time of 40 mins. was provided for working on the tasks. Eight high schools (Gymnasiums) and 27 classes from the South of Hessen took part in the study, with ninth (19 classes) and tenth (8 classes) graders. The resulting sample consisted of $N = 645$ students. The tasks were scored dichotomously on the basis of criteria established beforehand. We optimized the data set on the basis of a two-parameter logistic model, with regard to item-total correlations and p-values. To verify the various models of dimensional structure (1D, 2D, 5D) we applied the Bayesian information criterion (BIC) and the adjusted BIC.

The results showed that the 5-dimensional model can be assumed (see Nitsch et al. 2014). It was thus ascertained that translations between the graphical, numerical, situational, and algebraic forms of representation of a function (GA, GN, GS, NA, and SA) are essential when describing students' competencies in the area of functional relationships. It can be assumed that these translations include different aspects of competence. Hence, the translation process is not a one-dimensional construct in which the respective translations would be insignificant. The ability to translate between different forms of representations depends on the translations represented in the task. The consequence for mathematics classes is that all five translations would have to be considered. All translations represent different parts of the competence structure, and students should be given the opportunity to familiarize themselves with all translations in order to develop broad skills in the field of functional relationships.

In addition to an analysis of different translations, we also integrated different *cognitive actions* into the tasks. Cognitive actions are considered to characterize mathematical thinking processes (and thus are more specific than the cognitive process categories of Anderson and Krathwohl 2001). Up to this point, only a few studies have addressed students' cognitive actions during the process of translation between representations (e.g., Janvier 1987; Leinhardt et al. 1990). We considered four cognitive actions that were based on a conceptual system put forward by Bruder and Brückner (1989).

- **Identification (I):** When working with mathematical functions and their representations and translations, students have to identify the most important aspects of the depicted form(s) of representation(s) as a basic step.
- **Construction (C):** The student is asked to translate a given form of representation of the function into another one he/she will create, with no new parts given in the task.
- **Description (D)**: Either the student has solved the construction task and is then asked to describe his/her solution process, or the student describes generally what he/she would do if he/she had to solve such a task.
- **Explanation (E):** With regard to Description, the student is thus asked *what* he/she does (or would do), whereas with regard to Explanation, the student is asked to justify *why* the solution is (in)correct.

Previous research findings suggest that the difficulty of translation tasks depends on the translation action demanded (Bossé et al. 2011). Consequently, including the different types of translations and their related cognitive actions in one model could lead to a more adequate and more detailed modeling of the underlying competence structure. However, with regard to the data set in this study, combining the various types of translation and their cognitive actions within one competence structure model would result in far too many dimensions and would be very difficult to validate. Hence, we decided not to include the translation types and the cognitive actions in one model, but rather to separate our analyses into two different parts, so that the cognitive actions defined a separate model. Therefore, we restructured the

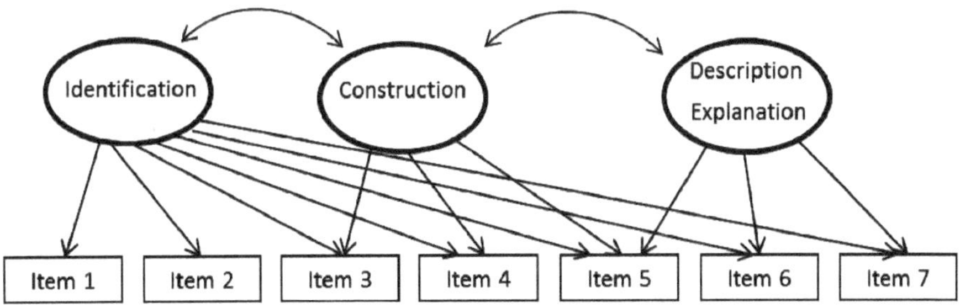

Fig. 23.3 A three-dimensional model based on cognitive actions

item pool and categorized the items with respect to the cognitive action, with the aim of testing whether these cognitive actions could be empirically separated.

We anticipated the following three-dimensional model: *Identification* (I) and *construction* (C) are considered to form two separate dimensions. In the third dimension, the cognitive actions *description* (D) and *explanation* (E) are summarized as a combined action (DE). In this model we assume that the dimensions of *identification* and *construction* differ in their cognitive demands, so that they cannot be represented in a single dimension. *Explanation* and *description* are combined, as both actions demand verbalization, which is not necessarily a requirement for *identification* and *construction*. Hence, these elements have a different type of requirement profile. Additionally, one item can be related to more than one dimension ("within-item-dimensionality"). *Identification* of important values or characteristics in the initial representation is essential for task solving, so that all items are related to this element of cognitive action. The cognitive action of *construction* is included in all items that require the student to construct the target representation of the function and/or to describe such an action. The third dimension, combining *description* and *explanation,* includes all items that demand a description of the solving process or an explanation of the identified form of representation (see Fig. 23.3).

A comparison of the three-dimensional model with several alternative models (one-, two- and four-dimensional models; for further information see Nitsch et al. 2014) showed that the three-dimensional model fits the data best. Hence, the cognitive actions considered cannot be viewed as a one-dimensional construct, as they include various requirements at the same time. An important finding is the separation of the elementary mathematical actions of *identification* and *construction.*

The *identification* of significant values or characteristics within one form of representation is essential for all other actions. Thus, this constitutes an elementary skill in mathematics and should be explicitly included in the exercises. *Construction* differs from *identification*, as no target representation is given; rather, it has to be built instead (e.g., Hattikudur et al. 2012). Hence, this has to be considered in mathematics classes separately.

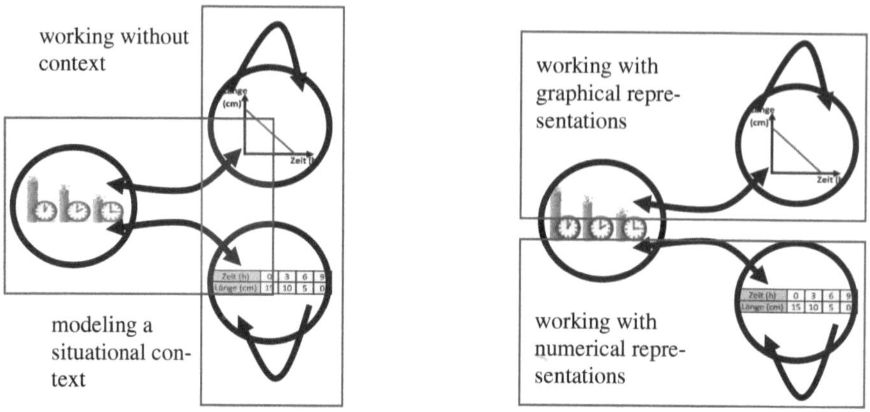

Fig. 23.4 Two models, representing different dominant factors

23.3.3 Extension: Hierarchical Models

Regarding the results of the first study (3.1) we assumed that it would be possible to empirically reveal a more differentiated competence structure and to achieve a deeper understanding of the competence area. Therefore, we set out to conceive of more sophisticated models drawing on theoretical deliberations, to optimize the operationalization and the assessment instrument, and to test the models empirically. Our main interest was to investigate the hierarchical structure of the representational and translational competencies in the area "problem solving with functions". The two central questions were: (1) Is the multidimensional structure of the competence area stable, when extending and revising the item pool and (2): Can we identify an aspect that has a larger impact on defining the competence structure than other aspects: that is, is there a predominant "higher dimension"? For theoretical reasons, it was plausible to hypothesize that either the situational aspect ("modeling within a situational context" vs. "working without context"; Fig. 23.4 l.h.s.) or the representational aspect (i.e. the type of representation—e.g., graphical vs. numerical) would be just such a dominant factor (see Fig. 23.4, r.h.s.).

For this goal, we restricted the item pool to the aforementioned dimension and extended it with respect to a broader coverage of task types within this subject matter area. 1351 students from Grade 7 ($n = 648$; 48 %) and Grade 8 ($n = 703$; 52 %) from 14 different grammar schools (Gymnasiums) in south western Germany participated in the study. They were distributed among 57 different classes (27 of Grade 7 and 30 of Grade 8). 695 of the students (51.4 %) were male and 655 (48.5 %) were female, with one student's gender unknown.

The average age of students was 12.8 years (ranging from 10 to 15, $SD = 0.7$). The study took place only in schools of type Gymnasium, to create a homogeneous student population in terms of verbal abilities. Due to the complex structure of the competence area a large number of items ($n = 103$) and a multi-matrix design were required. Every student worked on an average of 37 items (33 %), and every item was processed by 452 students on average.

Both two-dimensional models showed a better global model fit than a one-dimensional model (Naccarella et al. in prep.). This confirms the multidimensionality found in earlier studies (Bayrhuber et al. 2010; Elia et al. 2008). Furthermore, the two-dimensional model that distinguishes between problems with and without situational context described the data better than did the model that distinguishes between the mathematical representation types (graphical vs. numerical). This implies that the influence of the situational context is more important than the mathematical representation type.

23.4 Development and Evaluation of a Computerized Adaptive Testing Procedure

Following empirical validation of the psychometric models (see Sect. 23.3), the last part of the project cycle aimed at providing a reliable and—at the same time—efficient instrument for the assessment of student competencies, serving as a starting point for individual feedback on measured competencies in schools. Aligning the need for high reliability with the issue of practicability is a major concern in and a challenge for, the assessment of competencies in education. Technology-based assessment offers the possibility of making use of different information concerning students` abilities, and allowing for highly efficient measurement. In the field of competence diagnostics in particular, *adaptive testing* is considered an optimal approach to increase measurement efficiency (Frey and Seitz 2009), as item administration is constrained only to those items that provide a maximum gain in (test) information for a particular subject. Concretely, items are selected according to a (provisional) ability estimate, which is updated in response to the subjects` responses to the preceding items. The item selection criterion aims at a maximal increase in test information for a (provisional) unidimensional or multidimensional ability estimate, resulting in tests with low standard errors. As a consequence, adaptive testing can, compared to conventional tests with fixed or randomly selected items, either result in a reduction of testing time (i.e., shorter tests with the same accuracy), or result in a well-defined accuracy of estimation across a broad range of measures on the trait in question (i.e., a higher reliability for all students regardless of their true ability, given the same number of items; Ware et al. 2005).

23.4.1 Aims for the Development of the Adaptive Test

Considering several prerequisites for the development of a computerized adaptive test (CAT; see Veldkamp and Linden 2010; Weiss 2004), we decided to concentrate on a sub-model of our four-dimensional competence model, described in Sect. 23.3.1, comprising the dimensions SG and SN. We chose these two dimensions because the situational context was shown to be a (pre)dominant factor in the area of "problem solving with functions" (see Sect. 23.3.3).

To develop a two-dimensional CAT we aimed at (1) enhancing the item pool to $N > 60$ items for each of the two dimensions. The development of new items and item siblings was intended to result in a broad distribution of item difficulties, covering the whole range of latent abilities. As a necessary next step, we aimed (2) to computerize both the existing paper-based and the newly developed items; this was made possible by a project-specific extension of the Multidimensional Adaptive Testing Environment (MATE, Kroehne and Frey 2011) to the particular response formats used for the dimensions SG and SN. Furthermore, we aimed (3) to calibrate and empirically validate the enhanced computerized item pool and to estimate the latent correlation between SG and SN. Finally, (4) our goal was to specify a reasonable CAT-procedure for the assessment of students' competencies with the particular item pool, and to determine the properties of the resulting CAT with the help of a pre-operational simulation study.

23.4.2 Item Pool and Calibration

Drawing on existing items from our previous work (see Sect. 23.3.1), we initially enhanced the number of items in both dimensions (SG & SN) from 35 and 26 items to 96 and 81 items, respectively: that is, to a total of 177 items (Aim 1). Subsequently, the items with different response formats (e.g., multiple choice radio buttons, drop-down list boxes, text boxes to enter numbers, and grids for drawing graphs) were computerized. A prototypical extension of the available software was necessary to collect the students' individual responses for all response modes (Aim 2). The upper part of Fig. 23.5a shows an example item for the response mode "drawing", implemented to computerize various items of the dimension SG (i.e., translating between a situation and a graph).

To calibrate the enhanced item pool (Aim 3), in fall 2012 the computerized items of the two dimensions were administered to $N = 1729$ students, nested in 77 classes of Grades 7 and 8, at 13 German secondary schools. A multi-matrix-design was used, so that each student worked on a randomly selected booklet with about 35 items. Students worked on the test individually during regular classes, with one laptop for each student, and to assure a standardized testing procedure, students were instructed by trained test examiners. Within-test navigation was restricted in the calibration study in such a way that no backward navigation was allowed at all, although items could be skipped without answering. Responses were scored automatically according to pre-defined scoring rules.

IRT-based data analyses with the R package TAM (Kiefer et al. 2014) were conducted, to select the appropriate item response model under which item parameters (i.e. item difficulties and item discriminations) as well as person parameters (i.e. students' abilities) were estimated, and to select the final subset of items that fitted to the selected IRT model (see Henning et al., 2013).

In line with the theoretical model, the analyses showed a better data fit for a two-dimensional model with between-item multidimensionality that distinguishes

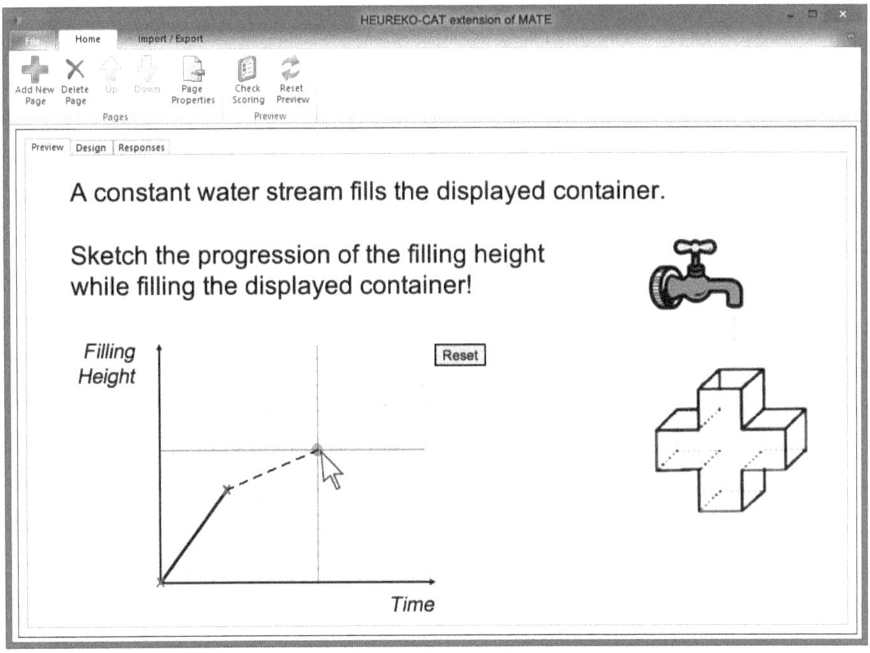

Fig. 23.5a Example item (dimension SG)

between different types of representations (SG vs. SN), compared to a one-dimensional model in which functional thinking is modeled as a representation-independent competence. We estimated a correlation of 0.863 between SG and SN.

Furthermore, comparative analyses revealed that a two-dimensional two-parameter logistic model (2-pl) including both a difficulty and a discrimination parameter for every item in the measurement model, had a better data fit than a two-dimensional one-parameter logistic model (1-pl) in terms of information criteria. For the resulting item pool, we found an almost homogenous distribution of difficulties covering a wide range of measures of the trait on both dimensions. However, we observed in particular that the more difficult items had larger estimated discrimination parameters. Nevertheless, with a mean item discrimination of 0.42 (SD = 0.11) the item pool had adequate psychometric properties to serve as the basis for adaptive testing.

23.4.3 Pre-operational Simulation Study

To conclude, the resulting calibrated item pool was used to concretize the CAT-procedure, which was then evaluated (Aim 4) with the help of a pre-operational CAT simulation, using the recently extended version of MATE (Kroehne and Frey 2013; see Frey et al. 2017, in this volume). For this purpose, N = 10.000 simulees

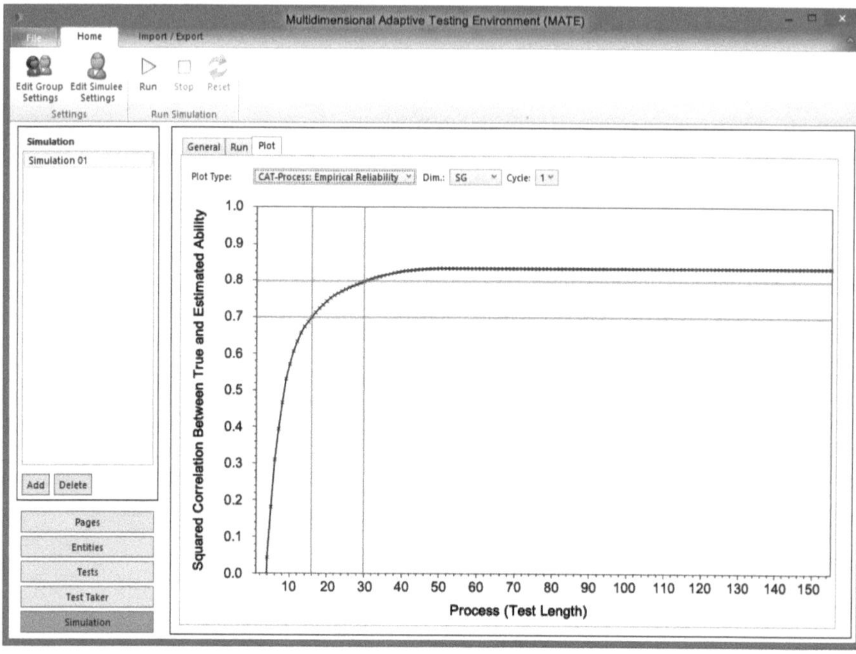

Fig. 23.5b Result of the pre-operational simulation study (correlation of true and estimated ability for dimension SG, conditional on test length)

were generated, with true abilities drawn from a multivariate normal distribution, incorporating the estimated correlation between SG and SN reported above as the true correlation. We also used this correlation as prior for the Bayes modal estimator, as described by Segall (1996). With MATE we simulated a two-dimensional adaptive test for SG and SN without any further restrictions (i.e., multidimensional adaptive tests were simulated for each of the simulees). Inspecting the estimated abilities from this simulation for tests of different test lengths allows for predicting the performance of the multidimensional adaptive test. We found a fast decrease of the average standard error, as well as a reliability (squared correlation of the true and estimated ability) greater than .70 for both dimensions, with only 16 items administered overall (see Fig. 23.5b for dimension SG) and greater than .80 for both dimensions with 30 items. These results imply that our development process was successful and the resulting CAT offers an individually tailored and highly efficient procedure for the assessment of student competencies in a central domain of mathematics education, a procedure that gains efficiency from incorporating the correlation of the two dimensions.

23.5 Discussion

The different sub-projects reported in this chapter systematically followed a multi-step program for modeling competencies in educational contexts (Klieme and Leutner 2006; Pellegrino et al. 2001). The competence area was chosen so that core competencies from the mathematics curriculum from Grades 7 to 10 were reflected—this decision proved pivotal for later practical use. In spite of this focus, the competence structures envisioned were still so complex that it was important to start from a framework model and to inspect partial models or sub-models in complementary studies. Following this strategy we gained empirical support for some of the main theoretical assumptions, without having created a model that covers all subcompetencies and relevant age groups. Nevertheless, one of the main insights derived is that when drawing on substantial theories of (mathematical) cognition, one can achieve assessment instruments that empirically reflect the theoretical structures (Rupp and Mislevy 2007). However, we do not claim that we have modeled cognitive processes, but only to have constructed coherent models to describe the interindividual differences that result from the learning trajectories of students within the given curriculum (Leuders and Sodian 2013; Renkl 2012).

Within this interpretational framework one can say that competence in using representations of functions depends on the type of translations represented in the task. Consequently, competence should be considered as a multi-dimensional construct rather that a one-dimensional construct in which the type of representation and its respective translations would be insignificant. A consequence for mathematics classes is that one can postulate that the different representations and their respective translations should be considered equally in curricula and textbooks. This contrasts with the frequent practice of overemphasizing certain representations (e.g., Leinhardt et al. 1990; Bossé et al. 2011).

Comparing the different sub-models that we examined in our study, it seems that the competence structure changes over time. Whereas in Grades 7 and 8, the translations within different forms of representation were considered, in Grades 9 and 10, translations between different representations were identified as the most relevant. This raises the question of how such changes can be helpful in modeling the development of competencies over time, and how these changes can be integrated into a psychometric model.

The development of the competence model was performed in close connection to curricular structures and to the classroom context. This was an asset in ensuring validity; in addition, it led to the use of project components in different practical contexts: Items from the project have been included in the statewide assessment of competencies at the end of Grade 7 in Baden-Württemberg across all school types. Members of the assessment developing group found it helpful to integrate items that had already proven empirically feasible. Furthermore, the test instrument was used as the basis for developing an accompanying diagnostic to identify students' learning difficulties in the competence area of functions (within the project CODI: Conceptual Difficulties in the field of functional relationships), where it inspired the construction of diagnostic items for qualitative error analysis (Ketterlin-Geller and Yovanoff 2009).

Acknowledgments The preparation of this chapter was supported by grants LE 2335/1, BR 2066/4, and WI 3210/2 from the German Research Foundation (DFG) in the Priority Program "Competence Models for Assessing Individual Learning Outcomes and Evaluating Educational Processes" (SPP 1293).

References

Adams, R. J., Wilson, M., & Wang, W. (1997). The multidimensional random coefficients multinomial logit model. *Applied Psychological Measurement, 21*, 1–23. doi:10.1177/0146621697211001.

Anderson, L. W., & Krathwohl, D. R. (Eds.). (2001). *A taxonomy for learning, teaching, and assessing. A revision of Bloom's taxonomy of educational objectives*. New York, NY: Addison-Wesley.

Bayrhuber, M., Leuders, T., Bruder, R., & Wirtz, M. (2010). Erfassung und Modellierung mathematischer Kompetenz: Aufdeckung kognitiver Strukturen anhand des Wechsels von Darstellungs- und Repräsentationsform [Capturing and modesling mathematical competencies: Revealing cognitive structures by means of change of representation]. *Zeitschrift für Pädagogik, Beiheft, 56*, 28–39.

Bossé, M. J., Adu-Gyamfi, K., & Cheetham, M. R. (2011). Assessing the difficulty of mathematical translations: synthesizing the literature and novel findings. *International Electronic Journal of Mathematics Education, 6*, 113–133.

Bruder, R., & Brückner, A. (1989). Zur Beschreibung von Schülertätigkeiten im Mathematikunterricht: Ein allgemeiner Ansatz [On the decription of students' actions: A general approach]. *Pädagogische Forschung, 30*(6), 72–82.

Elia, I., Panaoura, A., Gagatsis, A., Gravvani, K., & Spyrou, P. (2008). Exploring different aspects of the understanding of function: Toward a four-facet model. *Canadian Journal of Science, Mathematics, and Technology Education, 8*, 49–69. doi:10.1080/14926150802152277.

Frey, A., & Seitz, N.-N. (2009). Multidimensional adaptive testing in educational and psychological measurement: Current state and future challenges. *Studies in Educational Evaluation, 35*, 89–94. doi:10.1016/j.stueduc.2009.10.007.

Frey, A., Kroehne, U., Seitz, N.-N., Born, S. (2017). Multidimensional adaptive measurement of competencies. In D. Leutner, J. Fleischer, J. Grünkorn, E. Klieme, *Competence assessment in education: Research, models and instruments* (pp. 369–388). Berlin: Springer.

Gonzalez, E., & Rutkowski, L. (2010). Principles of multiple matrix booklet designs and parameter recovery in large-scale assessments. *IERI Monograph Series. Issues and Methodologies in Large-Scale Assessments, 3*, 125–156.

Hartig, J. (2007). Skalierung und Definition von Kompetenzniveaus [Scaling and defining competence levels]. In B. Beck & E. Klieme (Eds.), *Sprachliche Kompetenzen. Konzepte und Messung. DESI-Studie* (pp. 83–99). Weinheim: Beltz.

Hartig, J., Klieme, E., & Leutner, D. (Eds.). (2008). *Assessment of competencies in educational contexts*. Göttingen: Hogrefe.

Hattikudur, S., Prather, R. W., Asquith, P., Alibali, M. W., Knuth, E. J., & Nathan, M. (2012). Constructing graphical representations: Middle schoolers' intuitions and developing knowledge about slope and Y-intercept. *School Science and Mathematics, 112*, 230–240. doi:10.1111/j.1949-8594.2012.00138.x.

Henning, J., Naccarella, D., Kröhne, U., Leuders, T., Bruder, R., & Wirtz, M. (2013, August/September). *Development and validation of a computerized item pool as a prerequisite for adaptive testing*. Paper presented at the 15th Biennial Conference of the European Association for Research on Learning and Instruction (EARLI), Munich (Germany).

Janvier, C. (1987). Translation processes in mathematics education. In C. Janvier (Ed.), *Problems of representation in mathematics learning and problem solving* (pp. 27–32). Hillsdale: Erlbaum.

Ketterlin-Geller, L. R., & Yovanoff, P. (2009). Diagnostic assessments in mathematics to support instructional decision making. *Practical Assessment, Research and Evaluation, 14*, 1–11.

Kiefer, T., Robitzsch, A., Wu, M. (2014). *TAM: Test Analysis Modules*. R package version 1.0–1.

Klieme, E., & Leutner, D. (2006). Kompetenzmodelle zur Erfassung individueller Lernergebnisse und zur Bilanzierung von Bildungsprozessen: Beschreibung eines neu eingerichteten Schwerpunktprogramms der DFG [Competence models for assessing individual learning outcomes and evaluating educational processes]. *Zeitschrift für Pädagogik, 52*, 876–903.

KMK (Standing Conference of the Ministers of Education and Cultural Affairs of the States in the Federal Republic of Germany). (Ed.). (2003). *Bildungsstandards im Fach Mathematik für den Mittleren Schulabschluss. Beschluss vom 4.12.2003* [Education standards in mathematics for the secondary school qualification: Resolution approved by the Standing Conference on 4 December 2003]. Münster: Luchterhand.

Kroehne, U., & Frey, A. (2011, October). *Multidimensional adaptive testing environment (MATE): Software for the implementation of computerized adaptive tests*. Paper presented at the IACAT conference, Pacific Grove, CA.

Kroehne, U., & Frey, A. (2013). *Multidimensional adaptive testing environment (MATE)—Manual*. Frankfurt: German Institute for International Educational Research.

Lee, J., & Corter, J. E. (2011). Diagnosis of subtraction bugs using Bayesian networks. *Applied Psychological Measurement, 35*, 27–47. doi:10.1177/0146621610377079.

Leinhardt, G., Zaslavsky, O., & Stein, M. S. (1990). Functions, graphs and graphing: Tasks, learning and teaching. *Review of Educational Research, 66*, 1–64. doi:10.2307/1170224.

Lesh, R., Post, T., & Behr, M. (1987). Representations and translations among representations in mathematics learning and problem solving. In C. Janvier (Ed.), *Problems of representation in the teaching and learning of mathematics* (pp. 33–40). Hillsdale: Erlbaum.

Leuders, T. (2014). Modellierungen mathematischer Kompetenzen: Kriterien für eine Validitätsprüfung aus fachdidaktischer Sicht [Modeling of mathematical competencies: Criteria for a validity check]. *Journal für Mathematik-Didaktik, 35*, 7–48. doi:10.1007/s13138-013-0060-3.

Leuders, T., & Sodian., B. (2013). Inwiefern sind Kompetenzmodelle dazu geeignet kognitive Prozesse von Lernenden zu beschreiben [To what extent can competence models describe cognitive processes]? *Zeitschrift für Erziehungswissenschaft, 16*(Supplement 1), 27–33. doi:10.1007/s11618-013-0381-5.

Leutner, D., Fleischer, J., Grünkorn, J., Klieme, E. (2017). Competence assessment in education: An introduction. In D. Leutner, J. Fleischer, J. Grünkorn, E. Klieme (Eds.), *Competence assessment in education: Research, models and instruments* (pp. 1–6). Berlin: Springer.

Messick, S. (1995). Validity of psychological assessment: Validation of inferences from persons' responses and performances as scientific inquiry into score meaning. *American Psychologist, 50*, 741–749. doi:10.1037/0003-066X.50.9.741.

Niss, M. (2003). Mathematical competencies and the learning of mathematics: the Danish KOM project. In: A. Gagatsis, & S. Papastavridis (Eds.), *3rd Mediterranean Conference on Mathematical Education*. (pp. 115–123). Athens: Hellenic Mathematical Society.

Nitsch, R., Fredebohm, A., Bruder, R., Kelava, T., Naccarella, D., Leuders, T., & Wirtz, M. (2014). Students' competencies in working with functions in secondary mathematics education — Empirical examination of a competence structure model. *International Journal of Science and Mathematics Education*. doi:10.1007/s10763-013-9496-7.

OECD (Organisation for Economic Co-operation and Development). (1999). *Measuring student knowledge and skills: A new framework for assessment*. Paris: Author.

Pellegrino, J., Chudowsky, N., & Glaser, R. (Eds.). (2001). *Knowing what students know: The science and design of educational assessment*. Washington, DC: National Academy Press.

Renkl, A. (2012). Modellierung von Kompetenzen oder von interindividuellen Kompetenzunterschieden: Ein unterschätzter Unterschied [Modeling of competencies or inter-individual differences: An underestimated difference]? *Psychologische Rundschau, 63*, 50–53.

Rupp, A. A., & Mislevy, R. J. (2007). Cognitive foundations of structured item response theory models. In J. Leighton & M. Gierl (Eds.), *Cognitive diagnostic assessment in education: Theory and applications* (pp. 205–241). Cambridge: Cambridge University Press.

Rupp, A., Templin, J., & Henson, R. (2010). *Diagnostic measurement: Theory, methods, and applications*. New York, NY: Guilford.

Segall, D. O. (1996). Multidimensional adaptive testing. *Psychometrika, 61*, 331–354.

Südkamp, A., Kaiser, J., & Möller, J. (2012). Accuracy of teachers' judgments of students' academic achievement: A meta-analysis. *Journal of Educational Psychology, 104*, 743–762. doi:10.1037/a0027627.

Swan, M. (1985). *The language of functions and graphs*. Nottingham: Shell Centre for Mathematical Education.

Veldkamp, B. P., & van der Linden, W. J. (2010). Designing item pools for computerized adaptive testing. In W. J. van der Linden & C. A. W. Glas (Eds.), *Elements of adaptive testing* (pp. 231–245). New York: Springer.

Vollrath, H. J. (1989). Funktionales Denken [Functional thinking]. *Journal für Mathematikdidaktik, 1*, 3–37.

Ware, J. E., Gandek, B., Sinclair, S. J., & Bjorner, J. B. (2005). Item response theory and computerized adaptive testing: Implications for outcomes measurement in rehabilitation. *Rehabilitation Psychology, 50*, 71–78.

Weinert, F. E. (2001). Concept of competence: A conceptual clarification. In D. Rychen & L. Salganik (Eds.), *Defining and selecting key competencies* (pp. 45–66). Seattle: Hogrefe.

Weiss, J. (2004). Computerized adaptive testing for effective and efficient measurement in counseling and education. *Measurement and Evaluation in Counseling and Development, 37*, 70–84.

Wilson, M. (2005). *Constructing measures: An item response modeling approach*. Mahwah: Erlbaum.

Wilson, M., & Sloane, K. (2000). From principles to practice: An embedded assessment system. *Applied Measurement in Education, 13*, 181–208.

Chapter 24
Relating Product Data to Process Data from Computer-Based Competency Assessment

Frank Goldhammer, Johannes Naumann, Heiko Rölke, Annette Stelter, and Krisztina Tóth

Abstract Competency measurement typically focuses on task outcomes. Taking process data into account (i.e., processing time and steps) can provide new insights into construct-related solution behavior, or confirm assumptions that govern task design. This chapter summarizes four studies to illustrate the potential of behavioral process data for explaining task success. It also shows that generic process measures such as time on task may have different relations to task success, depending on the features of the task and the test-taker. The first study addresses differential effects of time on task on success across tasks used in the OECD Programme for the International Assessment of Adult Competencies (PIAAC). The second study, also based on PIAAC data, investigates at a fine-grained level, how the time spent on automatable subtasks in problem-solving tasks relates to task success. The third study addresses how the number of steps taken during problem solving predicts success in PIAAC problem-solving tasks. In a fourth study, we explore whether successful test-takers can be clustered on the basis of various behavioral process indicators that reflect information problem solving. Finally, we address how to handle unstructured and large sets of process data, and briefly present a process data extraction tool.

F. Goldhammer (✉)
German Institute for International Educational Research (DIPF), Centre for International Student Assessment (ZIB), Frankfurt/Main, Germany
e-mail: goldhammer@dipf.de

J. Naumann
Goethe University Frankfurt, Frankfurt/Main, Germany
e-mail: j.naumann@em.uni-frankfurt.de

H. Rölke • K. Tóth
German Institute for International Educational Research (DIPF), Frankfurt/Main, Germany
e-mail: roelke@dipf.de; toth@dipf.de

A. Stelter
Giessen University, Giessen, Germany
e-mail: Annette.Stelter@erziehung.uni-giessen.de

D. Leutner et al. (eds.), *Competence Assessment in Education*, Methodology of Educational Measurement and Assessment, DOI 10.1007/978-3-319-50030-0_24

Keywords Process data • Processing steps • Time on task • Explanatory modeling of success • Computer-based assessment

24.1 Introduction

The measurement and modeling of competencies is traditionally aimed at product data. This means that response patterns in a competency test serve as indicators of competency. Behavioral differences during task completion are usually not considered, and are difficult to observe in paper-pencil testing. Computer-based testing however, provides promising new directions. Besides increased construct validity (e.g., Sireci and Zenisky 2006) or improved test design (e.g., van der Linden 2005), computer-based testing can offer insights into behavioral processes of task completion by logging any test-taker interactions with the assessment system.

Taking into account individual differences in the process of task completion can enhance theoretical models of competencies and improve their measurement. Theoretical understanding of the construct and related individual differences can be extended, for instance, by exploring how construct-related solution behavior, as reflected by process data, predicts task success. Given a priori theoretical assumptions as to how behavioral processes relate to the task outcome, the construct interpretation of scores can be supported by evidence corroborating these assumptions. Furthermore, process data may be suitable for defining process-related latent variables such as "speed of performance", as indicated by item-response times (cf. Goldhammer and Klein Entink 2011).

In computer-based assessments, process data (e.g., clicks on a button, visits to a page) can be stored in log files. The granularity of process data depends on the level of interactivity that the item type requires from the test-taker. For traditional closed-response item types such as multiple-choice, only very generic process data is available, such as response time, change of response, and revisits. For item types requiring a higher level of interactivity, such as simulation-based items (presenting, e.g., a simulated computer environment), each interaction with the stimulus, and the related time stamp, can be observed. Thus, such complex item types are most promising for investigating the task completion process as reflected in behavioral process data.

With some inferences, process data can be used to infer cognitive processes (e.g., Goldman et al. 2012; Naumann et al. 2008; Richter et al. 2005; Salmerón et al. 2005). Process indicators serving as descriptors of information processing can be constructed on the basis of processing time, as well as processing steps—quantitative and/or qualitative aspects of a test-taker's interaction with the stimulus. Following the framework proposed by Naumann (2012), the completion process (i.e., the selection, sequence and duration of information processing elements) determines the result of task completion, which in turn provides the basis for ability estimation. The completion process itself depends on person-level characteristics (e.g., the availability of strategies or sub-skills) and task-level characteristics (e.g., cognitive requirements) and their interaction. Furthermore, task-level as well as person-level characteristics are assumed to moderate the relation between indicators of the task completion process (e.g., time on task), and the result of task completion. Examples for such moderation effects are research by Goldhammer et al. (2014) and Naumann et al. (2014), described below in Sects. 24.2 and 24.4, respectively.

In the following sections four studies are presented, to illustrate the potential of behavioral process data for explaining individual differences in task success. They take into account not only processing time, extending previous research on response times, but also processing steps, represented by interactions with the stimulus in complex simulation-based items. The first study, by Goldhammer et al. (2014) draws on process data from the OECD Programme for the International Assessment of Adult Competencies (PIAAC) to address the question of how the time spent on solving a task (i.e., time on task) in reading literacy and problem solving in technology-rich environments, is related to the respective task outcomes. In particular, this study investigates how this relation depends on the mode of processing (automatic vs. controlled).

The second study, by Stelter et al. (2015), also based on PIAAC data, extends the research by Goldhammer et al. (2014) by taking a closer look at time on task. Stelter et al. analyze the specific portion of time spent on basic subtasks within problem-solving tasks that can be completed through automatic cognitive processing. This measure is conceived as an indicator of individual automatization in solving basic subtasks. The idea here is that once basic subtasks in problem-solving are accomplished through automatic processing, cognitive capacity becomes available that benefits task performance and thus success.

The third study, by Naumann et al. (2014), moves from time taken to actions in simulation-based items, and asks how the number of steps taken during problem solving predicts success in PIAAC problem-solving tasks. The fourth study, by Tóth et al. (2013), uses multiple processing time and processing step indicators to explore whether a subset of test-takers who all eventually succeed in a problem-solving task can nevertheless be clustered according to the efficiency of their task engagement behavior.

The final section of this chapter addresses the research infrastructure that is needed to handle unstructured and large sets of process data, and briefly presents a process data extraction tool tailored to the extraction of PIAAC process data.

24.2 Study 1: The Effect of Time on Task Success Differs Across Persons and Tasks

Time presents a generic characteristic of the task completion process, and has different psychological interpretations, suggesting opposing associations with task outcomes. Spending more time may be positively related to the outcome, as the task is completed more carefully. However, the relation may be negative if working more fluently, and thus faster, reflects higher skill level. On the basis of the dual processing theory framework (Shiffrin and Schneider 1977), Goldhammer et al. (2014) argued that the strength and direction of the time on task effect depends on the mode of processing, which ranges from controlled to automatic processing. In the mode of controlled processing, long response times indicate thorough and engaged task completion, increasing the probability of task success (positive effect), whereas, in the mode of automatic processing, long response times indicate that the skill has not yet been automatized, which is associated with lower probability of task success (negative effect). From this it follows that the relative degree of controlled versus automatic cognitive processing determines the time on task effect.

24.2.1 Research Goal and Hypotheses

First, Goldhammer et al. (2014) claimed that problem solving, by definition, must rely on controlled processing (i.e., slow and serial processing under attentional control) to a substantial degree in each task. Therefore, a positive time on task effect was expected. A negative time on task effect was expected for reading tasks because, in reading tasks, a number of component cognitive processes are apt for automatization (Hypothesis 1). Second, within domains, the time on task effect was assumed to be moderated by task difficulty. That is, easy tasks were expected to be completed largely by means of automatic processing, whereas difficult tasks require controlled processing to a greater extent (Hypothesis 2). Third, for a given task, individuals were assumed to differ in the extent to which the information-processing elements that are amenable to automatic processing are actually automatized. More specifically, highly skilled individuals were expected to command well-automatized procedures within task solution subsystems that can pass to automatization. Goldhammer et al. (2014) therefore expected the time on task effect to vary across persons' level of skill (Hypothesis 3). Finally, for a particular problem-solving task, Goldhammer et al. (2014) expected positive time on task effects to be restricted to the completion of steps that are crucial for a correct solution, whereas for others, the effect is assumed to be negative (Hypothesis 4). Unlike the first three hypotheses, the fourth hypothesis goes beyond the (more traditional) analysis of total time spent on task. Instead, the total time was fractionated into pieces, representing qualitatively different aspects of the task completion process.

24.2.2 Methods

A total of 1020 persons aged from 16 to 65 years participated in the German Field Trial of the PIAAC study. Test-takers completed computer-based reading and problem-solving tasks. To investigate the heterogeneity of the association of time on task with task outcome at the between-person level, Goldhammer et al. (2014) used a response time modeling approach within the generalized linear mixed models (GLMM) framework (e.g., Baayen et al. 2008). The model included random intercepts for item (easiness) and person (ability), and a fixed intercept as predictors. Most importantly, the time on task effect was specified as a fixed effect that could be adjusted by item and person (random) effects. By modeling the effect of time on task as random across items and persons, the effects of the time components—that is, a person's speed and the task's time intensity (cf. van der Linden 2009)—can be disentangled (Goldhammer et al. 2014).

24.2.3 Results

As assumed in Hypothesis 1, in problem solving, which is assumed to require controlled processing, the time on task effect is positive, whereas in reading tasks, which require more routine processing, the time on task effect is negative. With regard to Hypothesis 2 (moderation by task), the already positive time on task effect for problem solving was substantially increased in difficult tasks, whereas the effect was less positive in easy tasks. Similarly, the negative time on task effect for reading became stronger in easier tasks, but was diminished in more difficult tasks. Regarding Hypothesis 3 (moderation by person), the positive time on task effect in problem solving decreased with higher skill level, and increased with lower skill level. In reading, the negative time on task effect became stronger with higher skill level and decreased with lower skill level. Figure 24.1 shows the by-task and the by-person adjustments to the time on task effect for selected tasks and persons. These curves indicate that positive time on task effects occurred especially in highly demanding situations (i.e., a less skilled person encounters a difficult task), and vice versa. Finally, to test Hypothesis 4, Goldhammer et al. (2014) predicted task success in the problem-solving task Job search (see Sect. 24.3 and Fig. 24.2) by fractions of the total time on task. As assumed only for time spent on the steps needed to solve the task—that is, on visiting and evaluating the target pages for multiple criteria—was a positive time on task effect observed. Negative or null effects were found for spending time on the non-informative search engine results page and the non-target pages.

24.2.4 Discussion

The heterogeneous effects of time on task on the task outcome suggest that time on task has no uniform interpretation, but is a function of task difficulty and individual skill. The results suggest that the time on task effect is mainly determined by differences in task difficulty and individual skill, which together can be conceived of as individual task difficulty or simply as an indicator of task success (for the related concept of Ability-Difficulty-Fit see Asseburg and Frey 2013). The next modeling step, therefore, would be to actually specify the effect of time on task as a function of this difference. Overall, the results are consistent with the notion that positive time on task effects reflect the strategic allocation of cognitive resources in controlled processing, whereas negative time on task effects reflect the degree of automatization. Nevertheless, time on task is ambiguous in respect of its interpretation in cognitive terms.

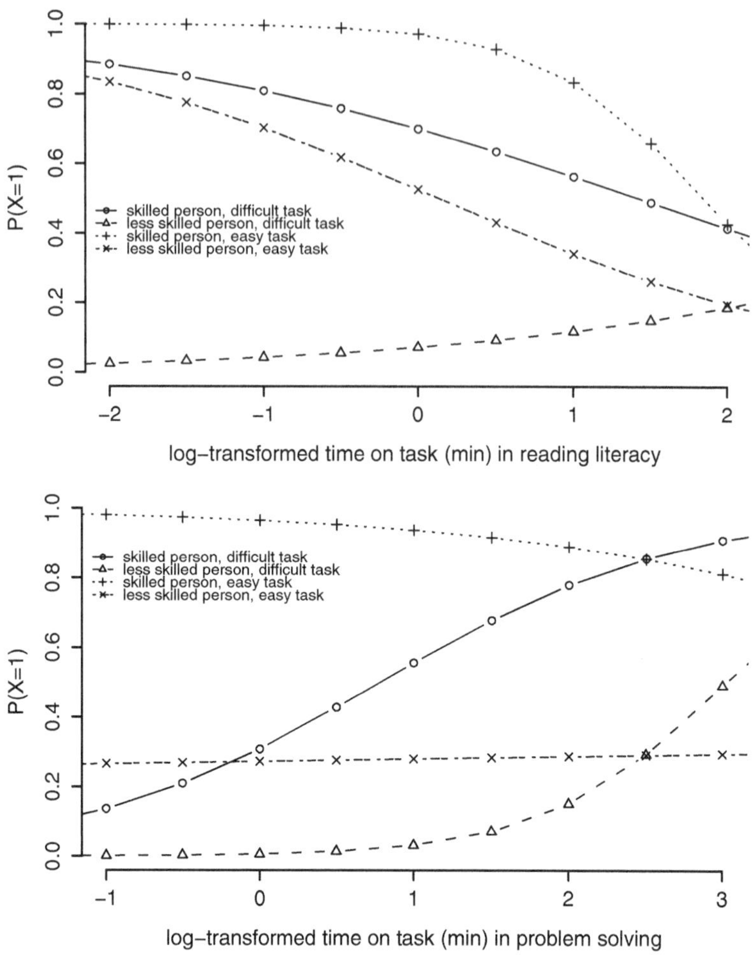

Fig. 24.1 Time on task effect by task difficulty and skill level for reading literacy (*upper part*) and problem solving in technology-rich environments (*lower part*). For combinations of two tasks (easy vs. difficult) with two persons (less skilled vs. skilled), the probability for success is plotted as a function of time on task (Goldhammer et al. 2014)

24.3 Study 2: Benefits for Task Completion from the Automatization of Subtasks

The automatization of cognitive processes occurs with practice, and is based on representations in long-term memory that fasten cognitive processes and actions (van Merriënboer and Sweller 2005). If subtasks of a complex task can be completed through automatic processing, the cognitive effort needed for a task is reduced (Ericsson and Kintsch 1995). For instance, solving information problems in a technology-rich environment involves not only subtasks requiring higher-order thinking, and coming up with new solutions, but also basic subtasks that are amenable to automatization. Stelter et al. (2015) argued that time spent on subtasks that can be automatized can be expected to show a negative time effect on the overall task result, since processing time is assumed to be an inverse indicator of automatization.

Thus, in this study, not the total time on task but, for each task, the time taken in required subtasks, was taken into account. This entailed identifying separable subtasks that represent coherent chunks of processing steps, and determining the time spent on these subtasks.

24.3.1 Research Goal and Hypotheses

Goldhammer et al. (2014) addressed time on task primarily on the level of whole tasks, and found a moderating function of the tasks' difficulty, presumably reflecting the proportion of subtasks amenable to automatization. Stelter et al. (2015) took a more direct approach. They identified subtasks within problem-solving tasks that can be automatized, and for these subtasks, estimated how the time required for their completion is related to task success. For automatable subtasks, time on task was expected to negatively predict task success, since time on task is assumed to reflect the degree of automatization (Hypothesis 1). In contrast, given that problem solving as such, *per definition*, requires controlled processing to a substantial degree (see Goldhammer et al. 2014, and Sect. 24.2), for the whole task, time on task was expected to predict task success positively (Hypothesis 2).

24.3.2 Methods

German field-trial data from the PIAAC study were analyzed ($N = 412$). Figure 24.2 illustrates a sample task, a job search where the test-taker was asked to bookmark web-pages that required neither registration nor fees. The test-taker began with a Google-like search page, then had to select a webpage from the search page and read the relevant information, to navigate through additional links and decide whether the page fulfilled the criteria. If so, the test-taker had to bookmark it and continue on the search page. For this sample task, the automatable subtask was to set a bookmark by clicking the bookmark button and confirming the bookmark settings. The degree of automatization was measured by the (log-transformed) time needed to operate the bookmarking commands.

For each of the six problem-solving tasks included in this analysis, subtasks were identified and judged with respect to the possible degree of automatization versus controlled processing. In this manner, across all six problem-solving tasks, three indicators of automatization were defined. These were (1) the time needed for drag

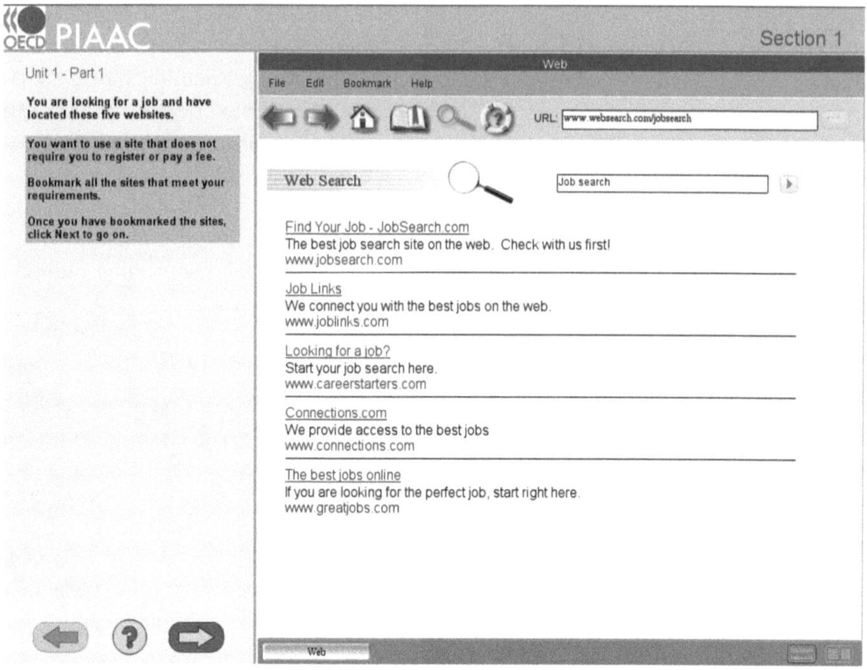

Fig. 24.2 Sample problem solving in a technology-rich environment task. See text for task description

& drop, (2) the time needed to close a popup window, and (3) the time needed to set a bookmark (as described for the sample task). Logistic regression analysis was used to test the relation of time on automatable subtasks to the probability of solving the task correctly. First, six regression models were estimated for six different PIAAC problem-solving tasks in a technology-rich environment, to test Hypothesis 1. In each task-specific regression model, the one task-specific measure of automatization was used as a predictor of task success (see Table 24.1, columns 2 and 3). Then, six regression models were estimated to test Hypothesis 2. In each of these models, the total time on task was used as a predictor of success on each of the six tasks respectively (see Table 24.1, column 4).

24.3.3 Results

The regression analyses confirmed Hypothesis 1. In four of the six regression models, a significant negative effect of the respective automatization indicator was found (see Table 24.1, columns 2–3). Thus, subjects who completed these subtasks faster were more likely to succeed on the task.

Table 24.1 Prediction of task success from automatization of subtasks (time taken) or total time on task[b]

Task	Automatization indicator	Effect β for the automatization indicator	Effect β for the total time on task	Task easiness (probability of success)
U1a	Drag&Drop	−1.25*	−0.44	.64
U1b	Drag&Drop	−2.03**	0.43	.56
U6a	PopUp	−0.27	0.40	.23
U10a	Bookmark	−0.43*	0.06	.37
U10b	PopUp	−1.67**	2.49**	.61
U11b	Drag&Drop	−0.78[a]	−1.13**	.28

[a]$p < .10$, * $p < .05$, ** $p < .01$
[b]Stelter et al. (2015)

Hypothesis 2 received only partial support. The assumed positive association of time on task with task success was found in one task, while in one other task, the association was negative. In all other tasks, no significant association was found between time on task and task success (see Table 24.1, column 4).

24.3.4 Discussion

These results confirm that time spent on subtasks amenable to automatization is negatively predictive of task success. The findings confirm the idea put forward in Goldhammer et al. (2014, see Sect. 24.2) that the relation of time on task to task success is conditional on a task's difficulty, which is a reflection of the proportion of potential automatic processing involved in task completion. This result also stands in contrast to the results found for total time on task. In each instance where time on subtasks amenable to automatization had a negative association with task success, no association or a positive association was found for the total time on task. This result is consistent with the idea that problem-solving in a technology-rich environment relies on different cognitive sub-processes that are automatable to different degrees. It is also consistent with a resource-allocation perspective that claims that when certain subtasks are automatized, more cognitive resources become available for controlled processing, which in turn benefits task success.

24.4 Study 3: Number of Interactions: More Is Not Always Better

In the past sections we have described how time on task measures, both global and specific, predict success in problem solving in technology-rich environments. These analyses provide evidence that time on task predicts task success, conditional on person characteristics (ability) and task characteristics: that is, both the task's difficulty (Sect. 24.2) and the degree to which subtasks are amenable to being automatized (Sect. 24.3). In this section, we move from the analysis of time on task to the analysis of actions as they can be observed in highly interactive simulation-based items.

24.4.1 Research Goal and Hypotheses

Naumann et al. (2014) started the analysis of actions as predictors of task success using a simple indicator: the total number of actions performed during task completion. They argued that different frequencies of taking an action, such as clicking a hyperlink, during the completion of a problem-solving task in technology-rich environments, can have different interpretations. They can mean goal-directed behavior, but can also however be the result of disorientation or helplessness. Depending on the interpretation, different associations will be expected between the number of actions and task success. Consider first a subject who fails to respond to task demands, who remains passive ("apathetic"; see the taxonomy of information problem solving suggested by Lawless and Kulikowich 1996). Such a subject will produce a low number of actions, and will likely fail on the task. Secondly, consider a subject who engages with the task: This subject will produce a moderate number of actions, and is likely to succeed on the task.

Thirdly, consider a subject who tries hard to complete the task, but gets disoriented (e.g., "lost in hyperspace" when solving an information problem; see, e.g., Schroeder and Grabowski 1995). This third subject will take a high number of actions, but is again likely to fail. Naumann et al. (2014) thus assume that the association between number of actions and task success takes the form of an inversely-shaped U: that is, with an increasing number of actions, from low to medium high levels, task success increases, whereas with a further increase of actions, task success no longer increases but rather decreases (see also OECD 2011, Ch. 3). In addition, the association of actions with task success can be assumed to be moderated by the task. In tasks that require long and complex action sequences, a strong positive association between the number of actions and task success can be assumed, but this association should be weak in tasks that require only few actions.

Three hypotheses directly follow from the above considerations: (1) The number of actions predicts task success in problem solving in technology-rich environments-tasks, (2) This relation is inversely U-shaped and (3), this relation is stronger in tasks that require more actions.

24.4.2 Methods

Naumann et al. (2014) used data from the German (N = 661) and Canadian (N = 411) PIAAC Field Trials. The association between number of actions and task success was assumed to be invariant across countries. Thus, the Canadian sample served to replicate the results expected for the German sample. Employing a GLMM-framework (see Sect. 24.2), the log odds of task success (success vs. failure) were regressed on the log-transformed and z-standardized number of actions taken by a subject, the length of the navigational path required by the task, and their interaction. To determine the length of the navigational path, all actions necessary for task completion were counted that resulted in a change in the stimulus displayed on screen. This variable was considered to reflect the complexity of information to be processed within a task. In addition, a quadratic effect was included for the number of actions taken. These predictors were entered as fixed effects.[1] In addition, random effects were modeled for persons and items, representing person skill and item easiness, respectively.

24.4.3 Results

Confirming their hypotheses, Naumann et al. (2014) found a significant positive effect for the number of actions. Also in accordance with the assumption of an inversely U-shaped relation between number of actions and task success, this effect was qualified by a quadratic trend that indicated that the positive effect of the number of actions was alleviated with increasing numbers of actions, and eventually reversed to negative (see the inversely U-shaped curves in Fig. 24.3). Across all tasks, the predicted probability of successfully solving a problem in a technology-rich environment reached its maximum for a number of actions of 1.64, or 2.54, standard deviations above the mean for the Canadian and German samples respectively. In addition to the quadratic trend, the association between number of actions and task success was moderated by task demands. A significant interaction was found between the length of the navigational path required by the task and the number of actions taken by a subject. In tasks that required long navigation paths (one standard deviation above the mean), a strong positive association emerged between the number of actions and the probability of task success. In tasks requiring short navigation paths, in contrast, the association was much weaker, and in the German sample, insignificant.

[1] Naumann et al. (2014) included a third predictor in their model: the openness of the task. For the results for this predictor, not reported here, please refer to the original source.

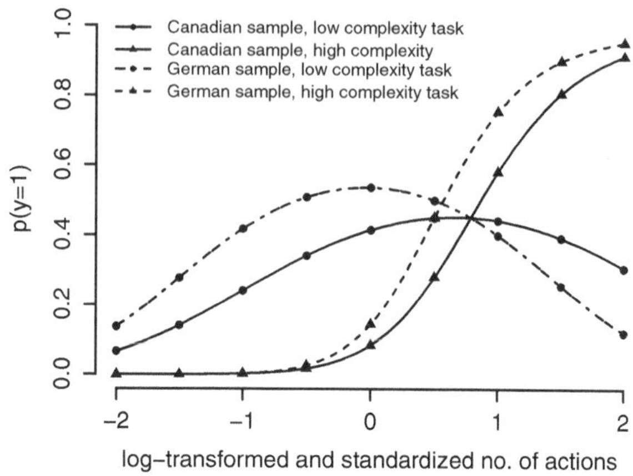

Fig. 24.3 Effect of the number of actions in low complexity and high complexity tasks for the Canadian and German PIAAC field trial data (Naumann et al. 2014)

24.4.4 Discussion

These results confirm that with problem solving in technology-rich environments, even a very basic indicator of the problem-solving process, such as the number of actions, is predictive of task success. They also show that the association is not simple, or linear. The number of actions, similarly to time on task (see Sect. 24.2 and 24.3), appears to correspond to different psychological processes, conditional on (1) the range of values, and (2) task features. The difference between taking few and taking a moderate number of actions appears to correspond to subjects being passive vs. subjects engaging with the task. Thus, this difference is associated with an increase in task success probability. In contrast, the difference between taking a moderate number and taking a very high number of actions appears to be associated with getting distracted, or disoriented within the task environment. As a consequence, this difference is then associated with a decrease in task success probability.

A similar consideration holds for task features. Taking a high number of actions is beneficial, especially in tasks that are complex. Interestingly, however, in one of two samples a positive association emerged also in tasks that required only few actions; in neither sample was a negative association found. This means that taking a high number of actions may not be beneficial, but is also not detrimental to succeeding in tasks of low complexity. Presumably, in these simple tasks, the probability of getting "lost" is low from the beginning. Taking a high number of actions might thus be indicative of exploration behavior that is not required by the task, and thus is not beneficial; it is however not harmful.

24.5 Study 4: Problem Solver Types: Different Ways to Success in Information Problems

In the first three sections of this chapter attempts have been made to identify individual variables, such as time on task, or the number of actions, that discriminate between successful and unsuccessful test-takers. In marked contrast to this, Tóth et al. (2013) looked at successful test-takers only and asked whether these might still differ from one another in how exactly they achieved success, taking into account different process measures simultaneously. The analyses of Goldhammer et al. (2014), described in Study 1 of this chapter, already offer some evidence that there may be multiple pathways to success. Goldhammer et al. (2014) found that positive time on task effects were especially strong in low-skilled students. This means also that low-skilled students can be successful in problem-solving tasks when they compensate for their lower skills by investing more time. In contrast to the previous three sections, in this section we look not at problem solving in technology-rich environments per se, but specifically at information problem-solving tasks (see e.g., Brand-Gruwel et al. 2009).

24.5.1 *Methods*

In the study by Tóth et al. (2013) the sample consisted of 189 German students with a mean age of 17.63 years ($SD = 0.78$). Just over half of the sample (57 %) was male. For the present analysis, one complex item was selected from the computer-based ICT literacy test designed by Pfaff and Goldhammer (2011). This complex item simulated a web search engine. It listed five web pages with short summaries (hits) on the opening screen that were accessible via hyperlinks. Six process measures (variables) that characterize students' interactions with the simulated web environment were taken into account, so that considered together, they would reflect the efficiency of the task completion process. These process measures were (1) the number of page visits, (2) the number of different pages visited, (3) the time spent on the relevant page, (4) the ratio of time spent on the relevant page to the total time on task, (5) the ratio of time spent on the opening screen to total time on task, and (6) total time on task. These variables were subjected to a K-means cluster analysis using the Euclidean Distance function.

24.5.2 *Results*

Two groups of students were identified by the K-means cluster algorithm. The first subgroup of students (Cluster 1: 44 %) solved the task in a more efficient way than the second group (Cluster 2: 56 %). Students in Cluster 1 required 53.88 seconds to successfully complete the task, compared to Cluster 2 members (87.94 s). On average, students in Cluster 1 visited a lower number of pages (3.33) than did those in Cluster 2 (7.77). In addition, the number of different pages visited was smaller in Cluster 1 (1.62) than in Cluster 2 (3.54). The latter finding means that Cluster 2 students were less selective in visiting web pages. Further, students in Cluster 1 spent less time on the relevant page containing the most credible information (8.79 s) than did students in Cluster 2 (16.86 s). This means that students in Cluster 1 required less time to inspect the relevant website and obtain the correct response. Furthermore, the mean values of the "ratio of time spent on the opening screen" variable of the two subgroups showed a significant difference: While students in Cluster 1 spent on average 75 % of their total time on task on the opening screen, students in Cluster 2 spent only 50 % of their total time on task on the opening screen. Thus, students in Cluster 1 took a greater percentage of their total time initially, but afterwards acted more efficiently than students in Cluster 2, who however were eventually successful as well.

24.5.3 Discussion

In this analysis, two subgroups of successful students were identified that differ according to their problem-solving efficiency. Members from Cluster 1 used the majority of their test completion time on the start page, in pre-selecting pages, in contrast to Cluster 2 members, who spent more time evaluating information sources on irrelevant websites. These results concur nicely with results reported by Goldhammer et al. (2014): Skilled students need less effort to succeed in problem solving in a technology-rich environment. However, lesser-skilled students can also come up with a successful solution to a task when they display a behavior that might compensate for their lesser skills. In this study, these lesser-skilled students presumably took more page visits, and more time, but eventually succeeded on the task as well.

24.6 How to Handle Unstructured Process Data?: The Log File Data Extraction Tool

Throughout this chapter, we have presented four studies based on process data. From a methodological perspective, these studies demonstrate the potential of taking into account task engagement process data. But these insights come at a price: Analyzing process data needs additional work, especially in the preparation phase.

The extra work starts with getting an overview of the process data available in log files and making it accessible to standard data analysis tools. The log files contain every interaction of the test person with the assessment system, as a sequence of log events, which rarely can be imported into standard data analysis software.

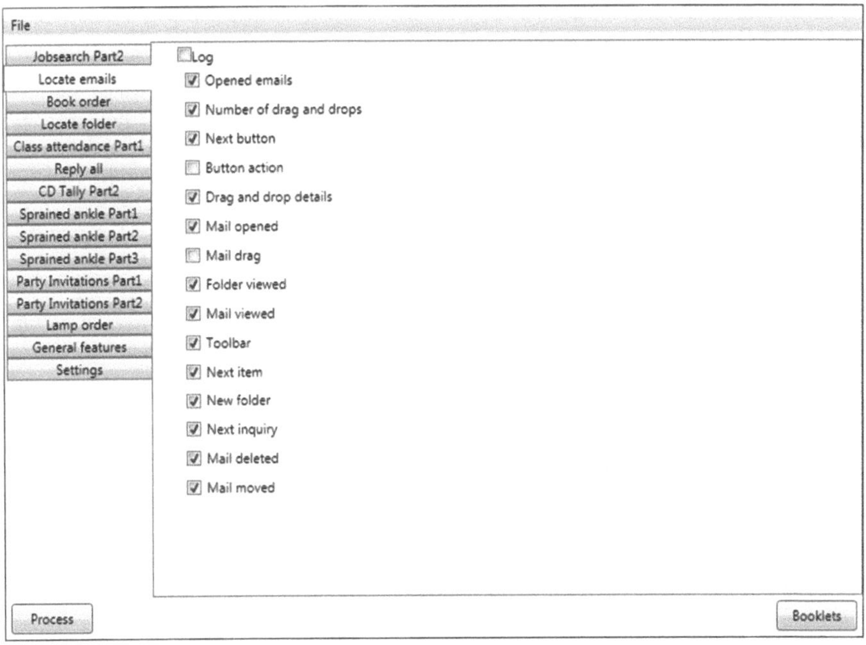

Fig. 24.4 Screenshot of the LDA prototype tool

First, this list of log events has to be transformed into a matrix form: for instance, in CSV format. Usually, only a small amount of the data is really necessary for a specific analysis. Thus, filtering the process data is a second important step. Frequently, a researcher might want to derive so-called *features*, variables combining certain log events, like the number of interactions, no matter what type. All these preparatory steps are cumbersome, error-prone, and have to be done performed repeatedly prior to each data analysis.

To improve the accessibility of the process data, we developed a software tool called "LogData Analyzer" (LDA), which is implemented in Microsoft's .NET technology and runs on Microsoft Windows systems. The current (prototype) version of the LDA is dedicated to extracting and transforming process data collected in the first round of the PIAAC study (OECD 2013). It was developed for researchers who want to prepare PIAAC process data for statistical analysis in a user-friendly way. Therefore, no programming skills are needed. Instead, the LDA offers a graphical user interface to import process data, to derive features, and to export tabulated log events and features.

Figure 24.4 shows a screenshot of the LDA tool. For one of the PIAAC example items (Locate Emails) the user selects features to be exported. Examples of features are the emails opened while working on the item, the number of drag-and-drop operations, the number of deleted mails, and many more. After selecting the appropriate variables (features) of all items to be inspected, the data is filtered and saved as a CSV file.

A complete process data set consisting of XML files by item block and person can be imported: that is, all log files of a PIAAC study. In the LDA, the process data information is presented item by item. The LDA allows for filtering the dataset by choosing first the item block, second the items included in the block and third, for each item to be analyzed, the events or features available, as shown in Fig. 24.4. Beyond the features already built-in, additional ones can easily be added to the LDA in a plug-in manner. For research purposes, the prototype version of the LDA is provided for free (contact: tba-info@dipf.de).

24.7 Conclusions and Final Remarks

The analysis and results presented in this chapter contribute to the broader theme of competency assessment: substantively, methodologically, and practically.

One major substantive conclusion that can be drawn from the present results is that problem solving in technology-rich environments draws not only upon controlled processes (by definition) but also upon automatic processes. This is indicated by the time on task effect being moderated by task difficulty, skill level, and the nature of subtasks under consideration; this concurs nicely with the framework proposed by Naumann (2012). For easy problem-solving tasks solved by skilled persons, or automatable subtasks of problem-solving tasks, we found negative time on task effects—suggesting automatic processes. This also means that successful problem-solving might be not only a result of careful deliberation and appropriate strategy selection (see Funke 2006, for an overview), but also the result of well-routinized component processes. A second major substantive conclusion is that weak problem solvers may compensate for their weaker skills by using appropriate task-engagement processes. This can mean taking more time overall (Goldhammer et al. 2014), or more time on specific actions (Tóth et al. 2013).

From a methodological perspective, the results reported in this chapter underscore both the potential for and the challenges of using process data from computer-based (large scale) assessments, to improve understanding of the assessed competency construct by considering process-related determinants of response behavior. The potential is illustrated by the fact that already very basic indicators, such as time on task (Goldhammer et al. 2014), or time on subtasks (Stelter et al. 2015) have proved strong predictors of task success. The analyses provided by Naumann et al. (2014) show that successful (i.e., "good") problem solvers are those who align their task engagement behavior (i.e., the number of actions) with task demands. In this vein, computer-based assessment, in particular when highly interactive and simulation-based items are included, provides opportunities not only to measure a "latent' variable by means of product data, but also the underlying processes that are otherwise empirically inaccessible (see Borsboom et al. 2004). The challenges however are illustrated by the fact that generic process measures that are defined task-unspecific, such as the number of actions or time on task, can have very different associations with task success, and presumably very different psychological interpretations, depending on the features both of the task and the test-taker. This is especially important to note, as psychometric models for response times such as Roskam's (1997) or van der Linden's (2007) models assume that time on task has a uniform interpretation across all tasks in the test. Our results show that, at least for complex domains, such as problem solving, this assumption may not hold. These considerations also make clear that ideally, to answer substantive research questions, analyzing process data from computer-based assessment must work together with small-scale laboratory and experimental research. While large-scale data sets may provide generalizability, in terms of samples being large and representative, laboratory research is needed to corroborate the interpretation of process measures by means of triangulation, using additional measures such as eye movements or think-aloud data.

Finally, from a more practical point of view, the analysis of process data starts with the definition of variables (features) that are extracted from log files and transformed into an importable database format. This log parsing process has to be supported by software tools. The challenge of data extraction is that various assessment systems produce log data in various log file formats. Standardized data formats would ease the access to data and enable a common and unified handling of log data coming from different sources.

Acknowledgments The preparation of this manuscript was supported by a grant from the German Research Foundation (DFG), awarded to Frank Goldhammer, Johannes Naumann, and Heiko Rölke (GO 1979/1-1) in the Priority Programme "Competence Models for Assessing Individual Learning Outcomes and Evaluating Educational Processes" (SPP 1293). Frank Goldhammer and Johannes Naumann contributed equally to this chapter.

References

Asseburg, R., & Frey, A. (2013). Too hard, too easy, or just right? The relationship between effort or boredom and ability-difficulty fit. *Psychological Test and Assessment Modeling, 55*, 92–104.

Baayen, R. H., Davidson, D. J., & Bates, D. M. (2008). Mixed-effects modeling with crossed random effects for subjects and items. *Journal of Memory and Language, 59*, 390–412. doi:10.1016/j.jml.2007.12.005.

Borsboom, D., Mellenbergh, G. J., & van Heerden, J. (2004). The concept of validty. *Psychological Review, 111*, 1061–1071. doi:10.1037/0033-295X.111.4.1061.

Brand-Gruwel, S., Wopereis, I., & Walraven, A. (2009). A descriptive model of information problem solving while using internet. *Computers & Education, 53*, 1207–1217. doi:10.1016/j.compedu.2009.06.004.

Ericsson, K. A., & Kintsch, W. (1995). Long-term working memory. *Psychological Review, 102*, 211–245. doi:10.1037/0033-295X.102.2.211.

Funke, J. (2006). Komplexes Problemlösen [Complex problem solving]. In J. Funke (Ed.), *Denken und Problemlösen (Enzyklopädie der Psychologie, Themenbereich C: Theorie und Forschung, Serie II: Kognition, Band 8)* (pp. 375–446). Göttingen: Hogrefe.

Goldhammer, F., & Klein Entink, R. H. (2011). Speed of reasoning and its relation to reasoning ability. *Intelligence, 39*, 108–119. doi:10.1016/j.intell.2011.02.001.

Goldhammer, F., Naumann, J., Stelter, A., Tóth, K., Rölke, H., & Klieme, E. (2014). The time on task effect in reading and problem solving is moderated by task difficulty and skill: Insights from a computer-based large-scale assessment. *Journal of Educational Psychology, 106*, 608–626. doi:10.1037/a0034716.

Goldman, S. R., Braasch, J. L. G., Wiley, J., Graesser, A. C., & Brodowinska, K. (2012). Comprehending and learning from Internet sources: Processing patterns of better and poorer learners. *Reading Research Quarterly, 47*, 356–381. doi:10.1002/RRQ.027.

Lawless, K. A., & Kulikowich, J. M. (1996). Understanding hypertext navigation through cluster analysis. *Journal of Educational Computing Research, 14*, 385–399. doi:10.2190/dvap-de23-3xmv-9mxh.

Naumann, J. (2012). *Belastungen und Ressourcen beim Lernen aus Text und Hypertext*. [Costs and resources in learning from text and hypertext]. (Unpublished habilitation thesis). Goethe Universität Frankfurt, Frankfurt, Germany.

Naumann, J., Goldhammer, F., Rölke, H., & Stelter, A. (2014). Erfolgreiches Problemlösen in technologiereichen Umgebungen: Wechselwirkungen zwischen Interaktionsschritten und Aufgabenkomplexität [Successful problem solving in technology-rich environments: Interactions between the number of actions and task complexity]. *Zeitschrift für Pädagogische Psychologie/German Journal of Educational Psychology, 28*, 193–203. doi:10.1024/1010-0652/a000134.

Naumann, J., Richter, T., Christmann, U., & Groeben, N. (2008). Working memory capacity and reading skill moderate the effectiveness of strategy training in learning from hypertext. *Learning and Individual Differences*, 18, 197–213.

OECD (Organisation for Economic Co-Operation and Development). (2011). *PISA 2009 results Vol VI: Student on line. Digital technologies and performance*. Paris: Author.

OECD (Organisation for Economic Co-Operation and Development). (2013). *OECD skills outlook 2013: First results from the survey of Adult Skills*. Paris: Author.

Pfaff, Y., & Goldhammer, F. (2011, September). *Measuring individual differences in ICT literacy: Evaluating online information*. Paper presented at the 14th biennial EARLI conference, Exeter, UK.

Richter, T., Naumann, J., Brunner, M., & Christmann, U. (2005). Strategische Verarbeitung beim Lernen mit Text und Hypertext [Strategic processing in learning from text and hypertext]. *German Journal of Educational Psychology, 19*, 5–22. doi:10.1024/1010-0652.19.12.5.

Roskam, E. E. (1997). Models for speed and time-limit tests. In W. J. van der Linden & R. K. Hambleton (Eds.), *Handbook of modern item response theory* (pp. 187–208). New York: Springer.

Salmerón, L., Cañas, J. J., Kintsch, W., & Fajardo, I. (2005). Reading strategies and hypertext comprehension. *Discourse Processes, 40*, 171–191. doi:10.1207/s15326950dp4003_1.

Schroeder, E. E., & Grabowski, B. L. (1995). Patterns of exploration and learning with hypermedia. *Journal of Educational Computing Research, 13*, 313–335.

Shiffrin, R. M., & Schneider, W. (1977). Controlled and automatic human information processing: II. Perceptual learning, automatic attending, and a general theory. *Psychological Review, 84*, 127–190. doi:10.1037/0033-295X.84.2.127.

Sireci, S. G., & Zenisky, A. L. (2006). Innovative item formats in computer-based testing: In pursuit of improved construct representation. In S. M. Downing & T. S. Haladyna (Eds.), *Handbook of test development* (pp. 329–348). Mahwah: Erlbaum.

Stelter, A., Goldhammer, F., Naumann, J., & Rölke, H. (2015). Die Automatisierung prozeduralen Wissens: Eine Analyse basierend auf Prozessdaten [The automation of procedural knowledge: An analysis based on process data]. In J. Stiller & C. Laschke (Eds.), *Berlin-Brandenburger Beitrage zur Bildungsforschung 2015: Herausforderungen, Befunde und Perspektiven Interdisziplinärer Bildungsforschung* (pp. 111–132). Frankfurt am Main: Lang.

Tóth, K., Rölke, H., Goldhammer, F. Kröhne, U. (2013, January/February). *Investigating students' ICT-skills with process data*. Paper presented at the DAILE13 workshop, Villard-de-Lans, France.

van der Linden, W. J. (2005). *Linear models for optimal test design*. New York: Springer.

van der Linden, W. J. (2007). A hierarchical framework for modeling speed and accuracy on test items. *Psychometrika, 72*, 287–308. doi:10.1007/s11336-006-1478-z.

van der Linden, W. J. (2009). Conceptual issues in response-time modeling. *Journal of Educational Measurement, 46*, 247–272. doi:10.1111/j.1745-3984.2009.00080.x.

van Merriënboer, J. J. G., & Sweller, J. (2005). Cognitive load theory and complex learning: Recent developments and future directions. *Educational Psychology Review, 17*, 147–177. doi:10.1007/s10648-005-3951.

Chapter 25
Dynamic Problem Solving: Multiple-Item Testing Based on Minimally Complex Systems

Joachim Funke and Samuel Greiff

Abstract Problem solving and thinking are important issues in contemporary research. With the advent of educational assessment, problem solving has been identified as a cross-curricular competence that plays an important role in educational and in occupational settings. Our research is connected to previous activities in the field of dynamic problem solving. On the basis of Dörner's "Theory of Operative Intelligence", we developed assessment instruments (called MicroDYN and MicroFIN) that allow for psychometrically acceptable measurements in the field of dynamic problem solving. MicroDYN is an approach based on linear structural equation systems and requires from the problem solver the identification of input-output connections in small dynamic systems with varying degrees of complexity. MicroFIN is an approach based on finite state automata and requires from the problem solver the identification of transitions of state in small simulated devices, within a variety of backgrounds. Besides developing of the test instruments, we checked the construct validity in relation to intelligence and working memory in a series of studies with pupils, students, and workers. Also, the internal relations between different facets of the global construct "dynamic problem solving" were analyzed.

Keywords Complex problem solving • Educational assessment • Dynamic decision making • MicroDYN • PISA 2012

J. Funke (✉)
Heidelberg University, Heidelberg, Germany
e-mail: funke@uni-hd.de

S. Greiff
University of Luxembourg, Esch-sur-Alzette, Luxembourg
e-mail: samuel.greiff@uni.lu

D. Leutner et al. (eds.), *Competence Assessment in Education*, Methodology of Educational Measurement and Assessment, DOI 10.1007/978-3-319-50030-0_25

25.1 Introduction

Problem solving research has changed its focus over the last 40 years. After the seminal paper of Dietrich Dörner (1980), which proposed a move from static to dynamic problems, a lot of research has been initiated in that area (for an overview, see: Frensch and Funke 1995; Sternberg and Frensch 1991), delivering new insights into phenomena such as intellectual emergency reaction (Dörner 1997) or the connection between emotion and complex problems (Barth and Funke 2010; Spering et al. 2005).

Our research goals are connected to this "young" tradition: (1) modeling of problem solving competencies based on Dörner's theoretical approach, (2) development of computer-based assessment instruments that allow for the measurement of different levels of proficiency and different facets of problem solving, and (3) empirical tests of the newly developed instruments within a context of educational assessment.

Our research started with questions resulting from basic research in problem solving but as the process developed (due to our collaboration with OECD on the PISA 2012 problem solving assessment), questions related to the applicability of our competence measurement in the context of large-scale assessments also became important.

This chapter presents information on all three issues in an overview format; some parts of this chapter have already been published, with more detailed information, in various publications (e.g., Fischer et al. 2012; Funke 2010, 2012; Greiff and Fischer 2013a, b; Greiff and Funke 2009; Greiff et al. 2013a, b; Greiff and Neubert 2014; Greiff et al. 2012; Wüstenberg et al. 2012; Wüstenberg et al. 2014).

25.2 Modeling of Problem Solving Competencies

In textbooks (e.g., Mayer and Wittrock 2006), problem solving is defined as cognitive processing directed at transforming a given situation into a goal situation when no obvious method of solution is available. This is very similar to the traditional definition of Duncker (1935), in his famous paper on the topic translated by Lynne Lees (Duncker 1945, p. 1): "A problem arises when a living creature has a goal but does not know how this goal is to be reached. Whenever one cannot go from the given situation to the desired situation simply by action, then there has to be recourse to thinking". Seventy years later, the definition of the problem situation has not changed substantially. What has changed drastically is the type of problem used in problem solving research: instead of static problem situations we now use dynamic situations that change in response to interventions and to time.

The Transition from Static to Dynamic Problems Dietrich Dörner (1975) was—independently of, but in line with, Donald Broadbent (1977), Andrew MacKinnon and Alex Wearing (1980)—convinced that the psychology of problem solving had to analyze how people deal with dynamics, intransparency, polytely, connectivity, and complexity as defining characteristics of problem situations. This is an issue mostly ignored in previous problem solving research that focused on static problems. But dynamic situations have tremendous consequences for the problem solver: they require the anticipation of future developments and of the short- and long-term consequences of decisions. The intransparency of a problem situation requires active information search and information generation, to gain transparency. The polytelic goal structure requires balancing goals that might compete with each other (antagonistic versus synergistic goals). The connectivity of a given system requires anticipation of even small, unintended side effects of interventions that in the end might adversely influence the intended main effects. The complexity of the problem situation requires reduction of information, so that limited cognitive resources ("bounded rationality" in the sense of Simon 1959) can deal with it.

The transition from static to dynamic problem situations was a turning point in problem solving research. The dynamics and complexities of everyday life problems, as well as those of societal challenges, became subject to theories and to empirical work (Dörner 1997; Frensch and Funke 1995; Sternberg and Frensch 1991; Verweij and Thompson 2006; Zsambok and Klein 1997). "Dynamic decision making" (Brehmer 1989) and "naturalistic decision making" (Klein 1997) were among the labels for the new movement. With his concept of *Operative Intelligence*, Dörner (1986) emphasized the importance of examining not only the speed and precision of some of the basic intellectual processes, but also the more formative aspects of problem solving: for example (1) *circumspection* (e.g., anticipation of future and side effects of interventions), (2) the ability to *regulate* cognitive operations (e.g., knowing when to do trial-and-error and when to systematically analyze the situation at hand; when to use exhaustive algorithms and when to rely on heuristics, when to incubate an idea, and so forth), or (3) the availability of *heuristics* (e.g., being able to build helpful subgoals, to constrain the problem space efficiently). It turns out that dynamic problems require these competencies in a greatly different way than static problems, which rely mainly on deduction.

This list of examples is not exhaustive, but it gives an idea of what is meant by the "operative" aspects that are not adequately addressed by traditional intelligence tests but may still be considered relevant for an organized course of intellectual processes (Dörner 1986). With its explicit focus on gaining and using information and knowledge about cognitive operations, adequate, operative intelligence can be considered one of the most relevant expansions of intelligence as it is measured with current measurement devices: Intelligence in a problem solving situation turns out to consist of being able to collect information, to integrate and structure goal-oriented information, to make prognoses, to plan and to make decisions, to set goals and to change them. To achieve all this, an individual has to be able to produce an organized series of information processing steps, flexibly adapting these steps to the demands of the situation—only then can it be considered intelligent (Dörner 1986, p. 292).

Table 25.1 The five facets and their relation to the five characteristic features of dynamic problem solving within the processes of representation and solution[a]

Model phase	Characteristic feature	Cognitive process
Representation	Complexity of the structure	Information reduction
Representation	Intransparency of the situation	Information generation
Representation	Interconnectedness of variables	Model building
Solution	Polytely of the task	Goal elaboration and balancing
Solution	Dynamics of the system	Prediction, planning and decision making

[a]Modified from Greiff and Fischer (2013b, p. 50)

A central premise of our research approach is its competence orientation (Weinert 2001). According to Klieme and Leutner (2006), competencies are defined as context-specific cognitive dispositions that are needed to successfully cope with certain situations or tasks in specific domains. In our case, we address the competence of dealing with problem situations from different domains that are complex, intransparent at the start of action, and that change their state over time.

The Five Facets of Dynamic Problems The facets of operative intelligence emphasized in this characterization closely resemble the facets of complex dynamic problems (Dörner 1997; Dörner et al. 1983; Funke 1992, 2001) that are most relevant for coping with these characteristic features: (1) the *complexity* of the structure (requiring information reduction), (2) the *intransparency* of the situation (requiring systematically generating information), (3) the *interconnectedness* of the variables (requiring building a model of the most relevant effects), (4) the *polytely* of the task (requiring goal elaboration and for setting priorities), and (5) the *dynamics* of the system (requiring planning and dynamic decision making). Table 25.1 shows these five facets and connects the first three of them to the representation of the problem solving situation (system exploration), whereas the last two are connected to solution approaches (system control).

These characteristic features of dynamic problems and the corresponding facets of *dynamic problem solving* (DPS; see Funke 2001) can be considered a fruitful starting point for measuring operative intelligence, which in turn might be the most important factor determining DPS performance. In the next section we present our ideas for assessing these facets of DPS with the help of computer-based assessment instruments.

25.3 Development of Computer-Based Assessment Instruments

Especially in the assessment of interactive, dynamic problem solving, much progress has been made in recent years. With the help of formalisms such as MicroDYN (problem situations based on linear structural equation systems, LSE approach) and MicroFIN (problem situations based on finite state automata, FSA approach), large-scale assessments such as the Programme for International Student Assessment (PISA; see e.g., OECD 2013) from the Organisation for Economic Cooperation and Development (OECD) have been directed to these competencies that will play an important role in the twenty-first century.

Why are these formalisms so helpful in designing assessment instruments? The answer lies in the fact that on the basis of some elementary building blocks, one can develop arbitrarily complex systems with different semantic embeddings. Figure 25.1 illustrates the modules that were used in our item construction: main effect, multiple effect, multiple dependence, eigendynamic, and side effects, describe different (and arbitrary) relations between an arbitrary number of inputs and an arbitrary number of output variables.

With the help of the building blocks shown in Fig. 25.1, one can design a large universe of MicroDYN systems, starting with a trivial 1x1 system and changing to infinitely complex NxM systems (N, M being the number of input and output variables, respectively) that have to be explored and controlled by our subjects. The building blocks of finite state automata are even simpler: they consist of states and transitions between states. One can build arbitrary complex MicroFIN systems that represent machineries with very different types of behavior (see the examples given by Buchner and Funke 1993). Behind the development of MicroDYN and MicroFIN stands the concept of minimal complexity, which has to be explained first.

The Concept of Minimal Complexity Inspired by ideas from Dörner, but coming from a psychometric perspective, Greiff and Funke (2010) introduced the following idea: rather than increasing problem complexity more and more, to start with *minimally complex systems*: that is, systems that are at the lower end of complexity.

The starting point of this concept is the idea that complex systems are needed in problem-solving research because their features differ markedly from simple static systems (in terms of complexity, connectivity, dynamics, intransparency, and

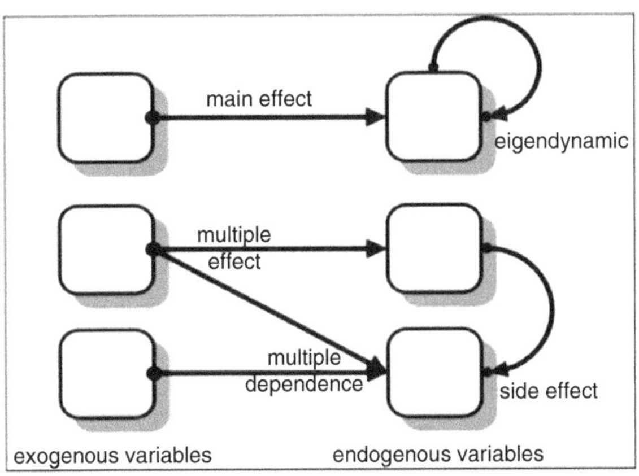

Fig. 25.1 Underlying elementary structure of a MicroDYN item displayed some possible effects between exogenous (input) and endogenous (output) variables (from Greiff and Funke, 2009, p. 159): The modules that were used in our item construction were main effect, multiple effect, multiple dependence, eigendynamic, and side effect

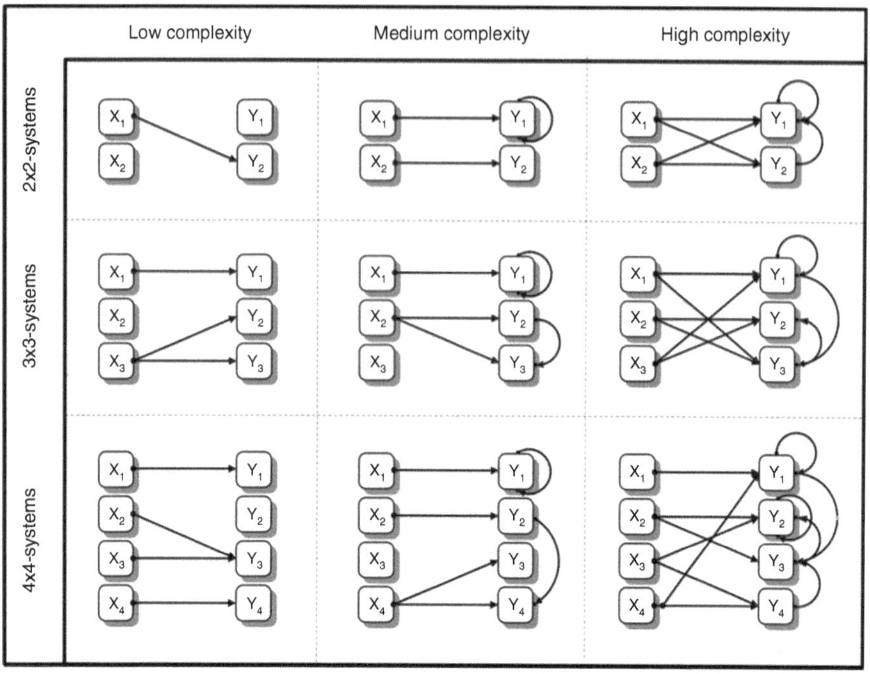

Fig. 25.2 Example of two independent complexity manipulations: (**a**) number of input and output variables (increasing from 2 to 4), (**b**) number of connections (increasing from 1 to 12)

polytely) and their solution requires not simply the addition of simple processes (Funke 2010). The conception of minimally complex systems uses a simple strategy: instead of realizing more and more complex systems (trying to reach for the greatest complexity) with questionable content validity, it instead seeks the minimum complexity. Complexity is a very unclear term—the upper limit of complexity is still open and yet, the lower limit of complexity must be somewhere between nothing and a small degree of complexity. Instead of searching for the upper bounds of complexity, we concentrate on the lower limits and introduce "complexifying elements"—to use a term introduced by MacKinnon and Wearing (1985, p. 170). Figure 25.2 illustrates two types of complexity manipulations for MicroDYN items, as described in Greiff and Funke (2009, p. 160).

This shift in focus to the perspective of minimally complex systems has some advantages for developers of psychometric tests, which can be characterized by the following four points: (1) the time spent on a single scenario is measured not in hours but in minutes, thereby increasing the economies of test application; (2) due to the short time required for item application, a series of items can be presented, rather than one-item testing, thereby increasing reliability; (3) because of our use of formalisms, arbitrary semantic embeddings become feasible, thereby increasing ecological validity; and, (4) a broad range of difficulty levels can be addressed, thereby increasing conceptual validity, as shown by Greiff et al. (2012).

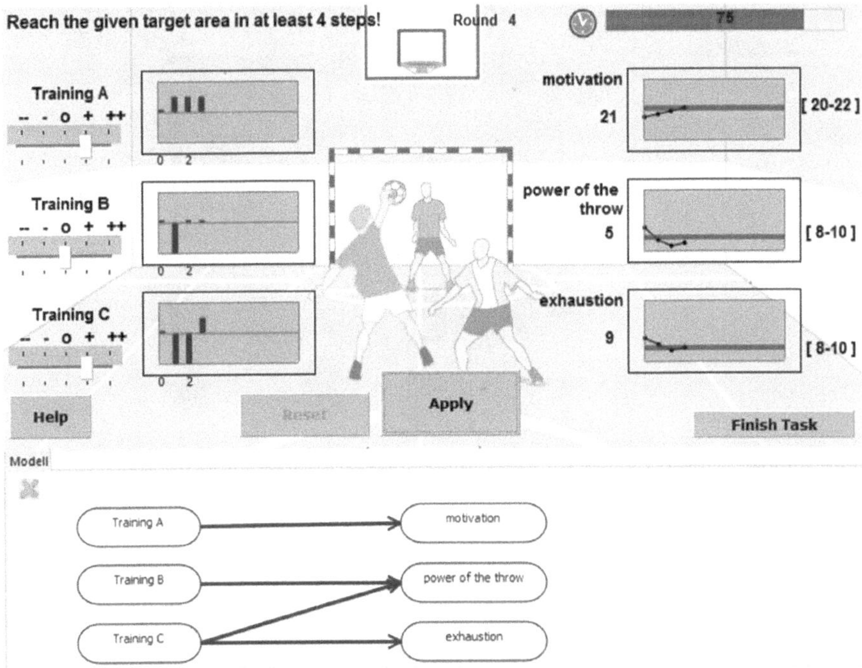

Fig. 25.3 Screenshot of the MicroDYN-item "handball training" (knowledge application phase). The controllers of the input variables (*upper left part*) range from "– –" to "++". The current values and the target values are displayed numerically and graphically (*upper part right*). The correct causal model is presented in the *lower part* (From Wüstenberg et al. 2012, p. 5)

What was the task for the subjects in our experiments? Firstly, a problem solver, who is only shown the values of the input and output variables (but not the underlying structure of the system), had to specify a series of input values in order to identify the system's structure (the problem solver could draw his or her model of the causal structure between the variables in a causal diagram). Secondly, the problem solver had to specify a series of input values in order to reach given target values (see Fig. 25.3 for an example within a MicroDYN task). In this phase ("rule application"), there is a specific goal for controlling the system, whereas in the first part ("rule identification"), there is the unspecific goal of exploring the system and drawing a causal model of the assumed relations ("rule knowledge").

The procedure in the MicroFIN task was very similar: First, participants had to explore the given automaton by pressing the available buttons and seeing what happens. After some time exploring self-selected state-transitions, in the second phase the task is to reach a specified goal state in the machine from a given state, with the least number of button presses. Figure 25.4 illustrates the interface for the "MP3-Player" developed for the PISA 2012 Study.

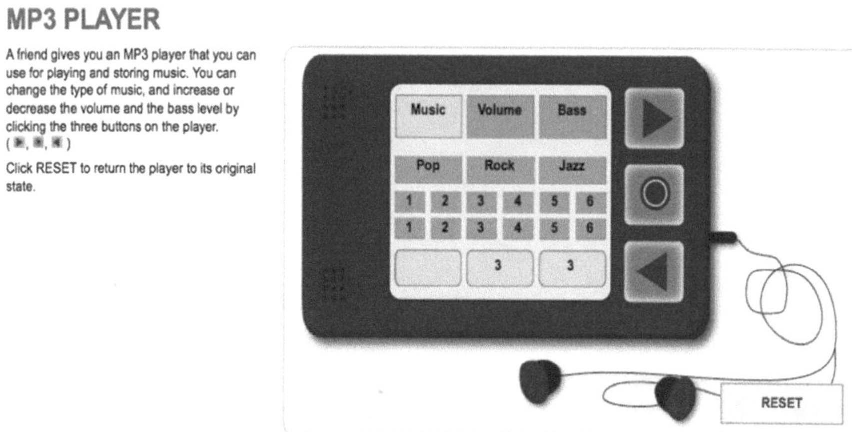

Fig. 25.4 MicroFIN item "MP3 Player" as an interactive problem-solving item example in PISA 2012. By pressing the buttons to the *right*, the MP3 player's state changes (indicated by the highlighted fields) (Version adapted from Greiff et al. 2013a, p. 78)

On the basis of the two formalisms, a large number of items (both for MicroDYN and MicroFIN) with different difficulty levels were developed and used in our studies.

Multiple Item Testing On the basis of the formal mechanisms of LSE and FSA, an additional feature of our approach comes into play, called multiple item testing. The idea comes from psychometrics and entails multiple items instead of single item testing. It is very easy to construct a universe of independent LSE and FSA tasks, each with varying degrees of difficulty. This procedure increases the reliability of measurement, compared to a situation in which one final data point after a long sequence of decisions is taken as a measure of performance (as is done, for example, in the standard procedure for the computer-simulated Tailorshop; see Danner et al. 2011).

Disadvantages of MicroDYN and MicroFIN The use of minimally complex systems and multiple item testing also has some disadvantages, the most important being the fact that dealing with complexity, in the sense of uncertainty management, is lost completely. In some cases, only main effects between three input and three output variables had to be identified—there were neither indirect effects nor delayed effects or goal conflicts. One could argue that—if no eigendynamic or side effects are implemented—these MicroDYN measurements mostly reflect the competence of the VOTAT strategy ("vary one thing at a time") or, in the phrasing of Klahr (2009) the CVS ("control of variables strategy"), but the set of strategies for dealing with complex systems is much larger. If broader strategies are to be assessed, different task requirements other than the identification of linear systems are needed. This has to do with the next point, stimulus sampling.

Stimulus Sampling of Problems For assessment purposes, a large item universe is needed. That is one of the advantages of formal systems (Funke 2001) such as linear structural equation systems or finite state automata. The disadvantage of using these formalisms is the restricted range of problems that follow all the same model. Subjects are confronted with changing semantics, but the deep structure of the problems does not change: one has to deal with linear combinations or with state transitions. After a short time, the problem situations become routine and the assessment runs the risk of no longer addressing problem-solving behavior. How long are subjects in those assessment situations problem solvers, and when do they learn from experience? Fiedler (2011, p. 166) warns against the consequences when stimulus sampling is not done broadly, namely, that "findings may reveal more about the stimuli chosen than the persons being tested".

Learning Effects A last problem of multiple-item testing consists in the fact that some generalizable strategies (e.g., VOTAT) can be learned during work on the first item of an item bundle, thus making the following items of that bundle easier, because problem-solving behavior changes from production to reproduction. Whereas learning within more complex tasks such as Tailorshop is part of the game, in a multiple item situation it could be a disadvantage, and would need to be controlled (see Funke 2014a).

25.4 Empirical Tests of the Newly Developed Instruments

During the active phase of our project, in cooperation with our partner institutions, we ran empirical tests of the newly developed instruments for the assessment of complex problem solving (CPS) based on multiple-item testing with MicroDYN. These tests addressed the following areas:

- Measurement model: What is the internal structure of our assumed competencies? Is it possible to identify the three postulated facets of (1) rule identification (adequateness of strategies), (2) rule knowledge (generated knowledge) and (3) rule application (ability to control a system)?
- Predictive and incremental validity: Do our constructs have validity in predicting external criteria like school grade point average (GPA), and is incremental prediction beyond IQ scores possible?
- Differences with respect to age, gender, culture: Is the data pattern with respect to differential variables (like the mentioned ones) plausible?

To answer these questions, some larger data collections at school were initiated by our research group: (1) school studies at the Heidelberg area, (2) school studies with a research group at Szeged University, and (3) school studies with a research group at Helsinki University. Reports about two of these data collections will be presented here in short (technical details can be found in the following publications: a paper from Wüstenberg et al. (2012) on the measurement model and on predictive and incremental validity (the Heidelberg School Study), and the paper from Wüstenberg et al. (2014) on individual differences with respect to age, gender, and cultural background [German-Hungarian School Comparison Study]).

Wüstenberg et al. (2012) analyzed the internal structure and construct validity of the newly developed MicroDYN items. The computer-based CPS test, with eight MicroDYN items, and the Raven Advanced Progressive Matrices, as traditional test of reasoning, were given to a sample of $N = 222$ university students.

Measurement model: Data analysis based on structural equation models showed that a two-dimensional model of CPS, including rule knowledge and rule application, fitted the data best. In this study, rule identification could not be established as a third facet on its own. Empirically, there was no difference between the two facets of rule identification and rule knowledge.

Predictive and incremental validity: Reasoning predicted performance in rule application only indirectly, through its influence on rule knowledge: This indicates that learning during system exploration is a prerequisite for controlling a system successfully. Also, MicroDYN scores explained variance in GPA even beyond reasoning, showing the incremental validity of our items. Our conclusion: MicroDYN items predict real life criteria such as GPA and therefore, measure important aspects of academic performance that go beyond reasoning.

Wüstenberg et al. (2014) analyzed cross-national and gender differences in complex problem solving. Six MicroDYN items were applied to a sample of 890 Hungarian and German high school students attending eighth to eleventh grade.

Differences with respect to gender and culture: Multi-group confirmatory factor analyses showed that measurement invariance of MicroDYN scores was found across gender and nationality. In regard to latent mean differences it showed that, on average, males outperformed females and German students outperformed Hungarian students. The main reason for these results was the comparatively poor performance of Hungarian females. Log files of process data showing the interaction of participants with the task illustrate that Hungarian females used the VOTAT strategy less often; as a consequence, they achieved less knowledge acquisition. A detailed log-file based analysis of such differences is therefore helpful for a better understanding of data from cross-national comparisons. We expect that such process analyses can also be helpful in better understanding group differences (between nations, gender, etc.) in large-scale assessments like PISA.

Summarizing: As can be seen from the empirical tests, our MicroDYN test development produced reliable data that were able to predict indicators like GPA, beyond IQ scores. Also, differential effects with respect to age, gender, and culture were mostly in line with our expectations and underline the usefulness of the new instruments for such comparisons.

25.5 Educational Application: PISA 2012

In educational contexts, measures of problem solving are useful if one is interested in cross-curricular competencies. The PISA 2012 definition of problem-solving competence is as follows:

> Problem-solving competency is an individual's capability to engage in cognitive processing to understand and resolve problem situations where a method of solutions is not immediately obvious. It includes the willingness to engage with such situations in order to achieve one's potential as a constructive and reflective citizen. (OECD 2013, p. 122)

In the PISA 2012 computer-based problem-solving assessment, with about 85,000 students from 44 countries and economies, over one half of the tasks were *interactive*. Examples of interactive problems encountered in everyday life include discovering how to use an unfamiliar mobile telephone or automatic vending machine. These PISA tasks were developed with the background described in this article; they were constructed on the basis of proposals from our Heidelberg research group.

PISA's *interactive* problems are intransparent (i.e., there is undisclosed information), but not necessarily dynamic or highly complex. *Static* problems are those in which all the information necessary to solve the problem is disclosed to the problem solver at the outset; by definition they are completely transparent.

Students' answers to the 42 problem-solving tasks in the assessment allowed the assignment of students into one of seven proficiency levels, including one that contained the students who performed below the first, and lowest, of six described proficiency levels. At the highest level, students should be able to do the following:

> At Level 6, students can develop complete, coherent mental models of diverse problem scenarios, enabling them to solve complex problems efficiently. They can explore a scenario in a highly strategic manner to understand all information pertaining to the problem. The information may be presented in different formats, requiring interpretation and integration of related parts. When confronted with very complex devices, such as home appliances that work in an unusual or unexpected manner, they quickly learn how to control the devices to achieve a goal in an optimal way. Level 6 problem-solvers can set up general hypotheses about a system and thoroughly test them. They can follow a premise through to a logical conclusion or recognize when there is not enough information available to reach one. In order to reach a solution, these highly proficient problem-solvers can create complex, flexible, multi-step plans that they continually monitor during execution. Where necessary, they modify their strategies, taking all constraints into account, both explicit and implicit. (OECD 2013, p. 122)

What are the educational and political consequences of this assessment? The OECD (2013, p. 122) report formulates:

> that today's 15-year-olds who lack advanced problem-solving skills face high risks of economic disadvantage as adults. They must compete for jobs in occupations where opportunities are becoming rare; and if they are unable to adapt to new circumstances and learn in unfamiliar contexts, they may find it particularly difficult to move to better jobs as economic and technological conditions evolve.

Training and teaching of problem-solving skills therefore becomes a task for schools.

25.5.1 Two Additional Issues: Optimization and Causal Diagrams

Use of Modern Mathematical Optimization Techniques As we have shown, important progress can be expected if the course of problem solving is evaluated quantitatively. Rather than merely evaluating the final solution, the concurrent evaluation of stepwise decision-making promises additional new insights, which can be achieved with the help of modern techniques of mixed-integer nonlinear optimization, as demonstrated by Sager et al. (2011) with the business scenario "Tailorshop". For that scenario, a process performance indicator can be computed under the label of "what is still possible": an indicator that shows the optimal solution at each point in time (during the round-based proceeding through the task), given all previous decisions and actions. For example, even for a subject who has played ten rounds of unsuccessful decision-making, there is still an optimal score for the last two rounds if, from now on, only the best decisions are made. This indicator allows a much more precise evaluation of a subject's solution path, compared to traditional indicators that measure the available money at the end of each round.

Causal Diagrams To measure knowledge acquisition by means of causal diagrams is a standard procedure in assessment procedures, and is used within MicroDYN. It leads to reliable measures of knowledge about causal relations, but it also has some disadvantages: On the one hand, considering causal connections between system variables stimulates thinking about causality that otherwise might not have been possible (see Blech and Funke 2006). On the other hand, Griffiths and Tenenbaum (2009, p. 670) point to an "inherent limitation in the expressive capacity of graphical models", due to the fact that they cannot discriminate between different types of causal entities or different functional relationships between variables, such as conditional links. Progress is needed, with respect to other ways of assessing structural knowledge. One has to be aware of the fact that this kind of mind-mapping turns out to be a secondary task that needs additional resources besides the identification task (see also Eseryel et al. 2013).

This issue relates also to an old question concerning implicit and explicit modes of knowledge about systems (see Berry and Broadbent 1988). Knowledge acquisition processes go for rule-abstraction, whereas knowledge application might be driven more by instance-based decision making (Gonzalez et al. 2003). Therefore, the question of adequate measurement of acquired knowledge is still open (also, learning curves would be helpful, to describe the process of acquisition in more detail).

25.6 Future Developments

Future developments could run along different, promising lines of research—we will explain two of them in more detail: (1) concerning the unit of analysis, an extension of complex problem-solving activities from the individual to the social dimension might occur, and (2) concerning methods, a more process-oriented use of log files resulting from computer-based assessments might reveal more process information. Further ideas for future research are described in Funke (2014b).

From the Individual to the Social Dimension The steep rise of communicative and team tasks in modern society (Autor et al. 2003) makes it evident that there is an inherently social aspect in any type of learning or problem solving (Lee and Smagorinsky 2000). To this end, collaborative problem solving—following Greiff et al. (2013a, p. 81)—is to be incorporated into an international large-scale assessment for the first time. In the PISA 2015 assessment framework (OECD 2012), collaborative problem solving is tentatively defined as "the capacity of an individual to effectively engage in a process whereby two or more agents attempt to solve a problem by sharing the understanding and effort required to come to a solution" (p. 7). In keeping with previous efforts to define collaborative problem solving (e.g., Griffin et al. 2011; Morgan et al. 1993; O'Neil et al. 2003), collaboration and problem solving are seen as correlated but sufficiently distinct dimensions. That is, for problem solving, the cognitive processes of interactive problem solving in the PISA 2012 framework will be retained, whereas a new assessment of social and collaborative skills will be added in the PISA 2015 framework.

Process-Oriented Use of Log files To quote Duncker (1945, p. 1, in italics in the original) once again: "How does the solution arise from the problem situation? In what ways is the solution of a problem attained?", is an important question in understanding the process of complex problem solving. To get answers on this old question, log files are promising a new era of process research (Schulte-Mecklenbeck and Huber 2003; Zoanetti 2010). Behavioral and process data of problem-solving patterns are now partly implemented in the PISA scoring procedures, and are directly connected to the emerging field of educational data mining, in which experimental and psychometric methods are applied to large educational data sets (Rupp et al. 2012). The promises of log-file analyses have been explored in recent work (see Goldhammer et al. 2014; Kupiainen et al. 2014) that gives deeper insights into problem-solving processes.

Optimistic Outlook Summarizing recent developments in problem-solving research under the auspices of what Stellan Ohlsson has correctly labeled the "Newell-Simon paradigm", Ohlsson (2012, p. 117) wrote:

> In summary, Newell and Simon's first concept of generality, codified in the General Problem Solver, failed as a psychological theory because it is not true: there is no single problem solving mechanism, no universal strategy that people apply across all domains and of which every task-specific strategy is a specific instance. Their second concept of generality initiated research on the cognitive architecture. The latter is a successful scientific concern with

> many accomplishments and a bright future. But it buys generality by focusing on a time band at which problem solving becomes invisible, like an elephant viewed from one inch away.

This pessimistic statement (specific problem solving research vanishes and ends up in general assumptions on cognitive architectures) is not our point of view. Within this priority program funded by the German Research Foundation, we have delivered some new ideas for psychometric sound assessment of problem solving (multiple item testing based on minimally complex systems from LSE and FSA formalisms). The competencies needed for these tasks are derived from Dörner's theory of operative intelligence. The measurement invariance, latent mean comparisons, and other psychometrically relevant data are documented in international large-scale studies beyond PISA (e.g., Wüstenberg et al. 2014). Therefore, as we have tried to show in this chapter, at least with respect to the assessment of problem solving competencies, some progress has been made in recent research activities, and will also be made in the future.

Acknowledgments The work reported here would not have been possible without the generous funding from the German Research Foundation (DFG) over so many years. Since 2007, continuous support (Fu 173/11, Fu 173/13, Fu 173/14) within the Priority Program (SPP 1293) "Competence Models for Assessing Individual Learning Outcomes and Evaluating Educational Processes" helped us to develop theory as well as assessment instruments, and to collect data. Additional, related funding from the German Ministry of Science (BMBF) supported these developments (FKZ 01JG1062: "Dynamisches Problemlösen als fachübergreifende Kompetenz", 2011–2014 to JF, and FKZ 012LSA004: "Validation and development of individual assessment devices to capture Dynamic Problem Solving", 2012–2015, to JF, together with Frank Goldhammer and SG). Also, DIPF (Frankfurt) and SoftCon (Munich) were extremely helpful in supporting the development of the ItemBuilder software.

Thanks are due not only to funding agencies but also to individual people. Andreas Fischer, Julia Hilse, Daniel Holt, André Kretzschmar, Jonas Neubert, and Sascha Wüstenberg are in the first line of acknowledgement; many Heidelberg student assistants are in the second line, our participants in the data collections in the third line. Colleagues from around the world have discussed our concepts with us intensively: Ray Adams, Esther Care, Beno Csapo, Michel Dorochevsky, John Dossey, Frank Goldhammer, Coty Gonzalez, Art Graesser, Patrick Griffin, Jarkko Hautamäki, Eckhart Klieme, Sirkku Kupiainen, Detlev Leutner, Romain Martin, Reinhold Nickolaus, Barry McCrae, Gyongyver Molnar, Markku Niemivirta, Magda Osman, Ray Philpot, Dara Ramalingam, Heiko Rölke, Andreas Schleicher, Alexander Siegmund, Philipp Sonnleitner, Robert Sternberg, David Tobinski, Mari-Pauliina Vainikainen, Kathrin Viehrig, Joachim Wirth—to mention only some of them. Thanks to all of you!

References

Autor, D. H., Levy, F., & Murnane, R. J. (2003). The skill content of recent technological change: An empirical exploration. *The Quarterly Journal of Economics, 118*, 1279–1333. doi:10.1162/003355303322552801.

Barth, C. M., & Funke, J. (2010). Negative affective environments improve complex solving performance. *Cognition & Emotion, 24*, 1259–1268. doi:10.1080/02699930903223766.

Berry, D. C., & Broadbent, D. E. (1988). Interactive tasks and the implicit-explicit distinction. *British Journal of Psychology, 79*, 251–272. doi:10.1111/j.2044-8295.1988.tb02286.x.
Blech, C., & Funke, J. (2006). Zur Reaktivität von Kausaldiagramm-Analysen beim komplexen Problemlösen [On the reactivity of causal diagram assessments in complex problem solving]. *Zeitschrift für Psychologie, 117*, 185–195. doi:10.1026/0044-3409.214.4.185.
Brehmer, B. (1989). Dynamic decision making. In A. P. Sage (Ed.), *Concise encyclopedia of information processing in systems and organizations* (pp. 144–149). New York, NY: Pergamon.
Broadbent, D. E. (1977). Levels, hierarchies, and the locus of control. *Quarterly Journal of Experimental Psychology, 29*, 181–201. doi:10.1080/14640747708400596.
Buchner, A., & Funke, J. (1993). Finite-state automata: Dynamic task environments in problem-solving research. *The Quarterly Journal of Experimental Psychology Section A, 46*, 83–118. doi:10.1080/14640749308401068.
Danner, D., Hagemann, D., Holt, D. V., Hager, M., Schankin, A., Wüstenberg, S., & Funke, J. (2011). Measuring performance in a complex problem solving task: Reliability and validity of the Tailorshop simulation. *Journal of Individual Differences, 32*, 225–233. doi:10.1027/1614-0001/a000055.
Dörner, D. (1975). Wie Menschen eine Welt verbessern wollten und sie dabei zerstörten [How people wanted to improve the world and destroyed it]. *Bild der Wissenschaft, 12*, 48–53.
Dörner, D. (1980). On the difficulty people have in dealing with complexity. *Simulations and Games, 11*, 87–106. doi:10.1177/104687818001100108.
Dörner, D. (1986). Diagnostik der operativen Intelligenz [Assessment of operative intelligence]. *Diagnostica, 32*, 290–308.
Dörner, D. (1997). *The logic of failure: Recognizing and avoiding error in complex situations*. New York, NY: Basic.
Dörner, D., Kreuzig, H. W., Reither, F., Stäudel, T. (1983). *Lohhausen. Vom Umgang mit Unbestimmtheit und Komplexität* [Lohhausen. On dealing with uncertainty and complexity]. Bern: Huber.
Duncker, K. (1935). *Zur Psychologie des produktiven Denkens [Psychology of productive thinking]*. Berlin: Springer.
Duncker, K. (1945). On problem-solving. *Psychological Monographs, 58*(5), 1–113.
Eseryel, D., Ifenthaler, D., & Ge, X. (2013). Validation study of a method for assessing complex ill-structured problem solving by using causal representations. *Educational Technology Research and Development, 61*, 443–463. doi:10.1007/s11423-013-9297-2.
Fiedler, K. (2011). Voodoo correlations are everywhere—Not only in neuroscience. *Perspectives on Psychological Science, 6*, 163–171. doi:10.1177/1745691611400237.
Fischer, A., Greiff, S., & Funke, J. (2012). The process of solving complex problems. *The Journal of Problem Solving, 4*(1), 19–42. doi:10.7771/1932-6246.1118.
Frensch, P. A., & Funke, J. (Eds.). (1995). *Complex problem solving: The European perspective*. Hillsdale: Erlbaum.
Funke, J. (1992). Dealing with dynamic systems: Research strategy, diagnostic approach and experimental results. *German Journal of Psychology, 16*, 24–43.
Funke, J. (2001). Dynamic systems as tools for analysing human judgement. *Thinking and Reasoning, 7*, 69–89. doi:10.1080/13546780042000046.
Funke, J. (2010). Complex problem solving: A case for complex cognition? *Cognitive Processing, 11*, 133–142. doi:10.1007/s10339-009-0345-0.
Funke, J. (2012). Complex problem solving. In N. M. Seel (Ed.), *Encyclopedia of the sciences of learning* (pp. 682–685). Heidelberg: Springer. doi:10.1007/978-1-4419-1428-6_685.
Funke, J. (2014a). Analysis of minimal complex systems and complex problem solving require different forms of causal cognition. *Frontiers in Psychology, 5*, 739. doi:10.3389/fpsyg.2014.00739.
Funke, J. (2014b). Problem solving: What are the important questions? In P. Bello, M. Guarini, M. McShane, & B. Scassellati (Eds.), *Proceedings of the 36th Annual Conference of the Cognitive Science Society* (pp. 493–498). Austin: Cognitive Science Society.

Goldhammer, F., Naumann, J., Stelter, A., Tóth, K., Rölke, H., & Klieme, E. (2014). The time on task effect in reading and problem solving is moderated by task difficulty and skill: Insights from a computer-based large-scale assessment. *Journal of Educational Psychology, 106*, 608–626. doi:10.1037/a0034716.

Gonzalez, C., Lerch, J. F., & Lebiere, C. (2003). Instance-based learning in dynamic decision making. *Cognitive Science, 27*, 591–635. doi:10.1016/S0364-0213(03)00031-4.

Greiff, S., & Fischer, A. (2013a). Der Nutzen einer komplexen Problemlösekompetenz: Theoretische Überlegungen und empirische Befunde [The value of complex problem-solving competence: Theoretical considerations and empirical results]. *Zeitschrift für Pädagogische Psychologie, 27*(1), 27–39. doi:10.1024/1010-0652/a000086.

Greiff, S., & Fischer, A. (2013b). Measuring complex problem solving: An educational application of psychological theories. *Journal for Educational Research Online, 5*(1), 38–58.

Greiff, S., & Funke, J. (2009). Measuring complex problem solving: The MicroDYN approach. In F. Scheuermann (Ed.), *The transition to computer-based assessment: Lessons learned from large-scale surveys and implications for testing* (pp. 157–163). Luxembourg: Office for Official Publications of the European Communities.

Greiff, S., & Funke, J. (2010). Systematische Erforschung komplexer Problemlösefähigkeit anhand minimal komplexer Systeme [Systematic research on complex problem solving by means of minimal complex systems]. *Zeitschrift für Pädagogik, Beiheft, 56*, 216–227.

Greiff, S., & Neubert, J. C. (2014). On the relation of complex problem solving, personality, fluid intelligence, and academic achievement. *Learning and Individual Differences, 36*, 37–48. doi:10.1016/j.lindif.2014.08.003.

Greiff, S., Wüstenberg, S., & Funke, J. (2012). Dynamic problem solving: A new assessment perspective. *Applied Psychological Measurement, 36*, 189–213. doi:10.1177/0146621612439620.

Greiff, S., Holt, D. V., & Funke, J. (2013a). Perspectives on problem solving in educational assessment: analytical, interactive, and collaborative problem solving. *The Journal of Problem Solving, 6*, 71–91. doi:10.7771/1932-6246.1153.

Greiff, S., Wüstenberg, S., Holt, D. V., Goldhammer, F., & Funke, J. (2013b). Computer-based assessment of complex problem solving: Concept, implementation, and application. *Educational Technology Research and Development, 61*, 407–421. doi:10.1007/s11423-013-9301-x.

Griffin, P., McGaw, B., & Care, E. (Eds.). (2011). *Assessment and teaching of 21st century skills*. New York, NY: Springer.

Griffiths, T. L., & Tenenbaum, J. B. (2009). Theory-based causal induction. *Psychological Review, 116*, 661–716. doi:10.1037/a0017201.

Klahr, D. (2009). "To every thing there is a season, and a time to every purpose under the heavens": What about direct instruction? In S. Tobias & T. M. Duffy (Eds.), *Constructivist theory applied to instruction: Success or failure?* (pp. 291–310). New York, NY: Taylor & Francis.

Klein, G. (1997). The current status of the naturalistic decision making framework. In R. H. Flin, E. Salas, M. Strub, & L. Martin (Eds.), *Decision making under stress: Emerging theories and applications* (pp. 11–28). Aldershot: Ashgate.

Klieme, E., & Leutner, D. (2006). Kompetenzmodelle zur Erfassung individueller Lernergebnisse und zur Bilanzierung von Bildungsprozessen. Beschreibung eines neu eingerichteten Schwerpunktprogramms der DFG [Competence models for assessing individual learning outcomes and evaluating of educational processes. Description of a new DFG priority program]. *Zeitschrift für Pädagogik, 52*, 876–903.

Kupiainen, S., Vainikainen, M.-P., Marjanen, J., & Hautamäki, J. (2014). The role of time on task in computer-based low-stakes assessment of cross-curricular skills. *Journal of Educational Psychology, 106*, 627–638. doi:10.1037/a0035507.

Lee, C. D., & Smagorinsky, P. (Eds.). (2000). *Vygotskian perspectives on literacy research: Constructing meaning through collaborative inquiry*. Cambridge: Cambridge University Press.

MacKinnon, A. J., & Wearing, A. J. (1980). Complexity and decision making. *Behavioral Science, 25*, 285–296. doi:10.1002/bs.3830250405.

MacKinnon, A. J., & Wearing, A. J. (1985). Systems analysis and dynamic decision making. *Acta Psychologica, 58*, 159–172. doi:10.1016/0001-6918(85)90005-8.

Mayer, R. E., & Wittrock, M. C. (2006). Problem solving. In P. A. Alexander & P. H. Winne (Eds.), *Handbook of educational psychology* (pp. 287–303). Mahwah: Erlbaum.

Morgan, B. B., Salas, E., & Glickman, A. S. (1993). An analysis of team evaluation and maturation. *Journal of General Psychology, 120*, 277–291. doi:10.1080/00221309.1993.9711148.

O'Neil, H. F., Chuang, S., & Chung, G. K. W. K. (2003). Issues in the computer-based assessment of collaborative problem solving. *Assessment in Education: Principles, Policy & Practice, 10*, 361–373. doi:10.1080/0969594032000148190.

OECD (Organisation for Economic Co-operation and Development). (2012, April). *PISA 2015 field trial collaborative problem solving framework*. Paper presented at the 33rd PISA Governing Board meeting, Tallinn, Estonia.

OECD (Organisation for Economic Co-operation and Development). (2013). *PISA 2012 assessment and analytical framework: Mathematics, reading, science, problem solving and financial literacy*. Paris: Author.

Ohlsson, S. (2012). The problems with problem solving: Reflections on the rise, current status, and possible future keywords. *The Journal of Problem Solving, 5*(1), 101–128. doi:10.7771/1932-6246.1144.

Rupp, A. A., Nugent, R., & Nelson, B. (2012). Evidence-centered design for diagnostic assessment within digital learning environments: Integrating modern psychometrics and educational data mining. *Journal of Educational Data Mining, 4*, 1–10.

Sager, S., Barth, C. M., Diedam, H., Engelhart, M., & Funke, J. (2011). Optimization as an analysis tool for human complex problem solving. *SIAM Journal on Optimization, 21*, 936–959. doi:10.1137/11082018X.

Schulte-Mecklenbeck, M., & Huber, O. (2003). Information search in the laboratory and on the web: With or without an experimenter. *Behavior Research Methods, Instruments, & Computers, 35*, 227–235.

Simon, H. A. (1959). Theories of decision making in economics and behavioural science. *American Economic Review, 49*, 253–283. doi:10.2307/1809901.

Spering, M., Wagener, D., & Funke, J. (2005). The role of emotions in complex problem-solving. *Cognition & Emotion, 19*, 1252–1261. doi:10.1080/02699930500304886.

Sternberg, R. J., & Frensch, P. A. (Eds.). (1991). *Complex problem solving: Principles and mechanisms*. Hillsdale: Erlbaum.

Verweij, M., & Thompson, M. (Eds.). (2006). *Clumsy solutions for a complex world: Governance, politics and plural perceptions*. Houndmills: Palgrave Macmillan.

Weinert, F. E. (Ed.). (2001). *Leistungsmessungen in Schulen [Assessment in schools]*. Weinheim: Beltz.

Wüstenberg, S., Greiff, S., & Funke, J. (2012). Complex problem solving—More than reasoning? *Intelligence, 40*, 1–14. doi:10.1016/j.intell.2011.11.003.

Wüstenberg, S., Greiff, S., Molnár, G., & Funke, J. (2014). Cross-national gender differences in complex problem solving and their determinants. *Learning and Individual Differences, 29*, 18–29. doi:10.1016/j.lindif.2013.10.006.

Zoanetti, N. (2010). Interactive computer based assessment tasks: How problem-solving process data can inform instruction. *Australasian Journal of Educational Technology, 26*, 585–606.

Zsambok, C. E., & Klein, G. A. (Eds.). (1997). *Naturalistic decision making*. Mahwah: Erlbaum.

Part VI
Feedback From Competency Assessment: Concepts, Conditions and Consequences

Chapter 26
Formative Assessment in Mathematics Instruction: Theoretical Considerations and Empirical Results of the Co²CA Project

Katrin Rakoczy, Eckhard Klieme, Dominik Leiß, and Werner Blum

Abstract Formative assessment is considered a promising approach to improving teaching and learning, especially in the Anglo-American literature. However, empirical evidence supporting this assumption is surprisingly weak. In this chapter, we introduce the concept of formative assessment by identifying the core components of formative assessment (assessment and feedback) and describing the way we assume formative assessment (via students' perception) affects learning processes and outcomes. Furthermore, we present the project "Conditions and Consequences of Classroom Assessment" (Co²CA), consisting of four studies in which we successively investigated the design and impact of formative assessment in mathematics instruction: (1) In a survey study, we described current practice of classroom assessment in mathematics, as perceived by teachers and students, and developed mathematical tasks as a basis for the assessment component in the following studies. (2) In an experimental study, we investigated the impact of written process-oriented feedback on learning in an internally valid setting. (3) In an intervention study, we implemented the instruments and results of the first two studies in mathematics instruction to analyze the impact of formative assessment in an ecologically valid setting. (4) Finally, we conducted a transfer study to make our results usable in educational practice: We developed a teacher training in formative assessment and investigated its impact on teachers' general pedagogical and pedagogical content knowledge. This chapter focuses on a description of the designs and selected results of Studies 3 and 4.

K. Rakoczy (✉) • E. Klieme
German Institute for International Educational Research (DIPF), Frankfurt/Main, Germany
e-mail: rakoczy@dipf.de; klieme@dipf.de

D. Leiß
University of Lüneburg, Lüneburg, Germany
e-mail: leiss@leuphana.de

W. Blum
University of Kassel, Kassel, Germany
e-mail: blum@mathematik.uni-kassel.de

D. Leutner et al. (eds.), *Competence Assessment in Education*, Methodology of Educational Measurement and Assessment, DOI 10.1007/978-3-319-50030-0_26

Keywords Mathematics instruction • Formative assessment • Feedback • Implementation • Transfer study

26.1 Formative Assessment: A Promising Approach to Improving Teaching and Learning?

26.1.1 Formative Assessment: State of the Art

The question whether and how performance assessment can be used productively in the classroom is an issue that has been addressed by educational research, school practice, and the professional public in Germany for years. On the basis of Anglo-American literature, formative assessment is described as a promising approach to improving teaching and learning (e.g., Black and Wiliam 2009; Stiggins 2006; Wiliam and Thompson 2008; for a detailed description that forms the basis of the present introduction see also Rakoczy et al. under revision). Probably the most frequently cited source supporting this assumption is the detailed synthesis of 250 studies on formative assessment published by Black and Wiliam (1998a, b, c). This synthesis made an indispensable contribution to research on formative assessment; however, the review's trustworthiness as a source of empirical evidence of the strong effect of formative assessment on learning can be challenged (Bennett 2011; Dunn and Mulvenon 2009; Kingston and Nash 2011).

Black and Wiliam (1998a) clearly stated that they did not perform any quantitative meta-analytic techniques on the data they gathered (see p. 53). However, they reported a range of effect sizes of classroom assessment on student achievement between .4 and .7 standard deviations in another paper (Black and Wiliam 1998b). Due to the broad definition of formative assessment used in the synthesis, it covered a very heterogeneous body of research: this did not allow for reliably answering the question whether formative assessment affected learning (Bennett 2011; Black and Wiliam 1998a; Kingston and Nash 2011). Accordingly, a more appropriate conclusion for Black and Wiliam (1998a) may have been to outline the need for more empirical research in the area of formative assessment (Dunn and Mulvenon 2009). More precisely, further empirical research on formative assessment should (1) take greater care in evaluating the sources of evidence and in the attributions made about them, and (2) develop a clearer definition of what is meant by formative assessment (Bennett 2011).

This first requirement was met by Kingston and Nash (2011), who provided a meta-analysis and used the following five strict criteria for inclusion of studies: (1) the intervention was described as formative or as assessment for learning, (2) participants were from an academic K-12 setting, (3) a control or comparison group design was used, (4) appropriate statistics were applied to calculate an effect size, and (5) publication was 1988 or later. Restricting studies according to these criteria resulted in a study base of only 13 studies with 42 effect sizes. Kingston and Nash found a much smaller but still meaningful mean effect size of.25 for formative assessment. The second requirement, a clearer definition of formative assessment, underlines the need to know more about what exactly constitutes effective formative assessment (see Sect. 26.1.2), and how the reported gains in student learning can be achieved (see Sect. 26.1.3) (Wiliam and Thompson 2008).

26.1.2 Components of Formative Assessment

According to Andrade (2010):

> any definition of formative assessment must be grounded in its purpose, which includes (1) providing information about students' learning to teachers and administrators in order to guide them in designing instruction; and (2) providing feedback to students about their progress in order to help them determine how to close any gaps between their performance and the targeted learning goals. (p. 344f; a similar definition can be found e.g., in Stiggins 2006)

To make assumptions how teachers and students should respond to the information received, a theory of action would be helpful (Bennett 2011). It would identify the characteristics and components of formative assessment and postulate how these characteristics and components work together to support learning (Bennett 2010). The framework of Wiliam and Thompson (2008) can be seen as a rudimentary theory of action for the second purpose mentioned by Andrade (2010). It suggests that formative assessment can be conceptualized as consisting of five key strategies: (1) clarifying and sharing learning intentions and criteria for success to determine where learners are going; (2) eliciting evidence of student understanding (assessment) to see where learners are; (3) providing feedback that moves learners forward; (4) activating students as instructional resources for one another; and (5) activating students as the owners of their own learning. The particular importance of the strategies of eliciting information and providing feedback is emphasized by many authors (e.g., Black and Wiliam 1998a; Black and Wiliam 2009; Hattie 2003; Harks 2013; Kingston and Nash 2011; Sadler 1998; Stiggins 2006), and we will focus on both as central components of formative assessment.

26.1.3 How Formative Assessment Affects Learning

To our knowledge, the question of how the reported gains in student learning are due to formative assessment during instruction, has not yet been the subject of empirical investigation. We tried to fill in this gap by referring to literature on feedback effects and conducting an experimental study on feedback effects (see Sect. 26.2.2). We combined our results with the assumption of Andrade (2010), who states that the essence of formative assessment is informed action. That is, students must be armed with strategies and the motivation needed to improve their work and

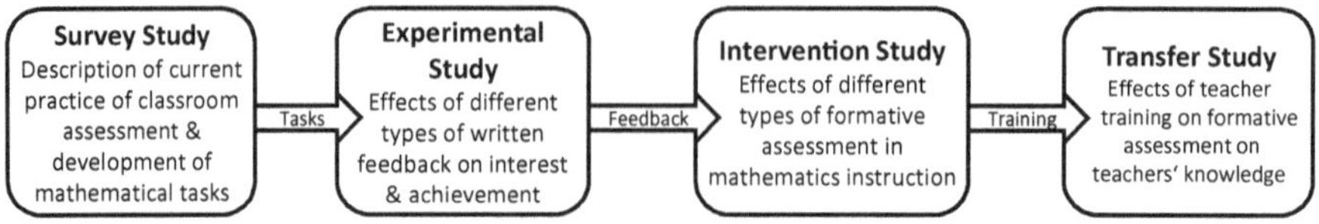

Fig. 26.1 Studies in the Co²CA project

deepen their learning after getting feedback. In other words, formative assessment does not simply result in better learning, but is also, drawing upon the theory of action, assumed to initiate particular actions that, in turn, lead to better learning outcomes (Bennett 2011). Regarding feedback, it cannot simply be assumed that students who are provided with it will know what to do with it (Sadler 1998). Rather, feedback has a certain functional significance for the learner depending on his or her perception and interpretation (Black and Wiliam 2009; Brookhart 1997). As perceived teacher behavior is considered an important intervening variable between actual teacher behavior and the learning outcome (Shuell 1996), it can be assumed that perceptions of feedback mediate the impact of feedback on learning outcomes (see Rakoczy et al. 2013).

26.2 The Four Studies of the Co²CA Project

The Co²CA project ("Conditions and Consequences of Classroom Assessment") has investigated in four successive studies how the two central components of formative assessment—assessment and feedback—should be designed to allow a precise and detailed assessment of performance and to influence student learning via their perception of feedback (see Fig. 26.1). In the following sections we will briefly describe the first two studies—a survey study and an experimental study—and provide references for further information and results on these studies. Then we will describe the design, and selected results, of the last two studies—an intervention study and a transfer study—in more detail. The intervention study, like the transfer study, was designed to investigate formative assessment in ecologically valid settings.

26.2.1 Survey Study

The first aim of the survey study, which took place in 2008 in 68 German middle track secondary school classes ($N = 46$ teachers, $N = 1480$ students) was to describe the current practice of performance assessment in mathematics classrooms. We wanted to learn more about how teachers elicit information in their classrooms, and what kind of information they give back to their students. In questionnaires, teachers reported on their assessment practice in the classroom (e.g., verbal, participative assessment or assessment by grades) and answered questions on further diagnostic issues. While participative and verbal assessment practices can be seen as formative assessment practices, assessment by grades reflects a summative character. Students' performance was assessed by a mathematics test, and they reported in questionnaires how motivated they were and how much effort they spent on mathematics (for more details see Bürgermeister 2014).

Concerning current assessment practices, Bürgermeister (2014) found, among other results, that verbal assessment dominated performance assessment in the classrooms, and was frequently combined with different teacher-centered forms of assessment or grades. Assessment that included students in the process of assessment (participative assessment) was seldom in total. The teachers who indicated use of this form of assessment also indicated that they were familiar with diagnostic issues. While assessment by grades was related to lower performance, motivation and student effort, verbal and participative assessment were connected to higher motivation. Moreover, teachers' assessment practice was related to the preciseness of their assessment: that is, participative assessment practices led to higher preciseness, which in turn affected performance, motivation, and student effort.

The second aim of this study was to develop and to calibrate the tasks needed for our subsequent studies. These tasks were partly taken from the DISUM project (see Blum and Leiß 2007b), partly from a Swiss-German study (Klieme et al. 2009), and partly were newly developed for the special purposes of our studies. The psychometric quality of the tasks was supported by applying item response theory to the data, and content-specific competence models were developed (for further information see, e.g., Bürgermeister et al. 2014; Klieme et al. 2010).

Additionally, specific research questions concerning psychometric issues were investigated on this database. Harks et al. (2014a) for example, investigated the empirical separability of (a) mathematical content domains, (b) cognitive domains, and (c) content-specific cognitive domains. A unidimensional item response theory model, two two-dimensional multidimensional item response theory (MIRT) models (dimensions: content domains and cognitive domains, respectively), and a four-dimensional MIRT model (dimensions: content-specific cognitive domains) were compared. Results indicated that a differentiation of content-specific cognitive domains showed the best fit to the empirical data.

26.2.2 Experimental Study

The second study focused on written feedback as a central component of formative assessment. In an experimental study conducted in 2009, three different types of written feedback—in addition to a control group with no feedback—were compared with regard to their impact on students' interest and achievement development: (a) process-oriented feedback that combines the supportive feedback characteristics known from the literature, (b) feedback by grades, which is the most frequently provided type of feedback in school, and (c) competence-oriented feedback, which provides students with information about the level of their performance with respect to a model of competence levels, which is the current state of the art in standards-based student assessment in Germany.

Three hundred and twenty nine 9th grade intermediate track students participated in the study, and each student worked in an individual testing session on a mathematics test consisting of selected tasks developed in the survey study. Then they received written feedback on their performance—process-oriented feedback, or grades or competence-oriented feedback, or no feedback in the control group. Focusing the analyses on specific mathematical tasks, process-oriented feedback had a positive impact on students' achievement (Besser et al. 2010). Taking the whole set of tasks into consideration, process-oriented feedback was perceived as being more useful for further task completion and as providing more competence support than grades. The positive perception, in turn, was connected with better achievement and interest development. Path analyses confirmed that process-oriented feedback had an indirect effect on achievement and interest development (Harks et al. 2014b; Rakoczy et al. 2013). Competence-oriented feedback was also perceived as more useful than grades, and affected achievement development and motivation indirectly via perceived usefulness (Harks et al. 2014c).

26.2.3 Intervention Study

26.2.3.1 Aims and Research Questions of the Intervention Study

Using tasks from the survey study, and building on results concerning the impact of different types of written feedback in the experimental study, the third study investigated the impact of formative assessment on student learning in an ecologically valid setting. Classroom formative assessment ranges on a continuum from informal to formal. That is, the formative assessment practices range from "on-the-fly" assessment, which arises when a "teachable moment" unexpectedly occurs, to formal curriculum-embedded assessment, which is planned in advance (Shavelson et al. 2008). In the present study we implemented two curriculum-embedded formative assessment interventions in mathematics instruction, which were based on the provision of written process-oriented feedback, and compared them to a control group, where no formative assessment techniques were applied. Among the research questions of the intervention study, the following will be treated in the present chapter:

Research Question 1 Do the two formative assessment interventions have a positive impact on students' achievement and interest development compared to instruction in a control group? Feedback has a certain functional significance for the learner, depending on his or her perception and interpretation (see also Black and Wiliam 2009; Brookhart 1997). The results of our experimental study underline the assumption that feedback fosters student learning only when the supportive feedback characteristics are recognized by the students (Harks et al. 2014b; Rakoczy et al. 2013). Therefore, we assumed indirect effects of the formative assessment interventions on achievement and interest development via students' perception of formative assessment practices in the classroom.

Research Question 2 As written process-oriented feedback is the core of our formative assessment interventions, we were interested in its implementation in instruction: How do teachers provide process-oriented feedback, with regard to the amount of feedback provided and the specificity of feedback comments? And how do these feedback characteristics affect students' math achievement and interest? We expected positive effects of both feedback characteristics—amount of feedback and specificity of feedback comments—on students' achievement and interest. This hypothesis was based on the assumption that in general, specific feedback, compared to global advice, is seen as more effective (for an overview see Shute 2008). Moreover, for complex tasks involving not only declarative knowledge but also procedural knowledge, more elaborated feedback has been shown to foster achievement and motivation (Narciss and Huth 2006). More feedback comments, and specifically formulated feedback about strengths, weaknesses and hints, were expected to provide the learners with a more detailed profile of their competencies and of knowledge of strategies for improvement. The detailed profile, in turn, should lead to informed adaption of the next steps in learning, increased sense of competence and self-efficacy, and consequently, to effects on achievement and interest (for a detailed description of the theoretical background see Pinger et al. 2016).

26.2.3.2 Design of the Intervention Study

Participants In the intervention study 39 teachers (64 % female) of 23 middle track schools in the German state of Hesse took part, with one 9th grade mathematics class each; 41 % of the 970 students were female and the mean age at the beginning of the study was 15.3 years ($SD = 7.73$ months). Participation in the study was voluntary.

Research Design We used a cluster randomized field trial with pre- and posttest in the school year 2010/2011. We implemented two different formative assessment interventions in mathematics instruction and compared their impact on student learning to the impact of instruction in a control group where no specific performance assessment and feedback practices were implemented. Classes were randomly assigned to one of the three conditions: Control Group (CG), Intervention Group 1 (written process-oriented feedback, IG1), and Intervention Group 2 (oral learning-process—accompanying feedback in addition to written process-oriented feedback, IG2). In all three groups the mathematical contents and the tasks the students worked on were standardized. Conditions were realized by teachers participating in respective teacher trainings (contents of the trainings are described in Sect. 2.3.2.4).

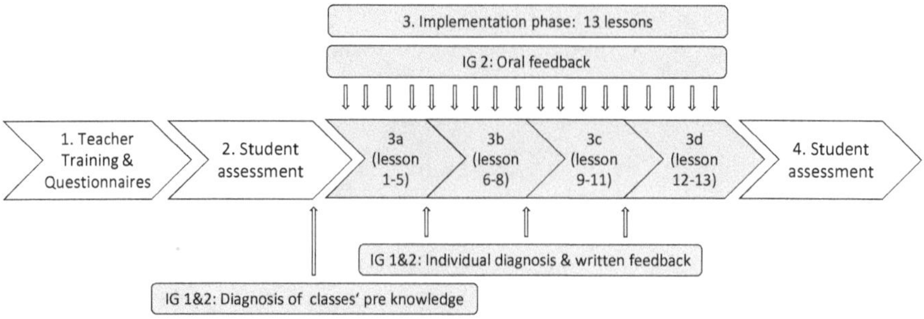

Fig. 26.2 Design of the Intervention Study (*IG 1* Intervention Group 1, *IG 2* Intervention Group 2)

Conception of Teaching Units The cluster randomized field trial covered the first 13 lessons of the teaching unit "Pythagoras' Theorem" and consisted of four phases (see Fig. 26.2). In Phase 1, teachers participated in the teacher training appropriate to the condition they had been assigned to. Before and after the training, teachers filled in questionnaires to assess their professional background, their beliefs and attitudes towards mathematics and instructional quality, their perception of the teacher training, and their plans to implement formative assessment in the future (for detailed information on the instruments see Bürgermeister et al. 2011). In Phase 2, students were assessed in four steps, in the lesson before the teaching unit started: first, students were informed about the content of a forthcoming mathematics test. Second, their interest in the forthcoming test was assessed by a questionnaire. Third, their pre-knowledge regarding Pythagoras was measured in a pretest, and fourth, their perception of instructional quality and of formative assessment practices in the classroom was examined by a questionnaire.
Phase 3 was the implementation phase: all teachers applied the didactical approach with the mathematical tasks they were provided with in the teacher training to implement four segments: (a) introduction, proof of Pythagoras' theorem, technical tasks (Lessons 1–5), (b) dressed-up word problems (Lessons 6–8), (c) modelling problems (Lessons 8–11), and (d) consolidation (Lessons 11–13). In both intervention groups the teachers received an overview of their students' pre-knowledge concerning Pythagoras, assessed in the pretest before they started with the teaching unit. Moreover, they assessed students' performance at the end of each phase with a semi-standardized tool (see Sect. 2.3.2.4) at three predefined time points (in the 5th, 8th, and 11th lessons) and provided written process-oriented feedback in the following lesson. In Phase 4, students were again assessed in four steps: first, they were provided with information about the content of a forthcoming post test. Second, their interest regarding the posttest was assessed by a questionnaire. Third, a posttest to measure students' mathematics achievement was administered, and fourth, their perception of instructional quality and formative assessment practices was assessed by a questionnaire.

In order to get a closer look at instructional quality and formative assessment practices in the participating classrooms the teachers' written feedback was collected, and two double lessons (1st/2nd and 9th/10th) were videotaped according to standardized guidelines (Klimczak and Rakoczy 2010).

Contents of the Teacher Training To ensure that the subject-specific content and the mathematical tasks during the 13 lessons of the study were comparable among all participating classes, all teachers took part in a half-day training session on mathematical content and tasks (Module 1). Teachers of both intervention groups additionally participated in another half-day training in written process-oriented feedback with our diagnosis and feedback tool, which has been shown previously, in our experimental study (see Sect. 26.2.2; Module 2) to foster achievement and interest development. Teachers of the Intervention Group 2 additionally participated in a third half-day training session on oral learning-process accompanying feedback (Module 3). Figure 26.3 gives an overview of the three modules and the participating teachers.

Module 1: Teacher Training on Contents and Mathematical Tasks Teachers of the intervention groups were introduced to subject-specific content and provided with the mathematical tasks for the first 13 lessons of the teaching unit "Pythagoras' Theorem". Teachers were also trained to use a didactic approach, one that is focused on students' ability to apply mathematical tools to real-world problems ("mathematical modeling"; see Blum and Leiß 2007a; Leiß et al. 2010). On the basis of this approach and its description of learning progression, the 13 lessons of the study were subdivided into four phases (see 3a–3d in Fig. 26.2). Tasks in the pre- and posttest, as well as the diagnostic tool for the intervention groups, were developed to assess students' achievement at different steps of the learning progression.

Module 2: Teacher Training on Written Process-Oriented Feedback Teachers of the Intervention Group 2 (in addition to the training in the contents and the didactical approach) were trained to assess students' performance at the end of Phases (a), (b), and (c), and to give written process-oriented feedback. To this end, teachers

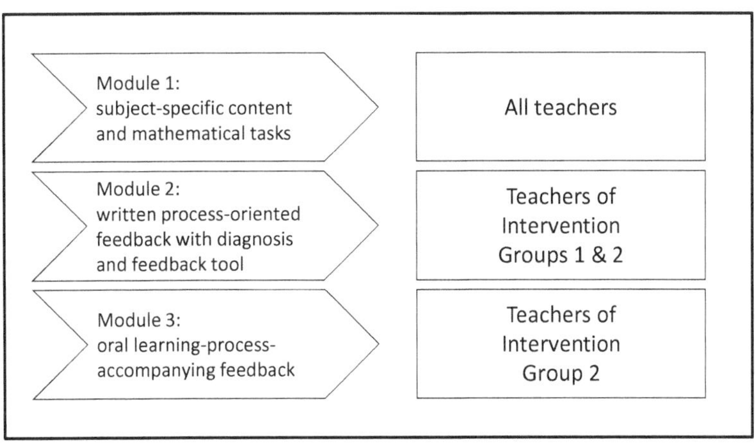

Fig. 26.3 Overview of the three teacher training modules and participating teachers

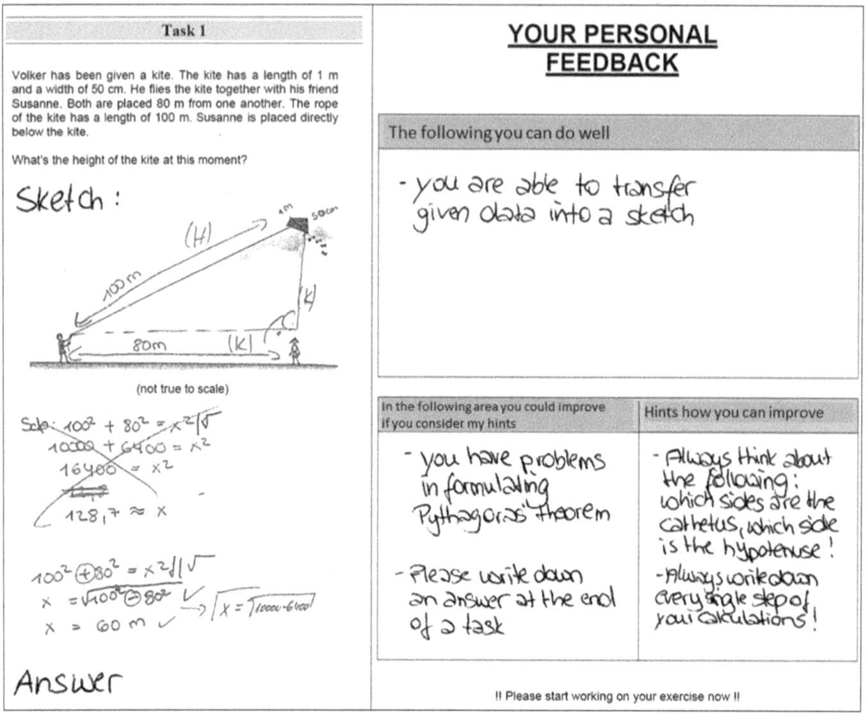

Fig. 26.4 Diagnostic and feedback tool of Phase b

were provided with a diagnostic and feedback tool that they were to apply according to a partly standardized procedure. The diagnostic and feedback tool (for an example see Fig. 26.4) consisted of an assessment part on the left-hand side and a feedback part on the right-hand side. The assessment part contained one or two mathematical tasks assessing the content that had been taught in the phase before (two technical tasks at the end of Phase (a), one dressed up word problem at the end of Phase (b), and one modeling problem at the end of Phase (c). At the end of the 5th, 8th, and 11th lessons, teachers asked the students to work on the task(s) for a maximum of 15 minutes. After the lesson the teachers collected the diagnostic and feedback tools. They corrected students' solutions before the next mathematics lesson and generated written feedback on the right-hand side of the sheet referring to students' strengths ("The following you can do well") and weaknesses ("In the following area you could improve if you consider my hints"), and to strategies for continuing ("Hints how you can improve").

To support teachers and to ensure quality, we partly standardized the procedure. On the basis of cognitive task analyses we developed a list of cognitive processes and operations that were necessary to solve the respective diagnostic task. Each process and operation could be fed back as a strength or a weakness, depending on whether the student mastered it or not. For each process and operation, a suggestion for a strategy or hint was provided that could be fed back when the respective process was not mastered. To keep the feedback economical and understandable, teachers were asked to summarize strengths across sub-competencies and to choose the weaknesses they believed to be most important.

Module 3: Teacher Training in Oral Learning-Process Accompanying Feedback In addition to the training in content and written process-oriented feedback, teachers were trained in providing students with oral feedback that was as adaptive as possible to the individual needs of each learner, as implemented in one of the conditions in the DISUM study (for the conception see Blum and Leiß 2007b; for results see, e.g., Leiß et al. 2010; Blum 2011). Teachers were especially prepared to intervene into students' working processes only by minimal-adaptive support, in order to let the students work on their own as much as possible (Leiß 2010). Specifically, the teachers were trained in respect of two central ideas of teacher interventions: Firstly, teachers should recognize that (oral) feedback on students' learning processes can focus on organizational, affective, metacognitive and/or content-specific levels of the learning process. Secondly, and with special regard to the topics students had to deal with, when they had to work on Pythagoras' theorem, teachers were trained intensively as to what content-specific oral feedback could look like if students were working on modeling problems in the classroom, and how such content-specific oral feedback could be used to support students' learning processes in a minimal-adaptive way.

Measures Here only the measures that are included in the analyses addressing Research Questions 1 and 2 are described. An overview of all scales in the project can be found in Bürgermeister et al. (2011).

The amount of feedback was measured by the number of feedback comments (the sum of strengths, weaknesses and hints for each student). For the evaluation of specificity, a coding scheme was applied in which specificity was judged separately for weaknesses and hints and then averaged (Code 0: no comment was specific; Code 1: at least one comment was specific). Two raters were trained on the basis of a manual. After the third coding round (60 feedback sheets each) the inter-rater reliability was sufficient, with Cohens-κ of .92 (weaknesses) and .97 (strategies).

Students' perception of formative assessment practices was assessed in the pre- and postquestionnaire using a newly developed five-item scale (Bürgermeister et al. 2011). Students were asked to indicate on a four-point scale, ranging from 0 (completely disagree) to 3 (completely agree) the extent to which feedback in the classroom helped them to learn what they already did well, where they can improve, and how they can improve. The key item was "During mathematics instruction I learned how I can improve what I am not yet good in". Internal consistency of the scale was $\alpha = .82$ in the prequestionnaire and $\alpha = .89$ in the postquestionnaire. The difference in perception between pre- and postquestionnaire was used as an indicator for the change in perception and was included as mediator in the analyses.

Students' interest was assessed with a four-item scale (Bürgermeister et al. 2011). Students were asked in the pre- and postquestionnaire to indicate on a four-point scale ranging from 0 (completely disagree) to 3 (completely agree) how interesting they found the topic of the forthcoming test. The key item was "I like the topic of the test". Internal consistency of the scale was $\alpha = .83$ in the prequestionnaire and $\alpha=.89$ in the postquestionnaire. Concerning the first research question, the difference in interest between pre- and postquestionnaire was used as an indicator for development of interest. Concerning the second research question, multilevel regression analyses included postquestionnaire scores as the dependent variable, controlled for prequestionnaire interest score.

Mathematics achievement was assessed with 19 pretest and 17 posttest items. Test items consisted of technical and modeling items in the content domain of Pythagoras' theorem (for examples see Besser et al. 2013) and had been analyzed previously on the basis of a scaling sample ($N = 1570$) in the survey study. A one-dimensional Rasch model was applied to the experimental data, and weighted likelihood estimators (WLE)-parameters (i.e., achievement scores) were estimated. Analyses were conducted in ConQuest (Wu et al. 1998). The estimated reliability (EAP/PV) was .66 for the pretest and.74 for the posttest. The difference between pretest and posttest WLE parameters was calculated as an indicator of development in mathematics achievement and was included in the path models to answer Research Question 1. The multilevel regression analyses to answer Research Question 2 included posttest WLE parameters as dependent variables, and controlled for pretest WLE parameters.

Data Analyses In order to address the first research question (the indirect effects of formative assessment on achievement and interest development via students' change in perception of assessment and feedback practices in the classroom), two multilevel path models according to Preacher et al. (2010) were applied to the data—one for achievement and one for interest development as outcomes. In both models, the intervention groups were entered as dummy-coded class-level predictor variables (0 = Control Group, 1 = Intervention Group 1, respectively Intervention Group 2). Perceived assessment and feedback practices in the classroom were entered as the manifest intervening variable at the individual level and (aggregated) at the class level, and z-standardized on the basis of its individual-level mean and standard deviation, and its class-level mean and standard deviation, respectively. Interest and achievement in mathematics were included as z-standardized manifest criteria at the student level. Random intercepts were estimated for these variables at the class level. We estimated total, direct, and indirect effects among predictor, intervening, and outcome variables.

Concerning the second research question (the effects of feedback characteristics), multilevel regression models were computed in Mplus7 (Muthén and Muthén 2012). For the analyses we used a subsample consisting of 17 teachers and 426 students (classes in which process-oriented feedback was provided as intended at all three predefined time points during the unit). Separate analyses were run for effects on achievement and interest and for each of the two feedback characteristics. The z-standardized pretest score for math achievement and the z-standardized prequestionnaire score for interest, as well as z-standardized scores for amount of feedback and specificity, were entered as level 1 predictors.

26.2.3.3 Selected Results of the Intervention Study

Indirect Effects of Formative Assessment on Learning (Research Question 1) The multilevel path analyses showed that students' perception of formative assessment practices became more positive following either intervention; this change was stronger than in the control group ($\beta = .34$, $p = .01$ for IG1; $\beta = .47$, $p = .00$ for IG2). The change in perception of formative assessment practices, in turn, was associated with a more positive interest development ($\beta = .53$, $p = .02$). The indirect effect of Intervention Group 1 (written process-oriented feedback) was marginally significant ($\beta = .17$, $p = .07$), while the indirect effect of Intervention Group 2 (written plus oral feedback) was significant ($\beta = .24$, $p = .00$). In contrast, no significant impact of perception on achievement development ($\beta = -.36$, $p = .30$), and consequently no indirect effect could be shown ($\beta = -.12$, $p = .23$ for IG1; $\beta = -.17$, $p = .30$ for IG2). So, we can conclude that our formative assessment based on written process-oriented feedback—whether provided alone or in combination with minimal-adaptive oral feedback—has the power to change the assessment and feedback practices from students' point of view, which then positively influences their interest in working on mathematics tasks, but that it does not foster students' achievement development via perceived assessment and feedback practices.

Effects of Feedback Characteristics (Research Question 2) Multilevel regression analyses revealed no significant effect of both feedback characteristics on interest. Moreover and contrary to our expectations, we found negative effects of the amount of feedback comments and the specificity of feedback on posttest achievement scores ($\beta = -.11$, $p = .02$ and $\beta = -.09$, $p = .03$, respectively). Negative correlations between the feedback characteristics and the pretest scores ($r = -.25$, $p = .00$ for amount of feedback and $r = -.13$, $p = .02$ for specificity, respectively) and the posttest scores ($r = -.22$, $p = .00$ and $r = -.14$, $p = .01$, respectively) indicate that students scoring low in the pretest received more feedback comments and more specific feedback than did students with high pretest scores and that those students, however, unfortunately did not benefit from the feedback received (see Pinger et al. 2016). More feedback comments might have increased the length and complexity of the feedback, resulting in the perception of feedback as less useful, or in processing the feedback message at a shallower level (Kulhavy et al. 1985).

26.2.4 Transfer Study

26.2.4.1 Aims and Research Questions of the Transfer Study

Previous studies in the Co^{2}Ca-project showed that written process-oriented feedback has the power to support student learning in an experimental setting, as well as in an ecologically valid setting. To make these results usable for educational practice, we conducted a transfer study (Besser et al. 2015a, b).

In the transfer study we referred to research on the quality of teaching, which identified teachers' knowledge as a crucial factor in explaining teacher behavior in the classroom (Bromme 2008). According to Shulman (1986), teachers' content knowledge (CK), teachers' pedagogical content knowledge (PCK) and teachers' general pedagogical knowledge (PK) are central aspects of teachers' expertise that help to explain the quality of teaching and student learning, and to understand the teacher's role in the classroom. Baumert and colleagues stress that:

> PCK—the area of knowledge relating specifically to the main activity of teachers, namely, communicating subject matter to students—makes the greatest contribution to explaining student progress. This knowledge cannot be picked up incidentally, but as our finding on different teacher-training programs show, it can be acquired in structured learning environments. One of the next great challenges for teacher research will be to determine how this knowledge can best be conveyed to both preservice and inservice teachers. (Baumert et al. 2010, p. 168).

Drawing on the results of our previous studies and on empirical evidence for the importance of teachers' knowledge in teaching, we developed a teacher training on formative assessment and investigated whether it fostered teachers' general pedagogical knowledge and pedagogical content knowledge on formative assessment in competence-oriented mathematics (with a focus on mathematical modeling). In order to evaluate this training, we needed to develop new tests for PCK and PK, with a focus on formative assessment. In detail, we investigated the following research questions:

1. Are our tests for assessing teachers' PCK and PK on formative assessment reliable and valid?
2. Does our teacher training on formative assessment foster teachers' PCK and PK on formative assessment in competence-oriented mathematics teaching dealing with modeling tasks?
3. Does our teacher training on formative assessment have an impact on the teachers' way of teaching and/or on their students' way of learning as reported by students' self-reports?

26.2.4.2 Design of the Transfer Study

Participants To answer the research questions we conducted an intervention study with pre- and posttests involving 67 teachers (66 % female) and their classes. Teachers could choose whether they participated in teacher training on formative assessment in competence-oriented mathematics instruction with a focus on mathematical modeling (Intervention Group [IG]) or teacher training in general questions regarding the implementation of competence-oriented mathematics instruction, with a focus on mathematical modeling and problem solving (Treatment Control Group [TCG]).

Procedure The teacher training covered a period of 10 weeks, including implementation in classrooms. Firstly, teachers filled in a pretest, to assess their PK and general PCK, and their students filled in a questionnaire about their perception of teaching quality and of formative assessment practices in the classroom. Secondly, teachers participated in a three-day teacher training, either on formative assessment (IG) or on problem solving and modeling (TCG). Thirdly, teachers were asked to implement the content of the teacher training in their competence-oriented mathematics instruction over 10 weeks. Fourthly, teachers participated in further three-day teacher training, either in formative assessment (IG) or in problem solving and modeling (TCG). Finally, they filled in a posttest on PK and PCK, and a questionnaire examining the perceived usefulness of the training they participated in (either on formative assessment [IG] or on problem solving and modeling [TCG]). Once again, the students filled in a questionnaire to assess their perception of teaching quality and of formative assessment practices in the classroom.

For organizational reasons, each intervention group was divided into two groups (IG1/IG2 and TCG1/TCG2), each consisting of a maximum of 20 teachers. IG1 and TCG1 participated in the study from February to March 2013, IG2 and TCG2 from September to December 2013. The contents of the teacher training for IG1/IG2 and TCG1/TCG2 were the same.

Contents of the Teacher Trainings In the teacher training for the Intervention Group (IG1/IG2), teachers were provided with theoretical considerations on formative assessment and with possibilities for implementing formative assessment in competence-oriented mathematics with a focus on mathematical modeling. In the training for the Treatment Control Group (TCG1/TCG2) teachers dealt with mathematical problem solving and mathematical modeling as a central element of competence-oriented mathematics instruction, and were provided with general didactical ideas and task analyses. Specifically, the teacher training concentrated on the topics shown in Table 26.1 (taken from Besser et al. 2015a, b).

Test of Teachers' General Pedagogical Knowledge and Pedagogical Content Knowledge To assess teachers' baseline pedagogical content knowledge before the teacher training, the PCK-test from the COACTIV-study (Krauss et al. 2011) was administered.

Table 26.1 Contents of the teacher training

Intervention Group (IG1/IG2)	Treatment Control Group (TCG1/TCG2)
(1) Diagnostis and feedback as central elements of formative assessment: A general psychological and pedagogical point of view	(1) Mathematical problem solving as a central element of competence-oriented mathematics: General didactical ideas and task-analyses
(2) Mathematical modeling as a central element of competence-oriented mathematics: Analyzing students' solution processes and giving feedback to the students	(2) Mathematical modeling as a central element of competence-oriented mathematics: General didactical ideas and task-analyses
(3) Implementing formative assessment in teaching mathematical modeling (written and oral)	(3) Implementing problem solving tasks and modeling problems in teaching competence-oriented mathematics

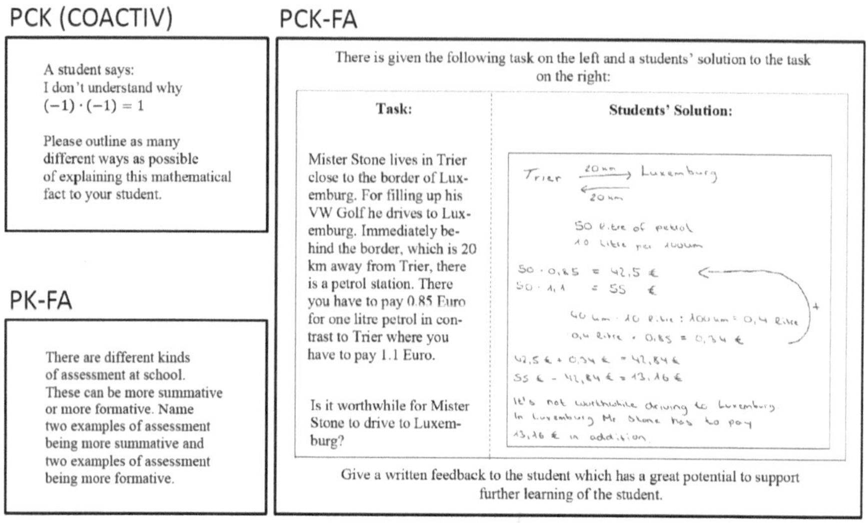

Fig. 26.5 Examples of items from the PCK-test of the COACTIV-study and the PCK-FA and PK-FA tests of the Co²CA project (*PCK-FA* pedagogical content knowledge on formative assessment, *PK-FA* pedagogical content knowledge on formative assessment)

To answer our research questions we developed the following tests of teachers' PK and PCK on formative assessment (FA) in competence-oriented mathematics (see Besser and Leiß 2014 and Besser et al. 2015a, b):

- Subtest of general pedagogical knowledge (PK-FA): 12 Items assessing theoretical pedagogical and psychological knowledge (1) about assessment in the classroom, (2) about ways to diagnose students' strengths and weaknesses, and (3) about how to give process-oriented feedback on students' strengths and weaknesses.
- Subtest on pedagogical content knowledge (PCK-FA): 10 Items assessing subject-specific knowledge (1) about modeling processes in mathematics, (2) about how to analyze students' solution processes in modeling tasks, (3) about how to implement core components of general ideas about formative assessment in competence-oriented teaching: that is, especially about how to give feedback to students when working on modeling tasks.

Examples of items assessing PCK at the beginning of the study by using the COACTIV-test (Krauss et al. 2011), as well as items assessing PK-FA and PCK-FA, are given in Fig. 26.5.

26.2.4.3 First Results of the Transfer Study

Concerning the quality of the tests for assessing general pedagogical and pedagogical content knowledge on formative assessment (Research Question 1) our results showed acceptable internal consistency in the 10 PCK-FA items (α =.78). The participating teachers achieved on average 10.15 ($SD = 4.54$) of a maximum of 21 points (Besser et al. 2015a, b).

Concerning the impact of our teacher training on pedagogical content knowledge (Research Question 2), our results show significant mean differences between both groups. While the teachers in the intervention group reached on average 13.33 points ($SD = 3.47$), teachers in the treatment control group reached on average 7.57 points ($SD = 3.57$; $t\,(65) = 6.66$, $p = .00$). The effect size for the independent samples is $d = 1.63$, so we can conclude that knowledge about formative assessment in competence-oriented mathematics instruction with a focus on mathematical modeling was significantly higher when teachers participated in our teacher training on formative assessment, compared to teachers trained in general aspects of competence-oriented mathematics instruction and problem solving (Besser et al. 2015a, b).

Concerning Research Question 3, preliminary analyses show that teachers' way of teaching, as reported by the students, did not increase after our teacher training on formative assessment: on the contrary, it decreased. However, analyses of variance with repeated measures showed that this change in the quality of teaching seems to be explained not by the teacher training but by "time". Examination of Research Question 3 is still work in progress, so we cannot as yet give any answer to the question how student learning develops after the teacher training.

However, the results we report so far are encouraging and underline the importance of teacher training to foster teachers' pedagogical content knowledge of formative assessment. The quality of the PK-FA test, the impact of the teacher training on teachers' pedagogical knowledge about formative assessment, and the impact of this pedagogical knowledge on students' perception of instruction, should be investigated in further analyses.

26.3 Summary

In the Co²CA project we analyzed, in four subsequent studies, how formative assessment should be designed and implemented to allow for a precise assessment of student performance, and to affect student learning. Assessment and feedback were identified as central components of formative assessment and were empirically analyzed with regard to their design and impact. Concerning the assessment component, we developed mathematical tasks that were appropriate for assessing students' technical competence and modeling competence in mathematics, and investigated psychometric issues of competence assessment, as well as teachers' assessment practice in the classroom (survey study). Concerning the feedback component, we developed a prototype of written feedback, called process-oriented feedback, and compared it in an experimental study to feedback as it is frequently used in classrooms (grades) or in standard-based testing (competence-oriented feedback). We found that process-oriented feedback was perceived by the students as more useful and competence-supportive, and that it affects achievement and interest development indirectly via students' perception (experimental study).

We implemented these results into classroom instruction and developed two formative assessment interventions (intervention study). First results showed that the formative assessment interventions changed students' perception of formative assessment practices in the classroom, as expected; perception, in turn, was related to better interest development but, unexpectedly, not to achievement development. The indirect effect of formative assessment on interest development via perception of formative assessment practices is in line with the assumptions we made according to the results of our experimental study on the effects of process-oriented feedback (see Sect. 26.2.2). This is a hint that we succeeded in implementing process-oriented feedback in mathematics instruction as an ecologically valid setting.

However, the change in perception of formative assessment practices did not lead to better achievement of the classes. As implementation quality might, among other factors, contribute to explaining the lack of achievement development (Furtak et al. 2008), further analyses were made on how teachers implemented the interventions, and whether the quality of implementation explained the impact on student learning. Pinger et al. (2016) found that the amount of written process-oriented feedback and specificity of feedback comments had no effect on students' interest, and even a negative effect on their achievement. The latter might be explained by the fact that students who scored lower in the pretest received more and more specific feedback comments. Moreover, if and how feedback is perceived and processed by the learner might depend not only on the feedback message itself but also on the way it is delivered to students. Analyses of the videotaped lessons show that in handing back the written feedback, stressing the importance of feedback utilization or emphasizing the performance evaluation affects students' math achievement and interest (see Pinger et al. 2016).

Finally, we extended our teacher training on formative assessment and made it available to a larger group of teachers (transfer study). The first, promising results show that teachers' pedagogical content knowledge on formative assessment was higher after they participated in the respective teacher training than when they participated in teacher training on general aspects of competence-oriented mathematics instruction and problem solving. Further analyses on the way formative assessment interventions were implemented, and how they impact teaching quality and student learning, are still in progress.

Acknowledgements The preparation of this chapter was supported by grants to Eckhard Klieme and Katrin Rakoczy (KL 1057/10), Werner Blum (BL 275/16) and Dominik Leiß (LE 2619/1), from the German Research Foundation (DFG) in the Priority Programme "Competence Models for Assessing Individual Learning Outcomes and Evaluating Educational Processes" (SPP 1293). The authors, who acted jointly as principal investigators, gratefully acknowledge the significant contributions made by (in alphabetical order) Michael Besser, Anika Bürgermeister, Birgit Harks, Malte Klimczak, Petra Pinger, Natalie Tropper and other members of staff.

References

Andrade, H. L. (2010). Summing up and moving forward: key challenges and future directions for research and development in formative assessment. In H. L. Andrade & G. J. Cizek (Eds.), *Handbook of formative assessment* (pp. 344–351). New York: Routledge.

Baumert, J., Kunter, M., Blum, W., Brunner, M., Dubberke, T., Jordan, & Tsai, Y. (2010). Teachers' mathematical knowledge, cognitive activation in the classroom, and student progress. *American Educational Research Journal, 47*, 133–180. doi:10.3102/0002831209345157.

Bennett, R. E. (2010). Cognitively based assessment of, for, and as learning: A preliminary theory of action for summative and formative assessment. *Measurement: Interdisciplinary Research and Perspectives, 8*, 70–91. doi:10.1080/15366367.2010.508686.

Bennett, R. E. (2011). Formative assessment: A critical review. *Assessment in Education: Principles, Policy & Practice, 18*, 5–25. doi:10.1080/0969594X.2010.513678.

Besser, M., & Leiß, D. (2014). The influence of teacher-training on in-service teachers' expertise: A teacher-training-study on formative assessment in competency-oriented mathematics. In S. Oesterle, P. Liljedahl, C. Nicol, & D. Allan (Eds.), *Proceedings of the 38th Conference of the International Group for the Psychology of Mathematics Education and the 36th Conference of the North American Chapter of the Psychology of Mathematics Education* (Vol. 2, pp. 129–136). PME: Vancouver.

Besser, M., Blum, W., & Klimczak, M. (2013). Formative assessment in every-day teaching of mathematical modelling: Implementation of written and oral feedback to competency-oriented tasks. In G. Stillman, G. Kaiser, W. Blum, & J. Brown (Eds.), *Teaching mathematical modelling: Connecting to research and practice* (pp. 469–478). New York: Springer.

Besser, M., Blum, W., & Leiß, D. (2015a). How to support teachers to give feedback to modelling tasks effectively? Results from a teacher-training-study in the Co²CA project. In G. A. Stillman, M. S. Biembengut, & W. Blum (Eds.), *Proceedings of ICTMA 16*. New York: Springer.

Besser, M., Leiß, D., & Klieme, E. (2015b). Wirkung von Lehrerfortbildungen auf Expertise von Lehrkräften zu formativem Assessment im kompetenzorientierten Mathematikunterricht [Impact of teacher training on teachers' expertise on formative assessment in competenc-oriented instruction]. *Zeitschrift für Entwicklungs- und Pädagogische Psychologie, 47*, 110–122. doi:10.1026/0049-8637/a000128.

Besser, M., Leiß, D., Harks, B., Rakoczy, K., Klieme, E., & Blum, W. (2010). Kompetenzorientiertes Feedback im Mathematikunterricht: Entwicklung und empirische Erprobung prozessbezogener, aufgabenbasierter Rückmeldesituationen [Competence-oriented feedback in mathematics instruction: Development and empirical test of process-oriented and task-based feedback situations]. *Empirische Pädagogik, 24*(4), 404–432.

Black, P., & Wiliam, D. (1998a). Assessment and classroom learning. *Assessment in Education: Principles, Policy & Practice, 5*, 7–75. doi:10.1080/0969595980050102.

Black, P., & Wiliam, D. (1998b). Inside the black box: Raising standards through classroom assessment. *Phi Delta Kappan, 80*, 139–148. doi:10.1177/003172171009200119.

Black, P., & Wiliam, D. (1998c). *Inside the black box: Raising standards through classroom assessment*. London: Kings College.

Black, P., & Wiliam, D. (2009). Developing the theory of formative assessment. *Educational Assessment, Evaluation and Accountability, 21*, 5–31. doi:10.1007/s11092-008-9068-5.

Blum, W. (2011). can modelling be taught and learnt? Some answers from empirical research. In G. Kaiser, W. Blum, R. Borromeo Ferri, & G. Stillman (Eds.), *Trends in teaching and learning of mathematical modelling* (pp. 15–30). New York: Springer.

Blum, W., & Leiß, D. (2007a). How do students and teachers deal with modelling problems? In C. Haines, W. Blum, P. Galbraith, & S. Khan (Eds.), *Mathematical modelling (ICTMA 12): education, engineering and economics* (pp. 222–231). Chichester: Horwood.

Blum, W., & Leiß, D. (2007b). Investigating quality mathematics teaching—the DISUM project. In C. Bergsten & B. Grevholm (Eds.), *Developing and Researching Quality in Mathematics Teaching and Learning: Proceedings of MADIF 5* (pp. 3–16). Linköping: SMDF.

Bromme, R. (2008). Lehrerexpertise [Teacher's skill]. In W. Schneider & M. Hasselhorn (Eds.), *Handbuch der Pädagogischen Psychologie* (pp. 159–167). Göttingen: Hogrefe.

Brookhart, S. M. (1997). A theoretical framework for the role of classroom assessment in motivating student effort and achievement. *Applied Measurement in Education, 10*, 161–180. doi:10.1207/s15324818ame1002_4.

Bürgermeister, A. (2014). *Leistungsbeurteilung im Mathematikunterricht: Bedingungen und Effekte von Beurteilungspraxis und Beurteilungsgenauigkeit [Performance assessment in mathematics instruction: Conditions and effects of judgement practice and judgement accuracy]*. Münster: Waxmann.

Bürgermeister, A., Kampa, M., Rakoczy, K., Harks, B., Besser, M., Klieme, E., Leiss, D. (2011). *Dokumentation der Befragungsinstrumente der Interventionsstudie im Projekt "Conditions and Consequences of Classroom Assessment"* (Co^2CA) [Documentation of the intervention study questionnaires in the project "Conditions and Consequences of Classroom Assessment"]. Frankfurt am Main: DIPF. - URN: urn:nbn:de:0111-opus-35284.

Bürgermeister, A., Klieme, E., Rakoczy, K., Harks, B., & Blum, W. (2014). Formative Leistungsbeurteilung im Unterricht [Formative assessment in instruction]. In M. Hasselhorn, W. Schneider, & U. Trautwein (Eds.), *Lernverlaufsdiagnostik* (pp. 41–60). Göttingen: Hogrefe.

Dunn, K. E., & Mulvenon, S. W. (2009). A critical review of research on formative assessment: The limited scientific evidence of the impact of formative assessment in education. *Practical Assessment, Research and Evaluation, 14*(7), 1–11.

Furtak, E. M., Ruiz-Primo, M. A., Shemwell, J. T., Ayala, C. C., Brandon, P. R., Shavelson, R. J., & Yin, Y. (2008). On the fidelity of implementing embedded formative assessments and its relation to student learning. *Applied Measurement in Education, 21*, 360–389. doi:10.1080/08957340802347852.

Harks, B. (2013). *Kompetenzdiagnostik und Rückmeldung: zwei Komponenten formativen Assessments* [Diagnostic of competencies and feedback: two components of formative assessment]. Doctoral Dissertation. Frankfurt/Main, Germany.

Harks, B., Klieme, E., Hartig, J., & Leiß, D. (2014a). Separating cognitive and content domains in mathematical competence. *Educational Assessment, 19*, 243–266. doi:10.1080/10627197.2014.964114.

Harks, B., Rakoczy, K., Hattie, J., Besser, M., & Klieme, E. (2014b). The effects of feedback on achievement, interest, and self-evaluation: The role of feedback's perceived usefulness. *Educational Psychology, 34*, 269–290. doi:10.1080/01443410.2013.785384.

Harks, B., Rakoczy, K., Klieme, E., Hattie, J., & Besser, M. (2014c). Indirekte und moderierte Effekte von Rückmeldung auf Leistung und Motivation [Indirect and moderated effects of feedback on achievement and motivation]. In H. Ditton & A. Müller (Eds.), *Feedback und Rückmeldungen: Theoretische Grundlagen, empirische Befunde, praktische Anwendungsfelder* (pp. 163–194). Münster: Waxmann.

Hattie, J. (2003). *Formative and summative interpretations of assessment information.* Retrieved from https://cdn.auckland.ac.nz/assets/education/hattie/docs/formative-and-summative-assessment-%282003%29.pdf.

Kingston, N., & Nash, B. (2011). Formative assessment: A meta-analysis and a call for research. *Educational Measurement: Issues and Practice, 30*(4), 28–37. doi:10.1111/j.1745-3992.2011.00220.x.

Klieme, E., Bürgermeister, A., Harks, B., Blum, W., Leiß, D., & Rakoczy, K. (2010). Leistungsbeurteilung und Kompetenzmodellierung im Mathematikunterricht [Assesment and modeling of competencies in mathematics instruction]. *Zeitschrift für Pädagogik, Beiheft, 56*, 64–74.

Klieme, E., Pauli, C., & Reusser, K. (2009). The Pythagoras study. In T. Janik & T. Seidel (Eds.), *The power of video studies in investigating teaching and learning in the classroom* (pp. 137–160). Münster: Waxmann.

Klimczak, M., & Rakoczy, K. (2010). *Richtlinien zur Aufzeichnung von Unterrichtsvideos im Projekt "Conditions and Consequences of Classroom Assessment" (Co2CA)* [Guidelines to videotape instruction in the project "Conditions and Consequences of Classroom Assessment"]. Unpublished manuscript.

Krauss, S., Blum, W., Brunner, M., Neubrand, M., Baumert, J., Kunter, M., et al. (2011). Konzeptualisierung und Testkonstruktion zum fachbezogenen Professionswissen von Mathematiklehrkräften [Conceptualisation and test construction of content-related knowledge of mathematics teachers]. In M. Kunter, J. Baumert, W. Blum, U. Klusmann, S. Krauss, & M. Neubrand (Eds.), *Professionelle Kompetenz von Lehrkräften: Ergebnisse des Forschungsprogramms COACTIV* (pp. 135–161). Waxmann: Münster.

Kulhavy, R. W., White, M. T., Topp, B. W., Chan, A. L., & Adams, J. (1985). Feedback complexity and corrective efficiency. *Contemporary Educational Psychology, 10*, 285–291. doi:10.1016/0361-476X(85)90025-6.

Leiß, D. (2010). Adaptive Lehrerinterventionen beim mathematischen Modellieren: empirische Befunde einer vergleichenden Labor- und Unterrichtsstudie [Adaptive teacher interventions for mathematical modeling: empirical results of a comparative experimental and field study]. *JMD, 31*, 197–226. doi:10.1007/s13138-010-0013-z.

Leiß, D., Schukajlow, S., Blum, W., Messner, R., & Pekrun, R. (2010). The role of the situation model in mathematical modelling: task analyses, student competencies, and teacher interventions. *JMD, 31*, 119–141. doi:10.1007/s13138-010-0006-y.

Muthén, L. K., & Muthén, B. O. (1998–2012). *Mplus (Version 7) [Computer Software]*. Los Angeles: Muthen & Muthen.

Narciss, S., & Huth, K. (2006). Fostering achievement and motivation with bug-related tutoring feedback in a computer-based training for written subtraction. *Learning and Instruction, 16*, 310–322. doi:10.1016/j.learninstruc.2006.07.003.

Pinger, P., Rakoczy, K., Besser, M., Klieme, E. (2016). Implementation of formative assessment: Effects of quality of program delivery on students' mathematics achievement and interest. *Assessment in Education: Principles, Policy and Practice*. Advance online publication. doi:10.1080/0969594X.2016.117066.

Preacher, K. J., Zyphur, M. J., & Zhang, Z. (2010). A general multilevel SEM framework for assessing multilevel mediation. *Psychological Methods, 15*, 209–233. doi:10.1037/a0020141.

Rakoczy, K., Harks, B., Klieme, E., Blum, W., & Hochweber, J. (2013). Written feedback in mathematics: Mediated by students' perception, moderated by goal orientation. *Learning and Instruction, 27*, 63–73. doi:10.1016/j.learninstruc.2013.03.002.

Rakoczy, K., Pinger, P., Harks, B., Besser, M., Klieme, E. (under revision). Formative assessment in mathematics instruction: Mediated by feedback's perceived usefulness and students' self-efficacy? *Learning and Instruction.*

Sadler, R. (1998). Formative assessment: Revisiting the territory. *Assessment in Education, 5*, 77–84. doi:10.1080/0969595980050104.

Shavelson, R. J., Young, D. B., Ayala, C. C., Brandon, P. R., Furtak, E. M., Ruiz-Primo, M. A., et al. (2008). On the impact of curriculum-embedded formative assessment on learning: A collaboration between curriculum and assessment developers. *Applied Measurement in Education, 21*, 295–314. doi:10.1080/08957340802347647.

Shuell, T. J. (1996). Teaching and learning in a classroom context. In D. C. Berliner & R. Calfee (Eds.), *Handbook of educational psychology* (pp. 726–764). New York: Macmillan.

Shulman, L. S. (1986). Those who understand: Knowledge growth in teaching. *Educational Researcher, 15*(2), 4–14. doi:10.3102/0013189X015002004.

Shute, V. (2008). Focus on formative feedback. *Review of Educational Research, 78*, 153–189. doi:10.3102/0034654307313795.

Stiggins, R. (2006). Assessment for learning: A key to motivation and achievement. *Edge, 2*(2), 3–19.

Wiliam, D., & Thompson, M. (2008). Integrating Assessment with Learning: What will it take to make it work? In C. A. Dwyer (Ed.), *The future of assessment: Shaping teaching and learning* (pp. 53–84). New York: Lawrence Erlbaum.

Wu, M. L., Adams, R. J., & Wilson, M. R. (1998). *ConQuest: Generalised item response modelling software*. Camberwell: Australian Council for Educational Research.

Chapter 27
Arguing Validity in Educational Assessment

Simon P. Tiffin-Richards and Hans Anand Pant

Abstract Interpreting test-scores in terms of whether examinees reach specific levels of achievement (e.g., below basic, basic, advanced), provides a means to assess and communicate whether educational goals are being reached and expectations are being met. Whether these interpretations of test-scores are informative, however, hinges on their validity. While validity plays an important role in educational assessment, it is rarely addressed in a systematic and comprehensive manner. Our aim is to detail a theoretical framework in which validation is considered in the context of practical test development. To this end, we apply Kane's (Psychol Bull 112:527–535, 1992; Rev Edu Res 64:425–461, 1994) interpretive argument approach and Toulmin's inference model (Kane, Lang Test 29:3–17, 2011; Toulmin, The uses of argument. Cambridge University Press, Cambridge) to the development of competence-based educational assessments and the interpretation of their results. A logical argument is presented to provide a theoretical framework for evaluating the rhetorical backing and empirical evidence supporting interpretations of educational assessment results. The discussion focusses on the role of standard setting procedures which define minimum passing scores on test-score scales in the evaluation of the validity of test-score interpretations.

Keywords Validity • Validation • Assessment • Standard Setting • Cut scores

S.P. Tiffin-Richards (✉)
Institute for Educational Quality Improvement (IQB), Berlin, Germany

Max Planck Institute for Human Development, Berlin, Germany
e-mail: tiffin-richards@mpib-berlin.mpg.de

H.A. Pant
Humboldt-Universität zu Berlin, Berlin, Germany

Institute for Educational Quality Improvement (IQB), Berlin, Germany
e-mail: hansanand.pant@hu-berlin.de

D. Leutner et al. (eds.), *Competence Assessment in Education*, Methodology of Educational Measurement and Assessment, DOI 10.1007/978-3-319-50030-0_27

27.1 Introduction

The assessment of competencies is an increasingly important tool to measure the outcomes of educational and qualification systems (Hartig et al. 2008; Klieme et al. 2010; Köller 2010; Koeppen et al. 2008). Competencies are conceptualized as context-specific cognitive dispositions in domains such as language, natural sciences and complex problem-solving that are acquired through experience and learning and can be directly influenced by educational institutions (Hartig et al. 2008; Klieme et al. 2010; Weinert 2001). The development of educational assessments that can measure the output and thus the success of such systems, consequently involves a set of complex procedures and considerations. These include the definition of competencies in terms of domain-specific knowledge, skills and abilities, and the development of measurement instruments to tap these competencies, as well as educational targets against which to measure success.

Setting educational goals requires the definition of criteria against which test-takers can be measured. Criterion-referenced assessments allow an examinee's test-score to be interpreted in terms of whether their performance satisfies criteria for reaching specific levels of proficiency. Examinee ability can then be described on a discrete ordinal scale with terms such as *basic*, *proficient*, and *advanced*, where each level is defined by content or criteria of increasing qualitative and quantitative demand. The continuous test-score scale is thus divided into an ordinal scale. It follows that "[a] criterion-referenced test is one that is deliberately constructed to yield measurements that are directly interpretable in terms of specified performance standards" (Glaser and Nitko 1971, p. 653). These performance standards can be interpreted as the success or failure to reach the prerequisites for specific qualifications, licensure or entry requirements. The methods used to set minimum test-scores for reaching specific levels of proficiency in a competence domain are referred to as standard-setting procedures. These procedures are typically based on expert judgments on what constitutes a sufficient score on a particular assessment to reach a particular level (Cizek and Bunch 2007). Importantly, these procedures provide the critical step in establishing the basis for the later communication of test results (see Pant et al. 2010), but have also been criticized as being largely arbitrary (Glass 1978).

This chapter focusses on the setting of minimum test-scores (henceforth referred to as *cut scores*) on educational assessments as a method of interpreting the results of competence-based assessments. To ensure that standards-based interpretations of student test-scores are sufficiently defensible as the basis for high- or low-stakes decisions (Decker and Bolt 2008), inferences based on student test-scores must be supported by evidence of their validity (Kane 1992, 2009; Messick 1989, 1995). The move towards standards-based assessment therefore makes the question of validity vitally important, as the results of standards-based testing can have consequences, both at the individual level of students and professionals, at the organizational level of schools and training programs, and at the system level of educational administration and policy. However, despite the central role of validity in interpreting test results, there is little consensus on the exact conceptualization of validity, how it is best evaluated, or indeed what constitutes *sufficient* validity (Lissitz 2009). Although some aspects of the current conceptualization of validity enjoy "fairly broad professional agreement" (Cizek 2011, p. 3), there remain disputes concerning the importance of different sources of validity evidence. The view is supported here that different sources of validity evidence are necessary, although not individually sufficient, to support criterion-referenced test-score interpretations.

We have divided the remainder of the chapter into three sections. In the first we provide a brief account of the development of the concept of validity in educational and psychological measurement. We next introduce standard-setting procedures as a necessary step in interpreting test results, in terms of reaching educational goals and minimum or target levels of proficiency in specific domains. In the third section we integrate the process of standard-setting in the theoretical frameworks of Kane (1992, 1994) and Toulmin (Kane 2011; Toulmin 1958) to construct a validity argument for test-score interpretations. We provide empirical evidence from studies conducted to examine the factors that may influence the validity of test-score interpretations following standard-setting procedures. The discussion focusses on the role of standard-setting, cut-score placement, and the importance of considering the evaluation of validity as the sequential weighing of rhetorical and empirical evidence supporting propositions of validity in interdisciplinary procedures, rather than a precise measurement procedure (see Nichols et al. 2010).

27.2 The Validity Concept

Standards for Educational and Psychological Testing (henceforth referred to as *Standards*) describe validity as "the most fundamental consideration in developing and evaluating tests", where validity is defined as "the degree to which evidence and theory support the interpretations of test scores entailed by the proposed uses of tests" (AERA et al. 1999, p. 9).

Although validity plays a central role in educational and psychological measurement, it has persistently eluded a straightforward and universally accepted definition (Cizek 2011). A simple, although arguably incomplete view of validity defines it as the degree to which a test measures what it is claimed to measure. The validity of test-score interpretations may consequently change, depending on what a test is claimed to measure (Sireci 2009).

The concept of validity has experienced a history of reconceptualization. As Sireci outlines in his chapter in Lissitz' (2009) *The Concept of Validity: Revisions, New Directions, and Applications*, validity has been defined both as a unitary construct and as a set of distinct elements described as types, aspects or categories. The *metamorphosis* of the concept of validity (Geisinger 1992) and the changing emphasis on various elements of validity can be traced back throughout the last century, both in scientific publications and in guidelines for professional standards (Geisinger 1992; Goodwin and Leech 2003; Lissitz and Samuelsen 2007; Sireci 2009).

Technical Recommendations for Psychological Tests and Diagnostic Techniques (henceforth referred to as the *Technical Recommendations*), published by the APA in 1954, proposed four types of validity: *concurrent*, *predictive*, *construct*, and *content*. In their seminal article, Cronbach and Meehl (1955) further elaborated this view and introduced *construct validity* into the validity concept. In a reorganization of the types of validity described by the *Technical Recommendations*, Cronbach and Meehl combined concurrent validity, which is concerned with the correlation of test-scores on independent assessments of a criterion measure, and predictive validity, concerned with the correlation of current test-scores with test-scores at a later date, to *criterion-oriented validity*. *Content validity* was considered to be the degree to which a sample of test items represents the universe of possible content that is of interest. Lastly, as Cronbach and Meehl (1955, p. 282) write, "construct validity is involved whenever a test is to be interpreted as a measure of some attribute or quality which is not operationally defined". Consideration of construct validity is therefore necessary "whenever no criterion or universe of content is accepted as entirely adequate to define the quality to be measured" (Cronbach and Meehl 1955, p. 282). The *process* of validation was viewed as evaluating the validity of the interpretation of test results: "one validates, not a test, but an interpretation of data arising from a specified procedure" (Cronbach 1971, p. 447). The view of validity as being comprised of these coexistent but independent types of *criterion*, *content* and *construct* validity has since been referred to as the *Holy Trinity* (Gorin 2007).

The *unitary concept* of validity stems from the argument that criterion or content universes are *never entirely adequate* to define the quality to be measured, which leads to the conclusion that all validity is necessarily construct validity (Messick 1998). Samuel Messick, one of the chief proponents of the unitary approach, provided a straightforward interpretation of the validity concept as: "[i]n its simplest terms, construct validity is the evidentiary basis for score interpretation" (Messick 1995, p. 743). Also, Loevinger (1957, p. 636) reasoned that, "since predictive, concurrent, and content validities are all essentially *ad hoc*, construct validity is the whole of validity from a scientific point of view". Construct validity is thus conceptualized as the integration of all evidence relevant to inferences based on test-scores that include sources of both content and criterion-related evidence. The defining characteristic of construct validity is the identification of cognitive processes, strategies, and knowledge relevant for task responses representing underlying functional models (Messick 1995). Having merged formerly coexistent types of validity into *construct validity*, Messick differentiated the unified concept into six distinguishable aspects (*content*, *substantive*, *structural*, *generalizable*, *external*, and *consequential*), which together form the basis for addressing validation procedures in educational and psychological measurement (Messick 1995, 1989). The inclusion of consequences in the evaluation of validity echoed earlier sentiments of Cronbach, (1971, p. 741), who stated that "in particular, what needs to be valid is the meaning or interpretation of the score; as well as any implications for action that this meaning entails".

27.2.1 The Place of Standard Setting in Educational Assessment

The aim of standard-setting procedures is to allow the interpretation of examinee test-scores in terms of whether specific levels of proficiency are reached. These can represent minimum and advanced educational goals students are expected to reach at specific stages of their education or qualification. Standard-setting methodologies typically involve panels of experts discussing the minimum requirements for reaching specific levels of proficiency on an assessment in consensus-building and iterative procedures, resulting in final recommendations for interpreting examinee test-scores (Cizek and Bunch 2007).

Standards-based interpretations of test-scores are argued to facilitate the communication of assessment results to non-technical stakeholders, such as policy-makers, teachers, and parents (Cizek et al. 2004). From a policy perspective, setting educational standards and assessing achievement towards them allows the definition of educational goals and the implementation of teaching practices that facilitate achievement towards these goals.

Test-centered standard-setting approaches focus on the items of an assessment and on how likely examinees are expected to be able to answer them correctly, depending on their level of proficiency. Popular methods include modifications of the Angoff (1971) and Bookmark methods (Mitzel et al. 2001). Test-centered standard-setting methods critically involve experts setting cut scores to differentiate proficiency levels, where the cut scores then define the minimum test-score required for reaching a proficiency level. Many of the methods currently employed combine expert judgment with psychometric analyses of item difficulty and examinee proficiency, allowing cut scores to be mapped directly onto item response theory (IRT)-derived metric scales (Cizek and Bunch 2007).

The significance attached to validating the inferences of test-scores based on cut scores and performance standards is also emphasized in the Standards:

> [C]ut scores embody the rules according to which tests are used or interpreted. Thus, in some situations the validity of test interpretations may hinge on the cut scores. There can be no single method for determining cut scores for all tests or for all purposes, nor can there be any single set of procedures for establishing their defensibility. (AERA et al. 1999, p. 53)

The guidelines provided by the Standards have two implications. First, cut scores must represent the characteristics and intended interpretations of a test—with regard to both content standards (construct representation) and performance standards (target levels of performance). Second, neither the method for placing cut scores, nor the procedure for evaluating the interpretations of test results in respect to cut scores is clearly specified; rather, each depends on the intended interpretations of test-scores. A further important notion is that cut scores and associated performance standards are concepts employed to interpret test-scores. Thus, there are no true cut scores that could be defined or applied, and therefore there is no method for establishing whether a cut-score is correct or not. Rather than establishing whether a cut-score is correct, the aim of validation procedures is to assess the degree to which there is "convincing evidence that the passing score does represent the intended performance standard and that this performance standard is appropriate, given the goals of the decision process" (Kane 1994, p. 443).

27.3 The Argument Approach to Evaluating Validity

The process of validation can be conceptualized as formulating an *argument* for the validity of interpretations derived from test-scores (Kane 1992), involving first the specification of the proposed interpretations and uses of test-scores and second, the evaluation of the plausibility of the proposed interpretations (Kane 2011). The first step is the construction of an *interpretive argument*, which builds the structure of the argumentative path from the observed performance to the inferred proficiency of an examinee in the domain of interest (e.g., proficiency in a foreign language). The interpretive argument hence "provides a framework for validation by outlining the inferences and assumptions to be evaluated" (Kane 2011, p. 9). The second step involves the construction of the *validity argument*, which appraises the evidence supporting the inferences that lead to the test-score interpretation and "provides an evaluation of the interpretive argument" (Kane 2011, p. 9). The notion of establishing an evidence-based case for an interpretation was shared by Messick (1989, p. 13) in his definition of validity as "an integrated evaluative judgment of the degree to which empirical evidence and theoretical rationales support the adequacy and appropriateness of inferences and actions based on test scores".

The attraction of the validity argument approach is that it is highly flexible. It is applicable to any kind of test use or interpretation, does not rely on any one preferred source of validity evidence, and is not limited to any specific type of test data. Validity is not considered a property of a test, but of the use of the test for a particular purpose. Kane emphasized the importance of a clear definition of the argument for the evaluation of the available evidence, or *sources of validity evidence*, in its support. There is, however, no assertion that the evidence supporting an interpretive argument can provide an absolute decision of validity. Validation is, rather, suggested to be a matter of degree. Importantly, Kane (1992, p. 528) also proposes that "[t]he plausibility of the argument as a whole is limited by its weakest assumptions and inferences". It is, therefore, important to identify the assumptions being made and to provide supporting evidence for the most questionable of these assumptions. The greatest attention should be directed towards evaluating the availability of evidence in support of weak assumptions, to rule out alternative interpretations of test-scores (Kane 1992).

A formal representation of the interpretive argument is presented by Kane (2011) in Toulmin's model of inference (Toulmin 1958). Toulmin's model provides a framework with which an interpretive argument can be structured and the validity evidence supporting a test-score interpretation can be evaluated. The basic structure of the model is described as the "*movement* from accepted *data*, through a *warrant*,

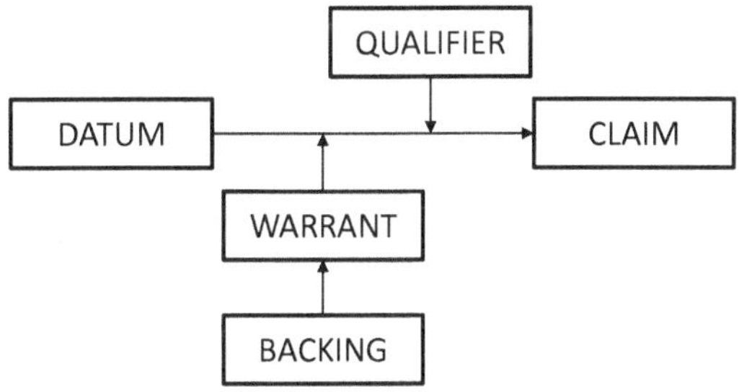

Fig. 27.1 Toulmin's model of inference

to a *claim*" (Brockriede and Ehninger 1960, p. 44), represented in Fig. 27.1. Kane (2011) summarizes three characteristics of such logical arguments. First, they represent disputable lines of argument that make substantive claims about the world and can be evaluated on the basis of empirical evidence, and in terms of how well they refute opposing arguments. Second, they provide arguments for probable or acceptable conclusions rather than certain facts, and may include an indication of their strength. Finally, informal arguments are *defeasible*, in the sense that they are subject to exceptions.

The movement from datum to claim is justified by a warrant, which is in turn supported by backing or evidence "designed to certify the assumption expressed in the warrant" (Brockriede and Ehninger 1960, p. 45). The notion of a warrant in the context of validation could for instance refer to empirical evidence of the concurrent validity of a newly developed reading comprehension test, compared to an older established comprehension test. The claim being made in this case is the classification of an examinee on a proficiency level (e.g., pass or fail on the reading comprehension test) on the basis of their test-score. A qualifier may be inserted if the claim is only valid under certain conditions. In the context of test-score interpretations the qualifier may relate to specific testing contexts (e.g., only suitable as a university entry requirement) and be designed to minimize unwanted consequences of testing.

27.3.1 A Structured Validity Argument

Criterion-referenced interpretations of test-scores are based on the claim that examinee performance on an assessment can be interpreted in terms of levels of proficiency in the domain of interest, such as foreign language proficiency. The goal is to be able to generalize an examinee's performance on a sample of test items from the domain of interest to their estimated proficiency across the domain. Hence, the score on an English as a Foreign Language exam is extrapolated to infer the general communicative language ability of the examinee (see Chapelle et al. 2010 for an application of the validity argument approach to the TOEFL). The argument that test-scores can be interpreted in this way can be evaluated on the basis of whether the propositions or warrants for this claim are met, being supported by sufficient

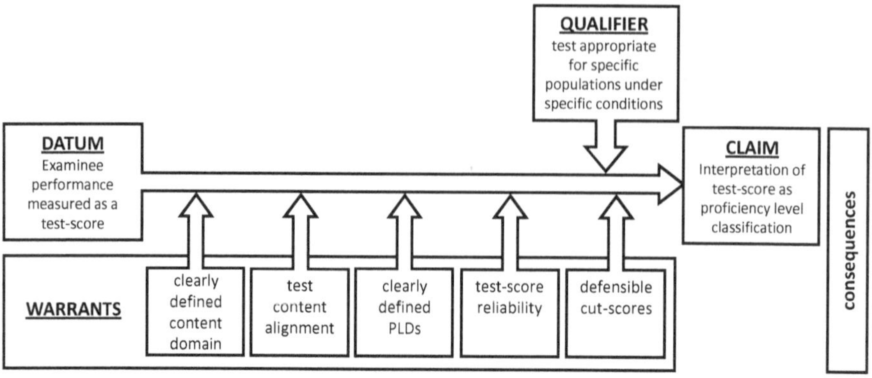

Fig. 27.2 Application of Toulmin's inference model and Kane's interpretive argument to the standards-based interpretation of test-scores

rhetorical backing and empirical evidence. In the example of a test of foreign language proficiency, these warrants could include evidence that the exam requires desired levels of vocabulary knowledge and text comprehension, that language skills can be applied in realistic communicative scenarios, and that the testing formats allow examinees to demonstrate their abilities adequately (e.g., productive as well as receptive language abilities).

The composition of the interpretive argument can be considered as a series of *propositions* of validity (Haertel 2002; Haertel and Lorié 2004), each of which must be supported by evidence of validity. Individually necessary—but not sufficient—propositions of validity can include (a) clear definition of the content standards detailing knowledge, skills and abilities relevant to the domain of interest, (b) representation of domain-relevant content in the assessment, (c) reliable and unbiased test-scores provided by the measurement instrument, (d) unambiguous definition of target performance standards, (e) defensible cut-score placements to differentiate proficiency levels with minimum test-scores, and (f) alignment of intended test use to defensible interpretations of test-scores provided by assessments.

In this context the datum is an examinee's observed performance in the content domain of interest, measured as a test-score on an assessment. The claim that examinee performance can be interpreted in terms of whether they satisfy the criteria for reaching a specific level of proficiency can be supported by five warrants or propositions that indicate that such a claim is appropriate. Each warrant is backed by rhetorical and empirical evidence (Fig. 27.2). A qualifier is inserted to detail the conditions under which the proposed claims are valid for a specified population. The qualifier thus accounts for concerns of *consequential validity* (Kane 2011) and is a *justification of test use* for specific purposes (Cizek 2011, 2012). The interpretive argument is represented by the path from datum to claim with all inherent warrants of validity and the qualification under which conditions the claim holds. The validity argument in turn appraises the backing for the warrants supporting the proposed interpretation of the test-scores.

27.3.1.1 Warrant of Well-Defined Content Standards

Content standards must be well-defined and must provide a description of "the kinds of things a student should know and be able to do in a subject area" (Messick 1995, p. 6) and thus define content domain-relevant knowledge, skills, and abilities (see Rychen and Salganik 2001, 2003). The definition of the content domain can be seen as the premise for any later test-score interpretation and "a necessary condition for criterion referencing since the idea is to generalize how well an examinee can perform in a broader class of behaviors" (Nitko 1980, p. 465). Domains that are poorly defined in terms of relevant behavioral objectives or defined solely by the characteristics of the items on an assessment are hence not well suited for criterion-referenced assessment (Nitko 1980). Clear definition of the content domain in the sense of *construct validity* (Messick 1995) has been described as problematic for complex constructs such as communicative language ability (Chapelle et al. 2010). However, a theoretical concept of the content domain as a starting point for the validity argument is important and "desirable for almost any test" (Cronbach and Meehl 1955, p. 282).

Backing for the warrant of a well-defined content domain may include the definition of educational *competencies* in terms of underlying cognitive processes and domain-relevant behaviors. The importance of considering cognition in educational assessment is stated in the National Research Council report *Knowing What Students Know* (Pellegrino et al. 2001), in their assertion that "[a]ll assessments will be more fruitful when based on an understanding of cognition in the domain and on the precept of reasoning from evidence" (Pellegrino et al. 2001, p. 178). The imbalance between the significance of cognitive process modeling and educational assessment practice is also emphasized by Embretson and Gorin (2001, p. 364) in that "[a]lthough cognitive psychology seemingly has tremendous potential for improving construct validity, actual applications have been lagging". Similarly, models of cognition have been described as the missing cornerstone of educational assessment (Brown and Wilson 2011). Understanding cognitive processes hence is seen as significant for educational assessment in three respects: first, to describe the construct of interest in terms of relevant mental processes; second, to provide clear construct-relevant criteria for item design; and third, to provide a theoretical framework to assess the construct validity (Messick 1995) of educational assessments, to ensure valid interpretations of test-scores.

27.3.1.2 Warrant of Test Alignment to the Content Domain

The tasks and items designed to assess examinee proficiency in a specific domain must be domain-relevant, and their solution must require the application of domain-relevant knowledge, skills and abilities. The evaluation of test alignment to the content domain can be considered as an evaluation of *construct-representation* (Embretson 1983).

Backing may include evidence of content validity (Messick 1995), as in construct-representation (Embretson 1983, 2007) and targeting of domain-relevant response processes (AERA et al. 1999). The method of *evidence-centered test design* (Mislevy et al. 2002) in test development can provide a clear basis for construct-representation. It is common practice in test development to conduct item construction guided by formal test specifications detailing construct-relevant content and item characteristics. These test-specifications have, however, been criticized for their often vague and generalized terminology (Embretson 2007; Embretson and Gorin 2006; Leighton and Gierl 2007), which may not provide item developers with adequate guidelines to translate content and performance standards into assessment tasks and items. Incorporating an explicit *item difficulty model* (IDM, Gorin 2006) of how construct-relevant item characteristics influence the cognitive complexity of items is argued to provide item developers clearer guidelines for designing content valid assessment items of target difficulty levels. Determining the effect of specific characteristics on the cognitive complexity of items allows the prediction of psychometric properties (e.g., IRT difficulty parameters) of items (Hartig and Frey 2012; Hartig et al. 2012).

27.3.1.3 Warrant of Well-Defined Performance Level Descriptors

Recent publications (Huff and Plake 2010; Nichols et al. 2010) stress the role of performance level descriptors (PLD) in operationalizing standards-based assessments. PLDs are the descriptive definitions of proficiency levels and are key to standard-setting procedures where expert panelists set cut scores on test-score scales.

Huff and Plake (2010, p. 132) suggest three preconditions to the use of PLDs: (a) they must be the product of research-based methodologies, (b) they should be derived from empirically-based learning progressions, and (c) they need to be integrated into test design. Hence, the warrant of clear PLDs requires evidence of explicit reference and relevance to the content domain, a model of underlying cognitive processes and their development, and the clear construct-representation of the assessment. This involves both a model of different levels of proficiency and a model of the development of proficiency as a result of learning and experience. The quality of the description of PLDs relies to a large extent on the prior definition of the content domain, relevant cognitive processes, etc. It should therefore become apparent here that the separate warrants of validity are not independent of one another, and that a poor foundation—that is, poor definition of the criterion measure—will lead to difficulties in constructing a strong validity argument for desired test-score interpretations.

27.3.1.4 Warrant of Reliable Test-Score Measurement

A criterion-referenced assessment must be able to produce reliable and unbiased measurements of examinee performance. Evidence for reliable and unbiased measurement can be derived from classical test theory and item response theory analyses, to rule out excessive measurement error, differential item functioning, or other sources of construct-irrelevant variance. As Borsboom et al. (2004, p. 1061) state: "[A] test is valid for measuring an attribute if and only if (a) the attribute exists and (b) variations in the attribute causally produce variations in the outcomes of the measurement procedure". As the issues of measurement reliability in the context of competence-based assessment are covered extensively elsewhere (see Hartig 2008), we will not go into further detail here.

27.3.1.5 Warrant of Defensible Cut-Score Placements

The process of standard-setting can be understood as a translation of policy decisions—such as the definition of educational standards or a passing criterion—through a process informed by expert judgment, stakeholder interests and technical expertise (Cizek and Bunch 2007; Kane 1998). This translation is achieved with the definition of cut scores by panels of experts, which differentiate discrete levels of proficiency on a continuous scale of examinee performance. The credibility of cut-score recommendations has been the subject of strong criticism (Glass 1978), and may be considered a critical but weak element in the interpretive argument.

Backing for the warrant of defensible cut scores can include sources of procedural, internal, external and consequential validity evidence (Cizek 1996; Kane 1994; Pant et al. 2009; Tiffin-Richards et al. 2013). *Procedural evidence* can include the selection and training of panelists, as well as their reported understanding of key concepts of the procedure (Raymond and Reid 2001), the psychometric calibration, selection, preparation, and presentation of materials, and the clear definition of performance standards (Cizek 1993). A central element of popular cut-score placement procedures such as the Bookmark method is the ordered item booklet, in which test items are arranged by increasing difficulty (Karantonis and Sireci 2006). Panelists make their cut-score recommendations by marking the boundaries between groups of items that represent the material an examinee is expected to have mastered at a specific level of proficiency. Tiffin-Richards et al. (2013) demonstrated that the selection of the items which are included in these item booklets can influence how expert panelists set their cut scores. In particular, items with a high mismatch between their content descriptions and their empirical difficulty presented panelists with difficulties in the standard-setting procedure, and in many cases resulted in more extreme cut scores for the highest and lowest proficiency levels (Tiffin-Richards et al. 2013). This indicates that the materials used in standard-setting procedures may have a significant influence on cut-score recommendations.

Internal evidence can be evaluated by assessing the inter- and intra-panelist consistency of cut scores across cut-score placement rounds, while *external evidence* can evaluate the consistency of cut scores across different standard-setting procedures or between parallel expert panels. A factor that may impact external evidence of validity was demonstrated by Pant et al. (2010), who showed that cut-score placement recommendations appeared to differ between expert panels with different constellations of participants. Expert panels, which included both educational practitioners and participants representing educational policy makers, set stricter minimum pass scores than did panels solely made up of educational practitioners. It appeared therefore that the experience panelists had of the examinee population, influenced their perception of what examinees could and should be expected to achieve. Of course, the nature of standard-setting studies, in which expert panels of highly qualified professionals are necessary, makes controlling for panelist experience and qualifications exceedingly difficult. Nevertheless, the constellation of expert panels may be critical in establishing both the appropriateness and the defensibility of cut-score recommendations.

Importantly, the warrant of appropriate cut-score recommendations for the operationalization of educational standards on assessments critically depends on the prior propositions of validity: well-defined content domain and performance standards, well-aligned assessment items, and reliable measurements of examinee performance. Without these preconditions, the cut-score placement procedure does not offer the basis to make appropriate recommendations for minimum test-scores on competence-based assessments.

27.4 Discussion

The argument approach to validation illustrates the complexity of the operationalization of competence-based testing programs, as well as the consequent complexity of the interpretive and validity arguments that can be constructed to provide a convincing case for the interpretation of test-scores. The perspective of considering validation as an argumentative case supporting a proposed interpretation of an examinee's test-score as an indication of their level of proficiency in the domain of interest, leads to two general conclusions.

First, it is evident from the sequential structure of the argument approach to validation that each element of the validity argument relies, at least in part, on preceding propositions of validity being met. Poor definition of the content domain and content standards will pose difficulties in the definition of clear PLDs, ambiguously defined PLDs provide a poor basis for cut-score placement procedures to differentiate proficiency levels, and so on. Deficits in rhetorical and empirical backing for a warrant supporting the proposed interpretation of test-scores can thus lead to weaker support for subsequent warrants, as well as weakening the overall support for the validity argument's claims. Being aware of the interdependence of the evidentiary support for each warrant of the argument's validity is therefore critical. This is particularly important for any institution or program responsible for the development and operationalization of educational standards, as validity evidence may need to be drawn from different groups of professionals at different stages (e.g., content domain experts and practitioners for construct definition, item developers for content alignment, psychometric experts for test reliability, etc.).

Second, cut-score placement procedures not only rely on the quality of prior propositions of validity, but also reflect expert opinions rather than exact measurement procedures. Cut-score placement procedures translate the descriptive PLDs onto the empirical test-score scale, to define numerical criteria for reaching proficiency levels on a particular assessment in a well-defined content domain. Cut-score recommendations represent expert judgments on how best to operationalize educational standards, based on the content of an assessment and PLD descriptions. Under ideal circumstances, content domains would be perfectly defined in terms of the cognitive processes required to complete domain-related tasks, test items would cover the entirety of the relevant content domain or represent a random sample of all its elements, and PLDs would perfectly describe examinee behaviors relevant to the content domain at each proficiency level. Expert panelists' intended cut scores would, in this ideal case, be as close to a *true* cut-score as possible. However, content domains and PLDs are usually described in general terms, item samples are limited and possibly not representative of the entire content domain, due to practical limitations. Cut-score recommendations are at best approximations of appropriate and defensible numerical criteria for reaching proficiency levels on assessments where the content domain and proficiency level descriptors are usually defined in generalized terms and there is a limited availability of assessment items and testing time.

The Weakest Link The logical argument framework for evaluating the rhetorical and empirical evidence supporting interpretations of educational assessment provides a useful structure for validation procedures. This approach involves the sequential weighing of rhetorical and empirical evidence supporting propositions of validity in interdisciplinary procedures. Cut-score placement procedures are arguably the weakest link in the validity argument for criterion-referenced interpretations of test-scores, and thus present a bottleneck for validity concerns. Cut-score placement procedures therefore require particular attention in the validation process and are particularly dependent on the quality of earlier stages of the validation process.

The argument approach to validation has both theoretical and practical value in the context of licensure, qualification and educational assessment. In all cases in which specific standards, minimum qualifications or passing scores are necessary, criteria for passing scores need to be defined. Cut-score placement procedures are one, arguably difficult and in parts arbitrary, approach to operationalizing these criteria. However, the focus of our efforts in validation should not necessarily only be on standard-setting procedures as the final stage of operationalizing educational standards. What the validity argument clearly demonstrates is that the validity of criteria-referenced test-score interpretation depends on a sequence of warrants of validity being met. A stronger focus on the definition of the constructs of interest (e.g., reading, writing, mathematics, natural science) in terms of underlying cognitive processes (e.g., word decoding, text comprehension, number sense, abstract reasoning) is the necessary basis for making standard-setting and cut-score placement procedures possible. The argument approach to validity provides a suitable framework for the challenging task of combining theoretical concepts and measurement procedures with practical considerations and policy aims, to develop and operationalize theoretically and psychometrically sound, practical and socially acceptable standards-based assessments.

The large programs that have followed the push towards competence-based assessment in the contexts of school education, higher education and vocational and professional qualification could profit from adopting a validity argument approach in appraising the assessment procedures which have been put in place in recent years. In this sense, validation procedures can be seen as quality control measures designed to evaluate whether the goals of an assessment program (i.e., distinguishing the levels of proficiency of examinees) have been successful. Validation should therefore be seen as an ongoing endeavor of quality monitoring, rather than a one-time procedure.

Acknowledgments This research was conducted at the Institute for Educational Quality Improvement (IQB) and supported in part by a grant (PA-1532/2-1) from the German Research Foundation (DFG) in the Priority Program "Competence Models for Assessing Individual Learning Outcomes and Evaluating Educational Processes" (SPP 1293).

References

AERA, APA, NCME (American Educational Research Association, American Psychological Association, National Council on Measurement in Education). (Eds.). (1999). *Standards for educational and psychological testing*. Washington, DC: American Educational Research Association.

Angoff, W. H. (1971). Scales, norms, and equivalent scores. In R. L. Thorndike (Ed.), *Educational measurement* (2nd ed., pp. 508–600). Washington, DC: American Council on Education.

Borsboom, D., Mellenbergh, G. J., & Van Heerden, J. (2004). The concept of validity. *Psychological Review, 111*, 1061–1071. doi:10.1037/0033-295X.111.4.1061.

Brockriede, W., & Ehninger, D. (1960). Toulmin on argument: An interpretation and application. *The Quarterly Journal of Speech, 46*, 44–53. doi:10.1080/00335636009382390.

Brown, N. J. S., & Wilson, M. (2011). A model of cognition: The missing cornerstone of assessment. *Educational Psychology Review, 23*, 221–234. doi:10.1007/s10648-011-9161-z.

Chapelle, C. A., Enright, M. K., & Jamieson, J. (2010). Does an argument-based approach to validity make a difference? *Educational Measurement: Issues and Practice, 29*(1), 3–13. doi:10.1111/j.1745-3992.2009.00165.x.

Cizek, G. J. (1993). Reconsidering standards and criteria. *Journal of Educational Measurement, 30*(2), 93–106.

Cizek, G. J. (1996). Standard-setting guidelines. *Educational Measurement: Issues and Practice, 15*(1), 13–21. doi:10.1111/j.1745-3992.1996.tb00802.x.

Cizek, G. J. (2011, April). *Reconceptualizing validity and the place of consequences*. Paper presented at the meeting of the NCME, New Orleans, LA.

Cizek, G. J. (2012). Defining and distinguishing validity: Interpretations of score meaning and justifications of test use. *Psychological Methods, 17*, 31–43. doi:10.1037/a0026975.
Cizek, G. J., & Bunch, M. B. (2007). *Standard setting: A guide to establishing and evaluating performance standards on test*. Thousand Oaks: Sage.
Cizek, G. J., Bunch, M. B., & Koons, H. (2004). Setting performance standards: Contemporary methods. *Educational Measurement: Issues and Practice, 23*(4), 31–50. doi:10.1111/j.1745-3992.2004.tb00166.x.
Cronbach, L. J. (1971). Test validation. In R. L. Thorndike (Ed.), *Educational measurement* (2nd ed., pp. 443–507). Washington, DC: American Council on Education.
Cronbach, L. J., & Meehl, P. E. (1955). Construct validity in psychological tests. *Psychological Bulletin, 52*, 281–302. doi:10.1037/h0040957.
Decker, D. M., & Bolt, S. E. (2008). Challenges and opportunities for promoting student achievement through large-scale assessment results: Research, reflections, and future directions. *Assessment for Effective Intervention, 34*, 43–51. doi:10.1177/1534508408314173.
Embretson, S. E. (1983). Construct validity: Construct representation versus nomothetic span. *Psychological Bulletin, 93*, 179–197. doi:10.1037/0033-2909.93.1.179.
Embretson, S. E. (2007). Construct validity: A universal validity system or just another test evaluation procedure? *Educational Researcher, 36*, 449–455. doi:10.3102/0013189X07311600.
Embretson, S. E., & Gorin, J. (2001). Improving construct validity with cognitive psychology principles. *Journal of Educational Measurement, 38*, 343–368. doi:10.1111/j.1745-3984.2001.tb01131.x.
Geisinger, K. F. (1992). The metamorphosis to test validation. *Educational Psychologist, 27*, 197–222. doi:10.1207/s15326985ep2702_5.
Glaser, R., & Nitko, A. J. (1971). Measurement in learning and instruction. In R. L. Thorndike (Ed.), *Educational measurement* (2nd ed., pp. 625–670). Washington, DC: American Council on Education.
Glass, G. V. (1978). Standards and criteria. *Journal of Educational Measurement, 15*, 237–261. doi:10.1111/j.1745-3984.1978.tb00072.x.
Goodwin, L. D., & Leech, N. L. (2003). The meaning of validity in the new standards for educational and psychological testing: Implications for measurement courses. *Measurement and Evaluation in Counseling and Development, 36*, 181–192.
Gorin, J. S. (2006). Test design with cognition in mind. *Educational Measurement: Issues and Practice, 25*(4), 21–35. doi:10.1111/j.1745-3992.2006.00076.x.
Gorin, J. S. (2007). Reconsidering issues in validity theory. *Educational Researcher, 36*, 456–462. doi:10.3102/0013189X07311607.
Haertel, E. H. (2002). Standard setting as a participatory process: Implications for validation of standards-based accountability programs. *Educational Measurement: Issues and Practice, 21*(1), 16–22. doi:10.1111/j.1745-3992.2002.tb00081.x.
Haertel, E. H., & Lorié, W. A. (2004). Validating standards-based test score interpretations. *Measurement: Interdisciplinary Research and Perspectives, 2*, 61–103. doi:10.1207/s15366359mea0202_1.
Hartig, J. (2008). Psychometric models for the assessment of competencies. In J. Hartig, E. Klieme, & D. Leutner (Eds.), *Assessment of competencies in educational contexts* (pp. 69–90). Göttingen: Hogrefe.
Hartig, J., & Frey, A. (2012). Konstruktvalidierung und Skalenbeschreibung in der Kompetenzdiagnostik durch die Vorhersage von Aufgabenschwierigkeiten [Using the prediction of item difficulties for construct validation and model-based proficiency scaling]. *Psychologische Rundschau, 63*, 43–49. doi:10.1026/0033-3042/a000109.
Hartig, J., Klieme, E., & Leutner, D. (Eds.). (2008). *Assessment of competencies in educational contexts*. Göttingen: Hogrefe.
Hartig, J., Frey, A., Nold, G., & Klieme, E. (2012). An application of explanatory item response modeling for model-based proficiency scaling. *Educational and Psychological Measurement, 72*, 665–686. doi:10.1177/0013164411430707.

Huff, K., & Plake, B. S. (2010). Innovations in setting performance standards for K-12 test-based accountability. *Measurement: Interdisciplinary Research and Perspective, 8*, 130–144. doi:10.1080/15366367.2010.508690.
Kane, M. T. (1992). Quantitative methods in psychology: An argument-based approach to validity. *Psychological Bulletin, 112*, 527–535. doi:10.1037/0033-2909.112.3.527.
Kane, M. T. (1994). Validating the performance standards associated with passing scores. *Review of Educational Research, 64*, 425–461. doi:10.3102/00346543064003425.
Kane, M. T. (1998). Choosing between examinee-centered and test-centered standard-setting methods. *Educational Assessment, 5*, 129–145. doi:10.1207/s15326977ea0503_1.
Kane, M. T. (2009). Validating the interpretations and uses of test scores. In R. W. Lissitz (Ed.), *The concept of validity: Revisions, new directions, and applications* (pp. 39–64). Charlotte: Information Age.
Kane, M. T. (2011). Validating score interpretations and uses. *Language Testing, 29*, 3–17. doi:10.1177/0265532211417210.
Karantonis, A., & Sireci, S. G. (2006). The bookmark standard-setting-method: A literature review. *Educational Measurement: Issues and Practice, 25*(1), 4–12. doi:10.1111/j.1745-3992.2006.00047.x.
Klieme, E., Leutner, D., Kenk, M. (Eds.). (2010). Kompetenzmodellierung: Zwischenbilanz des DFG-Schwerpunktprogramms und Perspektiven des Forschungsansatzes [Modelling of competencies: Interim results of the DFG priority program and perspectives of the research approach]. *Zeitschrift für Pädagogik, Beiheft, 56*, 1–312.
Koeppen, K., Hartig, J., Klieme, E., & Leutner, D. (2008). Current issues in competence modeling and assessment. *Journal of Psychology, 216*, 61–73. doi:10.1027/0044-3409.216.2.61.
Köller, O. (2010). Bildungsstandards [Educational standards]. In R. Tippelt & B. Schmidt (Eds.), *Handbuch Bildungsforschung* (3rd ed., pp. 529–550). Wiesbaden: VS.
Leighton, J. P., & Gierl, M. J. (2007). Defining and evaluating models of cognition used in educational measurement to make inferences about examinees' thinking processes. *Educational Measurement: Issues and Practice, 26*(2), 3–16. doi:10.1111/j.1745-3992.2007.00090.x.
Lissitz, R. W. (2009). *The concept of validity: Revisions, new directions, and applications.* Charlotte: Information Age.
Lissitz, R. W., & Samuelsen, K. (2007). Further clarification regarding validity and education. *Educational Researcher, 36*, 482–484. doi:10.3102/0013189X07311612.
Loevinger, J. (1957). Objective tests as instruments of psychological theory. *Psychological Reports, 3*, 635–694. doi:10.2466/PR0.3.7.635–694.
Messick, S. (1989). Validity. In R. L. Linn (Ed.), *Educational measurement* (pp. 13–103). New York: Macmillan.
Messick, S. (1995). Validity of psychological assessment: Validation of inferences from persons' responses and performances as scientific inquiry into score meaning. *American Psychologist, 50*, 741–749. doi:10.1037/0003-066X.50.9.741.
Messick, S. (1998). Test validity: A matter of consequence. *Social Indicators Research, 45*, 35–44. doi:10.1023/A:1006964925094.
Mislevy, R. J., Steinberg, L. S., & Almond, R. G. (2002). On the several roles of task model variables in assessment design. In S. Irvine & P. Kyllonen (Eds.), *Generating items for cognitive tests: Theory and practice* (pp. 97–128). Hillsdale: Erlbaum.
Mitzel, H. C., Lewis, D. M., Patz, R. J., & Green, D. R. (2001). The bookmark procedure: Psychological perspectives. In G. J. Cizek (Ed.), *Setting performance standards: Concepts, methods and perspectives* (pp. 249–281). Mahwah: Erlbaum.
Nichols, P., Twing, J., Mueller, C. D., & O'Malley, K. (2010). Standard-setting methods as measurement processes. *Educational Measurement: Issues and Practice, 29*(1), 14–24. doi:10.1111/j.1745-3992.2009.00166.x.
Nitko, A. J. (1980). Distinguishing the many varieties of criterion-referenced tests. *Review of Educational Research, 50*, 461–485. doi:10.3102/00346543050003461.

Pant, H. A., Rupp, A. A., Tiffin-Richards, S. P., & Köller, O. (2009). Validity issues in standard-setting studies. *Studies in Educational Evaluation, 35*, 95–101. doi:10.1016/j.stueduc.2009.10.008.

Pant, H. A., Tiffin-Richards, S. P., & Köller, O. (2010). Standard-setting für Kompetenztests im large-scale-assessment [Standard setting in large-scale assessment]. *Zeitschrift für Pädagogik*, Beiheft, *56*, 175–188.

Pellegrino, J., Chudowsky, N., & Glaser, R. (Eds.). (2001). *Knowing what students know: The science and design of educational assessment*. Washington, DC: National Academy Press.

Raymond, M. R., & Reid, J. B. (2001). Who made thee a judge? Selecting and training participants for standard setting. In G. J. Cizek (Ed.), *Standard setting: Concepts, methods, and perspectives* (pp. 119–157). Mahwah: Erlbaum.

Rychen, D. S., & Salganik, L. H. (Eds.). (2001). *Defining and selecting key competencies*. Kirkland: Hogrefe.

Rychen, D. S., & Salganik, L. H. (Eds.). (2003). *Key competencies for a successful life and a well-functioning society*. Cambridge, MA: Hogrefe.

Sireci, S. G. (2009). Packing and unpacking sources of validity evidence: History repeats itself again. In R. W. Lissitz (Ed.), *The concept of validity: Revisions, new directions, and applications* (pp. 19–37). Charlotte: Information Age.

Tiffin-Richards, S. P., Pant, H. A., & Köller, O. (2013). Setting standards for English foreign language assessment: Methodology, validation and a degree of arbitrariness. *Educational Measurement: Issues and Practice, 32*(2), 15–25. doi:10.1111/emip.12008.

Toulmin, S. E. (1958). *The uses of argument*. Cambridge: Cambridge University Press.

Weinert, F. E. (2001). Concept of competence: A conceptual clarification. In D. S. Rychen & L. H. Salganik (Eds.), *Defining and selecting key competencies* (pp. 45–65). Kirkland: Hogrefe.

Chapter 28
Evaluating Prerequisites for the Development of a Dynamic Test of Reading Competence: Feedback Effects on Reading Comprehension in Children

Tobias Dörfler, Stefanie Golke, and Cordula Artelt

Abstract Dynamic assessments are often assumed to produce more valid indicators of students' competencies than do static assessments. For the assessment of reading competence, there are only a few, and very specific, approaches to dynamic assessments available, and thus there is almost no support for the validity of dynamic measures, compared to static measures. Against this background, we explain the theoretical and practical prerequisites for a dynamic test of reading competence. After describing the concept of dynamic assessments (particularly for the area of reading competence), three computer-based experiments are presented that implemented the core principles of dynamic assessment in the domain of reading. In these experiments different, theoretically derived feedback and prompting conditions were varied systematically. The results show the benefits but also the costs and shortcomings of the implementation of a dynamic test of reading competence. Finally, further challenges and subsequent stages concerning the development of a dynamic assessment tool in this domain are outlined.

Keywords Dynamic assessment • Learning ability • Reading competence • Reading comprehension • Feedback

T. Dörfler (✉)
University of Education, Heidelberg, Germany
e-mail: doerfler@ph-heidelberg.de

S. Golke
University of Freiburg, Freiburg, Germany
e-mail: stefanie.golke@ezw.uni-freiburg.de

C. Artelt
University of Bamberg, Bamberg, Germany
e-mail: cordula.artelt@uni-bamberg.de

D. Leutner et al. (eds.), *Competence Assessment in Education*, Methodology of Educational Measurement and Assessment, DOI 10.1007/978-3-319-50030-0_28

28.1 Introduction

A major purpose of educational assessment is to measure and forecast academic achievement. The assessment of academic achievement most commonly consists of measuring students' current achievement levels. However, since the 1930s an alternative approach has developed in which the *learning potential* of a student is measured, in addition to his/her current achievement level. To measure the learning potential, feedback is provided to the students during the assessment; this procedure is known as dynamic assessment. How well students use this feedback to improve their performance is thought to reflect their learning potential.

Whereas dynamic assessments are quite common in the field of intelligence testing, the domain of reading has been neglected. However, according to findings from research on intelligence testing, a dynamic test of reading competence could help to identify students' capabilities and to inform educators about specific needs for training in the reading domain.

In the following, we first outline the concept of dynamic assessment in the field of reading competence and address its advantages as well as challenges. Second, the results of three experiments are presented and discussed. These experiments investigated what kind of feedback or (meta-)cognitive prompts are useful to understanding in a reading competence test. These experiments were a prerequisite to developing a dynamic reading competence test. Finally, a summative outlook on the dynamic assessment of reading competence will be afforded.

28.2 The Idea of Dynamic Assessments

Dynamic assessments are targeted to measure the current achievement level and students' responsiveness to intervention conditions—that is, instructions, feedbacks or prompts—at the same time (Embretson 2000). This responsiveness is considered to be the manifestation of learning potential. Due to the additional information gleaned, about the test person's potential, dynamic assessments should better determine and forecast achievement development. Modeling learning potential, in addition to ability assessment itself, is the major concern of dynamic assessments, regardless of the test format implemented or the labeling of the test. The best-established terms within the framework of dynamic assessment are *structural cognitive modifiability* (see Feuerstein et al. 1983), *learning potential assessment* (see Budoff 1987), *learning test* (see Guthke 1982) or *testing-the-limits* (see Carlson and Wiedl 1979). For comprehensive overviews, see Guthke and Wiedl (1996) or Poehner (2008).

Regardless of the terms applied to label the procedures, each implies the notion of learning potential, the understanding of which is usually based on Vygotsky (1964), who stressed the importance of the *zone of proximal development*, as compared to the *zone of current development*. The zone of current development represents the performance level an individual can achieve without external assistance. This is the outcome of conventional tests. Dynamic assessments represent the zone of proximal development, which "defines those functions that have not matured yet but are in the process of maturation, functions that will mature tomorrow but are currently in an embryonic state. These functions could be termed the 'buds' or 'flowers' of development rather than the 'fruits' of development" (Vygotsky 1978). Vygotsky assumed that under most circumstances, all flowers will produce fruit—meaning that what a child can do with assistance today, it will be able to do by itself tomorrow. Furthermore, Vygotsky has pointed out that the individual might improve their performance under the guidance of adults or more-capable peers. The distance between the current developmental level achieved without assistance and the level of potential development achieved through guidance, is defined as the zone of proximal development. This zone is assumed to provide additional information about individuals' learning ability in the respective domain, which is supposed to be predictive of upcoming developmental processes and the learning outcome. Thus, measures of the breadth of the zone of proximal development should render better prospective indications of subsequent courses of learning than do conventional test results. Consequently, the predictive validity of tests that measure the zone of proximal development should be greater than the predictive validity of tests that aim solely at the measurement of independent achievement (see Meijer and Elshout 2001). Studies addressing the validity of dynamic tests reveal modest but discernible superiority on a number of different criteria (e.g., school performance) over static tests (e.g., Beckmann 2001; Carlson and Wiedl 2000; Budoff 1987; Caffrey et al. 2008). The review of Caffrey et al. (2008), and studies from Fuchs et al. (2011) or Gilbert et al. (2013) provide some evidence for the incremental predictive power of dynamic assessment, especially for forecasting later reading competence.

Dynamic assessment, however, also brings challenges. This particularly applies to issues of scoring and scaling, since item responses to some extent (depending on the number of initial false responses) reflect changes induced by the dynamic assessment procedure itself. This implies that the intervention procedure itself needs to be scored (Embretson 1987; Guthke and Wiedl 1996), by means such as recording the correctness of responses and the number of provided aids that were needed to reach a specific criterion (Beckmann 2001). Convenient models for response data from dynamic assessments are based on item response theory. Scaling models for dynamic tests in complex, multi-dimensional performance domains have to account for the possible existence of multiple, domain-specific learning abilities (for an overview see Dörfler et al. 2009).

Within typical static tests, students' performance, assessed at one isolated time point (Cioffi and Carney 1983) is seen in relation to the distribution of achievement scores of all students in the reference group, which represents the standard. As described above, dynamic assessments also take into account how students respond to instruction during the assessment procedure. To this end, the emphasis is on collecting information related to the (probably maladaptive) strategies that students use during the process of solving test items (Carney and Cioffi 1992) and on identifying the student's learning potential, as defined by Vygotsky's zone of proximal development. From a diagnostic point of view, this responsiveness allows the examiner to improve interpretations of children's actual competence range and predictions of further development (Fuchs et al. 2011).

Two formats of dynamic assessment are commonly applied: the *test-train-test* design and the *train-within-test* design (see Dillon 1997). Both formats use some kind of educational assistance (e.g., instructions, feedback) to induce performance improvement in terms of Vygostsky's zone of proximal development. The extent of help provided, however, differs according to the dynamic assessment format. Dynamic tests in the test-train-test design provide one or more training sessions between a pretest and a posttest. In this approach, the degree of performance enhancement between pretest and posttest is seen as an indicator of a person's learning potential. In general, the test-train-test approach to dynamic assessments is similar in design to common training studies and therefore it is likely to produce greater gains.

Dynamic assessments in the train-within-test format, conduct performance testing within the intervention. Students respond to test items and receive some kind of assistance on their performance, which they can use to improve during the remainder of the test session. The assistance can be feedback or a (meta-)cognitive aid that is commonly provided immediately after an incorrect response. Students' responsiveness to the support given in this test session is assumed to reflect their learning potential. Hence, train-within-tests differ from test-train-tests in that they diagnose and predict performance on the basis of a single assessment. Expected performance gains are smaller than in the test-train-test format, but the focus of the current study rather is on estimating learning potential beyond the assessment of reading competence.

28.3 Dynamic Assessments of Reading Competence: Existing Approaches and Challenges

Dynamic assessment approaches have potential for everyday diagnostic practice in school (Elliott 2000). In particular, knowledge about individual learning deficits and potentials derived from curriculum-based dynamic assessment can be used for the development of individual learning plans for students with different learning requirements. Dynamic assessments have already been shown to be successful in the field of oral language proficiency for second language (L2) learners (e.g., Poehner and Lantolf 2013; Poehner and van Compernolle 2013). Convincing attempts to dynamically assess reading and language processing either use test-train-test settings (Kletzien and Bednar 1990) or focus on strategy instructions in L2 acquisition with English as a foreign language (Birjandi et al. 2013). There are quite a few test-train-test studies on reading competence, mostly focusing on training of cognitive and metacognitive strategies for text processing (Campione and Brown 1987). However, the results of these studies are often discussed as mere intervention/training studies (e.g., NICHD 2000) without an explicit focus on learning potentials. Dynamic assessment of reading competence in a computer-based train-within-test design is still missing, although such one-time assessments can be much more efficient than test-train-test designs. The lack of train-within-test designs for assessing reading competence might be due to a hesitation to assume a learning potential specific for the domain of reading (over and above a general learning potential that is measured via dynamic intelligence tests). It might also stem from the fact that reading for understanding is a rather complex cognitive ability that is oftentimes assumed not to be amenable to short term interventions, especially because poor performance on particular reading test items might be due to different reasons.

What makes reading comprehension a complex cognitive process, and what is challenging about providing learning aids within an assessment? Within assessments of reading competence, students are asked to read one or more texts and to answer questions related to the specific text that require the student to generate various text-based or knowledge-based inferences. Thus, for the development of a train-within-test of reading competence, a concept of relevant inferential processes and interventions for the construction of tasks and feedbacks is required. Dynamic assessments in the domain of reading often rely on instruction and practice in metacognitive knowledge (including strategies) that is specific to certain reading tasks and goals. In general, successful dynamic assessments further depend on the prompting of domain-specific processes, which are essential for the fulfillment of task requirements. The major goal of train-within-tests is an efficient assessment of reading competence and learning potential. The learning potential will be uncovered by the way students profit from feedback and prompts. Nevertheless, presumed competence improvements are small, due to the minimally invasive intervention of one test session. To foster learning and understanding in the focused domain to a substantial degree, instructions or hints and feedback are used to observe students' responsiveness to the given support.

The development of a dynamic reading competence test differs considerably from the construction of dynamic assessments in other cognitive domains. This claim can be illustrated by a comparison with the construction of dynamic tests for reasoning ability: Cognitive components of reasoning tasks are well investigated (Carpenter et al. 1990). For figural reasoning tasks, for example, difficulty is often associated with the number of varying criteria (e.g., shape, color, size etc.) that have to be taken into account. These task features are directly used to construct the feedback. In the case of unsuccessful trials, the assessment includes a sequence of feedback of increasing complexity and well-defined useful strategies that gradually lead to the correct solution.

In contrast, reading competence is a more complex construct, involving multilevel processes in which children often struggle (Cain 2009). In order to comprehend successfully—that is, to gain meaning from written text for a particular purpose—the reader must engage in various processes at the levels of words, sentences, and the text. The reader is required to identify a series of letters as a word, to access the meaning of words, and to integrate individual word meanings or sentence meanings. Generating inferences leads to text-based and knowledge-based connections, both within and across sentences (Singer et al. 1997). This involves connecting several idea units (propositions) distributed across the text and filling in missing information by activating prior knowledge from long-term memory, in an effort to construct global meaning from the text (Artelt et al. 2001; Graesser et al. 1994; Artelt et al. 2005; Graesser et al. 2003). In relation to constructing adequate help or feedback for dynamic assessments of reading competence in a train-within-test design, one has to take into account not only the specific constraints of the train-within-test format, as well as the specific cognitive processes of reading comprehension, but also general findings from feedback research.

As to the type of feedback, a general distinction can be made between verification and elaboration. Verification addresses the correctness of an answer, indicating the performance level achieved (e.g., "right/wrong"). This feedback type is the most common form of intervention provided in dynamic tests; certainly due to its simplicity, at least in the domain of intelligence (Beckmann et al. 2009). In contrast, elaborated feedback offers additional information by means of relevant cues. It can address the task or topic, particular errors, or responses. A large body of educational research shows that the effectiveness of feedback varies according to the type of feedback, with the greatest effects being achieved for elaborated feedback (Bangert-Drowns et al. 1991; Kluger and DeNisi 1996; Shute 2008). However, Kulhavy and Stock (1989) have argued that effective feedback should include both verification and elaboration.

A train-within-test calls for brief feedback interventions, due to the short test procedure. Feedback usually contains information on how to proceed, or why a specific response was incorrect or accurate. When conceptualizing a dynamic test of reading competence that focuses on (causal) inferences concerning processes at a shallow level (e.g., local coherence) as well as at deep levels of comprehension (e.g., global coherence, situational model), elaborated feedback might give error-specific explanations. That is, the learner is provided with an explanation of why his/her response is not an accurate inference or causal relation between several units of the text. Another feedback intervention might guide the learner to the correct solution without offering the correct answer. When test items refer to (causal) inferences, the feedback can provide a cognitive hint as to how the inference can be generated. A further intervention in a train-within-test of reading competence could address metacognitive processes, which are known to be highly relevant in the reading comprehension process. For example, learners might be prompted to reflect on their monitoring performance, or to evaluate the task requirements when responding to test items.

The development of different feedback types related to the complex demands of reading comprehension is not as straightforward as it is for reasoning tasks. Given that processes necessary for reading comprehension are less apparent than is the case in other domains, the implementation of a feedback sequence—as found in dynamic tests in other domains—is difficult to realize. Nevertheless, successful feedback that is suited to the purposes of dynamic assessment must take such domain-specific complexity into account. Thus, the systematic investigation of suitable feedback procedures for reading comprehension is a central requirement of our research.

28.4 Experiments on the Effectiveness of Feedback on Reading Comprehension in a Train-Within-Test Setting

Identifying effective feedback on reading comprehension was a prerequisite for the development of a train-within-test of reading competence. In a series of three experiments, we investigated the effectiveness of different aspects of feedback interventions on reading comprehension (Golke 2013; Golke et al. 2015). According to the logic of train-within-tests, these feedback interventions were provided on specific responses during a performance test on reading comprehension. The experiments focused the following aspects, which were derived from a literature review: feedback content (verification, [meta-]cognitive prompts), presentation-type feedback (computer/human-agent delivered), modality of feedback presentation (written/oral presentation), and motivational scaffolding, with the help of an agent and tokens. The basic research question for each of the three experiments was what type of feedback intervention enhances the comprehension of written texts. In general, it appears that feedback on reading comprehension in a train-within-test setting is a difficult endeavor to accomplish. The three experiments and their results are outlined in more detail in the following.

28.4.1 Experiment 1

The first experiment examined the effectiveness of the feedback content, because content is assumed to be the most influential feature of feedback itself (Bangert-Drowns et al. 1991). The experiment included three types of elaborated feedback and two control conditions. The elaborated types of feedback were: (1) prompts that referred to the required inference and how it can be generated (called inference-prompts in the following), (2) explanations for why a specific response to a test item is not correct, and (3) a metacognitive prompt that encouraged the participant to check his/her understanding of the text. These three types of elaborated feedback were chosen because they reflect different ways of supporting comprehension, and different levels of specificity. The two control conditions consisted of a condition without feedback and a condition with verification feedback. The no-feedback condition represented a traditional, static test. The verification feedback (i.e., "that's wrong") was implemented because it involved the same procedure as the elaborated feedback treatments, while it could be assumed to have relatively little impact on reading comprehension compared to more elaborate forms (Lee et al. 2009;

Schunk and Rice 1991, 1993). Feedback was provided on false initial responses to the test items in the treatment phase. Furthermore, all feedback was presented via computer. We hypothesized that all three types of elaborated feedback would enhance reading comprehension compared to both control conditions. Moreover, we specified that the elaborated feedback called inference-prompts would yield the highest effects on reading comprehension, and that feedback error-explanation would still be more effective than metacognitive prompts, due to its less-specific character. Children have to infer from metacognitive prompts how to handle their own deficits in understanding what is highly demanding. For this reason, we argue for error-explanation as a more direct and less demanding way of fostering students' ability to find the right answer.

A total of 566 sixth grade students participated in the first experiment ($M = 12.16$ years, $SD = 0.83$; 53.0 % girls). During the treatment phase of the experiment, the participants worked on five units. Each unit contained a text and on average seven multiple-choice items. The five texts were a mixture of two narratives and three expository texts. In all, the five units included 37 items. The items mainly asked for knowledge-based and text-based inferences that were implicitly contained in the text. The feedback procedure was as follows: When the first response to an item was incorrect, the participant was provided a feedback message via computer. Then, the participant was required to give a second response to the same item. After the second response, the next item was presented. When the first response to an item was correct, the next item appeared immediately. In this manner, the participants accomplished the five units of the treatment phase. In the control condition without feedback, participants responded only once to each item.

After the treatment phase, a posttest was conducted that was also computer-delivered. It contained two new units (one narrative, one expository text), with a total of 14 items. The posttest did not offer further assistance—all participants had one trial per item. Four weeks after the session with the experiment and the posttest, a follow-up test was administered in paper-and-pencil format. It included four new units (two narratives, two expository texts), with a total of 30 items.

The analyses of the effects of the feedback were based on measures of the posttest and the follow-up test, but also on performance within the treatment phase itself. Performance within the treatment phase was separated into initial responses to the test items and the second responses that followed after feedback was provided. The second responses therefore reflect the extent to which participants were able to successfully correct initially false responses. The results showed, however, that none of the feedback types had an effect on reading comprehension—neither on the first nor the second responses in the experiment, nor on the posttest or the follow-up (see Fig. 28.1).

The fact that none of the elaborated feedback forms had a learning effect was surprising, against the background of feedback research in the field of reading comprehension, and our own experiences from cognitive interviews. The cognitive interviews were conducted prior to the experiment, in an effort to get a first impression of how well feedback (and the texts and items) worked.

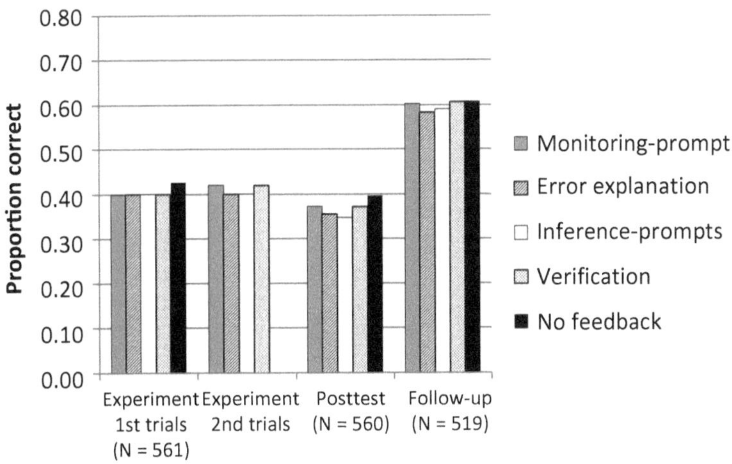

Fig. 28.1 Performance on the reading comprehension tests of Experiment 1

The setting of the cognitive interviews was, however, different from that of the experiment: the feedback was provided personally by the "experimenter" in a face-to-face situation. In discussing the results of Experiment 1, we speculated that the cooperative-like setting of the cognitive interviews was met by a stronger commitment of the students to engage in the feedback processing. In contrast, students working "anonymously" at the computer—as was the case in the reported experiment—may have experienced less motivation. Eventually we pursued the idea whether person-mediated feedback delivery in a face-to-face setting might support the participants' commitment to feedback processing, hence allowing elaborated feedback to become more effective.

28.4.2 *Experiment 2*

The second experiment contrasted computer-mediated and person-mediated elaborated feedback. The type of elaborated feedback was the inference-prompt. The control conditions remained the same: no feedback and verification feedback. We predicted that the person-mediated inference-prompts would enhance reading comprehension within the treatment phase as well as in the posttest (no follow-up in the second experiment). In line with the findings of the first experiment, the intervention with computer-mediated inference prompts was assumed to yield no performance improvement compared to the control conditions.

A total of 251 sixth grade students participated in the experiment (M = 12.42 years, SD = 0.58; 50.2 % girls). The methods were comparable to the first experiment. The feedback provision procedure was also the same as in the first experiment, whereas the person-mediated feedback condition had two new features: in

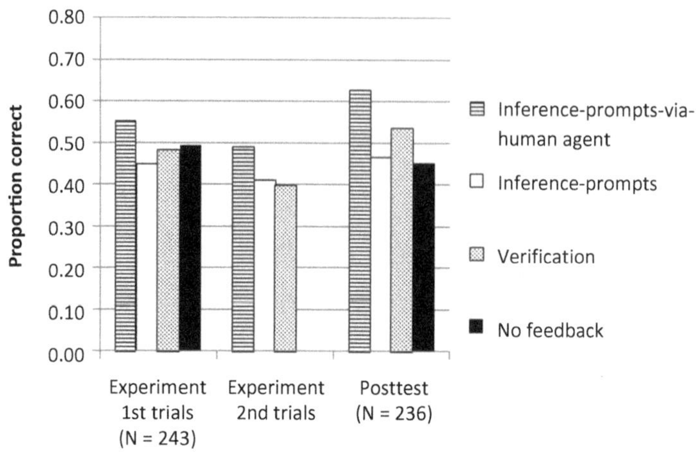

Fig. 28.2 Performance on the reading comprehension tests of Experiment 2

this condition the experimenter and the participant worked in a one-to-one setting in a room separate from the room in which the participants in the other conditions were tested. The experimenter sat next to the student. The student read the texts and answered the multiple-choice items on the computer, but when feedback was required, it was provided verbally by the experimenter. After verbally providing the feedback message to the participant, the experimenter placed a card with the same feedback message on the table. This procedure was implemented in order to prevent working memory influences.

The results (see Fig. 28.2) showed that the person-mediated inference-prompts yielded significantly higher performance than the other conditions. The significant positive effect showed in the second responses within the treatment phase, as well as in the posttest. The other three conditions (computer-mediated inference-prompts, verification feedback, and no feedback) did not differ from each other.

The latter result supports the assumption that computer-mediated elaborated feedback in a test setting like the one we used, is not suitable to enhance performance. However, when learners are sufficiently engaged in putting effort into the processing of the feedback messages, the inference-prompts are useful to successfully correcting the comprehension task at hand and to enhancing comprehension of further texts.

The second experiment therefore showed that inference-prompts can indeed improve comprehension of written texts; a conclusion that was not evident from the first experiment. However, with regard to the dynamic test, the feedback presentation type of the second experiment did not signify the end of our experimental studies. Person-mediated feedback provision is resource-intensive, and hence, further stages of development of the dynamic test of reading competence would hardly be achievable. The second experiment therefore raised the question of what features of the computer-based learning program ought to be changed, or what new aspects should be introduced, in order to allow motivated, engaged processing of the elaborated feedback.

28.4.3 Experiment 3

The computer-based learning program in the third experiment differed from the previous two experiments in that it contained a reward system for correct responses and an animated agent simulating personal feedback delivery. The latter was an attempt to implement a cooperative-like setting, which ought to enhance participants' involvement in the test and feedback procedure. All experimental conditions worked with the same altered learning program. Besides, we varied the modality of the feedback provision, contrasting an auditory-and-written format with an auditory-only format. According to the meta-analysis of Kluger and DeNisi (1996), oral feedback is less effective than written feedback, whereas the modality is confounded with the feedback source (i.e., person or computer). As person-mediated feedback had been linked to negative effects on students' performance, the impact of verbal feedback also diminished. However, modern technologies enable nearly every kind of feedback delivery via computer, removing person-induced negative effects on performance from the procedure. To our knowledge, the effect of the computer-provided feedback modality on reading comprehension has not yet been investigated. We saw the implementation of auditory feedback in a test environment, with an animated agent simulating personal feedback delivery, as an interesting possibility for modeling a motivating learning environment. To avoid working memory influences, the auditory feedback was also presented in written format on the screen. As to the type of elaborated feedback, we again drew upon inference-prompts, which were provided either in an auditory-and-written format or in written format. The third condition was verification feedback, also presented in the auditory-and-written format. Moreover, a control condition with no feedback was included. We predicted that the inference-prompts in the auditory-and-written format would result in higher performance scores than the inference-prompts in the written format, and that the latter would still improve performances compared to the control condition.

The experiment included 238 sixth grade students (*M* = 12.5 years, *SD* = 1.58; 50.0 % girls). The materials and the feedback procedure were the same as in the previous experiment.

The results (see Fig. 28.3) showed, however, that no effect could be obtained on reading comprehension, neither on the first nor on the second responses to the items in the treatment phase, nor on performance in the posttest.

Interpretation of these findings seems quite clear: auditory feedback presentation combined with rewards for correct responses and a cooperation-simulating learning program, is not sufficient to counter the motivational issues related to learning from computer-provided elaborated feedback on reading comprehension.

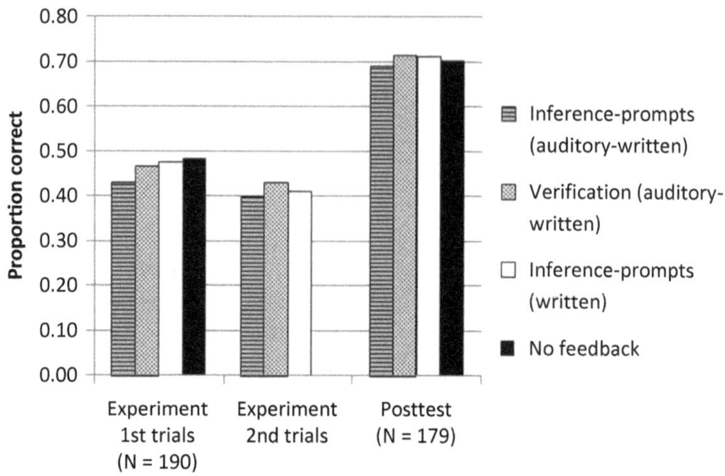

Fig. 28.3 Performance on the reading comprehension tests of Experiment 3

28.5 Effects of Feedback on Reading Comprehension Within a Computer-Delivered Test: Lessons Learned

Three experiments were conducted to test whether it is possible to induce learning improvement in reading comprehension during one test session, by means of feedbacks and prompts. This was considered a necessary first step for the development of a dynamic reading competence assessment. Taking the results of all three experiments into account, it can be inferred that elaborated feedback in the form of inference-prompts is effective for reading comprehension when it is provided personally in a face-to-face setting. The same feedback does not seem to work when provided by a device, rather than a human being. This is a rather awkward constraint for the development of a computer-delivered train-within-test. Hence, there is as yet no satisfying answer to the question of what type of feedback intervention produces sustainable effects on secondary school children's comprehension of texts in a computer-delivered test. However, the presented findings do not rule out the possibility that a train-within-test of reading competence can be created that serves the intended purpose within the framework of dynamic assessment.

Before elaborating in more detail on the idea of dynamic assessment in the domain of reading, two aspects of the reading assessment operationalizations used will be considered, which might have had consequences for the results of the experiments. The first aspect relates to the high demands and workload for the participating students, and the second aspect relates to the perceived value of the provided help, and thus the motivation to perform the reading test items as well as possible.

Processing Demands/Workload The reading tasks and materials used within our study apparently involved a high workload, as several texts had to be read and quite a number of test items had to be solved. Indeed, the procedure of having second responses after feedback on initially false responses further raised the workload. Moreover, the test items appeared to be rather difficult for the students, except with very good readers. Hence, most of the participants needed to work at a rather high level of processing. Thus it would seem worthwhile to reduce the reading task load, or to precisely align participants' reading competence level with treatment interventions.

Perceived Value of Feedback The reading task load is also connected to the perceived value of the provided feedback. If a student has to work on a unit that contains a text that is highly interesting to this student, it is likely that she or he would have specifically valued feedback messages on how to get the right answers to the test items. However, it is impossible to find texts that tap the diverse special interests of various students. Moreover, the value of the train-within-test should also reveal to the students that when they understand, they can gain relevant strategic knowledge that helps them to improve not only in the test, but in school lessons and everyday reading situations as well. To this end, more attention needs to be paid to the idea of the feedback intervention itself, and how its value and importance could be planted into the student's mind. Basically, learning in a train-within-test is learning from errors. In school, however, errors are commonly not much appreciated as learning instances. This might be accounted for in the train-within-test, for example, by including a practice task on how to use the feedback messages, or an instruction about why it is useful, quite beyond the confines of the test.

28.6 Prospects of Dynamic Tests of Reading Competence

Dynamic assessments of reading competence are supposed to provide incremental information about readers' skills, and particularly so for low performing students. For this reason, a reliable and valid—and, for reasons of efficiency, a train-within-format—test of reading competence seems a desirable goal. Nevertheless, as we have learned throughout the experiments, the construction of such a test is not trivial, and more effort must be invested to fulfill all requirements. Furthermore, on the basis of our experiments so far, we are not able to prove that a computer-delivered train-within-test of reading competence in fact yields added value compared to a conventional status test. This does at least apply to the theoretical assumption of a reading specific learning potential and its diagnostic value in a train-within-test format, alike used in the experiments above. However, even without this assumption, dynamic assessment in content domains yields added value since the tests in principle not only allow for fine grained analysis of errors within the process of reading comprehension, but also bear information about students' responsiveness to specific feedback/learning aids and thus, to interventions.

A possible implication of our findings is that fewer prerequisites have to be fulfilled to build a train-within-test assessment of reading competence that is delivered by a human agent rather than a technical device. However, investing further research effort into computer-delivered assessments seems worthwhile. It does not seem theoretically satisfying that the same kind of help provided by a human agent differs substantially in its effects when provided by a technical device. Further research is needed in order to understand, and possibly to work around, the specific constraints of computer-based tests. Thus it seems important to take into account recent developments in computer agents (Atkinson 2002; VanLehn et al. 2007; Sträfling et al. 2010). There are also other reasons for further elaborating the possibilities of computer-delivered dynamic assessments: Such tests are less vulnerable to interviewer effects, since the level of standardization is almost perfect. For train-within-test formats, standardization is obviously an issue that cannot easily be solved with face-to-face interaction. Furthermore, the implementation of feedback and prompts that are adapted to the specific responses of the test persons is vulnerable to interviewer errors.

Computer-based assessment also allows for adaptive or branched testing. Item administration thus varies as a function of prior performance, leading to a more efficient diagnostic process, since the number of items can at best be diminished, and the testing finished with a priorly settled reliability (Segall 2005). Students are confronted with as many items as needed for an appropriate assessment. In traditional adaptive tests, unidimensional models are used (Segall 2005). In contrast, multi-dimensional adaptive testing allows for the simultaneous utilization of test information provided by more than one construct (Frey and Seitz 2009). A possible implementation within the framework of dynamic assessment of reading competence would be to model reading competence as well as learning ability (related to reading competence) in a two-dimensional approach. For this sake, specific item response models need to be specified, to deal adequately with gain scores in reading competence induced by the test procedure itself (see also Dörfler et al. 2009).

Acknowledgements The preparation of this chapter was supported by Grants AR 307/7-1 and AR 307/7-2 from the German Research Foundation (DFG) in the Priority Program "Competence Models for Assessing Individual Learning Outcomes and Evaluating Educational Processes" (SPP 1293).

References

Artelt, C., Schiefele, U., & Schneider, W. (2001). Predictors of reading literacy. *European Journal of Psychology of Education, 16*, 363–383. doi:10.1007/BF03173188.

Artelt, C., McElvany, N., Christmann, U., Richter, T., Groeben, N., Köster, J., … Saalbach, H. (2005). *Expertise: Förderung von Lesekompetenz (Bildungsreform Band 17)* [Expertise: Fostering reading competence]. Bonn: BMBF.

Atkinson, R. K. (2002). Optimizing learning from examples: Using animated pedagogical agents. *Journal of Educational Psychology, 94*, 416–427. doi:10.1037/0022-0663.94.2.416.

Bangert-Drowns, R. L., Kulik, C.-L. C., Kulik, J. A., & Morgan, M. T. (1991). The instructional effect of feedback in test-like events. *Review of Educational Research, 61*, 213–238. doi:10.3102/00346543061002213.

Beckmann, J. F. (2001). *Zur Validierung des Konstrukts des intellektuellen Veränderungspotentials* [On validation of the construct of intellectual change potential]. Berlin: Logos.

Beckmann, N., Beckmann, J. F., & Elliott, J. G. (2009). Self-confidence and performance goal orientation interactively predict performance in a reasoning test with accuracy feedback. *Learning and Individual Differences, 19*, 277–282. doi:10.1016/j.lindif.2008.09.008.

Birjandi, P., Estaji, M., & Deyhim, T. (2013). The impact of dynamic assessment on reading comprehension and metacognitive awareness of reading strategy use in Iranian high school learners. *Iranian Journal of Language Testing, 3*, 60–77.

Budoff, M. (1987). The validity of learning potential assessment. In C. S. Lidz (Ed.), *Dynamic assessment: An interactional approach to evaluating learning potential* (pp. 53–81). New York: Guilford Press.

Caffrey, E., Fuchs, D., & Fuchs, L. S. (2008). The predictive validity of dynamic assessment: A review. *The Journal of Special Education, 41*, 254–270. doi:10.1177/0022466907310366.

Cain, K. (2009). Children's reading comprehension difficulties: A consideration of the precursors and consequences. In C. Wood & V. Connelly (Eds.), *Contemporary perspectives on reading and spelling* (pp. 59–75). New York: Routledge.

Campione, J. C., & Brown, A. L. (1987). Linking dynamic assessment with school achievement. In C. S. Lidz (Ed.), *Dynamic assesment: An international approach to evaluation learning potential* (pp. 82–140). New York: Guilford Press.

Carlson, J. S., & Wiedl, K. H. (1979). Towards a differential testing approach: Testing-the-limits employing the Raven Matrices. *Intelligence, 3*, 323–344. doi:10.1016/0160-2896(79)90002-3.

Carlson, J. S., & Wiedl, K. H. (2000). The validity of dynamic assessment. In C. S. Lidz & J. G. Elliott (Eds.), *Dynamic assessment:Prevailing models and applications* (Vol. 6, pp. 681–712). Oxford: Elsevier.

Carney, J. J., & Cioffi, G. (1992). The dynamic assessment of reading abilities. *International Journal of Disability, Development and Education, 39*, 107–114. doi:10.1080/0156655920390203.

Carpenter, P. A., Just, M. A., & Shell, P. (1990). What one intelligence test measures: A theoretical account of the processing in the Raven Progressive Matrices test. *Psychological Review, 97*, 404–431. doi:10.1037/0033-295X.97.3.404.

Cioffi, G., & Carney, J. (1983). Dynamic assessment of reading disabilities. *The Reading Teacher, 36*, 764–768.

Dillon, R. F. (1997). Dynamic testing. In R. F. Dillon (Ed.), *Handbook on testing* (pp. 164–186). Westport: Greenwood Press.

Dörfler, T., Golke, S., & Artelt, C. (2009). Dynamic assessment and its potential for the assessment of reading competence. *Studies in Educational Evaluation, 35*, 77–82. doi:10.1016/j.stueduc.2009.10.005.

Elliott, J. G. (2000). Dynamic assessment in educational contexts: Purpose and promise. In C. S. Lidz & J. G. Elliott (Eds.), *Dynamic assessment: Prevailing models and applications* (Vol. 6, pp. 713–740). Oxford: Elsevier.

Embretson, S. E. (1987). Toward development of a psychometric approach. In C. S. Lidz (Ed.), *Dynamic assessment: An interactional approach to evaluating learning potential* (pp. 141–170). New York: Guilford Press.

Embretson, S. E. (2000). Multidimensional measurement from dynamic tests: Abstract reasoning under stress. *Multivariate Behavioral Research, 35*, 505–542. doi:10.1207/S15327906MBR3504_05.

Feuerstein, R., Rand, Y., Haywood, H. C., Hoffmann, M., & Jensen, M. R. (1983). *Learning potential assessment device: Manual*. Jerusalem: HWCRI.

Frey, A., & Seitz, N. N. (2009). Multidimensional adaptive testing in educational and psychological measurement: Current state and future challenges. *Studies in Educational Evaluation, 35*, 89–94. doi:10.1016/j.stueduc.2009.10.007.

Fuchs, D., Compton, D. L., Fuchs, L. S., Bouton, B., & Caffrey, E. (2011). The construct and predictive validity of a dynamic assessment of young children learning to read: Implications for RTI frameworks. *Journal of Learning Disabilities, 44*, 339–347. doi:10.1177/0022219411407864.

Gilbert, J. K., Compton, D. L., Fuchs, D., Fuchs, L. S., Bouton, B., Barquero, L. A., & Cho, E. (2013). Efficacy of a first grade responsiveness-to-intervention prevention model for struggling readers. *Reading Research Quarterly, 48*, 135–154. doi:10.1002/rrq.45.

Golke, S. (2013). *Effekte elaborierter Feedbacks auf das Textverstehen: Untersuchungen zur Wirksamkeit von Feedbackinhalten unter Berücksichtigung des Präsentationsmodus in computerbasierten Testsettings* [The effects of elaborated feedback on text comprehension: Studies on the relevance of feedback content and feedback presentation type in a computer based assessment]. Bamberg: University of Bamberg Press.

Golke, S., Dörfler, T., Artelt, C. (2015). The impact of elaborated feedbacks on text comprehension within a computer-based assessment. *Learning and Instruction, 39*, 123–136. doi:dx.doi.org/10.1016/j.learninstruc.2015.05.009.

Graesser, A. C., Singer, M., & Trabasso, T. (1994). Constructing inferences during narrative text comprehension. *Psychological Review, 101*, 371–395.

Graesser, A. C., McNamara, D. S., & Louwerse, M. M. (2003). What do readers need to learn in order to process coherence relations in narrative and expository text? In A. P. Sweet & C. E. Snow (Eds.), *Rethinking reading comprehension* (pp. 82–98). New York: Guilford.

Guthke, J. (1982). The learning test concept: An alternative to the traditional static intelligence test. *The German Journal of Psychology, 6*, 306–324.

Guthke, J., & Wiedl, K. H. (1996). *Dynamisches Testen: Zur Psychodiagnostik der intraindividuellen Variabilität* [Dynamic testing]. Göttingen: Hogrefe.

Kletzien, S. B., & Bednar, M. R. (1990). Dynamic assessment for at-risk readers. *Journal of Reading, 33*, 528–533.

Kluger, A. N., & DeNisi, A. (1996). Effects of feedback intervention on performance: A historical review, a meta-analysis, and a preliminary feedback intervention theory. *Psychological Bulletin, 119*, 254–284. doi:10.1037/0033-2909.119.2.254.

Kulhavy, R. W., & Stock, W. A. (1989). Feedback in written instruction: The place of response certitude. *Educational Psychology Review, 1*, 279–308.

Lee, H. W., Lim, K. Y., & Grabowski, B. (2009). Generative learning strategies and metacognitive feedback to facilitate comprehension of complex science topics and self-regulation. *Journal of Educational Multimedia and Hypermedia, 18*, 5–25.

Meijer, J., & Elshout, J. J. (2001). The predictive and discriminant validity of the zone of proximal development. *British Journal of Educational Psychology, 7*, 93–113. doi:10.1348/000709901158415.

NICHD (National Institute of Child Health and Human Development). (2000). *Report of the national reading panel: "Teaching children to read": An evidence-based assessment of the scientific research literature on reading and its implications for reading instruction.* Washington, DC: U. S. Government Printing Office.

Poehner, M. E. (2008). *Dynamic assessment: A Vygotskian approach to understanding and promoting L2 development.* Berlin: Springer.

Poehner, M. E., & Lantolf, J. P. (2013). Bringing the ZPD into the equation: Capturing L2 development during computerized Dynamic Assessment. *Language Teaching Research, 17*, 323–342. doi:10.1177/1362168813482935.

Poehner, M. E., & van Compernolle, R. A. (2013). L2 development around tests. Learner response processes and dynamic assessment. *International Review of Applied Linguistics, 51*, 353–377. doi:10.1515/iral-2013-0015.

Schunk, D. H., & Rice, J. M. (1991). Learning goals and progress feedback during reading comprehension instruction. *Journal of Reading Behavior, 23*, 351–364. doi:10.1080/10862969109547746.

Schunk, D. H., & Rice, J. M. (1993). Strategy fading and progress feedback: Effects on self-efficacy and comprehension among students receiving remedial reading services. *Journal of Special Education, 27*, 257–276. doi:10.1177/002246699302700301.

Segall, D. O. (2005). Computerized adaptive testing. In K. Kempf-Leonard (Ed.), *Encyclopedia of social measurement* (pp. 429–438). Amsterdam: Elsevier.

Shute, V. J. (2008). Focus on formative feedback. *Review of Educational Research, 78*, 153–189. doi:10.3102/0034654307313795.

Singer, M., Harkness, D., & Stewart, S. T. (1997). Constructing inferences in expository text comprehension. *Discourse Processes, 24*, 199–228. doi:10.1080/01638539709545013.

Sträfling, N., Fleischer, I., Polzer, C., Leutner, D., & Krämer, N. C. (2010). Teaching learning strategies with a pedagogical agent. The effects of a virtual tutor and its appearance on learning and motivation. *Journal of Media Psychology, 22*, 73–83. doi:10.1027/1864-1105/a000010.

VanLehn, K., Graesser, A. C., Jackson, G. T., Jordan, P., Olney, A., & Rosé, C. P. (2007). When are tutorial dialogues more effective than reading? *Cognitive Science: A Multidisciplinary Journal, 31*, 3–62. doi:10.1080/03640210709336984.

Vygotsky, L. S. (1964). *Denken und Sprechen* [Thought and language]. Berlin: Akademie.

Vygotsky, L. S. (1978). *Mind in society: The development of higher psychological processes*. Cambridge, MA: Harvard University Press.

FSC
www.fsc.org
MIX
Papier | Fördert gute Waldnutzung
FSC® C083411

Kolibri 360 GmbH
Ferdinand-Jühlke-Straße 7
99095 Erfurt, Deutschland
produktsicherheit@kolibri360.de